History of the Canadian Peoples

Volume 2 | 1867 to the Present

Sixth Edition

Margaret Conrad · **Alvin Finkel** · **Donald Fyson**
University of New Brunswick · *Athabasca University* · *Université Laval*

PEARSON

Toronto

Vice-President, CMPS: Gary Bennett
Acquisitions Editor: Matthew Christian
Marketing Manager: Christine Cozens
Developmental Editor: Richard di Santo, with Stephen Kass
Project Manager: Richard di Santo
Production Services: Munesh Kumar, Aptara®, Inc.
Copyeditor: Janice Dyer
Proofreader: Karen Alliston
Permissions Project Manager: Erica Mojzes
Photo Permissions Clearance: Carly Bergey, Lumina Datamatics Inc.
Text Permissions Clearance: Mark Schaefer, Lumina Datamatics Inc.
Cover and Interior Design: Anthony Leung
Cover Image: Maintenance Jobs in the Hangar, by Paraskeva Clark, 14085. Beaverbrook Collection of War Art
© Canadian War Museum

Library and Archives Canada Cataloguing in Publication

Conrad, Margaret, author

    History of the Canadian Peoples / Margaret Conrad (University of New Brunswick), Alvin Finkel (Athabasca University), Donald Fyson (Université Laval).—Sixth edition.

Includes bibliographical references and indexes.
Contents: Volume 2. 1867 to the present.
ISBN 978-0-13-299197-1 (v. 2: pbk.)

    1. Canada—History.   I. Conrad, Margaret 1946–,   II. Finkel, Alvin, 1949–,
III. Fyson, Donald, 1967–.   Title.

FC165.C66 2014   971   C2013-907822-3

ISBN 978-0-13-299197-1

CONTENTS

LIST OF MAPS

LIST OF TABLES AND FIGURES

The first edition of the two-volume text *History of the Canadian Peoples* was published in 1993. Our objective was to write a survey of Canadian history that incorporated new research in Canadian social history and included developments in the lives of all Canadians, not just the rich and powerful. The stories of Aboriginal peoples, women, racial and ethnic minorities, the poor, and regions outside of the St Lawrence-Great Lakes heartland shared centre stage with the accounts of European explorers and colonial politicians and warriors. While it was enthusiastically endorsed, our text and many of the writings upon which it was based drew criticism from some historians who lamented the demise of a cohesive political narrative of the nation's history. Five editions later, we continue to draw upon an ever-expanding literature on Canada's rich and contested past to offer insights on the diverse peoples and regions of an evolving nation-state situated on the northern half of the North American continent.

History of the Canadian Peoples attempts to introduce readers to the complexity of the past—the conflicts and failures, common goals and successes that make Canada what it is today. We also want to expose students to the way history is constructed, using endnotes to document some of our sources and calling attention to conflicting interpretations of the past. By focusing on economic, political, social, and cultural themes, we hope to provide a balanced view of conditions that faced Canadians in the past. We, of course, recognize the limits of a national framework in assigning significance to events, but we stand firm in our conviction that a critical examination of the past helps to develop a historical consciousness and sense of human agency that serves us well in our efforts to shape the future.

Volume II is divided into five sections. In Part I, "Inventing Canada, 1867–1914," we explore the political processes that brought the scattered British colonies together to form a nation-state and outline the emergence of state institutions—federal, provincial, and municipal—that shaped the fledgling nation. Part II, "Economy and Society in the Industrial Age, 1867–1914," traces the ways in which Canadians in the early years of Confederation responded both to the creation of new state institutions and the rise of industrial capitalism in efforts to make the new political and economic order work better for members of their region, social class, gender, and ethnic group. In Part III, "The Transitional Years, 1914–1945," we study the impact of two world wars on Canadian political, economic, and social institutions, and observe how different groups of Canadians lived through a roller-coaster of economic ups and downs during a period of rapid industrialization that included a postwar recession, the "roaring twenties," and the crippling Depression of the 1930s. Part IV, "Reinventing Canada, 1945–1975," analyzes a period of dramatic economic growth, focusing on the development of the welfare state, the age of mass consumption, the Cold War, and challenges to Canadian identity resulting from increasing economic and social integration with the United States. Finally, Part V, "Post-Modern Canada, 1976–2014," evaluates changes and continuities in Canadian society in a period of economic "globalization," heated debates about the value of state interventionism as a means to improve the distribution of wealth, and a growing recognition that the future of our biosphere has been jeopardized by the ravages of fossil fuels and human greed.

In constructing and revising this text, we maintain the pedagogical features found in previous editions. "Historiographical Debates" alert readers to differing interpretations of key events in Canadian history. Other features, including "More to the Story," "Biography," and "Voices from the Past," supplement our narrative. A timeline appears at the beginning of each chapter to place events in chronological perspective, and maps and illustrations give visual support to the written word.

In this edition, we welcome a third member to our writing team: Donald Fyson, a historian of Quebec, is an equal partner with Margaret Conrad and Alvin Finkel, the authors of the five earlier editions. He has contributed to every chapter of this edition of the book and in all facets of its production.

Before tackling the sixth edition of *History of the Canadian Peoples*, the three of us prepared a third edition of its one-volume counterpart, *Canada: A History*. The sixth edition of *History of the Canadian Peoples* largely follows the organizational principles of *Canada: A History*, but with expanded coverage of major events and themes.

Margaret Conrad, Alvin Finkel, Donald Fyson

NEW TO THE SIXTH EDITION

- More coverage is given to Quebec and to Native peoples.
- The chapter structure has been changed to reduce the 23 chapters of the fifth edition to 18 chapters, better integrating materials that had been discussed separately in the earlier edition.
- The number of both historiographical essays and biographies has been increased to at least one of each per chapter.
- Recent events in the Canadian story have been added to make this as complete and up-to-date a survey history of Canada as possible.
- Full-colour maps prepared especially for the sixth edition help students to understand the geographical context of Canadian history, showing them key places, political divisions, and events. The maps were prepared by Renée Sénéchal-Huot and Émile Lapierre-Pintal of the Centre interuniversitaire d'études québécoises at Université Laval; our thanks to them and to the CIEQ. The sources used to create the maps are indicated in the Companion Website.
- New colour images draw students into visual representations for each time period.
- Offering a dynamic online experience, the Companion Website provides primary source documents and a comprehensive list of selected readings for each chapter.

STUDENT SUPPLEMENTS

The **Companion Website** provides an engaging online experience that personalizes learning. For *History of the Canadian Peoples*, students can access the following materials by visiting http://pearsoncanada.ca/conrad:

Selected Readings—We provide the most comprehensive reading list to accompany a survey history course that any Canadian history text has presented to date. While each chapter in the book provides a short list of especially helpful readings, the Selected Readings list in the Companion Website offers an extensive set of readings for almost any essay topic or topic of personal interest.

Primary Documents—We feature a wide range of material, including readings and images.

CourseSmart for Students: CourseSmart goes beyond traditional expectations, providing instant, online access to the required textbooks and course materials at an average savings of 60 percent. With instant access from any computer and the ability to search your text, you will find the content you need quickly, no matter where you are. And with online tools like highlighting and note-taking, you can save time and study efficiently. See all the benefits at www.coursesmart.com/students.

INSTRUCTOR SUPPLEMENTS

PowerPoints: PowerPoint presentations support each chapter of the text to facilitate the creation of stimulating lectures.

Image Library: Select from certain photos, figures, tables, and maps from the text to incorporate into your own PowerPoint presentations.

You can download the PowerPoints and the Image Library from a password-protected section of Pearson Canada's online catalogue at www.pearsoncanada.ca/highered by navigating to the text's catalogue page.

CourseSmart for Instructors: CourseSmart goes beyond traditional expectations, providing instant, online access to the textbooks and course materials you need at a lower cost for students. And even as students save money, you can save time and hassle with a digital eTextbook that allows you to search for the most relevant content at the very moment you need it. Whether you are evaluating textbooks or creating lecture notes to help students with difficult concepts, CourseSmart can make life a little easier. See how when you visit www.coursesmart.com/instructors.

Learning Solutions Managers: Pearson's Learning Solutions Managers work with faculty and campus course designers to ensure that Pearson technology products, assessment tools, and online course materials are tailored to meet your specific needs. This highly qualified team is dedicated to helping schools take full advantage of a wide range of educational resources, by assisting in the integration of a variety of instructional materials and media formats. Your local Pearson Canada Sales Representative can provide you with more details on this service program.

Pearson Custom Library: For enrollments of at least 25 students, you can create your own textbook by choosing the chapters that best suit your own course needs. To begin building your custom text, visit www.pearsoncustomlibrary.com. You may also work with a dedicated Pearson Custom Editor to create your ideal text—publishing your own original content or mixing and matching with Pearson content. Contact your local Pearson Representative to get started.

ACKNOWLEDGEMENTS

For their contributions to this edition, we extend thanks to the publishing team: Richard di Santo, Joel Gladstone, Matthew Christian, Janice Dyer, Karen Alliston, Munesh Kumar, and Stephen Kass. Thanks also to our permissions researchers Erica Mojzes, Carly Bergey, and Mark Schaefer. In earlier editions we also benefited from the editorial contributions of Karen Bennett, Robert Clarke, Gail Copeland, Dawn du Quesnay, Curtis Fahey, Sally Glover, Brian Henderson, Jeff Miller, Lisa Rahn, Adrienne Shiffman, and Barbara Tessman.

We are grateful to each of the following for providing formal reviews of parts of the manuscript during the development process for this edition of *History of the Canadian Peoples*: Alan Gordon, University of Guelph; Peter Russell, UBC Okanagan Campus; and Marty Wood, Laurentian University at Georgian. We also thank individuals who generously gave of their time when we consulted them on various issues: Jerry Bannister, Susan Blair, Yvon Desloges, Dan Horner, Talbot Imlay, Alain Laberge, Maude-Emmanuelle Lambert, Roch Legault, John G. Reid, Étienne Rivard, Marc St-Hilaire, Marc Vallières, and Thomas Wien.

We also thank reviewers and contributors to earlier editions of *History of the Canadian Peoples* as well as to various editions of its one-volume counterpart. These include: Douglas Baldwin, Stephanie Bangarth, Marilyn Barber, Matthew Barlow, Michael Behiels, John Belshaw, Rusty Bitterman, Clarence Bolt, Ruth Brouwer, Sean Cadigan, Shawn Cafferky, Robert Campbell, Cynthia Comacchio, Cecilia Danysk, George Davison, Graham Decarie, Catherine Desbarats, John Dickinson, Patricia Dirks, Darren Ferry, Gerald Friesen, Alan Gordon, Adam J. Green, David J. Hall, Roger Hall, Lorne Hammond, Larry Hannant, Jim Hiller, Norman Hillmer, Raymond Huel, Sharon Jaeger, Cornelius Jaenen, Kiera Ladner, Greg Kealey, Linda Kealey, Linda Kerr, Jeff Keshen, Larry Kulisek, Edward MacDonald, Heidi Macdonald, Greg Marquis, Mark McGowan, Sheila McManus, Kathryn McPherson, Carmen Miller, Jim Miller, David Mills, Wendy Mitchinson, Barry Moody, Peter Moogk, Suzanne Morton, Del Muise, Ken Munro, David Murray, Jan Noel, Peter Nunoda, Gillian Poulter, Jim Pritchard, Robert Rutherdale , Eric W. Sager, John Sandlos, Marda Schindeler, Adrien Shubert, Ron Stagg, Kori Street, Veronica Strong-Boag, Robert Sweeny, Georgina Taylor, Brian Young, and Suzanne Zeller.

NOTE ON STYLE

Throughout the text, we have generally italicized non-English words and phrases (but not the names of institutions or Aboriginal groups) only when they do not appear in either of the major English dictionaries, that is Oxford and Webster. We have limited capitalization to the full formal names of institutions, but do not capitalize when we use short forms such as "the church" or "the commission."

In 1829, Shanawdithit, the last surviving Beothuk on the island of Newfoundland, died of tuberculosis. Thirty-eight years later, three British North American colonies united to form the Dominion of Canada. The second of these two events has always had a central place in Canadian history textbooks. The first was largely ignored until the last decades of the twentieth century, when many historians began to recognize the need to research and write the history of Aboriginal peoples and the impact of European contact. For students of history, it is important to understand why the focus of historical analysis changes and what factors influence historians in their approaches to their craft.

WHAT IS HISTORY?

Simply stated, history is the study of the past—but the past is a slippery concept. In non-literate societies, people passed oral traditions from one generation to the next, with each generation fashioning the story to meet the needs of the time. When writing was invented, history became fixed in texts. The story of the past was often revised, but earlier texts could be used to show how interpretations changed over time. Although ordinary people continued to tell their stories, they were considered less important than "official" written histories that reflected the interests of the most powerful members of society. Some of the official texts, such as the Bible and the Koran, were deemed to be divinely inspired and therefore less subject to revision than the accounts of mere mortals.

In the nineteenth century, history became an academic discipline in Europe and North America. Scholars in universities began to collect primary historical documents, compare texts, develop standards of accuracy, and train students to become professional historians. While professional historians initially focused on political and military events that chronicled the evolution of empires and nation-states, they gradually broadened their scope to include economic, social, cultural, and environmental developments.

At the same time that professional historians were honing their craft, the production of history continued outside the academy. Oral transmission of historical knowledge flourished, especially in families and small communities, and enthusiastic amateur historians often proved as adept as their academic counterparts in finding, assessing, and interpreting historical sources. As literacy increased, the public interest in history grew, leading to the founding of local history societies, the publication of popular history books, and the commemoration of historical events. Meanwhile, governments at all levels tried to sustain historical memory for civic purposes by building monuments, museums, and historic sites, and by encouraging the teaching of Canadian history in the nation's schools.

In the twenty-first century, historians have many tools in their kit bag to help them understand the past. To fill the gaps in written documents, they draw upon other disciplines (including archaeology, anthropology, demography, and geography) to answer their questions. Oral traditions and the findings of archaeological excavations, for example, have enabled historians to explore the lives of the silent majority in past times. When personal computers became widely available in the 1970s, historians were able to more efficiently process large amounts of information found in such sources as censuses, immigration lists, and church registers. The science of demography, which analyzes population trends and draws upon vast quantities of data, has proven particularly useful in helping historians trace changes in family size, migration patterns, and life-cycle choices.

Writing history is a creative process. Even identical twins would not produce the same narrative when presented with the same set of historical sources to analyze. This truth has led some critics to conclude that history is just another branch of fiction, but this is not the case. Good historians, like good lawyers, must base their conclusions on solid evidence.

Whether they articulate it or not, historians are also influenced in their selection and interpretation of evidence by theories that help them to shape their thinking on the past. Scholars who study minorities, women, and the working class, for example, bring insights from multicultural studies, feminism, and Marxism to their analyses. The current scholarly preoccupation with the study of historical consciousness, historical memory, and public uses of the past suggests that we are entering a new phase in our understanding of history, one that not only acknowledges the limits to the truth-seeking goals of historical inquiry, but that also addresses—sometimes in unsettling ways—the role that history plays in shaping present identities and imagining future goals.

In short, history is a dynamic and evolving discipline. Debates rage, methods come and go, new sources are discovered, and different conclusions are drawn from the same body of evidence. We want students who use this text not only to learn about developments in Canada's past, but also to gain some understanding of how history is written. At the beginning of and at various points throughout each chapter, we cite from primary sources that historians use. We also discuss historiography—that is, reflections on historical interpretation—in sections entitled "A Historiographical Debate."

Ultimately, our goal in this textbook is to create a synthesis that helps readers to develop a clearer understanding of how the past unfolded in Canada. There is, we maintain, nothing inevitable about historical processes. At times in this text, the limitations on an individual's behaviour may appear to suggest that many—perhaps most—of our ancestors were hopeless victims of forces beyond their control. A closer reading reveals that people sought in various ways to transcend the limits placed on their lives. Social struggles of every sort changed, or at least sought to change, the course of history. As you read this book, we hope that you will gain a greater appreciation of how earlier generations of people in what is now called Canada responded to their environment and shaped their own history.

MORE TO THE STORY
What's in a Name?

Contemporary political movements that are changing the face of Canada are also forcing historians to think about the words they use. A half-century ago, most textbooks referred to people with black skin as *Negroes*. In the 1960s, the term was replaced by *black* and more recently by *African Canadian*. Similarly, the words used to describe Aboriginal peoples have changed in recent years. The term *savages* was quickly dropped from textbooks in the 1960s. The misnomer *Indian* has particular applications that seem as yet unavoidable. Since the adoption of the Constitution Act in 1982, the terms *Aboriginal peoples* and *First Nations* are more commonly used to encompass the "Indian," Inuit, and Métis peoples of Canada.

Women, too, have insisted on being described in more respectful terms. Feminists have objected strongly to the use of the word *girl* when adult women are being discussed, and dismiss *lady* as condescending or elitist. Because *man* was adequate for the male of the species, *woman*, they argued, was the most appropriate term, although some radical feminists prefer a different spelling, such as *wymyn*. Only the most hidebound of scholars still insist that the word *man* can be used to describe the entire human species.

Many scholars complained loudly about being asked to abandon words long established in their vocabularies. A few even argued that "political correctness" restricted freedom of speech. We do not hold such views. Since English is a living language and changes over time, we see no reason why it should not continue to reflect the new consciousness of groups in Canadian society. In our view, "politically conscious" more accurately describes attempts by groups to name their own experience.

Language, of course, is not only about naming things; it is also about power. Attempts by oppressed groups to find new words to fit their experiences should be seen in the context of their struggles for empowerment. In this text, we attempt to keep up with the changing times while bearing in mind that people in the past used a different terminology. We are also aware that in the future we may revise the words we use, as groups continue to reinvent their identities. Even the word *Canada* has changed its meaning over the past 500 years, and it is our job as historians to shed light on the way this term came to be applied, for a time at least, to all the people living on the northern half of the North American continent.

SELECTED READING

The following is a list of survey histories on Canadian regions, provinces, and territories; major subject areas; and key historiographical works that provide more information on topics covered in this text. A short list of more focused readings appears at the end of each chapter. The Companion Website includes a comprehensive list of readings for each chapter.

Baillargeon, Denyse. *A Brief History of Women in Quebec.* Waterloo: Wilfrid Laurier University Press, 2014.

Barman, Jean. *The West Beyond the West: A History of British Columbia.* Third edition. Toronto: University of Toronto Press, 2007.

Baskerville, Peter A. *Sites of Power: A Concise History of Ontario.* Don Mills: Oxford University Press, 2005.

Berger, Carl. *The Writing of Canadian History: Aspects of English-Canadian Historical Writing Since 1900.* Toronto: University of Toronto Press, 1986.

Brandt, Gail Cuthbert et al. *Canadian Women: A History.* Third edition. Toronto: Nelson Education, 2011.

Burnet, Jean R. with Howard Palmer. *Coming Canadians: An Introduction to a History of Canada's Peoples.* Toronto: McClelland & Stewart, 1988.

Cadigan, Sean T. *Newfoundland and Labrador: A History.* Toronto: University of Toronto Press, 2009.

Choquette, Robert. *Canada's Religions: An Historical Introduction.* Ottawa: University of Ottawa Press, 2004.

Clark, Penney, ed. *New Possibilities for the Past: Shaping History Education in Canada.* Vancouver: UBC Press, 2011.

Coates, Ken S. and William R. Morrison. *Land of the Midnight Sun: A History of the Yukon.* Montreal: McGill-Queen's University Press, 2005.

Conrad, Margaret and James K. Hiller. *Atlantic Canada: A History.* Second edition. Toronto: Oxford University Press, 2010.

Conrad, Margaret et al. *Canadians and Their Pasts: The Pasts Collective.* Toronto: University of Toronto Press, 2013.

Dickason, Olive Patricia with David T. McNab. *Canada's First Nations: A History of Founding Peoples from Earliest Times.* Fourth edition. Toronto: Oxford University Press, 2009.

Dickinson, John and Brian Young. *A Short History of Quebec.* Fourth edition. Montreal: McGill-Queen's University Press, 2008.

Dummitt, Christopher and Michael Dawson, eds. *Contesting Clio's Craft: New Directions and Debates in Canadian History.* Vancouver: UBC Press, 2008.

Finkel, Alvin. *Social Policy and Practice in Canada: A History.* Waterloo: Wilfrid Laurier University Press, 2006.

Forbes, E.R. and D.A. Muise. *The Atlantic Provinces in Confederation.* Toronto: University of Toronto Press, 1993.

Forkey, Neil S. *Canadians and the Natural Environment to the Twenty-First Century.* Toronto: University of Toronto Press, 2012.

Frenette, Yves. *Brève histoire des Canadiens français.* Montreal: Boréal, 1998.

Friesen, Gerald. *The Canadian Prairies: A History.* Toronto: University of Toronto Press, 1987.

Gossage, Peter and J.I. Little. *An Illustrated History of Quebec: Tradition and Modernity.* Toronto: Oxford University Press, 2012.

Granatstein, J.L. *Canada's Army: Waging War and Keeping the Peace.* Second edition. Toronto: University of Toronto Press, 2011.

Hallowell, Gerald, ed. *The Oxford Companion to Canadian History.* Toronto: Oxford University Press, 2004.

Harris, Cole et al., eds. *Historical Atlas of Canada.* Toronto: University of Toronto Press, 1987–1993.

Harris, Cole. *The Reluctant Land: Society, Space, and Environment in Canada Before Confederation*. Vancouver: UBC Press, 2008.

Heron, Craig. *The Canadian Labour Movement: A Short History*. Third edition. Toronto: Lorimer, 2012.

Hillmer, Norman and J.L. Granatstein. *For Better or for Worse: Canada and the United States into the Twenty-First Century*. Toronto: Thomson/Nelson, 2007.

Howells, Coral Ann and Eva-Marie Kröller, eds. *The Cambridge History of Canadian Literature*. Cambridge: Cambridge University Press, 2009.

Kalman, Harold. *A History of Canadian Architecture*. Toronto: Oxford University Press, 1994.

Kelley, Ninette and Michael Trebilcock. *The Making of the Mosaic: A History of Canadian Immigration Policy*. Second edition. Toronto: University of Toronto Press, 2010.

Landry, Nicolas and Nicole Lang. *Histoire de l'Acadie*. Sillery: Septentrion, 2001.

Leach, Jim. *Film in Canada*. Second edition. Toronto: Oxford University Press, 2011.

Li, Peter S. *The Chinese in Canada*. Toronto: Oxford University Press, 1998.

MacDonald, Edward. *If You're Stronghearted: Prince Edward Island in the Twentieth Century*. Charlottetown: Prince Edward Island Museum and Heritage Foundation, 2000.

MacDowell, Laurel Sefton. *An Environmental History of Canada*. Vancouver: UBC Press, 2012.

Magocsi, Paul R., ed. *Encyclopedia of Canada's Peoples*. Toronto: University of Toronto Press, 1999.

McMillan, Alan D. and Eldon Yellowhorn. *First Peoples in Canada*. Third edition. Vancouver: Douglas & McIntyre, 2004.

Mensah, Joseph. *Black Canadians: History, Experience, Social Conditions*. Second edition. Halifax: Fernwood, 2010.

Miller, J.R. *Skyscrapers Hide the Heavens: A History of Indian-White Relations in Canada*. Third edition. Toronto: University of Toronto Press, 2000.

Morrison, William R. *True North: The Yukon and Northwest Territories*. Toronto: Oxford University Press, 1998.

Morrow, Don and Kevin B. Wamsley. *Sport in Canada: A History*. Second edition. Toronto: Oxford University Press, 2009.

Morton, Desmond. *A Military History of Canada*. Fifth edition. Toronto: McClelland & Stewart, 2007.

Murphy, Terrence, ed. *A Concise History of Christianity in Canada*. Toronto: Oxford University Press, 1996.

Nischik, Reingard M., ed. *History of Literature in Canada: English-Canadian and French-Canadian*. Rochester: Camden House, 2008.

Norrie, Kenneth, Douglas Owram and J.C. Herbert Emery. *A History of the Canadian Economy*. Fourth edition. Toronto: Nelson Thomson, 2008.

Palmer, Bryan D. *Working-Class Experience: Rethinking the History of Canadian Labour, 1800–1991*. Toronto: McClelland & Stewart, 1992.

Payne, Michael, Donald Wetherell and Catherine Cavanaugh, eds. *Alberta Formed, Alberta Transformed*. Edmonton and Calgary: University of Alberta Press and University of Calgary Press, 2006.

Ray, Arthur J. *An Illustrated History of Canada's Native People: I Have Lived Here Since the World Began*. Revised and expanded edition. Montreal: McGill-Queen's University Press, 2011.

Rees, Ronald. *New Brunswick: An Illustrated History*. Halifax: Nimbus, 2014.

Reid, Dennis. *A Concise History of Canadian Painting*. Toronto: Oxford University Press, 1988.

Reid, John. *Nova Scotia: A Pocket History*. Black Point: Fernwood Publishing, 2009.

Roy, Patricia E. and John Herd Thompson. *British Columbia: Land of Promises*. Toronto: Oxford University Press, 2005.

Rudin, Ronald. *Making History in Twentieth-Century Quebec*. Toronto: University of Toronto Press, 1997.

Taylor, Graham D. *The Rise of Canadian Business*. Toronto: Oxford University Press, 2009.

Thompson, John Herd and Stephen J. Randall. *Canada and the United States: Ambivalent Allies*. Fourth edition. Montreal: McGill-Queen's University Press, 2008.

Thompson, John Herd. *Forging the Prairie West*. Toronto: Oxford University Press, 1998.

Tulchinsky, Gerald. *Canada's Jews: A People's Journey.* Toronto: University of Toronto Press, 2008.

Vance, Jonathan F. *A History of Canadian Culture.* Don Mills: Oxford University Press, 2009.

Vipond, Mary. *The Mass Media in Canada.* Fourth edition. Toronto: Lorimer, 2011.

Waiser, Bill. *Saskatchewan: A New History.* Calgary: Fifth House, 2005.

Winks, Robin W. *The Blacks in Canada: A History.* Second edition. Montreal: McGill-Queen's University Press, 1997.

Wright, Donald. *The Professionalization of History in English Canada.* Toronto: University of Toronto Press, 2005.

PART I
INVENTING CANADA, 1867–1914

Between 1867 and 1914, Canada was transformed from a string of isolated British colonies into a nation that was ready to make its mark on the world stage during the First World War (1914-1918). In this period, immigration, western settlement, the growth of cities, and new social values signalled the onset of what historians call "the modern age." Two trends are particularly noteworthy: first, the emergence of the state—federal, provincial, and municipal—as a major force in nation-building; and second, the role of industrial capitalism in defining Canada's economic and social realities. Together, the expanding state and vigorous industrial growth changed the lives of all Canadians and created a nation that was vastly different from the one that had come together so inauspiciously in 1867. Part I provides a bird's eye view of Canada in 1867 and describes the political processes that brought the scattered British colonies together to form an industrial nation. In Part II, we explore the economic and social impact of the new industrial order on Canadians.

CHAPTER 1
A PEOPLE IN SEARCH OF A NATION, 1867

On the roofs of houses and elsewhere, in all directions, flag-poles were being hoisted into the air to do their part in the celebration of Confederation Day. A programme of celebration arranged by the Government included a grand review of Her Majesty's Troops, regulars and volunteers, on the Bathurst Street Commons at ten A.M. At three o'clock there was a grand Balloon Ascension from Queen's Park. In the evening there were concerts given by the Bands of the Tenth Royal Regiment and the Grand Trunk Brigade in the form of a grand promenade at Queen's Park accompanied by the most magnificent display of fireworks ever exhibited in Canada.

This is how the *Globe* described the festivities in Toronto on 1 July 1867 in celebration of Confederation Day. Other communities marked the historic occasion differently. In Nova Scotia, the New Glasgow *Eastern Chronicle* captured the colony's strong opposition to the union with a satirical birth announcement: "Born: On Monday last, at 12:05 A.M. (premature) the Dominion of Canada—illegitimate. This prodigy is known as the infant monster Confederation."[1]

Regional and cultural tensions remained defining features of the Dominion of Canada, but the fledgling nation survived and even thrived in the half-century following its birth. By the 1880s, Canada's territorial jurisdiction had been extended to the Pacific and Arctic oceans, making it physically the second largest nation on Earth. In the twentieth century, Canada emerged as one of the world's industrial giants. Even the most optimistic supporters of Confederation would have been surprised by the success of their venture.

THE STATE OF THE UNION, 1867

Canada had a population of fewer than 3.5 million in 1867 (see Table 1.1). Clustered along the northeast coast of North America and the Great Lakes–St Lawrence waterway, the individual provinces were in closer communication with Great Britain and the United States, the two powers that dominated their existence, than they were with each other. They had very few links with the other British colonies in North America—British Columbia, Prince Edward Island, and Newfoundland and Labrador—or with the vast Northwest region, known as Rupert's Land, which had been claimed and nominally administered by the British-chartered Hudson's Bay Company since 1670. The Arctic

Archipelago, also claimed by Great Britain, was out of bounds for most "southerners," who tended to succumb to the rigours of its cold weather and difficult terrain.

In the settled areas, railroads were beginning to supplement the stagecoach services that linked major communities, but there was no direct rail communication, and only a poor excuse for a road, between Quebec and New Brunswick. Portland, Maine, was the eastern terminus and winter port of the Grand Trunk Railway, the longest rail line in Canada in 1867. When Canadians travelled to the Northwest, they usually did so through the United States, which boasted a transcontinental railroad by 1869. Even telegraph lines, the fastest form of communication, were often routed through the United States rather than directly from one colony to another.

Their isolation from each other notwithstanding, the citizens of the new nation were, willingly or not, all subjects of Great Britain, the world's most powerful empire

in the nineteenth century. As dependencies of Great Britain, the British North American colonies possessed, to a greater or lesser degree, the political, legal, and social institutions of their "mother country." Queen Victoria, who ascended the British throne in 1837, was popular in Canada. When she died in 1901, many Canadians looked back fondly on the Victorian Age, which they associated with material progress and social propriety. It was this shared heritage, and Great Britain's eagerness to relinquish direct involvement in the internal administration of its North American colonies, that enabled the Canadian government to move quickly in expanding its borders following Confederation.

Canada's closest neighbour, and the object of grudging admiration, was the United States. When 13 of Great Britain's colonies declared independence in 1776, they were not much larger in population and territory than Canada in 1867. The United States made good its claim to

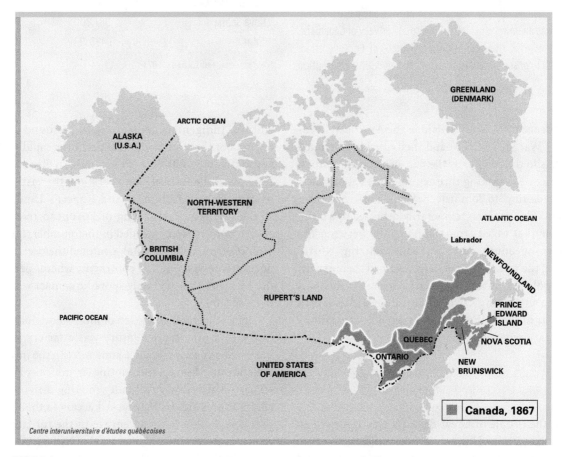

MAP 1.1

British North America in 1867. The map shows the initial extent of Canada following Confederation, along with the other existing colonies and territories of British North America

MORE TO THE STORY
Measuring the Canadian Population

In the nineteenth century, reformers argued that statistical tables revealed patterns that could help governments develop public policy. Section 91(6) of the BNA Act made census enumeration and vital statistics–that is, the record of births, marriages, and deaths–a responsibility of the federal government. Beginning in 1871, the Canadian government conducted census enumerations every 10 years and every five years after 1956. While all Canadians were required to provide basic information to census-takers in each census, in the late twentieth century, additional information was gathered through a so-called long-form census involving a subset of citizens. For the 2011 census, the federal government limited mandatory reporting to the short-form census to which all households were required to reply, claiming that an obligation to provide any more information was an unwelcome intrusion into the privacy of Canadians.

Covering the four original provinces of Confederation, the 1871 census provided a record of population distribution (see Table 1.1) and indicators of economic growth. The quality of the data depended to a large extent on the diligence and ability of the enumerators. Notwithstanding its flaws, the manuscript census remains one of the best sources available for historians and genealogists to gain information on the lives of ordinary Canadians at the time of Confederation.

TABLE 1.1
Population of Canada, 1871

Ontario	1 620 851
Quebec	1 191 516
New Brunswick	285 594
Nova Scotia	387 800
Total	3 485 761

Source: Census of Canada, 1871

independence from Great Britain in the American Revolutionary War (1775–1783) and then quickly expanded its borders to the Pacific. By the mid-nineteenth century, Americans were making threatening noises about their "manifest destiny" to dominate the whole North American continent. This goal was temporarily deflected by a bitter Civil War that raged from 1861 to 1865 between the slave-owning South and the industrializing North. Following the war, the Americans resumed their expansionary policies, purchasing Alaska from the Russians in 1867 and casting covetous eyes toward Rupert's Land. Fear of the United States played a key role in the Confederation movement.

CANADA'S PEOPLES

In 1867, the people of Great Britain's North American colonies were a mixed lot, scarcely the building blocks of a nation bound together by ties of a common history and culture. Indigenous peoples could be found in every region, but their numbers were declining rapidly. Of the approximately 130 000 Aboriginals in British North America at the time of Confederation, the vast majority lived in British Columbia and Rupert's Land. About 10 000 Métis, the offspring of European traders and Native women, were included in that number. Inuit peoples, close to 10 000 in total, confined themselves to the northern regions of the continent, where, perhaps to their benefit, they had only sporadic contact with European culture.

The vulnerable condition of most Aboriginal peoples in the mid-nineteenth century was a far cry from the independence they had once known. With the invasion of their farming, fishing, and hunting territories by European settlers, Natives had difficulty making a living. Their communities increasingly lacked access to the resources that would allow them to engage in the fur trade or to return to the traditional lifeways that had once sustained them. In the eastern colonies, about 20 000 Algonkian

At the time of Confederation, the artistic skills of Aboriginal peoples were highly prized. Christianne Morris, a Mi'kmaw from Halifax, made a good living from selling her needlework, quillwork, and splint baskets to collectors around the world. In 1860 her portrait, painted by William Gush, was presented to the Prince of Wales when he visited Halifax. This photograph of an "Indian Woman" from about 1864 is thought to be of Morris, who is shown holding a miniature quillwork canoe and displaying a small quilled box. SOURCE: NOVA SCOTIA ARCHIVES, NSARM ALBUM 5, NO. 76/NEGATIVE NO. 7288

and Iroquois peoples lived primarily on reserves and earned money by selling their crafts, including barrels, baskets, boxes, brooms, and canoes.

The legacy of the French regime in North America was present in the nearly one-third of Canadians whose first language was French. Concentrated in Quebec, the heartland of the old French empire, the population of French-speaking Canadians also included the Acadians in the Maritimes and a growing number of francophone settlers in the eastern sections of Ontario. The French-speaking Métis of Red River and other areas of the Northwest testified to the earlier influence of France in the fur trade.

Although it had been well over a century since the Acadian deportation (1755–1762) and the conquest of Quebec (1759–1760), the historical memory of the bitter conflict between Great Britain and France for ascendancy in North America was still very much alive. The creation of the Dominion of Canada in no way erased the francophone nationalism that was fast emerging in differing forms in Quebec and the Maritimes and was an important component of Métis identity in Rupert's Land.

British immigrants began settling the eastern seaboard more than a century before Great Britain officially gained control of the French colonies in North America by the Treaty of Utrecht (1713) and the Treaty of Paris (1763). Between 1713 and 1867 about 1 500 000 British subjects migrated to British North America. Many of these immigrants eventually drifted to the United States, but enough stayed in the colonies to ensure a British majority in every province except Quebec by 1867. British heritage did not guarantee a common culture or even a strong allegiance to the British Empire. The English, Welsh, Scots, and Irish differed from one another in significant ways and were divided by internal conflicts. People who traced their origins to Great Britain's former Thirteen Colonies—arriving as Loyalists following the American Revolutionary War or as the pioneers along the leading edge of the North American settlement frontier—added yet another ingredient to the "English" culture.

People who traced their origins to the German-speaking states—German unification was achieved only in 1871—comprised the largest ethnic group in Canada other than British and French at the time of Confederation. Although most Germans were not recent immigrants, they retained their cultural identity in areas where their settlements were concentrated, such as Lunenburg County, Nova Scotia, and Waterloo County, Ontario. In Waterloo County, the town of Berlin had Lutheran, Mennonite, Evangelical, and Roman Catholic churches and German-language newspapers and schools to serve its citizens. The close relationship of the British monarchy to Germany assured the place of Germans in the Canadian mosaic, at least until 1914 when antagonism between Germany and Great Britain erupted in war.

During the American Civil War, the British North American colonies feared an invasion from the United States. To help defend the colony, African Americans living in Victoria on Vancouver Island formed the Victoria Pioneer Rifle Corps (also known at the time as Sir James Douglas' Coloured Regiment), which is shown here in the 1860s. SOURCE: BC ARCHIVES F-641

About 30 000 people of African descent lived in Canada in 1867. Before 1763, most of the Africans living in the French and British colonies were slaves or indentured servants. Following the American Revolution and the War of 1812, African-American slaves who had won their freedom by supporting the British cause moved to British North America. Slavery was abolished in Upper Canada in 1793 and ceased elsewhere in British North America early in the nineteenth century. In 1833, Great Britain passed legislation abolishing slavery throughout the British Empire to take effect on 1 August 1834, thereafter known as Emancipation Day. As a result of this ruling, African Americans seeking to escape from the United States, where slavery was finally fully abolished in 1865, often turned their sights northward.

In the wake of the 1858 gold rush, the West Coast became home to some 7000 Chinese, the majority of whom came from the gold fields of California. Most Chinese immigrants were men who worked as merchants,

prospectors, and servants, but a few women worked with their merchant husbands or made a living as prostitutes. When the gold fields were depleted, fewer than 2000 Chinese remained to form the basis of Canada's oldest Chinese community. The hostility of the white majority, a lack of work, and difficulty finding marriage partners encouraged many Chinese to return either to California or to their homeland.

While more than 90 percent of Canadians in 1867 traced their origins to France or Great Britain, most had never set foot in Europe. Fully 93 percent of the inhabitants of Quebec and Nova Scotia had been born in Canada. The percentages were lower in New Brunswick and Ontario—87 percent and 73 percent, respectively—but it was clear that Canada was no longer a preferred destination for immigrants. By the mid-nineteenth century, large numbers of Canadians were moving to the United States, where frontier lands and industrial employment offered attractive opportunities.

LIFE AND DEATH

With more than half of its citizens under the age of 21, Canada was a young nation in 1867. Fertility—the number of births per thousand women between ages 15 and 49—was high, especially in francophone families and rural areas of the country. In urban centres, there was evidence of a dramatic decline in family size that demographers call the "fertility transition." People began limiting the size of their families for reasons that seem to be linked to a lower death rate and the adoption of new values associated with industrialism. On average, women born in 1825 gave birth to 7.8 children. The figure dropped to 6.3 for women born in 1845. By the end of the century, the average was under four.

Ninety-five percent of Canadians in 1867 were married or would enter into a marriage relationship at some point in their lives. Community proscriptions against pre-marital sex were part of a rigid sexual code that also included harsh legal penalties against intimate relations between people of the same sex. There were no doubt networks of gays and lesbians—terms that did not exist to describe same-sex relationships in 1867—but the legal system forced homosexuals to keep their intimate lives secret.

Average life expectancy in early Victorian Canada was 40 years. One in five children died before their first birthday, primarily as a result of diseases spread by impure water and contaminated milk. Those who survived childhood and adolescence had an average life expectancy of close to 60 years. At any age, death was a distinct possibility, and no Canadian could be assured of a long life or robust health. Illness was an ever-present threat, and cures were often worse than the disease. Epidemics of cholera killed thousands in cities, and diseases such as tuberculosis, smallpox, and diphtheria were common. Although some municipal jurisdictions had taken steps to improve sanitation, urban water and sewer systems were rudimentary. Cities were dangerous places to live in 1867 and were becoming more so as industrial processes increased the incidence of air and water pollution and created a receptive environment for the spread of diseases.

THE INDUSTRIAL AGE

The leading cities in the new dominion owed their growth to the Industrial Revolution that was fast transforming the lives of all Canadians. The term *Industrial Revolution* refers to changes in technology, transportation, and the organization of production that swept the North Atlantic world in the nineteenth century. Strongly influenced by Great Britain, the world's leader in industrial development, British North Americans were quick to adopt new transportation and production processes. Steam-propelled machines, trains, and ocean-going vessels changed the ways that people performed their most basic activities and created the context that made Confederation possible.

With its pivotal location on the St Lawrence trading system, Montreal was Canada's leading industrial city in 1867. Factories built along the Lachine Canal benefited from nearby hydraulic power and an abundant supply of cheap labour, enabling them to establish a dominant position in a variety of consumer and heavy industries. Between 1851 and 1871, Toronto was transformed from a city of independent artisans to one where over 70 percent of the labour force worked in shops employing more than 30 people. Saint John, thriving on its shipbuilding, foundry, footwear, and clothing industries, was the

Toronto Rolling Mills in 1864, drawn by William Armstrong. The size and complexity of operations associated with railway development elicited much comment and symbolized Canada's entry into the industrial age. SOURCE: TORONTO PUBLIC LIBRARY, J. ROSS ROBERTSON COLLECTION T10914

industrial leader in the Maritimes. Other smaller urban centres also embarked on the road to industrialization.

Railroad companies were Canada's largest corporations in 1867. With their personnel departments, complex accounting systems, quality control procedures, and specialized division of labour, they were at the forefront of practices associated with industrialization. Every community in Canada longed for a railroad to bring capital investment, quicken the pace of travel, and put them on the map. Significantly, Maritimers made an intercolonial railroad link one of their few conditions for joining Confederation, and the promise of a railway, or of assuming the debt of one already in existence, clinched the negotiations with British Columbia and Prince Edward Island.

Industrialism not only revolutionized production; it also changed the way that people related to each other and to their work. In pre-industrial society, artisans had controlled their workplace, making a product from start to finish and determining their own standards and prices. Machines, in contrast, encouraged the division of labour into repetitive tasks and the centralization of production in factories owned by a few wealthy capitalists who could finance such expensive ventures. Under the factory system, labourers lost control of their work and often found it difficult to make a living wage. In 1867, only a tiny minority of workers belonged to unions (which were still illegal), but, whether unionized or not, wage earners were determined not to become slaves to their capitalist masters. On 10 June 1867, just three weeks before the first Confederation Day, more than 10 000 workers in Montreal took to the streets in a show of worker solidarity.

In addition to transforming how people made a living, the Industrial Revolution prompted changes in the political structures governing the colonies. The British Empire had been built on a policy of mercantilism that required the colonies to trade exclusively with the mother country. As the world's industrial leader, Great Britain could now dominate global markets without imposing formal trade regulations. In 1846, Britain adopted a policy of global free trade and began dismantling the old mercantile system. The introduction of free trade alarmed colonial producers who believed that their fortunes depended on privileged access to the British market. A few merchants, especially those tied to the timber and wheat trades, even advocated annexation to the United States in 1849 as the only solution to economic chaos.

Although the crisis passed, it produced three new strategies that would have a profound impact on the British North American colonies. First, Great Britain negotiated a free trade treaty with the United States as a means of relieving some of the economic distress experienced by the colonies. In effect from 1854 to 1866, the Reciprocity Treaty applied only to primary products such as fish, timber, minerals, and agricultural products, but it proved particularly valuable when these commodities were in high demand during the American Civil War. Second, changing economic policy was accompanied by political reform. Between 1848 and 1855, the British North American colonies with elected assemblies were granted a limited form of colonial self-rule known as "responsible government." Armed with their new powers, the colonies embarked on a third strategy to meet the challenges facing them: free trade among themselves and tariff protection against imports from the rest of the world. Following Confederation, protectionism would become the cornerstone of Canada's national policy.

RURAL LIFE AND PRIMARY PURSUITS

The Industrial Revolution transformed Canadian society, but it is important not to overestimate the degree of social change it caused before 1867. According to the 1871 census, 80 percent of Canadians lived in communities of fewer than 1000 inhabitants and more than half of the working adult population made a living by farming, fishing, lumbering, and trapping animals (compared to fewer than five percent by the beginning of the twenty-first century). While some areas of the nation had been farmed for more than 200 years, huge sections, especially in more remote regions, were still at the frontier stage.

The goal of owning a farm had been within reach of many British North Americans in the century before Confederation. In 1871, fully 85 percent of farmers in Ontario over the age of 50 owned land. Those who remained tenants on the estates of others, as was the case of the Irish immigrants who lived on Amherst Island in Lake Ontario, often did so because it was profitable.

As Canada's frontier province, Ontario was exceptional in the degree of opportunity it offered its citizens. People living in areas where settlement had proceeded earlier and often under less liberal regimes faced difficult choices. In Quebec, seigneurialism, a system of

VOICES FROM THE PAST
Women's Work on a Canadian Farm, 1867

In 1868, when 27-year-old Juliana Horatia Ewing, an accomplished writer of children's literature and the wife of a British officer stationed in Fredericton, was asked to provide advice on a woman's domestic responsibilities to friends in England who were planning to emigrate to Canada, she wrote the following:

> She must learn to make her own soap & candles if not to spin her own yarn. She must get her neighbours to tell her if she ought to have her house banked for the winter with sawdust to keep the frost from the cellar. She must keep a strong (metal if she can get it) saucer or pot of water on her stove if she feels giddy from the stove heat. She must keep her wood ashes to make soft soap . . . & be very, very careful as to where she stores them till the heat has gone out because of fire. Wood ashes & water make ley [*sic*] to scrub the floors with. Hard soap is made with lime & grease–so she must save her bits of fat. In the winter the children had better wear 2 pairs of socks & moccasins instead of boots. She can learn to make them herself I think. What I should especially advise them to take are good seeds for next year. At least in Fredericton vegetable seeds were got out from England and dear. In the short & hot summer vegetation is wonderful. Squash & cucumbers & vegetable marrows will rampage over the ground. Everything is luxuriant. I advise plenty of carrots & beetroots, things that will store in a frost proof cellar for winter consumption as one gets a little tired of the monotony of winter fare. She will have to pack butter & eggs in autumn for winter consumption . . . I used to grease my eggs all over with butter & pack them in coarse salt the narrow end downwards. Meat is frozen and keeps any length of time, & is "thawed out" for cooking. It is best to thaw it gradually. Tell her not to frighten herself with thoughts of a barbarian outlandish life. I have gone through all of that & it is a great mistake.[2]

landholding that predated the conquest, had been abolished in 1854 but had left a legacy of small farms and long-term debt to former seigneurs. Prince Edward Island was still struggling to rid itself of the system of proprietary land ownership that had been imposed on the colony in 1767. Despite a generation of efforts to solve the "land question," some 60 percent of the Island's farmers in 1861 were either tenants or squatters. Because of the importance of the timber trade to the New Brunswick economy, much of the land there remained locked up in crown leases. Nova Scotia's land frontier was entirely gone, and the physical extent of settlement, much of it on marginal agricultural land, was greater in the 1860s than it is today.

Carlton House on the North Saskatchewan River, shown here in 1871, was a favourite stopping point for fur traders making the long trek between the Red River Colony and Edmonton. SOURCE: GLENBOW ARCHIVES NA-1408-8

The speed with which Canadians were gobbling up resources was evident to even the casual observer. In most settled regions, wild animals no longer lived in sufficient quantities to make the fur trade profitable, while several species of birds, such as the great auk, had become extinct from over-exploitation. The buffalo that had sustained Natives on the Prairies for millennia were rapidly disappearing under the pressure of the intense demand for hides to make belts for power-transmission systems in factories. The stands of white pine, much in demand for the shipbuilding industry, were also dwindling. In 1867, Canadians relied almost entirely on wood for their fuel, with the result that there was little forested land remaining near major cities. Coal made up less than 10 percent of energy production and the petroleum industry was still in its infancy.

This photograph, taken in 1867 by Frederick Dally, shows a mule team and a freight wagon at the Great Bluff along the Thompson River in British Columbia. SOURCE: BRITISH COLUMBIA ARCHIVES A-350

By 1867, farmers living on the best agricultural lands had moved well beyond the subsistence stage, producing significant surpluses for markets at home and abroad. Stimulated by mechanization, new seeds and breeds, better methods of transportation, and expanding markets, commercial agriculture grew dramatically in the mid-nineteenth century. Ontario was Canada's breadbasket, producing 84 percent of the nation's wheat, much of it destined for export. Ontario farmers also produced livestock, butter, milk, and wool in exportable quantities. Quebec specialized in livestock, potatoes, and coarse grains, most of which was consumed locally. Surplus grains, potatoes, apples, and other foodstuffs from Maritime farms found markets in Newfoundland and the Caribbean. Such sales increased a family's disposable income without threatening its primary goal of producing for subsistence.

In areas where farming alone could not sustain a family, members combined a number of activities to ensure survival. Fathers and older sons often worked in the fisheries or the woods for part of the year, while adolescent children moved to the cities to find work and wages to supplement the family income. When these strategies failed, entire families moved to industrial towns to work in factories. The family-based labour practices of rural farm life often worked effectively in the unregulated urban landscapes of Victorian Canada. If the income of the head of the household was insufficient for a family's needs, one or more children were sent out to work and, if space was available, boarders were taken in.

By 1867, the fur trade was experiencing a period of transition. The Hudson's Bay Company dominated the industry, but its days as a privileged monopoly were numbered. Although the depletion of fur-bearing animals posed some difficulties for the company, its major problems were economic and political. Competition from free traders and the eagerness of visionaries to convert the great Northwest to an agricultural frontier meant that the company had to expand its range of activities. As a result, the company transformed itself from a monopoly into a competitive corporation with its eye on agricultural land speculation rather than the fur trade.

The riches beneath the vast Canadian terrain offered exciting prospects for a nation on the verge of an industrial boom. A gold rush on the West Coast beginning in 1858 had accelerated settler occupation of Native lands.

While the gold rush in British Columbia was running down by 1863, a smaller rush in Nova Scotia peaked in 1867. The expansion of coal mining in Nova Scotia was one of the success stories of the decade. Between 1858, when the General Mining Association's monopoly over Nova Scotia coal was abolished, and 1865, 14 new coal mines were opened in Cape Breton and more on the mainland. Nova Scotia was the mineral capital of Canada in 1867, with more than 3000 men and boys employed in coal mines and another 700 in the gold industry.

FAMILY AND COMMUNITY

In 1867, the family was the basic unit of Canadian society. Most families worked together to ensure the survival of each individual member, but families were more than economic entities: they were the context in which children learned gender roles, heard stories of their ancestors, received their earliest lessons on the meaning of life, and were taught their "place" in society. That place was largely determined by socially constructed categories such as class, ethnicity, and religion. While an individual might move from one class to another, change religious affiliation, or lie about ethnic origins, it was rarely done. Colour, gender, and age could not be changed, but they also played a major role in determining individual destiny.

No distinction in Canadian society was more fundamental than that between the sexes. Men and women contributed different skills to the family economy and were treated separately under the law. Upon marriage, all personal property belonging to a wife and any wages she earned were under the absolute control of her husband. Husband and wife were declared to be one under British common law, which prevailed outside Quebec. In common law jurisdictions, it was impossible for a wife to sign a contract, sue or be sued in her own name, or testify against her husband in most cases. Nor could a married woman engage in business separate from her husband without his consent. The husband also had complete control over the children of the marriage and had easier access to divorce than did his wife. The civil law system in Quebec was no better, and also reinforced the inequality between men and women.

The subordination of women was based on the pre-industrial ideal of a male-headed household in which women, children, apprentices, and servants were provided for and protected. In practice, this ideal meant that women were excluded from the boards of banks and railways, professional and skilled occupations, university education, and formal politics. Despite the changes taking place around them, women were told that they must continue to take the status of their husbands and inhabit the private sphere of the home. Women who avoided their roles as wives and mothers to stay in the paid labour force, or who espoused the doctrines of "woman's rights," were the objects of criticism and ridicule. So, too, were men who failed to maintain their wives in a domestic setting.

Racial prejudices were also a source of individual and institutional discrimination. Notwithstanding the great range in ability and wealth among Aboriginal, African, and Asian peoples, they were all, virtually without exception, treated shabbily by the white majority of Canadians. Rather than disappearing following the abolition of slavery, racism became more deeply entrenched. New scientific theories about the origins of species were quickly adapted to make claims about the superiority of the white "race." Such ideas in turn fed prejudices against racial intermarriage that fuelled segregationist tendencies. As a result, people of African and Asian descent were often segregated into separate schools and churches, excluded from skilled trades and professions, and confined to the outskirts of communities dominated by whites.

In 1867, Aboriginal peoples could still be seen in the towns and cities of Canada, but they were being pressured to move to reserves, out of the sight of white communities. Native peoples living on reserves were denied the vote, allegedly on the grounds that they were wards of the state. They were also often forced to endure religious schooling and, on many occasions, were subjected to physical and sexual abuse from the very people who professed to be helping them. Because of such treatment, many Natives living in Canada questioned the wisdom of adapting to the world taking shape around them.

Hereditary privileges that existed in Europe failed to take root in North America, but people in Canada still managed to sort themselves on the basis of class. Tight cliques of businessmen, professionals, and politicians dominated all aspects of public life. With the exception of Quebec, where the elite was partly francophone and Roman Catholic, most members of Canada's ruling class were white, English-speaking, Protestant men. These men, along with their wives, imposed their values on Canadian society to a degree out of proportion to their numbers and in direct proportion to their wealth—and they were destined to increase in power as the century advanced.

The middle class of farmers and artisans constituted the backbone of the nation, but there were wide variations in wealth and status in this occupational group. While many families lived close to subsistence on the margins of society, others were poised to expand their operations and join the ranks of the economic elite. Most of the "middling sort" faced pressures that would result in the erosion of their status. In retrospect, they would view the mid-nineteenth century as a golden age, before the factory system, corporate management practices, and commercial agriculture completely undermined their imagined independence.

In both town and country, a class of propertyless labourers survived by doing manual work, often on a seasonal basis. This class was expanding rapidly and was anything but uniform in its composition. For some Canadians, wage labour was only a stage in their life cycle—a chance to earn a little money before returning to the family farm or setting up in a business or profession. Others who joined the working class were destined to stay there for the rest of their lives, their status defined by the skills they could acquire and the occupational choices that came their way.

Wealth, like power, was unevenly distributed in the new nation. For example, 20 percent of the farmers in Ontario owned 60 percent of the land, while in cities such as Toronto the wealthiest 10 percent of householders held well over half of the assessed estate and personal wealth. Among the middle class, it was becoming increasingly fashionable to display one's wealth in fine homes. The Victorian parlour—crammed with furniture, knick-knacks, photographs, and paintings—became a popular site for conspicuous consumption and a source of much grumbling by the growing army of domestic servants whose job it was to dust the objects that cluttered the room.

COMMUNITY AND CULTURE

In 1867, Canadians were moving quickly toward new ways of defining their sense of community. Older ways, based on local identities, face-to-face relationships, oral communication, and a holistic sense of community, were gradually being replaced by literate societies where written documents bound people through commercial, religious, and political institutions across greater expanses of time and space. As railways, newspapers, the telegraph, and state institutions diminished distance and accelerated the pace of change, people were wrenched from their local contexts of kin and community. Many Canadians were illiterate, but everyone was aware of written texts, such as the Bible, calendars, constitutions, laws, and contracts, and understood their importance.

Formal education, with its emphasis on teaching the skills of reading, writing, and arithmetic, offered the key for improving one's prospects in life. By the mid-nineteenth century, 60 percent of children claimed at least a few years of schooling. Once seen as the responsibility of parents and left to the voluntary sector, schooling was becoming a state responsibility in most provinces. Under new education acts, taxes were assessed on all property holders to finance state-operated schools. This policy was considered such an invasion of privacy that there were violent protests against it in some communities.

Despite the goals of school reformers, the common schools—or "free" schools as they were sometimes called—were not equally accessible to all children and were certainly not uniform in their curriculum and administration. In Quebec, Roman Catholics ran their own schools and shared government grants with Protestant schools. The Newfoundland government also provided assistance to a school system that was developed entirely along denominational lines. While school attendance under the new system increased impressively, many children attended erratically and for only a few years. Most parents viewed their children as contributors to the family economy and took them out of school to work in the fields, factories, and households. In the 1860s, the policy of compulsory school attendance was still too controversial to force upon reluctant citizens.

Religion played a central role in defining identity in Canada. In the mid-nineteenth century, the growth in membership and power of Christian churches was a trend of major significance. Nearly every individual claimed to be a Christian, and those who did not were under intense pressure to become one. Not only were religious leaders reaching out to the unconverted both at home and abroad, they were also mounting campaigns to build new churches, establish universities, and support social services. Churches had a higher profile than the state in most communities and were pivotal to the spiritual, economic, social, and political life of the nation.

Cull's schoolhouse in West Garafraxa, Ontario, in 1867. Many communities in Victorian Canada boasted new one-room schoolhouses, built to the latest specifications of heat, light, and ventilation and staffed by teachers hired by the government. SOURCE: WELLINGTON COUNTY MUSEUM AND ARCHIVES PH6130

The energy displayed by the institutional church was in part fuelled by competition among the various denominations. At the time of Confederation, more than 40 percent of Canadians were Roman Catholic (see Table 1.2). They were a majority in Quebec and Rupert's Land, and formed a significant minority nearly everywhere else. Roman Catholics had participated in the political life of most of the colonies before it was possible to do so in Great Britain, where "Catholic Emancipation" was achieved only in 1829. The deep roots of French Roman Catholicism in British North America, combined with a

TABLE 1.2

Religious Affiliation in Canada, 1871

DENOMINATION	PERCENTAGE
Church of England	14.00
Baptist	6.80
Jewish	0.03
Lutheran	1.00
Roman Catholic	43.00
Congregationalist	0.60
Methodist	16.30
Presbyterian	16.20
Other	2.07

Source: Census of Canada, 1871 (Statistics Canada)

reinvigorated papacy in Rome and the arrival of a large number of Irish Roman Catholics in the colonies, virtually guaranteed a growing rivalry with Protestants.

By the mid-nineteenth century, the Roman Catholic Church was asserting its authority everywhere, but especially in Quebec. Papal enthusiasts resisted the separation of church and state, maintained a tight control over social services and education, and intervened directly in political matters when secular authorities threatened their power. In social terms, the Roman Catholic Church touched the lives of its adherents at every level. The number of priests and nuns grew dramatically at mid-century, and church-sponsored institutions ran the gamut from day nurseries and orphanages to universities such as Laval in Quebec City.

At the time of Confederation, Ontario was the most Protestant province, with more than 80 percent of its population belonging to one of the Protestant denominations. There was little uniformity among Protestants except in their determined opposition to Roman Catholicism. By the mid-nineteenth century, the Church of England was rapidly losing ground to the Baptist, Methodist, and Presbyterian churches, whose evangelical message often had a greater appeal to ordinary folk. The diversity of religious beliefs in colonial society made separation of church and state and voluntary support for church organization the preferred option for the majority of Protestants.

Although Protestants subscribed to the voluntary principle in religious matters, it did not mean that they recoiled from political action. Protestant alliances came together during elections to ensure the defeat of Roman Catholic candidates, while organizations such as the Orange Order were devoted to the exclusion of Roman Catholics from all areas of public life. Initially organized by Irish Protestants, the Orange Order broadened its membership by offering assistance and camaraderie to anyone eager to fight papal influences. Violent clashes between Orange and Green (Irish Catholic) groups often accompanied parades marking important events in the history of Ireland, while a "mixed" marriage between a Protestant and a Roman Catholic might result in a noisy and even violent protest (known as a charivari) by disapproving neighbours.

Brute strength often outweighed notions of Christian charity in motivating individual behaviour in Victorian Canada, where political conflict, drunken brawls, and family violence were common. Many parents and teachers encouraged discipline in children by beating them, and social custom permitted husbands to use physical force to control their wives. Popular pastimes such as cockfighting, bear-baiting, wrestling, and fisticuffs carried violence into recreational activities. Along the waterfront in Quebec City's Lower Town and on Water Street in Halifax, drunkenness, prostitution, and violence were commonplace. While there were laws against fighting duels, upper-class men continued to challenge each other to physical contests to defend their honour against even the most trivial verbal slights.

By the time of Confederation, some people were raising the alarm about the ignorance and violence that characterized Canadian society. Middle-class reformers urged others to follow their lead in establishing "companionate" marriages, displaying good manners, and practising restraint in their public behaviour. In 1867, only a minority of Canadians were committed to such a degree of self-discipline, but as the middle class grew and gained power, demands for moderation and control became features of a set of "modern" values that would increasingly govern behaviour in Canada.

INTELLECTUAL REVOLUTIONS

The transformation sweeping Canada at the time of Confederation had an enormous impact on belief systems. As material wealth and technological innovation became the order of the day, people began to advance the view that human beings were essentially good and that worldly progress was a desirable end of human endeavours. This was in sharp contrast to the older Christian belief that humans were born in sin and that release from the pain of human existence came only in a heavenly afterlife. For those adopting the modern perspective, education and moral training were seen as key to creating a reformed society.

Middle-class reformers in the mid-nineteenth century turned their zeal on the poor, criminal, and insane. Once considered the world's unfortunate souls, less advantaged groups were now believed to be "curable." Reformers urged the establishment of Houses of Industry (where the poor

could be taught useful work habits), model prisons (where criminals could be reformed), and asylums (where the mentally ill could get remedial treatment). Like many other developments in this period, the reform impulse was documented by imposing buildings that testified to the public nature of the perceived solution to society's problems.

Concerned about the widespread consumption of alcoholic beverages, many reformers saw temperance as the single most effective solution to the complex problems facing a rapidly changing society. The Sons of Temperance was the largest temperance organization in 1867, with branches in every province. Not content to encourage individuals to discipline themselves in such matters as alcohol consumption, many temperance advocates urged the passage of laws prohibiting the manufacture and sale of liquor.

Nothing symbolized the progressive impulse of the Confederation period better than the promise and practice of science in Canada. Science stimulated industry, advanced civilization, filled hours of leisure time, and even, some believed, brought people closer to an understanding of God's purpose for the universe. By the 1860s, most Canadian universities had scientists on their faculties, and travelling lecturers could almost always guarantee a good audience if they spoke on a scientific subject. Practical inventions were the stock-in-trade of Canadians who, like their southern neighbours, were obsessed with finding better ways of doing things.

Most Canadians accepted new science as part of a larger movement toward a better society. In 1859, their complacency was shaken when British scientist Charles Darwin published *On the Origin of Species*. Darwin's view that all living things evolved from a single primitive form of life and had developed by a process of natural selection and survival of the fittest flew in the face of Christianity's human-centred view of creation and the notion of a God who, if not benevolent, was at least not deliberately cruel. Darwinism was hotly debated in intellectual circles, but did little to dampen religious enthusiasm or deflect the rage for reform.

In their quest for improvement, Canadians had laid the foundations for 17 universities by 1867. Most institutions of higher learning were sponsored by churches, and those claiming to be nondenominational, including Dalhousie, the University of New Brunswick, McGill, and the University of Toronto, often had close ties to one of the major churches. Open only to men, universities catered primarily to a small elite: about 1500 students attended Canadian universities in 1867. While law and medicine were taught in a few of the larger universities, the liberal arts—dominated by courses in Greek, Latin, and philosophy—was the most popular program of study.

In 1867, there was little that could be called a distinctive Canadian literary or artistic culture. Writers such as Susanna Moodie and Thomas Chandler Haliburton, who wrote humorous sketches of colonial life, had an international readership, but their British and American contemporaries such as Charles Dickens and Henry Wadsworth Longfellow were much more popular. While talented artists, including Paul Kane, Cornelius Krieghoff, and Joseph Legaré, produced scenes from colonial life, their craft was challenged by photography, a new technology that became

A snowshoeing party in Montreal in 1869–1870. Snowshoeing was one of the Aboriginal cultural practices appropriated by European elites in Canada and transformed into sport. This picture also illustrates a common photographic practice at the time: it was actually taken on a set in William Notman's studio. SOURCE: McCORD MUSEUM I-42976.1

practical and popular in the mid-nineteenth century. William Notman was Canada's most successful photographer at the time of Confederation. His studio in Montreal, founded in 1856, with branches throughout North America, provided the most enduring images of what mattered to Canadians.

In the Victorian era, organized sports, in which teams played by carefully prescribed rules and were encouraged to display good sportsmanship, became popular in Canada. Lacrosse and snowshoeing clubs, first organized in Montreal, had been inspired by the practices of Canada's Aboriginal peoples. By the 1860s, these activities were giving way to European leisure pursuits—cricket, curling, racing, rowing, skating, and yachting. Although a form of ice hockey was played in a few places before 1867, it was not the popular sport it would later become.

Other than by word of mouth, people received their information largely from newspapers. In 1867, 380 newspapers were published in British North America, one for every 10 000 people. Most newspapers appeared once or twice weekly and consisted of four pages crammed with editorials, shipping information, local items, serialized novels, advertisements, and news of the wider world. With the successful laying of the Atlantic cable in 1866, news from Europe was suddenly available in a few minutes rather than a week or two. Newspapers were sustained by political parties or religious denominations and by their subscribers, not by advertisements. As the purveyors of "knowledge," Canada's newspaper editors—men such as George Brown, Thomas D'Arcy McGee, and Joseph Howe—wielded considerable political power, and their high profiles often led them to careers in politics.

POLITICAL CHANGE

Political values in Victorian Canada reflected developments in the wider North Atlantic world. In Europe, the old order, in which power was concentrated in the hands of a small hereditary elite bolstered by a state-supported church and a standing army, was crumbling. The growing middle class demanded that power be shared by all men with a stake in society through elected representatives, rather than monopolized by appointed officials. These contrasting ways of organizing power, labelled "conservative" and "liberal," were challenged by a few people who argued that every man—and even every woman—should be given an equal political voice, and that equality of condition, not just equality of opportunity, should be the goal of public policy. Although such doctrines, labelled "radical" or "socialist," were quickly dismissed by the colonial elite, they developed a larger following as the Industrial Revolution gained ground.

The struggle between conservatives and liberals dominated colonial legislatures in British North America for the first half of the nineteenth century. Although there had been bloody rebellions in Upper and Lower Canada in 1837 and 1838, the transition to responsible government was a relatively peaceful affair. Political parties became the vehicle for choosing candidates to stand for election, and in most colonies they assumed the names of the theoretical positions they espoused: Conservative (Tory) and Liberal (Reform). In Quebec, these parties were often known by their colours: Bleu (conservative) and Rouge (liberal). In 1867, the federal Conservative Party, inspired less by liberal doctrines than by its ambition to undermine the opposition, sported the name Liberal–Conservative Party, one which it continued to use on official documents until the 1920s.

Following prevailing Vatican doctrine, the Roman Catholic Church in Quebec remained adamantly opposed to liberalism. It subscribed to the belief that the pope was infallible, proscribed controversial books listed on the papal Index, and excommunicated Catholics who became members of the liberal-inspired Institut canadien. Church leaders such as Ignace Bourget, Bishop of Montreal between 1850 and 1885, espoused the doctrine of ultramontanism, which sought to establish the supremacy of church dictates over political issues. Ultramontanes, for example, insisted on the church's right to control education. At election time, members of the Roman Catholic hierarchy usually threw their considerable weight behind Conservative candidates who, in their view, represented the best defence against liberalism.

Even outside the Roman Catholic hierarchy, there was only qualified support for liberalism in Canada. It might be acceptable to support public schools, provide government funding to railway companies, and dismantle proprietary property relations, but few were willing to take the notion of equality before the law too far. Colonial politicians toyed with the idea of adopting universal manhood suffrage, but fell back on property and rental qualifications as the basis for political citizenship. No public figure suggested that women should be granted suffrage. When elections were called for the Canadian parliament in 1867, only about 20 percent of the population was eligible to vote.

The blending of a liberal economic regime with a conservative social order was particularly evident in the way colonial politicians approached legal reform. In an effort to embrace the opportunities of the industrial age, new laws relating to contract, debt, and bankruptcy were adopted in most colonies before 1867. The acceptance of liberal principles in family law took much longer to achieve. Legal reform was particularly complicated in Quebec, where a new civil code (1866) and code of civil procedure (1867) introduced liberal thinking with respect to commercial relations, but maintained a more conservative approach to laws relating to family, marriage, inheritance, and the legal position of women.

The Confederation movement itself was inspired by a new idea—nationalism—that was modified to accommodate particular Canadian circumstances. In Europe, national independence became the goal of peoples who could point to a common cultural identity, often linguistic or religious. Nationalism was unleashed during the American and French Revolutions and quickly took hold in Latin America and Europe. In the mid-nineteenth century, British North Americans watched with growing interest the movements to unify the German and Italian states and efforts by Irish patriots to liberate Ireland from its hated union with Great Britain.

Many British North Americans saw nationalism as something that could spur the colonies to greater achievements, but nationalist sentiment posed problems in a society where culture divided rather than united its people. French Canadians, whose common language, religion, and history provided the basis for a separate national identity, were particularly leery of romantic talk about a larger British North American cultural identity. Safer ground for the new nationalism was the economic potential of the northern half of the continent, which stirred the hearts and imaginations of both the romantic idealist and the practical businessman. In the late 1850s, with the discovery of gold in British Columbia and scientific studies proclaiming the agricultural potential of the Prairies, the possibility of creating a transcontinental nation rivalling the United States suddenly seemed more than a pipe dream.

BIOGRAPHY

Thomas D'Arcy McGee

One of the most eloquent advocates of Canadian nationalism was Thomas D'Arcy McGee. A native of Ireland and a participant in the Irish rebellion of 1848, McGee moved to the United States and finally settled in Montreal in 1857. As editor of *New Era*, a newspaper that catered to the growing Irish community in Montreal, McGee quickly gained a high profile and was elected to the assembly of the Province of Canada. Rejecting the militant practices of his youth, he supported a new "northern nationality" for the British North American colonies within the larger imperial context.

For McGee, a moderate nationalism based on economic progress offered an alternative to the ethnic and sectional conflicts that he felt impeded the progress of the colonies, just as they had blunted the potential of his beloved Ireland. In a speech delivered to the assembly on 2 May 1860, McGee captured the enthusiasm that westward expansion and economic development inspired in many British North Americans:

> I look to the future of my adopted country with hope, though not without anxiety; I see in the not remote distance one nationality bound, like the shield of Achilles, by the blue rim of Ocean. I see it quartered into many communities, each disposing of its internal affairs, but all bound together by free institutions, free intercourse, and free commerce; I see within the round of that shield the peaks of the Western mountains and the crests of the eastern waves—the winding Assiniboine, the five-fold lakes, the St. Lawrence, the Ottawa, the Saguenay, the St. John, and the Basin of Minas—by all these flowing waters, in all the valleys they fertilize, in all the cities they visit on their courses, I see a generation of industrious, contented moral men, free in name and in fact—men capable of maintaining, in peace and in war, a Constitution worthy of such a Country.[3]

McGee's views were highly unpopular among militant Irish nationalists, who in the 1850s banded together to form the Irish Republican Brotherhood and Clan-na-Gael, popularly known as the Fenians. With supporters on both sides of the Atlantic, their goal was to lift the yoke of British oppression and secure independence for Ireland by any means possible—including violence. They were opposed to any plan whereby the British North American colonies willingly chose to remain part of the British Empire, and are believed to have been responsible for McGee's assassination in 1868.

Funeral procession of Thomas D'Arcy McGee in Montreal in 1868.
SOURCE: LIBRARY AND ARCHIVES CANADA C-84323

THE ROAD TO CONFEDERATION

Confederation was achieved relatively easily and without the violence and bloodshed typical of many national movements elsewhere. As with most successful undertakings, the context was critical to the final outcome. The revolution in imperial policy signalled by the adoption of free trade and the granting of responsible government was an important prerequisite. So, too, were the rapid advances in communication and transportation made possible by telegraph and the railroad. The Civil War in the United States (1861–1865) and its troubled aftermath added an air of urgency to constitutional discussions. Despite fierce provincial loyalties and long-held cultural identities, the fact that most people in 1867 had been born in British North America helped to make them more receptive to notions of homegrown nationalism.

Leadership, it could be argued, was also essential to the outcome of the Confederation movement. Both at centre stage and behind the scenes during the negotiations was a purposeful group of businessmen and politicians, many of them in the Province of Canada, who were determined to make their vision a reality. With a generation of experience behind them in colonial administration and capitalist development, they drew up the Confederation agreement, manoeuvred it through colonial and imperial legislatures, and played a central role in defining the policies that governed the new nation through its early years of development.

The event that set the ball rolling early in 1864 was the collapse of yet another administration in the Province of Canada. Engineered by Great Britain in 1840, before the colonies had been granted responsible government, the union of Upper and Lower Canada had been designed to solve the problems of ethnic antagonism, economic stagnation, and political conflict in the two colonies. It failed to produce the desired results. Instead, sectional politics became entrenched, with a predominantly Roman Catholic francophone population in Canada East (Lower Canada) aligned against a largely Protestant anglophone population in Canada West (Upper Canada).

Under the conditions laid down by the Act of Union, Canada East and Canada West had equal representation in the assembly. This situation became increasingly unacceptable to the rapidly growing population of Canada West. Policies favoured by one side were invariably imposed on the other, creating hard feelings on both sides. While Canada West tended to support public schools, ambitious economic programs, expansion of the militia, and a more democratic distribution of seats in the assembly, Canada East resisted such policies. By the late 1850s, the opposing parties in the assembly were so equally balanced that it became difficult to form a government. The resignation of another coalition government in March 1864 was the last in a long string of administrative failures that frustrated politicians and made capitalists uneasy about the investment potential of the colony.

By this time, too, the government of the Province of Canada was deeply in debt, much of it generated by the loan guarantees and massive subsidies given to the Grand Trunk Railway. Although the Grand Trunk linked the colony from Sarnia to Quebec City, it carried less traffic than was predicted, was badly administered, and threatened to take the government—and even some of the major banks in London—with it if it filed for bankruptcy. Investors in the Grand Trunk saw Confederation as the best way to recoup their failing fortunes. If the colonies united and expanded westward, the Grand Trunk could become a transcontinental railway carrying foodstuffs from a new agricultural frontier and products from Asia to markets in Great Britain. With this vision before them, some of the Grand Trunk's British investors bought controlling interest in the Hudson's Bay Company in 1863, planning to link the Northwest to the eastern colonies once, and if, Confederation was achieved.

George Brown, leader of the Reformers in Canada West, took the initiative in calling for a legislative committee with representatives from all parties to find a solution to the constitutional impasse. The committee met in May and early June of 1864. Although Brown had initially sought a smaller federation encompassing only Canada East and Canada West, he was prepared to accept the majority view that a larger federation should be attempted. When the government collapsed on 14 June—the very day the committee brought down its report—Brown became part of the so-called Great Coalition, which included his long-time rivals John A. Macdonald and George-Étienne Cartier. Its sole purpose was to settle the constitutional difficulties in the Province of Canada. The first step in achieving this goal was to approach the Maritime colonies with a proposal for the union of British North America.

FORGING AN AGREEMENT

The political crisis in the Province of Canada coincided with discussions in the Maritimes on the topic of Maritime union. Primarily of interest to Nova Scotians and New Brunswickers who were riding high on their success in shipbuilding and international trade, Maritime union had become a fallback position when the Canadians abruptly withdrew from discussions relating to an intercolonial railway in 1862. Maritime union offered the prospects of creating a larger stage for local politicians and the weight necessary to get British investors to look favourably on their railway proposals. The ice-free ports of Halifax and Saint John stood to benefit from any railway project the union could mount, and the region's rich reserves of coal would fuel the engines that ran the trains and factories.

When the Canadians sent letters asking to be invited to a proposed Maritime union conference, they initiated a chain of events that led to three conferences: one in Charlottetown in September 1864, a second a month later in Quebec City, and a final one in London in the fall and winter of 1866–1867. Prince Edward Island and Newfoundland opted out of negotiations after the Quebec Conference, but the advocates of Confederation in the other self-governing colonies persevered. At the end of March 1867, the British North America Act (BNA Act) passed in the British parliament.

The Canadians who had signed the act all had different expectations about what the new federation would accomplish, and therein lay seeds of discord. While Ontario businessmen and farmers saw it as a chance to expand their markets and take a lead in developing the Prairies, leaders of church and state in Quebec saw it as an opportunity to create a province with a francophone and Roman Catholic majority. Even the skeptical Maritimers sometimes allowed themselves to imagine a future in which their ports bulged with the imports and exports of a great transcontinental nation. The BNA Act reflected these diverse interests and the power relationships that prevailed in the colonies in the 1860s.

The Confederation agreement was largely the handiwork of politicians from the Province of Canada. For them, the most important goal was to preserve the liberal principle of majority rule while satisfying the demands of the francophone minority. This was achieved through the creation of a federal system by which the powers of the state were divided between national and provincial administrations. Canada West and Canada East would each have provincial status, thus ending once and for all the indignities imposed by the Act of Union. To protect the Protestant minority in Canada East, the separate school system in place there was specifically guaranteed. Representation by population, with seats being weighted slightly in favour of rural ridings, would prevail in the House of Commons. Sectional equality was the proposed

The Fathers of Confederation, by Robert Harris. This is a copy of Harris's 1884 painting of the Quebec Conference. The original painting was destroyed in the fire of the Parliament Buildings in 1916. SOURCE: LIBRARY AND ARCHIVES CANADA C-1466

basis for appointments to the Senate: Ontario and Quebec were each allotted 24 seats, the same number that the Canadians were prepared to let the Maritimers divide among themselves.

The Canadians presented this blueprint for union at the Charlottetown Conference and hammered out the details in resolutions adopted at the October meetings in Quebec City. So determined were they to adhere as closely as possible to their principles that they even refused Prince Edward Island's request for an extra seat in the House of Commons. According to the formula developed for representation by population, PEI received only five seats, an awkward number to divide among its three constituencies. The delegates were also unwilling to find a solution to the Island's "land question." With little inducement, Prince Edward Island withdrew from the negotiations to enter Confederation. New-foundlanders were equally unimpressed by the propos-als presented by the Canadians, whose interests in military protection, railways, and westward expansion were far removed from the issues that dominated the Newfoundland economy.

There were also dissenting voices in Nova Scotia and New Brunswick. Anti-Confederates in the Mari-times noted, with some justification, that Confederation was a scheme of Canadian politicians and business inter-ests who regarded the proposed new nation as an exten-sion of the boundaries of the Province of Canada. By virtue of the concentration of over three-quarters of the colonial population within its territory, it would domi-nate the new federation. Moreover, anti-Confederates argued, the financial proposals in the Quebec Resolu-tions gave the provinces inadequate income to pay for the responsibilities assigned to them, such as schools, roads, and social services. All customs duties, the main source of government funds in the 1860s, would be absorbed into the federal coffers, while the provinces would be forced to manage on a per capita grant. The small population base in the Maritimes meant that their provincial administrations would have little money to work with. Although Maritimers desperately wanted to be connected to the other colonies by an intercolonial railway, they saw little benefit coming their way from a line to the Pacific, or indeed from an agricultural fron-tier on the distant Prairies. Many Acadians and Irish Roman Catholics in the region were suspicious, on

principle, of any union that reflected British models in Ireland, Scotland, and Wales.

In Quebec, too, there were strong anti-Confederate arguments, such as those voiced by Rouge leader Antoine-Aimé Dorion. He maintained that the federal government, with control over trade, foreign affairs, interprovincial railways, justice, and defence, and armed with the right to take on extraordinary powers in times of emergency, would dictate to the provinces. Under such an arrangement Quebec would have little control over its destiny. Eventually its culture would be eroded and its people assimilated into an anglophone Protestant state. The Rouges pressed for an election or a referendum on Confederation, but to no avail. Despite tensions among its leaders, the Great Coalition held together. The Bleu majority from Canada East joined Reformers and Con-servatives from Canada West to give the Confederation proposals a comfortable majority in the legislature in the winter of 1865.

The opposition to Confederation in the Maritimes was not so easily brushed aside. Early in 1865, Samuel Leonard Tilley (who went by the name of Leonard) called an election in New Brunswick on the Confederation issue and was soundly defeated by the Anti-Confederates led by A.J. Smith. Resistance to Confederation in Nova Scotia developed so quickly under Joseph Howe's leadership that Conservative premier Dr Charles Tupper decided against introducing the Quebec Resolutions in the assem-bly for fear that they would be rejected. Since Prince Edward Island and Newfoundland also showed little interest in Confederation, it looked as if the Maritimes were out of the picture entirely.

CONFEDERATION ACHIEVED

Pro-Confederation forces soon showed their hand. By 1865, the colonial office was fully behind Confederation as a vehicle for reducing imperial commitments in North America, and it instructed its representatives in the colonies to use their influence to see that the scheme succeeded. Lieutenant-Governor Arthur Gordon in New Brunswick, demonstrating that imperial pressure could still be exercised in a colony that had responsible government, forced the resignation of his recently elected government and called another election. At the polls,

Tilley's pro-Confederation party, which promised to negotiate substantial alterations to the Quebec Resolutions to make them more acceptable to the voters, won a resounding victory.

Gordon's influence was not the only factor determining the outcome of the 1866 election. With the Reciprocity Treaty due to come to an end in 1866, timber interests in New Brunswick sought alternative economic strategies. The Roman Catholic hierarchy, originally opposed to Confederation, was also coming around to a more positive view. For those who were still wavering, money supplied by the Canadians and their Grand Trunk allies helped the Confederation cause. Further drama was added to the contest when, in the days leading up to the election, an American wing of the Fenian Brotherhood launched raids on New Brunswick and Canada West from their bases in the United States. Although easily deflected, the attacks gave emphasis to the pro-Confederate position that defence could be better handled by a strong federal government for all the colonies.

The end of reciprocity, which threatened markets for coal, timber, potatoes, and fish, also put Nova Scotia in a vulnerable position. In 1866, the prospects were so bleak that a few Nova Scotians even argued that annexation to the United States was the only sensible course of action. Tupper saw his main chance and took it. Unable to convince his own party to support the hated Quebec Resolutions, he managed to get the Nova Scotia assembly to authorize further negotiations on union. Since neither the Nova Scotian voters nor their elected representatives gave their approval to the proposals that ultimately became the basis of the BNA Act, there was certain to be trouble ahead.

At the meetings in London, the Canadians were adamant that the Quebec Resolutions remain the basis of negotiations. Assurances were provided that the Intercolonial Railway would be built and that subsidies to provincial governments would be improved, but no substantial changes were made to the federal structure to meet the concerns of the Maritimers. The pressure from the Roman Catholic hierarchy for protection of tax-funded separate schools outside Quebec was handled by including guarantees to separate schools legally in existence at the time the act went into effect and by the possibility of appeal to the federal government for remedial

legislation should any provincial government attempt to threaten their funding privileges.

Federal and provincial powers were defined in the BNA Act of 1867. Section 91 enumerated a wide range of federal powers—running the gamut from trade and commerce to patents and copyright—that were, in the words of the act, deemed to be in the interest of the "Peace, Order and Good Government" of Canada as a whole. The list of responsibilities delegated to the provinces in section 92 of the act seemed modest when it was drawn up in 1867. In later years, with the expansion of matters of a "local or private Nature," such as municipal institutions, social services, and education, the provinces faced the challenge of finding money to pay for the responsibilities that fell to them under the BNA Act.

The finishing touches to the agreement included giving the new union a title, name, and rank. It was decided to refer to the union as a "confederation" rather than a "federation" on the grounds that the latter term implied a loose political arrangement that many of the architects of Confederation sought to avoid. Agreement was quickly reached that it should be called Canada. Although suggestions were made that Canada should be ranked as a kingdom or viceroyalty, it was finally decided that it should be a "dominion," a term drawn, at Tilley's suggestion, from a biblical reference in Psalm 72: "He shall have dominion also from sea to sea, and from the river unto the ends of the earth."

CONCLUSION

Divided by culture and geography, the British North American colonies in the 1860s seemed unlikely candidates for national greatness. While external pressures—changes in British colonial policy, fear of the United States, and the social chaos accompanying the Industrial Revolution—were powerful inducements to political experimentation, it was unclear whether Natives and newcomers, English and French, Roman Catholic and Protestant, East and West, rich and poor could come together to produce anything more than unending conflict. Finding unity in diversity was the major challenge facing Canada's political leaders as they set about to create a transcontinental nation out of Great Britain's scattered North American colonies.

NOTES

1. *Eastern Chronicle* (New Glasgow), 3 July 1867.

2. Juliana Horatia Ewing's Canadian Pictures, 1867–1869. (Copyright © 1985 Donna McDonald. Reprinted with permission of Dundurn Press, 1985) 44–45.

3. David A. Wilson, *Thomas D'Arcy McGee: Passion, Reason, and Politics, 1825–1857* (Montreal: McGill-Queen's University Press, 2008) and *Thomas D'Arcy McGee: The Extreme Moderate, 1857–1868* (Montreal: McGill-Queen's University Press, 2011).

SELECTED READING

This chapter summarizes the later chapters of *History of the Canadian Peoples*, volume 1, which can be consulted for more information and sources relating to British North America in the mid-nineteenth century.

For a comprehensive list of readings for topics covered in this chapter, please visit http://pearsoncanada.ca/conrad.

CHAPTER 2
NATION-BUILDING, 1867–1896

In his Speech from the Throne opening Canada's first parliamentary session on 7 November 1867, Governor General Lord Monck expressed his gratification at being able to assist "at every step taken in the creation of this great Confederation." He congratulated his listeners "on the Legislative sanction which has been given by the Imperial Parliament to the Act of Union," and which, in his view, "laid the foundations for a new Nationality that I trust and believe will, ere long, extend its bounds from the Atlantic to the Pacific."[1]

Monck's optimism proved justified, but much effort would be required to make Canada an integrated nation-state stretching from sea to sea. To provide leadership in this daunting task, the governor general called upon John A. Macdonald. If anyone could bring the scattered elements of the new nation together, it would be "John A.," whose ability to charm his opponents and sustain the faithful with well-placed patronage was legendary.

CONSOLIDATING THE UNION

Macdonald had hoped to govern indefinitely with the Liberal–Conservative coalition that championed Confederation, but these plans were dashed when George Brown resigned in 1865 over the handling of negotiations to renew the reciprocity treaty with the United States. While the remaining Reform ministers in the coalition continued to support Macdonald's leadership until Confederation was achieved, they would be uncertain allies in the House of Commons. The Bleus led by George-Étienne Cartier held firm; Leonard Tilley, the Liberal premier of New Brunswick, and Charles Tupper, Conservative premier of Nova Scotia, also agreed to bring their pro-Confederation forces into Macdonald's Liberal–Conservative party.

The regional, religious, and cultural issues that plagued the colonies before Confederation lingered. When Macdonald created his first cabinet, he was obliged to accommodate various interests—Protestant and Catholic, French and English, province and nation. He did well enough that the new ministry carried 108 of the 180 seats in the first election, but almost half of the popular vote went to candidates opposed to the Liberal–Conservatives. Opposition benches included George Brown's Reformers, A.A. Dorion's Rouges, and the Maritime anti-Confederationists. In time, they would form a coalition that would become the basis of the Liberal Party.

Construction on Parliament Hill, 1863. In 1859, a year after Ottawa had been chosen as the new capital of the Province of Canada, ground was broken on the banks of the Rideau River for a building to house the legislature. Construction was delayed by cost overruns, scandals, and technical problems so that the Parliament Buildings were still unfinished when they became home to the administration of the Dominion of Canada in 1867. It was not until 1876 that they were largely completed, having been expanded to meet the needs of a rapidly growing country. SOURCE: LIBRARY AND ARCHIVES CANADA C-773

BIOGRAPHY

John A. Macdonald

Born in 1815 in Glasgow, Scotland, John A. Macdonald immigrated to Upper Canada with his parents five years later. He attended school and studied law in Kingston, where he established his practice and became involved in various business ventures. In 1844, at age 29, he was elected to the assembly and quickly became a leading figure in the Conservative Party. He helped engineer an alliance with the French-Canadian bloc, and in 1856 emerged as co-premier of the Province of Canada. During the negotiations leading to Confederation, it was clear that he had exceptional leadership skills.

As the first prime minister of the Dominion of Canada, Macdonald proved himself a quick-witted and practical politician. He kept close control over his party and used patronage to legitimize Confederation among those who resisted its charms. An innovator and a builder rather than an ideologue, he believed that it was essential that Canada maintain British institutions in the face of American influences and was tenacious in pursuing this goal. His accommodation of Quebec was based on political necessity rather than any liberal notion of minority rights.

An alcoholic, Macdonald's periodic binges caused embarrassment for his family and colleagues. His drinking may also have contributed to the mismanagement of the railway negotiations that resulted in the Pacific Scandal and the defeat of his government in 1873. Nevertheless, Macdonald remained leader of the Conservative Party and led it to victory in 1878. Championing a national policy of industrialization, railway building, and western settlement, he remained in office until his death in May 1891.[2]

Sir John A. Macdonald in 1868, a year after Confederation and a year after he was knighted. SOURCE: LIBRARY AND ARCHIVES CANADA PA-25335

MORE TO THE STORY
Voting in the New Dominion

Elections in the Confederation era were quite different from those held today. Outside of New Brunswick, which adopted the secret ballot in 1855, voters openly announced the candidate of their choice, under the watchful eyes of relatives, employers, and party workers. Violence between supporters of opposing sides was common. Indeed, in the Quebec riding of Kamouraska, no member was elected in 1867 because of riots that made polling impossible.

The lack of a national franchise policy also caused difficulties. From 1867 to 1884, provincial election lists determined who could vote. Except in Nova Scotia, where voting occurred simultaneously in all constituencies, elections were conducted at different times across the country. In 1867, voting took place from late July to September in the 180 constituencies electing members to the first Canadian House of Commons. As government leader, Macdonald could ensure that elections were held in the easy ridings first so that momentum could be used to sway votes in the constituencies where government support was uncertain.

The number of people eligible to cast ballots was relatively small. All provinces limited the vote to men over 21 years of age who owned or rented property of a certain value. Status Indians, regarded as wards of the state, had no vote, and property qualifications disenfranchised most unskilled workers and farm labourers. As a result of gender, property, and age restrictions, only 15 percent of the Quebec population, for example, could vote in the provincial or federal elections in 1867, and only about 20 percent had this right by 1900. Today, by contrast, under universal suffrage for people over 18, almost 70 percent of the population can vote. Most of the disenfranchised are now either children or immigrants who have not yet fulfilled the requirements for citizenship.[3]

NOVA SCOTIA'S SECESSIONIST MOVEMENT

The election results highlighted regional divisions. Although the Liberal–Conservatives won handily in Ontario and Quebec, pro-Confederation candidates won barely half the seats in New Brunswick, while Tupper was the only government candidate elected in Nova Scotia. The Conservative government was also badly mauled in the elections to the Nova Scotia assembly. With such a clear indication of discontent in his native province, Joseph Howe felt that he had a mandate to transform his anti-Confederation campaign into a demand for secession. A Repeal League quickly took shape, and Howe was dispatched to London to seek permission to take Nova Scotia out of Confederation.

Maritimers believed that they had every reason to feel aggrieved: the Liberal–Conservative Party proved to be little more than the old Conservative–Bleu alliance of the Province of Canada writ large; the federal cabinet was dominated by politicians from Ontario and Quebec who held nine of the 13 ministerial positions; and the nation's capital, Ottawa, was run by public servants who had formerly served the Province of Canada. Moreover, when parliament opened on 8 November 1867, it endorsed policies that fuelled Nova Scotia's discontent, among them a rise in the tariff rate from 10 to 15 percent, an affront to Maritime shippers dependent on international trade.

In London, Howe's request for repeal of the union fell on deaf ears. Accepting defeat, he began negotiating with Ottawa for policies that would address Nova Scotia's grievances. Howe's willingness to compromise was due in part to growing militancy among his anti-Confederate supporters. Neither a populist nor a republican, Howe was repulsed by talk of popular revolt or annexation to the United States, which many Repealers now saw as their only alternatives to the hated union. Howe reasoned that it was better to make the best of a bad bargain than risk the possibility of severing ties with Great Britain, and even of bloody conflict.

At meetings held in Portland, Maine, over the winter of 1868–1869, Howe and Finance Minister John Rose hammered out "better terms" for Nova Scotia. The federal government agreed to pay an additional $1 million of Nova Scotia's debt and to increase the province's annual grant by $82 698 per year for 10 years to help it meet the shortfall resulting from the loss of customs revenue. In a rare gesture of conciliation, Howe and Hugh McDonald,

another anti-Confederate from Nova Scotia, were given seats in the cabinet. The strategy was only partly successful. Despite his high profile, Howe had difficulty winning his own seat in a by-election and proved unable to convince many anti-Confederates from Nova Scotia to support the Macdonald government. In an effort to blunt Maritime discontent, Howe and Tupper urged Macdonald to move quickly on the construction of the Intercolonial Railway and to press for a new reciprocity treaty with the United States. Although all regions of Canada lamented the end of free trade with the United States in 1866, Maritimers were particularly eager to restore American markets.

The negotiations between the United States and Great Britain to resolve difficulties resulting from the Civil War provided Macdonald with an opportunity to pressure the Americans to accept free trade. As a member of the British delegation that met with their American counterparts in Washington in 1871, he quickly discovered that a Republican-dominated Congress would stand firm against major tariff reforms. The Treaty of Washington granted free entry of Canadian fish into the United States, but offered no other trade concessions. The Americans, meanwhile, continued to enjoy access to Canada's inshore waters, agreeing only to provide financial compensation—the amount to be determined by arbitration—for the privilege.

There were cries of "sell-out" in Nova Scotia, and many Canadians felt that British negotiators had put imperial interests in securing good relations with the United States ahead of Canada's well-being. Still, much of the energy had gone out of Nova Scotia's fight, at least for the time being. In the 1872 election, two-thirds of Nova Scotia's Members of Parliament (MPs) supported Macdonald.

THE RED RIVER RESISTANCE

The Macdonald government moved swiftly to bring the Northwest into Confederation. By 1869, an agreement had been reached with the Hudson's Bay Company to sell its land claims for £300 000 (about $1.5 million) and a grant to the company of one-twentieth of the land most suitable for farming. This agreement proved lucrative for the financiers who had bought control of the company in 1863 at a price of about $7.5 million. They retained their fur-trading operations and eventually netted $120 million from land sales.

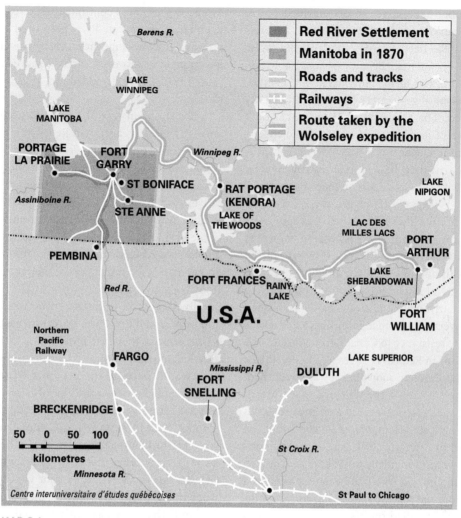

MAP 2.1
The Red River Settlement and the 1870 Wolseley Expedition

The Métis and Aboriginal peoples living in the Northwest were not included in these negotiations. Nor were they consulted when the federal government began to implement policies to integrate the region into the new nation. In August 1869, Ottawa sent land surveyors to the Red River colony to prepare for the influx of settlers expected when the official transfer of title occurred in December. Métis fears that they would lose possession of their unregistered land holdings seemed confirmed when the surveyors began measuring the land in square lots, ignoring the narrow river-lot system used by the Métis to mark off their property.

The behaviour of the Canadians living in the Red River area reinforced Métis anxieties. Unlike the fur traders, who were often paternalistic but rarely contemptuous toward Métis and Native peoples, the so-called "Canadian Party" regarded them as violent, uncivilized, and a major deterrent to European settlement. Canadians were a minority in the community—which according to the 1871 census, included 5757 French-speaking Métis, 4083 English-speaking people of mixed heritage, 1500 whites, and 558 Natives—but they had the ear of Ottawa. Many of them were land speculators who hoped to make their fortunes when Canada acquired the Northwest.

On 11 October 1869, a group of unarmed Métis stopped a road-building party from its work, angered that the contract had been awarded to an openly racist Canadian land speculator. Five days later, a Métis National Committee was formed to block Canada's takeover of Red River until guarantees for Métis land rights had been secured. The Métis chose 25-year-old Louis Riel, who had spent nearly 10 years in Catholic educational institutions in Quebec, as secretary to the committee. Literate and articulate, he was seen as someone who could negotiate with the Canadians on their own terms.

Meanwhile, William McDougall, the minister of Public Works in Macdonald's cabinet, had been appointed the first lieutenant-governor of what became known as the North-West Territories and travelled by way of the United States to his new job. When he attempted to enter the territory on 2 November, he was stopped by a group of armed Métis. Early in December, the Métis established a provisional government under John Bruce and Louis Riel to coordinate resistance to Canadian expansionism.

The Canadians in Red River attempted to overthrow the provisional government soon after it was established, but they were no match for the well-organized Métis. Sixty-five conspirators were captured and imprisoned in Fort Garry. Yet another attempt to seize control of the colony was foiled in February 1870. One of the militants captured in the second incident was Thomas Scott, an Orangeman from Ontario who had been employed as a road builder before the rebellion. Showing contempt for his Métis guards, he called on his fellow prisoners to

escape so they could continue their resistance to the provisional government. Riel, pressured by angry Métis guards bent on vengeance and by the challenge to his government's legitimacy, agreed to have Scott executed in March 1870. His death added fuel to sectarian fires across the country.

The situation was further complicated by the presence of American agents in Red River, who had expansionist goals of their own. Fearing that the United States would use the political crisis to seize control of the region, Macdonald reluctantly agreed to negotiate with representatives of the provisional government, led by Abbé N.J. Ritchot, who had the confidence not only of Riel but also of the Bishop of St Boniface, A.A. Taché. Church officials opposed the rebellion but supported the Métis land claims and demands for protection of the French language and Roman Catholic religion.

By May 1870, negotiations between the Canadian and provisional Red River governments concluded with an agreement that met most Métis demands: a small area encompassing the Red River colony and its environs would become the province of Manitoba; both English and French would be officially recognized in legislative and court proceedings; and denominational schools, both Protestant and Catholic, would be maintained. Unlike other provinces, Manitoba would have its land and other natural resources controlled by Ottawa. For the Métis, the major victory was the guarantee in the Manitoba Act that they would receive title for lands that they currently farmed and for an additional 1.4 million acres of farmland to be distributed to their children.

This victory proved hollow. Macdonald convinced British authorities to send a military expedition to Red River. Led by Colonel Garnet Wolseley, the army included in its ranks Ontario Orangemen who imposed a virtual reign of terror on the Métis. Riel fled to the United States, and other members of the provisional government went into hiding. In the wake of the army, white settlers poured into the province and received title for land, while the Métis were kept waiting for their grants. As immigrant hostility mounted, many Métis decided to move to territory that is now part of Saskatchewan, where they could establish communities under their own control.

Louis Riel (second row, centre) with his provisional government in 1870. SOURCE: LIBRARY AND ARCHIVES CANADA PA-12854

ABORIGINAL TREATIES

In an effort to avoid a similar confrontation with an estimated 34 000 Aboriginal people living on the Prairies, the Macdonald government negotiated seven treaties with them between 1871 and 1877. Natives agreed to the treaties because they wanted guarantees for their future well-being, which was threatened by the disappearance of the buffalo and the influx of settlers. Under the terms of the treaties, Natives were granted reserves where they could farm, and they were also promised implements, seed, and training to launch them in their agricultural endeavours. Treaties also recognized traditional hunting and fishing rights.

The government and Aboriginal peoples had diverging views of what treaties signified. In the government's view, a treaty meant a victory for Canadian imperialism: the signatures of the chiefs translated into surrender of all lands not set aside for reserves and acceptance of state control over the lives of those who lived on reserves. The expropriated land was then available for white settlers. By contrast, the Natives regarded treaties as agreements to share their lands with the newcomers in return for promises of aid. Negotiators for the government attempted to soothe their suspicions of white intentions by promising that European settlement would leave most of their hunting territories unscathed. What historian Arthur J. Ray calls "this duplicitous and very successful negotiating strategy" would later result in Native disillusionment, sometimes leading to acts of resistance, and later to court challenges.[4]

Given the discrepancies in their views of the purposes of treaties, misunderstandings inevitably developed. Indian commissioner Wemyss Simpson maintained that the Lower Fort Garry Treaty implied that implements and seed would be provided only when Natives had settled on reserves and built homes to demonstrate their readiness for an agricultural life. The distraught Lower Fort Garry Natives responded eloquently but with little impact: "We cannot tear down trees and build huts with our teeth, we cannot break the prairie with our hands, nor reap the harvest when we have grown it with our knives."[5]

THE INDIAN ACT

The political status of Native peoples on the Prairies was determined before the treaties were negotiated. Under the BNA Act, Aboriginal peoples throughout Canada were placed under the jurisdiction of the federal government. Those living on reserves in the eastern colonies were registered by the federal government, as were the "Treaty Indians" in the new areas acquired by Canada. In 1876, Ottawa consolidated its policies with respect to "Status Indians" in a comprehensive Indian Act. The act was revised periodically over the following century, but its basic premise—that Aboriginal peoples were still incapable of integrating into "civilized" society and therefore needed supervision in their economic, political, and social activities—remained unchanged.

The act made provision for replacing traditional political practices with elected band chiefs and councils, and subjected all reserve activities to the supervision of regional and national structures dominated by white bureaucrats. In defining Indian status, the act made gender distinctions: the wives and widows of registered men were declared Status Indians even if they had no Indian heritage, but an Aboriginal woman who married a white man lost her status as an Indian, as did her children. In later revisions to the act, Status Indians were denied the right to perform traditional religious practices or to drink alcohol. In theory, reserves were designed to isolate Aboriginal peoples so that they could learn European ways at their own pace and be introduced to white society when they were ready; in practice, reserves brought them together in closed political and social arrangements that made future integration highly unlikely.

As the provisions of the Indian treaties and Indian Act suggest, the government's priority in the Northwest was European settlement. In 1872, the Dominion Lands Act granted free homesteads of 160 acres to farmers who cleared 10 acres and built homes within three years of registering their intention to settle. In 1873, the North-West Mounted Police was established to maintain law and order in the Northwest. Although planning for the force was already in the works, its speedy approval by parliament was assured after the massacre of 22 Assiniboine in the Cypress Hills by American wolf hunters bent on avenging the alleged theft of horses. This atrocity emphasized the threat from Americans who coveted the lands claimed by Canada.

The North-West Mounted Police (NWMP) and its successors—the Royal North-West Mounted Police (1904) and the Royal Canadian Mounted Police (1920)—are often regarded as symbols of Canadian identity. For some observers, that identity is associated with British law and equal justice for all; for others, both the NWMP and the Canadian government that it served imposed an unjust social order.

In 2008, historian Walter Hildebrandt, summing up the evidence on both sides, concluded: "A careful examination of the acculturation process shows the police involved in both overt and subtle forms of cultural subjugation that reflected their belief in the superiority of the culture they represented and were to impose. They remained agents of the Anglo-Canadian hegemony over the West, often treating the local people as inferiors and sneering at their culture. This they did as much by ignoring the Native community as through overt acts of physical force."[6]

BRITISH COLUMBIA

Threats from the United States also stiffened Macdonald's resolve to negotiate the entry of British Columbia into Confederation. After the gold rush ended, both Vancouver Island and British Columbia faced growing deficits. The Colonial Office engineered their union in 1866, but, with combined debts of $1.3 million, the new colony of British Columbia was unable to initiate public projects. The jealousy between mainlanders and islanders further complicated the colony's politics. For two years, New Westminster and Victoria fought to be the capital before Victoria prevailed. By the 1870s, conditions were looking better. New economic activities had taken root in the colony, including coal mines in Nanaimo, sawmills along Alberni Canal and Burrard Inlet, a British naval base in Esquimalt, salmon canneries on the Fraser and Skeena rivers, and small agricultural settlements scattered through the colony.

The idea of Confederation had little appeal in British Columbia except among immigrants from the eastern colonies. They found the political system, which was dominated by appointed officials, oppressive and reasoned that Confederation would bring with it representative and responsible government. While a few business people in Victoria called for British Columbia to join the United States, the proposal was denounced by the dominant British interests in the colony, who supported continued membership in the Empire. In constructing their political visions, immigrants in British Columbia invariably excluded Aboriginal peoples who, if given the vote, could have controlled the elected institutions because they represented 80 percent of the population.

Amor de Cosmos in 1874. In 1852, William Smith left his job in a Halifax grocery business for the gold fields of California, where he changed his name to Amor de Cosmos, claiming that the name "tells what I love most . . . order, beauty, the world, the universe." Six years later, he moved to Victoria, where he established a newspaper—the *British Colonist*—and became involved in politics. A promoter of both responsible government and Confederation for British Columbia, he served as premier of the province from 1872 to 1874. He proved to be a poor politician and was defeated by the voters of Victoria in 1882 for advocating Canadian independence from Great Britain. SOURCE: LIBRARY AND ARCHIVES CANADA PA-25397

One of the major champions of Confederation was Amor de Cosmos, a colourful Victoria-based newspaper editor whose adopted name reflected his flamboyant style. In March 1867, de Cosmos countered annexationist proposals with a resolution in the Legislative Council that British Columbia be included as a province of Canada. Britain rejected the proposal at the time on the grounds that it was premature to incorporate the Pacific coast into the new federation before the Northwest had been acquired by Canada. Undaunted, de Cosmos and his allies established the Confederation League in 1868 to mobilize support for their cause. The Colonial Office sent Lieutenant-Governor Andrew Musgrave to British Columbia in 1869 to actively promote the union. The colony's Legislative Council established terms for British Columbia's entry into Confederation: a wagon road connecting New Westminster to Fort Garry, with a railroad to follow in due course; the assumption by Canada of British Columbia's existing debt; and an annual grant of $100 000.

During negotiations held in June 1870 with representatives from the Legislative Council, the Canadian delegation, led by George-Étienne Cartier, accepted the British Columbian conditions and even agreed to complete the railway within 10 years of British Columbia joining Confederation. These generous terms raised eyebrows in Ottawa. Given the colony's non-Aboriginal population of merely 10 500—8576 Europeans, 1548 Chinese, and 462 African-origin—the costs seemed to be excessive. Despite these concerns, the Macdonald government stood by the agreement. British Columbia would give Canada a Pacific Ocean boundary and fulfil the Confederation promise of a dominion from sea to sea.

Native peoples had no seat at the negotiating table. Under the terms of the Confederation agreement, the federal government assumed responsibility for "the Indians, and the trusteeship and management of the lands received for their use and benefit." Ottawa agreed to continue "a policy as liberal as that pursued by the British Columbia Government," and the province was required to release for reserves only "tracts of land of such extent that has hitherto been the practice of the British Columbia Government to appropriate for that purpose." As historical geographer Cole Harris has noted, this "dubious bargain" imposed a new constitutional rigidity on the province and resulted in ongoing federal–provincial conflict over the Native land question.[7]

Elections in November 1870 gave every seat in the British Columbia legislature to supporters of Confederation. In June 1871, British Columbia became the sixth province of Canada. Few people in British Columbia—and certainly not the disenfranchised Aboriginal peoples—felt much attachment to Canada. The economic stimulus of the proposed railway and Canadian government grants made Confederation seem a lucrative economic arrangement that should not be rejected.

PRINCE EDWARD ISLAND

Economic pressures also played a major role in bringing Prince Edward Island into Confederation in 1873. When the Conservatives under James Pope took office in 1870, the Island economy was stable, if not thriving. Its 94 021

people found export markets for the products of their farms and fisheries and, like other Maritimers, boasted a healthy shipbuilding industry. Only one thing seemed to be missing: railroads. An apostle of progress, Pope approved a costly line to link the Island's communities. Subsequently faced with huge public debt, Pope argued that only by joining Canada and letting that country assume the Island's debt could Islanders avoid financial disaster.

Again the Americans were on the scene. General Benjamin Butler of Massachusetts came to the Island in 1869 to negotiate a special trade deal, an apparent first step toward luring it into the American union. Although the American offers came to nothing, the Canadian government was spooked. Macdonald agreed not only to assume the railway debt and establish year-round communications between the Island and the mainland, but also to help buy out the remaining landlords so that tenants could become freeholders. With its interests thus addressed, Prince Edward Island became the seventh province of Canada in 1873.

NEWFOUNDLAND'S PERSPECTIVE

Unlike the other Atlantic colonies, Newfoundland faced neither an overwhelming debt nor intense British pressure to enter Confederation. The defence issue, which preoccupied leaders in the mainland colonies, inspired fears that the colony's young men would be conscripted to fight Canadian wars. Nevertheless, Conservative premier Frederick Carter supported Confederation. In the months preceding the 1869 election, he persuaded the assembly to pass draft terms for union, and negotiated an agreement with Canada.

Newfoundland voters were not persuaded. Led by merchant Charles Fox Bennett, anti-Confederationists won more than two-thirds of the legislative seats. Several generations would pass before Newfoundlanders debated the issue of Confederation again. In the 1880s, railway mania swept Newfoundland with the usual accompanying public debt. Although Canada again put out feelers, local politicians refused to touch the Confederation issue.

THE NORTH

In 1880, by an imperial order-in-council, the ͏ ͏ ͏ Archipelago was added to Canadian jurisdictic District of Franklin. This move was precipita

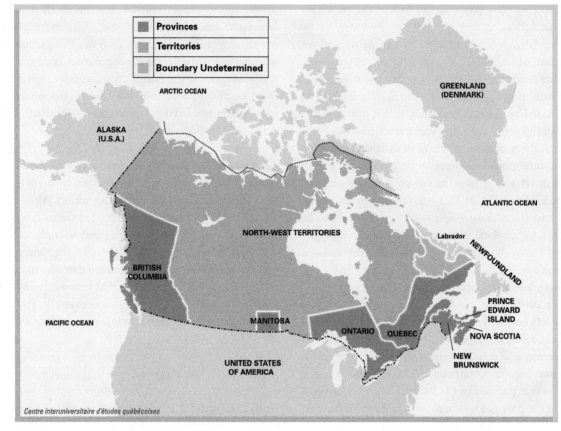

MAP 2.2

Canada in 1876. The map shows the new provinces and territories added to Canada between 1867 and 1873

American request in 1874 for mineral rights on Baffin Island. There was no thought of settling the region on the part of British or Canadian authorities. As one member of the Colonial Office remarked at the time, the main reason for turning the islands over to Canada was "to prevent the United States from claiming them, not from the likelihood of their being any value to Canada."[8]

CANADA FIRST

While economic imperatives drove the expansion of the Canadian state, it was viewed positively by idealists with a vision of a new nationality arising from the union of British North America. Thomas D'Arcy McGee was one of the most articulate proponents of national idealism and, following his assassination in 1868, a group calling itself Canada First formed to promote his vision. The leading Canada Firsters included Ottawa civil servant

and author Henry J. Morgan, Nova Scotia Coal Owners' Association lobbyist Robert Grant Haliburton, poet Charles Mair, militia officer and lawyer George Taylor Denison III, and lawyer W.A. Foster. They claimed as their mission the promotion of "national sentiment" worthy of a great transcontinental nation.

Canada Firsters presented Canada as a country peopled by robust northerners, disciplined by their efforts to survive in a harsh environment. In *Canadian Monthly and National Review* and *Nation*, two journals spawned by the expanding circle of Canada Firsters in the early 1870s, they expounded the notion of a new nationality based on a combination of race and geography. They took their cue from R.G. Haliburton, who in 1869 argued that the identifying feature of Canada "must ever be that it is a Northern country inhabited by the descendants of the Northern races." For Haliburton, the superiority of the "Northern races" was self-evident. "If climate has not had the effect of moulding races," he queried, "how is it that southern nations have almost invariably been inferior to and subjugated by the men of the north?"[9]

The place of French Canadians in the new nation was problematic. Although Haliburton and other Canada Firsters were willing in theory to include the "Norman French" among the Nordic elite, they failed in practice to demonstrate even this limited tolerance. Their bigoted attitudes toward French Canadians and complete contempt for Aboriginal peoples were fully exposed in their efforts to suppress the Red River Resistance. In Toronto, Denison threatened civil insurrection if Macdonald pardoned Riel and abandoned the West to the Métis. Mair, who had moved to the Red River Colony in 1869, was particularly outspoken, concluding that French Canadians were the principal "bar to progress, and to the extension of a great Anglo-Saxon Dominion across the continent."[10]

Racist and ethnocentric, Canada Firsters wanted white English Canadian values to prevail in the new dominion. Their movement was too narrowly based to be successful and, following the 1874 election, both the movement and the party it sponsored quickly collapsed. The views they expressed nevertheless continued to thrive.

THE PACIFIC SCANDAL

Macdonald's efforts to build a transcontinental nation did not win him widespread support in the 1872 election. Without the nine seats contributed by the new provinces of Manitoba and British Columbia, Macdonald would have had difficulty continuing to govern. Even Cartier lost his seat in Montreal East and only re-entered parliament through a by-election in Manitoba.

The biggest threat to Macdonald's government came from Ontario, where Alexander Mackenzie's Reformers—or Liberals, as they were increasingly called—revived criticisms of the Tories as corrupt spendthrifts and papist sympathizers. After the Red River uprising, sectarian issues intensified, and Ontario Liberals reminded Protestants that Macdonald had failed to bring the Métis murderers of Thomas Scott to justice. By contrast, opposition members from Quebec denounced Cartier for failing to settle Métis land claims or to win amnesty for Louis Riel.

Other issues surfaced during the campaign. Macdonald could not convince the United States to sign a new reciprocity agreement, a major item on the agenda of most primary producers. Nor, apparently, had his government determined

CONFEDERATION!
THE MUCH-FATHERED YOUNGSTER.

This 1876 spoof on Confederation is one of many drawn by one of Canada's great cartoonists, J.W. Bengough. Between 1873 and 1892, he produced the satirical weekly newspaper *Grip*, named for the raven in Charles Dickens's *Barnaby Rudge*. Born in Toronto in 1851, Bengough worked for the *Globe* before launching his own publication. The Pacific Scandal of 1873 gave him ample material for satire and launched him on a successful career as a newspaper editor, cartoonist, and public lecturer. SOURCE: LIBRARY AND ARCHIVES CANADA C-78676

who was to build the Pacific railway. Moreover, as a means of appealing to skilled workers, many of whom had sufficient property holdings to allow them to vote, Macdonald had legally recognized unions. George Brown, the éminence grise of the Ontario Liberals, was particularly outraged by this move, which put limits on the union-breaking tactics practised in his *Globe* newspaper offices.

Macdonald's desire to blunt growing opposition led him to engage in activities that ultimately led to the downfall of his government. In May 1871, the government introduced legislation to set the conditions for building a railway to the Pacific. The bill offered extensive cash and land incentives to the successful bidder. In the end, only two companies sought the lucrative contract. One was headed by Ontario Senator David Macpherson and included leaders of the Toronto business community. The other, led by Sir Hugh Allan, president of Allan Steamship Lines, represented Montreal business interests and had backing from the Northern Pacific Railway in the United States. Attempts by Macdonald to have these two Canadian groups merge, and keep the Americans out, proved futile.

Cartier was eager to see his city prevail in the contest with Toronto. Politically vulnerable, he also wanted to ensure a Liberal–Conservative Party victory at the polls in 1872. As the election approached, a beleaguered Cartier, suffering from Bright's disease that would take his life a year later, promised to do his utmost to deliver the contract to Allan in return for a major contribution to the party's election coffers.

In February 1873, the Macdonald government named Allan as president of the Canadian Pacific Railway Company. Two months later, Lucius Huntington, a Liberal MP from Quebec, rose in the House of Commons and charged that Allan had bought the charter with as much as $360 000 in donations to the Conservative Party. The Liberals apparently had a mole in the Conservative organization: incriminating letters and telegrams proved Cartier's corruption and left little doubt of Macdonald's. It was also revealed that behind Allan were American investors who would assume control of Canada's major railway company. Sensing that the government was doomed, many independents joined the Liberal opposition. On 5 November 1873, Macdonald resigned as prime minister.

Alexander Mackenzie in 1878, the year he lost power to Macdonald's resurgent Conservatives. SOURCE: LIBRARY AND ARCHIVES CANADA PA-26522

THE LIBERALS AT THE HELM

Governor General Lord Dufferin invited Alexander Mackenzie, member for Lanark, Ontario, to form a government. A Highland Scot, stonemason, and a Baptist, Mackenzie had left school at the age of 13 to contribute to the family economy. He was a teetotaller and had a tremendous capacity for hard work, but like many self-made men Mackenzie had little sympathy for anyone who was unable to succeed. He had taken the position of prime minister more out of duty than ambition after Edward Blake and A.-A. Dorion had turned it down. Mackenzie cobbled together a Liberal coalition out of Ontario Reformers, Quebec Rouges, moderate Liberals, and Maritimers of all political stripes disillusioned by Macdonald's government.

Hoping to use the Pacific Scandal to win a majority in support of his government, Mackenzie called an election for the winter of 1874. Macdonald, who remained Conservative leader, campaigned on a nationalist platform that emphasized the need for the Pacific railway to hold the Northwest and fulfil pledges to British Columbia. In keeping with the more cautious program favoured by his followers, Mackenzie focused on provincial rights and the need for economy, especially in extending grants to ambitious railway entrepreneurs. The Liberals won a majority of seats in every province except British Columbia, whose voters returned Conservatives in all six ridings.

Despite their strong mandate, the Liberals survived only one term in office. Canada was gripped in a worldwide recession in the 1870s, which meant less money for state initiatives. When the United States rejected the government's efforts to negotiate a reciprocity treaty, the Liberals had no economic strategy other than retrenchment. It inspired little enthusiasm. British Columbia threatened secession if Ottawa failed to build a railway within the time frame promised by their Confederation agreement, and Canadians continued to move to the United States to find work.

The Liberal interlude nevertheless left its mark on the new nation. In addition to introducing electoral reforms that included simultaneous voting, the secret ballot, and trial of disputed elections by the courts, the Liberals tried to enlarge the powers of Canada within the British Empire. This was the special goal of Edward Blake, who agreed to serve in a number of portfolios under Mackenzie's leadership. A brilliant but thin-skinned man, Blake had briefly associated himself with the Canada First movement, which tried to recruit him as leader of their short-lived political party, the Canadian National Association, founded in the wake of the Pacific Scandal. Although Blake rejected this overture, he remained sympathetic to their demand that Canada be given greater autonomy within the British Empire. As Mackenzie's minister of Justice, Blake extended the nation's powers to create admiralty courts, exercise authority over shipping on the Great Lakes, and pardon criminals. He also established the Supreme Court of Canada in 1875, but failed in his attempts to make it the final court of appeal, which remained the Judicial Committee of the Privy Council of Great Britain until 1949.

A Chinese work gang on the CPR in Glacier Park, BC, in 1889. In both Canada and the United States, railway companies employed Chinese labourers to do some of the most dangerous and back-breaking work. They were responsible for the jobs of tunnelling and handling explosives, which helps to account for the death of unknown hundreds of Chinese workers during the CPR construction process. In the words of the 1885 report of the Royal Commission on Chinese Immigration, they were "living machines" working for the benefit of the capitalists who employed them and the fragile nation that was bound together by iron rails. SOURCE: McCORD MUSEUM VIEW-2117

MACDONALD'S NATIONAL POLICY

It was widely conceded that the voters preferred Sir John A. drunk to Mackenzie sober, and the federal election of 1878 confirmed that verdict. Despite the Pacific Scandal and a weak performance in the House while the Liberals were in office, Macdonald's Conservatives won 142 of the 206 seats in the House of Commons and carried majorities in every province except New Brunswick.

During the campaign, Macdonald advocated a new national policy. Its centrepiece was the introduction of high tariffs to stimulate a strong manufacturing sector in the Canadian economy. To complement the tariff initiative,

Macdonald also supported the rapid completion of the Pacific railway and the promotion of population growth through immigration. Inspired by the slow economic climate of the 1870s, these policies would form the framework of national development under both Conservative and Liberal administrations until the First World War.

Following the election, the Macdonald government quickly implemented its ambitious program. In 1879, Finance Minister Tilley raised the tariff from 15 percent to levels ranging from 17.5 to 35 percent. Manufacturers welcomed a policy that they had long been promoting to fend off foreign competition. In 1880, the government approved a new Canadian Pacific Railway company. Headed by George Stephen, president of the Bank of Montreal, and Donald Smith, a major stakeholder in the Hudson's Bay Company, the company included American railway magnates Norman Kittson and James J. Hill. The CPR was from the outset a multinational enterprise with only about one-sixth of its stock held in Canada.

The Macdonald government offered the CPR syndicate generous support: $25 million in cash; 25 million acres of land (half of the land within 32 kilometres of the CPR's main line would be set aside until the company decided which parcels of land to claim); additional land for railway stations and road beds; 1100 kilometres of completed track built in the Mackenzie years; a 20-year monopoly on western rail traffic; exemption from tariffs on all materials required in railway construction; and a 20-year exemption for CPR properties from federal and provincial taxation and from taxation by municipalities not yet incorporated. More grants were required before the line was completed in 1885, and in 1888 the government guaranteed a $15 million bond issue in compensation for dropping the monopoly clause.

In the area of immigration, the Macdonald government was less successful. More than 900 000 immigrants arrived in Canada in the 1880s, but at least a million people left during the decade. The exodus from the Maritimes and Quebec to the United States caused alarm in both regions. Ontarians were most likely to take up the challenge of western settlement, but the numbers were modest. The Prairie population was about 400 000 by 1901, not the millions that optimists had predicted 20 years earlier.

TROUBLE IN THE NORTHWEST

Despite the relatively modest population growth, the old Northwest was entirely transformed during the period from 1870 to 1885. The disappearance of the buffalo, the signing of treaties, the building of the railway, the influx of white settlers, and the arrival of the federal government in the form of police, law courts, and legislatures were each occurrences of profound significance. Unfortunately, administrators in the Northwest and their political masters in Ottawa proved ill-equipped to handle the stresses that such rapid change produced.

Outside Manitoba, whose boundaries were extended in 1881, the Northwest remained under the jurisdiction of the federal government. The North-West Territories Act of 1875 determined that the area would be governed by an appointed council until such time as the population warranted the inclusion of elected officials. Since no provision was made

for responsible government, power was concentrated in the hands of the lieutenant-governor and his Ottawa advisers. The act guaranteed denominational schools and, by an amendment in 1877, French and English were made the official languages of the courts and council. The capital of the vast region was Battleford until 1882, when, with the arrival of the railway, it was moved to Regina.

The heavy hand of Ottawa was soon called into question. In 1879, the council, by then called the legislative assembly, resigned en masse, charging that Lieutenant-Governor Edgar Dewdney often ignored its advice. The federal government responded two years later by granting the assembly most powers held by provinces except the right to borrow money. Despite this concession, discontent continued to percolate.

Aboriginal peoples, who had no voice in the territorial government, were particularly discouraged. They experienced little acknowledgment of their needs, not even the promised government assistance to help them get established as farmers. In the early 1880s, Dewdney reduced government rations to destitute Natives as a cost-cutting measure. This policy was implemented in the early 1880s, just as the buffalo were disappearing from the Canadian Prairies—the last Canadian hunt occurred in 1879. The crisis facing the Aboriginal peoples was real: between 1880 and 1885, an estimated 3000 Natives in the Northwest died from starvation.

In desperation, some Natives stole cattle from settlers, provoking conflict with the NWMP. Cree chiefs such as Mistahimaskwa (Big Bear) and Pītikwahanapiwīyin (Poundmaker) played key roles in Aboriginal resistance. Big Bear had refused to sign Treaty 6 until starvation among his band forced his hand in 1882. In 1884, about 2000 Cree from several reserves gathered outside Battleford in an attempt to coordinate their efforts to bring pressure on the government. There was also growing discontent among the Métis living between the South and North Saskatchewan Rivers. While the Métis had accepted the need for a transition to a largely agricultural existence, they wanted the same support that white settlers received. Encouraged by the clergy, the Métis petitioned Ottawa for land, agricultural aid, schools, and a locally run police force.

When Ottawa ignored their petitions, the Métis decided in 1884 to invite Louis Riel to return to Canada from exile in the United States to lead his people. Initially, Riel attempted to pursue the peaceful route of pressuring the Macdonald government for concessions. This approach had the support of many white settlers in the region, who were growing impatient with their own treatment by Ottawa. Macdonald ignored Riel's petitions, with predictable results. On 18 March 1885, Riel proclaimed a provisional government and demanded that Ottawa grant the moderate demands outlined in a Bill of Rights. Riel still hoped for a peaceful settlement, but many Métis, including Riel's military adviser, Gabriel Dumont, felt that militant action was required.

Confrontations between Métis and NWMP at Batoche and Duck Lake resulted in more than 40 deaths and prompted the federal government to send a militia force under Major-General Frederick Middleton to the scene. Within two weeks, the first detachment of militia arrived on CPR trains. When word of the Métis rebellion reached Cree ears, the militants attacked the Hudson's Bay Company trading post at Frog Lake, killing a hated Indian agent and eight others. In another incident, two farming instructors regarded as hostile to Natives were murdered in the Battleford district. Riel withdrew his supporters to Batoche, where they held out against the army for six weeks before surrendering. At least 35 Natives and 53 non-Natives lost their lives in the confrontation. An all-white jury in Regina convicted Riel of treason and he was hanged in November 1885.

Aboriginal peoples paid dearly for their acts of resistance. Of 81 arrested, 44 were convicted. Eight of these were hanged, three were sentenced to life imprisonment, and many others were incarcerated for shorter periods. Even Big Bear and Poundmaker, who had tried to prevent violence, were sentenced to three-year prison terms on charges of felony-treason.

Following his capture in July 1885, illustrated in this photo, Big Bear was incarcerated in Stony Mountain penitentiary, north of Winnipeg. Like other prisoners, he had his hair cropped and was forced to do menial jobs. He was reported to have converted to Roman Catholicism while in prison. Released in 1887, he seemed broken in spirit and died within a year. SOURCE: LIBRARY AND ARCHIVES CANADA C-1873

BIOGRAPHY

Poundmaker (Pītikwahanapiwīyin)

Born around 1842, Poundmaker was the son of a Stony father and Métis mother of French and Cree descent. He was adopted by Crowfoot, chief of the Blackfoot, in 1873, and quickly rose to prominence. During the negotiations leading to Treaty 6 with the Canadian government, Poundmaker held out for better terms but ultimately signed the treaty on 23 August 1876. With the decline in the numbers of buffalo, he settled on a reserve near Battleford, Saskatchewan, and in 1881 was chosen to accompany Canada's governor general, the Marquis of Lorne, on a tour of the region.

In this address to his people on 1 January 1882, Poundmaker outlined the difficult situation facing the First Nations of the Plains:

> Next summer, or at the latest next fall, the railway will be close to us, and the whites will fill the country and they will dictate to us as they please. It is useless to dream that we can frighten them; that time has passed; our only resource is our work, our industry, our farms. The necessity of earning our bread by the sweat of our brows does not discourage me. There is only one thing that discourages me—what is it?—if we do not agree amongst ourselves; let us be like one man, and work will show quick, and there will be nothing too hard. Oh! Allow me to ask you all to love each other; that is not difficult. We have faced the bullets of our enemies more than once, and now we cannot hear a word from each other.[11]

During the Northwest Resistance, Poundmaker counselled restraint as his followers ransacked the abandoned village of Battleford and placed the fort under siege. He was also instrumental in preventing the warriors from pursuing Colonel William Dillon Otter's forces, who retreated under heavy fire after the bruising battle at Cut Knife Hill. Arrested and tried for treason in Regina, he told the court: "Everything I could do was done to stop the bloodshed. Had I wanted war, I would not be here now. I should be on the prairie. You did not catch me. I gave myself up. You have got me because I wanted justice." He was found guilty and sentenced to three years in prison. After serving less than a year in Stony Mountain Penitentiary near Winnipeg, he was released, broken in health and spirit. He died four months later in July 1886.[12]

The Surrender of Poundmaker to Major-General Middleton at Battleford in 1885, as depicted in an 1887 painting by Robert William Rutherford. SOURCE: LIBRARY AND ARCHIVES CANADA C-2769

THE LOST MÉTIS NATION

The Métis, whose sense of purpose was badly fractured in the years following the Northwest Resistance of 1885, fared little better than other Aboriginal peoples. Although they continued to demand lands as their Aboriginal right, the Métis met a brick wall of government indifference. They hunted, fished, and trapped in unsettled territories and moved on when white settlers arrived. Instead of the unified nation that the rebels of 1885 hoped to create, the Métis were dispersed across the Prairies in communities such as Green Lake, Saskatchewan, and Lac Ste Anne and Lac La Biche, Alberta. The Métis in Batoche finally won a land settlement in 1899–1900, receiving individual land grants rather than a reserve. Since farming required capital that the Métis lacked, many sold their lands.

In 1896, the Roman Catholic Church, spurred by the missionary Albert Lacombe, established a reserve, St Paul des Métis, 100 kilometres northeast of Edmonton. Promises of livestock and equipment failed to materialize, and it soon became clear that neither the church nor the federal government planned to invest much money in the enterprise. By 1908, most of the Métis farmers had moved away. For decades, the Métis remained a forgotten people, invisible even in the census until 1981 when, for the first time, "Métis" was recognized as an ethnic group.

VOICES FROM THE PAST
The "Bill of Rights," 1885

The Métis demands in the "Bill of Rights" suggest that Riel's program was neither separatist nor racist, as Canadian opponents of Riel charged at the time. While the concerns of the Métis were uppermost in Riel's mind, the "Bill of Rights" included calls for better treatment of all peoples in the North-West Territories. The following is a condensed version of the demands:

1. That the half-breeds of the North-West Territories be given grants similar to those accorded to the half-breeds of Manitoba by the Act of 1870.

2. That patents be issued to all half-breeds and white settlers who have fairly earned the right of possession to their farms; that the timber regulations be made more liberal; and that the settler be treated as having rights in the country.

3. That the provinces of Alberta and Saskatchewan be forthwith organized with legislatures of their own, so that the people may be no longer subject to the despotism of Lieutenant-Governor Dewdney; and, in the proposed new provincial legislatures, that the Métis shall have a fair and reasonable share of representation.

4. That the offices of trust throughout these provinces be given to residents of the country, as far as practicable, and that we denounce the appointment of disreputable outsiders and repudiate their authority.

5. That this region be administered for the benefit of the actual settler, and not for the advantage of the alien speculator; and that all lawful customs and usages which obtain among the Métis be respected.

6. That better provision be made for the Indians, the parliamentary grant to be increased, and lands set apart as an endowment for the establishment of hospitals and schools for the use of whites, half-breeds, and Indians, at such places as the provincial legislatures may determine.

7. That the Land Department of the Dominion Government be administered as far as practicable from Winnipeg, so that settlers may not be compelled, as heretofore to go to Ottawa for the settlement of questions in dispute between them and land commissioners.[13]

NEW BRUNSWICK SCHOOLS AND ACADIAN IDENTITY

Natives were not alone in questioning Macdonald's interpretation of Confederation. For francophones, Ottawa's handling of guarantees for French-language rights and denominational schools was disappointing. Both policies were resisted by provincial legislatures outside Quebec. Dominated by representatives of the English-speaking Protestant majority, the federal government also rejected pleas for legislation to protect francophone and Roman Catholic minorities throughout the country.

The first contest over denominational schools occurred in New Brunswick. The New Brunswick Common Schools Act of 1871 authorized municipalities to tax all ratepayers to support the public school system. The omission from the act of Roman Catholic schools, which had hitherto received public funding, though by convention rather than by law, was intentional. Regarding the law as unfair, Catholics in New Brunswick, who constituted one-third of the population, appealed to the courts. The legislation was declared valid, so they turned in vain to the federal government.

While most Catholic New Brunswickers vigorously opposed the school legislation, resistance was especially fierce among the province's Acadian population. They made up about half of provincial adherents to Roman Catholicism. Since only one Acadian child in six received any schooling, most Acadians balked at taxes to support any school, much less a school that excluded Catholic education.

Tensions came to a head in the village of Caraquet in January 1875, when violence erupted between Acadians and Anglo-Protestant police and volunteers. During the fracas, one volunteer and one Acadian were shot. The trial of nine Acadians for murder became a cause célèbre and forced the government to compromise. It dismissed charges against the accused Acadians, and permitted religious orders to teach Roman Catholics in areas where numbers warranted.

Confrontations over schools and language reflected the growing sense of political awareness among Acadians. By the time of Confederation, an Acadian sense of identity was

The Caraquet Riot of 1875 resulted in two deaths and encouraged leaders in church and government to compromise on the issue of school policy in New Brunswick. This engraving is from the *Canadian Illustrated News*. SOURCE: LIBRARY AND ARCHIVES CANADA C-62552

taking shape and their numbers, especially in New Brunswick, were growing rapidly. In 1880, Quebec's Société Saint-Jean-Baptiste invited all French-speaking communities in North America to send representatives to a "national congress" of French Canadians held at Quebec City. Acadians subsequently held their own congress at Collège Saint-Joseph in July 1881. More than 5000 people attended. In this and a subsequent congress in 1884 at Miscouche, Prince Edward Island, the Acadians chose a holiday, a flag, and a hymn to represent their sense of national purpose.

The emergence of a group identity and an expanding population base soon showed political results. In 1885, Macdonald appointed Pascal Poirier, a native of Shediac, as the first Acadian senator, and expanded Acadian representation in the provincial legislature in direct proportion to their growing numbers.

CONSERVATISM, ULTRAMONTANISM, AND NATIONALISM IN QUEBEC

In the years immediately following Confederation, Conservative politicians in Quebec could take comfort in the fact that Quebecers consistently supported them at both the provincial and the federal level. With the exception of the Mackenzie interlude in 1873–1878 and a very brief Liberal minority government led by Henri-Gustave Joly de Lotbinière in 1878–1879 (made possible only by the dubious intervention of Liberal lieutenant-governor Luc Letellier de Saint-Just), government in Quebec was dominated by the Conservative Party. The federal and provincial wings of the party collaborated extensively. Following the principle of double mandates (abolished in 1874), important Quebec Conservatives such as Cartier and Hector-Louis Langevin sat in both the House of Commons and the provincial legislature. Even the first premier of Quebec, Pierre-Joseph-Olivier Chauveau, was also a federal MP until 1873.

Liberal disorganization in Quebec helped solidify Conservative rule, as did support from the Roman Catholic Church. There were nonetheless challenges to Conservative dominance from Ultramontanes within the party who wanted to pull Quebec even more to the right. In 1871, the Ultramontanes published the *Programme catholique*, which called on voters to support Conservative candidates who acknowledged the pre-eminence of Roman Catholic doctrine in political matters, rather than more moderate, pragmatic candidates. After bitter fights, the more moderate wing finally won out, and the radical Ultramontanes quit the party in 1882.

Nationalist sentiment among francophone Quebecers remained strong, and all parties had to show themselves independent of Ottawa and of English, Protestant Canada. Nationalism surged in the 1880s, especially in the aftermath of Riel's hanging in 1885. Because the Métis rebels were primarily French-speaking Roman Catholics, Quebec nationalists, like Ontario Orangemen, took no account of the regional and Aboriginal concerns behind the uprising. Quebec Roman Catholics and nationalists saw Riel as a hero whose undoing proved that French-Canadian, Roman Catholic rights were trampled outside Quebec. After Riel's execution, an outpouring of grief and rage, including a demonstration in Montreal attended by more than 50 000 people, testified to the extent of French-Canadian alienation.

Building on francophone discontent, Honoré Mercier led the newly formed Parti national, which included Quebec's Liberals along with Conservative dissidents, to a provincial election victory in 1886. Mercier's success demonstrated the erosion of the political alliance between conservative politicians and the Roman Catholic Church that had prevailed in Quebec since the 1840s. By using the word *national* in the party name and portraying Quebec as French Canadians' motherland, Mercier also played to francophone sentiment in Quebec that they were a nation, even if it was submerged in the larger nation-state of Canada. Mercier was dismissed as premier in 1891 over a railroad scandal and the Conservatives returned to power provincially in 1892, but the heyday of Conservative domination in Quebec was over. They were definitively ousted from office by the reinvigorated Liberals in 1897.

ONTARIO FRANCOPHONES

French Canadians in Ontario, who numbered more than 100 000 by the 1880s, became hostages to the cultural bigotry spreading across the country. Although Ontario's denominational schools were protected by the constitution, French linguistic rights lacked similar guarantees. In the wake of the Northwest Resistance, the Ontario government limited hours of instruction in languages other than English. Local school boards initially often ignored this regulation, but Protestant anglophones were determined to impose conformity.

The Jesuit Estates Act of 1888 galvanized the anti-Roman Catholic forces of Ontario into more concerted action. When the Jesuits returned to Quebec in the 1840s, they demanded compensation for properties confiscated by Great Britain following the conquest of New France. The Quebec government invited Pope Leo XIII to arbitrate among the contending Roman Catholic claimants. Although the final settlement included funds for Protestant universities in Quebec, Protestant extremists in Ontario decried Vatican involvement in Canadian affairs and demanded that Quebec's Jesuit Estates Act be disallowed by the federal government. Only 13 MPs supported a motion for disallowance in the House of Commons, but anti-Catholic feelings continued to run high.

In June 1889, an Ontario-based group calling itself the Equal Rights Association (ERA) launched a campaign to rid the province and the nation of papal influences. D'Alton McCarthy, one of the Conservative Party's most able lieutenants, was a leading spokesman for the ERA. He urged the withdrawal of public funding for separate schools in Ontario, the abolition of language duality in the North-West Territories, and the assimilation of French Canadians. Eager to curry favour with its overwhelmingly English-speaking and Protestant electorate, the Liberal government of Ontario removed all French books from the authorized list of textbooks in 1889. Local school boards began to enforce the province's restrictions against French instruction. In short order, other jurisdictions also began to make changes to their educational policies.

THE MANITOBA SCHOOLS QUESTION

The Ontario approach to education was adopted in Manitoba, where extensive anglophone migration from Ontario had eliminated an earlier linguistic balance in the population. In 1890, Thomas Greenway's Liberal government, influenced by Ontario developments and the increasing dominance of anglophones in the province, eliminated official bilingualism and the separate schools system guaranteed by the Manitoba Act. Following Manitoba's lead, the North-West Territories in 1892 legislated an end to education in French after the third grade and removed French as an official language in legislative proceedings.

The Manitoba schools legislation quickly became a national issue. When the Judicial Committee of the Privy Council ruled that the federal government, under the provisions of the British North America Act, could pass remedial legislation to restore public funding for denominational schools, the Conservatives were torn between offering assistance to an aggrieved minority and defending education as an exclusively provincial matter. Macdonald died in 1891, leaving the decision to his successors.

EMPIRE ONTARIO

As the previous discussion suggests, the defence of provincial interests emerged as a major feature of the Canadian federal system. Macdonald favoured a strong federal state with the provinces as subordinate political entities.

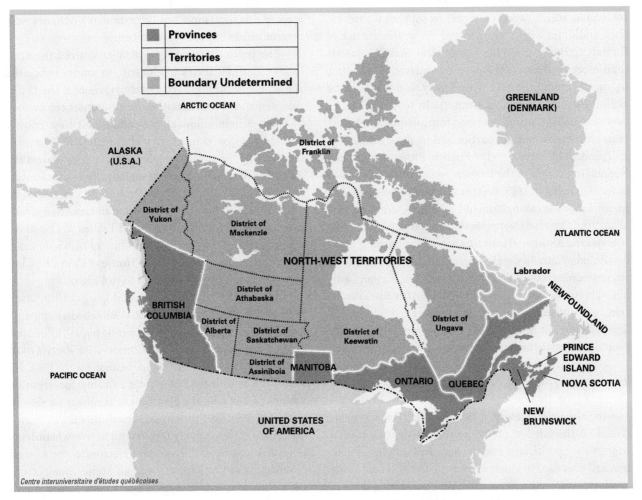

MAP 2.3

Canada in 1895. The map shows enlargement of Manitoba and the internal divisions of the North-West Territories

Instead, he was faced with ambitious principalities that claimed powers equal and even superior to those of the federal government in areas under their jurisdiction. Macdonald made extensive use of the power of disallowance, which enabled the federal government to set aside provincial legislation, but the provinces challenged his actions in the courts. Much to Macdonald's dismay, the Judicial Committee of the Privy Council of Great Britain often sustained the less centralized view of Confederation favoured by the provinces.

Oliver Mowat, Liberal premier of Ontario from 1872 to 1896, emerged as the undisputed champion of provincial rights. Mowat insisted that the British North America Act was an agreement among provinces and that the provinces retained the jurisdictions they had held before Confederation except for the specific responsibilities they had granted to the federal government. From this "provincial compact" point of view, there was no new "political nationality" formed in 1867. Such a reading of the constitution meant that the federal power to legislate for the "peace, order, and good government" of the nation should never intrude upon provincial jurisdiction in matters of a "local or private" nature.

Mowat believed that the federal government's frequent disallowances of provincial legislation amounted to unconstitutional interference in Ontario's sovereign areas of authority. He also resented Macdonald's favouritism toward provinces that supported Conservative administrations. When Macdonald attempted to have Ontario's boundaries restricted by placing territories north and west of Lake Superior in the province of Manitoba, Mowat challenged the decision in the courts and argued the case before the Privy Council in London. Only after several judicial decisions upholding Ontario's claim did Macdonald agree in 1889 to concede the boundary demanded by Ontario.

Macdonald's attempt to restrict Ontario's boundaries was motivated by more than his opposition to a Liberal premier. The discovery of rich mineral deposits in the disputed region, discovered while building the CPR, was a prize worth fighting for. Since Manitoba's public lands and natural resources were controlled by Ottawa—unlike those of Ontario—the federal government would benefit from a decision favouring Manitoba. Macdonald was no doubt also becoming uncomfortable with the growing wealth and population of Ontario, whose concerns increasingly dominated the national agenda.

THE PROVINCES IN REVOLT

The Ontario boundary dispute was in full swing when Quebec premier Honoré Mercier, who had a long list of grievances of his own against the federal government, suggested to the other premiers that they meet to discuss matters of common interest. Not surprisingly, Mowat was enthusiastic about the idea. In the Maritimes, provincial governments were also open to constitutional change. They were having difficulty managing on their federal subsidies and were alarmed by the impact of federal economic policies on their regional economies.

In May 1886, Liberal premier William S. Fielding introduced a resolution in the Nova Scotia legislature calling for repeal of the BNA Act and establishment of a Maritime union. The Liberal premier of New Brunswick, Andrew G. Blair, was not prepared to go that far, but he, like Fielding, was interested in cooperating with other premiers in a revision of the terms of Confederation. In Manitoba, economic growth encouraged plans for

Attendees of the first provincial premiers' conference in Quebec City in 1887. The premiers themselves are seated at the table: from left to right, Andrew George Blair (New Brunswick), Honoré Mercier (Quebec), Oliver Mowat (Ontario), William S. Fielding (Nova Scotia), and John Norquay (Manitoba). SOURCE: LIBRARY AND ARCHIVES CANADA C-11583

railways to the United States, but these were banned by the CPR's monopoly clause. John Norquay, Canada's first premier of Métis descent, was sued by the CPR and harassed by the federal government for his defiant approach to such matters. Although a Conservative, he, too, agreed to attend a conference of premiers.

Five of Canada's seven premiers—the Conservative premiers of Prince Edward Island and British Columbia stayed home—met in Quebec City in October 1887 to demand changes in federal–provincial relations and strengthening of provincial rights. The 22 resolutions passed by the premiers included calls for a million-dollar increase in subsidies to the provinces (which then stood at $3.2 million); the handing of the power of disallowance from the federal to the British government; provincial selection of half of all senators; provincial consent before local works could be placed under dominion control; and recognition of Ontario's boundary. Macdonald ignored the conference, accusing the four Liberal premiers of partisan mischief, but federal–provincial tensions would not disappear.

THE NORTH ATLANTIC TRIANGLE

The self-governing dominions and crown colonies in the British Empire accepted British primacy in the international arena and had little desire to establish foreign policy at odds with British interests. They also relied on British military force as the ultimate protection against foreign aggression. Nonetheless, Canada's leaders expected to be consulted by the British government on diplomatic initiatives that affected the new nation's interests. In the discussions leading to the Treaty of Washington in 1871 and on several occasions thereafter, Great Britain included Canadian representatives on its negotiating teams, but Canadians could never be certain that they would not be sacrificed to good international relations by British negotiators. Nor could Canadians necessarily rely on Great Britain for defence. Seeking to economize, the British army withdrew its garrisons from self-governing colonies in 1870–71, including the main Canadian garrison at Quebec City. This left only the naval bases at Halifax and Esquimalt. Canada thus had to tread carefully in its relations with its large, expansionist neighbour to the south.

Many of the problems between Canada and the United States revolved around fish. Fishing disputes grew out of the Anglo–American convention of 1818 that had excluded Americans from British North American inshore fisheries—defined as a three-mile limit from shore—and from access to the harbours, bays, and creeks of British North America except for shelter, repairs, and supplies of wood and water. During the periods in which the Reciprocity Treaty (1854–1866) and Treaty of Washington (1871–1883) prevailed, Americans had free access to the inshore fisheries.

When the terms of the Treaty of Washington came to an end, Americans showed little interest in coming to the bargaining table. As a result, Canada began enforcing measures to protect its fisheries. In 1886, nearly 700 vessels were boarded and some were seized for violations; the number doubled the following year. The Americans threatened to retaliate by cutting off all commercial relations with Canada if satisfactory redress for the seizures was not forthcoming.

In 1887, a British–American joint high commission was established to deal with the problem. Canada was invited by Great Britain to name a representative to the British delegation. Although Canada's delegate, Charles Tupper, was eager to secure Canadian access to the American market for fish and, if possible, a larger reciprocity agreement, he ran into a brick wall of American resistance. Even the limited arrangement negotiated by the British delegation, giving Canadians free access to the American market for fresh fish, was rejected by the American Senate. Americans paid a licence fee for access to Canadian ports, and Canadian fishermen were left high and dry.

Canada fared better with regard to its sealing industry in the North Pacific. After buying Alaska from the Russians in 1867, the Americans claimed exclusive rights to the Bering Sea. The United States leased sealing rights off the Pribilof Islands in the Bering Sea to the North American Commercial Company, which was enraged when British Columbia interests also began sealing in the region. The Americans charged that indiscriminate sealing was destroying the seal herd and seized Canadian vessels. Great Britain countered that the North American Commercial Company was the major perpetrator of the slaughter. In the face of a standoff, the two sides agreed to an arbitration panel, which met in Paris in 1893 and decided largely in Great Britain's favour. The slaughter of seals would continue, with all sides participating, until a moratorium on sealing in the Bering Sea was imposed in 1911.

CANADA IN QUESTION

Notwithstanding the protectionist sentiment in the United States, the Liberals, under their new leader Edward Blake, still clung to their free-trade agenda in the 1882 election. Macdonald, trumpeting the virtues of the National Policy, won handily. In Quebec, Blake's association with Protestantism and the strong support given by the Roman Catholic Church to the Conservatives resulted in the Liberals winning only seven of the province's 75 seats. Blake and Macdonald battled it out on the same issues in 1887 and again Macdonald won a majority. Since Blake had spoken against the hanging of Louis Riel, he had become more palatable to Quebec voters, and Quebec seats were split almost evenly between Liberals and Conservatives. With francophones now willing to vote for Liberals like Honoré Mercier, it was only a matter of time before the Liberal Party turned to Quebec to find a leader. Their choice was Wilfrid Laurier, who assumed leadership of the federal Liberal Party in June 1887. Over the next decade, he reshaped it into an election-winning machine, but first he had to deal with the free-trade issue.

The idea of closer trade relations with the United States was popular with many Liberal Party supporters. Among party radicals, there was even support for a commercial union, a policy that would harmonize the tariff structures of the two North American nations and open the border to trade in natural and manufactured products. Goldwin Smith, a British-born academic who had settled in Toronto in 1871, went further, arguing that annexation to the United States was the best option for Canada. In his book *Canada and the Canadian Question* (1891), Smith maintained that annexation would consolidate the peoples of North America into one progressive nation, enhance the global power of English-speaking peoples, and resolve, in one bold stroke, the nationalist issue in Quebec.

Although champions of the National Policy pointed out that a commercial union would compromise Canada's ability to determine its own economic policy, primary producers considered such concerns irrelevant. In 1887, the Conservatives tried to spike the Liberal guns by securing a limited trade agreement with the United States, but the Americans were moving in a more protectionist direction for reasons that had little to do with Canadian interests. When the United States introduced the McKinley Tariff Act in 1890, the latest in a series of tariff increases, Macdonald's hopes for a reciprocity treaty were completely dashed.

Opposition to reciprocity usually rested on economic arguments, but emotional issues also entered the debate. Among many Canadians, there was a lingering fear that overly close commercial ties with the United States would weaken economic and cultural relations with Great Britain. Even Canadians who were not of British origin recognized that the British connection and the institutions it represented were one of the main pillars of the Canadian identity. They argued that any policy threatening Canada's ties to the world's greatest empire should be avoided since British power and prestige gave

The Old Flag, The Old Policy, The Old Leader: a poster from Macdonald's 1891 electoral campaign. Brandishing a version of the Canadian Red Ensign, he is held aloft by the combined strength of agriculture and industry. SOURCE: LIBRARY AND ARCHIVES CANADA C-6536

Canada a higher international profile than its population and wealth warranted.

A scandal erupted during the 1891 election that seemed to confirm a conspiracy between members of the Liberal Party and American business interests to sever Canada's ties with Great Britain. The Conservative Party secured a copy of a private pamphlet written by Edward Farrer, editor of the *Globe*, which suggested ways of pressuring Canada into a union with its southern neighbour. The Conservatives used this seemingly clear evidence of treason to help them win the election, but they could not stop people from voting with their feet and moving to the United States.

In the 1891 election, Macdonald's last, the prime minister offered no new remedies for his divided country. The Conservative slogan—"The Old Flag, The Old Policy, The Old Leader"—said it all. The Liberals boldly declared their support for "unrestricted reciprocity." Such a position appealed to the radical wing of the party, but made many Canadians extremely nervous. It failed to deter francophones in Quebec who, for the first time since the Pacific Scandal, elected Liberals in a majority of their constituencies.

MORE TO THE STORY
Imperialist Enthusiasm

The rising tide of European imperialism at the end of the nineteenth century inevitably had an influence on Canada. When industrialized nations led by Great Britain and Germany began seizing control of the resources of Africa and Asia, definitions of Canadian nationhood became even more ethnocentric. As a result, the role of Canadians in supporting their "mother country" in their imperial enterprises created friction.

Many supporters of closer links between Canada and Great Britain ignored the exploitative character of imperialism, claiming that it was, at least potentially, a means of spreading the message of Christianity throughout the world. The Reverend George M. Grant, a Presbyterian clergyman from Nova Scotia, typified this brand of imperialism. Appointed principal of Queen's University in 1877, he remained in that post for more than two decades. Grant pressed for unity among Protestant churches and played a key role in the union of four previously independent Presbyterian denominations into the Presbyterian Church in Canada in 1875. The concepts of "Christian," "imperial," and "Canadian" unity were all part of the same organic whole for people like Grant, who believed that by helping to bring the spiritual and cultural benefits of Western civilization to "heathen" peoples around the world, Canadians were contributing to global progress.

During the 1880s, a groundswell of imperial sentiment swept across English Canada. This was encouraged in part by celebrations of the centenary of the Loyalist migration, but it also reflected a new enthusiasm in Great Britain for strengthening the bonds of an empire "on which the sun never set." In 1884, imperial enthusiasts in London established the Imperial Federation League and hosted a conference to celebrate Queen Victoria's Golden Jubilee in 1887. Thereafter, imperial conferences were held periodically and Canadians often played a leading role in these deliberations. Although imperialists disagreed among themselves about what form closer imperial ties should take, most discussions centred on a common imperial tariff, colonial representation in an imperial parliament, and cooperation in imperial defence.

Canada's most ardent imperial enthusiast was George Parkin. The self-styled "wandering evangelist of empire," he left his position as a teacher in Fredericton, New Brunswick, to become an employee of the Imperial Federation League. After taking his message of imperial unity to New Zealand and Australia in 1889, he settled in London for five years, where he continued to promote the imperialist cause. His book *Imperial Federation: The Problem of National Unity*, published in 1892, called for a single British imperial nation that would assume the burden of governing the world's "weak and alien races." It was a narrow-minded message, but it remained a significant element in Canada's political firmament.

In 1902, Parkin left his position as principal of Upper Canada College to become secretary of the scholarship trust established by Cecil Rhodes, a successful entrepreneur in South Africa. Rhodes had made provision in his will for young men throughout the empire to study at Oxford with the help of Rhodes scholarships.

THE TORIES IN TATTERS

When Sir John A. Macdonald died in June 1891, the Conservative Party fell into warring factions. John Sparrow Thompson (1845–1894), a highly respected Halifax lawyer, who had joined Macdonald's cabinet in 1885 as minister of Justice, was the most logical successor, but Thompson had a major strike against him. Raised a Methodist, he had converted to Roman Catholicism as an adult, and was passed over in 1891 in favour of John Abbott, who was a Protestant. Abbott had been a signatory to the Annexation Manifesto of 1849, but this indiscretion counted for less than his religious affiliation and the knowledge that Macdonald had considered him as the man most likely to hold the divided party together.

Never an enthusiastic politician, Abbott resigned in 1892 due to ill health. Thompson was finally accepted as the Conservative Party's leader, but his tenure as prime minister was also short-lived. In December 1893, at the age of 49, he died in Windsor Castle, a few hours after being sworn by Queen Victoria as a member of the Imperial Privy Council. He was succeeded by Mackenzie Bowell, an Orangeman from Montreal, who had a higher estimation of his own abilities than those around him did. On 4 January 1896, seven members of the cabinet resigned as a result of differing opinions on how to resolve the Manitoba Schools Question. Bowell was obliged to give way to the old war horse, Charles Tupper.

Under Tupper's leadership, the Conservative government introduced remedial legislation for the aggrieved Roman Catholic minority in Manitoba. It met stiff opposition in the House of Commons and became the focus of an election held in June 1896. Although the Conservatives won the popular vote, the Liberal landslide in Quebec gave Laurier a majority of seats. As the new prime minister, Laurier negotiated a compromise that conformed to the Liberal Party's support for provincial rights. The Manitoba legislation was allowed to stand in return for an agreement that permitted religious instruction and instruction in languages other than English where student numbers warranted such practices.

A HISTORIOGRAPHICAL DEBATE

The Métis Migrations

Following the Red River Resistance, between 1870 and 1885 about 40 percent of the Métis in the area moved farther west, either joining existing communities in the Northwest or founding new ones. The migrants, many of whom had figured among the rebels of 1869–70, also played key roles in the Northwest Resistance in 1885. Why did they move and why did they join in a second rebellion against Canadian authority?

For most historians before the 1970s, there was a simple answer: the Métis were "half-savages" with little interest in becoming part of the new agriculture-based European society that was emerging in Red River. They wanted to hunt, not farm, and moved to areas free of agricultural settlement. Disillusioned when their nomadic lifestyles again became threatened by settler society, they engaged in futile violence in 1885. From this perspective, the "pull" of a promised "primitive" life farther west explained the Métis migration.

In the 1980s, several historians suggested that "push" factors were more important than the lure of a pre-agricultural existence. Using archival evidence of government policy in this period, Douglas Sprague outlined the mistreatment of the Métis and the stalling tactics used by the federal government to deprive them of lands promised to them in 1870, to which both the federal and Manitoba governments turned a blind eye. This caused the Métis to give up in frustration and move farther west. As settlement and the railway again began to stretch into their new territories at the same time that the buffalo disappeared, the Métis demanded guarantees from Ottawa that they would not again be dispossessed. The government made a pretence of dealing with these demands, but its previous duplicity in Manitoba and continuing inaction in the North-West Territories provoked a violent Métis reaction.[14]

The dispossession thesis has been disputed by political scientist Thomas Flanagan and historian Gerhard Ens. Flanagan provided evidence to bolster the older view that the Métis did not want to farm. This, he argued, rather than government delays, official hostility, or mistreatment by European settlers, persuaded them to abandon or sell their land claims and move farther west. He also argued that delays in the Manitoba and Northwest land settlements resulted from disagreements and misunderstandings between the Métis and the federal government and not from deliberate stalling by the latter.[15]

Ens, meanwhile, suggested that a desire to participate in the flourishing trade of buffalo robes with American merchants informed the Métis decision to migrate. Ens used censuses of the population of older, established communities in Red River at different periods to demonstrate that the move west had begun before the rebellion, as hunters came to terms with declining numbers of buffalo in the Red River region. He inferred that many Métis, though once "peasants" content to eke out a living from hunting and small-scale farming, had become consumers on the European model, trading robes for consumer goods.[16]

In her study of the evolution of the Métis community of Batoche, Diane Payment took issue with Ens's suggestion that migrants to the territories were in search of buffalo robes and in retreat from a subsistence agriculture/hunting economy. Her research demonstrated that the Métis sought a settled, not a nomadic, life. They built stores, schools, and churches and started farms. Although they also hunted buffalo, the robe trade was only one of multiple strategies for making a living. Payment concluded that the "push" factors—the racism of the Manitoba settlers and the broken promises of governments regarding land—caused the Métis to migrate, since they established new communities much like those they had left behind.[17]

Payment also raised questions about the tendency of most historians of the Métis to leave gender out of the equation. Observing the important role of women in establishing institutions in Batoche, Payment argued that women's networks were central to the migration process and to community life. "The general resettlement pattern was organized according to extended family—grandparents, parents, brothers, sisters, cousins, and cross-cousins—but close analysis reveals a particularly strong female kinship tie."[18] Like many of the immigrants arriving on the Prairies, the Red River Métis moved because they were trying to escape oppression and were seeking a better future for their families.

In the late twentieth century, the debate about Métis migration patterns became entangled in Métis land claims. The Manitoba Métis Federation hired Sprague, who questioned some of Ens's findings, to make its case that the federal government has failed to fulfil its 1870 promises, while the federal Department of Justice contracted with both Flanagan and Ens to help prepare its case against the Métis claims.[19] In March 2013, the Supreme Court ruled in favour of the Métis, writing that "the Federal Crown failed to implement the land grant provision set out in s.31 of the Manitoba Act, 1870 in accordance with the honour of the Crown."[20]

CONCLUSION

Rounding out the borders of the Dominion of Canada proved to be the easy part of nation-building. Holding it together was more difficult. For many Canadians, the adjustment to new national policies as defined in the first three decades of Confederation brought only hardship and heartache. Aboriginal peoples and Métis experienced defeat and marginalization, while the outlying regions still wondered about their place in a Canadian firmament dominated by Ontario and Quebec. French Canadians also felt increasingly under attack, especially outside of Quebec. Throughout Canada, religious and cultural differences focusing on school and language policy made some people feel that imperial federation, annexation, or provincial independence were happier alternatives to being yoked in a federation where every national policy was ringed with compromise and bitterness. Perhaps most disappointing of all, the rapid economic growth that Canada's leaders sought proved elusive.

NOTES

1. Canada, *House of Commons Debates*, 1 November 1867, 5.

2. J.K. Johnson and P.B. Waite, "Sir John Alexander Macdonald," *Dictionary of Canadian Biography* http://www.biographi.ca.

3. Norman Ward, *The Canadian House of Commons: Representation* (Toronto: University of Toronto Press, 1963). See also Elections Canada, *A History of the Vote in Canada* http://www.elections.ca.

4. Arthur J. Ray, *I Have Lived Here Since the World Began: An Illustrated History of Canada's Native People* (Toronto: Key Porter, 2010) 214.

5. Quoted in Manitoba Indian Brotherhood, *Treaty Days: Centennial Commemorations Historical Pageant* (Winnipeg: Manitoba Indian Brotherhood, 1971) 24.

6. Walter Hildebrandt, *Views from Fort Battleford: Constructed Visions of an Anglo-Canadian West* (Edmonton: Athabasca University Press, 2008) 36.

7. Cole Harris, *Making Native Space: Colonialism, Resistance, and Reserves in British Columbia* (Vancouver: UBC Press, 2002) 73.

8. Cited in Shelagh D. Grant, *Sovereignty or Security: Government Policy in the Canadian North, 1936–1950* (Vancouver: UBC Press, 1988) 5.

9. Cited in Carl Berger, "The True North Strong and Free," in *Nationalism in Canada*, ed. Peter Russell (Toronto: McGraw-Hill, 1965) 6.

10. Cited in David P. Gagan, "The Relevance of Canada First," *Journal of Canadian Studies* 5 (1970) 38.

11. Cited in Don Gillmor, Achille Michaud, and Pierre Turgeon, *Canada: A People's History*, vol. 2 (Toronto: McClelland & Stewart, 2001) 19.

12. Hugh A. Dempsey, "Pitikwahanapiwiyin (Poundmaker)," *Dictionary of Canadian Biography* http://www.biographi.ca.

13. *Bill of Rights*, 13 April 1885, Provincial Archives of Alberta.

14. D.N. Sprague, *Canada and the Métis, 1869–1885* (Waterloo: Wilfrid Laurier University Press, 1988).

15. Thomas Flanagan, *Riel and the Rebellion: 1885 Reconsidered* (Saskatoon: Western Producer Prairie Books, 1983).

16. Gerhard J. Ens, *Homeland to Hinterland: The Changing Worlds of the Red River Métis in the Nineteenth Century* (Toronto: University of Toronto Press, 1996).

17. Diane Payment, *"The Free People—Otipemisiwak," Batoche, Saskatchewan, 1870–1930* (Ottawa: National Historic Parks and Sites, 1990).

18. Diane Payment, "'La Vie en Rose'? Métis Women at Batoche, 1870–1920," in *Women of the First Nations: Power, Wisdom and Strength*, eds. Christine Miller, Patricia Chuchryk, et al. (Winnipeg: University of Manitoba Press, 1996) 20. See also essays in Nicole St-Onge, Carolyn Podruchny, and Brenda Macdougall, eds., *Contours of a People: Metis Family, Mobility, and History* (Norman: University of Oklahoma Press, 2012).

19. D.N. Sprague, "Dispossession vs. Accommodation in Plaintiff vs. Defendant Accounts of Métis Dispersal from Manitoba, 1870–1881," *Prairie Forum* 16, 2 (Fall 1991) 137–56.

20. http://www.cbc.ca/news/politics/métis-celebrate-historic-supreme-court-land-ruling-1.1377827, accessed 24 April 2014.

SELECTED READING

Andersen, Chris. *"Métis": Race, Recognition, and the Struggle for Indigenous Peoplehood*. Vancouver: UBC Press, 2014

Armstrong, Christopher. *The Politics of Federalism: Ontario's Relations with the Federal Government, 1867–1942.* Toronto: University of Toronto Press, 1981

Berger, Carl. *The Sense of Power: Studies in the Ideas of Canadian Imperialism, 1867–1914.* Toronto: University of Toronto Press, 1970

Brown, Robert Craig. *Canada's National Policy, 1883–1900: A Study of American-Canadian Relations.* Princeton: Princeton University Press, 1964

Carter, Sarah. *Aboriginal People and Colonizers of Western Canada to 1900.* Toronto: University of Toronto Press, 1999

Curtis, Bruce. *The Politics of Population: State Formation, Statistics, and the Census of Canada, 1840–1875.* Toronto: University of Toronto Press, 2001

Darroch, Gordon and Lee Soltow. *Property and Inequality in Victorian Ontario: Structural Patterns and Cultural Communities in the 1871 Census.* Toronto: University of Toronto Press, 1994

Daschuk, James. *Clearing the Plains: Disease, Politics of Starvation, and the Loss of Aboriginal Life.* Regina: University of Regina Press, 2013

Gavigan, Shelley A.M. *Hunger, Horses, and Government Men: Criminal Law on the Aboriginal Plains.* Vancouver: UBC Press, 2012

Harris, Cole. *The Resettlement of British Columbia: Essays on Colonialism and Geographical Change.* Vancouver: UBC Press, 1997

Lamonde, Yvan. *Histoire sociale des idées au Québec,* vol. I, *1760–1896.* Saint-Laurent: Fides, 2000

Pennington, Christopher. *The Destiny of Canada: Macdonald, Laurier, and the Election of 1891.* Toronto: Penguin, 2011

Pryke, Kenneth G. *Nova Scotia and Confederation, 1864–74.* Toronto: University of Toronto Press, 1979

Silver, A.I. *The French-Canadian Idea of Confederation, 1864–1900.* Toronto: University of Toronto Press, 1997

Sprague, D.N. *Canada and the Métis, 1869–1885.* Waterloo: Wilfrid Laurier University Press, 1988

Stonechild, Blair and Bill Waiser. *Loyal till Death: Indians and the Northwest Rebellion.* Calgary: Fifth House, 1997

Stewart, Gordon T. *The Origins of Canadian Politics: A Comparative Approach.* Vancouver: UBC Press, 1986

Thomas, Lewis H. *The Struggle for Responsible Government in the Northwest Territories, 1870–97.* 2nd ed. Toronto: University of Toronto Press, 1978

For a comprehensive list of readings for topics covered in this chapter, please visit http://pearsoncanada.ca/conrad.

CHAPTER 3
ENTERING THE TWENTIETH CENTURY, 1896–1914

TIMELINE

1896–1911	Liberals under Wilfrid Laurier hold power in Ottawa
1896–1914	Nearly 3 million immigrants arrive in Canada
1897	Wheat boom begins; gold rush in the Yukon
1898	Treaties signed with the Dene; national referendum on prohibition
1899–1902	South African War
1903	Alaska Boundary decision; Ligue nationaliste canadienne established; two new transcontinental railways receive charters
1904	Founding of Association catholique de la jeunesse canadienne-française
1905	Saskatchewan and Alberta become provinces
1906	British troops withdraw from Esquimalt and Halifax
1908	Indian Act gives the federal government power to expropriate reserve lands
1909	Department of External Affairs established
1910	*Le Devoir* begins publication; Naval Service Bill
1911	Reciprocity Agreement negotiated with the United States rejected in federal election
1911–20	Conservatives under Robert Borden hold power in Ottawa
1913	Vilhjalmur Stefansson leads a Canadian expedition to the North
1913–14	Economic recession
1914–18	First World War

The more I advance in life . . . the more I thank Providence that my birth took place in the fair land of Canada. Canada has been modest in its history, although its history is heroic in many ways. But its history, in my estimation, is only commencing . . . in this century. The nineteenth century was the century of the United States. I think we can claim that it is Canada that shall fill the twentieth century.[1]

Wilfrid Laurier's comment during a speech to the Ottawa Canadian Club in 1904 reflected a growing optimism among Canadians. After three decades of uncertainty, the opening years of the twentieth century brought the economic growth that Canadian leaders had sought for their fledgling nation. Industries flourished, immigrants flocked to the West, two new provinces were created, and two more railways spanned the continent. When the United States finally agreed to the long-sought reciprocity agreement in 1911, the Liberals were convinced that it would buy them another victory at the polls. They were wrong. The Conservatives led by Robert Borden won the election and North American free trade was rejected by a nation that was increasingly confident of its future.

LAURIER LIBERALISM

Wilfrid Laurier became prime minister of Canada in 1896 at the age of 55. Trained in law, he joined the Rouges as a young man and edited a newspaper, *Le Défricheur*, in Quebec's Eastern Townships. Like many liberals in Quebec, Laurier initially opposed Confederation, but gradually became reconciled to the new political order. After a term in the Quebec legislature, he ran for a federal seat in 1874 and briefly served as minister of Inland Revenue in Mackenzie's cabinet. Laurier's opposition to the Ultramontanes in Quebec endeared him to many English Protestants. A stout defender of political liberalism and Canadian unity, Laurier was Edward Blake's choice as party leader after the party's defeat in 1887 despite the objections of a number of prominent Liberals, who wondered whether a Catholic from Quebec could win the hearts and votes of the majority of Canadians. Their fears were soon put to rest. Like Macdonald, Laurier had a personality for politics. He was a gifted orator and developed into a skillful politician who sought compromise among the discordant groups battling for ascendancy.[2]

Canadians voted for the Liberals in 1896 for a variety of reasons. Laurier's success in improving the party's organization was one of them. Another was the party's retreat in 1893 from its rigid free trade philosophy, which increasingly alienated voters in Ontario, where the tariff was credited with much of the province's recent economic growth. Laurier's talent for political management and his sensitivity to provincial aspirations no doubt also helped. These qualities were evident in the formation of his first cabinet. In it he included powerful local chieftains—William S. Fielding of Nova Scotia, Andrew G. Blair of New Brunswick, and Oliver Mowat of Ontario—and rising newcomers like Manitoba's Clifford Sifton, who in 1897 became minister of the Interior, responsible for development of the West.

Laurier's willingness to compromise was reflected in the tariff policy developed shortly after the Liberals came to power. In 1897, Finance Minister Fielding introduced the so-called "British preference," which applied lower tariffs to any country admitting Canadian products on a preferential basis. Since Great Britain had a

policy of global free trade, it was automatically granted tariff concessions. This measure pleased those with imperialist leanings and did little to hurt Canadian manufacturers, whose main competition came from the United States.

It was fortunate for the Liberals that they came into office just as international economic conditions were on the upswing and when most of the farmland on the American frontier had been taken up. Under Sifton's supervision, immigration was vigorously pursued, and the results were spectacular. More than two million people came to Canada between 1896 and 1911, a large proportion of them settling in the four western provinces.

In 1905, the Laurier government created two new provinces—Alberta and Saskatchewan—out of the North-West Territories. Laurier invited Liberals to form the government in both new provinces, giving his

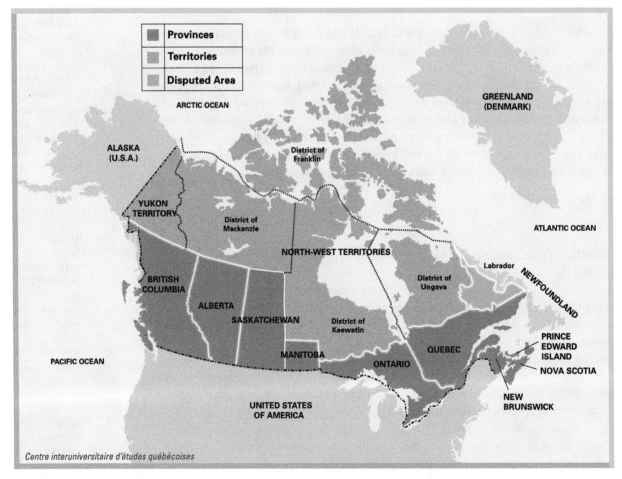

MAP 3.1

Canada in 1905. The map includes the new provinces of Alberta and Saskatchewan, carved out of the North-West Territories

MORE TO THE STORY
Railroading Canada

Encouraged by what seemed to be unending growth, Laurier decided to assist the eastern-based Grand Trunk Railway and the western-based Canadian Northern Railway companies to complete transcontinental lines. The vast sums of taxpayers' money invested in these projects meant that they, like the Canadian Pacific Railway Company (CPR), encouraged extravagance and political corruption. Unlike the CPR, the two new railways failed to make a profit and continued to be a drain on the federal budget long after Laurier had departed the scene.

The Canadian Northern Railway was the brainchild of Donald Mackenzie and Donald Mann, both originally subcontractors for the CPR. In 1895, the pair formed a partnership to build a railway to Hudson Bay. This project failed to materialize, but Mackenzie and Mann began buying short rail lines in Manitoba and soon had the basis for a second transcontinental railway. With bond guarantees and land grants from the Manitoba government, they marketed $14 million of securities in London and New York for their Canadian Northern Railway. Neither promoter put up any of his own money. A third of the capital was guaranteed by governments at various levels, while Mackenzie's Toronto associate, George Cox, added the financial muscle of the Canadian Bank of Commerce.

The Grand Trunk Railway, whose London-based directors saw their future survival as dependent on tapping the booming West, tried to buy the Canadian Northern Railway, but negotiations for a merger of the two companies failed. Under their new American general manager, Charles M. Hayes, the Grand Trunk embarked on a project to build its own new railway, incorporated as the National Transcontinental. Both companies would demand and get land grants, subsidies, and loan guarantees from the Laurier government. When Quebec and the Maritimes complained that they were left out of the investment in railways, the federal government agreed to build the Grand Trunk's Eastern Division from Moncton to Winnipeg and lease it to the company. Not to be outdone, Mackenzie and Mann knit together eastern lines to establish their claim to an Atlantic terminus.

Extravagance, greed, and patronage dogged the two ventures. When a royal commission was struck in 1911 to look into the skyrocketing costs of the Eastern Division, it was discovered that the project cost $70 million (out of $160 million) more than it should have. Nevertheless, the two companies pressed forward with construction, floating new security issues in London and demanding more subsidies and loan guarantees from Ottawa. Hayes was planning even grander schemes when he died in the sinking of the *Titanic* in 1912.

Mackenzie and Mann continued to expand their railroad empire, but their days were numbered. European investors were beginning to have second thoughts about investing in Canadian railways, and the outbreak of the First World War closed European financial markets completely. Faced with bankruptcy, Mackenzie and Mann were forced to let their railway empire be amalgamated with other government-owned railways into the Canadian National Railway system, which was created in a series of mergers between 1917 and 1923.[3]

party a substantial patronage advantage over his rival Conservatives. In deciding to keep public lands and natural resources under federal control, as Macdonald had in the case of Manitoba, Laurier perpetuated a continuing source of federal–provincial antagonism in the Prairie region. He also created a firestorm of complaint when he tried to include support for Roman Catholic schools in the autonomy bills creating the new provinces. In protest, Clifford Sifton resigned from the cabinet, thus depriving it of one of its most competent ministers.

THE KLONDIKE GOLD RUSH

The discovery of gold in the Klondike in 1896 coincided with Laurier's success at the polls. The latest in a series of discoveries that began with California in 1849 and

British Columbia in 1858, the Klondike gold rush began after California-born George Cormack, together with two Tagish brothers, Skookum Jim and Dawson Charlie, found gold nuggets at Rabbit Creek—soon rechristened Bonanza Creek. The three men and other prospectors in the region staked their claims well before the inrush of gold-seekers in 1897.

Most of the 40 000 people who flooded into Canada's new Eldorado returned home empty-handed. Still, there were fortunes to be made by those who knew how to take advantage of the situation. The shrewdest man of all was Joe Ladue, a trader and prospector who bought land in what would become the major settlement in the region. Two years after finding gold at Bonanza Creek, the lure of instant wealth had transformed Dawson from a tiny fur-trading post into western Canada's second-largest city. The land that Ladue had purchased for $10 an acre fetched as much as $1000 for a small building lot in 1898.

Getting to the Klondike proved an enormous challenge. For those with plenty of money, the trip could be made by a steamer that ran from Seattle or Victoria to the mouth of the Yukon River, and from there along the river to Dawson City. Some would-be prospectors travelled on the difficult and time-consuming overland route from Edmonton, while others climbed through the Chilkoot or White passes from the two Alaskan communities on the Lynn Canal, Dyea and Skagway, that sprang up to serve them. Although the trek through the passes was strenuous, it was not a formidable obstacle to reaching Dawson City. The problem was getting supplies to the region. The North-West Mounted Police (NWMP) decreed that no one could enter the Yukon without enough money or supplies to last six months.

At the height of the gold rush, Dawson City was a rough-and-ready place, with saloons and dance halls open 24 hours a day—though they closed on Sunday. Its reputation for lawlessness was nevertheless greatly exaggerated. Unlike Skagway, a roaring American frontier town ruled for a time by a gangster named Soapy Smith, Dawson was under the firm control of the NWMP, who

Gold-seekers on the Chilkoot Pass in 1898, at the height of the Klondike Gold Rush.
SOURCE: LIBRARY AND ARCHIVES CANADA C-14260

were dispatched to the Yukon as soon as the news of the gold discovery reached Ottawa. By 1898 there were 300 NWMP in Dawson in addition to 200 members of the Yukon Field Force, a military unit created to protect the newly established Yukon Territory.

Under Superintendent Sam Steele, the NWMP rigidly enforced the regulation banning firearms from being carried in town and handed out stiff penalties to those who broke the law. The police kept the three main routes to and from Dawson carefully guarded, not only to catch criminals, but also to make sure that the royalty on gold was paid. Between 1897 and 1911, gold worth more than $22 million (about $3.5 billion in today's dollars) was extracted from the Yukon, adding substantial sums in royalties to Ottawa's coffers. A railway connected the Yukon with Skagway on the Pacific coast in 1900, but by that time, the discovery of gold in Nome, Alaska, had shifted the attention of gold-seekers elsewhere.

Canada's gold rush frontier quickly settled into a more mundane existence. Individual prospectors gave way to international corporations, and the territorial government gradually became less authoritarian. Like other territorial governments, the Yukon was originally governed by a commissioner and appointed officials, backed by the NWMP. Elected officials were gradually added to the council.

Martha Munger Purdy Black

The Chicago socialite Martha Munger Purdy was one of the most remarkable participants in the Klondike gold rush. In 1898, she arranged for relatives to care for her two sons while she accompanied her husband, William Purdy, and her brother, George Munger Jr to Dawson. By the time they arrived in Seattle, William had decided to go to the Sandwich Islands (Hawaii) instead, resulting in the breakup of the marriage. George and Martha pressed on, hiring packers in Dyea, Alaska, to help them haul their supplies through the Chilkoot Pass. Martha was in the early stages of pregnancy at the time that she made the difficult trek to Dawson.

While her brother worked his claim, Martha made the best of the situation and gave birth to her third son in January 1899. Martha and her baby returned home in the spring, but Chicago offered few attractions for a woman of Martha's energy and ambition. By 1901, she was back in Dawson where she set up and managed a sawmill and a gold-ore crushing plant. In 1904,

she married lawyer George Black, a native of New Brunswick and a man seven years her junior. The Black family spent a few years in Vancouver, but returned to the Yukon when George was appointed commissioner of the territory in 1912.

George's decision to participate in the First World War prompted Martha to take another difficult journey, this time across dangerous Atlantic waters to England, where she worked as a volunteer in the war effort. During her overseas sojourn, she was elected a fellow of the Royal Geographical Society for her work on Yukon flora. George Black represented the Yukon for four terms as a Conservative member of the House of Commons, but was obliged to resign his seat due to illness before the 1935 election. Martha ran in his place and, at the age of 70, became Canada's second female Member of Parliament. She held the seat for one term before handing it back to her husband in 1940. Martha Munger Black died in Whitehorse in 1957 at age 91.[4]

Martha Munger Black with her husband, George. SOURCE: YUKON ARCHIVES, MARTHA LOUISE BLACK COLLECTION #3258

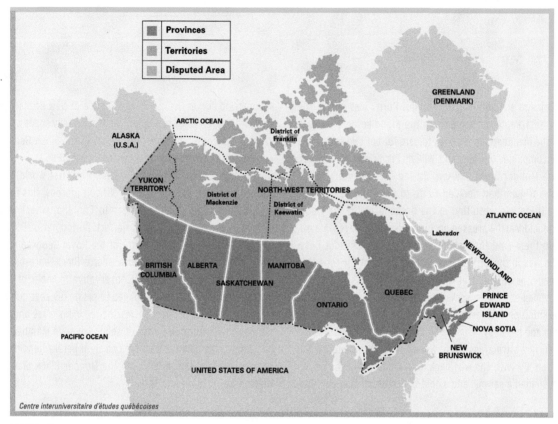

MAP 3.2
Canada in 1912. The map shows the northern expansion of the existing provinces to their present configuration

NOTHERN EXPOSURE

The Klondike gold rush had little impact on the North's Aboriginal residents, who still dominated the region north of the 60th parallel, the line that increasingly defined what Canadians believed to be "the true North." The area south of this boundary was gobbled up by the provinces of Quebec, Ontario, Manitoba, Saskatchewan, and Alberta, which only took on their present configuration in the early decades of the twentieth century.

As the southern areas of the old Northwest were opened to settlement, Aboriginal peoples in the North were increasingly drawn into the fur trade. This was particularly the case among the Dene who inhabited the Mackenzie River Valley. In the second half of the nineteenth century, free traders (many of them Métis), missionaries, and scientists (most of them associated with the Geological Survey and the Dominion Lands Branch of the Department of the Interior) increasingly encroached on the North. The Dene also became the

target for salvation by two missionary organizations, the Oblate Missionaries of Mary Immaculate and the Anglican Church Missionary Society. Like other Aboriginal peoples who became Christians, the Dene responded to the spiritual message of Christianity while shaping their religious practices to their own traditions and needs.

The potential wealth of the North, especially the oil-laden Athabasca tar sands and the iron-bearing rocks of Ungava, was gradually recognized by the federal government. In 1895 and 1897, orders-in-council finally affirmed the British cession of the Arctic to Canada, laid claim to all territory between 141 degrees west longitude and a vague line running west of Greenland, and created three new northern administrative districts—Mackenzie, Yukon, and Franklin. As early as 1891, the federal government declared its determination to negotiate treaties with the Dene, but it was slow to do so until the discovery of gold in the Klondike galvanized it into action. Treaties 8, 10, and 11 were signed with various Dene bands between 1898 and 1921.

Roman Catholic church at Fond du Lac, Saskatchewan, photographed by Joseph Burr Tyrrell of the Geological Survey of Canada in 1893. Fond du Lac, on the east end of Lake Athabasca, became the site of a Hudson's Bay Company post in 1853. Soon thereafter, the Oblates established a mission, named Our Lady of Seven Sorrows. Despite the ravages of European diseases and suspicions that priests were the source of their difficulties, the Dene gradually began to incorporate aspects of Roman Catholicism into their world view. SOURCE: THOMAS FISHER RARE BOOK LIBRARY, UNIVERSITY OF TORONTO, MS. COLL 26, BOX P143, FOLDER 8

Because Canada's claim to its Arctic sector was called into question by other nations, the federal government sponsored forays into the North by Captain Joseph Bernier between 1906 and 1911. Canada's pretensions notwithstanding, American explorer Robert Peary claimed the North Pole for the United States in 1909, but the Americans failed to follow up the claim. In 1913, Vilhjalmur Stefansson led an expedition under Canadian auspices to study the marine biology, oceanography, and Inuit people of the North. Soon after setting out, the primary government vessel, the *Karluk*, was crushed in the ice, and most of its crew, who had set out on foot, were never heard from again. A few managed to reach Wrangel Island, 180 kilometres off the coast of Siberia. Rumours that they had claimed the island for Canada set in motion a protracted sovereignty debate with the Soviet Union in the 1920s.

The Inuit of the eastern Arctic remained largely outside European influences until the 1930s, but the people living in the central and western Arctic were not so fortunate. The uncontrolled slaughter of whales and walrus from the 1860s to the 1880s left starvation in its wake among a population already weakened by European diseases. As a result, the Inuvialuit people disappeared from the region and were replaced by Alaskan Inuit.

PROVINCES AND REGIONS

While the prosperity that characterized the early years of the twentieth century helped cover up the cracks in Confederation, it failed to reduce the regional disparity that increasingly defined Canada. Nor did it stop the provinces from demanding that Ottawa pursue their interests, whether or not they conflicted with national policies. For better or for worse, federal–provincial tensions had become an enduring feature of the new nation.

Throughout the Prairies, a political storm was brewing over the high tariffs that favoured eastern manufacturers and forced farmers to pay higher prices for their agricultural machinery and supplies. After 1905, Manitoba became insistent that its northern boundary be pushed to the 60th parallel to give it a territorial base equal to Saskatchewan and Alberta. Westerners also wanted a railway to a Hudson Bay port to provide an alternative route to export markets. In British Columbia, the white majority were alarmed by the growing number of Asians arriving on their shores and insisted that Ottawa restrict Asian immigration.

In the Maritimes, resentment flourished as all three provinces fell behind the rest of the nation in economic growth. The expansion of industries related to coal and steel in the first decade of the twentieth century masked some of the deep structural problems facing the region's economy, but no one could deny that the Maritimes were generally losing power within Confederation. In 1867, the region held more than 20 percent of the seats in the House of Commons; by 1914, its representation had dropped to 13 percent. Declining representation made it difficult for the Maritime region to shape national policies to meet its needs.

Like Macdonald, Laurier built his success on support in Canada's two largest provinces, but he could not count on Ontario to keep him in office. Although the province's seats were split evenly between Conservatives and Liberals in 1896, thereafter the Conservatives won a majority of Ontario's seats in federal elections. James Whitney's Conservatives finally put an end to the 34-year reign of the Liberals in Ontario's provincial government in 1905. Holding more than a third of the seats in the House of Commons, Ontario wielded considerable influence in the corridors of power and caused Laurier as many problems as the other provinces put together. The strength of the province's industrial interests threatened the delicate balance between regional and national interests, while growing imperial sentiment among Ontario's overwhelmingly anglophone and Protestant population continued to clash with francophone nationalist sentiment in Quebec.

Laurier won large majorities in Quebec throughout his political career, but the nationalist movement remained an ongoing threat to his francophone support. Henri Bourassa, the grandson of Louis-Joseph Papineau—the Patriote leader in the rebellion of 1837–1838—emerged as the new spokesman for the nationalist cause. Although he was widely respected in his native province, Bourassa's vision of a bilingual and bicultural Canada put him at odds with some nationalists. Bourassa concentrated on influencing public opinion and existing parties rather than forming a new organization to promote his policies. His newspaper, *Le Devoir*, founded in 1910, emerged as a major force in developing public opinion in Quebec.

THE SOUTH AFRICAN WAR AND THE IMPERIAL QUESTION

The growing rivalry between Germany and Great Britain for imperial and industrial ascendancy inevitably created problems in Canada. So, too, did the jingoistic attitude of the United States, whose leaders continued to resist Canadian efforts to secure a free trade treaty or a generous

A one-time protégé of Wilfrid Laurier (left), Henri Bourassa (right) resigned from his seat in the House of Commons over Liberal policy on the South African War in 1899. He returned to parliament as an independent in 1900 and soon emerged as the intellectual and moral leader of French-Canadian nationalism. SOURCE: LIBRARY AND ARCHIVES CANADA C-27360 (LEFT) AND C-52291 (RIGHT)

settlement of the Alaska boundary. Laurier's genius for compromise was sorely tested in his efforts to steer a middle course in the conflicting demands generated by the two English-speaking empires that played a major role in Canada's political and economic life.

When Great Britain declared war against Dutch settlers—called Boers—in South Africa in 1899, many anglophone Canadians felt it was their war too. Laurier faced enormous pressure to send a Canadian contingent to South Africa, not only from imperialist-minded English Canadians, but also from Governor General Lord Minto and from Edward Hutton, the British-appointed general officer commanding the Canadian militia. In sharp contrast, Bourassa and other French-Canadian nationalists in Laurier's party were determined that Canada not be involved in the conflict. It had nothing to do with Canada's interests, they argued. Rather than seeing imperialism as another form of Canadian nationalism, French Canadians identified with the Boers, who were fleeing the clutches of an aggressive global empire.

True to form, Laurier offered a compromise: Ottawa would equip and raise volunteers, but once in South Africa they would be paid by the British. On the grounds that the effort would cost Canada little financially, he refused to debate the issue in the House of Commons. Laurier's compromise pleased neither side: it lost him the support of Bourassa, who resigned from the House of Commons in 1899 to protest the Liberal Party's policy on the war, and it did little to improve his image among the jingoistic imperialists.

More than 7000 Canadians eventually saw service in the South African War. Laurier's refusal to give more assistance to the British war effort encouraged a number of private initiatives. Donald Smith, raised to the British peerage as Lord Strathcona, funded an entire contingent. In Montreal, Margaret Polson Murray launched a patriotic organization of women, the Imperial Order Daughters of the Empire (IODE), to support empire unity and assist in the war effort. Its motto, "One flag, one throne, one country," appealed to many women who identified Canada's interests with those of Great Britain, and branches of the IODE sprang up across the country. The enormous interest that the war sparked on the home front also inspired the establishment of a Patriotic Fund, a Canadian branch of the

Group of Strathcona Horse on board S.S. *Monterey*, 1900. SOURCE: LIBRARY AND ARCHIVES CANADA PA-28917

Soldiers' Wives League, and the Canadian Memorial Association. The latter organization was dedicated to marking the graves of the 244 Canadian fatalities and erecting monuments to the men who fought in South Africa.

The South African War increased tensions between English and French Canadians, especially in Montreal, where anglophone imperialists and francophone nationalists lived in close proximity. On 5 March 1900, a group of McGill University students attacked the offices of two French-language newspapers and then paraded to the Montreal campus of Université Laval (now the Université de Montréal), where they tried to provoke the French students into retaliatory action. The following day, the Laval students held a peaceful demonstration to protest the behaviour of the McGill students, which, in turn, provoked a crowd of English-speaking students and townspeople, armed with sticks, clubs, and frozen potatoes, to march on the Laval campus. The mob was dispersed by police with water hoses, but the militia had to be called out to preserve public order in the ethnically divided city.

For those fighting in South Africa, the glamour of warfare quickly wore off. The Boers inflicted humiliating defeats on British forces in the first few weeks of the war, and when the empire finally threw enough troops into the field to win formal engagements, the Boers refused to surrender. Instead, they resorted to guerrilla warfare, which prolonged the war for two years. Most of the Canadian casualties were a result of the diseases that ravaged the military camps rather than of the shooting skills of the Boers.[5]

Empire Day in Canada

One expression of the growth of imperialist sentiment was the establishment of Empire Day as a national holiday. The idea was suggested by Clementine Fessenden, a prominent club member in Hamilton, and promoted in the wake of Queen Victoria's Diamond Jubilee in 1897 by Ontario's minister of Education, George Ross. First celebrated in Ontario, Nova Scotia, and the Protestant schools of Quebec on 23 May 1898–the day before Queen Victoria's birthday–it was designed to provide an opportunity to use public schools for the promotion of patriotic sentiments.

In his directive to all school inspectors, George Ross nicely blended national and imperial sentiments:

> Part of the forenoon might be occupied with a familiar talk by the teacher on the British Empire, its extent and resources; the relations of Canada to the Empire; the unity of the Empire and its advantages; the privileges which, as British subjects, we enjoy; the extent of Canada and its resources; readings by Canadian and British authors by the teacher; interesting historical incidents in connection with our own country. The aim of the teacher in all of his references to Canada and the empire should be to make Canadian patriotism intelligent, comprehensive and strong.
>
> The afternoon, commencing at 2:30 P.M., might be occupied with patriotic recitations, songs and readings by the pupils, and speeches by the trustees, clergymen and others as may be available. The trustees and public generally should be invited to be present at the exercises. During the day the British Flag or the Canadian Ensign should be hoisted over the school building.[6]

The Queen died in 1901, but Victoria Day is still celebrated, although in Quebec it has been replaced by the *Journée nationale des patriotes*. It has lost much of its imperial overtones, and busy school teachers often use the occasion to encourage civic engagement. For most Canadians, it marks the unofficial start of the cottage season and warmer weather–something everyone can celebrate.

DUELLING IMPERIALISMS

Following the South African War, Laurier was determined to find a middle ground between subordination to imperial authorities and total independence, but the task proved difficult. Canada still needed British support in negotiating with the Americans, who, like the British, seemed to be entering another expansionary phase. In 1898, the Americans trounced the Spanish in a nasty little war over Cuba and then took Puerto Rico, Guam, and the Philippines from the humiliated Spaniards. Would they use the same tactics with Canada?

The disputed boundary between Alaska and the Yukon became the testing ground. With the discovery of gold in the Klondike, the width of the Alaska Panhandle suddenly became important for determining who owned the ports through which people and goods entered the fabled gold fields. Canada's dependence on Great Britain in foreign affairs was reflected in the makeup of an international judicial tribunal established to decide the issue in 1903. The two Canadian delegates on the three-man British negotiating team (A.B. Aylesworth and Sir Louis Jetté) found an uncertain ally in the British appointee, Lord Alverstone. In their negotiations with three American commissioners, all loyal appointees of President Theodore Roosevelt, Alverstone sided with the United States, demonstrating, at least in the minds of many Canadians, that Anglo–American friendship was more important to Great Britain than were good relations with its senior dominion.

As a result of the meddling of British officers during the South African War and the bad feelings lingering from the Alaska boundary decision, the Laurier government began to assert more autonomy over the nation's foreign affairs. In 1904, Laurier insisted that the officer commanding the militia be appointed by the Canadian government rather than by Great Britain. Canada also theoretically assumed greater responsibility for its own defence in 1906, when Britain withdrew its troops from Halifax and Esquimalt, the last two British bases in Canada. In 1909,

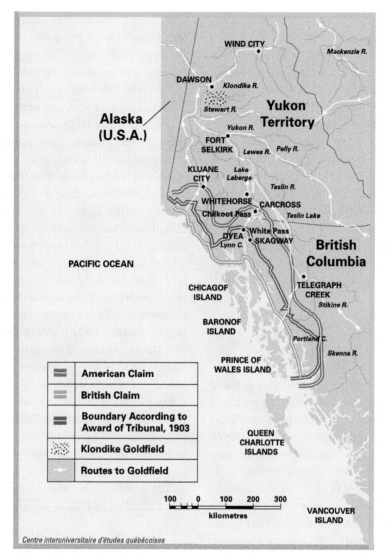

WIND CITY

Mackenzie R.

DAWSON

Klondike R.

Stewart R.

**Alaska
(U.S.A.)**

**Yukon
Territory**

Yukon R.

FORT
SELKIRK

Lewes R.   *Pelly R.*

KLUANE
CITY

Lake
Laberge

Teslin R.

WHITEHORSE   CARCROSS

Chilkoot Pass   *Teslin Lake*

White Pass

DYEA   SKAGWAY

Lynn C.

**British
Columbia**

PACIFIC OCEAN

CHICAGOF
ISLAND

TELEGRAPH
CREEK

Stikine R.

BARONOF
ISLAND

Portland C.

Skenna R.

PRINCE OF
WALES ISLAND

	American Claim
	British Claim
	Boundary According to Award of Tribunal, 1903
	Klondike Goldfield
	Routes to Goldfield

QUEEN
CHARLOTTE
ISLANDS

100 0 100 200 300
kilometres

VANCOUVER
ISLAND

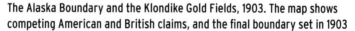
Centre interuniversitaire d'études québécoises

MAP 3.3

**The Alaska Boundary and the Klondike Gold Fields, 1903. The map shows
competing American and British claims, and the final boundary set in 1903**

John A. Macdonald's former secretary, Joseph Pope, was charged with the task of establishing a department of external affairs for Canada. Although Great Britain was still technically in control of international relations, the growing volume of paperwork surrounding trade, boundary disputes, and other matters pointed in the direction of better organization of foreign affairs. The same year, an International Joint Commission was established to settle questions relating to the boundaries between the United States and Canada and, in 1910, disputes between the two countries relating to the North Atlantic fisheries were submitted to arbitration at The Hague.

The major question facing Laurier as he entered his fourth mandate in 1908 was naval defence. Given the escalating Anglo–German naval rivalry, Canadians were pressed either to make a direct financial contribution to the British Admiralty or establish their own navy. Laurier again took a compromise position. His Naval Service Bill, introduced in 1910, proposed a Canadian navy that, in times of war, could be placed under imperial control. United in their disdain for Laurier's "tinpot navy," the Conservatives were nevertheless deeply divided between an English-Canadian majority demanding a direct contribution to the British Admiralty and a small band of

French Canadians who opposed any money being spent on naval defence.

In an age of competing imperialisms, there was little support for either Quebec or Canadian independence. Nevertheless, the idea of a separate Quebec was taken up by Jules-Paul Tardivel, a Franco-American who moved to Quebec in 1868. He advanced his idea of an independent French Catholic nation on the banks of the St Lawrence in his newspaper *La Vérité* as well as in a futuristic novel, *Pour La Patrie*, published in 1895. In English Canada, John S. Ewart, who served as legal counsel for the French-speaking minority of Manitoba, wrote a series of essays arguing for Canada to become constitutionally independent. There was little popular support for achieving such a goal until the First World War spurred Canadians to re-evaluate their lingering colonial relationship with Great Britain.

FRANCOPHONE NATIONALISM

Few francophones found much in the Canadian national identity debate that appealed to them. When Laurier gave way to pressure from imperialists in Canada and Great Britain to participate in the South African War in 1899, Bourassa embarked down an intellectual road that made him one of Canada's most original and controversial critics of Canadian public policy. In 1901, he introduced a bill into the House of Commons that would make the Canadian parliament the only authority that could declare war on behalf of Canada. Although the resolution was voted down, it signalled new thinking about Canada's status.

Bourassa also took the position that Canada should be an Anglo–French nation, with two cultures having equal rights throughout the country. During the debate surrounding the creation of the provinces of Alberta and Saskatchewan in 1905, he argued that Roman Catholics should have control of their own schools in the new provinces, warning that the equality of cultures was an absolute condition of French Canadians continuing to accept Confederation. Bourassa lost that battle and retreated from his notion of a bilingual, bicultural Canada because English Canada was so unreceptive to the idea. Instead, he began to emphasize the Roman Catholic nature of French-Canadian society and the need to protect Quebec's special identity, which, he felt,

was being threatened by secularism and materialism. Much troubled by the emergence of big corporations, Bourassa championed the rights of small business and farming families against the greed of corporate capitalism.

Bourassa emerged as a powerful spokesman for the nationalist forces that had been gaining momentum in Quebec since the 1880s. Following the defeat of Honoré Mercier's Parti national government in 1892, nationalist sentiment continued to thrive in a variety of voluntary organizations. The most important of these was the Ligue nationaliste canadienne, established in 1903. Bourassa was a leading figure in the Ligue, which stood for Canadian autonomy within the British Empire, provincial rights, linguistic dualism, separate Roman Catholic schools, and the economic development of Canada by and for Canadians. Although the Ligue had only a few active members, its doctrines were widely disseminated through its newspaper, *Le Nationaliste*, and the speeches and writings of Bourassa and his coterie of young followers.

The enthusiasm of young people for nationalist ideas was captured in the Association catholique de la jeunesse canadienne-française (ACJC), founded in 1904. Growing out of the determination of male college students to protect French-Canadian and Roman Catholic interests, it was encouraged by church officials and journalists who believed that French Canada was in the midst of a religious and national crisis. The ACJC's motto was "notre maître le passé" (our master the past), and its constitution embodied its idealistic goals:

1. The members of the Catholic Association of French-Canadian Youth believe that the French-Canadian race has a special mission to fulfil on this continent and that it must, for this end, guard its distinct character from that of other races.

2. They believe that the progress of the French-Canadian race is in a special fashion attached to the Catholic faith, which is one of the essential and specific elements.[7]

This approach was further developed by one of the organization's most prominent members, Lionel Groulx, a priest who taught at the Valleyfield Seminary. In his numerous publications, beginning with *Croisade d'adolescents* (1912), Groulx proclaimed a mission for French Canadians who, he argued, had been especially chosen by God to advance the cause of Roman Catholicism in North America. When he was appointed to teach history at Université Laval's Montreal campus in 1915, he had a platform from which to promote his providential view of French-Canadian history, an understanding of which he and other nationalists felt was essential to the struggle for cultural survival.

NATIVE PEOPLES AND THE DOMINANT CULTURE

Despite their presence in all provinces and territories, Aboriginal peoples throughout industrializing Canada found themselves largely outside of the national debate. Victims of blinding racism, their voices went unheard and their living conditions deteriorated. The combination of immigration and high death rates quickly reduced both the absolute and relative numbers of Aboriginal people, especially in western Canada. In Alberta, for example, Native peoples constituted a mere three percent of the population in 1911. Fifty years earlier, they had been the overwhelming majority in the territory. With overall numbers remaining around 150 000 at the beginning of the twentieth century, the very survival of Canada's First Nations seemed seriously in doubt.

Because white settlers tended to view Native peoples as a nuisance in the path of "progress," the major goal of federal policy became the removal of Aboriginal peoples from their lands without provoking a violent reaction. In 1908, Clifford Sifton's successor as minister of the Interior, Frank Oliver, introduced a measure that would allow Status Indians to be removed from reserves near towns with more than 8000 residents. Oliver won a further amendment to the Indian Act in 1911 that allowed portions of reserves to be expropriated by municipalities or companies for roads, railways, or other public purposes. Under this legislation, almost half of the Blackfoot (Siksika) reserve was sold for slightly over $1 million. The McKenna-McBride Commission, created in 1912 to resolve federal–provincial differences regarding Native land claims in British Columbia, ignored Aboriginal arguments, and exchanged more than 14 000 hectares of reserve land for larger but significantly less valuable holdings.

Education policies were similarly ill conceived. To save money, the federal government delegated responsibility for Native education to the churches that had sent missionaries to reserves to convert their charges to Christianity. Church administrators professed support for the assimilation of Aboriginal peoples into white society, but their school curricula suggested that they were welcome only in the lower ranks of the social hierarchy. Little time was devoted to academic subjects; instead, much of the teaching involved religious instruction and training in manual labour for boys and in household work for girls.

About two-thirds of the Aboriginal children enrolled in schools at the end of the nineteenth century attended day schools on their reserves, but the government's ideal for Native education was residential schools. In 1883, the cabinet minister introducing the legislation to build several federally financed residential schools expressed the government's philosophy: "If these schools are to succeed, we must not have them too near the bands; in order to educate the children properly we must separate them from their families. Some people may say that this is hard, but if we want to civilize them, we must do that."[8] In northern Ontario and the West, where few schools had been established before Confederation, residential schools became the norm as the Department of Indian Affairs routinely rejected requests for on-reserve schools in favour of church-controlled schools located sufficiently distant from reserves to limit the possibility of parental visits. Native parents complained that boarding schools separated children from their families, forbade the use of birth languages, and subjected youngsters to brutal and unhealthy living conditions, but their complaints fell on deaf ears.

Remedies for injustice did not come easily. As litigants in a European-based judicial system, Aboriginal peoples faced major social, cultural, and economic obstacles. They gradually responded by using the tactics of their adversaries: cooperation among themselves, organized protests, and demands that laws relating to property rights and personal freedom be applied equally to Native peoples. The Grand Indian Council of Ontario and Quebec, founded in 1870 by Iroquois and Ojibwa, protested Ottawa's legislation designed to expropriate their land near towns and cities. Land claims in British Columbia were the subject of a Squamish delegation to King Edward VII in London in 1906 and of a petition from the Nisga'a to the Judicial Committee of the Privy Council in 1913. Pan-Indian revival movements such as the Council of Tribes were even more outspoken, stating bluntly that whites had

Residential Schools

Residential schools exemplified a contradiction in European colonialist philosophy. While arguing that their goal was to "civilize" indigenous peoples, colonialists expressed the conviction that Natives were genetically and socially inferior. In practice, that contradiction was resolved by setting objectives to assimilate Aboriginal peoples to the lowest rungs of society and spending as little as possible to achieve such unambitious results.

The federal government's search for economy was reflected in its delegation of responsibility for Native schooling to Christian churches, a policy that had been phased out in most provincial jurisdictions. At any given time, the Roman Catholic Church operated about 60 percent of the residential schools, the Church of England about 25 percent, and the Methodist and Presbyterian Churches and, after 1925, the United Church most of the rest. Church officials repeatedly complained to the Department of Indian Affairs that they received too little funding to feed children properly, to provide them with adequate accommodation, to hire qualified teaching staff, or to make necessary building repairs, but with little effect. Dr Peter Bryce, the chief medical officer for Indian Affairs, reported in 1907 that only two or three of the 35 schools on the Prairies that he inspected had proper air circulation. Not surprisingly, the death rate for children sent to residential schools in the early years of the program was appallingly high.

The schools had little academic success. Only a small percentage of the residential school children received education beyond the elementary grades and, until the late 1940s, it was common for pupils to spend only half the day in the classroom. The other half consisted of domestic work and manual labour for the school. Discipline was harsh and the children were renamed, re-clothed, and forced to speak only English or French. Many parents resisted pressure from Indian Affairs and the churches to send their children to off-reserve schools, but legislation was passed in 1920 to make school attendance compulsory. Despite threats of criminal prosecution, many parents went into hiding with their children to prevent the RCMP from apprehending them.

Between 1948 and 1952, officials in Indian Affairs took advantage of the malnutrition that prevailed in residential schools and gave scientific and medical researchers the

Native industrial school students and their father, Saskatchewan, ca. 1900. SOURCE: LIBRARY AND ARCHIVES CANADA C-37113

opportunity to enlist children as test subjects for food supplements and vitamins. These experiments violated the Nuremberg Code requirements for informed consent, lack of coercion, and attention to the welfare of all participants in scientific research. The code had been proclaimed in 1947 by judges investigating Nazi experiments involving human beings.[9]

While residential schools were gradually phased out after the Second World War in southern Canada, they were imposed on the North in the 1950s and early 1960s. Between 1883 and 1996, when the last school closed, more than 150 Native residential schools operated in Canada, though the peak number at a given time was 80 in 1930. About 80 percent of all the schools were in the four western provinces or in the northern territories, but no region was spared the presence of Native boarding schools. It is estimated that about 150 000 Aboriginal and Métis children had a residential school experience.

The residential schools system collapsed in the wake of accusations that it fostered cultural genocide and of Native efforts to secure reparations in the courts for the unjust treatment. Attempting to limit the damage, both financial and political, the federal government signed an agreement in 2008 with Native complainants, offering to issue an apology on behalf of all Canadians to former residents of residential schools and to establish a Truth and Reconciliation Commission that would hear the stories of residential school survivors.

The commission's hearings from 2010 to 2014 painted a harrowing picture of young lives ruined by rampant physical and sexual abuse in the residential schools, and of the pain that children experienced as a result of being separated from their families and their communities. After leaving school, many of the students tried to drown their memories in alcohol and drugs, often telling no one what had happened to them because they accepted the claims of their harassers that no one would believe an "Indian" over a man or woman of the cloth. Residential school survivors suggested that after having experienced so much cruelty in their lives, they became abusive parents. Intergenerational harm also resulted from so many Native women becoming alcoholics and giving birth to children who suffered fetal alcohol damage.

Participants in the hearings described their determination to heal themselves, their families, and their communities, and to end the cycle of abuse that had begun with the residential schools and earlier colonial experiences. Many forgave their abusers, believing that their long years of being consumed by hatred and self-pity had immobilized them. Some also paid tribute to staff members at the schools whose kindness and educational prowess provided some compensation for the behaviour of more racist or predatory colleagues.

The residential schools tragedy forms only part of the story of Canada's dealings with its Native peoples. As historian James Daschuk, who has documented the dispossession of Native people in western Canada, comments: "As the skeletons in our collective closet are exposed to the light ... perhaps we will come to understand the uncomfortable truths that modern Canada is founded upon—ethnic cleansing and genocide—and push our leaders and ourselves to make a nation we can be proud to call home."[10]

demoralized and defrauded Native peoples, who should now fight back. Pressure from the Department of Indian Affairs, the indifference and outright hostility of most Canadians, and the military might of the majority doomed such protests.

As a last resort, Natives practised widespread defiance of measures taken to restrict their freedom. When a pass system was introduced on reserves in the North-West Territories after the rebellion of 1885, this regulation proved largely unenforceable. Attempts to ban the sun dances of the Prairie Natives in the 1890s simply drove them underground; the dances were an essential component of communion with the spirit world and, like all dances among Native peoples, were an expression of group solidarity. In British Columbia, Natives similarly defied the 1885 government ban on potlatches, elaborate gift-giving ceremonies widely practised in West Coast cultures.

In 1899, the Canadian government passed legislation to replace the community appointment of Aboriginal leaders in eastern Canada with a system of band council elections to be held every three years. Officials in Ottawa saw this as a progressive move designed to modernize political practices, but many bands ignored or amended the new rules imposed upon them. Traditional practices, including hereditary chiefdoms, continued to prevail in some communities, and there was little that overworked and poorly paid superintendents could or would do about it.

THE 1911 ELECTION

The plight of Canada's Aboriginal peoples was low on the list of Laurier's concerns on the eve of the 1911 election. With nationalist forces on the rise in Quebec, western alienation escalating, and charges of corruption dominating newspaper headlines, it was clear that the Liberals were in danger of defeat at the polls. A timely economic initiative by the Americans seemed to provide an issue that would unite the country and defeat the prime minister's opponents. Under President William

Howard Taft, the Americans proposed a comprehensive trade agreement that allowed the free entry of a wide range of natural products and set lower tariff rates on a number of manufactured goods, including agricultural implements dear to the hearts of Canadian farmers. Here, it seemed, was the solution to agrarian grievances and a means of satisfying those who had long worked for closer trade relations between Canada and the United States.

Although the reciprocity agreement passed easily in the American Congress, it was met with a firestorm of disapproval when it was introduced in the House of Commons in January 1911. The repercussions for the Liberal Party were immediate and extreme. On 20 February 1911, 18 Liberal Party members, industrialists, and financiers based in Toronto issued a manifesto decrying reciprocity. The so-called "Toronto 18" helped to establish the Canadian National League "to support such measures as will uphold Canadian Nationality and British connection, will preserve our Fiscal Independence and will continue to develop our current National policy of interprovincial and external trade, under which the Dominion has achieved its present prosperity." Augmented by these and other Liberal Party defectors, including Clifford Sifton, the Conservatives mounted such serious opposition that Laurier finally decided in July to call an election on the matter, despite having nearly two years left in his mandate.

At first glance, the phlegmatic Robert Laird Borden, federal Conservative leader since 1901, was not the man to challenge the charismatic Laurier. Yet this respectable Halifax lawyer had managed to rebuild a party shattered by the divisions of the 1890s. Like his predecessors, Borden was determined to pursue policies that would foster economic growth, but unlike Macdonald and Laurier, he was a progressive in his approach to policy. Borden emphasized morality, duty, and efficiency in government and struggled, in a way typical of progressives, to eliminate some of the worst abuses of the old patronage-ridden system. At a meeting in Halifax in 1907, the Conservatives unveiled a new platform designed to emphasize their progressive program. It included endorsement of policies such as free rural mail delivery, civil service reform, and federal aid to technical education. The Halifax platform failed to win many votes in 1908, but it remained the foundation for many

During the 1911 election campaign, companies opposed to free trade bought advertising space in their local newspapers to promote their opposition to free trade. This cartoon was by Donald McRitchie, who had previously published much of his work in the *Eye Opener*, a Calgary-based journal. SOURCE: THE GAZETTE (MONTREAL), 22 AND 23 SEPTEMBER 1911

of the policies promoted by the Conservatives in the 1911 campaign. By then, the Conservatives were also backed by effective local organizations.

The federal election of 1911 was preceded by months of heated debate and pamphleteering. Borden crisscrossed the country, promising to introduce the merit system into the civil service, establish a permanent tariff commission to set a "scientific tariff," create a board of grain commissioners to regulate the grain trade, implement free rural mail delivery, and provide subsidies to the provinces to improve roads and agricultural education. Prepared to accept increased state intervention in a number of areas, Borden was even quietly considering taking full control over the Liberal-sponsored Grand Trunk Pacific and Canadian Northern railways if they continued to sap the federal treasury. He also planned to scrap Laurier's "tinpot navy." In its place, he proposed to make an "emergency" $35-million contribution to Great Britain's efforts to keep the imperial navy—upon which Canada depended—strong and efficient. This would buy time, Borden argued, for Canadians to reflect more deeply on their defence policy. Borden also benefited from some support of Bourassa's nationalists, who damned Laurier's naval policy as a sell-out to English Canada.

Reciprocity and the naval policy, the two issues that more than any other posed the question of Canada's future, combined with the usual appeal of patronage, local issues, and individual candidates to defeat the Liberals. Although the popular vote was close, the distribution of seats was decisive. The Liberals won only 13 of Ontario's 86 constituencies, and altogether won only 87 ridings; the Conservatives took 134 seats, including 27 in Quebec. Neither Laurier's liberalism nor his efforts to steer a middle course between differing visions of Canada proved sufficient to address the problems of the day.

THE BORDEN ADMINISTRATION, 1911–1914

Born in Grand Pré, Nova Scotia, in 1854, Robert Borden had come far from his humble origins to become prime minister. After a brief education in nearby Acacia Villa Academy, he began a teaching career at the age of 14. He taught school for five years in Nova Scotia and New Jersey before articling in law with Weatherbe and Graham in Halifax. Called to the bar in 1878, he became a junior partner in the law firm of Graham, Tupper, and Borden in 1882. Close ties to Charles Tupper gave Borden opportunities to take cases to the Supreme Court of Canada in Ottawa and the Judicial Committee of the Privy Council in London. It also brought pressure on the loyal and hard-working Borden to run in the 1896 election.

The Conservative Party under Tupper's leadership went down to defeat, but Borden won his Halifax seat handily. When Tupper stepped down as leader after the party's defeat in 1900, there were few men willing to take his place. The dutiful Borden, after much pressure, agreed to do so. The leader and his party were defeated by the triumphant Liberals in 1904, but Borden refused to give up. He won a by-election in Carleton, Ontario, early in 1905 and moved with his wife, Laura, to Ottawa.

Forsaking his legal practice, Borden devoted his energies to reorganizing the party and developing a winning platform. Laurier whipped the Conservatives again in the 1908 election, but, after a decade in opposition, Borden finally tasted victory in 1911.

Having come to power in 1911 with the support of Quebec nationalists and the anti–free trade business community, Borden faced the challenge of keeping the Conservative coalition together. To make matters worse, the economy began to sink into a recession in 1913. People across the country were thrown out of work, and the unemployed began drifting to cities where they stretched municipal and charitable resources to the limit. Most frustrating for Borden was his inability to get some of his most innovative policies passed by parliament. Although the Conservatives had a majority in the House of Commons, the Liberal-dominated Senate rejected or severely amended much of the government's legislation.

Borden's cabinet included people who had not caught up with his style of progressive politics, but he had a strong ally in his minister of Finance, Thomas White. The vice-president of National Trust, White represented the Toronto Liberals who had defected from Laurier in 1911 and was a powerful figure in the Canadian financial community. Bourassa also supported Borden in 1911 and might have added a progressive voice to the cabinet, but he refused to consider such a role. The leader of the Quebec contingent of the cabinet, Frederick Debartzch Monk, a francophone, was uncomfortable in the predominantly anglophone milieu of Ottawa and, like Bourassa, held views on imperial policy that were diametrically opposed to those promoted by Borden and many of his imperialist-minded colleagues. Quebec nationalists had formed an alliance with the Conservatives in 1911 because they opposed Laurier, but a common enemy was not enough to keep them together once the party came to power. A little over a year after taking office as minister of Public Works, Monk resigned over the naval question. Like other Quebec nationalists, he was opposed to any policy that smacked of excessive subservience to the British.

Monk's defection from the cabinet made it harder to resolve the naval issue. When the Conservative Party's Naval Aid Bill was introduced into the House of Commons, it encountered such fierce opposition from the

Robert Borden in London with a young Winston Churchill, 1912.
SOURCE: LIBRARY AND ARCHIVES CANADA C-2082

Liberals that the government invoked closure, a manoeuvre designed to limit debate. This was the first time that such a procedure had been used in Canada, and Laurier pointed to it as justification for instructing the Liberals in the Senate to defeat the bill. In making this decision, Laurier undoubtedly took into consideration the views of the nationalists in his native province, but he was probably also taking revenge for Borden's scrapping of his naval program.

Bills creating the tariff commission and providing subsidies to provincial highways also fell victim to the Senate's powers to veto and amend bills. In justifying their obstructionism, Liberal senators argued that the Borden administration was usurping powers that were not authorized by the British North America Act. Even the Grain Act of 1912, which created the Board of Grain Commissioners and gave the federal government the power to own and operate terminal grain elevators, had to be carefully administered in order not to invoke the wrath of the Liberal senators.

Not all programs foundered on the rock of Senate intransigence. Borden's popularity soared on the Prairies when he agreed to support the construction of a railroad to Hudson Bay to provide another outlet for expanding grain exports. Farmers were doubtless also pleasantly surprised when many of the provisions of the aborted free trade agreement of 1911 were made available in the Underwood Tariff Act adopted by the United States in 1913. In 1912, Borden made good on his promise to Canada's most powerful provinces—Quebec, Ontario, and Manitoba—that he would grant them huge sections of federally administered territories on their northern borders. No effort was made to consult the largely Aboriginal populations who lived there. Maritime and western provinces, along with bankers and brokers, were relieved when the federal government saved the nation's two faltering railway companies from impending bankruptcy in 1914.

On the matter of civil service reform, the government was forced to move more slowly than it had planned. A commission headed by Sir George Murray, a British public servant with impeccable credentials, had been established in September 1912 to investigate the federal civil service. In his report, Murray recommended a complete overhaul of a system that had become top heavy, patronage-ridden, and inefficient. Borden's government took steps to introduce reforms, but the existing system was so inadequate that it was unable—and probably not all that eager—to preside over its own transformation.

Perhaps nothing was as disturbing in the long run as the economic recession that descended in 1913. While business and government leaders understood that a credit crunch and over-expansion had created the crisis, most people experienced it as bankruptcy, unemployment, and having inadequate income to purchase the necessities of life. The federal government responded by appointing a commission on the cost of living and by urging the railways to maintain high levels of employment. In the larger cities, municipal governments established employment bureaus. These efforts proved inadequate. Many people were facing real misery and, with immigrants still pouring into the country, there was every possibility that social unrest would be more than local police forces could manage. In May 1914, 2000 immigrants marched through the streets of downtown Winnipeg waving shovels and shouting, "Work or bread." This incident was a harbinger of what could come if economic conditions failed to improve.

The "Reciprocity Election" of 1911

At the time and in subsequent analyses, the federal election of 21 September 1911 was often viewed as a major milestone on Canada's road to nationhood. The issues fuelling the contest certainly seemed to be unusually clear-cut and even highly principled. While Laurier ran on a platform of reciprocity with the United States and the creation of an independent Canadian navy, Borden based his campaign on the national policy tariff and loyalty to the British Empire. Was the 1911 election really decided on the issue of reciprocity, or did other factors—including the inevitable grievances accumulated by a tired Liberal administration, the superior organizational capacity of the Conservative Party, and local matters—determine the outcome at the polls?[11]

There is no question that the Conservative Party played on well-honed anti-American sentiments, making reciprocity and Canada's identity as a member of the British Empire a central issue in their campaign. International commentators added weight to this position. Trumpeting the significance of the reciprocity agreement, US President William Taft opined that Canada was "at the parting of the ways," and British poet Rudyard Kipling issued a dire warning published in the *Montreal Daily Star* on 7 September: "It is her own soul that Canada risks today. Once that soul is pawned for any consideration, Canada must inevitably conform to the commercial, legal, financial, social and ethical standards which will be imposed on her by the sheer admitted weight of the United States."[12]

In many accounts, Laurier is seen as having blundered in embracing reciprocity in 1911. The historian W.L. Morton, writing in the early 1960s just as Canada was experiencing a new phase of anti-American sentiment, concluded that the Laurier administration was "shattered by a too easy return to the continentalism the Liberals had shed in the 1890s, and by one extreme of Canadian nationalism they would have been well advised to defend against the American approach." Morton also interpreted the election as testament to a maturing national identity, concluding that "the one note sounded throughout the campaign of 1911 by both the defenders and the opponents of reciprocity was the note of determination to maintain Canadian nationality."[13]

By the time that the second edition of Morton's *Kingdom of Canada* appeared in 1968, a new generation of political historians had begun to raise questions about the role that reciprocity played in determining the outcome of the 1911 election. These scholars focused on Ontario and Quebec, where the shift in voter preference made the most difference. While it had long been accepted that the tactical alliance of Henri Bourassa and his nationalists with the Conservative Party, rather than reciprocity, undermined Laurier's following there, Ontario presented a more complicated picture. Although the Toronto 18 and their fellow-travellers made headlines, Robert Cuff and Paul Stevens argued that a well-oiled Conservative Party apparatus and the collapse of Liberal Party organization in Ontario mattered more. Cuff stated categorically that "the Conservative Party swept the election of 1911 in Ontario by means of superior political organization. . . . No matter what public issue emerged in 1911, given the existing state of party machinery, the electoral results in Ontario would have remained substantially the same."[14]

Economists, meanwhile, took a closer look at voter self-interest in Ontario, noting that the election was not a simple matter of primary producers losing out to the corporate interests defending the national policy tariff. In some areas of the country, farmers voted for the Conservative Party, despite their long-standing support for reciprocity. Ontario pork producers, for example, feared competition from American processors under free trade.[15]

After a careful parsing of the election results, Patrice Dutil and David Mackenzie concluded in their monograph written on the centenary of the 1911 election that reciprocity did matter and that the election did have a long-lasting impact: "In the end, the vast, quasi existentialist debates about Canada and the Empire and Canada and reciprocity had changed the minds of only a few thousand men, but on an electoral map such as Canada's in 1911, that was enough to set the course for the next century."[16]

They also supported Cuff's conclusion that the Liberal Party would have lost the election without reciprocity being the issue.

Without reciprocity, many Canadians had less reason to vote for Laurier in 1911 than they had at any other time since 1896. Seen this way, Laurier's decision to fight his campaign on the reciprocity issue was not a political mistake. It was the one viable opportunity he had. Reciprocity probably helped bolster Liberal support in several areas of the country; it just was not enough in the end. He failed in 1911, therefore, not because he called the election too soon and chose to make reciprocity the issue of the campaign, and not because the opposition to reciprocity rose up to defeat him; it was more a case of reciprocity failing him and his attempt to save his government and his party from a likely, if not certain, defeat.[17]

Laurier's gamble failed, but the myth of an election fought on principle lived on in Canadian historiography. J.W. Dafoe, editor of the *Winnipeg Free Press*, perhaps best summed up the feelings of many Liberals in the week following the election:

> [W]hile I think the decision of the people of Canada on the issue submitted to them was idiotic and will so be adjudged by history, I am not, on other grounds, disposed to complain about the fate that has destroyed the Laurier Government. Regarded simply as an administration it has been growing weaker for some years, and, failing the reciprocity matter, it would probably have gone out of office at the next election. It is better that it should fall on a big issue, which covers its defeat with tragic dignity, than that it should have died of old age and incapacity.[18]

CONCLUSION

Borden's concerns over the economy and the Senate's obstructionism were quickly superseded by the outbreak of the First World War in the summer of 1914. Other concerns, some older than Confederation itself, would remain to complicate wartime planning. Despite impressive economic growth and successful political compromises, Canada was still a fragile nation-state. Alternative destinies, including provincial independence, union with the United States, and imperial federation, continued to attract those who were disappointed with what Canada had to offer. When wartime stresses were added to the curious brew called Canada, the very survival of the nation would be called into question.

NOTES

1. "First Annual Banquet," 18 January 1904, Addresses Delivered before the Canadian Club of Ottawa, 1903–1909 (1910), cited in *Colombo's Canadian Quotations*, ed. John Robert Colombo (Edmonton: Hurtig, 1974) 332.

2. Biographies of Laurier include Joseph Schull, *Laurier* (Toronto: Macmillan, 1965), Richard Clippendale, *Laurier: His Life and World* (Toronto: McGraw-Hill Ryerson, 1979), Réal Bélanger, *Wilfrid Laurier: quand la politique devient passion* (Quebec: Presses de l'Université Laval, 1986), and André Pratte, *Wilfrid Laurier* (Toronto: Penguin, 2011).

3. T.D. Regehr, *The Canadian Northern Railway: Pioneer Road of the Northern Prairies, 1895–1918*

(Toronto: Macmillan of Canada, 1976); G.R. Stevens, *History of the Canadian National Railways* (Toronto: Macmillan, 1973).

4. Carol Martin, *Martha Black: Gold Rush Pioneer* (Toronto: Anansi, 1996) and Martha Louise Black, *My Ninety Years* (Anchorage: Alaska Northwest Publishing Company, 1976).

5. On the South African War, see Carman Miller, *Painting the Map Red: Canada and the South African War, 1899–1902* (Montreal: McGill-Queen's University Press, 1993).

6. Cited in Robert Craig Brown and Ramsay Cook, *Canada, 1896–1921: A Nation Transformed* (Toronto: McClelland & Stewart, 1974) 316.

7. Brown and Cook, *Canada, 1896–1921*, 140.

8. Truth and Reconciliation Commission of Canada, *They Came for the Children: Canada, Aboriginal Peoples, and Residential Schools* (Winnipeg: Truth and Reconciliation Commission of Canada, 2012) i.

9. Ian Mosby, "Administering Colonial Science: Nutrition Research and Human Biomedical Experimentation in Aboriginal Communities and Residential Schools, 1942–1952." *Histoire sociale/Social History* 46. 91 (May 2013) 145–172.

10. James Daschuk, "When Canada used hunger to clear the West." *The Globe and Mail*, 19 July 2013, A11. See also J.R. Miller, *Shingwauk's Vision: A History of Native Residential Schools* (Toronto: University of Toronto Press, 1996).

11. The debates around the 1911 federal election are thoroughly aired in Patrice Dutil and David MacKenzie, *Canada 1911: The Decisive Election that Shaped the Country* (Toronto: Dundurn, 2011) and Paul Stevens, ed., *The 1911 General Election: A Study In Canadian Politics* (Toronto: Copp Clark, 1970).

12. Cited in Dutil and MacKenzie, *Canada 1911*, 211.

13. W.L. Morton, *The Kingdom of Canada*, 2nd. ed. (Toronto: McClelland & Stewart, 1968) 413.

14. Robert Cuff, "The Conservative Party Machine and the Election of 1911 in Ontario," *Ontario History* 57 (1965) 149–56 and Paul D. Stevens, "Laurier, Aylesworth, and the Decline of the Liberal Party in Ontario," *Historical Papers/Communications historiques* (1968) 94–113.

15. Richard Johnston and Michael Percy, "Reciprocity, Imperial Sentiment, and Party Politics in the 1911 Election," *Canadian Journal of Political Science*, 13 (April 1980) 711–29; M.B. Percy, K.H. Norrie, and R.G. Johnston, "Reciprocity and the Canadian General Election of 1911," *Explorations in Economic History* 19 (1982) 409–34; and Eugene Beaulieu and J.C. Herbert Emery, "Pork Packers, Reciprocity and Laurier's Defeat in the 1911 Canadian General Election," *Journal of Economic History* 62 (April 2001) 1083–1101.

16. Dutil and MacKenzie, *Canada 1911*, 279.

17. Dutil and MacKenzie, *Canada 1911*, 285–86.

18. Cited in Stevens, *The 1911 General Election*, 220.

SELECTED READING

Bouchard, Gérard. *La pensée impuissante: échecs et mythes nationaux canadiens–français, 1850–1960*. Montreal: Boréal, 2004

Brown, Robert Craig and Ramsay Cook. *Canada, 1896–1921: A Nation Transformed*. Toronto: McClelland & Stewart, 1974

Dutil, Patrice and David Mackenzie. *Canada 1911: The Decisive Election that Shaped the Country*. Toronto: Dundurn, 2011

English, John. *The Decline of Politics: The Conservatives and the Party System, 1901–20*. Toronto: University of Toronto Press, 1977

Levitt, Joseph. *Henri Bourassa and the Golden Calf: The Social Program of the Nationalists of Quebec (1900–1914)*. Ottawa: University of Ottawa Press, 1969

Miller, Carman. *Painting the Map Red: Canada and the South African War, 1899–1902*. Montreal: McGill-Queen's University Press, 1993

Miller, J.R. *Shingwauk's Vision: A History of Native Residential Schools*. Toronto: University of Toronto Press, 1996

Morrison, William R. *Showing the Flag: The Mounted Police and Canadian Sovereignty in the North, 1894–1925*. Vancouver: UBC Press, 1985

Porsild, Charlene. *Gamblers and Dreamers: Women, Men, and Community in the Klondike*. Vancouver: UBC Press, 1998

Stevens, Paul ed. *The 1911 General Election: A Study in Canadian Politics*. Toronto: Copp Clark, 1970

Truth and Reconciliation Commission of Canada. *They Came for the Children: Canada, Aboriginal Peoples, and Residential Schools*. Winnipeg: Truth and Reconciliation Commission of Canada, 2012

Zaslow, Morris. *The Opening of the Canadian North, 1870–1914*. Toronto: McClelland & Stewart, 1971

For a comprehensive list of readings for topics covered in this chapter, please visit http://pearsoncanada.ca/conrad.

PART II
ECONOMY AND SOCIETY IN THE INDUSTRIAL AGE, 1867–1914

Canadians who lived between 1867 and 1914 witnessed a transformation of their economy and society. While national policies designed to produce economic growth and industrial development at first seemed slow to bear fruit, by the turn of the century the economy was growing impressively. So, too, was the population, swelled at last by massive numbers of immigrants, most of them from Europe and the United States. Rapid growth created new problems in Canadian society and social movements to resolve them. Armed with a sense of their own ability to reform the industrial order, which heightened inequality while at the same time increasing material wealth, Canadians organized pressure groups, commissioned studies, collected signatures for petitions, buttonholed mayors and councillors, marched in the streets, and clashed with militias in an effort to make their demands known. There was also a new energy and complexity in cultural life. Everything from schools and universities to sports and fine arts adjusted to the challenges of the modern age and, in the process, laid the foundations for many of the institutions and values that still define Canadian society.

CHAPTER 4
THE NEW INDUSTRIAL ORDER, 1867–1914

In 1886, John A. Macdonald responded to criticism of labour conditions in Canadian factories by establishing a Royal Commission on the Relations of Labor and Capital. The commissioners held inquiries in Ontario, Quebec, and the Maritimes, and their report offered damning evidence of exploitative working conditions. In Montreal, the commissioners interrogated Théophile Charron, who at the age of 14 had been working in a cigar factory for three years. Charron testified that he had been paid "a dollar a week for the first year, $1.50 for the second year, and $2.00 for the third year." During that time of "seasoning," he and his fellow child labourers worked for eight to 10 hours a day. If they were late for work, talked too much, or otherwise misbehaved they were fined, beaten, and sometimes confined to a "black hole" in the basement of the factory. Charron was one of 282 "little boy" and 110 "little girl" apprentices among the 1264 workers listed as employed in the city's cigar factories. By hiring children as nearly a third of their labour force, cigar factory owners could achieve a competitive advantage in the cut-throat environment that characterized their industry.[1]

The rules and rhythms of work in Canada's factories differed considerably from those that prevailed on the family farm. Although most children had always been obliged to contribute to the family economy, the industrial age encouraged a level of exploitation that troubled many Canadians. School attendance and child labour laws eventually made it more difficult for employers to build their profits on the backs of the young, but not before a generation of children, such as Théophile Charron, were schooled in the harsh experiences of factory discipline.

ASSESSING THE NATIONAL POLICY

While not everyone had an easy ride on the rocky road to industrialization in Canada, the overall economic trends were encouraging. The total output of goods and services, known as the gross national product (GNP), multiplied several times between 1867 and 1921 as the population rose from 3.5 million to 8.5 million. By 1915, three rail lines stretched across the continent, linking cities, towns, and villages, many of which had not even existed in 1867. Wherever it went, the railway spurred economic growth and laid the foundations for a national economy dominated by the banks and businesses located in Montreal and Toronto.

Three policies—a protective tariff, transcontinental railways, and sponsored immigration—emerged as the cornerstones of the federal government's development

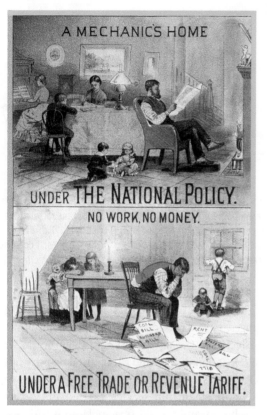

A Conservative Party election campaign poster against free trade, 1891. SOURCE: LIBRARY AND ARCHIVES CANADA C-95466

strategy, commonly labelled the National Policy. By linking the provinces, the railways enabled tariff-protected goods to find national markets. Immigration ensured passengers for railways and markets for Canadian products. Together, these policies were designed to bring Canada into an age of sustained industrial growth. In retrospect, these national policies look impressively integrated, but they actually developed in a piecemeal fashion and were challenged by regional, occupational, and individual agendas.

The importance of the National Policy in promoting industrial growth and economic expansion has long been debated. Detractors of the policy charge that the tariff benefited producers at the expense of consumers and encouraged investors to establish firms destined for failure. By protecting domestic manufacturers from foreign competition, they argue, high tariffs encouraged the development of industries that could never compete in international markets. Regional critics maintain that the policy encouraged economic development in central Canada to the detriment of the Maritimes and the West.

In contrast, supporters of the National Policy have argued that protection was necessary to allow infant industries to succeed against competition from established companies in other countries. Canada's model, after all, was the United States, where the importance of tariffs in promoting industrial development is generally conceded. Moreover, supporters point to statistics showing that, in the decade following the implementation of the National Policy tariff, capital investment increased 114 percent, total wages paid by manufacturers rose by 68 percent, and the number of manufacturing establishments grew by 52 percent over the previous decade. They also argue that, because of the National Policy, Canada was in a better position to take advantage of improved economic conditions in the late 1890s.

While the role of tariffs in Canadian economic development remains controversial, there are several points of agreement. It is clear, for example, that under the protective cloak of high tariffs, Canadian entrepreneurs moved to fill needs hitherto met by American imports. Southern Ontario, in particular, became the centre of specialized industries that served a national market. The agricultural implements industry is a good case in point. Using American patents in addition to developing their own lines, the firms of Massey Manufacturing of Toronto and A. Harris and Son of Brantford had emerged as leaders in the industry before Confederation. The implementation of a 35 percent tariff on imported agricultural machinery in 1883 gave them a tremendous boost in the Canadian market. In 1891, when the two companies merged as Massey-Harris, capitalized at $5 million, they formed Canada's largest corporation, controlling more than half the Canadian sales of agricultural machinery and accounting for 15 percent of the manufactured goods exported from Canada between 1890 and 1911.

There is also clear evidence that high tariffs laid the foundations for a branch-plant economy in Canada. Despite the success of such companies as Massey-Harris, many new companies, including Singer Sewing Machine, Gillette, Swift's, Coca-Cola, and Westinghouse, were American-owned. Their managers built factories in Canada to sell in a market that was protected from direct imports by tariff walls. In this period, the government welcomed foreign companies, and remained unconcerned about the nationality of company owners or the address to which profits were delivered.

The National Policy did little to shield Canada from dependence on foreign countries—primarily Great Britain and the United States—for capital and technology. Nor did it protect Canadians from international economic trends. Rising tariffs in the United States, fluctuating capital markets in Britain, and recessions in either country were immediately felt in Canada, and there was little Canadians could do economically or politically to alter that reality. International trends

Railway and construction accidents were all too frequent in the rapidly expanding transportation network. Boasting the longest cantilever span in the world, the Quebec Bridge, opened in 1919, was designed to carry trains across the St Lawrence and link Quebec City to the main Canadian rail lines. It collapsed twice during construction, killing 88 workers in all, 33 of them Mohawk high-steel workers from Kahnawake. This photo shows the second collapse, in 1916. SOURCE: LIBRARY AND ARCHIVES CANADA C-3623

meant that economic growth remained sluggish from 1867 to 1896, then soared until 1912. The First World War sent it soaring again. Shorter business cycles resulting in slowdowns in 1873–79, 1893–96, 1903–07, and 1913–14 were also felt in Canada.

It is impossible to determine whether another approach to economic development would have been more successful. No matter what they did, Canadians lived in a world dominated by the British Empire and situated on the border of the United States, an emerging industrial giant. When the Canadian economy was experiencing healthy growth, the American economy was often performing even better, encouraging people to move across the border to find work. In global terms, Canada's economic performance in this period was spectacular, but compared to the United States, the results seemed less impressive.

TRANSPORTATION AND COMMUNICATION

Railways played a major role in Canada's Industrial Revolution. By 1915, Canadians boasted more than 55 000 kilometres of track capable of shuffling goods and people from the Atlantic to the Pacific and even into the Yukon. By reducing transportation costs, railways expanded the geographic range in which products could be marketed. With the introduction of lower freight rates on eastbound grain under the Crow's Nest Pass Agreement of 1897 and competition resulting from the railway-building orgy of the early twentieth century, Prairie wheat farmers emerged

as highly competitive players in international grain exchanges. The increased efficiency of rail communication was reflected in the inauguration of daily postal service across the nation in 1886 and rural postal delivery in 1908.

Ocean travel was also improving in safety and capacity. Reliable steamship service carried Prairie wheat, Ontario bacon, and Nova Scotia apples to British markets on time and usually in good condition. Under the auspices of the federal government, which held responsibility for navigational aids, Canada's coasts and inland waterways sprouted lighthouses, channel markers, and wharves. When the *Titanic* was sunk by an iceberg in 1912, it shocked Canadians, who had become less accustomed to marine disasters than their grandparents had been. Increased capacity and lower rates also encouraged immigration.

The major threat to the supremacy of steam-powered transportation was the internal combustion engine, used in automobiles and aircraft. After the first manufacturing plant—a Ford branch plant—opened in 1904 in Windsor, Ontario, the auto industry thrived in Canada. By contrast, aircraft transportation was, literally, slow to get off the ground. Aeronautical experiments by J.A.D. McCurdy and F.W. Baldwin, under the auspices of Alexander Graham Bell's Aerial Experiment Association in Cape Breton, managed the first manned flight in the British Empire in 1909, with McCurdy at the controls, but it had few practical results.

Developments in transportation were matched by equally revolutionary advances in communication. Before he experimented in aviation, Alexander Graham Bell had become a household name with his highly publicized

The *Silver Dart* in 1908, at Badeck, Nova Scotia. In 1909, it flew the first manned flight. SOURCE: LIBRARY AND ARCHIVES CANADA PA-122520

telephone call between Brantford and Paris, Ontario, in 1876. Initially perceived as a novelty, the telephone quickly became a popular necessity for business and personal use. Another communication first occurred in 1901, when Guglielmo Marconi received a wireless signal from the other side of the Atlantic by hoisting an antenna on a kite on Signal Hill in St John's. Meanwhile, Canadian-born Reginald Fessenden was experimenting with wireless

telegraph and voice transmissions, conducting the first broadcast of the human voice by radio from his laboratory in Massachusetts in 1906.

This conquest of time and space through developments in transportation and communication made traditional ways of telling time awkward. In 1867, clocks were set by astronomical calculations in each major locality. This meant, for example, that 12:00 noon was 15 minutes

MORE TO THE STORY
Measuring the Canadian Economy

Economists divide the economy into three sectors: primary or staple industries such as hunting, fishing, forestry, farming, and mining; secondary or manufacturing industries that add value through the processing of primary resources; and tertiary or service industries that facilitate the use and development of primary and secondary resources. The tertiary sector includes financial services, trade, transportation, utilities, and public administration and services ranging from street cleaning to teaching. Together, the output of goods and services is called the gross national product (GNP).

In 1986, Statistics Canada adopted the gross domestic product (GDP) to measure the nation's economic performance. The GDP is calculated in the same way as the GNP except that it excludes payments on foreign investment. Since goods and services produced outside of the market economy, such as housework and voluntary labour, are not included in calculations of GNP, the national output is considerably greater than the official figures indicate. In 1996, Statistics Canada began collecting data on unpaid labour in and outside of the household, which accounts for much of the work performed by Canadians.

earlier in Halifax than in Moncton. The railway and telegraph demanded a more standardized approach, especially in a country as big as Canada. Appropriately, it was a Canadian, Sandford Fleming, who convinced those attending the International Prime Meridian Conference in 1884 in Washington to adopt a global system of telling time based on hourly variations from a standard mean, which is still in use today.

SECONDARY INDUSTRY

In the 50 years following Confederation, secondary industry went from strength to strength. The first phase of Canada's Industrial Revolution, which occurred roughly between 1850 and 1900, was characterized by a rapid expansion of consumer goods industries, such as textiles, clothing, footwear, and cigars. The second phase, beginning around 1900, was fuelled by a surge in capital goods industries, such as machinery and equipment, and new technologies that spurred development in mining, pulp and paper, and electrical and chemical industries. By 1921, nearly 30 percent of Canada's GNP was derived from manufacturing and construction (see Table 4.1), a proportion that remained virtually constant to the end of the twentieth century.

The emergence of a vigorous iron and steel industry at the turn of the century signalled Canada's arrival as an industrial nation. Located in convenient proximity to coal mines on Cape Breton Island and an abundant supply of iron ore shipped from Bell Island, Newfoundland, Sydney became home to two industrial giants: Nova Scotia Coal and Steel and Dominion Iron and Steel. After several false starts, the Hamilton Steel and Iron Company began pouring open-hearth steel in 1900 and established its dominance

TABLE 4.1

Percentage Sectoral Distribution of the GNP, 1880–1920

YEAR	PRIMARY	SECONDARY	TERTIARY	OTHER
1880	43.5	22.7	22.4	11.4
1890	36.6	28.1	26.7	8.6
1900	36.5	25.0	29.4	9.1
1910	30.2	27.8	33.6	8.4
1920	26.6	29.7	35.3	8.4

Source: William L. Marr and Donald Paterson, *Canada: An Economic History* (Toronto: Gage, 1980) 22

in the industry following its reorganization as Stelco in 1910. By that time, American visionary Francis Hector Clergue had capped his industrial empire at Sault Ste Marie with a massive steel and iron works. Between 1877 and 1900, Canadian iron production increased more than sixfold and multiplied tenfold again by 1913.

Canada's heavy industry expanded impressively during the first two decades of the twentieth century. In addition to the rails and rolling stock required for the railways, Canadian factories turned out binders and seed drills, bicycles and carriages, and furniture and appliances to supply the Canadian market. Stimulated by economic growth, construction materials such as lumber, bricks, glass, stone, and cement figured prominently in the secondary sector. The demand for factories, public buildings, homes, and tenements sustained a construction industry that accounted for more than five percent of the GNP by 1921.

As manufacturing became more complex, intermediate goods required in the production process became a larger segment of secondary industry. Among the most successful intermediate goods industries were those turning out products such as bolts, nails, nuts, and screws. Acids, alkalis, and heavy chemicals, essential ingredients in pulp and paper, iron and steel, oil refining, the electrical industry, and agriculture also experienced increased demand.

There was a clear geographical structure to the Canadian economy as it emerged under the National Policy. Neither the Maritimes nor the western provinces managed to emulate the manufacturing success of the central Canadian provinces, whose head start in the Industrial Revolution was evident even before Confederation. By 1901, Ontario accounted for fully half of the gross value of Canadian manufacturing, and Quebec for nearly a third. Once set, this pattern remained remarkably constant.

THE NEW FACE OF AGRICULTURE

Primary industries were also transformed in the industrial age. As agriculture evolved from a way of life to an industry, successful farms became larger and more highly mechanized, while subsistence farms on marginal lands were quickly abandoned. The decline in the relative importance of farming in this period reflects the fact that fewer farms were required to meet the Canadian and international demand for food.

Stimulated by local demand and the almost insatiable British market for staple foods, commercialized farming flourished in Ontario. With rail and steamship service offering more reliable transportation, cold storage facilities, and lower freight rates, huge quantities of Ontario bacon, cheese, butter, and eggs found their way to British larders by the end of the nineteenth century. Ontario farmers also branched into industrial crops such as sugar beets, grapes, and tobacco, and grew most of the fruit and vegetables that were canned in Canada before 1914. By the end of the century, the William Davies Company in Toronto slaughtered nearly 450 000 Canadian-grown hogs each year, employed 300 workers, and boasted annual export sales of more than $3.5 million. The export sales of Canadian cheese, much of it produced in Ontario, sky-rocketed from 8.3 million pounds in 1871 to 189.8 million

VOICES FROM THE PAST
Dairy Farming in Transition

Milk delivery wagon, Montreal, 1908. As Canada urbanized, farm families earned money by supplying creameries and city markets with milk, butter, eggs, and other foodstuffs. Before the age of the automobile, milk wagons pulled by horses or oxen were a common sight in city streets. SOURCE: McCORD MUSEUM MP-1991-40.1

Dairy farming became a major business enterprise at the end of the nineteenth century as farmers increasingly sold their milk to mechanized dairies. In 1905, F.E.A. Gagnon revealed his enthusiasm for modernization in his description of the dairy facilities at Sainte-Marie de la Beauce in Quebec.

> The centrifugal machine is truly marvelous: it separates the cream from the milk at a rate of 1000 pounds per hour. Thanks to its use, the one hundred and six farmers who supply the creamery, of which MM. Duchesnay, Lindsay, Chaperon, and others are the owners, need only transport their milk once a day. The evening milk is mixed with the morning milk. The light cream formed during the night is remixed with the milk during transport, but the centrifugal separator undoes all that.

> … The apparatus is put in motion by a six horse-power steam engine, a jewel! You must see the separator work, the mixer, the vacuum suction devices, etc. Above all, be sure to have everything explained to you by the intelligent director of the school-factory, Mr. Stanislas Barré.

> Go and see. I tell you just this, because one must always be careful not to promise more butter than bread.[2]

Gagnon's enthusiasm for the technological marvels of the industrial age was shared by many Canadians, who embraced the efficiency of new machinery and the promise of easily accomplishing tasks that had once involved back-breaking work. As mechanization increased across all sectors of the economy, it soon became clear that some benefited while others did not. People who once produced the necessities of life by hand lost their livelihoods, while the factory jobs created by mechanization were often organized to force workers to perform at inhuman speeds with endless repetition of the same tasks. Even the farm women, who rejoiced when the new creameries relieved them of the drudgery of separating cream and churning butter, soon realized that tasks they once controlled in the home were now managed by their husbands and sons in the public sphere.

in 1899. Although Canadian producers made their reputation with cheddar, they also invented processed cheese, upon which A.F. McLaren of Ingersoll built a thriving business. Following the First World War, he was bought out by another Canadian-born cheesemaker, J.L. Kraft, who had moved to Chicago in 1905 where he became the world's most successful cheesemaker.

Ontario's farms remained more productive than those of Quebec, where families were larger, mechanization slower, and farm surpluses less abundant. Nevertheless, cattle raising in Quebec's Eastern Townships proved a highly profitable venture, and Quebec farmers exported butter and cheese to Great Britain. The Maritimes, like Quebec, had a large number of marginal farms, but, in fertile areas such as the St John River Valley, the Annapolis Valley, and Prince Edward Island, farmers turned to commercial farming to take advantage of expanding urban markets at home and abroad. Potatoes were a successful crop throughout the region, and in the Annapolis Valley of Nova Scotia, the production of apples, destined primarily for the British market, increased nearly tenfold between 1881 and 1911.

The Prairie wheat boom was the most spectacular agricultural success story of this period. Between 1901 and 1913, wheat production expanded from 56 million to 224 million bushels, grain exports increased by 600 percent, and wheat soared from 14 to 42 percent of total Canadian exports. A variety of factors came together to make the wheat boom possible: faster maturing strains of wheat, the chill steel plough (which could handle the prairie sod), gas-driven tractors, rising world prices, lower transportation costs, a steady supply of immigrant labour, and encouragement from public and private agencies. Together, these factors transformed the Prairies from a fur-trade frontier into the breadbasket of the world, its wheat production second in volume only to that of the United States.

Although significant, wheat was by no means the only product of western agriculture. Dairy farming was important in Manitoba, as was mixed farming in the Park Belt of the Prairies and in British Columbia. Between 1885 and 1905, cattle ranching flourished in the Alberta foothills. Canada's "wild West" was developed by "gentlemen farmers" such as Senator Matthew Cochrane, a pioneer cattle breeder and successful shoe manufacturer from the Eastern Townships. With an embargo on American imports, generous terms for leasing land, and the completion of the CPR—all provided by the obliging Macdonald government in the 1880s—ranching fever gripped Alberta. Cattle ranching also expanded in the Okanagan Valley in the wake of the gold rush. Despite their initial success, ranchers in Alberta and British Columbia were soon fighting a rearguard action against farmers who, armed with dryland farming techniques, insisted on breaking up the cattle range.

Scientific and technological innovation had an enormous impact on agricultural production. It has been estimated that the development of the fast-maturing Marquis wheat by dominion cerealist Charles E. Saunders added more than $100 million to farm income between 1911 and 1918. While horse and human power continued to be the chief sources of energy on Canadian farms, engine power was introduced as early as 1877 when the first steam threshing machine was used in Woodbridge, Ontario. Steam threshers could process more in a day than the average farmer produced in a year, and they soon transformed the harvesting process. Gasoline engines and tractors became practical in the second decade of the twentieth century.

FISH, FOREST, AND FURS

East Coast fisheries, like agriculture, adjusted unevenly to the new economic order. In the second half of the nineteenth century, the inshore fisheries came under increasing competition from deep-sea fleets, while canning and cold storage emerged as new ways of preserving fish, supplementing salting, drying, and pickling. Investment poured into canning factories designed to process lobster, herring, and sardines, and into cold storage facilities to handle fresh fish. While technology and transportation dictated that the fresh fish industry would become centralized in a few communities, the canned and salt fishery remained dispersed and uncoordinated. Because virtually every fishing port had a cannery, the product varied widely in quality, and workers were relegated to seasonal employment. Quality control also plagued the saltfish industry, which was beginning to face stiff competition in its traditional Latin American and southern European markets.

On the Pacific Coast, the salmon fishery developed quickly in the final decades of the nineteenth century. By 1900, salmon had become the most profitable fishery

The influx of immigrants and the rapid spread of salmon canneries in British Columbia at the turn of the twentieth century resulted in a series of laws that restricted salmon-fishing licences in the interests of canning and recreational fisheries. Invariably, the laws had a negative impact on Native peoples, who were less likely than immigrants to own canning companies. This picture shows a federal fisheries officer (on the right-hand side above the chute) removing an "illegal" Kwakwaka'wakw salmon trap on the Marble River, Quatsino Sound, Vancouver Island, in 1912.
SOURCE: VANCOUVER PUBLIC LIBRARY 13904

in Canada, surpassing cod in the value of sales. Steveston became known as the sockeye capital of the world, exporting its canned salmon largely to a British market. In 1902, much of the industry was centralized under the British Columbia Packers Association. A company backed by eastern Canadian and American capital, it was based in New Jersey, a state whose loose incorporation laws made it a popular base for companies avoiding anti-trust legislation. The new company consolidated and mechanized the packing process, increasing its profits by reducing the costs of labour and fish supply. The Smith butchering machine, whose popular name, the "Iron Chink," reflected racist attitudes toward Asian cannery workers, processed 60 to 75 fish a minute and encouraged the mechanizing of filleting, salting, and weighing. When the sanitary can and double seamer were introduced in 1912, the automated assembly line became a reality.

Aboriginal peoples suffered most from the commercialization of the salmon fishery. For centuries, the economies and cultures of Natives on the Pacific coast had been based on salmon. Indeed, the commercial fishery in the early years depended on Natives' skills as fishers, processors, boat builders, and net makers. By the end of the nineteenth century, federal and provincial governments began passing legislation to control the fishery. Historian Dianne Newell has traced the process by which fishery regulations were used to deny Natives access to their traditional fishing sites and methods. She concludes: "As the industry spread and mechanized in the twentieth century, changes in labour supply, in markets for fish, in technology, and in government regulation rendered Indians less central to fishing, and eventually to fish processing."[3] By adapting to new technologies, new regulations, and white hostility, Native families and villages managed to maintain a toehold in the industry until the second half of the twentieth century, but they were no longer central to the industry they had once dominated.

British Columbia was also Canada's new timber frontier. By the 1880s, most of the white pine forests of eastern Canada had been laid to waste. The demand for lumber for construction in rapidly growing North American cities was met by the majestic Douglas fir and cedar trees of the West Coast. Between 1871 and 1880, some 350 million board feet of timber were cut in British Columbia; in the second decade of the twentieth century, the figure had risen to a staggering 13.5 billion, and lumbering had emerged as one of British Columbia's most lucrative industries. The forests of eastern Canada continued to produce lumber, fine woods for furniture, pit props for mines, railway ties, shakes, shingles, and laths, and contributed to the production of pulp and paper, an industry that expanded rapidly at the end of the nineteenth century.

New technology and modern business practices transformed the fur industry. By the first decade of the twentieth century, fur farming had begun to emerge as an alternative to hunting and trapping. Based primarily on Prince Edward Island, the raising of fox, mink, and other fur-bearing animals in captivity was made more practical by the introduction of woven wire enclosures in the late 1890s. Thereafter, the industry developed quickly, stimulated by improved breeding methods, the growing demand of the fashion industry, and the declining population of the world's wild fur-bearing animals. In the early twentieth century, Prince Edward Island breeders fetched as much as $15 000 a pair for their silver fox on the London market. Faced with this form of competition, the Hudson's Bay Company introduced bureaucratic management structures, used railways and steamships where possible, and pushed into new fur-trade frontiers.

Buildings, pit, and ore stockpile of the Moose Mountain iron mine, near Sudbury in Northern Ontario, about 1910. The environmental devastation is striking. SOURCE: McCORD MUSEUM MP-0000.794.1

THE MINING INDUSTRY

Canada's mining industry grew dramatically in the years following Confederation. Although the Klondike gold rush received plenty of publicity, it had relatively less impact on the Canadian economy than other mining ventures. The Industrial Revolution was built on resources of coal, iron, and other base metals. It was the discovery and exploitation of these resources that drew most of the investment, if not the popular attention.

Coal mining in the Maritimes, Alberta, and British Columbia expanded in the late nineteenth century to supply Canadian trains, factories, and homes. By the beginning of the twentieth century, huge quantities of coal and iron were processed in Canada's steel plants. Surveys conducted for the CPR and the Canadian Geological Survey revealed the potential wealth locked in the Canadian Shield and the western mountain ranges. When chemical and mechanical processes for separating complex ores were developed at the turn of the century, the nickel-copper deposits around Sudbury and zinc-lead-silver deposits in British Columbia became profitable fields for exploitation. Capital poured into Canada from all over the world to bring the vast storehouse of mineral wealth into production.

The discovery of copper-gold deposits at the base of Red Mountain in 1887 created an instant boom town at Rossland, British Columbia. By that time, an American promoter, F.A. Heinze, had built a smelter at Trail, which was connected to Rossland by a narrow-gauge railway. Following its decision to build a line through the Crowsnest Pass, the CPR bought Heinze's interests and incorporated them in the Consolidated Mining and Smelting Company of Canada (Cominco) in 1906. As a CPR subsidiary, Cominco had access to extensive capital resources, which were used to develop hydroelectric power in the region and to solve the metallurgical problem of separating ores. By 1910, British Columbia's mineral output was second in value only to Ontario's, much of it extracted from the Kootenay region.

Rich mineral resources were concentrated in "New Ontario," the area between Sudbury and Hudson Bay, which was granted in huge sections to Ontario by the federal government and the courts between 1874 and 1912. Following the discovery of copper sulphides in the Sudbury Basin in 1883, American promoter Samuel J. Ritchie established the Canadian Copper Company to develop Sudbury's deposits for refining by the Orford Copper Company in New Jersey. In 1888, a smelter was constructed at Copper Cliff to concentrate the nickel-copper matte prior to shipping. Canadian Copper and Orford merged in 1902 to form the International Nickel Company, or Inco, of New Jersey. Increasing demand for nickel-steel armour plate in a rapidly militarizing Europe led Mond Nickel of Wales to establish a base in Sudbury, which emerged as the world's major supplier of nickel. At the same time, discoveries of gold, silver, and cobalt along the route of the Timiskaming and Northern Ontario Railway put the names of Cobalt, Timmins, Kirkland Lake, and Porcupine on the map. The value of minerals produced in Ontario increased fourfold between 1900 and 1910 and nearly doubled again in the next decade, making Ontario Canada's leading province in the mining industry.

Quebec's rich mining frontier was slow to develop, but its extraordinary range of mineral resources inspired a variety of initiatives. At the end of the nineteenth century, foreign companies began working asbestos deposits in the Eastern Townships. Although Quebec quickly became the world's leading producer of this rare mineral, most of the processing was done outside of Canada, and the fierce competition between mining companies resulted in overproduction, gluts, and slowdowns that made the industry highly unstable. The copper and gold deposits of the Abitibi region of Quebec, though identified, were not seriously exploited until the 1920s.

With nearly 80 percent of Canada's electrical generating capacity, Ontario and Quebec dominated the second industrial revolution based on mining, chemicals, and pulp and paper, which relied on abundant energy resources. Ontario's initiative in developing Niagara Falls gave the province a massive source of hydroelectric power. In Quebec, American capital harnessed the mighty Shawinigan Falls on the Saint-Maurice River. Shawinigan soon attracted an aluminum smelter, pulp mill, and chemical factories. Unlike Ontario, which made hydro a government-run service in 1906, Quebec left the hydro industry to private enterprise. Whether publicly or privately owned, the abundant supply of hydroelectric power served as a magnet to industry.

SERVING THE INDUSTRIAL ECONOMY

The Industrial Revolution in Canada and elsewhere was carried forward by a growing army of clerks, cleaners, cab drivers, cooks, and secretaries, in addition to managers, bankers, lawyers, engineers, and civil servants. In 1921, as many people laboured in service industries as in the primary sector. They worked in jobs such as electrical repair, automobile sales, and switchboard operation, jobs which could scarcely have been imagined in 1867.

Clerical work was one of the fastest-growing occupations in an industrializing Canada, spurred by the introduction of the typewriter in the second half of the nineteenth century. While the general labour force grew by 10.4 percent between 1891 and 1901, the clerical sector rose 73.3 percent. This growth continued in the first decade of the twentieth century and reached an astounding 109.3 percent between 1911 and 1921. By the latter date, clerical workers represented nearly seven percent of the entire paid labour force. Another change also took place in this 30-year period. In 1891, women made up only 14.3 percent of those working in clerical positions; by 1921, 41.8 percent of clerical workers were women, and the trend toward the feminization of clerical work continued throughout the twentieth century.

As transportation improved and nationwide markets emerged, retail operations were transformed. The changes in retailing activity can be seen in the meteoric rise of the T. Eaton Company. In 1869, Timothy Eaton opened a dry-goods and clothing store on Yonge Street in Toronto. His method of selling, which included fixed prices, cash only, and money-back guarantees, proved so popular that he moved to larger premises, equipped with an elevator, in 1883. A year later, Eaton reached across the country to grab business from local retailers when he issued his first mail-order catalogue. The expansion in sales allowed Eaton's to manufacture its own merchandise, thus bypassing wholesalers and suppliers. In 1893, Eaton's established the first of a number of overseas operations in London. Eaton's also opened a branch in Winnipeg in 1905, the first in a chain-store business that would expand dramatically in the 1920s. Robert Simpson, also of Toronto, paralleled the Eaton's experience. No corner of Canada reached by the postal service was left unchanged by the rise of the great department stores and their dream-selling catalogues.

MASS PRODUCTION AND MODERN MANAGEMENT

Market expansion led to a reorganization of the structure of industry, encouraging small-scale, owner-operated businesses to evolve into bureaucratic, multipurpose, and multinational corporations. The limited liability corporation separated individual wealth from corporate wealth and made corporations independent legal entities. No longer tied to the fate of a single person or a few individuals, the corporation took on a life of its own. At the same time, ownership was divorced from management functions, which were increasingly carried out by salaried employees. No one individual, no matter how energetic or gifted, could keep on top of the details of such rapidly expanding businesses—nor was such control desirable. Chief executive officers needed their time to mobilize capital and plot long-range corporate strategy.

At the turn of the century, management techniques became the focus of attention for business people trying to maximize the profits of their enterprises. Scientific management, a term coined by American engineer Frederick W. Taylor, advocated that managers take responsibility for coordinating work processes and that employees be deprived of any initiative in deciding how to do their work. On the shop floor, this meant that the labour process was broken down into simple repetitive tasks and that employee output was closely monitored by supervisors. At the management level, rigid hierarchies with clear lines of authority were developed and new accounting procedures implemented to control production and labour costs. When American entrepreneur Henry Ford perfected the assembly line for his Model T in 1914, artisans who had once performed the most skilled of manufacturing operations—the assembly of complex machinery—were forced to submit to the dictates of management and the machine.

Driven by the Darwinian logic that held that only the fittest survived, corporate managers were forced to keep ahead of the competition or go to the wall. Not surprisingly, entrepreneurs were decidedly unenthusiastic about unrestrained competition. While giving lip service to free enterprise, they secretly agreed to fix prices and agitated publicly for policies that would guarantee them a "living profit." Nationwide associations, such as the Dominion Wholesale Grocers Guild, Retail Merchants Association, Canadian Manufacturers Association, and Canadian Bankers Association, tried to regulate the activities of their members, but restrictions on "unfair" trading practices often failed to bring order to the marketplace because it took only one entrepreneur to break an agreement.

For most businesses, growing bigger meant becoming more efficient, reaping the benefits of economies of scale, and gaining an edge over competitors. If a company could become big enough, it might be possible to sweep all competition aside and establish a monopoly over the marketplace. Although "monopoly" was a bad word in industrializing Canada, anti-combine laws, first introduced in 1889, had little impact on corporate practices. A spate of mergers in the 1880s was followed by an even bigger merger movement in the early twentieth century. Between 1909 and 1912, some 275 Canadian firms were consolidated into 52 enterprises, capitalized at nearly half a billion dollars.

The merger movement brought to the fore some of Canada's major corporate giants. Vertically integrated

What a difference a century made in the shoe industry, as this celebratory pair of prints trumpeted. The worker at the right, however, had far less control over his labour. SOURCE: McCORD MUSEUM M930.50.262 AND M930.50.5.142

companies were capable of handling all the functions of the industry, including supplying their own raw materials and shipping their products in company-owned boxcars. Their vast assets enabled them to mobilize capital on a scale hitherto unimaginable. Although such companies were not technically monopolies, their size gave them tremendous power in the reorganized marketplace. They could outbid and outlast their smaller competitors and make it difficult for new competitors to break into the industry. Many of the companies established at the turn of the twentieth century became household names in Canada—Imperial Oil, Bell Canada, General Electric, Stelco, and Canada Cement Company—visible testimony to their triumph over the "invisible forces" of the marketplace.

Consolidation was also the order of the day in banking. In 1871, Ottawa passed an act requiring banks to have assets of at least $500 000, resulting in the eventual dissolution of small banks. Between 1880 and 1920, while the number of branches rose from under 300 to 4676, the number of banks operating under dominion charter declined from 44 to 18. No longer simply vehicles for facilitating exchange, banks encouraged savings accounts by paying interest on deposited money, transferred funds from their many branches to profitable investment frontiers, and developed modern management structures. By 1920, four of the five Canadian banks that still tower over the business centres of most Canadian towns and cities—Scotia, Commerce, Montreal, and Royal—had established their positions in the financial firmament.

BIOGRAPHY
Max Aitken

Max Aitken was Canada's most flamboyant financier. The son of a Presbyterian minister, Aitken grew up in Miramichi, New Brunswick, and followed the money to Calgary and then to Halifax, where he became the protégé of Halifax businessman John Stairs. As manager of Stairs's new holding company, Royal Securities, founded in 1903, Aitken made his first fortune speculating in utilities in the Caribbean and Latin America. In 1907 he moved to Montreal, used Montreal Trust to take over Royal Securities, and became a key figure in the merger movement of 1909-12 that transformed Canada's corporate sector. His crowning achievement was putting together the Steel Company of Canada (Stelco) in 1910, a conglomerate that included Montreal Rolling Mills, Hamilton Steel and Iron, Canada Screw, and Canada Bolt and Nut. Rich and powerful, but embroiled in a financial scandal relating to his investments, Aitken moved to London, where he had marketed much of his speculative stock, became a member of parliament, bought himself a title–Lord Beaverbrook–and continued to keep an eye on his Canadian interests. Among Beaverbrook's merger-making associates was a future Canadian prime minister, R.B. Bennett, whose millions were earned in part by collaborating with Aitken to merge grain elevators and hydroelectric stations on the Prairies.[4]

Max Aitken c. 1914-1919. SOURCE: LIBRARY AND ARCHIVES CANADA PA-006478

PRIVATE INITIATIVE AND PUBLIC POLICY

In Canada, as in the United States and Great Britain, private capitalists were the preferred agents for undertaking risky economic ventures. Governments at all levels encouraged and assisted private enterprise, but became directly involved only as a last resort. Largely unfettered by government regulation before the First World War, capitalists also reaped most of the profit of their ambitious undertakings. Successful entrepreneurs paid no income tax before 1917, were subject to few estate or corporation taxes, and often benefited from huge government grants.

In the first decade of the twentieth century, entrepreneurs came under increasing criticism, and governments were encouraged to take action to protect the public against private greed. Regulatory commissions became a popular means of establishing some control over the activities of private corporations. In 1903, the Board of Railway Commissioners was set up to serve as a buffer between the disgruntled public and the railways. Federally chartered telephone companies came under the commission's jurisdiction in 1906.

The state played an enormous role in how Canadian industry developed. Public money provided much of the infrastructure, or basic services, upon which private fortunes were built. Apart from involvement in railways, Ottawa sponsored the Geological Survey of Canada, established a system of experimental farms, and subsidized cold storage facilities to enhance economic development. Most provinces passed legislation to encourage settlement and disposed of timber and mineral rights by sale or lease. From 1897 to 1900, Ontario imposed an excise tax on the export of unprocessed logs to encourage manufacturing in the province. As a result of this legislation, sawmills and pulp and paper plants were established in Ontario, leading other timber-producing provinces such as Quebec and New Brunswick to adopt similar legislative measures.

The Ontario government also took the dramatic step of establishing the provincially controlled Hydro-Electric Power Commission in 1906 to regulate private power companies, distribute power, and ultimately generate its own power. Promoted as a policy to bring "power to the people," Ontario Hydro was supported by entrepreneurs throughout southwestern sections of the province who wanted access to a cheap and reliable source of power for industrial purposes. Like Ontario, the Prairie provinces experimented with government-owned utilities, but most provincial administrations preferred to avoid the political pitfalls of direct government ownership.

Municipal governments also played their part. As cities grew and services became more complex, direct involvement seemed increasingly necessary. Private companies providing water, sewage, street lighting, communication, and transportation services in urban settings were often granted monopoly powers, and, in the opinion of consumers, many abused their privileged position. After the 1890s, many municipal governments either assumed direct control over utilities or created regulatory commissions to keep an eye on private corporations. The result of the spate of utility development in a burgeoning industrial economy was a typically Canadian system of mixed public and private services reflecting the circumstances of individual localities.

HUMAN CAPITAL

Life in the industrial workplace could be gruelling. In many occupations, 12-hour days were common. Conditions were sometimes better in small businesses where people worked with kin or in community settings, but in such cases there was even less recourse from a cruel or capricious boss. Children in the workforce were particularly vulnerable. Punishments were imposed to exact conformity, break children's independence, and ensure regular work habits. In families where children's income was critical to survival, it was not uncommon for parents to support employers in their efforts to "train" young workers.

Given their value to the family economy, many children no doubt preferred workplaces to schools. In Cumberland County, Nova Scotia, where children made up 16 percent of the coal-mining workforce in the 1880s, young boys were proud to be doing "a man's job." Coal miners, working with relatively uncomplicated technology, produced an indispensable product, and their ability to shut down a mine gave them power within the workplace and the community. Boys shared with men the dangers of the job. In 1891, the first of many mining disasters in Springhill, Nova Scotia, resulted in the deaths of 125 men and boys.

In keeping with the gendered notions of work that prevailed in industrializing Canada, skill—while arguably an objective concept—was also socially constructed. Certain jobs were treated as requiring special abilities or training, while others were not. For example, though it required little talent or training, printing was a well-paid "skilled" occupation that excluded women. Meanwhile, dressmaking, which required considerable skill, was a poorly paid "unskilled" task in which women were employed. Although women were the food manufacturers at home, in candy-making factories only men were confectioners. Women were hired at low wages to decorate and box prepared candies. As the structures of industrialization were gradually put in place, it became the ideal that married men earned incomes in the marketplace, while their wives stayed home to do housework and rear the children or, in middle-class families, supervise the servants who did this work.

Professionals and unionized craftsmen could often earn a wage sufficient to maintain a family, but the vast majority of wage earners could not. Nevertheless, the belief that the male head of household should earn enough to feed, clothe, and shelter a family was used to justify underpaying female workers. Writing in 1897 on the sweatshops of the clothing-manufacturing sector in Toronto, future prime minister William Lyon Mackenzie King quoted an owner who noted: "I don't treat the men bad, but I even up by taking advantage of the women. I have a girl who can do as much work, and as good work as a man; she gets $5 a week. The man who is standing next to her gets $11. The girls, however, average $3.50 a week, and some are as low as two dollars."[5]

On the railroads and in the highly mechanized manufacturing sectors, late-nineteenth-century employers capitulated to the demands of male workers that women and children not be hired as cheap labour. Such demands were often ignored in unskilled industries where competition to provide goods at the lowest possible cost occurred mainly on the backs of workers. The cigar makers of London, Ontario, for example, learned in the 1880s how easily a well-paid skilled occupation could be turned into a poorly paid "unskilled" job. While unionized cigar makers tried to maintain quality, restrict new entrants to the trade, and hold the line on wages, their employers were eager to reduce labour costs. When unionized workers refused to accept a cut in wages, their employers replaced most of them with women and children. By the mid-1880s, only 13 of the 150 cigar makers in town were adult men.

Company owners also kept Canadian labour in line by supporting an open-door policy for immigrants who agreed to work as strikebreakers or under conditions that Canadians found unacceptable. In response to demands from workers, the Laurier government passed an Alien Labour Act (1897) designed to make it unlawful to bring in foreign labourers. Despite its sweeping scope, the Alien Labour Act failed to prevent companies from importing contract labour and strikebreakers when they were determined to do so. The act was rarely enforced and applied only to the importation of labour from the United States.

Modern management techniques and hiring practices reduced the autonomy of many workers; so did the company-town phenomenon. Mining and textile-mill towns were frequently owned by companies, with homes, stores, schools, doctors, and even churches firmly under corporate control. Nova Scotia, Alberta, and British Columbia coal, Quebec asbestos, and Ontario gold, silver, and nickel were mined primarily by workers who lived in company towns. While some factory owners took a paternal attitude toward their workers, most resorted to authoritarian control if workers threatened to strike or otherwise stepped out of line.

The interior of a garment factory in London, Ontario, in about 1910. The photograph illustrates the cramped, dangerous working conditions of these women. SOURCE: LIBRARY AND ARCHIVES CANADA PA-803003

Disease and injury were often the fate of industrial workers. Although the 1889 Royal Commission on the Relations of Labor and Capital had reported dangerous working conditions and recommended reform, little action was taken. Workers stricken by injury were placed in the difficult position of having to prove employer negligence to be able to sue for compensation. In the second decade of the twentieth century, Ontario, Nova Scotia, British Columbia, Alberta, and New Brunswick passed Workmen's Compensation acts, which conceded a limited right to industrial compensation. Still, many employees found no protection from the high levels of zinc, mercury, asbestos, dry-cleaning fluids, dyes, and other chemicals that went unregulated. Coal miners and textile workers "retired" exhausted and prematurely aged, their lungs so damaged by coal dust and fabric fibres that they coughed themselves to death. Anonymous graves along rail tracks or near remote mines bear testimony to the immigrant labourers who worked under draconian conditions in industrializing Canada.

Provincial governments passed but rarely enforced legislation to improve industrial safety. In Canada's worst mining disaster, the explosion at the Hillcrest Coal and Coke Company mine on the Alberta side of the Crowsnest Pass in June 1914, the jury at the coroner's inquest noted that the company ignored the Mines Act regulation that required them to provide fresh air to each mine seam. That would have rendered harmless the noxious gases that killed 189 miners, but the company was never prosecuted for its refusal to follow the law.

VOICES FROM THE PAST
The Impact of Immigrant Labour

Canadian workers were opposed to a liberal immigration policy, which they saw as a means of keeping their wages depressed. For cities such as Montreal, where wages were relatively low to begin with, the arrival in the spring of 1904 of a large number of Italian men, many of them sojourners who planned to return home with their earnings, brought howls of complaint. The federal government felt obliged to respond to the uproar by appointing the Royal Commission on Immigration of Italian Labourers to Montreal and the Alleged Fraudulent Practices of Employment Agencies. Its report left little doubt about the impact of immigrant labourers.

Charles Hodgson Osler, a superintendent employed by the Montreal Light, Heat and Power company, testified that 100 of the roughly 250 men employed by the company were Italians and that wages had been reduced as a result of their arrival in the city.

Q. You remember the influx of Italian labour last April and May? – A. Yes.

Q. Would that affect the scale of labour for labourers? – A. Yes, I think it would.

Q. These Italians only received from $1.25 to $1.35 a day? – A. Yes.

Q. Are there others besides Italians only receiving that amount? – A. Yes, quite a number.

Q. Who are they? – A. Well, some English and some French speaking men.

Q. You get as many men as you require on your work without difficulty? – A. We have done it so far, we have had no trouble at all; we had a little trouble last year, but we increased the wages to $1.45. We got lots of men this year at $1.25, whereas we had to pay $1.45 last year.

Q. I suppose there are the same number employed this year as last? – A. No, I have nearly double the quantity this year.

Q. The wages then dropped 20 cents? – A. Yes, there was a large influx of men, and we took advantage of labour as it came in.[6]

THE UNION MOVEMENT

Both skilled and unskilled labour tried to control their working conditions, but they faced daunting challenges. In 1871, Toronto printers went on strike against all of the city's newspapers in an attempt to force the nine-hour day on the publishing industry. The publishers, led by Liberal Party notable George Brown, successfully prosecuted the strikers for seditious conspiracy, while 10 000 people paraded in support of the accused and their strike demands. Throughout 1872, the movement for the nine-hour day reverberated throughout industrial Canada, only to be quelled by the crushing recession of 1873.

John A. Macdonald, eager to embarrass Brown and to signal to skilled immigrants that Canada was a good place to work, passed a Trade Union Act in 1872, which removed common-law prohibitions against unions as combinations in restraint of trade. On the surface this was a major achievement for labour, but there were no provisions in the legislation to require employers to bargain collectively with their employees or to prevent employers from dismissing employees who supported unionization.

By the 1880s, the strike had become the chief method for addressing labour grievances. A key player in the strike wave was the Noble and Holy Order of the Knights of Labor. Originating in 1869 among Philadelphia garment cutters concerned about the loss of worker control in their industry, the Knights spread quickly across the United States and soon gained a foothold in Canada. Unlike craft unions, which organized workers according to their trade, the Knights were open to all workers regardless of skill, and encouraged workers to support each other's struggles.

It was not only employers who recoiled at the class consciousness promoted by the Knights. Craft union leaders claimed that the exclusive right of workers to practise certain trades would be whittled away if the Knights succeeded in developing all-inclusive "industrial" unions. By the late 1880s, craft unions began to force workers to choose between the Knights and separate craft unions. The Knights retained many locals, especially in Quebec, but their isolation increased as the Trades and Labour Congress (TLC), created in 1883, emerged as the major political voice of Canadian labour.

Dominated by craft-based unions, the TLC fought against industrial unions almost as hard as it did against employer intransigence. It also adopted the policy of its counterpart in the United States—the American Federation of Labor—of calling for higher wages and improved working conditions rather than for radical changes to the capitalist system. In 1902, at a meeting in Berlin, Ontario, the TLC formally affiliated with the American Federation of Labor. It then proceeded to expel industrial unions such as the Knights of Labor from its ranks and to consolidate its position as the dominant labour organization in the country. TLC exiles established a rival organization, the National Trades and Labour Congress, in 1907. Although its numbers were small, it offered a nationalist alternative for Canada's working men and women.

During Canada's rise to industrial maturity, labour organizations were fragmented along regional and cultural lines. In Nova Scotia, the Provincial Workmen's Association (PWA), established in 1879, emerged as the most powerful voice of the province's working class. Militant in its early years, the PWA shut down all the province's mines on two occasions, and its fiercely independent locals waged over 70 strikes before 1900. When strike activity increased during the first decade of the twentieth century, Maritime coal miners turned to the even more radical American-based United Mine Workers (UMW) of America to help them in their struggles.

Miner militancy on the East Coast was matched in British Columbia, where the Mutual Protective Society was established in 1877 among workers at Dunsmuir, Diggle and Company. The society protested wage cuts and the short-weighing of coal on company scales (the workers were paid by the ton), and closed down the Wellington mine on Vancouver Island. Robert Dunsmuir, British Columbia's leading capitalist, convinced the government to use the militia to force miners back to work, but a long history of miner organization and militancy in the province had begun. By 1905–06, the UMW had gained a foothold in the coal fields in both British Columbia and Alberta.

In Quebec, francophone workers were encouraged to look for assistance from the Roman Catholic Church rather than from secular unions, which the church condemned as foreign-dominated and materialistic. Church-sponsored unions were initially conservative in their approach to labour rights, but priests assigned to the unions soon became sensitive to the plight of working people. In 1921, Catholic unions came together as the

Bunkhouse men, like those in this undated photo, experienced some of the worst working and living conditions in industrializing Canada. SOURCE: LIBRARY AND ARCHIVES CANADA PA-115432

strike to protest a reduction in hourly rates for their highly skilled and physically taxing work. The strikers agreed to submit their grievances to a federal arbitration commission, whose members were more concerned about the impact of dangerous working conditions on the maternal potential of the women—most of whom were between the ages of 17 and 22—than the ability of the women to make a living wage.

Since most Asians and blacks were excluded from unions, they worked in manual jobs, many of them seasonal and part-time, which made it difficult for them to form their own unions. One exception was the occupation of railway porters. Although their hours were long and the pay low, working on the trains was almost a rite of passage for many African-Canadian men. In 1918, porters of the Canadian Northern Railway, then in the process of becoming part of the CNR system, organized Canada's first black union, the Order of Sleeping Car Porters. The Canadian Brotherhood of Railway Employees initially refused to accept the union but relented in 1919, thus becoming the first craft union to abolish racial restrictions on membership.

Unions made their presence felt during Canada's rise to industrial maturity, but they had little success in restructuring capitalist development in the interests of labour or in expanding their membership. Only 5.6 percent of the labour force in Ontario and 8.4 percent in Quebec was organized by 1911. While some of the difficulties can be attributed to the conservative agenda promoted by the international unionism of the TLC, this was only partly the cause. Union leaders were often overtly racist and sexist, thereby alienating a significant proportion of their potential membership. Many employers, harking back to the paternalism that they felt characterized pre-industrial relations, tried to earn the loyalty of their skilled and experienced employees by sponsoring company picnics, excursions to nearby tourist sites, and even company bands. When such inducements failed to work, employers used force, calling upon governments to send in police, militia, and troops to put down strikes and coerce labour into compliance.

Confédération des travailleurs catholiques du Canada with an outlook similar to that of the TLC.

While many unionized workers held their own in the workplace, the position of common labourers remained precarious. The most vulnerable among male wage labourers were the navvies—men who worked in construction gangs that built the railways and other public works. Living in grim bunkhouses and eating stale bread, a navvy had experiences of the work world far removed from those of the proud craftsman. Such workers were ripe for the message of Industrial Workers of the World (IWW), an American-based organization founded in 1905 that rejected both the parliamentary process and traditional unionism. The Wobblies, as they were called, focused on the strike as the most effective political weapon and urged their members to walk off the job collectively when a fellow worker was unjustly treated by an employer.

Women were largely excluded from labour organizations, but they nevertheless protested unfair labour practices in the trades they dominated. In 1900, female spoolers in the cotton industry in Valleyfield, Quebec, walked off the job when apprentices were hired to perform their work. The women had limited bargaining power because textile workers could easily be replaced, but women in more skilled occupations also fared poorly in their confrontations with management. In 1907, more than 400 Bell telephone operators in Toronto went on

As this photo of the 1914 Street Railway Strike in Saint John suggests, peaceful demonstrations sometimes led to violence when police tried to disperse demonstrators. SOURCE: PROVINCIAL ARCHIVES OF NEW BRUNSWICK HAROLD WRIGHT HERITAGE RESOURCES COLLECTION P338-200

WORK AND FAMILY LIFE

The shift to an industrial economy had an enormous impact on the Canadian family. While self-sufficiency was rare even in pre-industrial British North America, a majority of family units produced a substantial proportion of the goods they consumed, relying only peripherally on the sale of their products and labour in the marketplace. By the twentieth century, the market played a major role in the lives of virtually every Canadian. Urban dwellers, in particular, lacked the resources to produce most of their own food, clothing, or shelter, but even in the countryside, the fully subsistent farm family was becoming rare and was, in most cases, desperately poor.

Families responded to the new market economy in a gendered way. In many mid-nineteenth-century farming families, women began to increase their production for off-farm sales, becoming major producers in dairying, poultry raising, market gardening, and fruit growing. As these areas of farming expanded and wheat farming declined east of Ontario, men took over what had previously been considered women's work. Dairying was entirely transformed in the second half of the nineteenth century. Pasturing, feeding, calving, and milking, once regarded as women's work, were increasingly appropriated by men. For many women, this shift in farm responsibilities was welcomed as a reduction of the heavy physical labour that characterized their daily lives, but it also reduced their power in the family and community context.

Most families depended on the labour of all their members, including their children. Although a romantic view of childhood innocence was maintained by middle-class families who had the money to keep servants to perform household chores, the working classes could rarely afford to be sentimental about their children. Children in farm and factory households fetched water from wells, ran errands, and helped with the cooking, cleaning, gardening, babysitting, and care of the aged and infirm. In rural areas, children were frequently kept home from school during planting and

Alarmed by the growing class conflict, governments at all levels tried to find a "middle way" that would reduce the worst excesses of the capitalist system while leaving its structure largely intact. The Report of the Royal Commission on the Relations of Labor and Capital, submitted in 1889, provided a wealth of information on the shocking conditions in Canadian factories, but the commissioners' recommendations yielded few immediate reforms other than the declaration in 1894 of a national holiday—Labour Day—for Canada's working people.

In 1900, the federal Liberals established the Department of Labour and hired a university-trained labour relations expert, William Lyon Mackenzie King, to be its first deputy minister. In 1907, King helped to engineer the Industrial Disputes Investigation Act (Lemieux Act), which prohibited strikes and lockouts in public utilities and mines until the dispute had been investigated by a tripartite board of arbitration representing labour, capital, and government. By establishing a compulsory cooling-off period, the act deprived organized labour of its strongest weapon, the surprise strike, without any compensatory protection against retaliation by the employer, such as hiring strikebreakers. The TLC asked the Conservatives to repeal the act when they were elected to power in 1911, but Robert Borden let the legislation stand.

Farm children at work on the Prairies in about 1900. SOURCE: GLENBOW ARCHIVES NA 1148-11

before marrying. The 1871 census reported that 25 percent of boys and 10 percent of girls between the ages of 11 and 15 had occupations outside the home. Factory acts passed in Ontario and Quebec in the mid-1880s and later replicated in other provinces prohibited employment of boys under age 12 and girls under age 14 in factories, but these laws were poorly enforced and frequently circumvented by families facing destitution.

Most working-class families were poor at some stage in their evolution. Generally, at the time of marriage, savings and two incomes allowed a couple to enjoy an acceptable, if modest, standard of living, but poverty was especially pronounced for large families with children too young to work or be left unsupervised while their mothers entered the labour force. In such cases, the wife's marginal earnings from piecework, laundry, or boarders often meant the difference between a family's subsistence and destitution.

Families headed by women—those who had never married, who were widowed, or whose husbands had deserted them—and families where the husband was too ill to work were in a particularly precarious position. Legislation passed in 1869 made it a criminal offence for a man to refuse to provide his wife with food, clothes, and lodging, but few women were successful in pursuing their claims. Nor could a woman expect the state or private charity to offer anything more than temporary assistance, if that. Families and individuals in early industrializing Canada were largely left to sink or swim. In this respect there was little change from the pre-industrial era, when luck and good health played a greater role than planning in determining income levels.

harvesting seasons. When the household economy was faced with a crisis such as the death or illness of a parent, older children were called upon to take on adult roles.

As historian Bettina Bradbury explains in her research on Montreal, most working-class families needed at least two wage earners to make ends meet.[7] Children, rather than their mother, were the first to appear on the shop floor. Mothers were needed at home to attend to the young and old and to do the time-consuming domestic chores of cooking and cleaning. In the early years of industrialization, housewives sometimes kept animals in the backyard or planted a garden to supplement the family income, but these alternatives were soon denied them by restrictive municipal bylaws.

Working-class children often entered the paid labour force at age 11 or 12—and even younger—and lived with their parents for perhaps another 15 years

VOICES FROM THE PAST
One Hundred and Two Muffled Voices

The royal commissioners studying the relations concerning labour and capital in Canada between 1886 and 1889 heard the testimony of nearly 1800 witnesses. Only 102 of those who testified were women. Although women made up over 20 percent of the paid labour force in 1891, nobody on the commission was very interested in hearing from them. As historian Susan Mann Trofimenkoff revealed, it took a great deal of courage for working people generally, and women in particular, to speak before a formal body such as a royal commission.[8] Saying something that offended employers might threaten a worker's job. Nearly half of the women testified anonymously; only 30 out of nearly 1700 male witnesses did so.

The most dramatic testimony relating to women's work came from a woman identified as Georgina Loiselle. Beaten by her employer for her "impertinent" refusal to make a hundred extra cigars, she was still employed at the factory five years later when she gave her testimony. Her employer justified his behaviour to the commissioners on the grounds that "her mother had prayed me ... to correct her in the best way I could."

With three of Georgina's brothers also employed by the company, the factory's owner had assumed the role of disciplinarian to the fatherless Loiselle children. Georgina was 18 years old at the time of the beating, and no one, including Georgina herself, seemed particularly surprised by her employer's brutality.

When the commissioners submitted their report, they indicated much greater concern over the moral consequences of women working in unchaperoned settings and using common washrooms with men than they did about the poor salaries and working conditions that were uniformly the lot of wage-earning women in Victorian Canada.

NATIVES AND THE NEW ECONOMY

As we have seen in earlier chapters, Canada's Aboriginal peoples had difficulty embracing the opportunities that the new industrial order had to offer. They possessed neither the capital nor the networks to make capitalism work for their benefit. Nevertheless, they adapted as best they could to the changes taking place around them. Those lucky enough to hold on to good lands in the face of predatory settlers often prospered. In the Cowichan and Fraser River valleys and in many areas of the Prairie provinces, Natives raised livestock, cereals, and market produce. On many reserves, Natives made a reasonable living as carpenters, blacksmiths, and craftspeople; others owned trading schooners, hotels, inns, cafés, and small logging and sawmill operations.

Like many other Canadians facing the challenges of industrialization, Native peoples sought jobs in the industrial economy developing around them. The Iroquois of Kahnawake, near Montreal, were widely known as skilled construction workers. Cree

women and girls did laundry and cleaning for wages, while men worked on railway construction. In the Maritimes, a few Mi'kmaq worked in the coal mines, on the railroads, and in the steel mills. On the West Coast, women and men from Native communities found work in lumber mills, mines, canneries, and the commercial fishery. With the rise of tourism, many Natives worked as guides for recreational hunters and fishers. Unfortunately, the position of Aboriginal peoples in the industrial economy was often marginal, and grew even more so as economic growth became defined in terms of the immigrant population.

The introduction of manufactured goods eroded the advantage of Aboriginal peoples in most of their labour-intensive crafts. Snowshoes, however, remained a vital trade commodity for Native peoples in the North, who found a ready buyer in the Hudson's Bay Company. Here, a Native woman at Mackenzie River in the Northwest Territories threads snowshoes in the 1920s. SOURCE: LIBRARY AND ARCHIVES CANADA C-38174

The National Policy and Regional Development

It is a common belief in the Maritime and western provinces that the National Policy of the late nineteenth century was biased in favour of central Canada. Some historians confirm popular perceptions and suggest that central Canadian industrialization occurred at the expense of the outlying regions as a result of deliberate public policy. There are also scholars, past and present, who argue that the National Policy tariff had negligible impact on the economic fate of these two regions. Who is right?

S.A. Saunders argued in the 1930s that the economic problems of the Maritimes stemmed from a decline in demand or price for key staple exports. When British demand for timber and ships fell off in the 1880s, the region's economy began a decline from which it could not recover. The region's carrying trade, meanwhile, suffered a fatal blow from the competition of steam and steel ships.[9] This explanation, of course, does not address the issue of why the region's entrepreneurs did not adjust to changing economic times. According to T.W. Acheson, the failure of the Maritimes to generate a major metropolitan centre in the industrial age contributed to the region's drift to outside control and industrial stagnation. "With its powerful mercantile interests," Acheson argues, "Halifax could have most easily adapted to this role, but its merchants preferred, like their Boston counterparts, to invest their large fortunes in banks and American railroad stocks than to venture them on building a new order."[10] Historian E.R. Forbes points a finger at high freight rates for the problems facing Maritime producers in supplying Canadian markets, but it seems unlikely that lower freight rates alone would have changed the region's economic fate.[11]

Economist Ken Norrie and historian Doug Owram, authors of an economic history of Canada, are skeptical about the possibility of extensive industrialization of the Maritime region in the late nineteenth century. They are even more skeptical of attempts to pin the blame on the economic policies pursued by the federal government: "To find the argument credible, one would need to believe that fairly small changes in transportation rates or in Dominion subsidies could have had enormous effects on industrial prospects. Simply putting the issue in that manner suggests the probable answer."[12]

Norrie and Owram are equally skeptical of claims that the National Policy discriminated against western Canada. T.D. Regehr, for example, states, "[t]here has been deliberate and admitted freight-rate discrimination against the West."[13] Only constant battles by westerners resulted, over time, in partial amelioration of these rates, argues Regehr. In contrast, Norrie and Owram claim flatly that "rail freight rates in the development phase of the wheat economy were at least as low as they would have been under the next most likely alternative to the national policy."[14] Norrie rejects the view that federal tariff and freight-rate policies hindered western industrialization:

> In some instances, Prairie industrialization being perhaps the best example, the problem lies in being small and isolated rather than with discriminatory treatment. The present economic structure of the region is adequately explained by standard location theory concepts. It is incorrect to suggest that the federal government or other institutions have industrialized the East at the expense of the West. It must be recognized rather that any significant decentralization of industry in Canada can only be achieved by committing real resources to that end and that this means a subsidy for persons residing in the recipient regions at the expense of other Canadians.[15]

Norrie's argument perhaps makes too little allowance for the role the state has played in the marketplace, demonstrating a strong central Canadian bias in its purchasing policies, for example. But he correctly points out a fallacy in the claims of many who focus on alleged discrimination against the regions: the assumption that the free market, left to its own workings, would have produced a more equitable distribution of industry in Canada. The tendency of capital left on its own to concentrate in a few areas with transportation and population advantages is a universal phenomenon of the capitalist system. In some countries, the state has intervened to force industries to locate in less favoured areas, but there is little evidence that in late-nineteenth-century Canada there were significant sections of popular opinion in any region that favoured more draconian intervention in the marketplace than that envisaged by John A. Macdonald and his business community supporters.

CONCLUSION

By the turn of the century, few people could ignore the inequality that characterized the age of industry. American investigative journalist Gustavus Myers claimed in 1914 that fewer than 50 men controlled $4 billion, or a third, of Canada's wealth. Certainly no one could have made such a claim in 1867. The total estate of Nova Scotia's Enos Collins, who was reputed to have been one of the wealthiest men in Canada when he died in 1871, was little more than $6 million. The conflict between labour and capital was a troubling feature of the industrial age, but it was by no means the only problem facing the new nation. As we shall see in the next chapter, immigration and urbanization were changing Canada's social fabric in ways totally unanticipated by the Fathers of Confederation.

NOTES

1. Greg Kealey, ed., *Canada Investigates Industrialism: The Royal Commission on the Relations of Labor and Capital, 1889* (Toronto: University of Toronto Press, 1973) 214–16.

2. F.E.A. Gagnon, *Choses d'Autrefois, feuilles éparses* (Montreal, 1905) 51–53. Cited in B. Sinclair, N.R. Ball, and J.O. Petersen, eds., *Let Us Be Honest and Modest: Technology and Society in Canadian History* (Toronto: Oxford University Press, 1974) 133–34.

3. Dianne Newell, *The Tangled Webs of History: Indians and the Law in Canada's Pacific Coast Fisheries* (Toronto: University of Toronto Press, 1993) 206.

4. Gregory P. Marchildon, *Profits and Politics: Beaverbrook and the Gilded Age of Canadian Finance* (Toronto: University of Toronto Press, 1996).

5. Quoted in Ruth Frager, "Class and Ethnic Barriers to Feminist Perspectives in Toronto's Jewish Labour Movement, 1919–1939," *Studies in Political Economy* 30 (Autumn 1989) 148.

6. Report of the Royal Commission on Immigration of Italian Labourers to Montreal and the Alleged Fraudulent Practices of Employment Agencies, Canada, Sessional Papers 1905 (36b), cited in Jeffrey Keshen and Suzanne Morton, *Material Memory: Documents in Post-Confederation History* (Toronto: Addison-Wesley, 1998) 69.

7. Bettina Bradbury, *Working Families: Age, Gender, and Daily Survival in Industrializing Montreal* (Toronto: McClelland and Stewart, 1993).

8. Susan Mann Trofimenkoff, "One Hundred and Two Muffled Voices: Canada's Industrial Women in the 1880s," *Atlantis* 3, 1 (Fall 1977) 66–82.

9. S.A. Saunders, *Economic History of the Maritime Provinces* (Ottawa: Royal Commission on Dominion-Provincial Relations, 1940).

10. T.W. Acheson, "The National Policy and the Industrialization of the Maritimes, 1880–1910," *Acadiensis* I, 2 (Spring 1972) 27–28.

11. For a summary of the freight rate debate and the publications that fuelled it, see E.R. Forbes, "The Intercolonial Railway and the Decline of the Maritime Provinces Revisited," and Ken Cruikshank, "With Apologies to James: A Response to E.R. Forbes," in *Acadiensis* XXIV, 1 (Autumn 1994) 3–34.

12. Kenneth Norrie and Douglas Owram, *A History of the Canadian Economy* (Toronto: Harcourt Brace Jovanovich, 1991) 402.

13. T.D. Regehr, "Western Canada and the Burden of National Transportation Policies," in *Canada and the Burden of Unity*, ed. D.J. Bercuson (Toronto: Macmillan, 1977) 115.

14. Norrie and Owram, *A History of the Canadian Economy*, 327.

15. Kenneth H. Norrie, "Some Comments on Prairie Economic Alienation," *Canadian Public Policy* 2, 2 (Spring 1976) 222.

SELECTED READING

Armstrong, Christopher and H.V. Nelles. *Monopoly's Moment: The Organization and Regulation of Canadian Utilities, 1830–1930*. Toronto: University of Toronto Press, 1988

Baskerville, Peter and Eric W. Sager. *Unwilling Idlers: The Urban Unemployed and Their Families in Late Victorian Canada*. Toronto: University of Toronto Press, 1998

Belisle, Donica. *Retail Nation: Department Stores and the Making of Modern Canada*. Vancouver: UBC Press, 2011

Bliss, Michael. *A Living Profit: Studies in the Social History of Canadian Business, 1883–1911*. Toronto: McClelland & Stewart, 1974

Bradbury, Bettina. *Working Families: Age, Gender, and Daily Survival in Industrializing Montreal*. Toronto: McClelland & Stewart, 1993

Carter, Sarah. *Lost Harvests: Prairie Indian Reserve Farmers and Government Policy*. Montreal: McGill-Queen's University Press, 1990

Cohen, Marjorie Griffin. *Women's Work, Markets, and Economic Development in Nineteenth-Century Ontario*. Toronto: University of Toronto Press, 1988

Copp, Terry. *The Anatomy of Poverty: The Condition of the Working Class in Montreal, 1897–1929*. Toronto: McClelland & Stewart, 1974

Frank, David, ed. *Industrialization and Underdevelopment in the Maritimes, 1880–1930*. Toronto: Garamond, 1985

Goutor, David. *Guarding the Gates: The Canadian Labour Movement and Immigration, 1872–1934*. Vancouver: UBC Press, 2007

Heron, Craig. *Working in Steel: The Early Years in Canada, 1883–1935*. Toronto: McClelland & Stewart, 1988

Kealey, Gregory S. *Toronto Workers Respond to Industrial Capitalism, 1867–1892*. Toronto: University of Toronto Press, 1980

Linteau, Paul-André. *The Promoters' City: Building the Industrial Town of Maisonneuve, 1883–1918*. Toronto: James Lorimer, 1985

Mathieu, Sarah-Jane. *North of the Color Line: Migration and Black Resistance in Canada, 1870–1955*. Chapel Hill: University of North Carolina Press, 2010

Monod, David. *Store Wars: Shopkeepers and the Culture of Mass Marketing, 1890–1939*. Toronto: University of Toronto Press, 1996

Nelles, H.V. *The Politics of Development: Forests, Mines and Hydro-Electric Power in Ontario, 1849–1941*. Montreal: McGill-Queen's University Press, 2005

Newell, Dianne. *Tangled Webs of History: Indians and the Law in Canada's Pacific Coast Fisheries*. Toronto: University of Toronto Press, 1993

Palmer, Bryan D. *Working-Class Experience: Rethinking the History of Canadian Labour, 1800–1991*. Toronto: McClelland & Stewart, 1992

Parr, Joy. *Labouring Children: British Immigrant Apprentices to Canada, 1869–1924*. Montreal: McGill-Queen's University Press, 1980

Rens, Jean-Guy. *The Invisible Empire: A History of the Telecommunications Industry in Canada, 1846–1956*. Montreal: McGill-Queen's University Press, 2001

Rouillard, Jacques. *Le syndicalisme québécois: deux siècles d'histoire*. Montreal: Boréal, 2004

Russell, Peter A. *How Agriculture Made Canada: Farming in the Nineteenth Century*. Montreal: McGill-Queen's University Press, 2012

Walden, Keith. *Becoming Modern in Toronto: The Industrial Exhibition and the Shaping of a Late Victorian Culture*. Toronto: University of Toronto Press, 1997

For a comprehensive list of readings for topics covered in this chapter, please visit http://pearsoncanada.ca/conrad.

CHAPTER 5
A NATION ON THE MOVE, 1867–1914

In 1901, census-taker Charles P. McRosite arrived at the one-room home of a Chinese immigrant in Nelson, British Columbia. He recorded the name of its occupant as Juin Yen, noting that he was a 40-year-old man living with his son, Sing. Juin had arrived in 1898 and Sing in 1899. Sing's mother was nowhere in evidence, perhaps because immigration laws made it expensive for Yen to bring his wife to Canada. The lone-parent status of the Yen family was not unusual in industrializing Canada. In her research on the 1901 census, historian Bettina Bradbury found that 12 percent of Canadian families in which children were living in the home and where the parent was under 55 were headed by lone parents.[1]

Almost 5 million immigrants arrived in Canada between 1871 and 1921 (see Table 5.1). Some prospered; others clearly did not. The same could be said for most native-born Canadians, nearly 5 million of whom left Canada in the same period. Whatever their hopes and fears, Canadians were on the move in the half-century following Confederation. They struggled—sometimes individually, increasingly together—to come to terms with a country whose families, communities, and institutions were changing, often dramatically.

TABLE 5.1

Canada's Population (in thousands), 1861–1921

YEAR	NATURAL INCREASE	NET IMMIGRATION	EMIGRATION	MIGRATION	POPULATION
1861					3230
1861-71	650	186	376	−191	3689
1871-81	720	353	438	−85	4325
1881-91	714	903	1108	−205	4833
1891-01	719	326	507	−181	5371
1901-11	1120	1782	1066	716	7207
1911-21	1349	1592	1360	233	8788

Source: David C. Corbett, *Canada's Immigration Policy: A Critique* (Toronto: University of Toronto Press, 1957) 121

TIMELINE

1869	Canadian Immigration Act passed
1871–1921	5 million immigrants arrive in Canada
1872	Dominion Lands Act passed
1877	Disastrous fire in Saint John leaves 15 000 homeless
1885	Head tax imposed on Chinese immigrants
1892	St John's fire leaves 10 000 homeless
1897	Klondike gold rush begins
1906	Major revisions made to the Immigration Act
1907	Anti-Asian riots in Vancouver; Doukhobors in Saskatchewan have half their land confiscated
1908	Canada–Japan agreement to limit Japanese immigration
1914	*Komagata Maru* incident

THE PROBLEM OF OUTMIGRATION

In the early years of Confederation, the slow rate of population growth was as great a concern for Canadian leaders as railways and tariffs. Despite the passage of the Dominion Lands Act in 1872, most immigrants to North America in the late nineteenth century preferred to settle in the United States. So, too, it seemed, did many Canadians. Frontier lands, industrial jobs, and a better climate attracted Canadians like a magnet, and there seemed to be nothing that the nation's leaders could do to stop the exodus.

In Maritime Canada, close family ties and geographic proximity had long made New England a place to find work. Once the trend was set, other family members followed, producing what demographers describe as a "chain migration." Nearly half a million people left the Maritimes between 1880 and 1921, a number representing more than a third of the total population remaining in the region. Maritime carpenters thrown out of work by the collapse of the shipbuilding industry helped build the suburbs of American cities, former farm boys delivered milk in horse-drawn vans, and fishing families found the protected American markets easier to supply from Gloucester and Salem in Massachusetts than they did from Maritime ports. Women, who outnumbered men in the exodus, worked as domestics, factory hands, clerks, secretaries, teachers, and nurses.

Newfoundland experienced a similar trend. While most Newfoundlanders moved to Massachusetts or New York, a significant number also found work in the industrializing areas of the Maritimes, particularly Halifax and Cape Breton. The development of the iron reserves on Bell Island to supply Nova Scotia's steel industry led naturally to the migration of labour across the Cabot Strait to Cape Breton. From there, Newfoundlanders often joined Nova Scotians moving to better opportunities in the United States.

Large families and limited agricultural opportunities encouraged more than 600 000 Quebecers to leave Canada between Confederation and 1920, many of them destined for mill towns in New England. With factories employing men, women, and children, whole families joined the exodus and thereby became the founders of a Franco-American community that still retains its distinctiveness. Roman Catholic Church leaders were worried by the dangers of exposure to what they saw as an overly materialistic society. They tried to keep their flock at home by collaborating with the provincial government to develop colonization societies to settle frontier areas of the province, such as the Laurentians northwest of Montreal, but such efforts did little to stem the tide of French-Canadian emigration.

The Canadian West had little attraction for Quebec's rural migrants. Efforts by Bishop Taché and his successors in St Boniface to repatriate francophones from New England bore some fruit in the 1870s, but the numbers trickled off. Even attempts to maintain interest through a federally sponsored newspaper, *Le Colonisateur*, distributed throughout Quebec and New England in the 1880s, failed to have much impact on migration trends. In 1901, there were only 23 000 French-speaking settlers on the Prairies, many of them from France, Belgium, and Switzerland rather than Quebec. Francophones were scattered throughout the West in communities such as

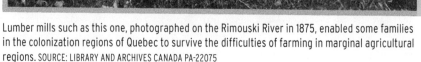

Lumber mills such as this one, photographed on the Rimouski River in 1875, enabled some families in the colonization regions of Quebec to survive the difficulties of farming in marginal agricultural regions. SOURCE: LIBRARY AND ARCHIVES CANADA PA-22075

St Albert, Grande Clairière, Montmartre, St Brieux, and Gravelbourg. Together they had an important influence on the culture and politics of the region, but they found their culture increasingly submerged in a flood of immigrants who spoke any language but French.

At the same time, the number of francophones living in Ontario and the Maritimes increased significantly in the half-century following Confederation. Quebecers crossed the border into eastern and northern Ontario to take advantage of employment opportunities in farming, resource development, and the federal bureaucracy. The number of Franco-Ontarians jumped from 102 743 in 1881 to 202 442 in 1911, an increase that brought their numbers to about eight percent of the provincial population. Although Acadians were attracted to jobs in New England, they were less likely than their anglophone neighbours to leave the Maritimes. They were also more likely than anglophones to have large families. As a result, those claiming a French heritage in New Brunswick rose from less than 16 percent of the population in 1871 to more than 31 percent in 1921. By the latter date, francophones had increased to 10.8 percent of the population in Nova Scotia and 13.5 percent in Prince Edward Island.

Rural Ontario lost population to the developing western territories and the urban and rural frontiers of the United States in the last three decades of the nineteenth century. Unlike the Maritimes and Quebec, where outmigration exceeded immigration until the 1930s, Ontario was able to stem the outward flow in the first decade of the twentieth century. Ontario's rapidly developing industrial economy and resource frontier employed not only the surplus population from the rural areas of the nation, but also a rising tide of immigrants who flooded into Canada in the early years of the twentieth century.

IMMIGRATION POLICY

Under the British North America Act, immigration was a responsibility shared by federal and provincial jurisdictions. Ottawa took an early lead with the passage of an act defining immigration and citizenship procedures in 1869. The Immigration Act established immigration offices in Great Britain and continental Europe, quarantine stations in Halifax, Saint John, and Quebec, and immigration branches in various Canadian cities. On paper, Canada's immigration policy was an open one; only criminals were

denied admission. In practice, people who were deemed destitute, physically unfit, or mentally disabled were required to post a bond and were often turned away.

In the first three decades following Confederation, Canada's ethnic balance changed very little. The 1901 census reported that 88 percent of Canadians were of British or French descent, just four percent fewer than in 1871. Although many Canadians were skeptical, Clifford Sifton, minister of the Interior from 1896 to 1905, was prepared to welcome eastern Europeans, assessing them as good prospects to survive the rigours of pioneering on the Canadian Prairies. "I think a stalwart peasant in a sheep-skin coat, born on the soil, whose forefathers have been farmers for ten generations, with a stout wife and a half-dozen children is good quality," Sifton declared.[2] Business people were similarly enthusiastic about such recruits, seeing them as ideal candidates for the hard, low-wage labour needed in factories, resource industries, and homes.

Under Sifton's direction, the Department of the Interior, in cooperation with transportation companies and other private recruitment agencies, advertised extensively in Europe and the United States for immigrants to settle the Prairies and work in Canada's expanding industries. These efforts coincided with a number of global trends that combined to make immigration an attractive option for many people. In Europe, ethnic and religious tensions, outright persecution, industrial upheaval, and the collapse of peasant farming systems "pushed" many potential emigrants to seek a new life in Canada. An upswing in the international economy, vigorous recruitment campaigns, improved transportation by steam and rail, technological breakthroughs in farming, and the relatively high wages in Canada "pulled" people to what was increasingly perceived as a land of opportunity.

Sifton's successor, Frank Oliver, who served as minister of the Interior from 1905 to 1911, pursued a much more restrictive immigration policy: "It is not merely a question of filling the country with people," he opined. "It is a question of the ultimate efforts put forward for the building up of a Canadian nationality. This can never be accomplished if the preponderance of the people should be of such a class and character as will deteriorate rather than elevate the condition of our people and our country at large." In 1906, the Immigration Act was revised to exclude the "feeble minded"; those "afflicted with a loathsome disease"; professional beggars, prostitutes, and those living off their

A 1907 poster designed to encourage immigrants to come to western Canada.
SOURCE: LIBRARY AND ARCHIVES CANADA C-56088

Britain, but enough came from other nations of the world to alter the ethnic composition of Canada. By 1920, more than 20 percent of Canadians traced their origins to countries other than Great Britain and France.

Between 1896 and 1914, nearly a million immigrant farmers arrived in Canada to work in the agricultural economy. Other immigrants found work as farm labourers, usually on a temporary basis. In 1891, 6300 seasonal workers were employed in the wheat harvest; by 1921, the number had increased tenfold. Many of the people employed on western farms came from the eastern provinces on "harvest trains," placed in service specifically to cater to the labour needs of the wheat economy. Immigrants were also attracted to the jobs opening up in Canada's industrial cities, on resource frontiers, and in the homes of the growing middle class.

Immigrant men were most likely to be found in the mining, lumbering, and railway camps scattered throughout industrializing Canada. With the assistance of the federal government and private agencies, company officials recruited Slavs, Scandinavians, and Italians for these jobs, but when their numbers proved insufficient, companies pressed the government to admit labourers from China, Japan, and India. Between 1907 and 1914, when all three of Canada's transcontinental railway systems were engaged in construction projects, 50 000 to 70 000 workers were required annually by the railway companies alone.

The three Prairie provinces, where 54 percent of the foreign-born settled, were entirely transformed by the newcomers. There, Canadian, British, and American settlers lived side by side with eastern and western Europeans, each of whom contributed about 20 percent to the population. On the Pacific coast, the cultural mix varied again. Sixty percent of the 40 000 Chinese and almost all of the 16 000 Japanese enumerated by the 1921 census were located in British Columbia, which otherwise was 60 percent British. Only the Maritime region, with its agricultural frontier long settled and its industrial base languishing, failed to attract a significant number of immigrants outside its coal-mining and steel-making communities.

avails; persons convicted of crimes of "moral turpitude"; and anyone "likely to become a public charge" or who "may become dangerous to the public health." Later amendments barred women or girls from coming to Canada for "any immoral purpose" and anyone suffering from alcoholism, mental or physical defects, or a condition of "constitutional psychopathic inferiority." Because these terms were vague, immigration officials had considerable latitude to make arbitrary judgments about the suitability of applicants.[3]

These laws failed to stem the tide of immigration before the First World War. From a low of 16 835 arrivals in 1896 to a high of 400 000 in 1913, immigrants came from Great Britain, Europe, the United States, and Asia, many of them settling in the four western provinces. As many as two-thirds arrived from the United States and Great

Because of the high birth rate among francophones, their percentage of the population of Canada dropped only marginally, from 31.1 percent in 1871 to 28.2 percent in 1921. The percentage of non-francophones and non-anglophones (generally referred to as allophones today) in Quebec rose from 1.6 percent in 1871 to 4.9 percent in 1921. While this increase did not represent a major demographic shift, its effect was particularly noticeable in Montreal, where 80 percent of the allophones—and 60 percent of the anglophones—lived.

By the second decade of the twentieth century, the population patterns of the "new" Canada were beginning to take shape. More than half of the population continued to live in Quebec and Ontario, but the proportion of Canadians living in these two provinces dropped from nearly 75 percent in 1891 to 60 percent in 1921. Maritimers accounted for only 11.4 percent, down from 18.2 percent three decades earlier. By contrast, the West registered explosive growth. Prairie populations rose from 7.8 percent to 22.3 percent of the Canadian total in the first two decades of the twentieth century, while British Columbians accounted for six percent by 1921.

Canadians harboured deep fears about immigration. For many English-speaking Canadians, the tide of foreigners threatened the dominance of British culture. Francophones were even more cautious. Since most immigrants came from English-speaking countries—and those who did not quickly assimilated to the Anglo-Canadian culture—French Canadians saw themselves disappearing in a sea of English-speaking North Americans. Between 1900 and 1940, virtually all nationalist organizations in Quebec went on record as opposing Canada's "open door" immigration policy. As a result of such views, there was little likelihood of Canada becoming a "mosaic" of different but equal peoples, or the "melting pot" favoured in the United States. Rather, the nation became a battleground for many cultures trying to establish their place in a rigid social pecking order.

VOICES FROM THE PAST
A Chief's Perspective on Settlement

Native peoples often expressed disbelief at the heavy-handedness by which they were dispossessed of their lands and resources when the new settlers arrived. This letter to the *Victoria Daily Colonist*, published on 15 May 1880, expressed views common among Native leaders.

I am an Indian chief and a Christian. "Do unto others as you wish others should do unto you" is Christian doctrine. Is the white man a Christian? This is a part of his creed—"take all you want if it belongs to an Indian"? He has taken all our land and all the salmon and we have nothing. He believes an Indian has a right to live if he can on nothing at all. . . .

Indians are now reduced to this condition—THEY MUST ROB OR STARVE. Which will they do? I need not answer. An Indian is a man; and he has eyes. If you stab him he will bleed; if you poison him he will die. If you wrong him shall he not seek revenge? If an Indian wrongs a white man what is his humility? Revenge. If want compels us to execute the villainy they teach they may discover when

it is TOO LATE that an Indian can imitate the lightning and strike in a thousand places at the same time. We are not beggars. In the middle of the magnificent country that was once our own we only ask for land enough to enable us to live like white men by working in the fields. If the Indians get no land this spring you MAY BE SURE the white man will have a very bad harvest this year, and the Indians will eat beef next winter. Fine talk won't feed an Indian. "Her Majesty's Indian subjects," whose rights are limited to living on nothing at all if they can, are prepared to face the worst—anything but death by starvation. In a court of justice we could prove that we are the only persons who have any right or title to this land. If the Queen has no power to aid us; if all the power belongs to the parliament, then I say again may the Lord have mercy on the Indians—AND ON THE WHITE-MEN.

WILLIAM,
Chief of the Williams Lake Indians[4]

SETTLERS AND SOJOURNERS

The federal government's early difficulties in attracting farmers to the West created an interest in sponsoring block settlements for ethnic minorities. In the 1870s, about 7400 German-speaking Mennonites left their homes in western Russia to settle in Manitoba, and their descendants gradually spread into the area that would become the province of Saskatchewan. The Mennonites proved to be excellent farmers, introducing crop rotation and planting trees as wind breaks. Because they were pacifists, farmed communally, and kept to themselves, they were initially viewed with suspicion by their neighbours. Despite their exclusiveness, the Mennonites created prosperous farming communities and soon established good relations with the people living around them.

Also in the 1870s, 2000 Icelanders settled in Gimli ("Paradise"), Manitoba, driven from their homeland by economic depression and volcanic eruptions. Just after the colony was founded, a devastating outbreak of smallpox resulted in an armed quarantine of the settlement and the deaths of 100 people, mainly young children. This tragedy was followed by floods in 1879 and 1880. Religious tensions between adherents of the Church of Iceland and more conservative Lutherans also racked the community and pushed a number of the settlers to move to the United States. Such difficulties notwithstanding, the colony thrived. Within a generation, its members had begun to adapt to English-Canadian culture while retaining pride in their distinctiveness, reflected in their own schools, churches, and Icelandic-language newspaper.

In the 1880s, the first wave of Jewish immigrants, fleeing persecution in the Russian Empire, established farming settlements in what would become Saskatchewan. It was a new experience for a people who had been barred by law from farming in their homeland. By the end of the century, Jews subjected to discriminatory policies in Poland, Austria-Hungary, and Germany also turned to Canada as a place of refuge, but found that Canada had its own discriminatory

The Cardston Temple of the Church of Jesus Christ of Latter-Day Saints, in 1927. SOURCE: GLENBOW ARCHIVES ND-27-12

practices. General hostility toward non-Christians forced Jewish immigrants to stick together, despite their diverse cultural backgrounds. At the same time, discrimination in employment and quotas restricting Jewish entrance into legal and medical schools focused them into a narrow range of occupations. In Winnipeg, Jews took up jobs as unskilled labourers, peddlers, and small shopkeepers and congregated in the city's north end. Wherever they settled, socialist political beliefs distinguished many Jewish settlers from their usually more conservative neighbours.

The Prairies were home to about 25 000 Jews by 1921. Even more could be found in Quebec and Ontario, which each counted almost 50 000 Jews in their populations in 1921. Because Montreal and Toronto had Jewish communities and offered urban employment, many Jews chose to make these cities their home, and Montreal's Jewish community quadrupled between 1901 and 1911. The Jewish presence in Quebec put tremendous pressure on Protestant English-language schools, which the Jews attended because they were excluded from Catholic schools and could not get provincial grants to create their own schools. By a 1903 ruling, Jews were considered Protestants for the purposes of school taxes, but they received few benefits from this ruling. By the 1920s, nearly 40 percent of the Protestant school board's students were Jewish, but there were no Jewish high school teachers. Protestant prayers and religious instruction were imposed upon Jewish children, and they were also denied the right to stay at home on Jewish holidays.

Not all group settlers came from Europe. In the 1880s, Mormons, adherents of the Church of Jesus Christ of Latter-Day Saints, began moving to Canada from their base in Utah. The first eight families of Mormons, under the leadership of Charles Ora Card, arrived in the North-West Territories in 1887. Using dryland farming techniques developed in Utah, the Mormons brought into agricultural production areas of the Prairies that had hitherto supported only open-range ranching. The aim of permanent settlement was reflected in one of Card's advertisements: "Come along with your capital and build our flouring mills, sugar refineries, electric railways and electric lights, and aid to establish other industries and grow up with an enterprising and healthy country. Don't forget to secure a good farm adjacent to one of the grandest irrigation systems of modern times."[5]

The Mormon population in Alberta rose to 7000 by 1912. In the following year, building began on a temple located in Cardston, Alberta. Completed 10 years later, it was distinctive not only for its size and style of architecture, but also because it was the first Mormon temple to be built outside the United States. Like other religiously defined cultural groups, the Mormons often felt the prejudice of neighbours who condemned their religious beliefs, most notably their advocacy of polygamy. Most Mormons abandoned this practice soon after their arrival in Canada, but Canadians were slow to forget that this had once been a distinguishing feature of Mormon culture.

One of the first groups to respond to Sifton's stepped-up recruitment program in the 1890s was a block of Doukhobors in Russia who were being persecuted by the

Doukhobor women winnowing grain in 1899. With their strongly held beliefs about appropriate spheres for men and women, middle-class Canadians objected to the hard physical labour performed by women in Doukhobor families and the extreme patriarchal control that Doukhobor men held over women and children. SOURCE: LIBRARY AND ARCHIVES CANADA C-8891

tsar for their ethnic traits and religious practices. Under an agreement negotiated in 1898 with the help of Russian intellectual Leo Tolstoy and University of Toronto professor James Mavor, some 7400 Doukhobors settled on 400 000 acres of land near Yorkton, Saskatchewan. Mainly followers of visionary leader Peter Veregin, who required his flock to live communally, they soon became divided over the degree of loyalty to their leader's beliefs the group should maintain.

The most fervent followers, called the Sons of Freedom, began to destroy their property in 1902 and conduct nude demonstrations as visible evidence of their faith. For shocked Canadians, such behaviour was visible evidence that the whole group should be brought into conformity with Anglo-Canadian practices. In 1906, the government began forcing Doukhobors to follow the strict letter of the homestead law with respect to their communal landholdings. About a third of the group agreed to abandon their communalism and remained in Saskatchewan under their leader Peter Makaroff. In 1912, the rest joined Veregin in the creation of a new utopia in the interior of British Columbia.

During the First World War, the Hutterites, a German-speaking pacifist group with communal practices, negotiated entry into Canada. Most of them had spent one or two generations in South Dakota before moving northward. Settling in Manitoba and Alberta, they established communities that resisted all efforts at assimilation. Their distinctive communal arrangements included a children's nursery, women's spinning hall, and common dining room. When a community reached a population of between 100 and 200 people, another one was established, which remained as self-sufficient and autonomous as its predecessor.

Canada also became the homeland for thousands of people from the Austro-Hungarian provinces of Galicia and Bukovina. Collectively known as Ukrainians, they were the largest and the most visible of all European peasant cultures to come to Canada. As many as 150 000 Ukrainians had arrived by 1914, and another 70 000 came in the interwar years. The exact numbers are difficult to determine since the newcomers were designated in a variety of ways in immigration records and came from countries whose boundaries were notoriously fluid. Often poor, illiterate, and oppressed in their homeland, they were the prototype of Sifton's peasant in a sheepskin coat.

Before 1910, the vast majority of Ukrainian migrants were men, the most destitute of whom began their Canadian experience clustered in tenements in the north end of Winnipeg and worked as railway navvies and farm labourers. As soon as they could, they moved to their own farms, many of them in the vicinity of Dauphin, Manitoba; Yorkton, Saskatchewan; or the Edna-Star district northeast of Edmonton. The Ukrainians quickly earned a reputation for hard work and determination, though their cultural practices brought widespread criticism from their Canadian-born neighbours.

The onion-shaped dome of their church architecture was the most visible symbol of Ukrainian presence in the dominion. Thatched-roof homes built by first-generation Ukrainians were also unlike any others found in the West,

Galicians at an immigration shed in Quebec City in the late nineteenth or early twentieth century. SOURCE: LIBRARY AND ARCHIVES CANADA C-4745

and they elicited much comment. Because of their numbers and varied political experiences, the Ukrainians were never a uniform cultural group. They held political views ranging from socialist to conservative and, while the majority of those who came to Canada before the First World War were Roman Catholics of the Byzantine Rite, about a third were Eastern Orthodox. As a group, Ukrainians left an indelible mark on Canada. In their insistence on maintaining their cultural distinctiveness, historian Gerald Friesen argues, Ukrainians, as much as any other single ethnic group, "were responsible for the official adoption of today's bilingual-multicultural definition of Canadian society."[6]

Although the majority of newcomers came to stay, another category of immigrant, called sojourners, planned to return to their homelands with money in their pockets. Most Chinese and Japanese immigrants fell into this category. So, too, did a number of eastern Europeans, including people from the mountain villages where the borders of Greece, Bulgaria, Serbia, and Albania meet. Now known as Macedonians, they began migrating to Canada to find work in the first decade of the twentieth century. Most of them were single or young married men, and many found jobs in Toronto's factories, abattoirs, and construction sites. While in Toronto, they lived in boarding houses located in ethnic enclaves such as Cabbagetown. During the recession of 1907, some 300 Macedonian sojourners were deported to prevent them from becoming objects of charity, but their numbers continued to grow. Mutual support soon found expression in the creation in 1910 of a "national" Eastern Orthodox parish centred in SS Cyril and Methody Church in Toronto. When the Balkan Wars in 1912–1913 divided their homeland, many Macedonian sojourners decided to become permanent settlers, a decision confirmed by the difficulties of returning to Europe during the First World War.

Italians came to Canada both as settlers and sojourners, their numbers swelling in the first two decades of the twentieth century when more than 120 000 Italians arrived. Like the Macedonians, most of the early Italian immigrants were young single men. They were often recruited by Italian labour agents (*padroni*) based in Montreal and Toronto who sponsored contract labour for railway and mining companies. The majority of the Italians who chose to stay in Canada lived in Montreal and Toronto; others settled in communities across the nation. The low proportion of women among them—10 834 out of a population of 45 411 in 1911—suggests one of the reasons why 10 years later only 66 769 people of Italian origin were reported living in Canada. Some men returned to their homeland once their work contracts expired; others moved to the United States, where the vast majority of Italian immigrants to North America chose to settle.

"WHITE CANADA FOREVER"

While eastern and southern Europeans were subjected to discrimination, non-white immigrants bore the brunt of Canadian hostility. The Chinese, who performed the most dangerous jobs in the construction of the Canadian Pacific Railway (CPR), were almost universally despised. In defending his policy of importing Chinese workers, John A. Macdonald revealed his contempt when he told a Toronto political meeting: "Well, they do come and so do rats. I am pledged to build the great Pacific Railroad in five years, and if I cannot obtain white labour, I must employ other."[8] Following the completion of the railway, many labourers stayed in Canada because their families in China depended on the money they sent home. Angry whites complained that they were unfair competition for jobs and lobbied for their deportation.

Chinatowns, such as this one in Victoria in 1886, were the products of racial segregation in Canada. SOURCE: LIBRARY AND ARCHIVES CANADA C-23415

William Peyton Hubbard

Canada's treatment of people with black skin was not always characterized by prejudice and exclusion. In 1894, William Peyton Hubbard was elected to the Toronto City Council; he continued to serve in this and other public capacities, including deputy mayor and justice of the peace, until 1915.

Born in 1842 in an area of Toronto known as "the bush," Hubbard was the son of Virginia slaves who had escaped to Canada West. He initially made his living as a baker and invented a commercial baker's oven, the Hubbard Portable. By the 1870s, he was married and working with his uncle's livery-cab chauffeur service. His career took a new turn when he rescued George Brown from drowning in the Don River after a carriage accident. Brown encouraged Hubbard to enter politics, but Hubbard resisted the idea until long after Brown's death in 1880.

In 1893, Hubbard finally ran for a seat on the city council in Ward 4, an affluent area of Toronto. Defeated in a tight race by just seven votes, he was elected the following year. He sat on the all-powerful four-member Board of Control and actively pursued a number of reforms, including the city-wide election of board members, improved waterworks, and better roads. In 1908, Hubbard was defeated, partly because private business interests resented his support of public control of hydro power. He returned to city council in 1913, only to retire at the end of the year due to his wife's ill health. On April 30, 1935, he died of a stroke at his home on Broadview Avenue. An official oil painting of him hangs in the mayor's office, a tribute to his determination and accomplishments as the city's first non-white elected official.[7]

Portrait of William Peyton Hubbard (1913), by W.A. Sherwood.
SOURCE: CITY OF TORONTO ART COLLECTION, CULTURAL SERVICES

Responding to pressure from the province of British Columbia, where most of the Chinese had settled, the federal government imposed a $50 head tax on Chinese immigrants in 1885. The tax was raised to $100 in 1901 and $500 in 1904, equivalent to a year's wages. The result was a gender imbalance in the Chinese-Canadian population. In the period before the First World War, most of the few Chinese women in the country were the wives of merchants who could afford to pay the tax or prostitutes who were already in Canada when the tax was instituted. Shunned by broader society, the Chinese lived in segregated Chinatowns, where support was available for the homeless, ill, and aged.

Like the Chinese, most Japanese immigrants to Canada (known as *Issei*) viewed themselves as sojourners who would return home after making some money. Many did so, but others established themselves in farming, fishing, and trade in the Vancouver and Steveston areas of British Columbia. Soon they began to bring in Japanese women and establish families. Known as "picture brides" because prospective husbands had only their pictures when they "proposed," the women were married by proxy in Japan after negotiations between the couple's families. The economic success of the Japanese drew the ire of their racist neighbours, who made no secret of the fact that they wanted to keep British Columbia "white forever."

Whether immigrant or Canadian-born, Chinese and Japanese were denied the franchise in the western provinces, barred from access to the professions, subjected to discriminatory housing covenants, and segregated in public places. They were also threatened with physical violence. In 1907, whites marched through Japanese and Chinese sections of Vancouver, breaking windows and shouting racist slogans. The incident indicated the depth of the hostility faced by Asian immigrants. The federal government responded to these racist sentiments by negotiating an agreement with Japan in 1908 that restricted the number of Japanese allowed to enter the country to 400 annually.

While it was difficult for Canadians to impose restrictions on immigrants from India, which, like Canada, was a colony of the British Empire, it did not stop them from trying. The federal government passed an order-in-council in 1908 requiring East Indians to come to Canada by continuous passage from India. Since there was no direct steamship line between the two countries, the regulation virtually precluded immigration. In 1913, a group of 38 Sikhs contested the restriction and were admitted. This experience encouraged others to charter the *Komagata Maru*, a Japanese-owned freighter, to bring 376 Punjabis, mostly Sikhs, to Canada in 1914. Detained on board for two months in Vancouver harbour while their case was heard before the courts, the would-be immigrants were eventually ordered to leave. To give point to the court order, the Royal Canadian Navy cruiser *Rainbow* was sent to the scene. Due to such policies, only 1016 East Indians were enumerated in Canada in 1921, down from 2342 (2315 men and 27 women) 10 years earlier.

By the late nineteenth century, most white Canadians had become adherents of racist beliefs that held blacks to be mentally and morally inferior. Even Wilfrid Laurier was heard to proclaim in 1910 that "[W]e see in the United States what grave problems may arise from the presence of a race unable to become full members of the same social family as ourselves."[9] Thus the arrival between 1910 and 1912 of some 1300 African-American homesteaders from Oklahoma, where statehood brought deteriorating conditions for blacks, caused a major uproar. Because they were healthy American citizens and held property, immigration regulations could not be used to keep them out.

Public petitions from all three Prairie provinces urged Ottawa to ban further admission of black immigrants and the federal government prepared an order-in-council to do so for a year, but it was never proclaimed. Fears that relations with the United States would be damaged and that black voters in Ontario and the Maritimes would be alienated apparently caused politicians to exercise restraint. Instead, agents were sent into the United States to discourage black immigrants, and border officials were rewarded for the rigorous application of immigration regulations against blacks trying to enter the country—policies that, sadly, had the effect that was intended.

REINFORCING THE DOMINANT CULTURE

The majority of immigrants to Canada in this period came from Great Britain and the United States. Because most of them were Caucasian, spoke English, and came as individuals, they attracted less attention from nativistic Canadians. This was especially the case with the English-speaking Canadians living in the United States who took advantage of the incentives offered in the Canadian West to return to the land of their birth. Not only were they better able to adapt to institutions that were familiar to them, they were also likely to have extended family members in Canada upon whom they could draw for assistance.

Between 1904 and 1914, some 90 000 British women came to Canada to work in domestic service: 60 percent came from England, 29 percent from Scotland, and 10 percent from Ireland. This breakdown meant that the Irish servant typical of the 1870s had almost vanished by the early twentieth century. British sources made up about three-quarters of the immigrants who came to work as domestic servants in this period, while others came from Scandinavia and central and eastern Europe. Domestic servants were believed to be especially desirable immigrants because they made the most likely marriage partners for the male farmers and labourers who were the majority of newcomers in the migration process. Not surprisingly, the open door for domestics and wives did not include African, West Indian, or Asian women.

Nearly 100 000 poor and orphaned children from Great Britain were sent to Canada between the 1860s and the 1920s. They were known as "home children" because they came from British orphanages, commonly called

VOICES FROM THE PAST
Home Children

Maggie Hall was one of the home children shipped to Canada to begin a new life. She described a typical work day in a letter to her friend in 1890:

> I have to get my morning's work done by 12 o'clock every day to take the children for a walk then I have to get the table laid for lunch when I come in then after dinner I help to wash up then I have to give the little boy his lessons then for the rest of the afternoon I sew till it is time to get afternoon tea and shut up and light the gas then by that time it is time for our tea after which I clear away get the table ready for Miss Smith's dinner then put the little boy to bed & after Miss Smith's dinner I help wash up which does not take very long then I do what I like for the rest of the evening till half-past nine when we have Prayers then I take Miss Smith's hot water & hot bottle, the basket of silver & glass of milk to her bedroom shut up & go to bed which by the time I have done all it is just about ten.[10]

Maggie's responsibilities were essentially those of an all-purpose maid, but she, like most home children, received no remuneration for her labours. Little wonder that both urban and rural families eagerly applied for a "home child" to lighten the drudgery of domestic life.

In the second half of the twentieth century, people who immigrated to Canada and elsewhere as home children began to tell their stories and to press governments for an apology for their treatment. On 16 November 2009, Immigration Minister Jason Kenney announced that Canada would not follow the Australian example of issuing an apology for the exploitation of home children. Instead, the Canadian government proclaimed 2010 the "Year of the British Home Child" and Canada Post issued a commemorative stamp in their honour.

"homes," which sponsored their placement overseas. While their experiences in Canada varied widely, most home children were indentured to farm families as cheap labour and seldom received the love and care they were promised. Scottish philanthropist and child welfare advocate Emma Stirling, who brought more than 200 children to her Hillfoot Farm in Aylesford, Nova Scotia, between 1886 and 1895, discovered this truth to her disgust. In 1895 she fought a court case on behalf of Grace Fagan, one of her home children who was obliged by the reputed father to have an abortion that nearly cost her life. Shortly thereafter, Hillfoot Farm was destroyed in a suspicious fire, an indication, perhaps, that the citizens in the community wanted all evidence of this embarrassing episode expunged. Given the vulnerability of home children, Grace Fagan's experience was likely not unusual.

Despite their talk about keeping the country British, Anglo-Canadians were not always welcoming of immigrants from their imperial homeland. Many Canadians found the superior attitude adopted by some British immigrants particularly hard to swallow. An even greater cause for concern, especially for employers,

was the socialist perspective held by those who had been associated with labour politics in Great Britain. Because many British immigrants came from urban backgrounds, they often made disgruntled homesteaders. Dubbed "green Englishmen" by their neighbours, they drifted to Prairie towns to find work, where they were sometimes met with signs indicating that "No Englishmen need apply."

While many British immigrants came as single men looking for work in Canadian towns and cities, in at least one instance it was British women who were actively sought as factory operatives. John Penman, the owner of Penman's woollen factories in Paris, Ontario, recruited 700 skilled hosiery workers from the East Midlands of England between 1907 and 1928. Many were single women who were accustomed to lifelong wage earning. In her investigation of these women, Joy Parr found that they maintained this tradition in Paris, relying on female networks, public services, and family practices to sustain their continued labour-force participation. The commercial provision of laundry services, the hours for Saturday shopping, and early school-leaving laws all reflected that Paris was a "woman's town."

SETTLING IN

Immigrants faced special challenges in establishing a sense of community. Whether they settled in rural or urban areas or came as individuals, families, or in groups, they were caught between their old world and the new. Their lot might have been marginally easier than that of pre-Confederation immigrants, but both faced hostility from native-born Canadians and the difficult task of making a living in a rapidly changing economy. The *Missionary Outlook* in 1910 embodied an attitude that was all too general across Canada: "Every large city on this continent has its fourfold problem of the slum, the saloons, the foreign colony and the districts of vice. The foreign colony may not properly be called a slum, but it represents a community that is about to become an important factor in our social life and will become a menace in our civilization unless it learns to assimilate the moral and religious ideals and the standards of citizenship."[11]

Despite such views, immigrants at the turn of the twentieth century almost always had an easier experience settling in than did earlier immigrants. Atlantic crossings, while not always pleasant, usually lasted less than two weeks and rarely resulted in marine disaster. Train travel, even in roughly fitted colonist cars, was vastly better than the discomfort of crossing the country before the advent of the railway. All the same, survival in Canada proved a good deal harder than settlers

and sojourners had been led to expect by the optimistic pamphlets, films, and lectures supplied by recruitment agencies. Once at their destination, immigrants were left to fend for themselves, without public assistance. On the Prairies, new arrivals faced the back-breaking work, poor living conditions, and homesickness that pioneers in other regions had experienced in an earlier era. Historians estimate that as many as 40 percent of those who filed for homesteads eventually sold or abandoned their claims.

The Canadian homestead policy of 160 acres for a $10 fee and minor settlement duties seemed a bonanza to many people, but families settling on the land needed more than hope and industry to succeed. The minimum investment required in ploughs, oxen, cattle, poultry, wagons, and basic household utensils, in addition to seed and sufficient supplies to tide families over until the first harvest, was reckoned to cost even thrifty families close to $1000. Few came with such a sum; it had to be earned in Canada. Many immigrants worked as labourers and domestics on more prosperous farms or took jobs with the railways or in mines before taking up farming. While husbands and older sons and daughters worked elsewhere to earn the cash to guarantee the family's future, married women regularly maintained homesteads, living for long, lonely winter months in what were often little more than shacks—or in the somewhat less uncomfortable "soddies" constructed out of the prairie land itself—caring for young children and tending livestock.

MORE TO THE STORY
The Pioneering Experience

The Prairie pioneering experience offered singular hardship. One of the sons of Maria Aho, a founding settler of a Finnish community established in southwest Saskatchewan in 1888, recalled how difficult the early years were for his family:

> My mother was so homesick, she never allowed us to dismantle her trunk insisting that she would not stay in this bush with no roads, nothing, just a small two-room hut with branches as a roof. The roof leaked. But every second year she had a new baby until there were twelve of

us. She worked all the time, I never saw her sleep and still she kept insisting we act civilized. I was not allowed out to the nearest town till I could read and write. She taught us all that and she told us about Finland, her hometown Lapua. We dug a well by hand, but it kept drying up. Still we had a sauna every week and we were all scrubbed. Then we read the Bible and sang from the hymn book. . . . Mother never saw Finland again, she died at seventy-six, and I have never seen that country, but still if people ask me I tell them that I am a Finn.[12]

Belonging to the dominant Anglo-Canadian culture did not always make matters better. For example, Roy and Verna Benson, who settled in Munson, Alberta, were less than enthusiastic about their experience. Roy wrote in January 1911:

> I suppose you are wondering what kind of country we have struck well there are a lot of people right here that are doing the same thing wondering. This past year has made a lot of them sit up and notice. Some have left the country, some couldn't. . . . I had a 10 a[cres] broke a year ago (cost me $50) last July. Last spring I let a fellow put in on shares and put $20 into a fence–this fall I told him he could have it all but the fence.

In May of the same year, Verna offered her perspective:

> I surely don't care anything about putting in another winter like last winter. I went to one of the neighbours New Years day and I wasn't away from home again until the last of April. There was two months last winter I never saw a woman and in fact the only persons I did see during that time was Roy and our bachelor neighbor. Then the men all wonder why the women don't like it here and the women all wonder what there is about the country that the men like so well.[13]

Verna's bachelor neighbour probably also suffered from loneliness. In her study of male labour in Prairie agriculture, Cecilia Danysk cites the case of Ebe Koeppen from Germany, who recorded in his diary that he had reached a "very sad point." For Koeppen, life without a wife was "slow spiritual death." He admitted that he did not write home about such things because "the staggering drearyness of such existence is too difficult to make understandable." A popular Prairie song, "The Alberta Homesteader," made light of this familiar lament of single men:

> My clothes are all ragged, my language is rough,
> My bread is case-hardened and solid and tough
> My dishes are scattered all over the room
> My floor gets afraid of the sight of a broom.[14]

"Hot meals served at all hours": These harvesters in Saskatchewan around 1910 were fed at all hours to fuel them in their back-breaking work. Farm women, meanwhile, worked all day preparing the meals.
SOURCE: SASKATCHEWAN ARCHIVES BOARD R-A8634-1/S-B1157

Despite the hard times, uncertain reception, and lack of family, newcomers found encouragement and support in both rural and urban settings. Mutual aid societies, church organizations, cooperatives, and just plain neighbourliness rescued many families and individuals from destitution and despair. Ethnic solidarities proved invaluable. Minority communities such as Vancouver's "Little Tokyo" and Saskatchewan's Jewish agricultural colonies near Wapella,

Hirsch, Cupar, Lipton, and Sonnenfeld gave inhabitants opportunities to share cherished customs and to work out collective ways of dealing with life's many hardships. In the Ukrainian settlements of east-central Alberta, more than 90 community halls had been built by 1913 to host meetings, lectures, plays, concerts, dances, and choir practices. For navvies and sojourners, the fellowship found in the boarding houses, stores, cafés, and restaurants run by their compatriots sometimes helped to compensate for Canadian inhospitality.

This is not to say that ethnic solidarity was an entirely positive experience. Among immigrant Italians, for example, the *padroni* often extorted substantial commissions from their desperate clients. On the West Coast, Chinese prostitutes were sometimes virtual slaves of the merchants who sold their sexual services to Chinese and white customers. Police records of Canadian cities show a high incidence of crime, especially assault and theft, within immigrant communities. While this evidence perhaps reflects the fact that immigrants were more likely to be singled out by the forces of law and order, it also testifies to the tensions that, not surprisingly, surfaced among unhappy immigrants thrown together in less than ideal circumstances.

URBANIZATION

Emigration, immigration, and the growth of population in the western and northern frontiers were paralleled by an unprecedented movement of people from rural to urban areas of the country. In the boom years from 1901 to 1921, the population of Montreal nearly doubled and that of Toronto increased by about 150 percent. Even this growth paled in comparison with that of Winnipeg, Calgary, Edmonton, and Vancouver. Urbanization changed the way people thought about community and left rural areas scrambling to respond to the loss of population. Despite the problems surfacing in congested cities, they were exciting places to live, offering amenities and opportunities that rural folk were hard-pressed to emulate.

Cities in western Canada grew out of nowhere to dominate their rural hinterlands. A sleepy village in 1871, Winnipeg would have remained a backwater except for the determination of local merchants to have the CPR put its main line through the town and construct its western yards and shops there. The CPR Syndicate had planned to build through Selkirk, northeast of Winnipeg, but the railway directors could always be persuaded to change their minds.

By building a bridge across the Red River and securing two rail loops that could link a Pacific railway with the United States, Winnipeg had something other locations lacked. It offered the CPR free passage on the bridge, a $200 000 bonus, free land for its station, and a permanent exemption from municipal taxes on railway property.

With the railway in place and Prairie agriculture under way, Winnipeg grew quickly and emerged as the third-largest city in Canada by 1911. Other Prairie cities, including Edmonton, Calgary, Saskatoon, and Regina, had begun to expand by the end of the century, but the railyards and Winnipeg's position as the main distribution point for the region gave it an advantage in attracting new industry. It became the home of the grain exchange, whose speculators bid on the wheat crop, and developed a substantial manufacturing sector, including clothing, furniture, and food processing firms and metal shops dependent on the railway.

Jasper Avenue in Edmonton, 1890 (top) and 1910 (below). SOURCE: PROVINCIAL ARCHIVES OF ALBERTA, E. BROWN COLLECTION B4755 AND LIBRARY AND ARCHIVES CANADA C-7911

Like Winnipeg, Vancouver owed its growth to the CPR. Vancouver became the terminus of the company's transcontinental line, a decision sealed by subsidies and tax holidays. In competition with Victoria, whose commission merchants continued to control trade with Great Britain and California for another 20 years, Vancouver's merchants sought to dominate the British Columbia economy. They convinced city council to provide a $300 000 subsidy to local promoters of a railway to the Upper Fraser Valley, to spend $150 000 on a bridge across False Creek to connect the city with roads to the Fraser Valley, and to offer subsidies to the initiators of a sugar refinery and graving dock.

CANADIAN CITIES IN TRANSITION

Wherever they were located, cities harboured the worst features of uncontrolled growth in this period. Noise, overcrowding, poor sewage systems, pollution from smokestacks, and inadequate roads combined to make life unpleasant for most city dwellers. Despite the problems experienced in Canada's congested cities, some people lived in much better circumstances than others. The gap between rich and poor was evident in the stark contrast between the spectacular homes and office buildings of the wealthy and the substandard housing and dust-ridden factories of workers.

Montreal, Canada's largest city, was a textbook case of the problems caused by industrialization. By the end of the nineteenth century, most of its working-class citizens lived in rundown tenements, its infant mortality rate among the highest in the Western world. In 1896, Herbert Brown Ames, a businessman and social reformer, conducted a survey of living conditions in Montreal. Ames focused on two areas of the city, which he labelled "the city below the hill" and "the city above the hill." The former consisted of the industrial area in west-end Montreal, around the Lachine Canal; the latter encompassed the high terraces along the base of Mount Royal, later known as the Golden Square Mile. Ames's city below the hill was home to about 38 000 people—divided into an almost equal number of French, English, and Irish Canadians; the city above the hill was peopled largely by those of English and Scottish background.

Above the hill, Ames noted, there were "tall and handsome houses, stately churches and well-built schools," while below the hill "the tenement house replaces the single residence, and the factory with its smoking chimney is in evidence on every side." Beautiful parks and abundant greenery added to the charms of the homes in the upper city, and all the homes had modern plumbing and looked out on wide, well-paved, clean streets. Below the hill, half the houses lacked running water and were served by pit-in-the-ground privies, while "one paltry plot of ground, scarce an acre in extent, dignified by the title of Richmond Square, is the only spot where green grass can be seen free of charge." Below the hill, population density was more than double the city average, and residents suffered disproportionately from disease, crime, drunkenness, poverty, and early death. Summing up the conditions below the hill, Ames noted that for every 10 families in the area, "One family might secure an entire house to itself, but nine families must needs share theirs with another."[15]

Later studies have confirmed the view that there were two cities in Montreal, with the rich and poor living completely different lives. Even in the 1920s, children of Montreal's wealthier families, the majority of them of English and Scottish Protestant backgrounds, still had a much higher life expectancy than those who were born into poor families, most of them French and Irish Roman Catholics. The continuing high infant mortality rate in poor districts of Montreal can be traced in large part to contaminated milk and water. While affluent families could afford to purchase milk that was certified pure, 90 percent of the milk shipped to Montreal in freight cars was unfit for human consumption. The elite were also more likely to be able to afford better food and live in areas served by adequate water, sewage mains, and municipal parks. Moreover, when bad weather or epidemics rendered urban life especially unsafe or uncomfortable, they could escape to hideaways outside the city, like those in Ontario's Kawarthas, along Quebec's North Shore, or in St Andrews in New Brunswick.

Because the rich could avoid most of the problems created by poverty, urban improvements were often a long time coming. It was not until 1926 that the province of Quebec made the pasteurization of milk mandatory, and only the threat posed to wealthy residents by disease helped to encourage some early public health efforts such as compulsory vaccination for smallpox in 1903 and a water filtration plant in 1914.

Toronto, Canada's second-largest city, was only marginally better off than Montreal. Although falling land prices made home ownership possible for an increasing number of Toronto's working families, slum conditions prevailed in the back-lane cottages of St John's Ward and in areas close to railyards, factories, and packing houses. As in Montreal, Toronto's leading citizens spent as much energy bemoaning the morality of those living in poverty as the economic and political conditions that produced their sad condition.

A one-room dwelling in Winnipeg, c. 1915. SOURCE: PROVINCIAL ARCHIVES OF MANITOBA N2438

The requirement that a person had to own property to acquire the municipal franchise ensured that local governments attended mainly to the needs of ratepayers in Canadian cities. Even in small cities such as Charlottetown, where waterworks, sewerage, and improved sanitation appeared in the last two decades of the century, the *Patriot*, a local newspaper, complained in 1874:

> The rich citizen can have his residence in the suburbs where the air and water are both pure, or if he chooses to live in the city he can afford to buy spring water, and he has always a doctor at hand to attend to any of his family who shows any symptoms of being unwell. [The poor man] must bring up his family in the neighbourhood of reeking cesspools and filthy pigsties. He can not well afford to buy pure water at a very expensive rate; and he has to think twice before he calls in a doctor.[16]

Despite the general recognition by the 1870s of the role of polluted water in carrying disease, many city governments were slow to install better water systems outside wealthy neighbourhoods. Vancouver was an ugly, smelly city without sewers or any hint of planned development in the 1880s. By the late 1890s, the city had acquired a waterworks and extended water mains to most areas. With the mountains supplying pure water, Vancouver's water-related disease problems were minor compared with most cities.

In Winnipeg, just 10 percent of the population had sewers and waterworks in 1890. Only in central Winnipeg, where the commercial elite lived and conducted their business, was the water supply adequate. In the working-class north end, water was delivered to homes but the sewage system emptied into the river, with the result that deadly Red River fever (typhoid) was a continuing problem in the area. The combination of wooden buildings and a poor water supply translated into uncontrolled fires that destroyed many homes. Winnipeg was not unique in this regard. A major fire left 15 000 people homeless in Saint John in 1877, and 15 years later the homes of 10 000 people were destroyed by fire in St John's.

The nation's capital was not immune to problems facing urban dwellers. While the city named a health officer in 1874 to demand that householders dispose of garbage, Ottawa had no dump. Smallpox spread through the tenements of Lower Town in 1875. It has been estimated that a quarter of the population of Ottawa were working poor—people able to find work during part of the year, but unemployed and often destitute during the winter. There were also people who could not find work at all: men maimed in mill, construction, and bush accidents; pregnant serving girls; the handicapped and those ill with diseases such as tuberculosis. Both the working poor and the unemployables required aid from private charities to survive when relatives or friends were unable or unavailable to help.

Halifax, with its military base, was unique among Canadian cities. When the British withdrew their troops from Canada in 1871, they retained their garrison in Halifax, which served as Great Britain's naval and military base for the North Atlantic. The bishop of the Church of England declared in 1889 that "the military were a curse to this city and were the cause of a great deal of demoralization among the poor."[17] Since cities without military

In the 1890s, Halifax, like most Canadian cities, switched from horse-drawn streetcars such as those in this 1894 photograph to electric streetcars. SOURCE: PUBLIC ARCHIVES OF NOVA SCOTIA N-0405

bases also had demoralized poor in their midst, it is doubtful that the good bishop was correct in laying the entire blame on the military. It was nevertheless the case that grog shops, brothels, and disreputable boarding houses thrived on Barrack Street just below the Citadel and helped sustain the lifestyle of the repeat offenders

committed to Rockhead Prison, a substantial octagonal building located in the north end of the city. After Barrack Street was closed to the military and its name changed to South Brunswick in the early 1870s, "soldier-town" drifted to adjacent areas and continued to be a major cause for concern among urban reformers.

A HISTORIOGRAPHICAL DEBATE
Urban Poverty During the Laurier Boom

While most historians agree that the period coinciding with Wilfrid Laurier's term of office (1896-1911) was one of economic growth, there are various opinions about its impact on the people who flocked to Canadian cities to take up industrial and service jobs. Until the 1970s, most scholars, following the inter-pretations of those who lived through the period, claimed that all Canadians benefited, although perhaps at differing rates, from the unparalleled prosperity created by immigration,

industrial development, and western settlement. By the 1970s, social historians who studied the working-class experience in the industrial cities came to different conclusions, arguing that the standard of living of the working poor improved very little during the Laurier boom. What factors prompted this revisionist perspective?

One of the most positive descriptions of this period in Canadian history was penned by Liberal Party partisan

O.D. Skelton in the multi-volume study *Canada and Its Provinces* (1913).[18] Because Skelton and his contemporaries were gripped by the drama of western settlement and resource development, they were less likely to take into account the conditions in industrial cities, where the majority of immigrants and many rural-born Canadians eventually settled. Social gospellers such as Methodist minister J.S. Woodsworth, who worked among the urban poor in Winnipeg's north end, were more aware of the growing inequality that characterized the age of industry. "In country districts people are to a large extent on a level," he asserted in 1909, "but in the cities we have the rich and the poor, the classes and the masses, with all that these distinctions involve."[19]

In the 1970s, historians returned to Woodsworth's theme of social inequality. Terry Copp examined the standard of living of Montreal's working class at the turn of the twentieth century and concluded that "as far as real income is concerned the average wage earner in Montreal was less well off during the period of economic expansion than during the 'depression' of the late 19th C."[20] Michael Piva reached a similar conclusion in his study of working-class conditions in Toronto.[21] The story was the same in the Maritimes. In his study of industrial workers in Amherst, Sydney, and Yarmouth, Nova Scotia, Del Muise revealed that the earnings of both men and women were suppressed in the first two decades of the twentieth century. This situation contributed to the continuing outmigration that further weakened the region's industrial potential.[22]

Further research showed that age, culture, and gender determined who suffered most from the growing gap between rich and poor. Howard Palmer documented the discrimination that immigrants without capital or skills faced in both urban and rural settings. For many immigrants, Palmer argued, stereotypes emphasizing peasant origins "played a role in determining job opportunities and functioned to disparage those who would climb out of their place."[23] Discrimination not only forced many immigrants to take gruelling and low-paying jobs as navvies, bunkhouse men, and farm labourers in remote areas; it also helped to create urban ghettos with names such as "Little Italy" and "Little Africa."

The standard of living of working-class women stagnated during the Laurier boom. As Joan Sangster discovered during her research on the 1907 Bell Telephone strike in Toronto, women were not only systematically paid less than men for their labour, they were also less likely to be unionized and therefore generally unsuccessful in their efforts to resist wage reductions and oppressive working conditions.[24] In her study of the "girl problem" in Toronto, Carolyn Strange notes that "Toronto's service and light manufacturing industries were built on the back of working girls," whose low wages were justified on the basis of "their age, their marital status and their sex."[25] By encouraging young women to seek security in "respectability" and family life, social reformers made it highly unlikely that female workers would find equality in the public sphere of work and wages.

By the 1990s, as the gap between rich and poor steadily widened even as the economy was growing, it became easier to understand that statistics indicating overall economic growth do not always translate into better living conditions for everyone. Some people benefit more than others in periods of rapid economic change, and often an "underclass" bears the brunt of "progress."

CONCLUSION

By the turn of the twentieth century, immigration and urbanization were changing the face of Canada. The influx of settlers, who made their homes primarily in cities and in the western provinces, helped fuel the economic boom that characterized the early 1900s and performed much of the back-breaking labour that made economic growth possible. Immigrants also made Canada a more culturally diverse nation, forcing English, French, and Aboriginal Canadians to reassess their own identities and adjust to the values and practices of newcomers who brought their own ways of doing things. In the end, native-born and immigrant Canadians faced a similar challenge: how to make a living and create a sense of community in a nation in a state of rapid transition.

NOTES

1. Bettina Bradbury, "Children Who Lived with One Parent in 1901," in *Household Counts: Canadian Households and Families in 1901*, eds. Eric W. Sager and Peter Baskerville (Toronto: University of Toronto Press, 2007) 247–248.

2. Cited in J.W. Dafoe, *Clifford Sifton in Relation to His Times* (Toronto: Macmillan, 1931) 142.

3. Cited in Reg Whitaker, *Canadian Immigration Policy Since Confederation* (Ottawa: Canadian Historical Association, 1991) 8, 11.

4. Cited in Penny Petrone, ed., *First People, First Voices* (Toronto: University of Toronto Press, 1983) 68–69.

5. Cited in Jacqueline Hucker, "Temple of the Church of Jesus Christ of the Latter-Day Saints" (Agenda Paper No. 32, Historic Sites and Monuments Board, November 6–7, 1992) 163.

6. Gerald Friesen, *The Canadian Prairies: A History* (Toronto: University of Toronto Press, 1984) 265.

7. Kevin Plummer, "Historicist: Public History and William Peyton Hubbard," *Torontoist*, February 2009 http://torontoist.com/2009/02/historicist_public_history_and_william_peyton_hubbard

8. *Daily Globe*, 7 June 1882.

9. Cited in James W. St. G. Walker, *Racial Discrimination in Canada: The Black Experience* (Ottawa: Canadian Historical Association, 1985) 4.

10. Cited in John Bullen, "Hidden Workers: Child Labour and the Family Economy in Late Nineteenth Urban Ontario," *Labour/Le Travail* 18 (Fall 1986) 181.

11. Cited in Robert Harney, "Ethnicity and Neighbourhoods," in *Cities and Urbanization: Canadian Historical Perspectives*, ed. Gilbert A. Stelter (Toronto: Copp Clark Pitman, 1990) 228.

12. Varpu Lindström-Best, *Defiant Sisters: A Social History of Finnish Immigrant Women in Canada* (Toronto: Multicultural History Society of Ontario, 1988) 27.

13. Cited in John W. Bennett and Seena B. Kohl, *Settling the Canadian-American West, 1890–1915: Pioneer Adaptation and Community Building* (Lincoln: University of Nebraska Press, 1995) 68.

14. Cecilia Danysk, *Hired Hands: Labour and the Development of Prairie Agriculture, 1880–1930* (Toronto: McClelland & Stewart, 1995), 71–72.

15. Herbert Brown Ames, *The City Below the Hill* (1897; Toronto: University of Toronto Press, 1972) 103, 105, 48.

16. Quoted in Douglas Baldwin, "'But Not a Drop to Drink': The Struggle for Pure Water," in *Gaslights, Epidemics and Vagabond Cows: Charlottetown in the Victorian Era*, eds. Douglas Baldwin and Thomas Spira (Charlottetown: Ragweed Press, 1988) 110.

17. Cited in Judith Fingard, *The Dark Side of Life in Victorian Halifax* (Porters Lake: Pottersfield Press, 1989) 16.

18. O.D. Skelton, "General Economic History, 1867–1912," in *Canada and Its Provinces*, vol. 9, eds. Adam Short and Arthur G. Doughty (Toronto: Glasgow, Brook, 1913).

19. Cited in Paul W. Bennett and Cornelius Jaenen, *Emerging Identities: Selected Problems and Interpretations in Canadian History* (Scarborough: Prentice-Hall, 1986) 355.

20. J.T. Copp, "The Condition of the Working Class in Montreal, 1867–1920," *Historical Papers* (1972) 172.

21. Michael J. Piva, *The Condition of the Working Class in Toronto, 1900–1920* (Ottawa: University of Ottawa Press, 1979).

22. D.A. Muise, "The Industrial Context of Inequality: Female Participation in Nova Scotia's Paid Labour Force, 1871–1921," *Acadiensis* 20, 2 (Spring 1991) 3–31.

23. Howard Palmer, "Reluctant Hosts: Anglo-Canadian Views of Multiculturalism in the Twentieth Century," in *Multiculturalism as State Policy* (Ottawa: Canadian Consultative Council on Multiculturalism and Supply and Services Canada, 1976) 96.

24. Joan Sangster, "The 1907 Bell Telephone Strike: Organizing Women Workers," *Labour/Le Travaillleur* 3 (1978) 109–30.

25. Carolyn Strange, *Toronto's Girl Problem: The Perils and Pleasures of the City, 1880–1930* (Toronto: University of Toronto Press, 1993) 39, 41.

SELECTED READING

Avery, Donald H. *Reluctant Host: Canada's Response to Immigrant Workers, 1896–1994.* Toronto: McClelland & Stewart, 1995

Bagnell, Kenneth. *The Little Immigrants: The Orphans Who Came to Canada.* Toronto: Dundurn, 2001

Baskerville, Peter and Eric Sager, eds. *Household Counts: Canadian Households and Families in 1901.* Toronto: University of Toronto Press, 2007

Copp, Terry. *The Anatomy of Poverty: The Condition of the Working Class in Montreal, 1897–1929.* Toronto: McClelland & Stewart, 1974

Fingard, Judith. *The Dark Side of Life in Victorian Halifax.* Porters Lake: Pottersfield Press, 1989

Friesen, Gerald. *Citizens and Nation: An Essay on History, Communication, and Canada.* Toronto: University of Toronto Press, 2000

Iacovetta, Franca with Paula Draper and Robert Ventresca, eds. *A Nation of Immigrants: Women, Workers, and Communities in Canadian History, 1840s–1960s.* Toronto: University of Toronto Press, 1998

Johnston, Hugh. *The Voyage of the* Komagata Maru: *The Sikh Challenge to Canada's Colour Bar.* Vancouver: University of British Columbia Press, 1989

Kelley, Ninette and Michael Trebilcock. *The Making of the Mosaic: A History of Canadian Immigration Policy.* Toronto: University of Toronto Press, 2010

Linteau, Paul-André. *Maisonneuve: comment des promoteurs fabriquent une ville.* Montreal: Boréal Express, 1981

Olson, Sherry and Patricia A. Thornton. *Peopling the North American City: Montreal, 1840–1900.* Montreal: McGill-Queen's University Press, 2011

Parr, Joy. *The Gender of Breadwinners: Women, Men, and Change in Two Industrial Towns, 1880–1950.* Toronto: University of Toronto Press, 1990

Piva, Michael J. *The Condition of the Working Class in Toronto, 1900–1920.* Ottawa: University of Ottawa Press, 1979

Strange, Carolyn and Tina Loo. *Making Good: Law and Moral Regulation in Canada, 1867–1939.* Toronto: University of Toronto Press, 1997

Strong-Boag, Veronica, et al., eds. *Painting the Maple: Essays on Race, Gender, and the Construction of Canada.* Vancouver: UBC Press, 1998

For a comprehensive list of readings for topics covered in this chapter, please visit http://pearsoncanada.ca/conrad.

CHAPTER 6
SOCIETY AND CULTURE IN THE AGE OF INDUSTRY, 1867–1914

In March 1888, Jessie McQueen, a 27-year-old teacher from Pictou County, Nova Scotia, took the Canadian Pacific Railway to British Columbia, where she had been hired to teach school. Her younger sister, Annie, had made the same journey a year earlier and a cousin, Jessie Olding, would soon join them. As this letter from Jessie's brother, George, who was working in the United States, suggests, the McQueens carried their Scottish Presbyterian values with them when they moved in search of work.

> So you and Jessie Olding and I suppose several more would-be cow girl maidens are going to storm the home of the deceitful mustang and lordly wheat. Are you all going to buy revolvers like the small boys in the novels . . . ? It was awful for that harum scarum George to go away off to New York 60 hours from home, but it's nothing for the little birdlings to go clean across the Continent. One word of advice don't marry a man unless he's three quarters Scotch & one quarter English and has been brought up a Scotch Presbyterian. It's the best mixture in the world and we says it who ought to know.[1]

Drawn to British Columbia by higher salaries than they could earn in the Maritimes, Jessie and Annie McQueen played a role as important as that of businessmen and politicians in determining the shape of the new nation. Historian Jean Barman argues that, by laying the foundations for family life, Christian churches, common schools, and myriad voluntary organizations, these women and others like them Canadianized what at the time was perceived as a "Wild West."[2]

THE PROGRESSIVES

Women such as the McQueen sisters had been raised to respect the values of self-help and Christian charity. As a result, they were susceptible to various movements for reform that swept across the nation in the second half of the nineteenth century. Labour organizers joined professionals, church leaders, journalists, and women's rights activists in an impressive coalition to demand a growing list of reforms. Dubbed by historian Ramsay Cook as "the regenerators," they were inspired by a vision of progressive reform in which scientific expertise, efficient management, and government oversight would transform capitalist society from a Darwinian battle of the survival of the fittest to a paradise on Earth.[3]

Alcohol was a favoured target of progressive reformers, who saw it as the cause of many of Canada's social problems. Over the course of the nineteenth century, the movement to encourage temperance in the use of alcohol had given way to a demand that the state impose laws to prohibit its manufacture, sale, and consumption. This transition from the personal to the political prompted the Protestant churches, led by the Baptists, Methodists, and Presbyterians, and voluntary organizations such as the Sons of Temperance and the Woman's Christian Temperance Union, to forge a formidable alliance that no politician could ignore.

Pressed by the mounting support for action, the Mackenzie government passed the Canada Temperance Act in 1878. Known as the Scott Act, it allowed municipalities to hold plebiscites to determine whether liquor could be sold within their boundaries. Many areas of Canada voted "dry," and the consumption of alcohol actually declined, but it never stopped. What separated the "wets" from the "drys" was not the problem of alcohol abuse, which nearly everyone agreed was a cause for concern, but the means of addressing it. For many people, the demand for state intervention went too far. This was the position taken in Quebec, where the Roman

Catholic Church resisted the growing power of the state while at the same time strongly encouraging Catholics to reduce or eliminate their alcohol consumption through church-led temperance movements.

Prime Minister Laurier tried to avoid federal action by agreeing to a national referendum on the issue. Held in 1898, it yielded a predictable result: a majority for the drys in every province except Quebec, where a combination of distillery interests and Catholic Church opposition ensured the failure of the initiative. The relatively small overall majority and a low voter turnout allowed Laurier to sidestep the issue that bitterly divided the country. For the time being, Prohibition advocates had to be content with the existing system of local option, but their forces were not yet spent. They turned to their provincial governments to pass legislation prohibiting the liquor trade. They also demanded a wholesale reform of the political system, including giving women, who were believed to be more supportive of the temperance cause, the right to vote.

Many reformers focused on the moral issues associated with social problems. This approach was diligently pursued in Toronto, which was dubbed "Toronto the Good" for its earnest efforts to legislate and enforce morality. In 1886, Toronto's reforming mayor, William Howland, established a Morality Department in the city police force. People involved in prostitution, the illicit sale of liquor, gambling, and the mistreatment of children and animals were hauled into court by the new morality squad. By using a broad interpretation of the

Beer parlour, Boisetown, New Brunswick, 1912. SOURCE: PROVINCIAL ARCHIVES OF NEW BRUNSWICK, NASHWAAK FAMILY BICENTENNIAL ASSOCIATION COLLECTION P145-61

Women in Action

To be an active member of the Woman's Christian Temperance Union (WCTU), a woman needed a strong will. The *Ottawa Daily Citizen* published this account of a WCTU action on 5 February 1890:

> A Band of evangelistic workers announced a few days ago by handbills distributed throughout Hull, that meetings would be held every Tuesday evening in that city in a hall on the corner of Duke and Queen Streets.... It seems that preparations were made by a gang of roughs, headed by an unlicensed saloon keeper, to give the new-comers a warm reception; in fact, the intention was more or less openly expressed to "clean them out." The band of evangelists was composed of Miss Bertha Wright, accompanied by a considerable number of young ladies. . . . On opening the doors of the Hall a crowd of about TWO HUNDRED MEN well primed with liquor rushed in and filled the place. For a time, their interruptions were confined to noises, etc., but on being remonstrated with they made an attack on the speaker and singers. For a time everything was in confusion, and there was reason to fear the worst, missiles being thrown and blows freely given, but not returned. The young women then joined hands and formed a circle around the speakers, and the roughs refrained from striking them but confined their efforts to separating the little band. . . . Finally the police managed to clear the hall and took the Ottawa people to the station, fighting off the crowd with their batons all the way. At this time some of the young women were badly hurt by the missiles that were thrown.[4]

Despite the "warm reception," Bertha Wright and her "little band" from the Ottawa Young Woman's Christian Temperance Union were back in Hull the following week, this time to take on an angry mob of 400 "roughs."

vagrancy laws, young women innocently walking on the streets at night could be interrogated by the morality police. Women and children were the special concern of moral reformers, who had difficulty accepting the freedom from parental and patriarchal control that city life encouraged.

At the forefront of the movement for progressive reform was an army of health professionals led by medical doctors and nurses. They argued that public health should be a priority of reform, and provided municipal officials and school boards with scientific evidence of the need for vaccinations, medical inspection, and better nutrition. Throughout the country, energies were marshalled to train doctors and nurses, build new hospitals, establish clinics for young mothers and their babies, and teach schoolchildren that "Cleanliness is next to Godliness." Campaigns against smoking and spitting—both connected for those who pursued the popular pastime of chewing tobacco—encouraged habits

In 1913, Toronto's Medical Health Department established well-baby clinics, like this one at St Christopher House, to instruct new mothers on how to care for their infants. Similar clinics were instituted in many larger cities. SOURCE: CITY OF TORONTO ARCHIVES, FONDS 200, SERIES 372, SUBSERIES 32, ITEM 234

that would lead to healthier Canadians. By urging restrictions on untrained practitioners, they also cornered the market on legal medical services, putting patent medicine promoters, herbalists, and midwives on the defensive.

Churches were central to progressive reform efforts in many communities. By the turn of the century, many Protestant denominations had adopted what is termed the "social gospel" approach to their work. While still concerned with spiritual salvation and social purity, they expanded their charitable activities to address the appalling conditions created by the industrial system. Canada's Protestant churches sponsored missions, labour churches, and settlement houses in the inner city to minister to the spiritual and physical needs of the working class. One of the most prominent social gospellers was Methodist minister J.S. Woodsworth, who from 1907 to 1913 served as superintendent of Winnipeg's All People's Mission, which catered to the city's culturally diverse immigrant population.

While the Catholic Church would never consider itself progressive, it too was spurred to respond to the miseries caused by rapid urbanization and industrialization. It relied mainly on traditional structures based on religious orders and on the parish, adapted to the urban, industrial context. In Quebec, the network of Catholic hospitals, schools, orphanages, and other charities launched in the decades before Confederation expanded dramatically and came increasingly under direct church control. By the 1870s, almost all charitable institutions in the province that had previously been operated by lay Catholics were run by religious orders. At the same time, the multiplication of Catholic parishes in urban areas led to the rapid growth of voluntary associations dedicated to raising money for parish charities through activities such as bazaars, musical shows, raffles, and even lotteries, all designed to encourage devotional practices that solidified the church's hold over its parishioners.

While its influence remained greatest in Quebec, the Roman Catholic Church expanded its presence throughout Canada to serve its increasingly diverse membership. In the case of Polish immigrants, Catholicism was closely allied to Polish nationalism, a connection that in 1901 turned the congregation of the Winnipeg Holy Ghost parish against the German-speaking Oblate Fathers. At the same time that it was suppressing Native languages in its residential schools, the Catholic Church played an essential role in maintaining minority eastern European languages through its networks of parochial schools. By 1916, for instance, there were 11 Polish and Ukrainian Catholic schools in Manitoba.

In 1888, Protestant churches founded the Lord's Day Alliance to fight for respect of the Sabbath. In cooperation with union leaders and the Catholic hierarchy, they pressured the federal government to legislate Sunday observance. Passed in 1907, the Lord's Day Act banned paid employment, shopping, and commercial leisure activities on Sunday—policies that the churches argued not only conformed to Canada's Christian beliefs, but also gave working people a day of rest. Buoyed by this success, the Methodists and Presbyterians collaborated in the founding in 1907 of the Moral and Social Reform Council of Canada (its name was changed to the Social Service Council of Canada in 1913) to pursue an ambitious reform agenda.

The Methodist Church also took a lead in educating English Canadians on issues of sexual hygiene. Since the 1892 Criminal Code prohibited the promotion and sale of aborficients and contraceptives, the church was eager to counsel self-control in sexual matters and distributed sex manuals targeted at various age levels for women and men. While criticized today as moralistic and wrongheaded, the manuals incorporated the thinking of the time in the field of "sexology" and moved some distance from the puritanical approach to sex typical of the period. Some progressives went even further and advocated a program of eugenics. Drawing on scientific findings related to reproduction in the plant and animal world, eugenicists argued that society could be improved by preventing people with undesirable mental and physical traits from reproducing.

The desire for social control and scientific analysis led to same-sex relationships being labelled "homosexual" and deemed unnatural. There were both gays and lesbians in Canada at the time, but the prevailing theories depicted women as sexually passive and thus unlikely to desire sex with other women. The law therefore targeted only male same-sex relations. Although sexual intercourse between men had been illegal since the colonial period, an 1890 law extended the ban to "gross indecency" between men in any public or private setting. Such vague language greatly expanded the scope of police surveillance and state repression of intimacy between men. While social purity advocates insisted on

MORE TO THE STORY
The Grenfell Mission

In Newfoundland, the social gospel movement was represented in a dramatic way by the mission of Wilfred Grenfell. Born in England in 1865, Grenfell was a student at London Medical School when he was converted to active Christianity by American evangelist Dwight L. Moody. He subsequently joined the Royal National Mission to Deep Sea Fishermen. He visited the coasts of Newfoundland and Labrador in 1892, where he saw a great opportunity to combine medical and missionary work among people who rarely saw a doctor or a minister. The following year, he opened a hospital in Battle Harbour, Labrador, and by the end of the century had established his mission headquarters at St Anthony's on the northern tip of Newfoundland.

Backed by supporters in the United States, Canada, and Great Britain, Grenfell expanded his activities to include nursing stations, schools, cooperatives, and an orphanage. His well-publicized efforts to bring services to isolated areas–including a close brush with death on an ice floe in 1908–made him a popular hero and enabled him to earn money for his mission through the lecture circuit. Following his marriage to a Chicago heiress in 1909, Grenfell spent less time in missionary work, which was carried on by dedicated men and women inspired by Grenfell's pioneering efforts.[5]

Staff at the Battle Harbour Hospital, c. 1909. Wilfred Grenfell is seated at the left. SOURCE: THE ROOMS PROVINCIAL ARCHIVES VA 118-69.5

jail sentences for homosexuals, the medical profession began describing same-sex attraction as a form of insanity requiring confinement in a "lunatic" asylum rather than a prison. Practising homosexuals could face either fate in a society that subscribed to the view that sex should be confined to married couples. In Victoria, two men convicted of sodomy in 1891 were each sentenced to

15 years in prison, a sentence later commuted to seven years. Sentences of a year or two were more common.

Progressives also took up the cause of environmental reform, arguing that Canada lagged behind other industrialized nations in attending to the problems of pollution and resource depletion. The example of the United States inspired the federal government to set aside

Banff Hot Springs Reserve (the ancestor of Banff National Park) for public use in 1885. Following the North American Conservation Conference convened by President Theodore Roosevelt in 1909, the federal government established a Canadian Commission of Conservation (CCC). Under the energetic direction of Clifford Sifton, the CCC investigated everything from fur farming and migratory birds to power development and urban planning.

The "city beautiful" movement, with its notions of rational planning, elegant buildings, and public spaces, appealed to many progressives. Originating in Europe and the United States, the movement soon had Canadian converts, including Herbert Ames who catalogued Montreal's problems in his book *The City Below the Hill*, published in 1897. Urban reformers established their own voluntary associations, such as Montreal's City Improvement League, and enlisted the support of the Union of Canadian Municipalities. Urban planning experts argued that changing cities would also change the people who lived in them.

Suspicious of private utilities in water, power, telephones, and transport, progressives argued for government control of such essential services. Municipal and provincial governments in the first decade of the twentieth century often responded to pressure from reformers to take over the utilities from private developers. While most of Montreal's private utilities weathered the tide of consumer grievance, Edmonton's streetcars, electricity, and telephones all became publicly owned. In Toronto, Bell survived as a private telephone monopoly, but the Toronto Transit Commission assumed control of the street railways.

As progressives encountered resistance from municipal governments, they became critical of political processes. The ratepayers, critics argued, had become passive pawns in the hands of corrupt developers who could influence voting in the poorer wards. To curb the power of "special interests," cities were urged to establish boards of control, elected on a city-wide franchise. Because middle-class voters were more likely to vote than the working class, they could influence the results in a city-wide election, thereby putting an end to ward politics. Boards of control were adopted in a number of cities including Winnipeg (1906), Ottawa (1907), Montreal (1909), Hamilton (1910), and London (1914). Another way of wresting power from the masses was to delegate authority to "expert" city managers and appointed commissioners, policies adopted in Edmonton in 1904, Saint John in 1908, and a few years later in Regina, Saskatoon, and Prince Albert.

THE RADICAL RESPONSE

By 1914, a growing number of Canadians were pursuing visions more radical than those championed by the progressives, whose main goal was to impose regulation on capitalist development. Socialists were in the forefront of an international movement to abolish a system that they believed put property ahead of people and pitted labour against capital in an uneven struggle refereed by a state clearly biased in favour of the rich. Although socialists disagreed on the best means of achieving a society where each would receive according to his or her needs, their goal had wide appeal in early industrializing Canada.

The socialist movement that took root in Canada was an uneasy amalgam of Marxism, Christian socialism, and reformism. At one end of the spectrum, radicals such as the Industrial Workers of the World preached syndicalism, the view that labourers should join forces to overthrow the yoke of capitalism. These hardliners argued that a cataclysmic conflict between labour and capital was the only way the new order would be given birth. In contrast, the Christian Socialist League, whose leading spokesman was G. Weston Wrigley, maintained that Christ was the first socialist and advocated a more gradual and constitutional approach to a socialist utopia.

One of the earliest spokesmen for the gradual approach was T. Phillips Thompson, a journalist based in Toronto. Unlike most Anglo-Canadians, he sympathized with the francophone and Métis minorities and advocated the abolition of the monarchy. A free thinker, he was influenced by the work of American critic Henry George, whose book *Progress and Poverty*, published in 1879, caused a stir throughout Canada. George's message—that industrialism had unleashed an insupportable burden of poverty and distress—was not new, but his solution was a tax on the property of the rich. Dubbed the "single tax," it had the virtue of simplicity.

With the arrival of thousands of immigrants bearing a tradition of socialist politics, efforts to achieve unity in the socialist cause became highly complicated. No sooner had socialist groups in British Columbia come together to produce the Socialist Party of Canada in 1904 than they were weakened by the defection of members who founded the more moderate Social Democratic Party (SDP) in 1907. With its language locals, the SDP appealed to some in the Finnish, Ukrainian, and Russian communities on the Prairies, who felt excluded from the established political parties. The SDP also proved more open to women's issues, including the problems of unpaid domestic labour and Prohibition, than the Socialist Party of Canada, whose leaders considered such issues as detracting from "scientific" socialist goals.

Many Canadian workers followed the example of their counterparts in Great Britain who were throwing their support behind the Independent Labour Party. While socialists initially preached the total abolition of capitalism, the British Labour Party focused on improving the lot of workers within the capitalist system. In addition to supporting public ownership of railways, banks, and utilities, its leaders urged state enforcement of safe working conditions and the introduction of social insurance programs such as unemployment and health insurance and old-age pensions. Labour candidates and labour parties soon began to appear on the Canadian scene. The first to win a seat in the House of Commons was Alphonse-Télesphore Lépine, a Montreal member of the Knights of Labor elected in 1888. He was followed by others, including A.W. Puttee, a founder of the Winnipeg Labour Party, and Ralph Smith, president of the Trades and Labour Congress, both elected in 1900.

THE RURAL RESPONSE

While cities served as a focus for reform, people living in rural communities were far from passively resigned to the changes taking place around them. Western farmers were particularly suspicious of the power of eastern-controlled railways, banks, and governments, but rural people elsewhere were disturbed by the growing dominance of urban-based institutions. Their concerns focused on the depopulation of rural areas and the lack of amenities available to their city neighbours.

The impact of commercialization on rural life and the flight of large numbers of people to the city also troubled many urban dwellers. In Montreal, Henri Bourassa wrote frequently and eloquently about the danger to society of

abandoning the values associated with rural life, reflecting the prevailing view of conservative nationalists in Quebec. Similarly, Andrew Macphail, a Montreal-based medical doctor who edited *University Magazine* between 1907 and 1920, looked back nostalgically upon his childhood in rural Prince Edward Island. He lamented the rapid disappearance of what he saw as a superior way of life. For these men, rural living was as crucial to the moral and spiritual well-being of the nation as it was to physical survival and food production.

The flight of women from the farm was a particular concern of reformers. When markets became the focus of production, the balance of power in the family enterprise shifted in favour of men. Profits from farming, if there were any, were more likely to be invested in farm machinery than in appliances to relieve domestic drudgery. Discouraged by discriminatory homestead laws, unequal inheritance patterns, and the unending domestic toil that confronted them, young women deserted the farm for jobs in the city. Industrial wages were lower for women than men, but at least in the cities women had access to an income that was often denied them on the farm.

Rural discontent blossomed into a full-blown movement that demanded major changes in Canada's political structures. In the 1870s, the Dominion Grange Movement in the Maritimes and Ontario paralleled efforts by labour and capital to use collective action to achieve their goals. The Grange movement focused on educational activities and avoided direct political action, but another American import, the Patrons of Industry, led to the election of candidates to the Ontario and Manitoba legislatures as well as to the House of Commons in the 1890s. The Patrons were succeeded by the Ontario Farmers' Association, which in 1902 emerged as a critic of high transportation costs and the protective tariff. By 1907, it had joined with the Grange to form the United Farmers of Ontario. Led by E.C. Drury and J.J. Morrison, it was determined to make Ottawa listen to the concerns of the farming community.

On the Prairies, agrarian discontent led to the founding of the Territorial Grain Growers' Association in 1901, which became the basis for provincial associations following the creation of the provinces of Saskatchewan and Alberta in 1905. The Manitoba Grain Growers' Association was founded in 1902. In 1908, the *Grain Growers' Guide*, a newspaper based in Winnipeg, was established as a mouthpiece for agrarian discontent. Francis Marion

Beynon's column in the *Guide* gave women plenty to think about. Recognition of women's contribution to farm life led to the creation of women's auxiliaries to the prairie farm organizations and to support for female suffrage.

Rural areas of Newfoundland were also ripe for the message of social reform. Under the dynamic leadership of William Coaker, the Fishermen's Protective Union (FPU), founded in 1909, swept through the outports, gaining support from the workers in the fishing and forest industries. The FPU demanded state intervention to ensure a fair return to the people who caught and processed the fish, improvements in education and health care in the outports, and implementation of an old-age pension program. In alliance with the Liberal Party, the FPU won eight seats in the Newfoundland legislature in 1913 and applied pressure on the government to legislate reforms.

One of the most significant challenges to capitalist development came from the cooperative movement, which was particularly strong in rural Canada. Originating in Britain in the early nineteenth century, cooperatives were organized on the principle of cooperation rather than competition and were owned by their members rather than by anonymous investors. Between 1860 and 1900, farmers in the Maritimes, Quebec, and Ontario developed more than 1200 cooperative creameries and cheese factories. They also organized insurance companies to provide protection against crop failure and fires. In Quebec, Alphonse Desjardins used cooperative principles to establish a system of largely rural credit unions, the caisses populaires, which provided services where banks would not. Grain farmers in western Canada, led by E.A. Partridge, organized the Grain Growers' Grain Company in 1906 to market directly to buyers in Europe.

The creation of the Cooperative Union of Canada in 1909 brought like-minded cooperators together for education and lobbying activities. In the same year, Ontario farmers and western grain growers established the Canadian Council of Agriculture. Reform of tariff policy was high on their agenda. Roundly condemned as a charge on society's producers for the benefits of manufacturers, tariffs were seen by the farmers as an instrument of oppression by a class of businessmen who were sucking the nation dry through their greed and corruption.

In June 1910, Prime Minister Laurier set out on a three-month tour of the western provinces and was besieged by petitions from well-organized farmers. Later in the year, nearly 1000 farmers from all across the country descended on Parliament Hill demanding lower tariffs, better rail and grain elevator service, and legislation supporting cooperative enterprises. When the Laurier government negotiated a free trade treaty with the United States in the winter of 1911, it did so because a clear majority of rural Canadians demanded an end to high tariffs. The defeat of the Liberals later that year only confirmed the belief held by farmers that industrial interests controlled the levers of power in the nation.

THE "WOMAN MOVEMENT"

Women's involvement in Canada's reform movements was fuelled by the enormous changes in their lives and by new ideas about the role of women in society. With the introduction of manufactured clothes, foodstuffs, and household products, and the tendencies toward smaller families and educating children in public schools, much of what was considered women's work moved into the public sphere. At the same time, middle-class women were told that their only place was in the home. To reinforce that injunction, women were denied access to higher education, professions, boardrooms, and political office.

The doctrine of separate spheres led middle-class women to organize separately from men in a variety of voluntary organizations. In the 1870s, Women's Missionary Aid Societies sprouted in various Protestant churches. Designed to spread the gospel at home and abroad, missionary aid societies sponsored single women for overseas service in countries such as India and China and taught women valuable organizational skills. While consistent with women's long-standing role in charitable activities, missionary work provided a source of employment for women in the public sphere, often in areas such as medicine and administration largely denied to them at home.

Two of the earliest women's organizations, the Young Women's Christian Association (YWCA) and the Woman's Christian Temperance Union (WCTU), took middle-class women another step down the road to public service. Founded in Great Britain as a counterpart to the YMCA, the Canadian YWCA was first established in Saint John in 1870. The "Y" provided both lodging and job training, largely in domestic service, for girls

A group of women in front of a YWCA boarding house in Toronto, c. 1913-1917. Organizations such as the YWCA brought together women from a wide range of backgrounds to discuss issues relating to their status and well-being in Canadian society. SOURCE: LIBRARY AND ARCHIVES CANADA PA-126710

arriving in the "dangerous" urban environment. The first Canadian branch of the American-based WCTU was founded by Letitia Youmans in Picton, Ontario, in 1874. The WCTU focused women's energies on achieving Prohibition, but it soon took on other reform causes. Spreading quickly throughout the nation, the WCTU formed a Dominion Union in 1883, and by the 1890s claimed more than 10 000 members.

While many of the voluntary organizations that appealed to women originated in Great Britain and the United States, Canada made its own contribution in the form of the Women's Institutes, the first of which was established in Stoney Creek, Ontario, in 1897 by Adelaide Hoodless, whose youngest child died as a result of drinking contaminated milk. Hoodless pushed for domestic science courses in the schools, pure milk legislation, and public health reforms. These goals were taken up with zeal by the Women's Institutes after the Ontario government began

subsidizing their efforts in 1900. By the 1920s, the Women's Institutes had spread throughout Canada and had taken root in rural areas of Great Britain and around the world.

In Quebec, francophone women found an outlet for their energies in religious orders that had responsibility for education, health care, and social services. Between 1837 and 1899, 34 new female religious communities were established in Quebec. By 1901, 6.1 percent of the province's single women over 20 years of age were nuns. Nuns took up many reform causes. For example, the Grey Nuns in Montreal organized daycare centres for working-class families in the early 1870s. By the turn of the century, lay women in Quebec began to resist the conservative injunctions of their clerical leaders. In 1907, Marie Lacoste-Gérin-Lajoie played a leading role in founding the Fédération nationale Saint-Jean-Baptiste, an organization that pushed for access to higher education for women, improvements in their legal status, and reform of working conditions.

The Hospice of the Soeurs de la Charité in Rimouski, 1890. The imposing building in a small town, with its ranks of staff and residents, illustrates the institutional power of the Roman Catholic Church in Quebec. SOURCE: BIBLIOTHÈQUE ET ARCHIVES NATIONALES DU QUÉBEC, CENTRE D'ARCHIVES DE QUÉBEC P600,S6,D5,P567

The growth in Canadian women's activism was capped by the formation of a national federation of women's clubs in 1893. Known as the National Council of Women of Canada (NCWC), it was the brainchild of Lady Aberdeen, the wife of the governor general. An enthusiastic supporter of reform causes, Lady Aberdeen was a founder of the Aberdeen Association (1890), which distributed reading material to isolated settlers, and of the Victorian Order of Nurses (1897), an organization that provided nursing services in areas where trained medical help was not available. The NCWC began cautiously but soon encompassed a wide range of reforms, including temperance, child welfare, and professional advancement for women. In 1910, the NCWC endorsed women's suffrage, the final step in recognizing women as having public power in their own right.

By the 1890s, an increasing number of reformers supported what was known at the time as "woman suffrage." People came to the cause in a variety of ways: from lengthy struggles to open universities, professions, and businesses on an equal basis to women; from groups condemning women's subordination under the law; and from reform movements that felt their goals might be advanced by the support of women. Two feminist perspectives were evident in the suffragists' arguments: equal rights and maternal, or social, feminism. Equal rights advocates were determined to eliminate the unfair laws and attitudes that encouraged discrimination against women. Maternal feminists wanted laws to support women in their roles as wives and mothers. In both lines of thinking, women's suffrage became a key element in the struggle for reform.

The hardships of the suffrage campaign wore out several generations of women and deterred the less courageous from publicly expressing their opinions. Misogyny and anti-feminism were widely expressed both orally and in print by people determined to keep women in their place. In Quebec, Henri Bourassa lashed out against feminism as a dangerous import from a godless Anglo-Saxon culture that would destroy Roman Catholic

Quebec. While tolerating the founding of the first French-Canadian feminist umbrella group in 1907, the Fédération nationale Saint-Jean-Baptiste, the archbishop of Montreal, Paul Bruchési, clearly established the limits of Catholic feminist action: "Because the word feminism had been introduced into our language, I accept it, but I claim a Christian meaning for it. . . : woman's zeal for all noble causes in the sphere which Divine Providence has assigned to her." Bruchési continued by specifying that "good" feminism must not concern itself with female emancipation and women's participation in the public and professional spheres.[6]

English-Canadian intellectuals such as Stephen Leacock were equally appalled by the notion of equality for women, and resorted to the comfortable view that because women were superior to men they should be shielded from the realities of the public sphere. Canada's union leaders were no better than their middle-class employers, arguing that women should be segregated in the workforce and receive lower wages. When immigrants brought with them traditional views about the subordination of women, they added further weight to the patriarchal perspective. Even Protestant church leaders, whose congregations were increasingly dominated by women, preached against defying the divinely sanctioned subordination of women.

Not surprisingly, given their education and sense of purpose, many of the first generation of professional women became active in the suffrage movement. Dr Emily Howard Stowe, who was forced to go to the United States to get a medical degree, took the lead in establishing Canada's first women's suffrage organization in 1876, whose purpose was concealed under the name the Toronto Women's Literary Club. By 1883, the group felt confident enough to change its name to the Toronto Women's Suffrage Association and at the same time to launch the Canadian Women's Suffrage Association. Pressure from women's organizations led

to gradual municipal enfranchisement of unmarried and widowed women who met the property qualification. Ontario granted this right in 1884, New Brunswick in 1886, Nova Scotia in 1887, and Prince Edward Island in 1888, but many municipalities still refused women the right to hold public office.

The right of women to vote in provincial and national elections was steadfastly resisted. In Nova Scotia, the lobbying of women's groups produced a narrow majority in favour of women's suffrage in the legislative assembly in 1893, but the bill was scuttled in committee by the anti-suffrage attorney-general, James W. Longley. Women's franchise bills in other provincial jurisdictions were invariably voted down. By the end of the century, the tide seemed to have turned firmly against women's suffrage, in part because so many reforms, including Prohibition, were predicted to succeed if women ever got a chance to clean up the political system.

In this discouraging context, Nellie McClung emerged as Canada's most prominent leader of the suffrage cause. Born in Grey County, Ontario, she migrated to Manitoba as a young girl, married a druggist, raised five children, and had a successful career as a fiction writer. Her sense of humour and clever repartee enabled her to survive the many taunts that came her way. In 1914, she packed Winnipeg's Walker Theatre for a

British suffragist Emmeline Pankhurst (first row, fifth from left) stands beside Nellie McClung (left of Pankhurst, in the striped dress) at McClung's house in Edmonton, during Pankhurst's 1917 tour of North America. SOURCE: BC ARCHIVES B-06786

performance of "How the Vote Was Won." To thundering applause, she played the role of premier of a women's parliament and punctured the pretensions of Conservative premier Sir Rodmond Roblin with her speech to an imaginary group of franchise-seeking men: "We wish to compliment this delegation on their splendid gentlemanly appearance. If, without exercising the vote, such splendid specimens of manhood can be produced, such a system of affairs should not be interfered with. . . . If men start to vote, they will vote too much. Politics unsettles men, and unsettled men means unsettled bills, broken furniture, broken vows, divorce."[7] Such events put the anti-suffrage forces on the defensive and paved the way for opposition parties to embrace a cause whose time had come.

INTELLECTUAL CHALLENGES

The changing intellectual climate of the late nineteenth century had a profound impact on Canadians. As the revolutionary ideas of Karl Marx, Charles Darwin, Sigmund Freud, and other European intellectuals percolated among the chattering classes, they undercut the Christian and conservative social values that had dominated the Victorian Age and played into a growing secularism that made many people nervous.

Following the publication of Charles Darwin's works on evolution, the literal truth of church teachings was called sharply into question. Many church leaders responded to the Darwinian challenge by rejecting the theory of evolution as speculative nonsense. Others argued that Biblical stories were figuratively rather than literally true. Protestant "higher critics" borrowed critical methods from contemporary German and British scholars, treating the Bible like any other literary work, and interpreting its truths in mythical rather than literal terms. By the end of the nineteenth century, a widening gulf was developing between church leaders who accepted higher criticism and those who remained faithful to the literal teachings of the Bible.

The social problems accompanying industrialization sparked major debates in most Canadian churches. While many religious leaders continued to ascribe poverty to personal failings, others began to criticize the new economic order. By focusing on the physical and material condition of people on earth, social gospellers moved away from the evangelical preoccupation with individual spiritual development and life after death. This direction troubled many church members, who became concerned about the abandonment of what they believed to be the fundamental issues of Christianity.

The mainstream churches also faced competition from new religious organizations. The Salvation Army, which took root in Canada in the 1880s, was the most successful and enduring of the new evangelical churches, especially among the urban working class. At the turn of the century, a variety of millenarian groups, which believed in the imminent return of Christ, attracted

John Joseph Lynch, archbishop of the Roman Catholic Church in Toronto, who tried to stop his parishioners from attending free-thought meetings, is portrayed here in 1880 by caricaturist J.W. Bengough as slaying the serpent of free thought with the sword of faith. SOURCE: LIBRARY AND ARCHIVES CANADA R13244-0-1-E

followers who were disillusioned with the apparent secularization of the established churches. These groups, in turn, often disillusioned their followers when the predicted Second Coming failed to occur. By the late nineteenth century, skepticism about the teachings of mainstream churches was evident in the spread of spiritualism and theosophy. Most shocking to the churches were the "free-thought" societies founded by intellectuals who equated Christianity with superstition and promoted atheism and agnosticism.

Although the Roman Catholic Church was not without its skeptics and was well aware of the difficulties caused by rapid urbanization and industrialization, the clerical hierarchy was limited in how far it could deviate from the injunctions of papal pronouncements. The church banned books that it considered irreligious and forbade the faithful from joining secular organizations, such as the Knights of Labor, that it felt distracted people from their religious duties. Nowhere was clerical control more successful than in Quebec, where 85 percent of the population was Catholic.

A celebrated case of the church's confrontation with its critics occurred in 1869 when it refused to allow the burial of Joseph Guibord, an activist of the Institut canadien, in a Catholic cemetery. Founded in Montreal in 1844, the Institut championed freedom of conscience and had a library that included publications placed on the church's index of forbidden books. Clerical leaders in Quebec had the Institut condemned by Rome in 1868. Guibord explicitly refused to renounce his membership and, when he died in 1869, Bishop Bourget of Montreal denied him burial in consecrated ground. Guibord's widow took the case to court. In 1874, after a series of appeals, the Judicial Committee of the Privy Council ordered that Bourget's ruling be overturned. Because feelings ran so high over the issue, Guibord's body, which had rested in a Protestant cemetery for five years, had to be accompanied by an armed military escort when it was transferred to its final resting place. Even then, Bishop Bourget had the last word: he immediately deconsecrated the ground where Guibord's body lay.

By the end of the nineteenth century, the Roman Catholic Church became more receptive to reform ideals. Pope Leo XIII lifted an ineffectual ban on the Knights of Labor in 1887, and in his encyclical of 1891, *Rerum Novarum*, he condemned an uncontrolled market economy. The pope's position that "some opportune

remedy must be found quickly for the misery and wretchedness pressing so unjustly on the majority of the working class" eventually spurred a Catholic social action movement that was more directly concerned with social reform than the more traditional charitable institutions. In Quebec, this led to institutions such as the Montreal-based École sociale populaire, established in 1911, which trained Catholic activists to work in the community.

SCHOOLING AND SOCIETY

During the second half of the nineteenth century, school attendance increased dramatically. It also varied according to region and culture. By 1891, it was estimated that only six percent of Ontario residents and 13 percent of Maritime Canadians were totally illiterate. In Quebec, where compulsory schooling was enacted only in 1943, 26 percent of the population was deemed unable either to read or write; in Newfoundland, the figure was 32 percent.

In all Canadian provinces except Quebec, the education system was under a state-directed department of education, which set minimum standards for schools. Quebec had two systems, one Catholic and one Protestant, each eligible for provincial subsidies. Although committed to basic education for both boys and girls, the Catholic Church in Quebec nevertheless opposed compulsory, state-run education. The trade union movement in the province battled for free, compulsory schooling, but the church's position was supported by the textile, tobacco, and shoe industries, which employed many older children. Poor working-class and farm families also tended to regard the labour and wages of their older children as necessary for family survival.

Elsewhere in Canada, education was experiencing a rapid transformation. Faith in the value of education, fear of social breakdown, and conviction that new skills were required in the industrial labour market contributed to the growth of schools and changes in curriculum. Beginning in Ontario in 1871, the introduction of high schools offered parents who could afford it a chance to further educate their children. By 1905, with the exception of Quebec, all provinces had legislated free schooling and compulsory attendance for youngsters under the age of 12. Between 1891 and 1922, elementary and secondary

By the end of the nineteenth century, multi-room schools such as the Lunenburg Academy, shown here soon after being built in 1894-1895, were emerging in towns and cities as monuments to the faith in education as a panacea for society's ills. SOURCE: NOVA SCOTIA ARCHIVES AND RECORD MANAGEMENT 1985-562 NO. 11

Schools served as a vehicle for assimilating new Canadians, especially on the Prairies. As the region filled up with people from diverse cultures, educational systems based on the cultural conditions of eastern Canada faced serious challenges. The 1897 compromise in Manitoba over French and Catholic schools, for example, had permitted a limited number of Catholic teachers, religious instruction at the end of the day, and bilingual teaching in English and any other language spoken by at least 10 pupils in the school. What was not anticipated in 1897 was the flood of new Canadians who would take advantage of the right to bilingual schooling. Immigrant parents, who spoke a variety of languages, proved intensely interested in both preserving their culture and securing the best schooling possible for their children.

enrollments in Canada more than doubled from 942 500 to 1 939 700. The number of teachers grew still faster, from 21 149 in 1890 to 54 691 in 1920. Teachers' qualifications improved steadily, and women increased their numerical predominance to over 82 percent of the profession in 1921.

Under pressure from parents, teachers, and administrators, schools became more humane and child-centred, as well as more practical and relevant. Kindergartens, with their goal to improve the family life of the poor and to nurture creativity and independence in the child, expanded slowly from their Ontario urban base. To respond to pressures that the curriculum be made more applicable to the world of work, courses in household science and manual training were introduced. Pressure also increased for the establishment of minimum standards of health and safety in the schools. Montreal's schools set the pace in 1906 with Canada's first regular and systematic medical inspection of pupils. As an integral part of the health-reform effort, formal instruction in physical education was introduced in many schools. For boys this often meant cadet training, an option that regularly pitted peace advocates against more militaristically inclined nationalists.

The English majority in the Prairie provinces refused to accommodate linguistic pluralism in their schools. Despite strong opposition from French-Canadian, Polish, Mennonite, and Ukrainian communities, the Manitoba government withdrew funding from all bilingual schools in 1916. Flying in the face of the compromise of 1905, Saskatchewan abolished instruction in languages other than English beyond the first grade in 1918. The Catholic clergy in Alberta had made separate schools, not language, its cause in 1905. The result was that, officially anyway, there were no bilingual schools to outlaw. Nor were there any bilingual schools in British Columbia.

In Ontario, Anglo-Canadians also resisted efforts of the growing francophone minority to secure education in its own language. The ultra-Protestant Orange Lodges and English-speaking Catholics worked together to push Ontario's Department of Education to enact Regulation 17 in 1912. Under this law, only schools with English-speaking teachers, where English instruction was begun upon admission, and where French was not used beyond the second year, could be eligible for government funding. Public protests were staged and legal challenges were launched, but the courts supported the Ontario government.

UNIVERSITIES IN THE INDUSTRIAL AGE

Universities served a much smaller clientele than schools, but they were important barometers of change in post-Confederation Canada. In 1867, most of Canada's 17 degree-granting institutions managed on meagre endowments, tuition fees, and small government grants. Despite pressure from provincial governments in Nova Scotia and Ontario for consolidation, denominational colleges survived, and more were founded, including the Anglican-inspired University of Western Ontario in 1878, and McMaster Baptist University in 1887. In Quebec, francophone university education finally spread to Montreal in 1878, when Université Laval opened a branch there. In the western provinces, governments asserted control over universities from the beginning. Manitoba combined Saint Boniface (Catholic), St John's (Anglican), Manitoba College (Presbyterian), and Wesley College (Methodist) under the umbrella of the University of Manitoba in 1877. In each of the other western provinces, a single provincial university was established: the universities of Alberta (1906), Saskatchewan (1907), and British Columbia (1908).

Most Canadian anglophone universities opened their doors to women in the 1880s and 1890s, but female students remained a minority in the student body and were often discouraged from enrolling in science and professional programs. By 1921, women made up about 15 percent of the professoriate, but they could be found primarily in the bottom ranks and in arts faculties. Cultural and racial minorities, such as Jews and blacks, were rarely welcomed as students or professors.

Notwithstanding their reputation for conservatism, universities were changing. Areas of study were expanding to include natural and social sciences; students were less preoccupied with piety than with social issues and participated in a wide range of extracurricular activities; and ornate buildings, housing laboratories, lecture theatres, and lounges proliferated on expanding, landscaped campuses. The growth of professional schools in universities reflected a growing demand for career-related education.

In their efforts to restrict entry into their fields, professionals pressured the state to grant them self-regulation. Increasingly, a specific university degree became a condition for receiving a licence to practise a profession. Physicians, lawyers, and engineers succeeded in winning self-regulation in most jurisdictions by the end of the century and required university training as a condition of licensing. As well, specialized technical and agricultural colleges were established in most provinces to bring academic rigour to practical pursuits. Like other professionals, university professors expanded their training and increasingly turned to research as the basis for their academic credentials. The PhD, a German innovation, was emerging as the most coveted degree in arts and sciences, though few Canadian universities yet offered it.

REINVENTING NATURE

Industrialization led Canadians to approach the natural environment in a different way. No longer only a wilderness to be tamed or a rich storehouse of resources to be exploited, nature was increasingly seen as a respite from the competition and anxiety of modern society. In organizations such as the Alpine Club and Field-Naturalists' Club, urban adults were initiated into nature's mysteries, while foundations were established to fund summer vacations in rural areas for slum children. Even religious leaders incorporated the romantic view of nature into their teachings. Among theologians, it became fashionable to refer to nature as a medium whereby people could communicate with God, and poets wrote eloquently about the kinship between people and nature. In many towns and cities, branches of the Society for the Prevention of Cruelty to Animals gave practical focus to the growing sympathy for their "four-legged friends."

With urban life increasingly redefining what it meant to be a man, boys became the particular focus of reformers who saw nature as the vehicle for inculcating survival skills and manly virtues. Ernest Thompson Seton, who achieved fame as a naturalist and animal-story writer, inspired a club movement dedicated to teaching boys the skills of tracking, camping, canoe-ing, and woodcraft. Hundreds of Woodcraft Clubs sprang up throughout North America in the first decade of the twentieth century before they were superseded in Canada by the Boy Scout movement. Founded in Britain in 1908 by South African War veteran Robert Baden-Powell, the Boy Scout movement was based on the view that the frontier experience toughened boys up so that they would make better men—and better soldiers.

Baden-Powell launched the Girl Guides in 1909 as a counterpart to the Boy Scouts, and by January 1910 Canada had its first Guide group in St Catharines, Ontario. Even more popular among girls was the Cana-dian Girls in Training (CGIT), an organization estab-lished by the YWCA in cooperation with the major Protestant denominations in 1915. Dedicated to training young women between the ages of 12 and 17 in Chris-tian leadership, the outdoor experience was prominent in CGIT activities.

Nature enthusiasts also became converts to conser-vation. Under pressure from environmentalists, govern-ments in most provinces passed Game Acts, although these often served mainly to protect and manage game for wealthy hunters. In 1904, Jack Miner established his first bird sanctuary in Kingsville, Ontario, thereby launching a lifelong career devoted to the preservation of birds. The federal government followed up its initiative in Banff by creating more federally designated national parks, including Yoho (1886) and Jasper (1907); the Ontario government established the first provincial park reserve, Algonquin, in 1893. Although Canadians contin-ued to gobble up resources at an alarming rate, there was a growing sense that some control over their exploitation was necessary.

The idea of nature as a refuge from the city led those who could afford it to buy or rent summer cot-tages in attractive rural areas outside the city. With rail-ways providing access to hitherto remote areas, people flocked to the Lake of the Woods, Georgian Bay, and Muskoka regions of Ontario, and the Lower Lakes region and the Charlevoix and Gaspé areas in Quebec. In the Maritimes, St Andrews, New Brunswick, Caven-dish Beach, Prince Edward Island, and the Bras d'Or Lakes in Cape Breton became favourite haunts of the rich and famous from all over North America. For many well-heeled tourists, hunting and fishing with a Native

guide was the ultimate wilderness experience, taking them back to simpler times when survival in the great outdoors, rather than in some stifling office, was what life was all about.

ORGANIZED SPORTS

As with tourism, sporting activities were shaped by the opportunities and values of the industrial age. Competi-tive games, the codification of rules regulating play, and commercialization paralleled trends in the marketplace and sparked debates about the purpose of games. The expansion of railway and road networks enabled teams to develop regular schedules of intercommunity, interre-gional, and even international play. By the 1890s, special-ized sports pages had become common to most newspapers, an indication that such activities were becoming commercially viable. Electrically lit indoor facilities, such as ice rinks, tracks, and gymnasia, made conditions more predictable for those sports that could be played indoors.

The middle class clung tenaciously to the amateur ideal, with its prohibition of payment to participants and its gentlemanly codes of conduct. Amateurism became the defining feature of the Olympic Games when they were reinstated in 1896 (Canada sent its first team in 1904) and also prevailed in athletic programs established in schools, universities, and most social clubs before 1914. The Montreal Amateur Athletic Association (1881), an essentially elite, anglophone club, was the first organization to serve as an umbrella for amateur sports enthusiasts, and it became the driving force behind the Amateur Athletics Association of Canada, founded in 1884. In 1893, the governor general, Lord Stanley, donated a cup to the Canadian amateur hockey champi-ons, and in 1909 another governor general, the Earl Grey, provided a trophy for the football champions on the con-dition that the "cup must remain always under purely amateur conditions."

Canada ultimately followed the United States down the slippery slope toward the professionalization of sports. The Montreal Wanderers, after winning the last amateur Stanley Cup in 1908, immediately turned professional. In the same year the Eastern Canada Hockey Association turned professional, and in 1909 the rival National Hockey Association was formed. Although football and hockey inspired enthusiastic fans, professional baseball emerged as the most popular spectator sport in this period, attracting working-class audiences throughout English and French Canada.

For many Canadians the rise of professionalism not only violated their much-cherished ideal of amateurism, it also opened the door to other undesirable, even "un-Canadian," practices. The issues were addressed by Toronto lawyer W.A. Frost in a letter to the editor of *The Varsity*, the University of Toronto's student newspaper. According to Frost, baseball "has been degraded by Yankee professionalism until the name of baseball cannot fail to suggest a tobacco-chewing, loud-voiced, twang-nosed bar-tender, with a large diamond pin and elaborately oiled hair."[8] Despite such views, professional sports continued to attract a wide following.

The Royals Baseball Club of Saint John, New Brunswick, Intermediate Champions, 1921. SOURCE: PROVINCIAL ARCHIVES OF NEW BRUNSWICK, HAROLD WRIGHT COLLECTION P338-2, #3575

Given the migration of so many Canadians to the United States in this period, and the lure of professional salaries, it is not surprising that some Canadians earned their sporting reputations in events sponsored south of the border. Nat Butler, a native of Halifax, began his career in bicycle racing in Boston and broke all records at the Winter Velodrome in Paris in 1905. Although basketball was developed by a Canadian— James Naismith from Almonte, Ontario—it was pioneered at the YMCA International Training School in Springfield, Massachusetts, where Naismith was a student and later a teacher.

Sports were often closed to racial minorities because whites would not allow them to join their teams and clubs. In the Maritimes, blacks began forming their own baseball teams in the 1880s, and by the 1890s were hosting an annual regional championship. Tom Longboat, a rare exception to the increasing exclusion of Native peoples from competitive athletics, came first in the 1907 Boston Marathon. Like whites, individuals from racial minorities often found sporting opportunities in the United States. Gabriel Dumont, for example, toured in the United States as a crack marksman in Buffalo Bill's Wild West show in the 1880s, and two black boxers from Nova Scotia, George Dixon and Sam Langford, won acclaim at home as well as in the United States for their successes in the ring.

Sporting activities were also beginning to open up for women. In the 1880s, bicycling joined tennis, curling, and skating as amusements for middle-class women and as a cause for worry among those who identified an increase in women's physical freedom and scandalously scant sporting attire with moral laxity and, worse still, feminist sympathies. The participation of women in school and university sports, such as basketball, field hockey, and ice hockey, helped to break down proscriptions against female participation in competitive play.

By 1914, the prevalence of school athletics and the multitude of programs run by groups such as the YWCA, YMCA, CGIT, Girl Guides, and Boy Scouts had given sports an unprecedented place in the lives of most Canadians. The discovery by sports promoters that good money could be made presenting professional baseball, football, and hockey on a regular basis meant that Canadian sport was well on its way to becoming a major North American industry. And, for all the predominance of middle-class anglophones, a shared interest in sporting activity may well have helped to begin to knit together diverse groups of Canadians.

THE ARTS IN THE AGE OF INDUSTRY

In the half-century following Confederation, Canadians lamented their lack of a distinctive artistic and literary culture. The dominion's youth, colonial inheritance, and proximity to the United States were advanced as reasons why Canadian writers, painters, and sculptors rarely achieved international recognition. In retrospect, we can see that Canadians were planting the seeds of a distinct cultural identity, but it would take some time for those seeds to bear fruit.[9]

In Quebec, where the Roman Catholic Church remained powerful, most authors stuck to conservative narratives. Quebec was represented in this literature as a devout Catholic nation with a mission to spread the Catholic word throughout the world. With its idealization of country life, the peasant novel, a popular European genre, took firm root among francophones. Its most enduring example is Louis Hémon's *Maria Chapdelaine* (1913), which dealt with the difficult choice for many French Quebecers of moving either to New England to find work or to communities on Quebec's agricultural frontier. A few writers resisted clerical dictates. Influenced by French modernists like Baudelaire and Rimbaud, bohemian Montreal poets such as Émile Nelligan and members of the École littéraire de Montréal espoused a highly individualistic literature preoccupied with the meaning of life, death, and love. Such writers risked clerical censure and faced minuscule markets for their work.

In the late nineteenth century, English-Canadian literary production was, on the whole, as conservative and prone to romanticizing the past as was its French-Canadian counterpart. Loyalist themes, common in works from the 1820s onward, remained popular and were reinforced by centennial celebrations of Loyalist settlement. Both the initial Loyalist flight from the mad republic to the south and the defence of the Canadas in 1812 were mythologized in Egerton Ryerson's *The Loyalists of America and Their Times* (1880). In 1876, Sarah Curzon, a Toronto suffrage and temperance advocate, produced a play called *Laura Secord, the Heroine of 1812*, which used popular Loyalist mythologies to promote a positive view of women's abilities. Canada Firster Charles Mair won praise for his poems drawing on the history of the Loyalists. Ironically, Mair, who harboured racist attitudes toward Riel and his Métis followers, presented the Native leader, Tecumseh, who had supported the British in 1812, as a hero in an 1886 drama. By the end of the twentieth century, a group of poets born in the 1860s, including Charles G.D. Roberts, Bliss Carman, Archibald Lampman, and Duncan Campbell Scott, were beginning to make a reputation beyond the borders of Canada.

Novelists and poets found that the centres of English-language publishing were located in London, and, increasingly, New York and Boston, where there was only a limited market for Canadian themes. Indeed, one of the reasons why Canadians remained mired in the romantic literary tradition after other countries had abandoned it was that the popular demand for stories about New France, Acadia, Aboriginal peoples, and rural life remained strong in foreign markets. Dramatic readings by Pauline Johnson, Canada's "Mohawk Princess," on stages in and outside Canada drew on her Native heritage to conjure up a distinctive northern nationality that was far removed from the experience of most of her listeners.

By the end of the nineteenth century, literary production began to increase in range and output, fuelled in part by the growing tendency of newspapers to run serialized novels. Women, who were sometimes able to make a living as writers or journalists, particularly excelled as novelists. In *Roland Graeme: Knight*, Agnes Machar fused her reformist, feminist, religious, and patriotic concerns in her highly romantic portrayal of a Knight of Labor and the woman who loved him. Margaret Marshall Saunders, the daughter of a Nova Scotia Baptist minister, published *Beautiful Joe*, the story of an abused dog, in 1893. After winning first prize in an American Humane Society competition, *Beautiful Joe* became a best-seller, reputedly the first work by a Canadian author to sell a million copies. One of Canada's best-known writers was Lucy Maud Montgomery, whose first published novel, *Anne of Green Gables*, became an instant international success when it appeared in 1908.

A new realistic tradition was reflected in the work of Sara Jeannette Duncan, a disciple of the American novelist Henry James and the first woman to be hired as a full-time journalist at the Toronto *Globe*. Her novel, *The Imperialist* (1904), dissected small-town Ontario life and explored the need to balance British sentiment with the reality of North American living. Only one major popular writer, Stephen Leacock, in heavily ironic volumes like *Sunshine Sketches of a Little Town* (1912) and *Arcadian*

Adventures of the Idle Rich (1914), questioned the values and virtues of North American liberal capitalism. Leading periodicals of the day such as *Saturday Night* (established 1887), *Busy Man's Magazine* (1896–1911), which became *Maclean's*, and *Canadian Magazine* (1893–1939) were somewhat more inclined to express liberal sentiments, but they were often narrowly provincial in their focus.

WRITING CANADA'S HISTORY

In the nineteenth century, history emerged as a popular vehicle for "inventing" Canadian identity. Historians drew on the past to provide support for nation-building efforts, while public commemorations encouraged a common, if selective, understanding of what happened in the past. In this context, Samuel de Champlain, Dollard des Ormeaux, Madeleine de Verchères, Tecumseh, and Laura Secord, among others, became heroic, larger-than-life figures who stood for virtues that they might not have possessed. By the early twentieth century, commemorations such as the one held to mark the ter-centenary of Quebec City in 1908 were attended by

thousands of people and left in their wake statues, monuments, and plaques to remind Canadians of their debt to the past.

Efforts to bring Canadians together around a common understanding of their past proved to be a major challenge. English-Canadian historians tended to portray Canada as a collection of peaceful, crown-loving, moderately liberal colonies. In such texts as John Charles Dent's *The Last Forty Years: Canada Since the Union of 1841* (1881) and *The Story of the Upper Canadian Rebellion* (1885), both oligarchies and radical reformers were given short shrift, while those who supported responsible government, such as Robert Baldwin and Louis-Hippolyte LaFontaine, were portrayed more positively. These historians subscribed to what is known as a Whig view of history—the notion that history is the story of events that reveal the progress of human development.

Nowhere was this view of history more explicitly revealed than in the popular 10-volume *History of Canada*, published by civil engineer William Kingsford between 1887 and 1898. Kingsford was touted as English Canada's counterpart to the famous French-Canadian

In the late nineteenth century, an important cultural event in most black communities across Canada was Emancipation Day, an annual celebration of the freeing of slaves in the British Empire on 1 August 1834. The parade depicted here took place in 1894 in Amherstburg, Ontario. SOURCE: LIBRARY AND ARCHIVES CANADA PA-163923

nationalist historian François-Xavier Garneau, whose multi-volume *Histoire du Canada*, published in the 1840s, extolled the history and culture of his people. Although both historians shared a progressive view of history, they differed in their interpretation of events. Garneau regretted the conquest, while Kingsford and most English-Canadian historical writers regarded it as a blessing in disguise for French Canadians and a necessary step in the march toward civilization.

In French Canada, the liberal, anti-clerical perspective typified by Garneau gave way to histories that emphasized the role of the clergy in developing French-Canadian society. Abbé Jean-Baptiste-Antoine Ferland's histories in the 1860s, for example, painted a portrait of

BIOGRAPHY

E. Pauline Johnson/Tekahionwake

In the period before the First World War, E. Pauline Johnson was one of only a handful of Canadian authors who achieved an international audience for their work. The youngest child of an English mother (Susanna Howells) and a Mohawk father (George Johnson), Johnson was born in 1861 and grew up in Chiefswood, an elegant home on the Grand River's Six Nations Reserve near Brantford, Ontario. Educated in both Native and Euro-Canadian cultures, she drew upon her mixed heritage to produce poetry and prose that addressed such issues as racism, feminism, and Canadian national identity.

Johnson began writing to support herself following the death of her father in 1884, and was soon signing her works with both her European name and her Native name, Tekahionwake. In 1892, she launched a career as a performance artist, reading her poems to primarily white audiences in Canada, the United States, and Great Britain. Wearing Native costume for the first half of her program and a drawing-room gown for the second half, "the Mohawk Princess" thrilled audiences with dramatic recitations of such poems as "The Song My Paddle Sings," "A Cry from an Indian Wife," and "As Red Men Die." Her first book of poems, *The White Wampum*, appeared in 1895 and her second collection, *Canadian Born*, in 1903.

In 1906, while touring in England, she met Joseph Capilano (Su-á-pu-luck) and his delegation who were protesting to Edward VII about recent hunting and fishing restrictions on Natives in British Columbia. Johnson's friendship with "Chief Joe" reinforced her growing attraction to the west coast and its Native history, which was being ignored by new immigrants to the region. In 1909, ill with breast cancer, she retired to Vancouver. There, editor Lionel Waterloo Makovski and journalist Isabel McLean established a committee that included representatives of the Canadian Women's Press Club and the local Women's Canadian Club to raise money for Johnson's care and also to help with the publication of her work. She produced *Legends of Vancouver* in 1911 and a collection, *Flint and Feather*, in 1912. Johnson died in 1913 and, as she requested, was buried in Stanley Park within sight of Siwash Rock.[10]

Pauline Johnson/Tekahionwake in about 1895. SOURCE: LIBRARY AND ARCHIVES CANADA PA-111473

New France as a missionary colony whose history was guided by providence and its earthly representatives in the form of self-sacrificing bishops, nuns, and priests. Even Garneau modified his earlier views in light of the clerical assault. While a few anti-clerical historians such as Benjamin Sulte championed secular forces, they tended to glorify rural life and paid little attention to the economic history of French Canada.

By the end of the nineteenth century, the historian's craft was being taught in universities. The naming of George Wrong to the chair of history at the University of Toronto and the introduction at Queen's University of Adam Shortt's lectures on the economic and social history of Canada, both in 1894, marked the beginning of more rigorous academic approaches to the nation's past. Between 1913 and 1917, Adam Shortt teamed up with Arthur Doughty to produce the multi-volume series *Canada and Its Provinces*. While Shortt and Doughty shared the progressive view of history, they abandoned the romanticism of earlier writers for a detailed analysis of the nation's social and economic development. Abbé Lionel Groulx's lectures in Canadian history at the Montreal campus of Université Laval in 1915 led to his appointment as the first full-time professor of Canadian history at a francophone university.

These men were not charting new directions in a vacuum. In 1872, the founding of the Dominion Archives (now Library and Archives Canada) under the direction of Douglas Brymner testified to a growing interest in the collection of historical documents, which could be used by historians to develop a more accurate view of past developments. A decade later, the formation of the Royal Society of Canada gave academic historians a forum in which to disseminate their scholarly research.

While university-based historians were preoccupied with national themes, amateurs continued to practise their craft, producing county, community, and regimental histories. Female historians, some of them university-trained but denied university postings, served as custodians of local history, worked as unacknowledged writers and research assistants for their male relatives and employers, and chronicled social and cultural topics neglected by professional historians. Throughout the nation, Canadians whose stories were not reflected in the dominant narratives and public commemorations passed on oral and written traditions about their experiences.

PAINTING AND SCULPTURE

Academic art tended to follow the international trends, though often at some distance. In 1868, a Society of Canadian Artists was established to promote formal Canadian artwork in a variety of exhibits. The Royal Academy of Arts and the National Gallery of Canada were created in 1880 at the urging of the governor general, the Marquis of Lorne. Before the end of the century, a number of art schools had been established in urban centres. Overwhelmingly, professional artists were either

In Quebec, large-scale public sculpture often commemorated major historical figures, as in this 1898 monument to Champlain in Quebec City, by French sculptor Paul Chevré. Here, the nationalist Association catholique de la jeunesse canadienne-française hold a rally in front of the monument in 1908, during the celebrations of the 300th anniversary of the founding of Quebec. SOURCE: ARCHIVES DE LA VILLE DE QUEBEC #5465

Old Union Station, Toronto, Ontario (c. 1908), and miners' cabins at the Union Mine, Cumberland, British Columbia (1889). While cities were becoming architectural monuments to the industrial age, company towns on the resource frontier bore a remarkable similarity to one another in their undistinguished architecture and lack of amenities. SOURCES: CITY OF TORONTO ARCHIVES, FONDS 1244, ITEM 594, BRITISH COLUMBIA ARCHIVES A-04531

men such as William Brymner, Robert Harris, and George Reid, who trained in the academic style of the Paris Salon school, or those such as Edmund Morris and Curtis Williamson, who later found inspiration in the atmospheric Hague school. An exception to the habit of European training was Homer Watson, who, like the Quebecer Ozias Leduc, was self-taught and visited Europe only later in life.

As a major sponsor of painting, sculpture, and architecture in its great cathedrals, the Roman Catholic Church encouraged some of the most impressive religious art produced anywhere in the world. A combination of church and private commissions supported fine contributions in the art nouveau tradition by painters such as Ozias Leduc and sculptors such as Alfred Laliberté. Louis-Philippe Hébert's monuments to George-Étienne Cartier (in Ottawa) and Maisonneuve (in Montreal) stand out as some of the best sculpture produced in Canada. Outside of the commissions sponsored by the church, Quebec painters of the late Victorian period focused on landscapes and romanticized portraits of people's lives. Before the First World War, Quebecers in search of more liberated artistic expression moved to Paris.

Secular artists regularly took up identifiably Canadian subjects, particularly landscapes of settled areas of the country. In 1907, the creation of the Canadian Art Club (CAC) encouraged showings by early Canadian impressionists. These painters, who focused their attention on light, colour, and mood in their work, were roundly criticized by traditionalists who felt that art, like photographs, should strive to represent objects as they were, not as imagined. By the time of its last exhibition in 1915, the CAC was being overtaken by men such as Lawren Harris and J.E.H. MacDonald, who along with Tom Thomson, Frank Carmichael, Frank Johnston, Arthur Lismer, Fred Varley, and A.Y. Jackson, began applying new approaches to art in their sketches of Algonquin Park. The war and the death of Thomson in 1917 postponed the public arrival of the painters who came to be known as the Group of Seven, but they were part of a significant pre-war effort to find artistic expression for what was deemed uniquely Canadian.

On the west coast, Emily Carr developed her own powerful, post-impressionist style to convey the majesty of Native life and the coastal landscape. Lacking the sympathetic community available to her eastern male contemporaries, she was forced to support herself by running a boarding house. Both Carr and the Algonquin Group, like the great majority of earlier Canadian painters, tended to avoid the city and its problems. Their world, like that of many writers, most often symbolized an effort to come to terms with the natural rather than the human world of early twentieth-century Canada.

Like sports, the interest in literature, music, and art extended beyond professional artists and organizations to embrace a wide range of amateur activities. Historian Maria Tippett has observed that almost everyone was organized in song throughout the country on Sundays. In Toronto, choirmaster A.S. Voigt enlarged his Jarvis Street Baptist Church choir to 250 voices and formed the Toronto Mendelssohn Choir in 1894, soon to be known throughout North America for its *a cappella* singing. From Bella Bella and Metlakatla to Glace Bay and St John's, brass bands performed at funerals, weddings, and village feasts.

Throughout this period, people met in each other's homes at regular intervals to make music, read poetry, and perform plays. The Cavendish Literary Society, founded in 1886 for "the mutual improvement of its members," gave a young Lucy Maud Montgomery a place to test her ideas, while the Vagabond Club of Vancouver, established in 1914, offered men "an outlet for whatever small talents we possessed in a city in which buying and selling of real-estate was the preoccupation of the majority of inhabitants."

THE DRAMATIC ARTS

Canadians were enthusiastic spectators of a host of foreign and domestic touring theatre companies that crossed the country on the expanding railway networks. In 1897, Corliss Powers Walker, an impresario with a string of small theatres in North Dakota, settled in

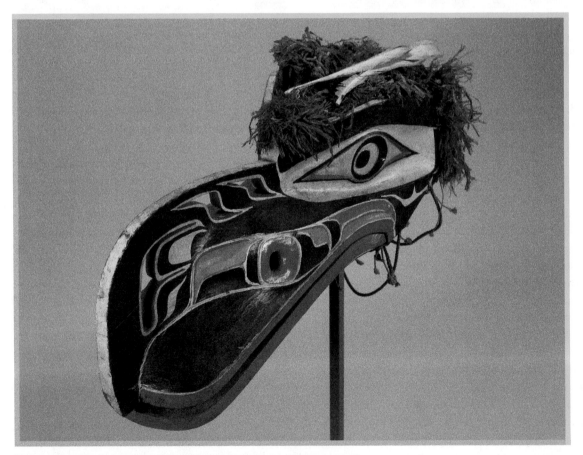

Raven mask, by Charlie George Sr., 1899. SOURCE: UBC MUSEUM OF ANTHROPOLOGY A4250

Clarence Gagnon, *Matinée d'hiver à Baie-Saint-Paul*, c. 1930. SOURCE: MUSÉE NATIONAL DES BEAUX-ARTS DU QUÉBEC 34.148

Winnipeg, which he used as a base for controlling bookings and theatre management throughout the West. His flagship theatre seated 2000 people and hosted productions, some of them direct from Broadway, six nights a week, 52 weeks a year. The touring companies of the Perth, Ontario-based Marks Brothers entertained in small towns across the dominion.

In the 1890s, the first homegrown professional French-language companies were founded, following on the phenomenal success of Parisian companies that toured Quebec. The British Canadian Theatrical Organization Society (1912) attempted to balance extensive American influence by organizing tours of British theatrical troupes. Although the Trans-Canada Theatre Society (1915) was Canadian-owned, it stayed in business by organizing tours of foreign companies. Britons and Americans gradually acquired controlling interests in Canadian theatres, effectively monopolizing the booking of entertainment by 1914.

The difficulties faced by Canadian talent did not escape notice. In 1907, Governor General Earl Grey created the Earl Grey Musical and Dramatic Competition for the dramatic arts, but this venture collapsed in 1911 and had only a minimal influence. There was significant progress in amateur little theatre, notably with the creation in 1905 of the Toronto Arts and Letters Players and in 1913 of the Ottawa Drama League. With the opening of the Hart House Theatre at the University of Toronto in 1919, financed by the Massey family, many distinguished Canadian actors, directors, and playwrights had a forum for their talents.

Canadian audiences were also introduced to the international world of dance, though not without earning the disapproval of church leaders. Acclaimed dancers Lois Fuller and Anna Pavlova, as well as Vaslav Nijinsky and the Diaghilev Ballet Russe, all made Canadian appearances. Many dance performances were aimed at more well-to-do audiences, but the crowds they drew included Canadians from many walks of life. Spectators also found much to entertain them in dance halls, burlesque theatres, and taverns, where hypnotists, magicians, circuses, and vaudeville shows drew audiences into a rich world of political satire, popular music, risqué dancing, and bawdy comedy.

These years also saw the appearance of the "movie," a popular form of entertainment that would soon outdraw all others. In 1896, 1200 citizens of Ottawa paid 10 cents each to watch a production of Thomas Edison's

J.E.H. MacDonald, *Morning Shadows*, 1912. SOURCE: ART GALLERY OF ONTARIO

James Wilson Morrice, *Ice Bridge over the Saint-Charles River*, 1908. SOURCE: MONTREAL MUSEUM OF FINE ARTS

"Vitascope." Because of the obvious potential of the medium to attract viewers, the Department of the Interior experimented with film in their efforts to promote western settlement. By 1914, sporadic screenings were beginning to give way to regular shows offered in movie theatres that charged each enthusiastic customer a nickel: hence the name *nickelodeon*. With more comfortable theatres, better story lines, and higher prices, films were also appealing to the middle class, who had at first scorned the medium's reputed vulgarity.

CONCLUSION

When Canada went to war in 1914, there was still little consensus on what it meant to be a Canadian. There was no distinctive Canadian flag and, while the beaver and the maple leaf seemed to sum up what was distinctive about Canada, they were not adopted as official symbols of the country. Calixa Lavallée, a composer born in Quebec, penned the words to "O Canada" in 1880, but the song was not heard in English Canada until the turn of the century. Outside of Quebec, "The Maple Leaf Forever," with its triumphant imperialist lyrics, was much more popular. Growing cultural diversity and rapid economic development in the first decade of the twentieth century only compounded the natural tendency to emphasize differences. As participants in the new industrial order, however, Canadians shared more than they realized, including an expanding literacy, a rich popular culture, and a small but growing number of nationwide organizations. Whether these cultural trends were sufficient to hold the nation together under the impact of a world war would remain to be seen.

The English-Canadian Suffragists

English-Canadian middle-class reformers, imbued with the progressive spirit of the age, were convinced that political action and social reform could eliminate many of the "social evils" that they saw around them. For many historians, these reformers have become the heroes of Canadian history, and people such as feminist Nellie McClung have been praised for their clarity of vision. Other historians have taken a more critical approach to reformers, viewing them less as people of vision than as a privileged group who tried to impose their narrow middle-class values on all Canadians. The clash of opinion is clearly drawn around the women's movement, which culminated in the granting of suffrage to women in Canada outside of Quebec during and immediately following the First World War.

In her pioneering study of the Canadian women's suffrage movement, published in 1950, Catherine Cleverdon argued: "Political equality is a prize not to be lightly held. Though it came to Canadian women without the harshness and bitterness of the struggle in Great Britain, it was won by the hard work and heartaches of small groups of women throughout the dominion who had the courage and vision to seek it."[11] Cleverdon's perspective was shaped by her strong commitment to the democratic process and her identification with the suffrage leaders, many of whom she interviewed while conducting her research.

When interest in women's history resurfaced in the 1970s and 1980s, Carol Lee Bacchi, following the direction taken by feminist scholars internationally, was less inclined to see English-Canadian suffragists only as women with courage and vision. She concluded from her study of some 200 suffrage leaders that most of them were elite women who wanted to impose Protestant morality, sobriety, and family order on Canadian society. In many suffrage circles, it was revealed, racist and class-bound solutions—including eugenics, exclusive immigration laws, and restrictive voting practices—were openly advocated. Even more damning, especially from the point of view of left-wing scholars, was the fact that many middle-class suffrage leaders had the time to devote to "good causes" because they exploited an underclass of household servants. Since a narrow maternal feminist vision—many suffrage leaders saw women's primary role and rationale for public action as rooted in their status as mothers—seemed to motivate most Canadian suffragists, they were ultimately seen as unworthy predecessors to the more purposeful feminists of the modern women's movement. To quote Bacchi, "[t]he female suffragist did not fail to effect a social revolution for women; the majority never had a revolution in mind."[12]

The rejection of the early suffrage leaders as "foremothers" to modern feminism has elicited a vigorous response. In a critique of Bacchi's book, historian E. R. Forbes used the experience of women in Halifax, who were described by both Cleverdon and Bacchi as being invariably "conservative" in their approach to female suffrage, to expose the parochialism and present-mindedness of such a position. Halifax suffrage leaders took on a whole range of feminist reforms, Forbes argued, and used any available argument to promote their clearly radical goals. "Reading only the leaders' statements in the newspapers one might conclude that the scheme was motivated chiefly by class interests and social control. Having read the minutes [of the Local Council of Women] I do not believe it. Neither, apparently, did the men who rejected their proposals."[13] In her study of women involved in left-wing organizations such as the Social Democratic Party of Canada before 1914, Janice Newton found that many socialist women also espoused maternal feminist goals, often in defiance of their male colleagues. Newton maintains that there was nothing inherently conservative about maternal feminism in this period because many women on the left wanted "nothing less than the socialist transformation of women's maternal and domestic roles."[14]

Contemporary political concern about what constitutes modern feminism motivates such a debate and may obscure more important questions that should be asked about the suffrage movement. Australian scholar Judith Allen, for instance, has called upon scholars to adopt a comparative and international approach to suffrage. By looking at such issues as temperance and sexual consent laws in the context of women's suffrage, Allen shows that feminist causes were rooted in time and place. For example, the reforms that followed the granting of the vote to women in New Zealand and parts of Australia in the 1890s were different from those that followed the success of suffrage in Great Britain, Canada, and the United States, where women's enfranchisement was achieved a generation later.[15]

By analyzing suffrage and other reform activities in the context of the larger changes taking place in society and in comparison with developments elsewhere, historians can understand individual reform leaders on their own terms. The question then becomes not whether suffrage leaders were heroes or villains, or whether their policies were right or wrong, but why they responded to their world in the way they did.

NOTES

1. George McQueen to Jessie McQueen, 7 January 1888, Greenville, The McQueen Family Papers, Atlantic Canada Virtual Archives, no. 3347_05_02. University of New Brunswick, Fredericton, NB, Canada. Original: The McQueen Lowden Fonds, vol. 3347, folder 5, letter 2. Nova Scotia Archives and Records Management, Halifax, Nova Scotia.

2. Jean Barman, *Sojourning Sisters: The Lives and Letters of Jessie and Annie McQueen* (Toronto: University of Toronto Press, 2003).

3. Ramsay Cook, *The Regenerators: Social Critisism in Late Victorian English Canada* (Toronto: University of Toronto Press, 1985).

4. Cited in Sharon Anne Cook, "*Through Sunshine and Shadow*": *The Woman's Christian Temperance Union, Evangelicalism and Reform in Ontario, 1874–1930* (Montreal: McGill-Queen's University Press, 1995) 3.

5. Ronald Romkey, *Grenfell of Labrador: A Biography* (Toronto: University of Toronto Press, 1991).

6. *Premier Congrès de la Fédération Nationale Saint-Jean-Baptiste* (Montreal: Paradis, Vincent & Cie, 1907), 123 (author's translation).

7. Cited in Catherine Cleverdon, *The Woman Sufffrage Movement in Canada* (2nd ed.) (Toronto: University of Toronto Press, 1974) 59.

8. Cited in Colin D. Howell, *Northern Sandlots: A Social History of Maritime Baseball* (Toronto: University of Toronto Press, 1995) 55.

9. Cited in Maria Tippett, *Making Culture: English-Canadian Institutions and the Arts Before the Massey Commission* (Toronto: University of Toronto Press, 1990) 6.

10. Veronica Strong-Boag and Carole Gerson, *Pulling Her Own Canoe: The Times and Texts of E. Pauline Johnson* (Toronto: University of Toronto Press, 2000) 1.

11. Cleverdon, *The Woman Sufffrage Movement*, 67.

12. Carol Lee Bacchi, *Liberation Deferred? The Ideas of the English Canadian Suffragists, 1877–1918* (Toronto: University of Toronto Press, 1983) 148.

13. Ernest R. Forbes, "The Ideas of Carol Bacchi and the Suffragists of Halifax," *Atlantis* 10, 2 (Spring 1985) 122.

14. Janice Newton, *The Feminist Challenge to the Canadian Left, 1900–1918* (Montreal: McGill-Queen's University Press, 1995) 13.

15. Judith Allen, "Contextualizing Late Nineteenth-Century Feminism: Problems and Comparisons," *Journal of the Canadian Historical Association*, n.s., 1 (1990) 17–39.

SELECTED READING

Bacchi, Carol Lee. *Liberation Deferred? The Ideas of the English Canadian Suffragists, 1877–1918*. Toronto: University of Toronto Press, 1983

Cook, Ramsay. *The Regenerators: Social Criticism in Late Victorian English Canada*. Toronto: University of Toronto Press, 1985

Cook, Sharon Anne. *"Through Sunshine and Shadow": The Woman's Christian Temperance Union, Evangelicalism and Reform in Ontario, 1874–1930*. Montreal: McGill-Queen's University Press, 1995

Fecteau, Jean-Marie. *La liberté du pauvre: sur la régulation du crime et de la pauvreté au XIXe siècle québécois*. Montreal: VLB, 2004

Gidney, R.D. and W.P.J. Millar. *How Schools Worked: Public Education in English Canada, 1900–1940*. Montreal: McGill-Queen's University Press, 2012

Harper, J. Russell. *Painting in Canada: A History*. 2nd ed. Toronto: University of Toronto Press, 1977

Howell, Colin D. *Blood, Sweat, and Cheers: Sport and the Making of Modern Canada*. Toronto: University of Toronto Press, 2001

Jasen, Patricia. *Wild Things: Nature, Culture, and Tourism in Ontario, 1790–1914*. Toronto: University of Toronto Press, 1995

Kealey, Linda. *Enlisting Women for the Cause: Women, Labour, and the Left in Canada, 1890–1920*. Toronto: University of Toronto Press, 1998

Lafferty, Renée N. *The Guardianship of Best Interests: Institutional Care for the Children of the Poor in Halifax, 1850–1960*. Montreal: McGill-Queen's University Press, 2012

Lamonde, Yvan, Patricia Lockhart Fleming, and Fiona Black, eds. *History of the Book in Canada*, vol. II, *1840–1918*. Toronto: University of Toronto Press, 2005

Marks, Lynne. *Revivals and Roller Rinks: Religion, Leisure, and Identity in Late-Nineteenth-Century Small-Town Ontario*. Toronto: University of Toronto Press, 1996

McCormack, A. Ross. *Reformers, Rebels, and Revolutionaries: The Western Canadian Radical Movement, 1899–1919*. Toronto: University of Toronto Press, 1977

McKay, Ian. *Reasoning Otherwise: Leftists and the People's Enlightenment in Canada, 1890–1920*. Toronto: Between the Lines, 2008

McKillop, A.B. *A Disciplined Intelligence: Critical Inquiry and Canadian Thought in the Victorian Era*. Montreal: McGill-Queen's University Press, 1979

Strange, Carolyn and Tina Loo. *Making Good: Law and Moral Regulation in Canada, 1867–1939*. Toronto: University of Toronto Press, 1997

Tippett, Maria. *Making Culture: English-Canadian Institutions and the Arts Before the Massey Commission*. Toronto: University of Toronto Press, 1990

Valverde, Mariana. *The Age of Light, Soap, and Water: Moral Reform in English Canada, 1885–1925*. Toronto: University of Toronto Press, 2008

Zeller, Suzanne. *Inventing Canada: Early Victorian Science and the Idea of a Transcontinental Nation*. Toronto: University of Toronto Press, 1987

For a comprehensive list of readings for topics covered in this chapter, please visit http://pearsoncanada.ca/conrad.

PART III
BOOMS, BUSTS, AND WARS, 1914–1945

Canadians were active participants in the Great War, which raged from 1914 to 1918 and took the lives of 65 000 Canadians, most of them young men. At the end of the war, almost 50 000 Canadians died in a virulent influenza pandemic. These tragedies helped to exacerbate social divisions and served as a catalyst for the trends emerging in the prewar period. In the 1920s, many Canadians embraced mass consumer culture, defining their success by the extent to which they could purchase the cars, radios, household appliances, and fashions produced in the nation's factories. Mass production seemed to promise a greater abundance for all, but many people were left behind in the rush for material well-being. The problem of poverty in the midst of plenty was exposed during the postwar recession that prevailed until 1924, and even more starkly during the Great Depression of the 1930s. Although movements to create a "welfare state" or usher in a socialist transformation of the capitalist system failed in the interwar years, the federal government's success in mobilizing the nation's resources in the Second World War between 1939 and 1945 paved the way for dramatic changes in Canadian government and society following the war.

CHAPTER 7
THE GREAT WAR AND RECONSTRUCTION, 1914–1921

Ahead of me I see men running. Suddenly their legs double up and they sink to the ground. Here's a body with the head shot off. I jump over it. Here's a poor devil with both legs gone, but still alive.[1]

Until the outbreak of the Second World War in 1939, the earlier conflict was known as the Great War, and its impact on Canada was deep and long lasting. Out of a population of only 8 million, more than 600 000 Canadians were involved in military service, 430 000 of them serving overseas. More than 60 000 Canadians died and another 134 000 were wounded in battle, some of them maimed for life. In addition, 34 000 military personnel were injured in accidents of various kinds, and another 5000 died within three years of war's end, many as a result of their wounds, both mental and physical. At home, nearly everyone grieved the loss of a relative or friend, bore the brunt of restrictive wartime regulations, and experienced the soul-searching that accompanied the imposition of conscription for military service in 1917. The war also marked a major turning point in the political history of Canada, propelling it along the road to greater independence.[2]

PREPARING FOR WAR

The assassination of Austrian archduke Franz Ferdinand and his wife in Sarajevo by a Serb nationalist in June 1914 seemed at first to be a remote tragedy. What led to war was not the murder of a future head of state, but rather the system of military alliances among European nations, which produced a domino effect when efforts were made to redress the outrage. Looking for revenge after the assassination, Austria-Hungary declared war on Serbia, and turned to its German ally for support. Germany, jealous of the power of France and Great Britain, embraced the crisis as an opportunity to show the world its military prowess. This, in turn, led Russia, an ally of Serbia, to mobilize its army; France, an ally of Russia, shortly did the same. As Germany prepared to invade neutral Belgium en route to an attack on France, Great Britain felt compelled to intervene. Italy and Romania eventually joined the effort to stop the German alliance, as did the United States in April 1917. The Ottoman Empire entered the war on the side of Germany in 1915.

As a member of the British Empire, Canada was automatically involved when Great Britain declared war. Canadians nevertheless had a choice about how to participate in the fighting in Europe, or, indeed, whether to participate at all. In August 1914, most people,

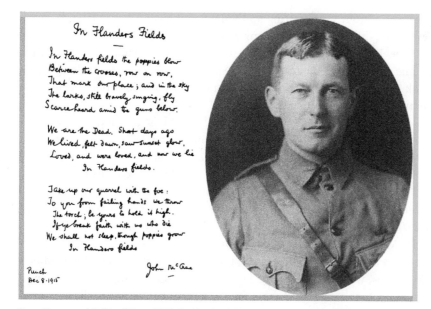

In Flanders Fields
—

In Flanders fields the poppies blow
Between the crosses, row on row,
That mark our place; and in the sky
The larks, still bravely singing, fly
Scarce heard amid the guns below.

We are the Dead. Short days ago
We lived, felt dawn, saw sunset glow,
Loved, and were loved, and now we lie
      In Flanders fields.

Take up our quarrel with the foe:
To you from failing hands we throw
The torch; be yours to hold it high.
If ye break faith with us who die
We shall not sleep, though poppies grow
      In Flanders fields

Punch
Dec 8·1915   John McCrae
—

It was the second Battle of Ypres (1915) that inspired Lieutenant-Colonel John McCrae, a Canadian doctor, to write the poem "In Flanders Fields," a moving call to keep faith with the soldiers who had given up their lives. By the time that McCrae died in Europe in 1918, his poem had become one of the most popular symbols of the Allied war effort and generations of schoolchildren were required to memorize it. SOURCES: LIBRARY AND ARCHIVES CANADA C-26561/GUELPH MUSEUMS, McCRAE HOUSE COLLECTION

turn, were organized into regiments, brigades, and divisions for what became known as the Canadian Expeditionary Force (CEF).

As soon as war was declared, Borden's minister of Militia, Sam Hughes, telegraphed his 226 unit commanders, appealing for volunteers for a division of 25 000 men. He was swamped with replies. When the volunteers arrived at the army's new military base at Valcartier a few kilometres outside Quebec City, they found construction and confusion all around. More by good luck than good management, 31 000 men, 8000 horses, and sundry equipment, much of it useless, were loaded onto transports and dispatched to Europe on 3 October. Among those travelling with the First Division were 101 nurses under the direction of Matron Margaret MacDonald, all full-fledged members of the CEF.

including Wilfrid Laurier and Henri Bourassa, saw Germany as the aggressor and thought it prudent to support Great Britain. Neither the Canadian state nor individual citizens were prepared for what this decision meant.

Struggling to deal with the demands of war, Conservatives and Liberals in the House of Commons united to pass the War Measures Act early in August 1914. This act gave the federal government authority to do everything it deemed "necessary for the security, defence, peace, order and welfare of Canada." Under the provisions of the act, Ottawa imposed tough censorship laws, intervened in the marketplace, stripped many people of their democratic rights, and overrode provincial claims to jurisdiction.

Canada entered the war with a standing army of just 3110 men and a navy consisting of two aging vessels, the *Niobe* and the *Rainbow*. Since the end of the nineteenth century, most of Canada's defence expenditures had been channelled to the militia, whose budget had risen from $1.6 million in 1898 to $11 million in 1914. Militia strength stood at more than 74 000 in the summer of 1914, and it was from these part-time soldiers that Canada would draw many of its first eager recruits. Instead of staying in their militia units, volunteers were grouped in numbered battalions of about 1000 men. Battalions, in

Because no Canadian had sufficient military experience, a British officer, Major-General E.A.H. Alderson, took command. Under Alderson's leadership, soldiers were organized into the 1st Canadian Infantry Division and drilled into fighting form in England. The division moved to France in February 1915. At Ypres, Belgium, in mid-April, they had their first real test when they experienced a chlorine gas attack. The Canadians refused to break lines when others around them, who had taken the brunt of the attack, fell back. It soon became clear that the war would be long and that Great Britain needed all the help it could get from the empire. Great Britain's Lord Kitchener, who was in charge of the War Office, had shocked his cabinet colleagues in the early days of the war by calling for a million soldiers. In the end, Great Britain needed five times that number.

While men and matériel continued to move across the Atlantic, there were difficulties at every turn. Many of the problems, such as inadequate facilities and bottlenecks in military supplies, would have occurred no matter who was in charge, but Hughes turned even the smallest problem into a major crisis. Patronage and corruption riddled the Militia Department's massive purchasing program, and the command structure of the

Canadian forces was a shambles. Hughes was a stout defender of Canadian-made Ross rifles, even though the gun had a tendency to jam in the heat of battle. In 1916, they were replaced by British-made Lee-Enfields, but in the meantime Canadian soldiers often took Lee-Enfield rifles off their dead British comrades because the Ross rifle was so unreliable. Although he was knighted in 1915, Hughes was finally dismissed from his portfolio in 1916. By that time, his administrative incompetence had brought an avalanche of criticism against the government's mishandling of the war effort.

Even before Hughes's dismissal, Borden had begun the process of bringing efficiency to the war effort. A variety of committees, including the Imperial Munitions Board (IMB), War Purchasing Board, National Service Board, and Ministry of Overseas Military Forces, were established and staffed by people with administrative experience. Since the government lacked professional civil servants capable of managing an economy suddenly on a war footing, Ottawa was critically dependent on the expertise and good will of businessmen such as Joseph Flavelle, general manager of the William Davies Packing Company, who became chair of the IMB. Flavelle spurred private firms to new levels of productivity, enticed American companies to locate in Canada, and, when all else failed, created government-run factories to produce everything from acetone to airplanes. By 1917, the IMB was the biggest business in Canada with 600 factories, 150 000 workers, and a turnover of $2 million a day.

THE WARTIME ECONOMY

Although it did not change the direction of the Canadian economy in any major way, the First World War sped Canadians a little faster down the road to industrial maturity. Markets expanded, at least temporarily, and the value of Canadian exports doubled in the first three years of the war and doubled again by 1919. In 1913, only seven percent of Canadian manufactures were sold overseas, a figure that rose to 40 percent during the final two years of the war. Factories ran full-tilt producing for the war effort, grain acreage soared, and mines operated at full capacity.

Canada's wartime economy, like that of peacetime, depended on private initiative, but the government found it necessary to intervene in a variety of ways. In addition to setting up the IMB and related committees to ensure that the army was properly equipped, Ottawa brought a wide range of supplies and services under its control. The Board of Grain Supervisors became the sole agent for Canadian wheat sales; the Fuel Controller decided the price and use of coal, wood, and gas; and the Food Board determined policy relating to the cost and distribution of food. In an effort to increase agricultural efficiency, the Food Board purchased 100 tractors from the Henry Ford Motor Company to distribute at cost to farmers. The same board urged Canadians to eat more fish so that beef and bacon could be released for overseas armies. Children were encouraged to grow "victory gardens" as their contribution to the war effort.

Inevitably, there were complaints about government policy. The Food Board's "anti-loafing law," threatening punishment for any man or boy not gainfully employed, was understandably not very popular, and no one enjoyed the discomfort that resulted from the "fuelless days" mandated by the Fuel Controller. The IMB's pattern of granting contracts sparked accusations that Flavelle and his associates favoured central Canadian firms over those from the less industrialized regions of the nation. When companies producing war supplies recorded huge profits, Canadians became increasingly skeptical about the patriotic claims of corporations. People like Flavelle prospered, while servicemen's families, without any resources to sustain them, were often forced to rely on charity.

By 1916, the Canadian economy was fully geared for war. Hostilities rejuvenated the Canadian shipbuilding industry, but in the industrial heartland rather than the Maritime ports. During the war, the British-owned Vickers Company employed more than 15 000 people in its shipyards near Montreal, while Davie Shipbuilding near Quebec City produced anti-submarine vessels and steel barges. Between 1914 and 1918, Canada's steel mills doubled their capacity to meet British demands for shells, supplying as much as a third of British artillery needs. Supplemented by the domestic labours of women and children who knit socks, preserved jam, and rolled bandages for the men at the front, farm and factory production increased to meet the demand for food, clothing, and footwear.

Notwithstanding the enhanced role of government and industry, voluntary activities remained essential to the war effort. The 1200 branches of the Red Cross in Canada served as essentially an auxiliary of the Army

Medical Corps. In many communities, the Imperial Order Daughters of the Empire and the Women's Institutes collected money and packed parcels for men overseas. A range of other organizations—the Great War Veterans' Association, the War Veterans' Next-of-Kin Association, the YMCA and YWCA, Consumers' Leagues, Women's Patriotic Leagues, Vacant Lot Garden Clubs, and the Women's Volunteer Army Division—all "did their bit."

Much of the work of caring for the families of soldiers and men who returned wounded to Canada was managed by volunteer groups. In the early days of the war, the federal government established a Canadian Patriotic Fund, an organization staffed largely by volunteers whose role was to help the families of soldiers overseas, a growing number of which were dependent on charity. An enlisted man was required to sign over a portion of his pay to his wife or dependent mother, but this did not always happen. Volunteers in the Patriotic Fund helped dependents apply for financial assistance—as much as $50 a month by the end of the war—and also arranged services for veterans who returned sick, wounded, insane, or addicted to alcohol.

The twin demand for workers and soldiers resulted in a labour shortage. To address the problem, the federal government created the National Service Board in 1916 to mobilize the nation's resources, and women were recruited into transportation and metal trades that were previously the preserve of men. More than 30 000 women were hired in munitions factories during the war, and many more positions temporarily opened to women. Although women were paid less than the men they replaced and were fired from their "untraditional" jobs at the end of the hostilities, they got a sense of what they could do when given a chance.

As the economy moved into high gear, Canadians confronted inflation and a soaring cost of living. Wages, controlled by wartime regulation, failed to follow the upward spiral of prices, and many people got caught in the financial squeeze. In the last two years of the war, Canada's productive capacity was threatened by rising levels of strike activity and political unrest. Canada's War Labour Policy, which was proclaimed in 1918, prohibited strikes and lockouts while affirming the right to organize and to receive fair wages and equal pay for equal work. Nevertheless, labour shortages blunted the efforts by governments

Women working in a wartime munitions factory in Verdun, Quebec, c. 1915-1917. SOURCE: LIBRARY AND ARCHIVES CANADA C-18734

and employers to prevent strikes and protests. There was no desperate reserve army of labour willing to take the jobs of striking workers, who recognized their potential power in bringing employers to heel. Union membership increased dramatically, and support for labour parties grew.

FINANCING THE WAR

Under the sweeping provisions of the War Measures Act, the federal government took a variety of economic initiatives that would have been unthinkable prior to the outbreak of hostilities. It suspended the gold standard, expanded the money supply, and engaged in deficit financing. When British financial markets closed, Ottawa floated loans in the New York bond market for the first time. Canadians also extended credit to Great Britain for the purchase of the necessities of war.

The federal government raised money at home by selling Victory Bonds, War Savings Certificates, and, for children, War Savings Stamps, generating nearly $2 billion in loans. In 1917, Ottawa began the process of nationalizing half the country's railway capacity by taking control of the Grand Trunk Pacific and Canadian Northern and amalgamating them with other government-controlled railways, including the Intercolonial, to create the Canadian National Railways system. The government also used the wartime emergency to build a more effective civil service. In 1918, Ottawa placed some 40 000 government workers under the Civil Service Commission, which was responsible for ensuring that people were hired on the basis of merit rather than patronage.

In response to demands that wealth be conscripted along with manpower, the federal government implemented a war profits tax in 1916. It was pegged at 25 percent on all profits greater than 7 percent of capital for corporations and 10 percent of capital for other businesses with a capitalization of $50 000 or more. In 1917, Ottawa imposed personal income taxes for the first time. The tax affected only single persons earning more than $1500 and married men with family incomes of $3000, a small minority of Canadians. The tax was graduated, with incomes above the exempted amount rising from a mere 4 percent on income up to $6000, to 29 percent on income

above $100 000. Difficult to collect, the new taxes played a negligible role in funding the war effort. Eighty-four percent of wartime revenues were raised through customs and excise duties, while less than one percent came from personal income taxes. The "temporary" income and corporate taxes imposed during the war outlived the crisis that sparked them, and by 1939 were generating nearly a third of the federal government's revenues.

THE WAR IN EUROPE

Canadian men enlisted in the armed forces for a variety of reasons, among them patriotism, adventure, and unemployment. As Larry Nelson, a Toronto enlistee in 1914, recalled, "most of us were young and saw it as a wonderful opportunity to throw off the shackles of working in an office or a factory or on a farm or what-have-you."[3] Emotional attachment to Britain was also a key factor: more than 65 percent of the first wave of volunteers consisted of recent British

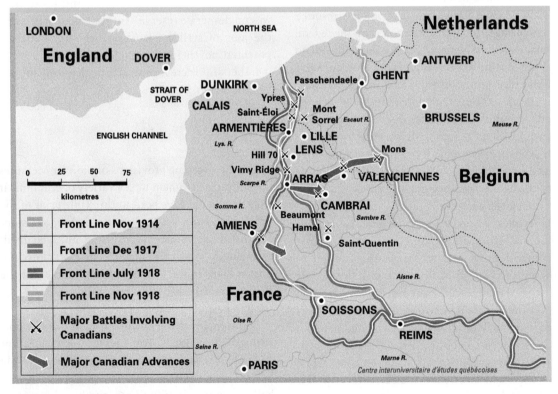

MAP 7.1

The European Front, 1914-1918. The map shows the main actions of Canadian troops during the First World War

immigrants, and one-half of all enlistees in Canadian forces in the First World War were British-born.

The 6000 Canadians killed or injured in April 1915 at Ypres were only the first in a long list of battle casualties. On 1 July 1916, the first day of the Allied offensive on the Somme, the British suffered 21 000 casualties, including nearly 700 members of the Newfoundland Regiment, who fought at Beaumont Hamel. The Canadian Corps, now four divisions strong, suffered more than 24 000 casualties in the Somme offensive—but the worst was not over. With the Russian front crumbling, the Dardanelles taken by the Turks, and the Germans holding the line in Europe, it seemed possible that the Allies might lose the war. There were mutinies in the French army, and some Canadian soldiers were shot for desertion as a warning to anyone else contemplating such a move.

Jack Turner and Lee Allan from Prince Edward Island taking a break from battle in 1917. Allan reads *The Island Patriot* while Turner holds *Jack Canuck*, a comic strip showing the heroics of soldier life. A photography buff who enlisted in 1915, Turner concealed his camera under his clothes and documented the war from the perspective of an ordinary soldier. SOURCE: PRINCE EDWARD ISLAND PUBLIC ARCHIVES AND RECORDS OFFICE ACC2767/107

In April 1917, the Canadian Corps took Vimy Ridge after a fiercely fought battle in which there were more than 10 000 Canadian casualties. It proved to be a turning point for Canadians in the war. Until 1917, the soldiers of the CEF fought as "imperials" under Britain's Army Act. This did not always go over well with the troops or the folks at home. By the fall of 1916, Borden was determined to give Canadians more control over their own war effort. He created a Ministry of Overseas Military Forces under the control of Sir George Perley, the Canadian High Commissioner in London, and redefined the CEF as an overseas contingent of the Canadian militia. Many of the British officers were gradually replaced by Canadians and, after Vimy Ridge, the process accelerated until June 1917, when Arthur Currie, the Canadian commander of the First Canadian Infantry Division, was made commander of the entire Canadian Corps. Under the methodical Currie, Canadians developed a reputation for bravery and determination. In October 1917, the Canadians were dispatched to Passchendaele, in Belgium,

where the British Fifth Army had already lost 68 000 men. In October and November, the Canadian Corps broke through the German lines, but the price—15 000 casualties—was high.

Canadian Gunners in the Mud, Passchendaele, by Lieutenant Alfred Bastien (1917). Bastien was a Belgian war artist working for the Canadians. SOURCE: BEAVERBROOK COLLECTION OF WAR ART, CANADIAN WAR MUSEUM 19710261-0093

BIOGRAPHY
Arthur Currie

Born in Ontario in 1875, Arthur Currie taught school for a time before heading west. When war was declared, he was a real-estate and insurance broker living in Victoria. The recession that descended in 1913 left him with crippling debts, and the war brought a welcome opportunity. As an officer in the local militia since 1897, he had developed a reputation both as a crack marksman and able administrator. Minister of Militia Sam Hughes offered Currie the command of one of the infantry brigades being formed for overseas service in the fall of 1914. Currie accepted the offer, but not before he took more than $10 000 from the funds from his regiment to pay off his debts.

In the field of battle, Currie quickly became recognized as a highly capable officer, most notably during the gas attack at the second battle of Ypres. Promotions followed. As commander of the 1st Canadian Division, he played a major role in the assault against Vimy Ridge in April 1917, and was appointed lieutenant-general in command of the Canadian Corps in June. The Canadian Corps continued to score successes at the front until the end of the war. In the meantime, rumours of Currie's financial indiscretion reached Borden and the cabinet. Currie was forced to borrow money from two senior subordinates to repay the funds. Not surprisingly, this revelation raised a few eyebrows in Ottawa.

Currie was knighted in 1917 and received a number of honours, but his reputation as a Canadian military hero was slow to develop. As the war came to an end, rumours spread among his men—who called him "guts and garters" due to his aloof manner—that he had sacrificed lives to enhance his image. In 1919, these accusations were announced to the House of Commons by Sam Hughes, who harboured a grudge against Currie for his part in having Hughes dismissed from the cabinet in 1916. Unlike high-ranking British officers who received cash payments after the war, Currie received no such compensation and his postwar position as inspector-general of the army was so unfulfilling that he resigned to become principal of McGill.

Lieutenant-General Sir Arthur Currie at the Canadian front in June 1917. SOURCE: LIBRARY AND ARCHIVES CANADA PA-1370

Although Hughes died in 1921, the rumours around Currie's allegedly brutal wartime command would not go away. Currie finally sued a small-town newspaper, the Port Hope *Evening Guide*, which on 13 June 1927 repeated the substance of Hughes's charges. Currie won the highly publicized court case, but suffered a stroke shortly after the trial and died in 1933. In the final years of his life, he became reconciled with the Canadian Legion, lobbied for the establishment of the Canadian Pension Commission, and embraced disarmament, the latter a policy supported by many veterans who had survived the horrors of war at close range.[4]

While the vast majority of Canadian military personnel served in the land forces, significant numbers also saw action at sea and in the air. The unexpected success of German submarines (U-boats) in sinking the merchant ships that carried North American war supplies to Britain and Europe brought a new dimension to naval warfare. As a result, nearly 10 000 Canadians served in the navy. Most of them operated Canadian-built anti-submarine craft on the east coast, but about 1000 served with the British fleet in European waters.

MORE TO THE STORY
The Realities of War

I am terrified. I hug the earth, digging my fingers into every crevice, every hole. A blinding flash and an explosive howl a few feet in front of the trench. My bowels liquify. Acrid smoke bites the throat, parches the mouth. I am beyond mere fright. I am frozen with an insane fear that keeps me cowering in the bottom of the trench. I lie flat on my belly waiting. . . .[5]

Charles Yale Harrison, an American soldier in the Canadian Expeditionary Force (CEF), was far from alone in his reaction to a German shelling. Nor was the heat of battle the only challenge facing Canadian soldiers on the European front. While on duty they lived in trenches that stretched from Switzerland to the English Channel. Their dugouts were pits of thick mud infested with fleas, lice, rats, and germs. Soldiers devoured their rations of corned beef, biscuits, bread, and tea, but it was not a healthy diet and it left them constantly hungry and susceptible to diseases. If the enemy missed his mark, dysentery, pneumonia, and "trench fever" might be just as deadly. Chemical warfare was an entirely new and horrifying experience. To survive their first attack of chlorine gas at Ypres, men urinated in their handkerchiefs and held them to their noses. Rats nibbled the corpses of fallen comrades, while those soldiers who were still alive dug new trenches and maintained existing ones, moved supplies, and tried not to think of their hunger and fear.

Fear was justified. More than 65 000 Canadians died as a result of their involvement in the First World War, and as many were so severely wounded, physically or mentally, that they were unable to resume a normal life. The mentally wounded, or "shell-shocked" as they came to be known, returned to a society that was ill-prepared for such casualties. While a soldier whose wounds put him in a wheelchair received a government pension and the sympathy of other Canadians, there was little

Men remained in the trenches for a week or more at a time in all kinds of weather before they were relieved briefly to go to makeshift rest camps. This picture shows Canadian soldiers in France in 1917, sheltering as best they could in what were known as "funk holes" dug into the sides of the trenches. SOURCE: LIBRARY AND ARCHIVES CANADA PA-1326

comfort for the emotionally disabled who remained unfit to resume their work and family life and who stared vacantly into space or sought comfort in the bottle.

Following the war, Canadians tried to find ways to come to terms with the sacrifice of so many men in the prime of their lives. Jonathan Vance, in his book *Death So Noble*, describes how the death and dismemberment of ordinary soldiers became idealized through monuments in town squares and reflections on the war that highlighted its role in fostering a national spirit. Such views, he argues, conveniently glossed over the horror of war and the divisions it created among Canadians.[6]

Thousands of Canadian sailors also served the war effort in the merchant marine, ferrying vital military supplies to Europe. In the summer and fall of 1918, three German U-boats hunted off Nova Scotia and Newfoundland. The Canadian anti-submarine vessels, which escorted merchant ship convoys, helped keep losses of major vessels to only two. It was more difficult to protect the widely scattered fishing fleets, and more than 30 schooners and trawlers were destroyed in Canadian and Newfoundland waters.

Canada authorized a tiny air unit early in the war, but airmen were encouraged to participate in British units. More than 20 000 Canadians served in the Royal Flying Corps (RFC), the Royal Naval Air Service, or, after 1 April 1918, the Royal Air Force. Lieutenant-Colonel W.A. "Billy" Bishop, who shot down 72 enemy planes, was one of Canada's most famous fighting pilots. Unlike the more than 1500 other Canadians killed while pioneering the use of the "aeroplane" in wartime, he lived to tell about it. The achievements of Canadian airmen such as Bishop, combined with the expertise Canadians gained in the British flying services and the tremendous growth of aircraft technology, helped to ensure advances in aviation after the war.

Only once were Canadians at home offered a real taste of what it was like to have their world devastated by the horrors of war. Shortly after nine o'clock on the morning of 6 December 1917, the French munitions ship *Mont Blanc*, laden with explosives, collided with the Belgian relief ship *Imo* in Halifax harbour, producing one of the largest explosions in human history up to that time. More than 1600 people were killed outright, another 9000 were injured—including 200 blinded by flying glass—and 20 000 were left without adequate shelter for the coming winter. Homes, factories, train stations, churches, and a great sweep of harbour facilities disappeared in the blast or the subsequent fires and tidal wave that engulfed the city. Makeshift mortuaries, hospitals, and shelters were set up in surviving churches, schools, and rinks, while people wandered aimlessly about the smoking rubble looking for lost loved ones.

As soon as word of the tragedy got out, help poured in from surrounding communities, from other provinces, from Ottawa, from Newfoundland, and eventually from around the world. The people of Massachusetts, where so many Maritime-born Canadians lived and worked, immediately dispatched a train equipped with medical personnel, money, and supplies, and Sir John Eaton, president of the T. Eaton Company, arrived in Halifax with his own train, food, sleeping car, staff, and medical unit. Some $30 million, more than half of it from the federal government, was provided to help Halifax and its sister town Dartmouth, which had also suffered from the blast, recover from the devastation.

A view of the devastation following the 1917 Halifax Explosion, looking south along the railway track. SOURCE: LIBRARY AND ARCHIVES CANADA C-19948

THE WAR AT HOME

The slaughter on the European front spread panic in the British War Office and led to the demand for more troops. Prime Minister Borden had pushed the approved strength of the CEF up to 500 000 in his New Year's message for 1916, but lagging voluntary enlistments and high casualty rates at the front were already making it difficult to keep units up to strength. Where would the new recruits come from?

In the early months of the war, it had looked as if voluntary enlistment would sustain the Canadian war effort. Overall, one in six Canadian men between the ages of 15 and 54, or nearly 233 000 individuals, had volunteered for the infantry by 1917. Canadians had also joined other branches of the CEF, such as the artillery, engineer, medical, and army service corps, or had responded to appeals to join British forces, bringing the numbers almost up to the half-million demanded by Borden.

Most men of military age never volunteered, but the success of recruiting efforts varied dramatically by region and culture. Perhaps 15 000 to 20 000 volunteers were francophones,[7] but they formed a much smaller proportion of recruits than their percentage of the Canadian population. Men in Ontario and the West were also more likely to sign up than those from the Maritimes and Quebec. The attachment of recent immigrants to their European homelands to some extent explains the lower recruitment rates in the longer-settled eastern provinces, but there were other factors determining who decided to volunteer.

French Canadians were initially sympathetic to the Allied cause, but this feeling waned as the war progressed. During the first year of the war, French Canadians were dispersed among various units, creating language difficulties. The only entirely French unit, the Royal 22nd Battalion, was established in October 1914. Anger at Ontario's 1912 legislation restricting French-language instruction in public schools reinforced feelings of estrangement from a cause that was identified with Great Britain and English Canada. As wartime tensions mounted, provincial governments outside Quebec intensified their efforts to suppress French-language education in their jurisdictions, and English Canadians began accusing French Canadians of shirking their duty. French Canadians, meanwhile, began to wonder why they should volunteer for overseas duty when they had battles to fight at home.

Borden tried to maintain volunteer strength by stepping up recruitment efforts, conducting a National Registration of all able-bodied men and creating a Canadian Defence Force that would relieve soldiers stationed in Canada for European service. None of these measures worked. In May 1917, the Prime Minister announced his intention to impose conscription, or compulsory military service, on a war-weary nation. The Military Service Act, which was stick-handled through the House of Commons by Solicitor General Arthur Meighen, drafted single men between the ages of 20 and 35. Opposition to the measure was high, especially in Quebec and among farmers and labourers. Although Borden had postponed calling an election in wartime, he

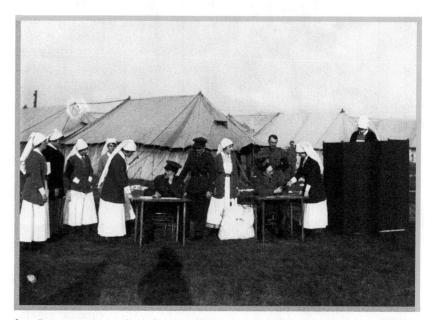

Canadian nurses at a hospital in France vote in the 1917 election. SOURCE: LIBRARY AND ARCHIVES CANADA PA-2279

now changed his mind. An election would clear the air about the issue of conscription and give the government a mandate to carry on.

Before dissolving Parliament on 6 October, Borden approached Liberal opposition leader Sir Wilfrid Laurier to join him in a coalition to support an all-out war effort. Laurier rejected the offer, fearing the loss of Quebec to Bourassa's nationalists, who were adamantly opposed to conscription. Defying Laurier's decision, a rump of Liberals primarily from the West and Ontario joined with the Conservatives to create a Union government that campaigned on a platform of conscription, Prohibition, and abolition of party patronage.

To ensure a victory for his unstable coalition, Borden saw to it that the right people got the vote. A Military

As this campaign poster produced by the Union Government Publicity Bureau suggests, the 1917 election campaign was bitterly fought, with Laurier being accused of pleasing Kaiser Wilhelm of Germany by refusing to support conscription. SOURCE: LIBRARY AND ARCHIVES CANADA C-93224

Voters' Act enfranchised every man and woman in the CEF, while the Wartime Elections Act gave the vote to mothers, wives, and sisters of soldiers—dead or alive—and took it away from citizens of enemy origin naturalized after 1902. The only compensation for those who were disenfranchised was an exemption from conscription. Even these draconian measures failed to convince Unionists that they would carry the day. Running scared during the election campaign, they promised sons of farmers an exemption from conscription, a promise that was later broken.

The results of the election held on 17 December surprised few people: the Union government won 153 seats, while the Liberals won 82. Sixty-two of Quebec's 65 seats went to Laurier, but the Liberals carried only 10 of 28 seats in the Maritimes, 8 of 82 in Ontario, and 2 of 57 in the West. The popular vote suggested greater division outside Quebec than the seat totals suggest. Civilian voters in the Maritimes gave a slight majority of their votes to anti-conscription candidates; even in Ontario, anti-conscriptionist parties won nearly 40 percent of the civilian vote.

Anti-conscriptionists constituted a substantial part of the electorate in English Canada, but they were the overwhelming majority in Quebec, where feelings continued to run high after the election. In 1918, the Quebec legislature debated a resolution on secession from Canada. When conscription tribunals began hearing applications for military exemptions in Quebec, violence erupted. The worst incident occurred in Quebec City, where, in March 1918, furious crowds attacked the military service registry and trashed businesses. Ottawa sent in troops, many of them English-Canadian. After a series of clashes with the rioters, the troops opened fire, killing four people and injuring many more.

Whether conscription served its military purpose has been much debated. Defaults and desertions were common, and tribunals were often sympathetic to local boys. Of the more than 400 000 men who registered under the legislation, only 24 000 went to France. Because of the difficulty of raising conscripts, the Fifth Division in Britain was dissolved and its soldiers distributed among the thinning ranks of other divisions. The war ended a year after conscription had been imposed, but its effects were felt for a long time, especially in national politics, where the Liberal Party could claim that it had been Quebec's champion in a time of need.

ENEMIES WITHIN

The Wartime Elections Act revealed another source of tension for a nation at war: the roughly half a million people living in Canada who traced their origins to enemy countries. Since many of the 100 000 "enemy aliens"—people who were born in enemy countries—had arrived in the decade before the outbreak of war, they were viewed with suspicion by Canadians who had been apprehensive about the number of immigrants pouring into the country even before the war began.

Internees at their compound located at Castle Mountain in Banff, July 1915. SOURCE: GLENBOW ARCHIVES NA1870-6

Enemy aliens in urban centres were forced to register with police authorities and were forbidden to carry arms. If unemployed, they were interned as prisoners of war in 26 camps scattered across the country. Internment camps were initially established in northern Ontario and Quebec, out of the way of nervous civilians. Between 1915 and 1917, some 900 men worked for six days a week at 25 cents a day, clearing land and building roads in various national parks. Others were contracted to private corporations to work as miners or farm labourers. Ultimately, 8579 enemy aliens were interned, including more than 3000 Canadian citizens.

Harassment of people who traced their origins to enemy countries went beyond official sanctions and internment. Universities fired German professors, judges threw cases brought by alien plaintiffs out of court, and angry mobs attacked businesses owned by Germans and Austro-Hungarians. Even people whose families were deeply rooted in Canada, such as the Germans of Lunenburg County, Nova Scotia, and Waterloo County, Ontario, felt the wrath of wartime prejudice. In an effort to demonstrate their patriotism, the citizens of Berlin, Ontario, changed the name of their city to Kitchener in 1916, while many people in Lunenburg County claimed their origins to be "Dutch" rather than German in the 1921 census.

Following the Bolshevik Revolution in Russia in the fall of 1917, radicals became the focus of attention in Ottawa. The Union government issued an order-in-council

making it an offence to print or possess any publication in an enemy language without a licence from the secretary of state. "Foreign" organizations, including the Industrial Workers of the World, were banned, as were meetings in which enemy languages were used. In British Columbia, tensions ran high when socialist labour leader "Ginger" Goodwin was shot by the police in 1918, ostensibly because he was evading the draft.

People who espoused pacifist views were also subjected to harassment. Francis Marion Beynon lost her job as a columnist for the *Grain Growers' Guide* because of her pacifist stance, and J.S. Woodsworth resigned from the Methodist Church in 1918 when it could no longer tolerate his pacifist and left-wing views. Groups such as the Mennonites and Hutterites, whose religious convictions included a rigorous pacifism, experienced both official and unofficial sanctions in a country that increasingly defined citizenship by the extent of one's military participation.

Acrimonious debates over commitment to the war effort tore apart friendships, families, and organizations. Suffragist and novelist Nellie McClung recalled in 1945:

> The fall of 1914 blurs in my memory like a troubled dream. The war dominated everything. Some of my friends were pacifists and resented Canada's participation in a war of which we knew so little. . . . Chief among the Empire's defenders among the women was

Miss Cora Hind. Her views were clear cut and definite. We were British and must follow the tradition of our fathers. She would have gone herself if women were accepted. Miss Hind saw only one side of the question and there were times when I envied her, though I resented her denunciations of those who thought otherwise. The old crowd began to break up, and our good times were over.[8]

A WHITE MAN'S WAR

Prejudices based on gender and race, in large measure, determined who could participate in the fighting. Although women might keep the home fires burning and serve behind the lines as nurses, no serious thought was given to allowing them to be combatants. Women, it was believed, were too weak and emotional to stand the rigours of battle and, in any event, it was men's role to protect them.

A few women, such as the Yukon's Martha Black, managed to get to Great Britain at their own expense. While they waited for word of their loved ones at the front, these women worked as volunteers in British hospitals and other service institutions. Most of the more than 3000 women who joined the Canadian Army Nursing Service went overseas. Forty-seven died on duty, and many received distinguished service awards, including Matron Ethel Ridley, who was invested a Commander of the Order of the British Empire for her work as principal matron in France.

For visible minorities, as for women, pervasive perceptions of their inferiority limited the roles they were allowed to play in wartime. Only Aboriginal peoples were specifically denied admission to the army from the outset, on the spurious grounds that "Germans might refuse to extend to them the privileges of civilized warfare." Not widely publicized, the directive was ignored by some militia officers. Throughout the war, officials repeatedly insisted that there was no "colour line," but when visible minorities offered their services, they were invariably turned down by militia officers. Fifty blacks from Sydney, Nova Scotia, who arrived at the recruitment office, were advised: "This is not for you fellows, this is a white man's war."[9]

Many members of Canada's visible minorities believed that participation in the war would help them to improve the status of their people. So determined were they to be accepted that, in the face of rejection by recruitment offices, they formed their own segregated units and offered their services. On the west coast, the Canadian Japanese Association enlisted 227 volunteers who drilled at their own expense. African Canadians were persistent in their demands that they be allowed to enlist for overseas service.

The crisis in recruitment helped to crack the wall of racial prejudice. In the fall of 1915, the directive against Native Canadians was lifted, and thereafter they were recruited for the 114th Battalion and accepted into other units. African Canadians had champions in Conservative Party MPs from the Maritimes, including the Prime

Commanded by white officers, the No. 2 Construction Battalion, formed in 1916, included blacks from across Canada as well as 145 African Americans who crossed the border to participate in the war. The battalion was attached to the Canadian Forestry Corps, a labour unit whose job was to support the men fighting at the front. This picture was taken in England. SOURCE: ROY STATES COLLECTION, RARE BOOKS AND SPECIAL COLLECTIONS, McGILL UNIVERSITY LIBRARY

Minister. In April 1916, with Borden presiding, the Militia Council decided to form a black battalion—the No. 2 Construction Battalion—headquartered in Nova Scotia. By the summer of 1916, Japanese men who had received basic training were admitted to 11 different battalions. Chinese men were also grudgingly accepted. When conscription was imposed, Natives and Asians were exempted because they were disenfranchised, and little effort was made to recruit black conscripts. In all, about 3500 Natives, more than 1000 African Canadians, and several hundred Chinese and Japanese Canadians served in the Canadian forces.

Prejudice did not stop once they were in the army. Units composed of visible minorities were likely to be shunted into forestry and construction activities, and they were segregated whenever possible from whites. Nor did their service in the war change their status once they returned home. It had remained a white man's war to the end, and the service of visible minorities was largely forgotten in accounts of the war effort.

CANADA ON THE WORLD STAGE

Borden's willingness to pursue an all-out war effort despite the opposition in Quebec owed much to his faith that Canada would emerge from the war with a new international status. From the beginning, he pressed British authorities to give the dominion a voice in war planning, but his efforts bore little fruit until David Lloyd George became British prime minister in late 1916. Influenced by Max Aitken, Canada's London-based champion and a leading figure in the political manoeuvring that had made him prime minister, Lloyd George wanted help from the dominions in a war that was going badly. In 1917, he called an Imperial War Conference and created the Imperial War Cabinet—the British War Cabinet with dominion representation. These bodies gave Borden more information and the opportunity to express his views, but the British remained firmly in control of their empire's war effort.

In April 1917, the United States entered the war against Germany. The presence of fresh American troops provided welcome support for the war-weary Allied forces. By August 1918, the tide had turned. The final Hundred Days Offensive leading to the armistice on 11 November 1918 began with the battle of Amiens, spearheaded by Canadian troops. The Canadian Corps played a major role in bringing Germany to its knees in the last days of the fighting. The cost was great—more than 30 000 casualties—but at least the bloody war was over.

Canada was represented in the British Empire delegation to the Paris Peace Conference and separately signed the Treaty of Versailles with Germany, the first time Canadians signed a multilateral treaty. Canada also became a member of the new League of Nations, established to keep the peace, and the International Labour Organization, designed to maintain international labour standards. Despite these accomplishments, Canada was still technically a colony, a point that American president Woodrow Wilson raised when he opposed the status accorded to the British dominions at Versailles.

DEMOBILIZATION AND RECONSTRUCTION

The task of bringing back the combatants and reintegrating them into civil society was almost as difficult as fighting the war. In October 1917 the government formed a cabinet committee on reconstruction, and a few months later created a new Department of Soldiers' Civil Re-Establishment to oversee demobilization. Its minister, Senator James Lougheed, was charged with responsibility for the Board of Pension Commissioners, the Soldiers' Land Settlement Scheme, hospital treatment and vocational training for the returned men, and the re-employment of munitions workers. Under Lougheed, the new department began building hospitals, nursing homes, and sanatoria, and helped to establish programs to retrain the disabled. In 1919, a new Department of Health took over many of the responsibilities formerly handled by the provinces and volunteers.

Health reform came too late to ward off yet another disaster associated with the war years. In the final months of the war, an influenza epidemic swept across the world. It killed almost as many Canadians as had died in the trenches, leaving citizens everywhere reeling with shock. Already stretched to the limit by the war effort, Canadians and their government had few resources with which to fight this new enemy. The epidemic finally receded, but it contributed to a wave of discontent that swept the nation as the war came to an end.

What the cabinet did not predict, though it should have, was the rising tempers of soldiers when they were left hanging around Europe and Great Britain following the signing of the armistice. The lack of suitable transport and the inability of Canada's rail lines to carry more than

MORE TO THE STORY
The Influenza Pandemic of 1918–1919

When a significant proportion of the world's population becomes infected with a virus at roughly the same time, the result is called a pandemic. The influenza pandemic of 1918 was particularly deadly, killing as many as 100 million people worldwide. Why the influenza virus was so deadly remains a mystery, and the origins of the virus are also difficult to determine. At the time, it was called the "Spanish flu," but only because the press in Spain, which was not a combatant in the war, was the first to publish accounts of the disease. One seemingly logical explanation, and the one usually given by Canadian scholars, is that the virus originated in the European trenches and quickly spread around the world as troops returned home.

By carefully tracking the progress of the disease, historian Mark Osborne Humphries provides convincing evidence to support another source of the deadly virus.[10] He argues that the flu arrived in Canada from the United States in the second and third weeks of September 1918, primarily with American soldiers on their way overseas to the battlefields of Europe. Although the virus seems to have originated in Kansas in the winter of 1918, it was not until the end of August that it reached pandemic proportions in the eastern United States. In mid-September, it appeared in Canada almost simultaneously in four separate locations. At Niagara-on-the-Lake, Ontario, Saint-Jean, Quebec, and Sydney, Nova Scotia, it arrived with recruits from the United States en route to the Allied offence in Europe. It was spread to Victoriaville, Quebec, at the same time by American visitors to a Eucharist Congress.

The disease was then efficiently dispersed throughout the country by the Siberian Expeditionary Force (SEF) assembled to support the "White Russian" forces against the Bolsheviks, who had seized power in 1917. Recruits for the SEF were drawn from across

Canada and converged on Vancouver late in September and early October 1918. As soldiers travelling from points east fell ill, they were removed from the troop trains and deposited in local hospitals. Thus, influenza was spread not by soldiers returning home from the battlefields of Europe, but by recruits bound for a new front in Asia.

Since the government was more focused on the war effort than on public health, it made little effort to contain the disease, which killed at least 50 000 Canadians before it ran its course in 1919. As a study of the impact of the epidemic in Winnipeg demonstrates, working-class neighbourhoods were harder hit than middle-class areas that enjoyed better civic services and medical facilities. In the city's north end, 6.3 per 1000 residents succumbed to the Spanish flu, compared to 4 per 1000 in wealthier parts of town.[11] Aboriginal peoples proved particularly vulnerable. When the mission ship *Harmony* brought the flu to Labrador late in 1918, nearly a third of the Inuit population in the area of the Moravian missions died within three months.

Among the hardest hit by influenza in 1918-1919 were those who tended to the victims, such as these Soeurs du Bon-Pasteur in Quebec City. SOURCE: SOEURS DU BON-PASTEUR DE QUÉBEC

20 000 troops a month from the nation's only major ice-free winter ports—Halifax and Saint John—created an explosive situation. In March 1919, discontent among Canadian soldiers stationed in Wales burst into violent

protest when a black guard arrested a white soldier and placed him under a "coloured" escort. White soldiers attacked their black compatriots, and in the ensuing melee 5 people were killed and 27 injured. More riots followed in

May. Determined to rid themselves of the troublesome Canadians, the British managed to find extra shipping capacity, and most Canadians were home by July 1919.

The Great War Veterans' Association (GWVA), founded in Winnipeg in 1917, emerged as the voice of the former members of the CEF. At the war's end, the organization was dominated by able-bodied men who demanded their rights and would brook no opposition from Conservative ministers. By 1925, the GWVA was amalgamated with a number of other smaller organizations into the Canadian Legion, which was more cautious and non-partisan in its approach.

The long-term costs of helping returned men and their families were immense. In 1920, more than 6500 men were still in hospital, while 20 000 parents, wives, and children of dead soldiers qualified for pensions in 1925. As health problems surfaced, the number of people qualifying for disability pensions rose from nearly 28 000 in 1919 to 43 000 in 1933. The total cost of these and other programs for veterans ranked second after the national debt in government expenditures, with accumulated costs of over $1 billion by 1935.

With the costs of reconstruction mounting alarmingly, the government decided to demobilize its armed forces as quickly as possible. Only three warships, two submarines, and the Royal Naval College survived from the larger wartime military establishment. In 1923, the militia, navy, and air force were amalgamated under a new Department of Defence. The government created a small Permanent Force to provide a modicum of defence but there would be no massive standing army to serve as a legacy of Canada's role in the Great War.

FEMALE SUFFRAGE

For many Canadians, the new era of liberal democracy offered potential for major reform. The Union government in 1918 followed up the Wartime Elections Act with legislation that gave the federal franchise to women on the same basis as men. During the war, the wall of opposition to female suffrage collapsed: in 1916, the three Prairie provinces adopted female suffrage, followed by Ontario and British Columbia in 1917, and Nova Scotia in 1918. New Brunswick extended the vote to women in 1919, but they were not allowed to hold public office in that province until 1934. Prince Edward Island granted women the vote in 1922, and Newfoundland in 1925. The latter based its legislation on British policy, which gave

the vote to women over the age of 25—not, as for men, 21. By 1920, most of the property and income restrictions placed on federal and provincial voting rights had also been swept away. Nonetheless, status Indians, Asians in British Columbia, women in Quebec's provincial elections, and conscientious objectors, including Mennonites and Hutterites, were denied the right to vote.

Women's suffrage advocates had the pleasure not only of seeing the franchise question resolved outside of Quebec, but also of witnessing the implementation of programs that were specifically designated "women's issues," such as Prohibition, mothers' allowances, and minimum-wage legislation. Under the provisions of the War Measures Act, the federal government legislated full Prohibition in 1918, and following the war all provinces except for Quebec and British Columbia maintained the policy, at least for a few years. In 1917, Alberta was the first jurisdiction to pass a minimum-wage law for women, a policy adopted during the 1920s by all provinces except New Brunswick and Prince Edward Island.

For many women, the franchise served primarily as a means of pressing politicians to pass reform legislation. The National Council of Women developed a policy of adopting a Canadian Women's Platform to identify issues to be pursued through the established political parties. In 1920, the platform included demands for equal pay for equal work, the female minimum wage, and political equality of the sexes. Party organizations successfully resisted attempts to integrate women fully into their activities, much to the disappointment of some suffrage leaders who had hoped that the vote would transform Canadian political life.

LABOUR REVOLT

Suffragists were not alone in being disillusioned by the failure of the war to usher in a major transformation in society. Higher profits for a few were accompanied by low wages, repressive working conditions, and a crushing cost of living for many. Desperate to mobilize resources for war, and with few close ties to labour, governments did little to rectify abuses. This failure set the groundwork for a level of class conflict unprecedented in Canadian history.

The Bolshevik Revolution in Russia in 1917 and the rising tide of socialist and communist protest in Europe and the United States inspired many Canadians, just as it terrified Canadian capitalists. In the fall of 1918, Borden called up more than 4000 Canadian recruits, many of them French Canadians, to participate in a Siberian Expeditionary Force (SEF), an Allied effort to support the so-called "White Russians" against the Bolsheviks. The labour movement was inevitably highly critical of this move, as were many of the recruits involved in the SEF, a third of whom were conscripted. On 21 December 1918, two companies of troops in the 259th Battalion (Canadian Rifles) mutinied in the streets of Victoria. The mutineers were whipped back into line by their loyal comrades, and two days later the expedition embarked for Vladivostok, minus a dozen ringleaders detained in prison cells.

Unhappy as it might have been with the Union government, the labour movement was also deeply divided. Conservative eastern craft unionism maintained control of the Trades and Labour Congress at the 1918 convention, but the Western Labour Conference held shortly thereafter in Calgary broke with TLC policies of conciliation and restraint. Those attending the conference resolved to create a single industrial union, the One Big Union (OBU), to challenge conservative unionists, hostile employers, and unsympathetic governments. Before the fledgling OBU could hold its founding

VOICES FROM THE PAST
Bloody Saturday

Labour and capital viewed the events of 21 June 1919 in Winnipeg in entirely different ways. Following is the official strikers' view of the events of that afternoon as reported in *Strike Bulletin*, the newspaper published by the Strike Committee.

> One is dead and a number injured, probably thirty or more, as [a] result of the forcible prevention of the "silent parade" which had been planned by returned men to start at 2.30 o'clock last Saturday afternoon. Apparently the bloody business was carefully planned, for Mayor Gray issued a proclamation in the morning stating that "Any women taking part in a parade do so at their own risk." Nevertheless a vast crowd of men, women and children assembled to witness the "silent parade." . . . On Saturday, about 2.30 P.M., just the time when the parade was scheduled to start, some 50 mounted men swinging baseball bats rode down Main Street. Half were red-coated R.N.W.M.P., the others wore khaki. They quickened pace as they passed the Union Bank. The crowd opened, let them through and closed in behind them. They turned and charged through the crowd again, greeted by hisses, boos, and some stones. There were two riderless horses with the squad when it emerged and galloped up Main Street. The men in khaki disappeared at this juncture, but the red-coats reined their horses and reformed opposite the old

Demonstrators during the Winnipeg General Strike, June 1919. SOURCE: ARCHIVES OF MANITOBA N12299

> post office. Then, with revolvers drawn, they galloped down Main Street, turned, and charged right into the crowd on William Avenue, firing as they charged. One man, standing on the sidewalk, thought the mounties were firing blank cartridges until a spectator standing beside him dropped with a bullet through his breast. Another standing nearby was shot through the head. We have no exact information about the total number of casualties, but there were not less than thirty. The crowd dispersed as quickly as possible when the shooting began.[12]

convention, its strike philosophy had an unanticipated practice run.

On 15 May 1919, the Winnipeg Trades and Labour Council called a general strike following the breakdown of negotiations between management and labour in the metal and building trades in the city. At stake were the principles of collective bargaining and better wages and working conditions. Only 12 000 of Winnipeg's workers belonged to a union of any kind, but 30 000 workers joined the strike within hours of the call for action. They included telephone operators and department store clerks who had waged successful wartime strikes and hoped to consolidate their gains by working to strengthen the labour movement as a whole.

Winnipeg's strike sparked a series of general strikes of varying lengths across the country. Although these strikes were ostensibly held in support of the Winnipeg workers, local grievances came to the fore everywhere. The Winnipeg strike was the longest, stretching from 15 May to 26 June. While its leaders made every effort to keep it orderly, agreeing to have essential services such as milk delivery continue throughout the strike, it faced formidable obstacles. Opponents of the strike, drawn mainly from employer and professional groups in the city, organized a committee to crush the strike and discredit its leadership. Insisting that the strike was Bolshevik-inspired, the Citizens' Committee of One Thousand refused to let the issue of employees' right to collective bargaining become the sole focus of the debate.

Convinced that they had a revolution on their hands, the federal government sent the Royal North-West Mounted Police to Winnipeg, allegedly to maintain order. On 21 June—a day that became known as Bloody Saturday—the Mounties attempted to disperse protesters by firing a volley of shots into the crowd. By the end of the day, two men were dead and many others were injured. Following the confrontation, strikers were arrested by the score. Among those jailed were two Winnipeg aldermen and a member of the Manitoba legislature. Recognizing the state's determination to crush the strike, those leaders who had not yet been imprisoned capitulated on 26 June. Winnipeg would remain a class-divided city for generations to come.

The federal government moved quickly to make radical protest difficult, if not impossible. Even attending a meeting, advocating the principles, or distributing the literature of such an organization could result in charges under section 98 of the Criminal Code.

EXPANDING POLITICAL HORIZONS

Like the differences that increasingly separated French and English Canada, a heightened awareness of class division was a long-term legacy of the Great War. Left-wing parties benefited from such divisions, including labour parties, which managed to win two seats in the 1921 election: J.S. Woodsworth, briefly imprisoned for his role as editor of the strike newspaper, was elected as an MP in a working class riding in Winnipeg, and William Irvine, a Scottish-born Unitarian minister, won a seat in Calgary. Labour radicalism also found a home when the Communist Party of Canada was founded at a secret meeting in Guelph, Ontario, in 1921.

Farmers, too, had reform on their minds. In 1916, the Canadian Council of Agriculture developed the Farmers' Platform, which included a call for free trade; graduated income, inheritance, and corporation taxes; nationalization of railway, telegraph, and express companies; and reform of the political process to eliminate the problems created by patronage, corruption, and centralized party discipline. Farmer candidates ran in the 1917 election on the Union ticket, but when the promised exemption from conscription for farmers' sons was cancelled in April 1918, most of them drifted away from the Conservatives. The Farmers' Platform was fleshed out and rechristened the New National Policy, which became the platform for the national Progressive Party established in 1920.

In Newfoundland, as in Canada, politics lost their prewar simplicity. Labour shortages led to a spread of industrial unionism, with the Newfoundland Industrial Workers' Association organizing railway shops, longshoremen, street railway workers, and factory workers. In the outports, fishing families got better prices for their fish, but felt that the war effort was very much a St John's affair. When Fishermen's Protective Union leader William Coaker supported the government's efforts to form a coalition and impose military conscription, outport families felt betrayed. The economic recession following the war resulted in a wave of bankruptcies and escalating unemployment, but the cash-strapped government had difficulty responding to the mounting crisis. In 1919, the National Government collapsed. It was replaced by a Liberal–Fishermen's Protective Union (FPU) alliance led by Richard Squires, but it, too, failed to find a solution to the postwar crisis. Demonstrations in

Conscription 1917

Historians have long debated whether conscription was necessary for the effective conduct of the war, and, if so, whether it served its purpose. According to one perspective, political pressure from English Canada forced the government's hand on a policy that was more political than military in its intent. Authors of an influential history of Quebec argue that Prime Minister Robert Borden was "responding to the will of the English-speaking majority."[13]

Most historians agree that there was pressure on the government for conscription, but add that the government was aware that English Canadians were divided on the issue and feared that conscription might lose votes for a government already in difficulties.[14] Borden and his key ministers, they argue, imposed conscription because of British pressure for a greater Canadian commitment to the war effort. Moreover, Borden's own conviction that Canada should do more left the government few options when voluntary recruitment failed to meet the government's targets for fighting men. From this viewpoint, conscription was a military necessity. Military historian A.M. Willms claims that, proportionate to its population, Canada before 1917 had contributed fewer military recruits than the other dominions in the British Empire. More recruits were necessary because of the heavy casualties of war.[15] Quebec historians have long argued that this interpretation accepts the Allied view that a peace treaty was not negotiable. Robert Rumilly's biography of Henri Bourassa stresses the view that negotiations were possible if both sides gave up the idea that there had to be a clear victor.[16]

Rumilly and other francophone Quebec historians have generally accepted Bourassa's view that no great principles were at stake in the war, but most English-Canadian historians have rejected the view that Canada simply subordinated itself to British imperialism. Ramsay Cook, explaining the support for conscription by *Winnipeg Free Press* editor John W. Dafoe, suggests that many English Canadians who fought for greater Canadian autonomy from Britain believed the war was being fought over "cherished values" of democracy and not from motives of "sycophantic colonialism or aggressive imperialism."[17] In their history of the First World War, published in 1989, J.L. Granatstein and Desmond Morton maintain that the members of Borden's cabinet did indeed believe that they were fighting a battle for "Canadian liberty and autonomy."[18]

Most historians agree that the Wartime Elections Act failed to respect the liberty of all citizens. There is less agreement about the extent to which the government resorted to ethnocentric appeals in its attempts to overcome anglophone divisions about the fairness of imposing conscription. Roger Graham, who wrote a biography on the influential cabinet minister and later prime minister Arthur Meighen, claims that the government attempted to avoid having the election contribute to national disunity.[19] Many Quebec historians dismiss this claim, noting that one important purpose of conscription was to assuage English-Canadian opinion that French Canadians were not doing their share. They also note the virulent anti-French-Canadian language adopted in much of the English-Canadian press. Recently, Quebec historians have also begun to pay more attention to those who actively resisted conscription, shifting the focus away from the political struggles.[20] Some anglophone historians also disagree with Graham's suggestion that the government took the high road in the election of 1917. J.L. Granatstein and J.M. Hitsman conclude: "The Union Government campaign, founded on the Military Service Act and the Wartime Elections Act, deliberately set out to create an English-Canadian nationalism, separate from and opposed to both French Canada and naturalized Canadians. No other conclusion can be drawn from this election campaign, one of the few in Canadian history deliberately conducted on racist grounds."[21]

In 2005, J.L. Granatstein, writing as Canadians were debating their military contribution to the war against the Taliban in Afghanistan, acknowledged that he had underplayed the military side of the equation in his earlier publications. He now argues that there was, indeed, a need for more soldiers to replace the casualties of the fierce fighting on the European front, and that military concerns were central to the federal government's difficult decision to introduce the Military Service Act. Further, he maintains that his earlier conclusion, that "[c]onscription had not worked in Canada," was wrong.[22] The more than 24 000 soldiers who fought overseas as a result of the act "kept the units up to strength, allowed for the Canadian Corps to function with great effectiveness and efficiency in the final decisive battles of the Great War and helped to minimize casualties."[23]

St John's underscored the social tensions that were unlikely to be resolved by any government.

CONCLUSION

Anyone surveying the Canadian scene in 1919 must have wondered if the nation could survive the challenges facing it. So much had changed since 1911, the last time that Canadians had voted in a peacetime election. Rather than bringing people together, the war had widened the gulf between Quebec and the rest of Canada and exposed deep regional and class divisions. A generation of young men had been lost in the trenches, and even those who survived were often scarred for life. With the enfranchisement of women, the potential electorate had doubled; so, too, had the number of political parties. Canada's status as an independent nation had been further advanced by its involvement in the war, but decisions made in Great Britain and the United States still determined the nation's well-being. Would Canada, like many nation-states cobbled together in the nineteenth century, simply dissolve into chaos? Or would the sacrifices and conflicts generated by the Great War inspire Canadians to work harder to develop a sense of national purpose?

NOTES

1. Quoted in Tim Cook, *At the Sharp End: Canadians Fighting the Great War, 1914–1916* (Toronto: Viking Canada, 2007) 129. See also Cook, *Shock Troops: Canadians Fighting the Great War, 1917–1918* (Toronto: Viking Canada, 2008).

2. For a survey on the war at home and abroad, see Desmond Morton and J.L. Granatstein, *Marching to Armageddon: Canadians and the Great War, 1914–1919* (Toronto: Lester and Orpen Dennys, 1989). On the fortunes of the expeditionary force sent to Russia, see Benjamin Isitt, *From Victoria to Vladivostok: Canada's Siberian Expedition, 1917–19* (Vancouver: University of British Columbia Press, 2010).

3. Daphne Read, ed., *The Great War and Canadian Society: An Oral History* (Toronto: New Hogtown Press, 1978) 100.

4. Tim Cook, *The Madman and the Butcher: The Sensational Wars of Sam Hughes and General Arthur Currie* (Toronto: University of Toronto Press, 2010) and "Currie, Sir Arthur," in the *Dictionary of Canadian Biography*, http://www.biographi.ca.

5. Cited in Morton and Granatstein, *Marching to Armageddon*, 5–6.

6. Jonathan Vance, *Death So Noble: Memory, Meaning, and the First World War* (Vancouver: UBC Press, 1997).

7. Elizabeth Armstrong, *The Crisis of Quebec, 1914–1918* (Toronto: McClelland & Stewart, 1974) 247–50.

8. Cited in Alison Prentice et al., *Canadian Women: A History* (Toronto: Harcourt, Brace Jovanovich, 1988) 207.

9. Cited in James W. St G. Walker, "Race and Recruitment in World War I: Enlistment of Visible Minorities in the Canadian Expeditionary Force," *Canadian Historical Review* 70, 1 (March 1989) 1–26.

10. Mark Osborne Humphries, "The Horror at Home: The Canadian Military and the 'Great' Influenza Pandemic of 1918," *Journal of the Canadian Historical Association* 16 (2005) 235–61.

11. Esyllt W. Jones, *Influenza 1918: Disease, Death, and Struggle in Winnipeg* (Toronto: University of Toronto Press, 2007) 61.

12. Defense Committee, *The Winnipeg General Sympathetic Strike, May-June 1919* (Winnipeg: Wallingford Press, 1919) 184–6.

13. Paul-André Linteau, René Durocher, and Jean-Claude Robert, *Quebec: A History, 1867–1929* (Toronto: Lorimer, 1983) 524.

14. See, for example, J.L. Granatstein and J.M. Hitsman, *Broken Promises: A History of Conscription in Canada* (Toronto: Oxford University Press, 1977) 67.

15. A.M. Willms, "Conscription 1917: A Brief for the Defence," in *Conscription 1917*, ed. Ramsay Cook, Craig Brown, and Carl Berger (Toronto: University of Toronto Press, 1969) 1–14.

16. Robert Rumilly, *Henri Bourassa: la vie publique d'un grand canadien* (Montreal: Éditions Chantecler, 1953) 544.

17. Ramsay Cook, "Dafoe, Laurier and the Formation of the Union Government," in *Conscription 1917*, ed. Cook, Brown, and Berger, 15–38.

18. Morton and Granatstein, *Marching to Armageddon*, 145.

19. Roger Graham, *Arthur Meighen*, vol. 1, *The Door of Opportunity* (Toronto: Clark, Irwin, 1960) 194–95.

20. See, for example, Linteau, Durocher, and Robert, *Quebec: A History, 1867–1929*, 524; Robert Comeau, "L'opposition à la conscription au Québec," in *La Première Guerre mondiale et le Canada: contributions socio-militaires québécoises*, ed. Roch Legault and Jean Lamarre (Montreal: Méridien, 1999) 91–109; and Patrick Bouvier, *Déserteurs et insoumis: Les Canadiens français et la justice militaire, 1914–1918* (Outremont: Athéna éditions, 2003).

21. Granatstein and Hitsman, *Broken Promises*, 78.

22. Granatstein and Hitsman, *Broken Promises*, 269.

23. J.L. Granatstein, "Conscription in the Great War," in *Canada and the First World War: Essays in Honour of Robert Craig Brown*, ed. David Mackenzie (Toronto: University of Toronto Press, 2005) 74.

SELECTED READING

Cook, Tim. *At the Sharp End: Canadians Fighting the Great War, 1914–1916*. Toronto: Viking Canada, 2007

_____. *Shock Troops: Canadians Fighting the Great War, 1917-1918*. Toronto: Penguin, 2008

_____. *Clio's Wars: Canadian Historians and the Writing of the World Wars*. Vancouver: UBC Press, 2006

Friedland, Judith. *Restoring the Spirit: The Beginnings of Occupational Therapy in Canada, 1890–1930*. Montreal: McGill-Queen's University Press, 2011

Glassford, Sarah and Amy J. Shaw, eds. *A Sisterhood of Suffering and Service: Women and Girls of Canada and Newfoundland During the First World War*. Vancouver: UBC Press, 2011

Hadley, Michael L. and Roger Sarty. *Tin-Pots and Pirate Ships: Canadian Naval Forces and German Sea Raiders, 1880–1918*. Montreal: McGill-Queen's University Press, 1991

Hayes, Geoffrey, Andrew Iarocci, and Mike Bechthold, eds. *Vimy Ridge: A Canadian Reassessment*. Waterloo: Wilfrid Laurier University Press, 2007

Heron, Craig, ed. *The Workers' Revolt in Canada, 1917–1925*. Toronto: University of Toronto Press, 1998

Humphries, Mark Osborne. *Spanish Influenza and the Politics of Public Health in Canada*. Toronto: University of Toronto Press, 2012

Isitt, Benjamin. *From Victoria to Vladivostok: Canada's Siberian Expedition, 1917–19*. Vancouver: UBC Press, 2010

Jones, Esyllt. *Influenza 1918: Disease, Death, and Struggle in Winnipeg*. Toronto: University of Toronto Press, 2007

Kordan, Bohdan S. *Enemy Aliens, Prisoners of War: Internment in Canada During the Great War*. Montreal: McGill-Queen's University Press, 2002

Mackenzie, David, ed. *Canada and the First World War: Essays in Honour of Robert Craig Brown*. Toronto: University of Toronto Press, 2005

Mann, Susan. *Margaret Macdonald: Imperial Daughter*. Montreal: McGill-Queen's University Press, 2005

Morton, Desmond. *Fight or Pay: Soldiers' Families in the Great War*. Vancouver: UBC Press, 2004

Morton, Desmond and J.L. Granatstein. *Marching to Armageddon: Canadians and the Great War, 1914–1918*. Toronto: Lester and Orpen Dennys, 1989

Morton, Desmond and Glenn Wright. *Winning the Second Battle: Canadian Veterans and the Return to Civilian Life, 1915–1930*. Toronto: University of Toronto Press, 1987

Oliver, Dean and Laura Brandon. *Canvas of War: Painting the Canadian Experience, 1914–1945*. Vancouver: Douglas and McIntyre/Canadian War Museum, 2000

Rawling, Bill. *Surviving Trench Warfare: Technology and the Canadian Corps, 1914–1918*. Toronto: University of Toronto Press, 1992

Ruffman, Alan and Colin D. Howell, eds. *Ground Zero: A Reassessment of the 1917 Explosion in Halifax Harbour*. Halifax: Nimbus, 1994

Rutherdale, Robert. *Hometown Horizons: Local Responses to Canada's Great War*. Vancouver: UBC Press, 2004

Vance, Jonathan F. *Death So Noble: Meaning, Memory and the First World War*. Vancouver: UBC Press, 1997

Whitaker, Reg, Gregory S. Kealey, and Andrew Parnaby. *Secret Service: Political Policing in Canada from the Fenians to Fortress America*. Toronto: University of Toronto Press, 2012

Wise, S.F. *Canadian Airmen and the First World War*. Toronto: University of Toronto Press, 1980

For a comprehensive list of readings for topics covered in this chapter, please visit http://pearsoncanada.ca/conrad.

CHAPTER 8
THE TURBULENT TWENTIES

In the 1920s, "experts" on children's health joined appliance manufacturers and utility companies to convince Canadian mothers to make purchases that would improve the health of their families. Writing in the *Grain Growers' Guide* in 1920, Dr. Laura S. Hamilton boasted that "from the provincial governments down to the daily papers, inquirers can get directions as to the best literature on the subject, and in many cases that literature will be supplied free."[1] Electric stoves and mechanical refrigerators, she argued, would allow women to pasteurize milk and keep it cold; electric heating and boiled water would provide babies with warm rooms, sterilized bottles, and germ-free laundered clothing.

While most Canadians heard such promising messages, few had the money to heed the advice. City dwellers might get jobs manufacturing these miraculous new products, but the wages of factory workers were rarely enough to buy what they made. Farm families were even less likely to make such purchases. A survey of Manitoba farm homes in 1922 suggested that 60 percent had wood-burning or coal-burning stoves, and few had mechanical refrigerators or even iceboxes. A decade later, only two percent of the province's farm homes had running water.

The discrepancy between industrial production and purchasing power suggests that the "Roaring Twenties" roared for industrialists and a growing middle class, but largely

It is easy to overestimate the distribution of new labour-saving devices for the home in the interwar period. Mary Tidd had neither running water nor electricity in her home in Ross River, Yukon. For her, wash day continued to involve a great deal of physical labour, particularly the constant hauling of water from a well and arduous scrubbing on a washboard. SOURCE: YUKON ARCHIVES, CLAUDE B. TIDD COLLECTION 8533

bypassed the majority of Canadians. This chapter explores the experiences of winners and losers in the 1920s and traces the turbulent politics that accompanied the onset of mass consumer society.

RIDING THE ECONOMIC ROLLER COASTER

Canada, like most nations involved in the First World War, had trouble adjusting its economy to peacetime production. After the armistice, the Union government reduced state spending, slashing defence budgets and resisting pressures to enact social programs. Although veterans received some consideration, the government argued that market forces must make up for the slack resulting from the transition to peacetime conditions. When the Liberals came to power in 1921, they, like their predecessors, focused on reducing the deficit accumulated during the war rather than on stimulating the economy.

Canada's principal trade partners, the United States and Great Britain, followed similar economic policies. As a result, they experienced economic slowdowns that reduced their demand for Canada's exports, which had accounted for a third of the value of Canadian economic output before the war ended. In 1920, near-drought conditions in the southern Prairies and a precipitous drop in wheat prices spelled disaster for the wheat economy. The United States responded to its own economic woes by raising its tariff levels, which had a particularly detrimental effect on Canadian primary producers. In 1921, manufacturing, construction, and transportation industries stagnated, and the GNP dipped an ominous 20.1 percent. As the effects of the slump reverberated throughout the economy, company bankruptcies, unemployment, and migration to the United States rose in tandem.

Recovery began slowly after the trough of the recession in 1922, and by 1924 the cloud of recession in most regions had lifted. From then until 1929 there was significant economic growth. As in the first two decades of the twentieth century, much of the growth in the Canadian economy came from the staples of wheat, pulp and paper, minerals, and hydroelectric power, but the manufacturing sector, protected by tariffs, also expanded impressively, stimulated by a growing demand for automobiles and electrical appliances.

The spectacular expansion of the American economy in the 1920s contributed significantly to investment in Canada and accelerated the long-established tendency of North American economic integration. With their factories running full tilt, the United States became increasingly dependent on foreign resources. By 1924, American capital investment in Canada had exceeded British investment, while trade with the United States was greater than that with Great Britain—although trade with the entire British Empire still exceeded American trade. Surpluses in trade with Britain served to offset Canada's deficit in trade with the United States.

During the recovery, Canadians found their lives reshaped by the acceleration of the Industrial Revolution based on the internal combustion engine, resource development, electrical power, and new chemical processes. These developments continued the long-term decline in the relative number of Canadians employed in primary industries. While secondary industry held its own, employment and investment growth was concentrated in the tertiary, or service, sector, which accounted for more than 50 percent of GNP in 1929

Clerical employment expanded in the postwar period with the growth of the service sector. As this 1924 photograph of an office in Montreal illustrates, many of the new clerical employees were women. While office hierarchies reserved senior administrative posts and better salaries for men, an increasing number of women found employment as secretaries, stenographers, and file clerks. SOURCE: McCORD MUSEUM VIEW-21089

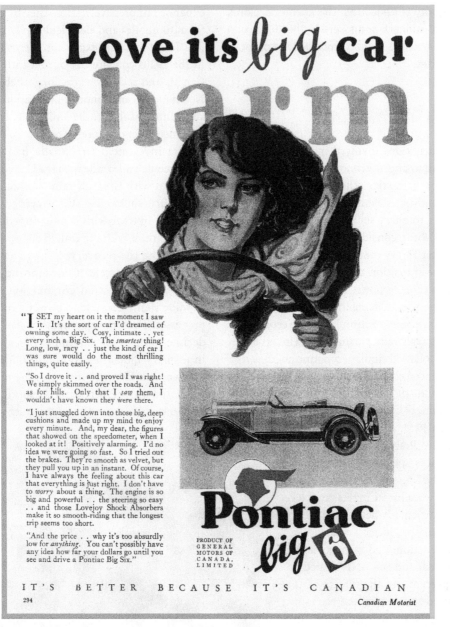

This General Motors of Canada advertisement attempted to appeal both to middle-class women's nationalism and their desire for independence. Pontiac, the Aboriginal leader who tried to expel the British from Native territory in the early 1760s, is presented as a fierce warrior, suggesting that a Pontiac car provided modern, civilized women with the possibility of experiencing the unlimited freedom of an uncivilized, pre-modern man. SOURCE: CANADIAN MOTORIST, JULY 1929

(see Table 8.1). Wholesaling, retailing, banking, and insurance expanded dramatically, while the paperwork associated with corporate enterprise kept offices growing. These trends resulted in continued migration from rural to urban areas and transformed the lives of many Canadians.

Automobiles, the symbol of the modern age, demonstrate why the service sector expanded the most. By

TABLE 8.1

Percentage Sectoral Distribution of the GNP, 1920–1930

YEAR	PRIMARY	SECONDARY	TERTIARY	OTHER
1920	26.6	29.7	35.3	8.4
1930	15.9	26.1	52.3	5.7

Source: William L. Marr and Donald Paterson, *Canada: An Economic History* (Toronto: Gage, 1980) 22

the 1920s, a few Ontario cities had cornered the lion's share of the employment created in the manufacture of automobiles. Nevertheless, every city and most towns across Canada had car dealerships, gas stations, repair shops, auto insurance firms, and tire stores. Public demand for better roads led provincial governments to construct hard-surfaced highways along much-travelled routes. Taxes levied on gasoline and cars helped finance the ribbons of asphalt that cost even more to build and maintain than railway lines. No longer tied to train routes, entrepreneurs built restaurants and cabins along busy highways to cater to the motoring public. Tourism developed to new levels and required more service workers, many of them on a seasonal basis. Governments tested prospective new drivers and issued drivers' licences and vehicle licence plates, and hired police to enforce road and highway regulations. An emerging credit industry benefited from the demand for a product that only the wealthiest consumers could dream of purchasing with ready cash. Advertising firms hired public relations staff to weave the narratives for automobile companies that persuaded families to put themselves in debt to make a status symbol purchase.

Advertising, along with low prices achieved through mass purchases, allowed chain store operations to grab more than 20 percent of the Canadian retail market by the end of the 1920s. Chains became the symbol of consumer society, promoting mass taste and uniformity in culture. Eaton's and Simpson's expanded their operations throughout the country, and outlets of such American companies as Woolworth, Kresge, and Metropolitan stores could be found on the main streets of most Canadian towns. In the grocery business, Dominion and Safeway emerged as prominent names. Direct sales by such companies as Imperial Oil, Kodak, and Singer also emerged as a feature of the retailing scene in the 1920s.

PRIMARY AND SECONDARY INDUSTRIES

As markets for wheat in Great Britain and Europe rebounded, Prairie farmers expanded their acreage and immigration to the West resumed. Between 1925 and 1929, the Prairie provinces produced more than 400 million bushels of wheat annually, and supplied 40 percent of the world's export market. After three decades of expansion, the wheat economy was a complex network of growing, harvesting, and marketing mechanisms.

Vancouver was a major beneficiary of the expanding grain economy. With the opening in 1914 of the Panama Canal, which connected the Pacific and Atlantic oceans for shipping, Vancouver became a major port for selling goods to Europe. Not content to limit its new markets to the products of British Columbia forests and mines, the Pacific coastal metropolis challenged the prewar practice of sending all western grain to Europe via eastern Canada. From 1921 to 1928, Vancouver's annual shipments of grain leaped from 1 million to 100 million bushels. In 1929, 40 percent of Canadian grain shipped abroad left from British Columbia ports. Meanwhile, Winnipeg's economy stagnated as the city lost its status as the warehouse for all the grain going to Europe.

Encouraged by orderly marketing procedures established during the war, western farmers experimented with a system of wheat pools in the 1920s. Producers agreed to sell their wheat to a common pool and share the returns rather than gamble individually on the Winnipeg Grain Exchange. With high prices in the late 1920s, the system worked well, and just over half of the wheat crop was sold through co-ops in 1929. When markets became glutted and prices fell in the 1930s, neither the pools nor private companies could save farmers from ruin.

During the 1920s, pulp and newsprint began to rival "King Wheat" as Canada's principal export. Following the abolition of the American tariff on imported newsprint in 1913, Canadian output grew more than sevenfold to 2 985 000 tons in 1930, making Canada the world's largest producer of newsprint. Much of the investment in pulp and paper came from the United States, which absorbed the bulk of the output. The demand for pulp and paper breathed new life into the forestry industry of the Ottawa, Saint-Maurice, Saguenay, Miramichi, and Humber rivers and animated declining communities such as Liverpool, Nova Scotia, and Kapuskasing, Ontario.

Sir Edward Beatty and Sir Henry Thornton

Edward Wentworth Beatty in 1931 (left) and Sir Henry Thornton in 1927 (right). SOURCES: McCORD MUSEUM II-298323 AND LIBRARY AND ARCHIVES CANADA R231-2263-9-E

During the 1920s, two railway titans became locked in a dramatic battle to capture customers with more railway lines, hotels, ships, and commuter services. Before the Roaring Twenties had passed, additions to Canada's spiffiest hotels included the CPR's Royal York in Toronto and the Lord Nelson in Halifax, along with the CNR's Jasper Park Lodge, the Bessborough Hotel in Saskatoon, and the Nova Scotian in Halifax. The two company presidents responsible for these new facilities provided contrasting personalities and business philosophies.

Born in Thorold, Ontario, in 1877, Edward Wentworth Beatty was appointed president of the CPR in 1918. The son of a wealthy CPR manager, Beatty joined the company's legal department in Montreal in 1901, shortly after being called to the bar in Ontario. A bachelor workaholic, he became the choice of long-time CPR president Lord Shaughnessy to be his successor. Both men were livid that the Canadian

government, rather than allowing the CPR's main competitors to go into bankruptcy or be bought up by the CPR, created the Canadian National Railways to ensure competition in railway services.

Throughout the 1920s, Beatty, with the support of most leading bankers and corporate magnates in Montreal, waged an expensive public relations campaign to persuade politicians that the CPR should be allowed to manage the CNR. He claimed that the competition between the two companies was ruinous to both and was contributing to a huge increase in Canada's national debt. He also argued that, as president of the CPR, he was mainly responsible to company shareholders and that it was his duty to battle unions and to lobby against competition from a government railway that forced the CPR to be cautious in its pricing policies. Until the Depression, both railways posted impressive earnings, and the CPR was able to distribute over 350 million dollars in dividends between 1918 and 1930.

Sir Henry Thornton, the flamboyant president of the CNR, was cut from a different cloth. Born in Logansport, Indiana, in 1871, he had initially been a private railway executive, but he became more supportive of government-owned services after being hired as inspector-general of Allied Transportation in Britain during the Great War. He received a knighthood for his services. As CNR president, Thornton sought close relations with unions and welcomed government input in determining company priorities, arguing that the CNR needed to be as concerned about the public interest as it was with turning a profit. Thornton lived lavishly, enjoyed the nightlife, and scandalized some of Canada's political elite by divorcing his first wife to marry a much younger woman.

The two men clashed frequently, but never more so than during the Great Depression when both railways faced financial difficulties. With ruthless competition threatening ruin, the two presidents suggested ways to save Canada's railways. Thornton proposed a supervisory board composed of politicians and a labour representative that would oversee the operations of the two railways and enforce cooperation when that appeared desirable. In contrast, Beatty proposed "unification" of the two railways under CPR control, arguing that "some of the most efficient, most widely administered and most public-spirited public corporations on this continent are monopolies."[2]

Although Beatty persuaded most Canadian senators to champion his cause as early as 1925, elected MPs of all parties recognized that they would face the wrath of voters if they supported a private monopoly in the railway sector. Thornton felt compelled to resign as CNR president in 1932 because the Conservative government was hostile to him as a Liberal appointee and blamed him for the company's problems. He died the following year. Beatty hoped that the fall of his nemesis would help his unification plan, but it was not to be. Angry that elected politicians refused to stand up to the masses, Beatty, joined by many corporate leaders, attempted to persuade the Liberals and Conservatives to end political competition by forming a "National Government" that would hand him the CNR on a silver platter. The Liberals would have none of it and Beatty's plan went nowhere. He was knighted in 1935 and continued to play a leadership role in the business community until he died in 1943.

Unplanned growth in the newsprint industry resulted in cut-throat competition and unstable market conditions. Six companies controlled 86 percent of Canada's newsprint industry, but were unable to bring order to the market. Between 1920 and 1926, the price of newsprint dropped from $136 to $65 a ton. Efforts by Quebec premier Louis-Alexandre Taschereau to encourage price fixing proved futile because the big American publishers, demanding low prices, proved more than a match for the newsprint producers. By the end of the decade, over half of the productive capacity was located in Quebec, where abundant and accessible forest resources, cheap labour, and low power rates attracted capital.

Quebec also accounted for nearly 50 percent of Canada's hydroelectric energy production. Other provinces lagged far behind Quebec and Ontario, although British Columbia had huge hydro potential and, together with the Yukon, produced nearly 10 percent of Canada's hydroelectric power. Because of the availability of abundant hydroelectric resources, Canada became the site of aluminum manufacture. Bauxite from the West Indies was imported to Quebec, where intensive electrolysis isolated aluminum for industrial use. By the 1930s, the Aluminum Company of Canada had emerged as the world's second-largest aluminum producer. Its new reduction plant in Arvida, Quebec, was one of the marvels of Canada's industrial age.

Canada's mining frontier continued to attract investment. New developments during the 1920s included gold and copper mines in the Abitibi region of Quebec and copper-zinc mines in Flin Flon, Manitoba. Sudbury's nickel mines enjoyed exploding demand, while markets for British Columbia's silver, copper, lead, and zinc more than replaced slumping demand for its coal. Alberta's oil fields witnessed significant development, but only five percent of Canadian petroleum consumption was supplied by Canadian wells. The rest was imported from the United States, the Caribbean, Latin America, and Borneo.

In the manufacturing sector, consumer durables—automobiles, radios, household appliances, and furniture—were the big success story of the 1920s. Automobile and household appliance prices fell during the 1920s, coming increasingly within reach of the middle-class consumer. As home to the largest concentration of consumers, Ontario was also home to most plants producing consumer durables. Between 1920 and 1930, the number of cars jumped from 1 for every 22 Canadians to 1 for every 8.5. Ford's economic Model T was particularly popular until GM's Chevrolet managed to capture the fancy of consumers in the late 1920s.

Canada's independent automobile manufacturers were left in the dust by the "Big Three" American firms—Ford, General Motors, and Chrysler—which controlled two-thirds of the Canadian market. High tariffs on imported cars encouraged the American giants to establish branch plants to supply the Canadian market as well as the British Empire, in which Canada had a tariff advantage. By the 1920s, Canada's automobile industry was the second-largest in the world, and exports accounted for more than a third of its output. The spectacular growth of Oshawa, Windsor, and Walkerville, where the assembly plants of the big automobile manufacturers were located, was proof enough of the significance of "the great god Car." By 1928, automobile manufacturing employed more than 16 000 people directly, and many more in parts and service. The burgeoning industry gobbled up iron, rubber, plate glass, leather, aluminum, lead, nickel, tin, and, of course, gasoline. In 1926–1927, the federal government reduced tariffs on automobiles in an effort to bring down prices and introduced Canadian content rules to encourage more parts manufacturing in Canada.

Demand for radios as an essential home entertainment gadget led the postwar expansion in the electrical appliance industry, which was also fuelled by the new popularity of washing machines, toasters, electric ranges, and vacuum cleaners in middle-class urban households. Canadian General Electric and Westinghouse were the giants of appliance manufacturing, and during the decade, Hoover, Philco, and Phillips became household names. Only a few Canadian-owned companies, such as Moffatt and Rogers Majestic, managed to carve out a niche for themselves in the rapidly expanding appliance market.

ECONOMIC COLLAPSE

The impressive growth in some consumer durable, service, and staple industries masked problems in other areas of the Canadian economy. In agriculture and the fisheries, export markets were often blocked by tariffs, soft markets, and stiff competition. Primary producers across the country experimented with cooperative marketing organizations and attempted to improve their efficiency by investing in new machinery, but they were always at the mercy of market forces over which they had little control. At the same time, many industries that defined the first phase of the Industrial Revolution, including railways, coal, and iron and steel, were forced to restructure. Only the Hamilton-based companies Stelco and Dofasco, fattened by the demands of the automobile industry, survived the 1920s unscathed. It was a measure of the limited number of high-paying jobs available in the 1920s that workers used pull or bribes to find work in a steel plant.

A few Canadians made fortunes by riding the waves of opportunity that emerged in the 1920s, but the economic transition brought only hardship to many. Historian Michiel Horn suggests that during the interwar period, "it is likely that more than half of the Canadian people were never anything but poor."[3] In 1929, the average wage of $1200 per year was $230 below what social workers estimated a family required to live above poverty level. The Roaring Twenties did not even purr for many Canadians, but worse was yet to come.

By late 1929, the problems experienced in a few industries and in some regions throughout the 1920s were becoming nation-wide. The crash of the New York stock market on 29 October 1929 signalled the beginning of the Great Depression that lasted until the outbreak of the Second World War in 1939. A symbol of the underlying problems in the international economy, the crash reflected the shaky foundations upon which the prosperity of the period from 1924 to 1929 had been based. The unprecedented productivity made possible by new technologies was unmatched by gains in consumer purchasing power. In most countries, the workers' and farmers' incomes lagged far behind the availability of new goods. Economic growth was unsustainable without markets. Unable to have much of an impact on international trade, Canadian politicians were deeply divided about how to promote prosperity and economic stability.

King and Canada

The career of William Lyon Mackenzie King sheds some light on the changing economic and social scene in Canada in the interwar years. The grandson of the leader of the Upper Canada Rebellion of 1837, King had been a prominent civil servant and served as Canada's first minister of labour in the final years of the Laurier regime. During the First World War, he amassed a fortune as a consultant for American corporations attempting to dampen labour radicalism, beginning with John D. Rockefeller's coal-mining interests in Colorado. In 1918, King published a book entitled *Industry and Humanity: A Study in the Principles Underlying Industrial Reconstruction*, in which he emphasized the role of the state in reconciling what he saw as the ultimately common interests of labour and capital.

When Laurier died early in 1919, the Liberal Party decided to hold a leadership convention in Ottawa to secure maximum publicity. Previously, both national parties had allowed a few insiders to choose the leader. In response to postwar labour and farmer radicalism, the Liberals adopted a platform that included promises of state-funded old-age pensions, unemployment insurance, and health care. Liberal power brokers viewed King as a logical candidate to convince Canadians of the party's reformist intentions, while reassuring vested interests that they would not be unduly disrupted. When he agreed to run for the Liberal Party leadership, wealthy Canadians, headed by the heir to the Salada Tea fortune, assembled a trust fund to ensure that King's decision to enter political life would not affect his standard of living. King easily bested his only rival for the party leadership, the aging former minister of finance in Laurier's cabinet, William S. Fielding.

The Liberals won the 1921 federal election and King moved cautiously, acting on social policy only when convinced that popular pressure gave him no other choice. Throughout his political career, he felt constrained in his liberal tendencies by the combined pressures of big corporations, conservative elements in his party, and provincial premiers determined to protect their constitutional jurisdictions. Depression and wartime radicalism gradually pushed him to implement a variety of reforms, including means-tested old-age pensions, national unemployment insurance, and family allowances.

The Prime Minister's caution in domestic policy was equalled on the international front. He believed firmly that

William Lyon Mackenzie King governed the country from 1921 to 1930 and again from 1935 to 1948. This photo was taken in 1926, the year he formed his first majority government. SOURCE: LIBRARY AND ARCHIVES CANADA C-9062

national unity and Liberal Party unity depended upon accommodating Quebec, which had turned firmly against the Conservative Party as a result of the imposition of conscription in 1917. Although King supported Canada's membership in the League of Nations and had a sentimental attachment to Great Britain, he emphasized Canada's North American character and was reluctant to commit the country to European wars. He joined the leaders of Ireland and South Africa in pressing Great Britain for recognition of the dominions as autonomous nations. An independent Canada might choose to support Britain if it went to war, but would not automatically be involved as was the case in 1914. For King, the League was a place where the world's nations could discuss contentious issues rather than a body to impose collective action against individual nations accused of having acted aggressively against other members.

King's contemporaries had difficulty following the twists and turns of his political thought. After his death, he became even more of an enigma when his diaries revealed a side of Canada's longest-running prime minister known only to his closest friends. In the pages of these intensely intimate documents, King is shown as a mystic, a believer in numerology, and a devotee of séances and fortune tellers. He provided a sycophantic account of his meeting with Adolf Hitler in Berlin in June 1937, giving no indication of unhappiness with either Hitler's treatment of the Jews or his arming of the Spanish fascists who were battling the elected government of Spain. He also made a variety of anti-Semitic remarks, which might help to explain his government's unwillingness to provide a haven for Jews attempting to flee fascist regimes in Europe.

THE CHANGING POLITICAL LANDSCAPE

The 1921 federal election set the stage for a new era in Canadian political life. Not only did new political parties win seats, but the result also produced the country's first minority government. The Conservative defeat came as no surprise. The Union government had begun to disintegrate shortly after the armistice, with its Liberal members either returning to their old political home or joining the new Progressive Party. While Arthur Meighen brought new leadership to the Conservative Party following Borden's retirement in 1920, he was unpopular. An arch-defender of the Tory policies of high tariffs, he also had to live down his involvement in imposing conscription in 1917 and in sending the Mounties to quash the Winnipeg strikers in 1919. He faced the new leader of the Liberal Party, William Lyon Mackenzie King, who had played no role in the Union government and who accused the Unionists of mismanaging the economy and being responsible for the recession. Although the Liberal convention of 1919 had called for deep tariff cuts and the legislation of social insurance programs, King made few promises during the election, wanting the Tory record and not his promises to become the election issue.

The Conservatives were reduced to only 50 seats; the Liberals won 116. The Liberal sweep of Quebec's 65 ridings was expected, given the province's lingering hostility to conscription. The real surprise was the success of the Progressive Party, which had come second to the Liberals with 65 seats. Calling for the public ownership of utilities and a speedy elimination of all tariffs, the Progressives apparently struck a responsive chord among rural residents in English Canada, winning seats in Ontario and the West and one in New Brunswick.

The result followed a provincial trend that began in Ontario in 1919 with the election of a minority government headed by the United Farmers in coalition with the Independent Labour Party. The following year, a Farmer–Labour coalition emerged as the opposition in Nova Scotia. In 1921, the United Farmers of Alberta headed a majority government even though they had run candidates only in rural seats and had won just 28 percent of the popular vote. In 1922, Manitoba also elected a Farmers' government. Yet by 1929, the national Progressive Party was on life support and would be swept away entirely by the Depression. The United Farmers of Ontario enjoyed only one term of office, their Manitoba counterparts merged with the Liberals in 1932, and Alberta's Farmers were eviscerated by Social Credit in 1935. In Quebec, though the party participated in the 1923 provincial elections, it only managed to field four candidates, none of whom were elected, and it quickly disappeared thereafter. Divisions within the farm movement and an effort by the old-line parties to respond to issues raised by the Progressives caused this occupation-based movement to collapse within two decades of its founding.

THE PROGRESSIVE PARTY

The Progressive Party arose as an attempt by the organized farm movement to unite farmers around a political program and elect members of Parliament who would speak for farmers' interests. Frustrated by their declining political power and business dominance in the Liberal and Conservative parties, many farmers found the idea of a new political party attractive.

Despite the widespread discontent in most farming communities, the Progressive Party faced real obstacles in becoming a truly national party. Its first leader, Thomas A. Crerar, had been a conscriptionist Liberal and a cabinet minister in Borden's Union government, which limited his appeal in rural Quebec. Like Canadians generally, the Progressives were divided on questions of economic restructuring. Opposition to tariffs held party supporters together, but there were strong disagreements on the merits of public control of railways, utilities, and the marketing of grain.

At best, Progressives were a loose coalition of provincial organizations. On the conservative side, disenchanted imperialist Liberals, mostly from Ontario and Manitoba, focused on the party's reform agenda and rejected any notion of transforming the economic and political system. A more radical wing, based primarily in Alberta and led by Henry Wise Wood, rejected the party system altogether and claimed that elected representatives should be free to vote as their constituents wished rather than forced to support the party line. Wood felt that the party system subordinated local MPs to the urban central Canadian party leadership.

Although many Progressives were committed to more democratic, participatory politics, most party leaders simply wanted the Liberal Party to get rid of tariffs. First Crerar, and then his successor as Progressive leader, Robert Forke, accepted the wily King's invitations to join his party and cabinet when the radicals had frustrated their attempts to create a traditional party machine. In an effort to lure moderate Progressives into the Liberal fold, King lowered tariffs on farm machinery and equipment and acceded to Prairie demands to complete a rail link to the port of Churchill. King also restored the Crow rate (the favourable freight rates on grain negotiated with the CPR in 1897, and later applied to all railways), which had been suspended in wartime. In the late 1920s, he surrendered federal control over the natural resources of the Prairie provinces.

THE KING–BYNG AFFAIR

Prime Minister King's political manoeuvring also played a role in reducing the impact of the Progressive Party. In the 1925 election, the Liberals carried 101 seats, with the resurgent Conservatives taking 116 thanks to Maritime discontent and solid support from Ontario. King formed another minority government by wooing the low-tariff Progressives, who had been reduced to 24 seats, almost all in western Canada, and conceding a means-tested old-age pension (introduced in 1927) for the support of the two Labour MPs.

The Progressives and Labour joined the Conservatives in defeating the government in June 1926 with a motion of censure regarding widespread corruption in the Customs Department. When King asked Governor General Byng to dissolve Parliament and call another election, Byng exercised his prerogative to ask Arthur Meighen to form a government. Meighen's ministry lasted less than three days, making it the shortest-lived government in Canadian history, but it gave King the opportunity he needed to shift the emphasis of the 1926 election away from the customs scandal.

During the campaign, King made political hay out of Byng's refusal to accept his advice to dissolve Parliament, advancing the questionable claim that the governor general had violated the principle of responsible government. In the end, the customs issue and the King–Byng disagreement may have cancelled each other out, allowing King to aim specific promises to the West and the Maritimes, conceding only tariff-hungry Ontario to the Conservatives. Westerners seemed particularly keen to abandon the Progressives in order to keep Arthur Meighen, viewed as the high priest of protection, out of office. On 14 September 1926, the Liberals won enough seats to give King his first majority government.

POLITICAL WOMEN

For women who had been recently enfranchised, the interwar period failed to yield significant political progress. Only nine women sat in provincial legislatures before 1940, with none outside the western provinces, and only two won seats in the House of Commons. The reasons for this unimpressive showing are complex. Following the granting of suffrage, the women's movement lost its single focus, and women sorted themselves according to class, regional, and cultural interests. Professional women on the edge of the male-dominated public world continued to argue for equality of opportunity, especially in the context of blatantly discriminatory hiring practices, but they framed their arguments in the language of human, not women's, rights.

Their caution was understandable. In the interwar years, popular culture equated feminism and women's rights with "man-hating" and the promotion of "sex wars" to such an extent that many women in public life were quick to deny any association with feminist doctrines. A feminist agenda had to be disguised as an effort to strengthen the family or the nation to avoid immediate condemnation from the men who headed the country's political organizations. In some cases, even this was not enough. In Quebec, despite the efforts of maternal feminists such as Marie Gérin-Lajoie, Idola Saint-Jean, and Thérèse Casgrain to show that conceding voting rights to women was in no way contrary to Catholic doctrine or to the survival of the French-Canadian "race," the province's male politicians and clergy remained on the whole adamantly opposed to the measure.

The women's sections of farm organizations demonstrated the strengths and weaknesses of 1920s feminism. Having won the battle for the vote, women's organizations used their political influence to convince governments to spend money to improve community services. Irene Parlby, president of the United Farm Women of Alberta (UFWA) from 1917 to 1921 and later the first female member of the Alberta cabinet, argued that rural homes could be strong only if their residents worked together to provide health, educational, and recreational facilities in their communities. Saskatchewan farm women, led by Violet McNaughton, spearheaded a movement to have municipalities hire salaried doctors and work together to create "union hospitals" that served a large agricultural district. This constituted the first step in Saskatchewan's march toward becoming the first jurisdiction in North America to provide public hospital insurance (1947) and medical insurance (1962). Farm women's organizations also fought for better protection of women's property rights both within marriage and during divorce. The UFWA attempted to persuade the provincial government to establish family planning clinics, but it made little headway on "women's issues" with the largely male UFA cabinet.

One concession won by the women's movement in most provinces was mothers' allowances. Beginning in Manitoba in 1916, mothers' allowances had been instituted in all the western provinces and Ontario by 1920. Other provinces, such as Quebec which acted only in 1937, dragged their heels. The allowance programs provided funds to some women in desperate need, but their detailed regulations in most provinces reflected a conservative gender ideology. There was close surveillance of recipients to ensure that they lived chaste lives and spent the allowances on necessities. Only widows and, in some provinces, wives of men unable to support their families

for medical reasons were eligible. Never-married, single mothers need not apply. The allowances were too small to keep a woman-headed family with no other income out of poverty.

While women achieved little electoral representation in the 1920s and lacked the vote in Quebec provincial elections until 1940, they made some progress toward political equality. In 1929, five Alberta women were instrumental in convincing the Judicial Committee of the Privy Council that women were "persons" under the law. Without this recognition, women had been excluded from appointment to the Senate and other privileged institutions. The five women who took up the so-called Persons Case were Nellie McClung, suffrage activist, writer, and former Liberal MLA; Emily Murphy,

Agnes Macphail in 1934, while she was a United Farmers of Ontario MP and a member of the Progressive caucus. Elected in 1921, Agnes Macphail was Canada's first female MP. A teacher from Grey County, Ontario, she sat as a Progressive and soon made her mark as a defender of farmers, workers, women, and prisoners. After her defeat in the federal election of 1940, she served as a CCF member in the Ontario legislature from 1943 to 1945 and 1948 to 1951, during which time she was responsible for the enactment of the first equal-pay legislation in Canada. SOURCE: LIBRARY AND ARCHIVES CANADA C-21562

Violet Clara McNaughton

In the early twentieth century Violet McNaughton emerged as the leading voice for Prairie farm women. Her biographer, Georgina M. Taylor, classifies her as an "agrarian feminist," one of a large number of women working in agriculture who emphasized both the need for the farm to be treated as a production unit in which gender equality was practised, and for improvements to "the poor conditions in which farm women and their families lived by using the principles of agrarian co-operation."[4]

Born in north Kent in England in 1879, Violet Clara Jackson was a schoolteacher before moving to Canada in 1909 to join her brother and father, who were already homesteading about 100 kilometres southwest of Saskatoon in the Hillview farm district. Appalled by the lack of hospitals, medical personnel, and midwives in rural Saskatchewan, Jackson, who had married homesteader John McNaughton in 1910, decided to devote her life to improving the lot of farm women and farm families after a hysterectomy in 1911 deprived her of her hopes of starting a family.

Organizing local farm women and eventually all women across Saskatchewan, McNaughton was the founder and first president in 1914 of the Women Grain Growers (WGG) and played an important role in the founding of its equivalents in the other two Prairie provinces and Ontario. Under McNaughton, the WGG not only participated in a successful effort to win the vote for women in Saskatchewan in 1916, but also won legislation that allowed rural municipalities to collect taxes to establish hospitals and hire municipal doctors and nurses. This government insurance model of medical coverage caught on and became the basis for Saskatchewan's pioneering provincial efforts, most associated with the name of Premier Tommy Douglas, to insure the medical needs of citizens province-wide. McNaughton is sometimes called the "mother of medicare," though she has received far less attention than Douglas, the "father of medicare."

After the war, McNaughton worked to organize wheat pools and the women-dominated Saskatchewan Egg and Poultry Pool, and served as president of the Council of Farm Women and the Women's Section of the Canadian Council of Agricul-

Violet McNaughton in about 1920. SOURCE: SASKATCHEWAN ARCHIVES BOARD S-B 2042

ture from 1919 to 1923. Politically active in the Progressive Party, she was one of the organizers of the United Farmers of Canada (Saskatchewan section), which became the major founding group of the Cooperative Commonwealth Federation in Saskatchewan in 1932. As women's editor of *The Western Producer* from 1925 to 1950, she campaigned for ethnic harmony, peace, women's inclusion in all spheres of public life, and eventually for an end to discrimination against Native people in Canada. Short of stature, the "mighty atom," as some of her supporters called her, remained a tireless campaigner for the rights of farm women until her death in Saskatoon in 1968.

writer and, in 1916, the first woman magistrate in the British Empire; Irene Parlby; former MLA Louise McKinney; and Henrietta Muir Edwards, a founding member of the National Council of Women of Canada

and the Victorian Order of Nurses. In 1930 King appointed Cairine Wilson, a mother of nine children and a prominent Liberal Party organizer, as the first woman senator in Canada.

FIRST NATIONS IN THE AGE OF DEMOCRACY

In the 1920s, Canada's Aboriginal peoples also began to organize more systematically to reform the political structures that kept them dependent on white authorities. They faced an uphill battle. Status Indians, that is, Aboriginal people whose names appeared on the band register of the Department of Indian Affairs, were still denied the franchise unless they were war veterans, and amendments to the Indian Act in 1920 gave the Department of Indian Affairs the explicit right to ban hereditary chiefdoms and other forms of Native governance.

Interference with Native political practices was a long-standing grievance among status Indians. Prior to the First World War, Chief Deskaheh, a Cayuga, had begun a movement to achieve independence for the Six Nations of Grand River, Ontario. He argued unsuccessfully before the League of Nations in 1923 that they should recognize his people as a sovereign nation. Despite this campaign, Indian Affairs imposed an elective council on the Six Nations in 1924 and banned the hereditary council. Women, who had hitherto preserved their traditional veto in the selection of chiefs, had no vote on the elected council.

Another Six Nations member, Fred O. Loft, founded the League of Indians of Canada in 1918, Canada's first national organization of Aboriginal people. It included representatives from the three Prairie provinces, Ontario, and Quebec. Loft was a well-educated Mohawk from the Six Nations reserve who spent 40 years in the Ontario civil service, mostly as an accountant. The League stressed the importance of improved educational opportunities on reserves and greater cooperation among Native peoples. As Loft observed, "The day is past when one band or a few bands can successfully . . . free themselves from official-dom and from being ever the prey and victims of unscrupulous means of depriving us of our lands and homes and even deny[ing] us the rights we are entitled to as free men under the British flag."[5] Government harassment and police surveillance limited the League's success.

VOICES FROM THE PAST
Indian Affairs' Top Official Speaks His Mind

The Indian Act was amended in 1920 to require that all Native children attend school, even if that forced them to go to residential school, and to give the government the power to "enfranchise" Native people, that is, to revoke their status as an Indian. Duncan Campbell Scott, the deputy superintendent general of the Department of Indian Affairs, spoke to a parliamentary committee that discussed these proposed changes several times in March and April of that year. Scott, a famous Canadian poet whose poetry ironically romanticized the Canadian wilderness and traditional Native ways, was a lifelong bureaucrat in Indian Affairs, and served as the top civil servant in the department from 1913 to 1932.

> The difficulty in the West is with the almost savage people we have there, to get them to realize the benefit of education and to send their children voluntarily. . . . I have endeavoured to mitigate the separation as much as possible by providing that there shall be a holiday every year, and that the Department shall pay the expenses of sending their children home and bringing them back so that the Indian parents will be assured of seeing their children running around the Teepee for a month or six weeks every summer at least.

> . . . I want to get rid of the Indian problem. I do not think as a matter of fact, that this country ought to continuously protect a class of people who are able to stand alone. That is my whole point. I do not want to pass into the citizens' class people who are paupers. That is not the intention of the Bill. But after one hundred years, after being in close contact with civilization it is enervating to the individual or to a band to continue in that state of tutelage, when he or they are able to take their position as British citizens or Canadian citizens, to support themselves, and stand alone. That has been the whole purpose of Indian education and advancement since the earliest times. One of the very earliest enactments was to provide for the enfranchisement of the Indian. So it is written in our law that the Indian was eventually to become enfranchised. It will be many years before this will apply to the Indians in the West. . . .[6]

In the Northwest Territories, the discovery of oil at Norman Wells in 1920 led to greater southern interest in the region. The federal government quickly signed treaty number 11 with representatives of the Dene and the Métis in the region and established a council to support the Northwest Territories' commissioner in his efforts to impose southern control. Treaty 11 Natives soon complained that the federal government was violating guarantees of Native rights to hunt, fish, and trap, and had failed to grant all the reserve lands promised. In 1976, the federal government conceded that the treaty obligations had not been fulfilled, thereby opening the door to new land claims negotiations in the Mackenzie Valley. The Inuit meanwhile were largely ignored by the federal government until the courts ruled in 1939 that the welfare of the Inuit was a federal responsibility.

LABOUR POLITICS

During the 1920s, labour parties steered an uneasy course between socialism and reform. Several provincial labour parties espoused gradual nationalization of major industries and greater labour control of the workplace, but the struggle for immediate reforms for workers—minimum wages for women, improved workers' compensation, federal unemployment insurance—absorbed most of the time of elected Labour representatives. Organized provincially, the labour parties elected few federal members of Parliament during the 1920s, and only the popular J.S. Woodsworth was able to hold his seat for the entire decade.

Within the labour movement, craft union leaders reasserted their supremacy and forestalled the advance of industrial unions. The increased conservatism of labour was partly a result of state repression following the Winnipeg General Strike, but it was also reinforced by the postwar recession. A marked contrast to this trend was the Communist Party of Canada (CPC). Organized furtively in a barn outside Guelph in 1921, the CPC included many of the nation's most committed labour radicals. Communist leadership in the coal fields, garment shops, hard-rock mines, and among northern Ontario bushworkers brought a spirit of militancy to groups either ignored or poorly represented by established unions. Immigrant unskilled labour, particularly Ukrainians, Finns, and Jews, formed the backbone of Canada's Communist Party.

Communist doctrines appealed to Scottish immigrant J.B. McLachlan, whose uncompromising organizational work among the coal miners of Cape Breton brought him into conflict with both company bosses and the

Women's Labour League members in Winnipeg sew dresses for the children of striking Cape Breton coal miners in 1925. SOURCE: PROVINCIAL ARCHIVES OF MANITOBA N13141

conservative American leadership of the United Mine Workers. Convicted in court of seditious libel, McLachlan spent a few months in prison before returning to Cape Breton in 1924 to edit the *Maritime Labour Herald*. The following year, a bitter strike by Cape Breton coal miners focused widespread attention on the troubled island. McLachlan described the efforts of the British Empire Steel Corporation (BESCO) to starve the miners into submission in a letter to J.S. Woodsworth on 6 March 1925:

> Besco cut off all credit to all miners who are idle, that affected about 2500 families. Their jobs gone, their little bit of credit gone, left miners no alternative. The utmost gloom is settling over the mining towns and many of the men are talking the most desperate kind of talk.... The coal company is taking the horses and pumps out of the mines and the local government is allowing this dismantling to take place without a word of protest.[7]

Before the strike ended, one miner, William Davis, had been killed by company police, and Cape Breton miners had become renowned throughout Canada and around the world for their resistance to capitalist exploitation.

THE MARITIME RIGHTS MOVEMENT

Labour unrest in Cape Breton was only one chapter in a large volume of woes facing people in the Maritime provinces. Manufacturing declined by 40 percent between 1917 and 1921, and the recession that gripped the national economy in the early 1920s never entirely lifted in the region. Nearly 150 000 people drifted to greener pastures to find work in the 1920s. Maritimers watched with dismay as national leaders ignored their problems—too busy, they bitterly concluded, catering to central Canada and the West. Particularly galling was the policy of railway consolidation that merged the Intercolonial into the CNR and moved its head office to Toronto. Not only were jobs lost and freight rates

dramatically increased, but Saint John and Halifax were also abandoned as major terminals of international trade.

The hope of redressing grievances seemed remote. As the population of the Maritimes declined relative to the rest of the nation, the political power of the region, including their representation in Parliament, plummeted. Convinced that their interests, already largely ignored, would be shunted aside completely, Maritimers of all classes and interests came together to fight for "Maritime rights." The Maritime Rights Movement was led by business and professional interests who hoped that by adopting a regional rather than a provincial approach they could force Ottawa to respond to their concerns. Within the movement, Maritimers demanded larger federal subsidies, national transportation policies that took the region's needs into account, and tariff policies that offered protection for the Maritime coal and steel industries.

The federal Liberal Party had won most of the Maritime constituencies in the 1921 election, but when King subsequently dismissed the concerns of his Maritime backbenchers, the region turned to the Conservative Party as a vehicle for promoting its interests. Needing all the help

Lawren Harris (1885-1970), *Miners' Houses, Glace Bay*, c. 1925. This grim representation of life in a mining town depicts the miners' lives and work as one. The pollution over the town and the rows of identical, stark-looking homes combine to make the miners' town look much like the underground of a coal mine, as well as a cemetery. SOURCE: ART GALLERY OF ONTARIO

he could get in the 1925 and 1926 elections, King promised action. He set up the Royal Commission on Maritime Claims in 1926, naming as its head British lawyer-industrialist Sir Andrew Rae Duncan. Recognizing that Maritime governments were forced to tax their citizens more than other provincial governments to maintain a minimal level of services, Duncan called for a series of provincial subsidies based on need. He also recommended a revision of freight rates, assistance to the region's coal and steel industries, better ferry connections to Prince Edward Island, and improvements to port facilities at Halifax and Saint John to encourage international trade through the region.

While King appeared to embrace the Duncan Report, his government refused to fully implement its recommendations. The Maritime Freight Rates Act of 1927 helped the region's producers compete more effectively in central Canadian markets, but provincial subsidies based on need proved too hot a concept for the government to handle. So, too, was the plight of the region's fisheries, which became the subject for yet another commission of inquiry. Some assistance was provided to move Maritime coal to Quebec markets, but further aid to the coal and steel industries was deferred.

NEWFOUNDLAND'S DILEMMA

Newfoundland, like the Maritimes, saw little prosperity in the 1920s and sought political solutions to the dilemma of poverty in the midst of plenty. When Richard Anderson Squires became premier in November 1919, he headed a coalition government made up of members of the Liberal Reform Party allied with William Coaker's Fishermen's Protective Union. As minister responsible for the fisheries, Coaker set minimum market prices for cod and penalties for exporters who attempted to undersell. He also established a government-controlled fish-culling system, with trade agents hired in foreign markets. In 1921, the regulations were repealed because exporters simply ignored them. The fisheries failed to make the transition to an industrial economy, with results that would prove disastrous.

Although Newfoundland already carried a heavy debt load from earlier railway construction and the financing of the war effort, Premier Squires borrowed more money. He used it for projects designed to make Newfoundland a more attractive site for investors as well as to oil his party's patronage machine. One bright spot during the decade

was the decision by the Judicial Committee of the Privy Council in 1927 in Newfoundland's favour in the long-standing border dispute between Labrador and Quebec. The government was so indebted that Squires tried to sell its resource-rich windfall, but no one was interested.

ONTARIO AND QUEBEC: POLITICS AND IDEOLOGY

The Farmer–Labour government of Ontario, formed after the 1919 election, lasted only one term. Unlucky to have their entire period in office marked by recession, this government alienated urban residents with its puritanical stances on liquor, gambling, and Sunday entertainments. George H. Ferguson's Conservatives roared back to power in 1923. Buoyed by a reviving economy, they succeeded in marginalizing the upstart class-based parties that had emerged so forcefully after the war.

Ferguson invested public funds in a provincial highway system, promoting in particular roads linking the region's northern forestry and mining communities with southern Ontario. He established the Liquor Control Board of Ontario to replace Prohibition with state regulation, and the Department of Public Welfare to increase the state's presence in the lives of the poor. A lifelong member of the Orange Order, Ferguson could not be accused of being part of a French Catholic plot when he repealed the contentious Regulation 17 and legislated a limited right to French-language education in elementary grades. While continuing Ontario's long-standing efforts to limit federal intervention in areas of provincial jurisdiction, he brought Ontario into the federal means-tested pension plan legislated in 1927.

Quebec remained a Liberal fiefdom under Louis-Alexandre Taschereau, premier from 1920 to 1936. Like other provincial leaders, Taschereau embarked on a program of building roads and encouraging foreign investment. He also proposed educational and welfare reforms, but was forced to compromise in the face of church opposition to any weakening of its long-standing control over education and social services. Despite church opposition, his government passed a law in 1921 which provided limited assistance for the hospitalization of indigent patients and is often seen as the first major incursion of the Quebec state into social welfare. Even more resistant to federal intrusions than his Ontario counterpart, Taschereau refused until 1936 to participate in Ottawa's pension system. A member of the board of directors of an array of large corporations, even as he served as premier, Taschereau had little sympathy with either clerical or labour critiques of the practices of increasingly powerful companies in the province.

The Liberal Party's stranglehold on provincial politics in Quebec was facilitated by the weakness of the provincial Conservative Party, tainted by its association with the federal Conservatives and by a change in tactics by the conservative nationalist movement founded by Bourassa. In the 1920s, conservative nationalist intellectuals, now led by historian and clergyman Abbé Lionel Groulx, largely abandoned electoral politics and focused instead on intellectual avenues, such as the journal *Action française* (founded in 1917) and groups such as the Association catholique de la jeunesse canadienne-française (founded in 1904). Like Bourassa, they continued to preach the fundamental importance of the family and the Catholic Church as guardians of the French-Canadian race, and to denounce the evils caused by industrialization and urbanization, advocating a return to agriculture.

In the aftermath of conscription and discriminatory language legislation in anglophone provinces, Henri Bourassa's pan-Canadian nationalist vision for francophones gradually gave way to a focus on Quebec alone as the homeland of francophone Catholic culture. Groulx and other nationalists even flirted with the idea of independence for their beloved province. Nationalists denounced the control of Quebec's economy by foreign capital and the economic marginalization of francophones in the province, and some came to see the Quebec state as part of the solution to francophone economic inferiority.

While the ideas of conservative nationalists were largely shared by the powerful clergy and were disseminated by Catholic newspapers such as *Le Devoir* (Montreal) and *L'Action catholique* (Quebec City), their influence over Quebec society was far from hegemonic. Even within the nationalist movement itself, there were more progressive streams, such as those involved in the École sociale populaire (founded in 1911), which focused on how Catholicism and the new social order could be reconciled. And though the Quebec Conservative Party increasingly allied itself with conservative nationalists, it was unable to dislodge the Taschereau Liberals.

CONCLUSION

The 1920s ended as they had begun in Canada, with the country mired in economic recession, but much had changed during the decade, which had provided a tantalizing glimpse of technology-induced prosperity. By the late twenties, Canadians who could afford to do so drove cars, listened to radios, and bought electrical appliances for their homes. Those without enough money to buy such luxuries began to gravitate toward movements and organizations that promised to spread the wealth more equitably. Although economic and political policy remained in the hands of free-market supporters, they would have a lot of explaining to do when the Great Depression descended in 1929.

A HISTORIOGRAPHICAL DEBATE
In Search of William Lyon Mackenzie King

William Lyon Mackenzie King has generated more divisive assessments from Canadian historians than perhaps any other prime minister. Cautious to a fault in his public persona, King no doubt contributed to the controversies by keeping a capacious daily diary that he intended to draw upon when he wrote his memoirs. In the end he produced no memoirs, but his expressed wishes to have most of the diary material destroyed when he died were ignored by his literary executors. They recognized the significance of such a rich source of historical information on Canada's longest-serving prime minister and made their decision on the grounds that his instructions were imprecise. Filled with contradictory sentiments on many topics, along with mean-spirited attacks on allies and opponents alike, the diaries also often appear to contradict King's public actions and speeches.[8]

The historians chosen by the King estate to write biographies of his life focused on King's knack for reconciling perspectives that threatened to tear the country apart. For Blair Neatby, writing about King in the interwar period, the Liberal prime minister proved able to provide just enough support to French-Canadian nationalists, British imperialists, and free traders and pacifists attracted to North American continentalism to create a governing coalition that held Canada together. Neatby credited King with understanding in particular the depths of alienation from the national government felt in Quebec and western Canada, and following policies that appeased both regions.[9]

Donald Creighton, the famed biographer of John A. Macdonald, rejected the notion of King as compromiser. Studying King's policies from 1939 to his retirement in 1948, Creighton alleged that King had contempt for Britain and the British Empire, and followed policies that inextricably linked Canada's economy, along with its foreign and defence policies, with the United States. For Creighton, King's appeasement of the regions reflected the lack of a true national vision.[10] Creighton's defence of the British Empire has, in turn, been treated as quaint and unfair to King by historians such as J.L. Granatstein, who recognized King's skill as a political operator.[11]

While Creighton is the historian most critical of King's alleged lack of national purpose, C.P. Stacey, a military historian, raised troubling questions about the personality of the Prime Minister. Stacey suggested that King was an embarrassment to Canadians with his visits to prostitutes to reform them, his flirtations with married women, and, above all, his séances with his dead mother, politicians, and his dog Pat.[12] Writing almost four decades later, Christopher Dummitt suggests that Stacey judged King through the prism of a particular vision of manhood that was prevalent in Stacey's generation to which King failed to measure up. In Dummitt's view, the military-minded and fairly conventional Stacey failed to grasp that King's attitudes and behaviour fit in well with those of many Victorian gentlemen, and that King needs to be viewed in the light of the times that shaped him, not judged as bizarre because he seemed that way to men of the generation that followed him.[13]

King presented himself publicly as a reformer, and many historians praise his introduction of new social programs, suggesting that he sincerely wished to create a more advanced welfare state than the federal Liberals under his leadership managed to implement. Resistance from conservative and small-minded provincial premiers, they say, stood in King's way.[14] Often making use of King's diaries, others argue that King was in no way a radical reformer and that he manufactured clashes with the premiers so that he could renege on electoral promises that he thought would require too much taxation of corporations and the wealthy.[15]

Given the rich sources of information on King, it is likely that he will continue to generate differing views on his fascinating and complicated life.

NOTES

1. Quoted in Nadine I. Kozak, "Advice Ideals and Rural Prairie Realities: National and Prairie Scientific Motherhood Advice, 1920–29," in *Unsettled Pasts: Reconceiving the West Through Women's History,* eds. Sarah Carter, Lesley Erickson, Patricia Roome, and Char Smith (Calgary: University of Calgary Press, 2005) 182–183.

2. Don Nerbas, *The Dominion of Capital: The Politics of Big Business and the Crisis of the Canadian Bourgeoisie, 1914–1947* (Toronto: University of Toronto Press, 2013) 133.

3. Michiel Horn, ed., *The Dirty Thirties: Canadians in the Great Depression* (Toronto: Copp Clark Pitman, 1972) 14.

4. Georgina M. Taylor, "'Ground for Common Action': Violet McNaughton's Agrarian Feminism and the Origins of the Farm Women's Movement in Canada," unpublished PhD thesis, Carleton University, 1997.

5. Donald B. Smith, "Fred Loft and the Future of the First Nations: A Report on Work in Progress" (unpublished paper).

6. "Testimony of Duncan Campbell Scott Before 1920 House of Commons Committee on Bill 14, 'An Act to Revise the Indian Act,'" in *Reconciling Canada: Critical Perspectives on the Culture of Redress,* eds. Jennifer Henderson and Pauline Wakeham (Toronto: University of Toronto Press, 2013) 305, 312.

7. Quoted in David Frank, *J.B. McLachlan: A Biography* (Toronto: James Lorimer, 1999) 373.

8. The Diaries of William Lyon Mackenzie King are deposited at Library and Archives Canada and are available online in searchable form at http://www.bac-lac.gc.ca/eng/discover/politics-government/prime-ministers/william-lyon-mackenzie-king.

9. H. Blair Neatby, *William Lyon Mackenzie King: The Lonely Heights* (Toronto: University of Toronto Press, 1963); and *William Lyon Mackenzie King 1932–1939: The Prism of Unity* (Toronto: University of Toronto Press, 1976).

10. Donald Creighton, *The Forked Road: Canada 1939–1957* (Toronto: McClelland & Stewart, 1976).

11. J.L. Granatstein, *How Britain's Weakness Forced Canada into the Arms of the United States* (Toronto: University of Toronto Press, 1989).

12. C.P. Stacey, *A Very Double Life: The Private World of Mackenzie King* (Toronto: Macmillan of Canada, 1976).

13. Christopher P. Dummitt, "The Importance of Not Being Earnest: Postwar Canadians Rethink Mackenzie King's Christian Manhood," in *Canadian Men and Masculinities: Historical and Contemporary Perspectives*, eds. Christopher J. Grieg and Wayne J. Martino (Toronto: Canadian Scholars' Press, 2012) 61–75.

14. See particularly Robert Bothwell, Ian Drummond, and John English, *Canada Since 1945: Power, Politics, and Provincialism* (Toronto: University of Toronto Press, 1990).

15. For example, see Alvin Finkel, "Paradise Postponed: A Re-examination of the Green Book Proposals of 1945," *Journal of the Canadian Historical Association*, n.s.4 (Ottawa 1993) 120–142.

SELECTED READING

Badgley, Kerry. *Ringing in the Common Love of Good: The United Farmers of Ontario, 1914–26.* Montreal: McGill-Queen's University Press, 2000

Bélanger, Damien-Claude. *Prejudice and Pride: Canadian Intellectuals Confront the United States, 1891–1945.* Toronto: University of Toronto Press, 2011

Cadigan, Sean. *Death on Two Fronts: Newfoundland Tragedies and the Fate of Democracy in Newfoundland, 1914–1934.* Toronto: Allan Lane, 2013

Forbes, Ernest R. *Maritime Rights: The Maritime Rights Movement, 1919–1927.* Montreal: McGill-Queen's University Press, 1979

Frager, Ruth A. and Carmela K. Patrias. *Discounted Labour: Women Workers in Canada, 1870–1939.* Toronto: University of Toronto Press, 2005

Frank, David. *J.B. McLachlan: A Biography.* Toronto: James Lorimer, 1999

Morton, W.L. *The Progressive Party in Canada.* Toronto: University of Toronto Press, 1989

Neatby, H. Blair. *William Lyon Mackenzie King: The Lonely Heights, 1924–1932.* Toronto: University of Toronto Press, 1963

Nerbas, Don. *The Dominion of Capital: The Politics of Big Business and the Crisis of the Canadian Bourgeoisie, 1914–1947.* Toronto: University of Toronto Press, 2013

Parnaby, Andrew. *Citizen Docker: Making a New Deal on the Vancouver Waterfront, 1919–1939.* Toronto: University of Toronto Press, 2008

Pulkingham, Jane, ed. *Human Welfare, Rights, and Social Activism: Rethinking the Legacy of J.S. Woodsworth.* Toronto: University of Toronto Press, 2010

Sharpe, Robert J. and Patricia McMahon. *The Persons Case: The Origins and the Legacy of the Fight for Legal Personhood.* Toronto: University of Toronto Press, 2007

Snell, James G. *The Citizen's Wage: The State and the Elderly in Canada, 1900–1951.* Toronto: University of Toronto Press, 1996

Strong-Boag, Veronica. *The New Day Recalled: Lives of Girls and Women in English Canada, 1919–1939.* Toronto: Copp Clark Pitman, 1988

Struthers, James. *The Limits of Affluence: Welfare in Ontario, 1920–1970.* Toronto: University of Toronto Press, 1994

Thompson, John Herd with Alan Seager. *Canada, 1922–1939: Decades of Discord.* Toronto: McClelland & Stewart, 1985

Vigod, Bernard L. *Quebec Before Duplessis: The Political Career of Louis-Alexandre Taschereau.* Montreal: McGill-Queen's University Press, 1986

Wardhaugh, Robert A. *Mackenzie King and the Prairie West.* Toronto: University of Toronto Press, 2000

For a comprehensive list of readings for topics covered in this chapter, please visit http://pearsoncanada.ca/conrad.

CHAPTER 9
THE GREAT DEPRESSION

As the 1930s Depression descended, Ed Bates, a butcher in Glidden, Saskatchewan, faced with bankruptcy, moved his family and business to Vancouver. There, too, work was scarce and the Bates family was forced to seek relief. Denied welfare by the Vancouver authorities because of their recent arrival in that city, they attempted to get social assistance in Saskatoon, only to be told they must return to Glidden to apply for help. Too proud to return home to live on welfare, they rented a car and attempted suicide by carbon monoxide poisoning. Ed and his wife, Rose, survived, but their son Jack died, and they were charged with his murder. While the Bates's actions had caused Jack's death, local citizens blamed the politicians for the tragedy. A defence committee was formed, and a coroner's jury found Ed and Rose Bates not guilty in the death of their son.[1]

The Bates family tragedy occurred during the Great Depression, an economic catastrophe unprecedented in its intensity. As the human misery mounted, ever-increasing numbers of people came to blame the political and economic system, rather than the individual, for widespread poverty. Movements for reform and even revolution led to the creation of new political parties, and to demands for social insurance and state regulation of industries so that ordinary people would never again be reduced to desperate measures because they could not find work.

Despite the prevalence of such views, the continued conservatism of many Canadians, particularly politicians at all levels, meant that change was slow in coming and the poor suffered terribly. In the rural municipality of Montcalm, Manitoba, for example, unemployed single men were expected to board with area farmers. The municipality provided money for their food to the farmer, not the unemployed individual. As in many other municipalities, families requiring assistance in Montcalm received no direct money, their relief instead given to a grocer, and assistance was provided only to long-time residents. Recent arrivals to the area had to shift for themselves.[2]

In remote areas, particularly Aboriginal communities, many people starved to death. The Hudson's Bay Company responded to sagging markets and profits by cutting off credit to its Native suppliers. Ralph Pearson, fur trade commissioner for the company, reported that a "score" of Inuit died of starvation at Great Whale River in the far north of Quebec in 1931. Their diet had consisted of roots, tree bark, and water. In Rupert's House, also in northern Quebec, an entire Cree family of 13 children died of malnutrition while 10 of the 12 children in another family perished.[3]

THE DIRTY THIRTIES

The panic that began with the Wall Street crash of October 1929 produced a virtual halt in new investments in the Western world that endured through most of the next decade. Once the global downward spiral started, it took on a life of its own. Prices dropped dramatically and then dropped again and again, as producers tried to convince someone to buy their products at any price.

Canada was especially hard hit by the Depression. Its small and open economy was buoyed by exports of primary products, which the world now decided it no longer could afford. High American tariffs implemented in 1930 meant disaster for Canadian sellers to the country's major trading partner. Competition from Argentine and Australian wheat contributed to wheat prices dropping to their lowest in more than a century. As the price of basic foods eroded, the market for fresh and salt fish collapsed. Automobile sales dropped to less than a quarter of their 1929 level, the contraction of the British Empire market compounding a shrinking domestic demand. By 1933, the real value of Canada's exports was about 60 percent of what it had been in 1929. Although export volumes resumed their earlier levels by the late 1930s, values remained below the 1929 figure (see Table 9.1).

With companies collapsing, and those that survived firing workers, unemployment reached unprecedented levels. Although unemployment figures are elusive for this period, nearly 20 percent of the labour force was officially classified as unemployed in 1933, the worst year of the Depression. Many more Canadians were underemployed, working part-time and in menial jobs that did not use their skills and training. As had always been the case in Canada, seasonal unemployment added greatly to the poverty of working people. Hidden unemployment was rife in the 1930s as women were forced into unwanted retirement, and, in the case of married women, actually fired from their jobs, ostensibly to provide more work for men supporting families. Since unemployment among married men was also high, many families were left with no income earner at all.

In cities, the unemployed were dependent upon social assistance, or "relief," from the municipal authorities. Rates varied across the country, but everywhere they were low, and dozens of regulations existed to restrict funds to recipients deemed morally worthy. Both the low rates of relief and the demeaning regulations provoked mass demonstrations and relief strikes across the country, which often met with success in convincing municipal councils to treat the unemployed less parsimoniously. For example, in Saskatoon in 1932, a sit-down strike by

TABLE 9.1
The Canadian Economy, 1926-1939

	1926	1929	1933	1937	1939
GNP*	5 152	6 134	3 510	5 257	5 636
Exports*	1 261	1 152	529	997	925
Farm income*	609	392	66	280	362
Gross fixed capital formation*	808	1 344	319	809	746
Automobile sales (thousands)	159	205	45	149	126
Common stock prices (1935-39 = 100)	200.6	203.4	97.3	122.4	86.1
Unemployment (thousands)	108	116	826	411	529
Unemployment (percent of labour force)	3.0	2.8	19.3	9.1	11.4
Cost of living index (1935-39 = 100)	121.7	121.6	94.3	101.2	101.5
Wage rates (1939 = 100)	46.1	48.5	41.6	47.3	48.9
Corporation profits ($ millions pretax)	325	396	73	280	362

* Millions, dollar values unadjusted for inflation and deflation

Source: Michael Bliss, *Northern Enterprise: Five Centuries of Canadian Business* (Toronto: McClelland & Stewart, 1987) 418–19. Reprinted by permission of Michael Bliss.

48 women and their children at city hall ended after two days when the council agreed to their demands: to reduce the amount of money that relief recipients had to pay back when they found work; to close the relief store where social assistance recipients were segregated as shoppers; and to limit the powers of bureaucrats regulating relief.

The lives of all unemployed people were grim, but marital status, gender, and race determined just how grim. While families received relief vouchers that allowed them to buy necessities, single men were obliged to eat in state-supported mass food kitchens. Most cities made no provision for single unemployed women without dependants, or for never-married women with dependants. In November 1930, the Vancouver relief rolls included 4513 married men and 5244 single men. Only 155 women were listed by their own names, and they appear to have been mainly widows and deserted wives with dependants. Charity organizations were left to establish a women's hostel in the city. Reforms came gradually, mainly in response to a concerted campaign by the Women's Labour League and the Unemployed Women and Girls Club. At various times in 1933, the city provided milk to women with babies, relief for ill single women, medical care for pregnant women, clothing allowances for married women and their children, and assistance to needy Japanese and Chinese families.

Asian and African Canadians were more likely to be denied relief than their European-origin counterparts among the unemployed. In British Columbia, relief rates for Asian-origin recipients were set at half the rate for whites. In Calgary, only a spirited campaign by the Communist Party resulted in the city's destitute Chinese citizens becoming eligible for social assistance.

What added insult to injury for the poor, both employed and unemployed, were the great disparities in income that prevailed during the Depression. For example, Gray Miller, chief executive officer of Imperial Tobacco, earned on average $69 000 a year in salary and bonuses between 1929 and 1933, at the same time that clerks in the company's United Cigar Stores earned as little as $1300 a year for a 54-hour week.

In the first four years of the Depression, per capita income dropped sharply throughout Canada. Saskatchewan, staggering under the double assault of the collapse of the wheat economy and massive crop failures, experienced the greatest descent in income. Drought plagued the southern Prairies for most of the decade and raised fears that the region might swirl away with the dust storms that characterized the hot, dry summers. Gophers, which flourished in this climate, provided food for many poor families. Saskatchewan's net farm income—that is, receipts minus costs of operation—was a negative figure from 1931 to 1933. Without federal relief, there would have been mass starvation or mass migration away from rural western Canada during the Depression. Even with federal aid, approximately 250 000 people left the Prairies between 1931 and 1941.

The Maritime provinces could ill afford to sink any lower, but they did. Dependent on primary industries and international trade, the Maritimes, like the Prairies, were devastated by the Depression. Even their major source of relief—out-migration—was closed as Maritimers who fell on hard times elsewhere

Destitute family in Saskatchewan, 1934. The Fehr family is shown here in Edmonton, returning to Saskatoon from the Peace River country. SOURCE: GLENBOW ARCHIVES ND 3-6742

returned home in the 1930s. The Depression highlighted the underdeveloped state of municipal and social services in the Maritimes, as well as the utter inadequacy of the region's rapidly shrinking tax base.

Unable to find the money to participate in federal cost-sharing programs to help the destitute, the region's governments were responsible for some of the most mean-spirited relief policies in the nation. Unemployed miners in Cape Breton received less than a dollar a week to feed their families and, in New Brunswick, officials prosecuted relief recipients who produced a child out of wedlock. Without the aid of relatives, neighbours, and charitable organizations, many of the region's dependent citizens would have succumbed to starvation. As it was, an untold number of people on relief died because hospital services were denied them until they were too far gone to be cured.

Crowds in front of the Colonial Building in St John's, 5 April 1932. The final chapter in Newfoundland history under responsible government was precipitated by a public demonstration outside the Colonial Building, which escalated into a riot involving 10 000 people. Prime Minister Sir Richard Squires escaped from the building with a police escort, but was voted out of office in an ensuing election.
SOURCE: THE ROOMS PROVINCIAL ARCHIVES A-19-23

In Quebec, government response to the crisis was as inadequate as elsewhere. The Depression was, however, a boon to conservative nationalists and especially to their call for a return to agriculture to counter what they saw as the threat of urban life. New programs, including the joint federal–provincial Gordon Plan and the 1935 Plan Vautrin, encouraged the urban unemployed to become colonists in new, often marginal agricultural regions in Quebec, such as the Abitibi-Témiscamingue. While the colonists endured miserable hardships and some abandoned their farms, many stayed to found new settlements in these more remote regions of the province.

NEWFOUNDLAND ON THE ROCKS

In Newfoundland, the impact of the loss of external markets, so devastating for Canada's resource-extracting regions, was even more dramatic. Newfoundland's efforts to preserve its political independence collapsed with its economy. With 98 percent of its exports coming from the fish, forestry, and mineral sectors, Newfoundland could neither repay its debts nor provide social assistance to destitute citizens. In April 1932, a demonstration of unemployed workers in St John's deteriorated into a riot that gutted the legislature and forced Prime Minister Squires to call an election. The United Newfoundland Party, led by Frederick Alderdice, won an overwhelming victory, but it had no solutions to the financial crisis. In desperation, the new government turned to Great Britain for help.

Britain established a commission of inquiry into Newfoundland's future. Headed by Lord Amulree, the commission recommended the suspension of Newfoundland democracy and the handing over of power to a British-appointed commission of government headed by a governor. While humiliated, the members of the House of Assembly felt they had no choice but to acquiesce. The commission of government, which came into operation in February 1934, brought an injection of British funds to pay off interest on debts, and began programs to encourage cooperatives and a cottage hospital system in the outports.

HANGING ON BY THE FINGERNAILS

The Canadian economy managed to weather the storm somewhat better than Newfoundland, but there were some tense moments. To pay its bills, the federal government resorted to wartime precedents of borrowing from the public. A National Service Loan of $150 million—oversubscribed by $72 million—helped to pull Canada through the crisis. Ottawa also came to the rescue of the provincial governments, most of which were deeply in debt.

Some industries recovered relatively quickly from Depression conditions after 1934. While most entrepreneurs were slow to gamble on new investment, the automobile industry rebounded quickly. Radio stations, cinemas, and oil and gas companies showed steady growth. After the price of gold was artificially raised from $20 to $35 in 1934, mining companies had little difficulty attracting investors. Ontario and British Columbia were the main beneficiaries of the gold-mining boom, but many provinces—and the territories—experienced their

MORE TO THE STORY
Environmental Catastrophe

The misery of the farmers of the southern Prairies during the Depression provides one of the enduring images of the decade. Southern Saskatchewan, southeastern Alberta, and southwestern Manitoba turned into a dust bowl, where farmers' attempts to grow their cereal crops were mocked by drought, dust, and wind. "The Wind Our Enemy," by Anne Marriott, gave poetic voice to the farmers' disillusionment with nature's attack on their livelihood.

Prairie farmers liked to think of themselves as stewards of the soil. Arguably, though, at the root of the farmers' problems was a futile attempt to dominate the natural environment rather than to respect its limitations. Dryland farmers ignored warnings from government experts about the dangers of one-crop farming, presuming that science and new technologies could conquer all obstacles. With wheat prices rising in the 1920s, farmers opted for short-term financial gains rather than for the longer-term security that might come from diversification of crops and animal husbandry.

A disastrous drought from 1917 to 1921, accompanied by an invasion of grasshoppers, was followed by frequent and devastating attacks of rust and smut. Sawflies, cutworms, and wireworms caused millions of dollars of damage annually to repeatedly sown cropland. In Saskatchewan alone, 57 percent of all homesteaders were forced to abandon their land between 1911 and 1931. By that time, there were few traces of the buffalo landscape that had characterized the region in the mid-nineteenth century.

Natural predators had been eliminated or reduced to small populations, and the vegetation was changed by cattle and horses overgrazing on fenced-in ranches.

The monoculture of wheat had transformed the environment, and farmers' language testified to their view that this transformation represented "progress." As historian Barry Potyondi notes: "The everyday terminology of the farmers depreciated the value of the natural world and hinted at the artificiality of their intrusion: 'cultivated' crops and 'tame' grass replaced 'wild' hay; machinery replaced horsepower; 'correction' lines replaced ancient trails that followed natural contours. This was a collision of natural and human forces on a grand scale, legislated into being and mediated by science and technology."[4]

Dust storm at Twin River, Alberta, in the 1930s. SOURCE: GLENBOW ARCHIVES NA-4235-1

own gold rushes in the 1930s. Discoveries of the mineral pitchblende near Great Bear Lake made Eldorado Gold Mines one of the success stories of the Depression. The source of radium used in the treatment of cancer, pitchblende also contains uranium, initially considered a useless by-product of the mining process, but ultimately an essential component of atomic energy.

As British war production increased, the demand for gold, nickel, zinc, copper, and other minerals strengthened the mining industry in northern Ontario, producing growth and a degree of prosperity in such communities as Sudbury and Timmins. Toronto was the financial capital for this mining expansion, and in the late 1930s, for the first time, the Ontario metropolis surpassed Montreal as the major source of financial capital in the nation. While the gross national product (GNP) had almost regained the levels of the late 1920s by 1939, the effects of the Depression lingered on in the form of an unemployment rate that hovered around 11 percent. Only with the economic demand created by the Second World War did the economic clouds finally lift entirely.

TRADE UNIONS AND HARD TIMES

Not everyone was content to deal individually with Depression-imposed hardships. Huge demonstrations of the unemployed and violent strikes by workers trying to limit wage reductions rocked many communities in the 1930s. Under the leadership of the Communist Party, the Workers Unity League (WUL), dedicated to the creation of militant industrial unions, was founded in 1929 and soon took root among miners, loggers, and garment workers.

In the United States, meanwhile, workers began to join a brash new federation of industrial unions, the Congress of Industrial Organizations (CIO), which soon also had branches in Canada. Many of the early CIO organizers in Canada were activists in the WUL, which disbanded in accordance with orders from the international organization of Communist unions for radicals to work inside the mainstream union movement. Gaining an early stronghold in Sydney's steel plant, the CIO played a role in convincing Nova Scotia's Liberal premier, Angus L. Macdonald, to pass Canada's first provincial law establishing rules for state recognition of a union in a particular firm or industry in 1937. The law also forced employers

to engage in collective bargaining with certified unions. Alberta quickly followed suit.

Mitchell Hepburn, Ontario's Liberal premier from 1934 to 1942, was less open to accommodation. When the CIO-inspired United Auto Workers (UAW) called a strike in 1937 against General Motors in Oshawa, the union brought 4000 workers onto the streets, and Hepburn organized a special police force, which was quickly dubbed "Hepburn's hussars." Afraid that the strike would get out of hand, General Motors negotiated an agreement with the UAW, though it withheld formal union recognition.

Female industrial workers were as keen to join unions as their male counterparts, and just as likely to be confronted by state and employer repression when they struggled to receive better pay. In 1937, Peterborough's two Dominion Woolens plants participated in a CIO-led strike. The determination of the police, particularly the Ontario Provincial Police, to help the employer keep the plants running with strikebreakers led to clashes with the striking workers. "Dorothy," one of the women arrested during the conflict, recalled a half-century later:

> I remember being on picket line. That's all I was doing, I was really surprised how wild [the police] were. . . . The chief of police came and grabbed me from behind with fingernails in my neck—you could see the marks. I was trying to kick out at him: I couldn't figure out why he was picking on me. He shoved me under the gate. . . . By that time I was crying and . . . started to run out. . . . Another girl came to rescue me from Chief Newall, and they threw her in [to the paddywagon] too. They made us go to city jail and we had "a bit of a trial." . . . The chief of police charged me with throwing pepper in his face, and I never even had any pepper.[5]

In 1939, on orders from the American Federation of Labor, CIO affiliates were expelled from the crafts-dominated Trades and Labour Congress. Undeterred, they joined a group of Canadian-controlled unions to form the Canadian Congress of Labour (CCL). The unions were biding their time. Only the high rate of unemployment gave employers and the state the power to prevent willing workers from unionizing. When and if the economy turned around, the unions would be ready to assert themselves.

In Quebec, the Confédération des travailleurs catholiques du Canada, formed in 1921, continued to be a strong force within the trade union movement. Associating strikes with socialism, church leaders believed that international unions were promoting an adversarial model that pitted class against class. In practice, the Catholic unions and many of the chaplains associated with their operations soon came to the view that workers needed the weapon of the strike to deal with those intransigent employers who could not otherwise be persuaded to treat their workers fairly.

Montreal was fertile ground for labour activists with more radical views, such as Jeanne Corbin and Léa Roback, members of the Communist Party of Canada. In the early 1930s, Corbin produced and distributed Communist literature in French in Montreal, and became a key organizer for the Workers Unity League among francophone workers. Roback opened the first Communist bookstore in Montreal in 1935. In 1936–1937, she helped unionize female garment workers in the city under the auspices of the CIO-affiliated International Ladies' Garment Workers' Union, leading a strike of some 5000 women and men.

In Newfoundland, as in Canada, the Depression provided a spur to union organization. The Newfoundland Lumbermen's Association was formed in 1935 by 12 000 loggers to fight for a just piece rate for the wood that they cut. Railway clerks unionized, and when both their employer and the commission of government refused to recognize the union, they took their case to Britain, which granted recognition of their rights as workers.

Western Canadian workers continued to prove receptive to radical labour leadership during the Depression. The WUL spearheaded strikes among New Westminster sawmill workers, Vancouver island loggers, and fishers on the Skeena and Nass Rivers, but repression limited labour's gains in the region. The Royal Canadian Mounted Police (RCMP) was used to suppress strikes such as the Estevan coal miners' strike in 1931, during which three miners were killed. Such repression highlighted the apparent league of the state with employers against workers.

THE BENNETT YEARS, 1930–1935

Slow to grasp the seriousness of the situation as Canada faced its first Depression winter, Prime Minister William Lyon Mackenzie King lost his temper during a parliamentary debate and said that he would not provide so much as "a five-cent piece" to help any province with a Tory government. The "five-cent piece speech" became the theme of Conservative candidates stumping the country in the July 1930 election campaign. Under their new leader Richard Bedford Bennett, the Conservatives won a resounding victory, carrying 137 seats to 91 for the Liberals, 12 for the United Farmers of Alberta and the Progressives, and three for Labour. The Conservatives won every province and territory apart from Alberta, Saskatchewan, and Quebec. Like King, Bennett remained a bachelor and tried to compensate for the lack of female candidates running for the Conservatives by campaigning with his sister Mildred, who proved to be more effective on the hustings than her sometimes over-earnest brother.

Born in 1870 in Albert County, New Brunswick, R.B. Bennett was proud of his alleged Loyalist roots, his Methodist values, and his rise to prominence from humble origins. After teaching school, Bennett studied law at Dalhousie University and, in 1897, moved to Calgary to work as a

A "Bennett buggy" on the campus of the University of Saskatchewan, c. 1935. Farmers too poor to buy gas during the Depression gave that derisive name to their horse-drawn automobiles.
SOURCE: UNIVERSITY OF SASKATCHEWAN ARCHIVES A-3412

junior partner in Senator James Lougheed's legal firm. Bennett became wealthy working for powerful clients such as the CPR and through wise investments. In 1911, he won the Calgary seat in the House of Commons, but he refused to run for the Union government in the 1917 election. A "progressive" Conservative who supported both old-age pensions and unemployment insurance, he was chosen to succeed Meighen at the Conservative Party's first national leadership convention held in Winnipeg in 1927.

Eager to make good on his election promise to address the problems created by the Depression, Bennett called a special session of Parliament soon after taking power. The government introduced the Unemployment Relief Act to provide $20 million—an unprecedented sum—to help people get back to work, and

Prime Minister R.B. Bennett (left) in Toronto in 1934 in a somewhat contrived picture of political friendship with opposition leader W.L.M. King. SOURCE: LIBRARY AND ARCHIVES CANADA PA-148532

embarked on a program of tariff increases designed to protect languishing Canadian industries from foreign competition. It was not enough. Bread lines lengthened, prices continued to plummet, and municipal and charitable

VOICES FROM THE PAST
Making Ends Meet

For Canadians of all ages, the poverty and unemployment of the 1930s often meant puzzlement and anger. People spent their savings, if they had any, and then were forced to make ends meet as best they could. Letters written to Prime Minister R.B. Bennett provided a flavour of the challenges that were faced.[6] A Saskatchewan teenager reminded him of the meaning of destitution for many children.

DEAR SIR

I am a girl thirteen years old, and I have to go to school every day its very cold now already and I haven't got a coat to put on. My parents can't afford to buy me anything this winter. I have to walk to school four and a half mile

every morning and night and I'm awfully cold every day. Would you be so kind as to send me enough money . . . so that I could get one.

My name is,   EDWINA ABBOTT

Working-age adults felt the pressures of poverty in their own way. Housewives, who had little recourse when the family breadwinner lost his job, also turned to the Prime Minister. As one Saskatchewan woman explained to Bennett in 1933: "I really dont know what to do. We have never asked for anything of anybody before. We seem to be shut out of the world altogether we have no telephone Radio or newspaper. For this last couple of years we have felt we could not afford to have them." Nor could this woman afford underwear for her husband who worked outside in the cold Saskatchewan winter: "I have patched and darned his old underwear for the last two years, but they are completely done now." As a last resort, she wrote to the Prime Minister to ask him to "send for the underwear in the Eaton order made out and enclosed in this letter," a request to which he acceded.

Even old age offered little relief. The means-tested old-age pension was cost-shared by the provinces with the federal government on a 50-50 basis, causing poorer provinces to set rates well below the $20 maximum and to establish tough conditions that deprived all but the poorest or best connected politically from collecting. This letter, written by a man from New Brunswick to Bennett in 1935, suggests the precarious lives of many elderly Canadians forced to rely on stringent poor relief.

DEAR SIR

I am writing you a few lines to ask if you will be kind enough to let me know the Law of the Direct Relieved, I am an Old man of 73 years old cant hardly help myself nearly cripple of both hands and my wife 68 years old I went to see the man who is appointed to give the Relieved this morning and I had a hard time to get $3.00 worth I got a bag of flour and a gallon of Paraphine oil I couldn't not get no tea or anything else long as we cant get no tea we will have to eat that bag of flour with cold water indeed it is a hard way to live so long in the party conservative and to be used that way.

---

organizations collapsed under the weight of the demands placed upon them. At a loss as to how to stem the crisis, Bennett resorted to desperate measures and soon found his party embattled from without and divided from within.

PROTEST FROM THE LEFT

Bennett's biggest challenge was finding ways to prevent discontent from coalescing into a movement to overthrow the economic system that created such misery. During the 1920s, communism had attracted little support, but it thrived in the appalling conditions of Depression Canada. In 1931, the Bennett government instructed the RCMP to join with provincial and municipal police to arrest and charge the Communist Party's national leadership in Toronto with participation in a criminal organization. Under the sweeping provisions of Section 98 of the Criminal Code, it was illegal to join, participate in, or defend any organization that advocated or defended force to achieve economic or political change. The courts determined that the Communist Party fit the bill and imprisoned seven leading Communists, including leader Tim Buck, effectively rendering all Communist activities illegal in Canada. The use of state violence to protect the established order was not new in Canada, but the intensity of the repression, which included jail sentences, beatings, and, for those who were not Canadian citizens, deportation,

reached a new level in the hysteria fostered by hard times. Section 98 was rescinded in 1936, although Quebec responded in 1937 with its own anti-Communist law.

In 1932, the Bennett government established relief camps under military control to house the single, unemployed men who had been riding the rails from city to city in search of work. From the government's perspective, these unfortunate people were a potentially explosive group who should be segregated from society until the economy improved. The transients were to be denied welfare unless they agreed to live in the camps, where they would labour on public works for their board and receive an allowance of 20 cents a day. As Irene Baird's powerful novel *Waste Heritage* (1939) vividly illustrated, Communist organizers had little difficulty convincing these desperate young men to organize to demand "work and wages" and the closing of the camps.

While there were several tragic instances in the 1930s of strikers being killed by the police, the clash between the authorities and the victims of the Depression that gained the most national attention occurred in Regina in 1935. Relief camp workers, fed up with their lot, were enthusiastic recruits to the Relief Camp Workers Union (RCWU) organized by the Workers Unity League. In April 1935, the RCWU led nearly half of the 7000 relief camp inmates in British Columbia on a strike for work and wages. Early in June, 1200 of the strikers boarded freight trains heading east. Picking up support along the way, they planned to converge on Ottawa and put their demands directly to the Prime Minister.

The On-to-Ottawa Trek, as it became known, quickly attracted the nation's attention. Bennett responded by calling on the RCMP to stop the demonstrators in Regina. One constable was killed and hundreds of strikers and constables were injured in the melee that ensued as the strikers resisted RCMP orders to disperse. One of the strikers later died of his wounds. The next year, King abolished the relief camps, which by that time had provided temporary homes and education in radical politics to about 170 000 Canadians.

Communists and socialists led marches of unemployed men and women demanding better treatment of those unable to find work and more efforts on the part of the state to create work. In 1935, the United Married Men's Association marched in Calgary, carrying a banner that read, "We stand behind 12 000 on relief." SOURCE: GLENBOW ARCHIVES NA-2800-12

With as much as one-third of the nation facing destitution by 1932, many Canadians looked to new political parties to find a solution to their problems. The Co-operative Commonwealth Federation, Social Credit, and the Union nationale were all born in the Dirty Thirties, each with its own formula for preventing capitalist boom-bust economic cycles.

THE CCF

The Co-operative Commonwealth Federation (CCF) was formed as the result of grassroots pressure to unite the disparate left-wing labour and farm organizations to challenge the exiting order. In 1932 a small contingent of Labour and Progressive MPs, along with a reform organization known as the League for Social Reconstruction,

BIOGRAPHY

James Shaver Woodsworth: From Social Gospel to Socialism

Born in Etobicoke, Ontario, in 1874 and raised there and in Brandon, Manitoba, J.S. (James Shaver) Woodsworth appeared destined to become a man of the cloth. His father was a Methodist minister who became that church's superintendent of missions in western Canada in 1882. J.S. followed in his father's footsteps but he was plagued with doubt about Christian teachings.

Between 1907 and 1913, Woodsworth served as superintendent of All People's Mission in the North End of Winnipeg.

He was appalled by the poverty of his clients and reflected on the causes of their destitution. In 1909 he published an account of ethnic immigrants in Canada entitled *Strangers Within Our Gates*. It was replete with every ethnic stereotype promoted by conservative church missionaries who were determined to "Canadianize" immigrants, that is, to encourage them to embrace British Protestant values and behaviours. This perspective implied that immigrant poverty was the result of their character flaws.

J.S. Woodsworth in 1935. While the CCF leader won a great deal of respect from Canadians, his party was vilified by the mainstream media and made only minor electoral inroads before the Second World War.
SOURCE: LIBRARY AND ARCHIVES CANADA C-3940

While he still believed in social reform, Woodsworth became convinced that social justice could only be achieved when capitalism had been replaced by government ownership, which would ensure a fairer distribution of the nation's wealth. He left the Methodist Church in 1918 in protest against its support for Canada's war effort and worked briefly as a stevedore in British Columbia. A supporter of the Winnipeg General Strike, he briefly edited the strikers' newspaper after its editor was charged with seditious libel and jailed. Woodsworth was also imprisoned, but the charges were dropped against him when it became clear that the passages cited as seditious came from the Bible.

Like all of those arrested for their roles during the strike, Woodsworth was regarded as a martyr by Winnipeg workers, who elected him as the Independent Labour Party MP for Winnipeg Centre in 1921. Re-elected in Winnipeg North Centre in 1925, Woodsworth remained an MP until his death in 1942. Although few other Labour members were elected in the 1920s, Woodsworth, supported by the more socialist-inclined members of the Progressive Party, became an influential voice in Parliament. Together, they formed an informal caucus referred to as the Ginger Group. Woodsworth used his clout in the minority government that emerged after the 1925 election to extract a promise from Prime Minister King to introduce old-age pension legislation.

The onset of the Depression convinced Woodsworth that the time had come to create a democratic socialist party in Canada along the lines of the British Labour Party. The Ginger Group was of the same mind, as were many people disturbed by the misery generated by hard times. As leader of the Co-operative Commonwealth Federation, Woodsworth campaigned for an array of social reforms to alleviate the worst effects of the Depression. A man of principle, he voted against Canada's entry into the Second World War. He nevertheless was re-elected in September 1940, but soon thereafter suffered a stroke and died in 1942.

Over the next few years, Woodsworth adopted the views of social gospellers who argued that exploitation by employers and inaction by governments were to blame for the poverty of hard-working immigrants. He campaigned for social reforms that would reduce exploitation and produce a better social order. By the beginning of the First World War, Woodsworth had become a socialist and pacifist.

brought farmers, labourers, and socialists together in Calgary where they established their new party and chose J.S. Woodsworth, a Labour MP from Winnipeg, as its leader.

The following year, CCF supporters met in Regina where they adopted a manifesto outlining their platform.

The Regina Manifesto proclaimed the possibility of a parliamentary road to socialism, recommending state planning as the best route to social justice. Propelled by a sense of mission, the authors of the manifesto declared that "No CCF Government will rest content until it has eradicated capitalism and put into operation the full pro-gramme of socialized planning which will lead to the establishment in Canada of the Co-operative Common-wealth." Although this economic vision had much in common with the Communists, Woodsworth was deeply committed to parliamentary government and opposed to the use of violence to achieve social change. He purged individuals from the CCF who called for a common front of socialists and Communists.

The CCF inherited the often contradictory traditions of labourism, socialism, social gospelism, and farm radi-calism, but it offered a bold alternative to the mainline political parties. Early election results demonstrated that, outside of industrial Cape Breton, the CCF had taken root mainly in the West, though it did have its supporters in Ontario and Quebec. By 1939, it had formed the oppo-sition in British Columbia, Saskatchewan, and Manitoba.

SOCIAL CREDIT

Not all western Canadians who rejected the mainstream political parties turned toward socialism for a solution to economic ills. When popular Alberta radio evangelist William "Bible Bill" Aberhart began in 1932 to inject "social credit" into his weekly radio broadcasts, he found a receptive audience. Aberhart adapted doctrines espoused by a British engineer, Major C.H. Douglas, to Alberta con-ditions and built on traditional provincial suspicion toward central Canadian financial institutions. Claiming that the Depression had been caused by the failure of the banks to print enough money so that consumer spending could match industrial production, Aberhart offered a blueprint for getting monetary policy back on track. To many free enterprisers disillusioned by the severity of the Depression, Aberhart's nostrums proved appealing. If only the banks could be forced to supply consumers with money, they believed, prosperity could be restored.

Social credit meant that governments would replace financial institutions as the vehicle for deciding how much money should be in circulation and in whose hands. It claimed to offer a scientific formula to deter-mine the shortfall in purchasing power, advocating that the government simply credit all citizens equally with a share of this shortfall to keep the economy healthy.

Aberhart turned the social credit study clubs spawned by his radio appeals into a political movement that won 56

of 63 seats in the provincial election of 1935. Once in power, he failed to deliver on his promises to issue social dividends or to control prices, and he only attempted to regulate banks and currency when a revolt by backbench-ers in the party forced him to stop procrastinating. Legis-lation to this end was disallowed by the federal government and ultimately by the courts, which upheld federal juris-diction over banking and currency. Aberhart was thus able to blame the federal government for his failure to imple-ment his election promises and could maintain provincial support for his party with his strong stand against Ottawa.

THE UNION NATIONALE

In Quebec, the reform movement resulted less from pop-ular pressure than from clerical responses to Pope Pius XI's 1931 encyclical *Quadragesimo Anno*, which sup-ported state intervention to achieve social justice. The Jesuit-sponsored École sociale populaire, an organization that promoted church teachings, assembled representa-tives of lay Catholic organizations—including unions, caisses populaires, and professional groups—to produce a document on social reforms that conformed to papal thinking. In 1933, they published the *Programme de res-tauration sociale*, a program of non-socialist reforms including government regulation of monopolies, improved working conditions in industry, a system of farm credits, and a variety of social insurance measures.

The business-oriented Liberal regime of Louis-Alexandre Taschereau proved resistant to reform. In frus-tration, progressive Liberals, led by Paul Gouin, formed a breakaway party, the Action libérale nationale. Maurice Duplessis, a Trois-Rivières lawyer who led the province's almost-moribund Conservative Party, sensed a political opportunity and formed an electoral alliance with the renegade Liberals. In 1935, the rechristened Union natio-nale contested the provincial election, with the *Programme de restauration sociale* as its platform and with its two component parties maintaining organizational autonomy.

Disillusionment with the long-governing Liberals produced a close result: 48 Liberal and 42 Union natio-nale seats. Shortly after the election, the Union nationale was able to capitalize on evidence of government corrup-tion and nepotism to force Taschereau's resignation. The hastily formed new government, forced to call an election in 1936, was badly mauled by the Union nationale, which

Maurice Duplessis and Mitchell Hepburn, the two premiers of central Canada, worked together for several years, resisting federal social programs and economic regulation. While both men were economic conservatives, their motives for opposing the federal government differed in important respects. Hepburn wanted to avoid a redistribution of wealth away from the country's richest province, while Duplessis was leery of any proposals that might threaten the French-speaking, Catholic character of Quebec. They are shown here in 1938.
SOURCE: LIBRARY AND ARCHIVES CANADA C-19518

made corruption rather than reform the focus of its campaign. Duplessis out-manoeuvred Gouin to take full control of the Union nationale, merging its two founding parties into a new organization under his personal control and becoming the new political chief of the province.

In power, the Union nationale delivered only on its promises to help farmers with cheap loans and to expand programs to settle the unemployed in remote areas of the province, consistent with its conservative nationalist ideals. Employers, not labour, received a sympathetic ear from the government, and the broader reform program was abandoned. In 1937, Duplessis demonstrated how far he would go in repressing dissent when he passed the Padlock Law. Ostensibly designed to suppress "communism" and "bolshevism," the law was frequently invoked to intimidate any labour organization that the government considered undesirable and, indeed, any group that threatened the Catholic, conservative coalition that underpinned Duplessis's regime.

THE EXTREME RIGHT

By no means all of the opponents of the status quo during the Depression responded by embracing social reform. A minority embraced the world view of the fascist leaders of Germany and Italy, and some were prepared to use violence to bring fascism to Canada. Hitler's glorification of violence, white supremacy, and hatred of Jews, Communists, and homosexuals inspired Canadian Nazis and fascists to fight pitched battles with Communists and union groups and make efforts to keep Jews off beaches and away from other public places. Their intended victims sometimes fought back. On 16 August 1933, as a mainly Jewish softball team played a wholly gentile team in Toronto's Christie Pits, Nazis from the Balmy Beach Swastika Club unfurled a swastika. The result was a race riot, with Jewish players and spectators battling the racists through the night. Toronto police proved helpless to restore order as thousands of young people joined one side or the other in the conflict.

Le cirage à chaussures merveilleux

SUPREME SINCE 1896

CIRAGE A CHAUSSURES **FABIEN** SHOE POLISH

LE MEILLEUR DEPUIS 1896

Vous ne trouverez pas ce cirage chez les Juifs, mais vous pourrez vous le procurer chez tous les marchands chrétiens.

Les marchands chrétiens sont invités à donner leurs commandes par téléphone.

B. FABIEN Enrg.

MONTREAL.

2350 Delorimier.   AMherst 6361

This advertisement from the back of a fascist propaganda brochure reveals how anti-Semitism penetrated even to the level of shoe polish. The manufacturer, B. Fabien, declares that his polish is available only in Christian stores, not in Jewish ones. The brochure was published in 1934 by the *Patriote* newspaper, associated with Adrien Arcand. It reproduced a virulently anti-Semitic speech by Conservative MP Samuel Gobeil, who in 1935 briefly became postmaster general in R.B. Bennett's cabinet. The ad also appeared on the back of the founding platform of Arcand's Parti national social chrétien. SOURCE: SAMUEL GOBEIL, *LA GRIFFE ROUGE SUR L'UNIVERSITÉ DE MONTRÉAL* (1934)

militancy of labour movements, and the strength of parties on the left, many Roman Catholics found comfort in the state repression and heightened sense of nationalism advocated by the fascists. While church leaders rarely condoned violent attacks on minorities, some urged Catholics to boycott Jewish stores, Hollywood movies, and liberal-leaning newspapers such as Montreal's *La Presse*. Most French-Canadians ignored such advice along with calls to abstain from drinking and gambling, and Arcand's party remained very much a fringe movement.

While there was a Nazi-inspired fascist movement under the leadership of William Whittaker in western Canada, anti-Catholic zealots made up much of the violent right wing. They were led by the Ku Klux Klan, the secretive, violent brotherhood of hooded white men who took up the cause of white supremacy in the American South after the Civil War. Although details of its operations were sketchy, the KKK was active in many areas of Canada in the 1920s and early 1930s. Since there were few blacks to terrorize, the Canadian KKK became a Protestant extremist organization with Roman Catholics as its target. They called for an end to non-Protestant immigration and deportation of Roman Catholics born outside Canada.

By the late 1920s, the KKK's membership in Saskatchewan reached between 10 000 and 15 000 and it was able to exercise influence on the provincial Conservative Party, which led a coalition government from 1929 to 1934. KKK

In Quebec, fascists banded together in 1934 in the Nazi-inspired Parti national social chrétien, under the leadership of Adrien Arcand. They claimed to represent the last stand of Roman Catholicism against the forces of decadence. Many conservative religious leaders in the province turned a blind eye to fascist attempts to use the church to promote racism and anti-Semitism, and some Conservative politicians in Quebec openly espoused anti-Semitic views. Alarmed by rising secularism, the

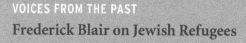

VOICES FROM THE PAST
Frederick Blair on Jewish Refugees

Prime Minister William Lyon Mackenzie King appointed Frederick Blair to the position of director of the Immigration Branch of the Department of Mines and Resources in 1935. Under Blair's leadership, Canada's immigration policies toward Jews tightened. In 1938, he argued that only non-Jewish immigrants from Germany should be welcomed in Canada. He wrote:

> It is apparent that so far as Jewish political refugees are concerned, there is a growing disposition [in Germany] to take from them both capital and citizenship[:] in our view two essentials of immigration. Without capital there is little hope of absorption in immigration countries and without a recognition of citizenship which will allow return to country of origin in the event of trouble arising shortly after migration, the acceptance of immigrants becomes almost impossible. It is suggested that immigration countries could well afford to stand together in refusing to accept immigrants without either capital or recognized citizenship.... If the political refugees were of the agricultural class and the manner of capital and citizenship could be adjusted, we could show much greater consideration in their admission to this country. Since Confederation, and indeed before that date, encouragement of immigration has been limited to the agricultural classes....
>
> ... According to the census of 1931 about 1 1/2% of our Jewish population was connected in some way with agricultural pursuits. It is a curious fact in view of the present relations existing between German and Jew that the former should be at the top of the agricultural list and the latter at the bottom.[7]

Ultimately for Blair, one Jew was too many and he proved steadfast in holding the line on the entry of Jewish refugees into Canada. Between 1933 and 1939, Canada granted entry to only 4000 Jews, while a total of 800 000 had escaped Europe in that period.

---

pressures contributed to the government's decision to end French-language instruction in the early grades of school and to dismiss nuns teaching in public schools.

Only a minority of Canadians believed that the Depression could be ended and further economic crises averted by deporting or persecuting Catholics, Jews, and Communists. Racial prejudices among influential people and organizations nevertheless proved enduring enough that Canada did virtually nothing to help Jewish and other victims of the Nazi terror after Hitler came to power in Germany in 1933. Only about 4000 Jews were allowed entry into Canada during the 1930s, almost all of them under family reunification clauses in the Immigration Act.

Although he harboured anti-Semitic prejudices, Prime Minister King eventually recognized that Germany had become a dangerous country for Jews. Still, he remained unwilling to stand up to opponents of Jewish immigration into Canada, particularly the Roman Catholic hierarchy in Quebec and officers in the federal government's immigration bureaucracy. A sad chapter in Canadian history occurred in 1939, when an ocean liner, the S.S. *St Louis*, sailing from Hamburg and carrying more than 900 German Jewish refugees, searched for somewhere in the Americas to land. Like the Latin American countries and the United States, Canada said no. Most found refuge in Europe, but mainly in countries subsequently occupied by the Nazis. A large number of the S.S. *St Louis* passengers died in Nazi death camps.

BENNETT'S NEW DEAL

Not immune to the mounting pressures for action, Bennett's first instinct was to turn to the traditional Tory nostrum: the tariff. He promised to create jobs by raising tariffs as a means of forcing Canada's trading partners to sue for mercy. Great Britain was the first to respond to Bennett's initiative, agreeing to preferential treatment for Canadian agricultural and forest products at the Imperial Economic Conference held in Ottawa in 1932. Although the agreement did little to help Canada's floundering manufacturing sector or the devastated wheat economy, it was welcome news to apple growers in Nova Scotia, lumbermen in British Columbia, and Ontario's beef and dairy farmers. In 1935, the United States began its retreat from high tariffs when it signed a comprehensive trade treaty with Canada.

Pressure also mounted to manipulate the money supply as a means of stimulating the economy. Bennett resisted most of the "soft money" proposals that circulated during the decade, but did provide relief to hard-pressed farmers through the Farmers' Creditors Arrangement Act. As banking practices became increasingly restrictive, there was widespread agreement that Canada needed a central bank, like the Bank of England or the Federal Reserve Bank in the United States, to convince the public that someone was in control. In 1934, the Bank of Canada Act made provision for a central bank. Its major function, in the words of the preamble to the act, was "to regulate credit and currency in the best interests of the economic life of the nation."

The bank's first governor, Graham Towers, was recruited from the Royal Bank. Towers pursued a policy of modest growth in the money supply in order to cut interest rates and stimulate the economy. Bankers' commitment to "sound money" was too strong for him to undertake bolder efforts to make credit available to most Canadians. Although the economy remained sluggish, conservative economists and bankers worried that an increase in the money supply would result in an unacceptable level of inflation.

Responding to pressing problems relating to wheat exports, municipal funding, and housing, Ottawa pumped money into the economy through programs established under the Prairie Farm Rehabilitation Act, the Municipal Improvement Assistance Act, and the Dominion Housing Act. The federal government also passed the Natural Products Marketing Act, providing a legal framework for marketing boards, and created the Canadian Wheat Board to manage the sale of Canada's most troubled staple. Given the magnitude of the crisis, it no longer seemed wrong to fix prices and regulate output in the farming sector.

The notion of a government-sponsored social security system also gained wider support. In 1935, R.B. Bennett, facing an election, introduced legislation to regulate hours of work, minimum wages, and working conditions, and to provide unemployment insurance. Much of the inspiration for Bennett's program, as well as the name "New Deal," came from reforms undertaken in the United States by President Franklin Delano Roosevelt. Despite popular support for Bennett's proposed reform measures,

many voters remained unimpressed. Only contributors to the unemployment insurance fund were eligible for benefits, which excluded those already unemployed. Skeptics claimed that the courts would reject Bennett's new laws. Most of Bennett's New Deal pronounced on matters that the BNA Act placed under provincial control and would surely be declared unconstitutional.

THE 1935 ELECTION

Whatever his motives, Bennett received few benefits from his conversion to social security. He not only lost the 1935 election, but also watched his party split into warring factions. One revolt was led by Trade and Commerce Minister H.H. Stevens in response to public outrage against the apparent callousness of big corporations in the face of widespread human misery.

In 1934, Stevens headed a parliamentary committee established by the government to investigate the gap between what producers were receiving and what consumers were required to pay for necessities of life. Testimony in the committee hearings revealed damning evidence that big meat-packing companies, such as Canada Packers, made huge profits while farmers who raised the cattle and hogs had been paid "ruinous" prices. Similarly, seamstresses who did piece work for big department stores were paid a few pennies for dresses that sold for $1.59 at Eaton's or Simpson's.

When Bennett resisted taking the captains of industry to task for their exploitative policies, Stevens resigned and established the Reconstruction Party. While the party of "the little man" won only one seat—its leader won his Vancouver riding—it split the Conservative vote in constituencies from Nova Scotia to British Columbia. King, also resisting pressure to adopt new policies for new times, campaigned under the slogan "King or chaos," and won the largest majority of his political career.

As had been predicted, much of Bennett's New Deal was declared unconstitutional, and even marketing boards were deemed by the courts to be a matter for provincial rather than national legislation. King resisted appeals for dramatic action. In typical King fashion, he had the situation studied, appointing a National Employment Commission to investigate and recommend policy on unemployment and relief, and forming a Royal Commission on Dominion–Provincial Relations as a means of resolving the constitutional impasse. Only time would tell if Ottawa could introduce legislation to expand its role in the social and economic lives of Canadians.

CANADA AND THE WORLD

King's efforts, along with those of leaders of other white dominions, had led to informal British recognition of virtual sovereignty for the dominions. By the Statute of Westminster, passed by the British Parliament in 1931, Canada and the other dominions were given full legal freedom to exercise their independence in domestic and foreign affairs. While Canadian autonomy was not complete—amendments to the BNA Act still had to be approved by the British Parliament, and the Judicial Committee of the Privy Council remained the final court of appeal—the Statute of Westminster paved the way to complete independence for Canada in foreign affairs.

Canada proved cautious in its approach to world events, unwilling to do much to defend either sovereignty or democracy for other nations. It was hardly alone. The ambivalence of League of Nations members ensured an ineffectual response to the aggressive behaviour of Japan, Germany, and Italy in the 1930s. When Walter Riddell, Canada's representative at the League, called for stronger measures against Italy after its invasion of Ethiopia in 1935, he was ordered by the King administration to change his position: Canada had no interest in the fate of Ethiopia.

Canada was equally unwilling to provide aid to the Spanish republic when its armed forces, led by General Franco—supported by German and Italian arms— overthrew the country's elected government during a bloody three-year civil war (1936–39). Ordinary people, nevertheless, came to the defence of Spanish democracy. Nearly 1700 Canadians fought for the Spanish republic as volunteers. Most of them were in the Mackenzie-Papineau Battalion, named after William Lyon Mackenzie and Louis-Joseph Papineau, leaders of the 1837–1838 rebellions in Upper and Lower Canada. Dr. Norman Bethune, a Canadian doctor and Communist who had offered free medical care to the poor in Montreal, set up a mobile blood transfusion system for Spanish freedom fighters. Later, Bethune offered his medical talents to the Chinese Communists who were fighting a Japanese invasion of their country. He died of an infection incurred while treating soldiers on the battlefield.

The Canadian government regarded those who fought for the Spanish republic with suspicion, and the Roman Catholic hierarchy in Quebec was openly sympathetic to Franco and the fascists. When Hitler annexed Austria and dismembered Czechoslovakia, Ottawa made no official protest. Even after Germany invaded Poland and imposed a murderous regime, King suggested to the British government that he try to mediate between the Allies and Nazi Germany.

CONCLUSION

Canadians emerged from the Depression with few political illusions. Although Canada had become a player in its own right on the international stage, the game of global politics was a dangerous one that threatened to engulf Canadians in another world war. Nor did Canada's new international status do anything to inspire a new national identity. Canadians were divided as never before along class, regional, and cultural lines, and many had abandoned the old two-party system to support new political parties that promised to address these interests. If there was cause for hope, it was that all parties professed to seek a solution to the problem of poverty in the midst of plenty and to make Canada a better place for all Canadians. Time would tell whether such democratic idealism would survive in the new era of mass consumer culture.

A HISTORIOGRAPHICAL DEBATE
Populism, Right and Left

The Co-operative Commonwealth Federation and Social Credit are sometimes seen as polar opposites, but not all scholars view them in this manner. Some point to the similarity in origin of these movements: both had urban roots but found a mass audience among prairie farmers; both claimed a national platform but focused on regional and provincial strategies for political change; and neither had an important base outside western Canada in the 1930s. Both parties were populist—that is, they claimed to be people's movements against the interests of the entrenched political and economic elites who dominated the country.

The CCF's populism was directed against all big capitalists, while Social Credit's populist attack targeted only financial institutions. The CCF may therefore be described as a "left-wing populist" movement because it identified farmers' interests with workers' interests against the interests of big business. Social Credit may be described as "right-wing populist" because it was suspicious of unions and suggested that workers and farmers had interests in common with capitalists other than bankers.

But were these two parties very different in practice? Some scholars say yes.[8]

When the CCF assumed office in Saskatchewan in 1944, it nationalized auto insurance and the distribution of natural gas and established a provincial intercity bus company. By contrast, the Alberta government denounced all state ventures in the economy. The CCF pioneered universal free hospital and medical care insurance in Saskatchewan; the Social Credit regime in Alberta insisted that medical care schemes must be voluntary and must involve some direct payment for services by subscribers to prevent abuse of the program. The CCF passed labour legislation that favoured union organization in

Saskatchewan, while Social Credit produced a labour code that made unionization difficult. Welfare recipients were subjected to mean-spirited treatment in Alberta, but received some sympathy in Saskatchewan.

Despite these contrasts, many scholars believe that the gap in performance between the CCF in Saskatchewan and Social Credit in Alberta has been exaggerated.[9] They claim that the farm programs of the two governments were similar and that, whatever philosophical differences existed between them, both governments spent lavishly on health, education, and roads. The provincial takeovers in Saskatchewan are held to have had a negligible impact on overall private ownership and direction of the provincial economy.

The claims of the two sides are difficult to adjudicate, in part because the Alberta government, awash in oil revenues by the 1950s, had a vastly superior financial base compared to its Saskatchewan counterpart. It could afford to spend extravagantly, all the while deploring the tendencies of governments generally to spend more than they earned. Nonetheless, left-wing critics of Alberta Social Credit suggest that the poor in Alberta were largely passed over in the orgy of public spending. Their point of comparison is usually Saskatchewan, which they allege had more humanitarian social policies. Meanwhile, left-wing critics of the Saskatchewan CCF suggest that, in office, the party attempted to appease elite interests at the ultimate expense of the poor.

NOTES

1. James Struthers, *No Fault of Their Own: Unemployment and the Canadian Welfare State, 1914–1941* (Toronto: University of Toronto Press, 1983) 83–84.

2. Kenneth Michael Sylvester, *The Limits of Rural Capitalism: Family, Culture, and Markets in Montcalm, Manitoba, 1870–1940* (Toronto: University of Toronto Press, 2001) 128–129.

3. Tina Loo, *States of Nature: Conserving Canada's Wildlife in the Twentieth Century* (Vancouver: UBC Press, 2006) 103.

4. Barry Potyondi, "Loss and Substitution: The Ecology of Production in Southwestern Saskatchewan, 1860–1930," *Journal of the Canadian Historical Association* 5 (1994) 235.

5. Joan Sangster, *Earning Respect: The Lives of Working Women in Small-Town Ontario, 1920–1960* (Toronto: University of Toronto Press, 1995) 178.

6. L.M. Grayson and Michael Bliss, eds., *The Wretched of Canada: Letters to R.B. Bennett, 1930–1935* (Toronto: University of Toronto Press, 1971) 53–56, 111.

7. Library and Archives Canada, Department of Employment and Immigration fonds RG 76, vol. 432, file 644452, pt. 1.

8. The view that there are sharp differences between Social Credit's performance in Alberta and the CCF performance in Saskatchewan is defended in Alvin Finkel, *The Social Credit Phenomenon in Alberta* (Toronto: University of Toronto Press, 1989) 202–13, and Walter D. Young, *Democracy and Discontent: Progressivism, Socialism and Social Credit in the Canadian West* (Toronto: McGraw-Hill Ryerson, 1978). On the general distinction between left and right variants of populism, see John Richards, "Populism: A Qualified Defence," *Studies in Political Economy* 5 (Spring 1981) 5–27.

9. The best case for the convergence in the behaviour of the two parties in office is made in John F. Conway, "To Seek a Goodly Heritage: The Prairie Populist Responses to the National Policy" (PhD diss., Simon Fraser University, 1978). Peter R. Sinclair argues that the Saskatchewan CCF had lost its early radicalism before winning office. See "The Saskatchewan CCF: Ascent to Power and the Decline of Socialism," *Canadian Historical Review* 54, 4 (Dec. 1973) 419–33. An opposite view is found in Lewis H. Thomas, "The CCF Victory in Saskatchewan, 1944," *Saskatchewan History* 28, 2 (Spring 1975) 52–64.

SELECTED READING

Abella, Irving and Harold Troper. *None Is Too Many: Canada and the Jews of Europe, 1933–1948.* Toronto: University of Toronto Press, 2012

Baillargeon, Denyse. *Making Do: Women, Family, and Home in Montreal During the Great Depression.* Waterloo: Wilfrid Laurier University Press, 1999

Betcherman, Lita-Rose. *The Swastika and the Maple Leaf: Fascist Movements in Canada in the Thirties.* Toronto: Fitzhenry & Whiteside, 1975

Campbell, Lara. *Respectable Citizens: Gender, Family, and Unemployment in Ontario's Great Depression.* Toronto: University of Toronto Press, 2009

Evans, Clinton L. *The War on Weeds in the Prairie West: An Environmental History.* Calgary: University of Calgary Press, 2002

Finkel, Alvin. *The Social Credit Phenomenon in Alberta.* Toronto: University of Toronto Press, 1989

Frank, David. *J.B. McLachlan: A Biography.* Toronto: James Lorimer, 1999

Lévesque, Andrée. *Red Travellers: Jeanne Corbin and Her Comrades.* Montreal: McGill-Queen's University Press, 2006

McCallum, Todd. *Hobohemia and the Crucifixion Machine: Rival Images of a New World in 1930s Vancouver.* Edmonton: AU Press, 2014

Pulkingham, Jane, ed. *Human Welfare, Rights, and Social Activism: Rethinking the Legacy of J.S. Woodsworth.* Toronto: University of Toronto Press, 2010

Safarian, A.E. *The Canadian Economy in the Great Depression.* Montreal: McGill-Queen's University Press, 2009

Saywell, John T. *"Just Call Me Mitch": The Life of Mitchell F. Hepburn.* Toronto: University of Toronto Press, 1991

Strikwerda, Eric. *The Wages of Relief: Cities and the Unemployed in Prairie Canada, 1929–39.* Edmonton: AU Press, 2013

Waiser, Bill. *All Hell Can't Stop Us: The On-to-Ottawa Trek and Regina Riot.* Calgary: Fifth House, 2003

Waite, P.B. *In Search of R.B. Bennett.* Montreal: McGill-Queen's University Press, 2012

For a comprehensive list of readings for topics covered in this chapter, please visit http://pearsoncanada.ca/conrad.

CHAPTER 10
SOCIETY AND CULTURE: THE SEARCH FOR IDENTITY, 1919–1939

During the Christmas season one Depression year, an Eaton's saleswoman witnessed throngs of little girls admiring Shirley Temple dolls. Priced at between nine and 16 dollars, the dolls cost a month's income for a family on welfare.

> Some used to come at opening time and just stand there looking at those pink-cheeked, golden-haired lovely Shirley Temples. Little faces, they needed food. You could see a lot who needed a pint of milk a day a thousand times more than they needed a Shirley doll. They'd stare for hours. We tried to shush them away, but it didn't do any good. . . . One [clerk] had a crying fit over just that, those hundreds of poor kids who would never own a Shirley Temple in a hundred years. They were lucky if they had breakfast that morning, or soup and bread that night.[1]

This moving account of would-be juvenile consumers speaks volumes about Canada in the interwar years. By creating desire through advertising, corporate capitalism touched most people, including children. The commercial media, dominated by radio, movies, magazines, and newspapers, focused on the good life and encouraged people to indulge the whims of the moment. Defying the sexual and social taboos of the prewar period, many women wore shorter skirts and displayed a devil-may-care attitude. Men returning from the trenches in Europe ignored the petty conventions that had characterized polite society in the prewar years. Prohibition, poverty, and a domestic ideal in which gender roles were rigidly prescribed also marked the interwar years. The clash of old and new values created tensions and sparked debates about many issues, including how families should raise children and what it meant to be a man or woman in the modern age.

POPULATION

In 1941, Canada's population was more than 11 500 000. Immigration peaked during the late 1920s but dried up during the Depression (see Table 10.1). In the interwar years, Canada still gave preferential treatment to immigrants from Great Britain and the United States. The federal government bowed to pressure from railway companies, manufacturers, and farmers—all facing labour shortages—and opened the doors to wider European

TABLE 10.1

Canada's Population (in thousands), 1911-1941

YEAR	NATURAL INCREASE	IMMIGRATION	EMIGRATION	NET MIGRATION	POPULATION
1911-21	1270	1400	1089	311	8 788
1921-31	1360	1200	970	230	10 377
1931-41	1222	149	241	-92	11 507

Source: Statistics Canada

immigration after the postwar recession began to ease. Southern Ontario, largely an Anglo-Celtic preserve before 1920, joined the West in becoming home to tens of thousands of southern and eastern European immigrants.

Some of Canada's new immigrants had fled religious persecution at home. Between 1922 and 1930, more than 20 000 Mennonites arrived from the Soviet Union. Most settled on prairie farms, reliving the harsh lives of earlier generations of settlers. Ukrainian-Canadian politics of the interwar period was strongly influenced by the debate about the future of Ukraine. While radicals supported the Soviet Union, conservative Ukrainians wanted an independent, non-Communist Ukraine.

Racism continued to dog many new Canadians. In 1923, federal legislation excluded Chinese nationals from immigrating to Canada. This policy prevented men working in Canada from bringing their families from China, and unemployment, especially during the Depression, meant there was no money to send home to the family. Many accepted Vancouver City Council's offer of a free one-way ticket to China on condition that they never return. The Japanese invasion of China in 1937 cut communications between China and Canada, leaving Chinese Canadians without knowledge of the fate of their loved ones back home.

The Japanese in Canada were also caught up in the web of international developments. Since most were second-generation Canadians, or *Nisei*, they spoke English and shared the liberal democratic outlook of other Canadians. Nevertheless, they continued to face discrimination in educational and job opportunities, and were subject to growing hostility as Japan began its military assault in Asia. An articulate minority of Nisei formed associations to discuss their mutual problems and founded

English-language newspapers such as *The New Canadian*. Their elders, by contrast, clung to the language and traditions of their Japanese homeland.

While the gates were open to continental Europeans during the 1920s, 28 000 of them were deported during the Depression, most because they were unable to find work and applied for relief. A significant minority were expelled because they participated in left-wing politics or union activity in their adopted country.

CANADA'S NATIVE PEOPLES

In the interwar years, the living conditions of most Natives continued to deteriorate. Courts, dominated by whites, rejected Native efforts to establish land claims. A 1928 decision in the case of *R. v. Sylliboy* found that eighteenth-century treaties in the Maritimes were invalid because the Mi'kmaq had allegedly not been competent to sign. After receiving jurisdiction over their natural resources in 1930, the Prairie provinces tended to ignore treaties with the federal government that granted hunting and fishing rights in Native territories.

In the North, southern trappers similarly ignored Native hunting rights, and overtrapping led to resource

These Métis trappers at their winter camp in the foothills of the Rockies in the 1930s barely eked out a living for their efforts. SOURCE: GLENBOW ARCHIVES PA-2218-985

depletion. The Inuit, drawn into the whaling industry off Herschel Island in the western Arctic, suffered massive epidemics. The population began to rise only in the 1930s as the Inuit developed immunities to European diseases. Ultimately, a new northern society emerged that was characterized, in the words of Kenneth Coates, by "limited growth, federal government neglect, dependence on a small number of mines, a vibrant fur trade, and a bicultural society."[2]

Without treaties of any kind, the Métis lived in appalling conditions. A provincial commission in Alberta heard shocking medical evidence suggesting that 90 percent of the Métis population was infected with tuberculosis. The province responded in 1939 by establishing six Métis colonies where schools and health care were provided, but the colonies lacked an economic base. In Saskatchewan and Manitoba, the Métis were almost completely ignored by their provincial governments.

ENVIRONMENTAL ATTITUDES

Government interference in Aboriginal trapping and hunting practices was often justified on the grounds of conservation of game. Wood Buffalo National Park, for example, was established after the First World War on the traditional hunting territory of the Chipewyan with a mandate to increase buffalo numbers. Park managers ordered the Chipewyan, who depended on the bison to supply most of their food, clothing, and trade needs, to drastically reduce their kill. The Chipewyan resisted the new policy, but they were hardly alone in resisting the demands of game wardens. Rural residents generally regarded them with suspicion and often threatened them with violence, occasionally murdering wardens who persisted in enforcing conservation measures.

Some Natives benefited from the desire of wealthy Canadian and American sportsmen to have wilderness experiences. Seeing an opportunity to earn some much-needed income, they offered their services as hunting and fishing guides. For example, Johnnie Johns, a successful Yukon entrepreneur of Tagish and Tlingit heritage, began a long guiding career in the 1920s. Along the way he accepted "enfranchisement"—that is, he relinquished his Indian status, likely to improve his chances of being licensed as a chief guide.

Governments were slow to impose conservation measures unless a species or resource was threatened. For example, the soil-destroying practices of Prairie farmers received little attention before the 1930s. Only when drought aggravated the problem to the point that wheat cultivation seemed to be in jeopardy was action taken. Beginning in 1935, the federal government's new Prairie Farm Rehabilitation Administration (PFRA) organized Agricultural Improvement Associations to encourage better farming practices. Community pasture programs and water development projects soon followed. The PFRA also worked with Ducks Unlimited to establish wildlife conservation areas. Established in 1938, Ducks Unlimited Canada consisted mainly of wealthy members who were also sportsmen, whose efforts were focused on preserving wetlands without challenging private property rights.

SEXUALITY AND RESPECTABILITY

As Canadians moved to cities, and movies and radio vied with churches and schools for the minds of the masses, fears spread of a moral breakdown in society. Established church leaders, in particular, regarded modern culture as hedonistic, violent, and profane. Traditionalists countered modernism by reaffirming long-standing moral conventions that sex was only acceptable if it was heterosexual, infrequent, and confined to married couples. They also railed against dancing, drinking, gambling, smoking, and swearing—behaviour associated with the Roaring Twenties.

Heterosexual men who violated this moral code faced few penalties, but women risked their reputations if they became sexually available "flappers." A pregnant unwed woman lost all claims to "respectability" and, if she could afford it, concealed her condition. Both public and private institutions were prepared to exploit her for their own ends. In Chester, Nova Scotia, the Ideal Maternity Home charged hefty fees both for unwed pregnant women who stayed in the home and for would-be parents who adopted the babies. Many of the babies born in the home died. Their bodies were packed in empty butter boxes and hastily buried behind the home.

In Montreal and Quebec City, unwed mothers could give birth at hospitals run by religious congregations such as the Soeurs de la Miséricorde and the Soeurs du Bon-Pasteur, in return for labour in the hospitals. Poverty forced most of them to allow their children to be adopted. In Montreal, more than a third of the children died in the homes during their first year, mostly from preventable diseases. So deep was the social disapproval that haunted "illegitimate" children that a nun wrote to the grandfather of one of the children in 1934: "Dear Sir: We regret to say that the baby born to E.C. is dead. Thank God for this great favour."[3] When the Duplessis government introduced mothers' allowances in 1937, it forbade municipalities from providing social assistance to single mothers, which prompted municipal authorities in Montreal to remove these mothers from its welfare rolls.

In the interwar years, the birth-control movement gained widespread support in English Canada. New attitudes toward sex made the 1892 criminalization of the provision of birth-control information seem antiquated, standing in the way of "modern" values. When the Depression descended, limiting family size became an essential survival strategy for the growing number of people experiencing hard times. A few birth-control clinics, beginning in Hamilton in 1932, began offering advice about planned parenthood, and in 1935 Alvin Kaufman, a wealthy businessman from Kitchener, Ontario, founded the Parents' Information Bureau to distribute birth-control information more broadly.

Such blatant defiance of the law against counselling contraception resulted in a test case before the courts. In 1936, Dorothea Palmer, a field worker for the Bureau, was arrested for distributing birth-control information in the French-Canadian, Catholic working-class suburb of Eastview in Ottawa. She was tried and acquitted in 1937 on the grounds that her work was done for the public good. Resolute resistance from the Quebec government and the Roman Catholic Church prevented the federal government from following up this landmark decision by making birth-control devices legal.

The Eastview birth-control trial also had eugenic undertones: the judge's ruling asserted that the children of poor mothers were a burden on the public. This darker side of the birth-control movement found its ultimate expression in the idea that the human race would be improved by sterilizing people deemed physically and mentally inferior to some defined standard.

Nazi Germany's grim implementation of this policy eventually discredited eugenics, but in the interwar years it had the support of many Canadians. In 1928, Alberta established a Eugenics Board with the power to authorize the sexual sterilization of individuals deemed "psychotic" or "mentally defective." The Board approved 4725 cases for sterilization, and 2822 were carried out before the legislation was finally repealed in 1972. In British Columbia, where similar legislation was in place between 1933 and 1973, such drastic measures were less likely to be imposed.

Women who were victims of sexual assaults were wary of using the courts to have their assailants punished. Any suggestion of sexual impropriety in her life could turn the trial against the victim rather than the rapist. Women who laid complaints against rapists not only risked disbelief and ostracism within their communities, but they also experienced low self-esteem in a society that was so wary of sexual impropriety.

Apart from condemning as immoral women who transgressed the sexual conventions, respectability required that a married woman be seen as a good mother, frugal consumer, tidy housekeeper, and devoted wife. Similarly, men wanted to reflect the image of good providers who turned over enough wages to their wives for the family to live decently. Poverty caused many men to become hopelessly depressed, to commit suicide, or to desert their families as it became impossible to fulfil their breadwinning roles.

Meeting the ideal of respectability eluded many people. A letter written by a Mrs Richards to her landlord, the Halifax Relief Commission, in 1926, illustrates efforts to cling to an image of respectability in the face of extreme poverty. Asking for time to make up back rent, she argued that her husband's limited income made it "pretty hard to be respectable a[nd] to keep up under the conditions we are living." This family of six had one bed, where the father and three children slept while the mother and baby slept on a mattress with a broken spring. There was too little money for food and fuel, but Mrs Richards wrote that she would go to prison before going on the streets. Her father-in-law had offered to help in exchange for sex. "I'm an English-woman and I'd not touch one cent of money belonging to that man," she declared.[4]

Divorce remained uncommon in interwar Canada, even in provinces where it was legally recognized. The

1931 census indicated that fewer than 8000 Canadians were legally divorced. Husbands were more likely than wives to desert their marriages. While some women left abusive husbands, sometimes taking the children with them, most accepted the economic logic that fleeing simply plunged the family into permanent poverty. The judicial system continued to be unsympathetic to most women's accusations of battering and deaf to claims from children about abuse by relatives. Mothers' allowances, introduced in all provinces except New Brunswick and Prince Edward Island during the First World War or in the interwar period, were modest and restricted in most provinces to widows.

MOTHERHOOD IN THE MODERN AGE

In the interwar years, mothers became the particular focus of a campaign to reform and homogenize child-rearing practices. Mass-circulation magazines and government-sponsored child welfare departments dispensed "scientific" advice on how to be a better mother. "Old-fashioned" methods and "maternal instinct" came under harsh criticism. While reformers worked to reduce infant mortality through better hygiene, dietary practices, and prenatal care, there was a tendency to medicalize motherhood. In 1926, only 17.6 percent of births took place in hospitals, a figure that rose steadily to 94.6 percent in 1960.

Experts increasingly intruded in the nursery, with middle-class families leading the way in embracing new methods of bringing up baby. Funded by private sources, two nursery schools, one in Montreal, one in Toronto, were established to study children. The University of Toronto's Institute of Child Study became world-famous under Dr William Blatz for its pioneering work on child development.

Views about raising children departed dramatically from the prewar period. Reflecting new notions of behavioural science pioneered by American psychologists, families were encouraged to teach their children good habits from an early age by establishing fixed schedules for every activity. At its height, the trend toward regimentation included toilet training at the age of two weeks. "If the time and place are always the same and the mother shows her approval of the first successes," one 1943 pamphlet suggested, "the baby will soon learn what is expected of him."[5]

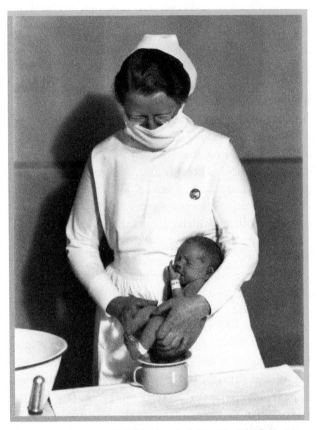

Child-care experts opined that regimentation was best for both mother and baby. Such advice was reflected in attempts to "toilet train" infants almost immediately after birth, as in this 1939 photo of a nurse and newborn in Ottawa. SOURCE: LIBRARY AND ARCHIVES CANADA PA-803178

WOMEN, WORK, AND THE FAMILY

Work, including waged work, meant different things to men and women. Gendered attitudes about work were reinforced by the different socialization that girls and boys received. As historian Joy Parr notes:

> Through waged work, boys learned manliness; they mastered disciplines and discriminations, ways of appraising their work and one another, which they would practice through their adult lives; varied though these ways of being manly were, they shared one trait: they were lessons males alone might learn. Girls did not learn womanliness through their paid employment. Their experience of waged work was important in their growing into womanhood because it became them to remain under the protection of male kin while they waited for their life's work, in marriage and outside the market, to begin.[7]

MORE TO THE STORY
The Dionne Quintuplets

The five girls born to a poor rural francophone couple on 28 May 1934 in Corbeil, Ontario, illustrate the impact of show business on Canadian society. They also reveal the increasing power of the state and medical experts in the lives of Canadian families. From the moment they were born, Annette, Emilie, Yvonne, Cecile, and Marie Dionne were famous. The media immediately focused on what was indeed a remarkable event—the birth and survival of quintuplets. Almost as quickly, the state removed the infants from the care of their parents, who were already raising five older children. Two months after their birth, the Ontario government placed the girls under the control of a local board of guardians and moved the babies to a specially equipped hospital where their upbringing was overseen by Dr Allan Roy Dafoe, who had helped to deliver them. Only after a long battle were the girls restored to their outraged parents.

It was little wonder that everyone wanted custody of "the Quints," who had become a major economic asset. They had endorsements of more than $1 million, were the subjects of Hollywood films, and became a major tourist attraction—three million curiosity-seekers flocked to view them from behind a one-way screen. The girls never recovered from their first traumatic years and felt little bond with their parents or older siblings after their return to the family home. Emilie died in a convent in 1954, and the four survivors recorded their unhappy stories in *We Were Five* (1965). In 1995, the survivors charged that their father had sexually abused them, offering yet another wrinkle to their tragic story. The willingness of the state, the media, the medical profession, and even their own family to exploit the girls provides a telling glimpse into the values of the modern age.[6]

Ontario cabinet minister David Croll (left) poses in 1934 with Dr A.R. Dafoe (centre) and "the Quints." SOURCE: ARCHIVES OF ONTARIO S801

Many rural women dreamed of escaping to the city and many of them sought waged labour there. As their diaries and letters attest, they went to movies, dances, and shops with friends whom they had met at work and in boarding houses, but their work lives were rarely glamorous. Most were underpaid store clerks, office workers, and domestics. Immigrant women whose first language was not English were clustered in the lowest-wage occupations, such as home sewing by the piece, cleaning, and laundering.

Women's work created a sense of community in new single-industry towns such as Powell River, British Columbia,

Montreal Housewives and the Great Depression

In the 1980s, historian Denyse Baillargeon interviewed working-class Montreal women who had married between 1919 and 1934 about their Great Depression experiences. While these women described remarkable hardships, they also revealed a great deal about how they had managed to survive long periods when their husbands could find no work, and about the dreams they had held for their future.

One woman recollected how relatives helped to tide her family over during hard times.

> They helped us out a lot because they brought us lots of vegetables from the country. One of my sisters was married to a farmer, so she could bring me lots of vegetables. . . . We used to walk to my mother's place sometimes for weeks at a time. When we didn't go, she sent for us. She said: "Come on over, I was worried." . . . Then when we were at her place, we made many little things. Sewing, knitting . . . we were fortunate because we always had my mother-in-law . . . if we were lacking food, we went to eat there, and that was the end of that . . . as soon as my little girl ate, I knew that everything would work out. Sometimes she kept her for three or four days.

When family aid was not available or was insufficient, families had recourse to charitable organizations such as the Société Saint-Vincent de Paul or the Salvation Army for food, clothing, and furniture. The completely destitute qualified for relief from the city, but it was minimal. Credit with the grocer, doctor, and small shopkeepers was available to some, but those who could avoid indebtedness often chose simply to go without. As a housewife explained:

> We never had debts. I never bought anything on credit because I told myself that if I had no money today, I would have no more tomorrow. . . . If we had had debts, I do not

know how we would have paid them. In those days, we always thought that the day after we might have no wages. There was nothing then, you know (no social measures). It was necessary not to rely on anyone. It was necessary to rely on ourselves. That is why many times we went without many things we would have liked to have. But you couldn't, you didn't, that was it.

Some women violated the taboo against married women working outside the home in order to supplement family income, but only if their families were small—one or two children—and babysitting could be arranged. One recalled:

> He earned ten bucks a week. We couldn't get by. So I worked. I sewed for people, knit, I did everything to make ends meet . . . 15 cents for knitted mittens, 35 cents for stockings . . . it was no fortune. But for me, it helped a lot.

Since most of these women had been poor before the Great Depression, the Depression seemed only an intensification of the poverty they largely took for granted. But they were not all fatalistic. Some women talked, for example, about how they ignored Roman Catholic teachings favouring large families and resorted to contraception. They believed that with fewer mouths to feed, they and their children would be better off. A housewife summed up her feelings at the time:

> I told myself that the Good Lord sent me children but I did not want them to suffer later on. The big families always had miseries. . . . So I said that my kids, if they wanted to study, they were going to study and I was going to help them and that is what I did. You have to plan. I said I prefer to have a small family and to be able to give them what they want. It was the education that I was looking to for later on.[9]

and Timmins, Ontario. While the men toiled in the town's main industry, their wives established community facilities. A woman who arrived in Flin Flon, Manitoba, in 1926 when the town was still a bush camp, later recalled: "Women organized the community centre, the schools, the hospital. . . . Women looked after the home

and that's what makes this town great. It's a family town."[8]

Female single parents faced dismal prospects. Rose and Edith Biscun were nine and six when their widowed Russian mother placed them in the Winnipeg Jewish Orphanage in 1931. Until 1936, she worked all week in a *shmata* (garment) factory, seeing them only occasionally.

Children in single-parent families enjoyed few opportunities, as their labour was needed for financial support. In 1931 Halifax, 25 percent of 15- to 19-year-olds were in school, versus 12 percent for children of widows.

HOUSING CANADIANS

By international standards of the period, Canadians were relatively well-housed. While individual home ownership was the ideal, this varied considerably across the country. Toronto in 1921 had the highest rate of home ownership of the 20 largest North American cities, whereas Montreal had one of the highest proportions of tenants on the continent. Housing conditions were not always ideal. During the Second World War, a government-sponsored report provided a detailed picture of the shelter available to Canadians that highlighted deficiencies. The report concluded that 10 percent of existing dwellings should be demolished, while another 25 percent required major repairs. There was overcrowding in one in five dwellings.

Ethnicity influenced housing options. Land titles often had restrictions that kept non-whites, Jews, and eastern Europeans out of new developments. French Canadians and eastern European immigrants were far more likely than Anglo-Canadians to be living in overcrowded conditions. Visible minorities fared worst, being easy targets for prejudiced realtors and landlords. Natives on reserves often lived in unheated shacks. Families in the Chinese business quarters east of Dewdney Street in Vancouver lived shabbily, and single Chinese males lived in crowded, poorly lit, poorly ventilated boarding houses. This was hardly surprising since British Columbia gave Chinese men an accommodation voucher worth a third of white men's vouchers.

In the early 1920s, both workers and the middle class lived in the heart of the cities, though the middle class had larger lots and better access to sewer and water services. Many workers escaped the pollution, noise,

and squalor of the neighbourhoods where they could afford to rent by building homes on the urban fringes. By the mid-1920s, middle-class families, now in possession of cars, viewed the previously unattractive urban fringes as ideal places to raise families. Urban planners and developers alike pressed city councils to implement regulations requiring that suburban homes meet certain building standards and be subject to municipal taxes. These measures often forced the original low-income suburbanites to return to the city centres. Following the planners' models, the new suburbs were residential oases separated from commercial and industrial life and characterized by curved streets, large parks, and generous-sized lots.

Wherever they lived, Canadians of the interwar period were influenced by the new domestic ideal propagated in the media. This ideal suggested that, along with the church and community hall, the home should be a major site for entertainment. Radios, gramophones, and fine furnishings were necessary accoutrements for a satisfactory middle-class home life. As "labour-saving devices" such as electric stoves, vacuum cleaners, and washing machines began to replace servants, wives increasingly did all their own housework, often in isolation from other women. Men were expected to spend less time in public places and more time with their families.

Tenants being evicted in Montreal during the Depression. In 1931, only 15 percent of Montrealers lived in homes they or their families owned, one of the lowest rates in North America; by 1941, this had dropped even further, to 12 percent. SOURCE: LIBRARY AND ARCHIVES CANADA C-30811

Some Canadians paid outrageous rents to secure an accommodation that could help them approximate the goals of the new cult of domesticity.

RURAL LIFE

As late as 1921, a majority of Canadians lived in communities of less than 20 000 people, and even in 1941, more than two out of five Canadians were rural residents. Most farmers depended on the sale of their produce to buy farm implements and consumer goods. When hard times descended, they could survive by subsistence farming, an option unavailable to most city-dwellers. This was particularly true for farmers in the fertile belt of southern Ontario, Quebec, and the Maritimes. Many farmers' sons and daughters returned to farms during the 1930s to wait out the Depression.

More than ever before, rural Canadians were connected to metropolitan centres. By the late 1920s, 40 percent of Alberta farmers owned an automobile and used it to shop in the larger towns and cities. Small-town merchants lost business and often closed shop, leaving their towns to languish, a trend that would continue throughout the twentieth century.

In the interwar period, the farm population of Ontario and Quebec declined, but it remained stable in the Maritimes and increased on the Prairies. More farms were created in northern Saskatchewan and Alberta, as well as in the foothills of the Rocky Mountains. These provided an alternative to unproductive areas on the southern Prairies, the driest of which were abandoned after homesteaders had made heartbreaking efforts to turn deserts into productive farmlands.

During the 1930s, provincial governments settled landless families without income on infertile lands where it was hoped that they could eke out a subsistence. The "back-to-the-land" movement of the 1930s suggested the strength of agrarian ideology in Canada, which held that it remained possible in the industrial age for families to live off the land without help from the state. In Quebec, provincial expenditures on rural roads and church emphasis on sustaining parish institutions kept many communities alive. Elsewhere, the bleakness of life in some of the new farming areas disillusioned those who had been resettled, and many families relocated to cities and towns when the Second World War offered them employment. Outside of portions of southern Ontario, electrification was slow to reach rural Canadians. As late as 1949, only one percent of Saskatchewan farms had electric power.

THE COMMUNICATIONS REVOLUTION

The automobile transformed transportation in the interwar years, but it was not alone in shattering the isolation of even the remotest rural community. For most people, airplanes were the wonder of the age. Canadians eagerly awaited news of aviation pioneers, such as Americans Charles Lindbergh and Amelia Earhart, as they made daring attempts to cross the Atlantic or to fly around the world. The commercial potential of air flight was especially obvious in the Canadian North, which attracted "bush pilots" willing to fly to remote areas. In 1936, the federal government established Trans-Canada Airlines (the precursor to Air Canada) as a Crown corporation to help bridge the great distances that defined Canada.

Although the technology for radios, recordings, and movies pre-dated the First World War, they came into their own in the 1920s, precipitating a revolution in the ways that Canadians created and consumed culture. Radio made its first appearance in Canada in 1920 and became wildly popular. By 1941, four in five Canadian households owned a radio. Farmers in areas without electricity might buy a crystal radio set in the 1920s, which required only an antenna to pick up radio waves. In the 1930s, battery-operated radios, whose sound was less likely to fade in and out, became more popular than crystal sets.

Most of the early Canadian radio stations were owned by appliance retailers or newspapers. Advertising provided revenues to owners while selling products and dreams to a largely uncritical and unsuspecting audience. American stations and programs dominated the early Canadian radio scene, both English and French. Fears that unregulated radio would contribute to the Americanization of Canadian culture sparked the formation of the Canadian Radio League. Taking its inspiration from the state-owned British Broadcasting Corporation, the League declared that, in broadcasting, it was "the state or the United States."

In 1928, the federal government created a royal commission to advise on the future control, organization, and financing of radio broadcasting. Sir John Aird, president of the Bank of Commerce, chaired the commission, which recommended the creation of a public broadcasting company to own and operate all radio stations and to build seven stations across the country. In 1932, Prime Minister R.B. Bennett established the Canadian Radio Broadcasting Commission, which in 1936 was reorganized as the Canadian Broadcasting Corporation. The CBC was to supervise the operations of the private stations and use its own stations to foster a "national spirit." Limited funding left the CBC largely unable to create programs that would lure audiences away from the American-dominated private stations. Apart from airing American shows, these stations focused on recorded music from New York's Tin Pan Alley and Nashville's Grand Ole Opry.

Canadians also watched American movies. After the First World War, movies had become a favourite pastime for Canadians of all social classes. The average Canadian went to 12 movies a year in 1936, and children in cities watched far more. Most of the movies were made in Hollywood, even those watched by francophones in Quebec. Marginalization of the Canadian film industry was apparent by the early 1920s as major American studios came to dominate the distribution as well as production of films. By 1930, Famous Players distributed about 90 percent of all feature pictures shown in Canada.

Movies defined the material desires of mass consumer society. The silver screen shaped individual fantasies, established trends in clothing and hairstyles, and encouraged new patterns of leisure and recreation. Canadian politicians recognized that film was a powerful medium. In 1939, the National Film Board was created with a mandate to interpret Canada to Canadians and to the larger world. Quickly swept up in producing wartime propaganda, the NFB thrived under its first commissioner, John Grierson, a British film producer.

Magazines also helped to establish standards of taste and behaviour. In 1925, American magazines outsold their Canadian counterparts in the country by eight to one. Tariff protection in the Bennett years reduced the gap to three to two, but by the end of the Depression, as trade agreements removed tariff protection for made-in-Canada magazines, American magazines regained their former market share. Nevertheless, *Chatelaine*, *Maclean's*, and *Saturday Night* magazines survived the competition, while in French Canada, publications such as *La Revue populaire* and *La Revue moderne* catered to francophone audiences.

Interwar governments had little interest in legislating greater Canadian content in the popular media. They focused instead on censoring materials deemed unsuitable, especially in movies. Quebec's censorship board was the most aggressive, but not alone in snipping scenes depicting sex, burglaries, gambling, divorce, suicide, and unpatriotic behaviour. A prime reason for much of this censorship was that the new mass culture was corrupting the younger generation. If radio, movies, and dance halls took up all the time of young people, it was argued, they would soon reject the moral values and religious convictions of their elders.

THE CHRISTIAN CHURCHES IN A SECULAR AGE

The Protestant churches, concerned about the worldly focus of modern society, often tried to turn back the tide of modernism. In 1925, the leaderships of the Methodist, Presbyterian, and Congregationalist churches agreed to merge their denominations into the United Church of Canada in an effort to support the cause of ecumenism and to increase their influence. United Church leaders were motivated by lofty notions of the Christian mission in Canada, but many Presbyterians, particularly in Ontario and the Maritimes, were more concerned with preserving Scots and Scots–Irish cultural traditions than in pursuing the exalted goals of their clergy. A large minority of Presbyterians rejected the union and maintained the Presbyterian Church as a separate entity.

The founders of the United Church hoped to influence legislators in such areas as temperance, censorship, Sunday observance, and gambling. The Prohibition issue illustrates their limited success. The federal government had yielded to distiller pressure after the war to abandon national Prohibition, leaving the fate of "demon rum" to the provinces. Soon the Prohibition front began to crumble, beginning with a vote by British Columbians in 1920 to create a government monopoly on hard liquor sales, with beer to be sold in grocery stores. By the end of the 1920s, only Prince Edward Island clung to Prohibition.

The conservatism of Canadian churches was evident in attitudes to women. Although the majority of active church members were women, they were not welcome in the pulpit. The United Church ordained Canada's first female minister, Lydia Gruchy, in the 1930s, but few women were encouraged to follow in her footsteps. For some Canadians, the mainline Protestant churches remained too liberal and lacking in fervour. The

MORE TO THE STORY
Booze and Drugs

Liquor was big business in the interwar period. Both large-scale and mom-and-pop bootlegging operations sprouted everywhere during Prohibition to serve both the illicit alcohol trade at home and the lucrative American market, fuelled by the rigorous policy of Prohibition south of the border from 1920 to 1933. As Canadian jurisdictions eased their restrictions against alcohol, the larger bootleggers often became legitimate big business operators in Canada, while continuing their illegal operations in the United States.

Liquor empires could be found in all regions. In New Brunswick's Madawaska County, Albenie Violette, also known as Joe Walnut, worked in tandem with American crime syndicates to smuggle liquor into the United States, assembling gun-toting groups of former lumberjacks and sailors to staff his large-scale interests in distilling, rum-running, and bootlegging. The Bronfman family made their early fortune with an illegal distillery in Saskatchewan that similarly cooperated with American crime syndicates to smuggle booze into the United States. In 1924, they used their profits to open up the Distillers' Corporation in Montreal, and in 1926, with Ontario about to end Prohibition, they bought control of Seagram in Waterloo.

Men and women line up to buy alcohol at a Commission des liqueurs branch in a francophone area of Montreal in 1937. Despite its long-standing reputation for social conservatism and resistance to state intervention, Quebec in 1921 joined British Columbia as one of the first two Canadian jurisdictions to institute a government monopoly on alcohol sales. SOURCE: BIBLIOTHÈQUE ET ARCHIVES NATIONALES DU QUÉBEC, CENTRE D'ARCHIVES DE MONTRÉAL P48,S1,P1892

While bootleggers were mainly men, a few women participated in the trade. Women were even more prominent as the operators of "blind pigs," illegal drinking establishments, whose female owners were generally known by a combination of "Ma" and their surnames.

Ironically, just as the Canadian provinces were winding down their efforts to make the manufacture and sale of liquor illegal, the federal government strengthened the laws regarding the sale and use of "narcotic" drugs. In British Columbia, opponents of Asian immigration campaigned hysterically against the supposed degeneracy of the Chinese, for which opium use was allegedly emblematic. Responding to the general moral panic about drug use, the federal government increased the penalties for "trafficking" and possession of opium and banned the use of marijuana in 1923, making a moral rather than a medical judgment of its harmfulness. The Royal Canadian Mounted Police (RCMP) quickly earned a reputation for its vigilance in cracking down on drug users and political radicals, both of whom conservatives regarded as violators of Christian morality. Formed in 1920 by a merger of the Royal North-West Mounted Police and the Dominion Police, the RCMP cultivated an image of moral rectitude and efficient policing that limited debates about its often high-handed interference in Canadians' civil rights.[11]

Pentecostals and the Jehovah's Witnesses were among the religious sects that grew in the interwar period and that focused almost exclusively on the individual's relationship with God.

The Roman Catholic Church was, if anything, more conservative than the major Protestant denominations on women's issues. While the Protestant churches cautiously endorsed mechanical contraceptives to limit family size in the 1930s, the Catholic hierarchy would only endorse the use of the unreliable rhythm method. It was also implacably against divorce and most efforts to foster equality for women.

Even in Quebec, where the church enjoyed considerable success in its efforts to stem the tide of modernism, new values began to have an impact. As historian Michael Gauvreau has pointed out, in church-sponsored institutions, such as the popular Action catholique youth movements, the "more personalist, egalitarian, and cultural interpretations that posited the relationship between husband and wife as involving reciprocal understanding of each partner's imagination, will, and sensibility, rather than legalistic notions of hierarchy and subordination, began to appear in the waning years of the Depression."[10]

In the Maritimes, the Roman Catholic Church sponsored the Antigonish Movement, a unique combination of cooperatives and adult education to help producers escape exploitation by middlemen. The movement was led by Father Moses Coady, the founding director of the Extension Department of St Francis Xavier University in Antigonish, Nova Scotia. Beginning in 1928, cooperatives were established in many communities dependent on farming, fishing, coal mining, and steel production. The movement was particularly successful among Acadians, who responded enthusiastically to Coady's message of community cooperation.

EDUCATION

By the 1920s, parents who could afford to delay their children's entry into the workforce generally encouraged them to complete as many years of secondary schooling as possible. The Ontario government endorsed this goal by extending the school-leaving age to 16 in 1921, a move that most other provinces gradually copied. As the value of academic skills was increasingly recognized, high school matriculation became a prerequisite for many jobs. Public schools reinforced gender stereotypes in the workforce, streaming boys who were not academically minded into trades programs while girls received commercial or domestic training. In keeping with the gender stereotype, elementary education remained primarily in the hands of poorly paid single women, while men predominated among the higher-paid high school teachers.

Quebec francophones, indeed francophones generally, lagged in the trend toward increased schooling. As late as 1926, only six percent of Quebec francophones attended school beyond the elementary level. The Catholic Church in the province still resisted pressure to force children to remain in school, its leaders arguing that higher education was needed only for future priests,

MORE TO THE STORY
Medical Research in Canada

C.H. Best (left) with Dr. Frederick Banting (right), co-discoverers of insulin, on the roof of the University of Toronto Medical Building in 1921. The dog, "Dog 408," was one of those used in the experiments that led to the discovery. SOURCE: UNIVERSITY OF TORONTO, FISHER LIBRARY P10077

Canadian universities were not only teaching institutions; they also sponsored research. Canadians made headlines in the field of medicine in the early 1920s when a team at the University of Toronto, headed by Frederick Banting, discovered insulin, a life-saving therapy for diabetes mellitus. Banting and one of his co-researchers, J.J.R. McLeod, shared the 1923 Nobel Prize for their efforts. Banting gave half of his prize money to C.H. Best, a key researcher on the investigative team.

At McGill University's Medical Museum, Maude Abbott's authoritative cataloguing of the types of congenital heart disease led to the eventual development of surgical therapies for its treatment. Surgical intervention saved the lives of countless "blue babies," whose fate in earlier years had been almost certain death. Although Abbott was recognized as one of the world's leading authorities in her field, McGill never promoted her beyond the level of assistant professor.

In 1934, Wilder Penfield established the Montreal Neurological Institute, which rapidly became internationally renowned for its research, teaching, and treatment related to diseases of the nervous system. Penfield established the "Montreal procedure" for the treatment of epilepsy and was a tireless student of the brain, which he argued was the most important unexplored field of scientific inquiry.

teachers, and professionals. Since the labour of older children often kept families out of poverty, many were pleased that schooling was not compulsory. By the early 1940s, reformist elements within the church joined with trade unions and liberal women's organizations in recognizing the need for a better-educated citizenry. Finally, in 1943, the Liberal government of Adélard Godbout passed

legislation making education compulsory for children from ages six to 15.

Outside Quebec, only New Brunswick resisted restrictions on French-language education. Poor educational opportunities and an association of French with poverty encouraged many francophones outside Quebec to assimilate to the anglophone culture. In 1931, the percentage of Ontarians whose first language was French but who later became primarily English speakers was reported as 22.1 percent. Acadians in the Maritimes were also finding it difficult to resist assimilation in the age of mass consumer culture, which was overwhelmingly delivered in the English language.

Enthusiasm for schooling extended slowly to the post-secondary sector. With university education generally still confined to an elite minority, provincial governments were reluctant to increase spending on universities. Between 1929 and 1940, Canadian university enrolment increased from 23 418 to 37 225. Women's participation jumped from 16 to 24 percent of all enrolment, but their increase was concentrated in areas stereotyped as women's professions: nursing, household science, library science, and physical and occupational therapy. Women were rarely hired as professors outside of the departments offering training in "women's professions." In the interwar years, women seeking educational challenges or career training became an important part of the audience for adult education programs. Several universities established extension programs aimed first at rural areas, and eventually at the non-university population of the cities.

Nor was adult education restricted to universities. At the turn of the century, Frontier College had been founded by Alfred Fitzpatrick, a Nova Scotia–born Presbyterian minister, to provide basic education to workers, particularly immigrants. In the interwar years, university students flocked to work sites on the industrial frontier to teach people with little other hope of receiving formal education. Trade unions and political parties of the left ran schools in an attempt to counter the information dispensed by the media, which the left viewed as tools of the capitalist class. In Montreal, for example, labour activist Albert Saint-Martin founded the Université ouvrière in 1925. Its Sunday lectures on subjects ranging from communist doctrine and anticlericalism to astronomy and history attracted hundreds of participants.

LITERATURE AND ART

A better-educated public provided an increasing market for the arts, despite the overwhelming influence of American popular culture. The creation of the Canadian Authors' Association in 1921 testified to a new sense of national identity among Canadian writers. With 800 members and a French-Canadian branch, it sponsored an annual book week and encouraged sales of the works of Canadian authors.

In Quebec, novels written by francophones remained preoccupied with the idealization of rural life, but a few writers, led by Ringuet (pseudonym for Philippe Panneton), stressed that the traditional Quebec was disappearing and could not be restored. Social realism marked much of the literature of English Canada. From Irene Baird's *Waste Heritage*, chronicling class strife in British Columbia during the Depression, to Martha Ostenso's *Wild Geese*, with its portrait of a tyrannical Manitoba farm patriarch, the writing of this period reflected the critical perspectives that had emerged after the First World War. Such perspectives were often unappreciated. Frank Parker Day's *Rockbound* (1928) portrayed a small fishing village headed by a tyrant whom the hard-working but insular local people failed to resist. The people of Ironbound, Nova Scotia, recognizing that their village had provided the inspiration for the novel,

Emily Carr, *Kispiax Village*, c. 1929. SOURCE: ART GALLERY OF ONTARIO 2420

demanded and received an apology from Day in 1929 for casting them, in their view, in an unfavourable light.

In the interwar years, many Canadian painters were in revolt against conventional subject matter and styles. Emily Carr's work was enriched by Native art forms and themes. In New Brunswick, Miller Brittain was a leading member of a group of artists who abandoned idyllic landscape art to portray the harsher side of Maritime life, while in Quebec, modernist approaches influenced francophone artists such as Marc-Aurèle Fortin and Adrien Hébert in their depictions of Montreal. Perhaps the most influential art of the period was the work produced by the Group of Seven. Although originally based in Toronto, members of the group worked across the country. More popular than the new experimental art, their work contributed to a nature-based Canadian nationalism. Over the years, A.Y. Jackson and Arthur Lismer remained especially faithful to the Group of Seven's original work, while Lawren Harris's art became more abstract, and Fred Varley, through Emily Carr, discovered Native art.

MUSIC AND THEATRE IN THE INTERWAR YEARS

When film and radio reduced the audience for the popular prewar vaudeville shows, many music halls became cinemas. Movies posed a threat to touring theatre troupes, but community theatre groups flourished. In 1933, the first Canadian Drama Festival was held in which community theatre groups competed for prizes in acting, directing, design, and production after a series of regional run-offs. This annual event stimulated amateur theatre across Canada.

Radio and records increased the audience for live bands, and a variety of nightclubs sprang up in Canadian cities. Guy Lombardo and His Royal Canadians and Wilf Carter (who had morphed into Montana Slim) were among the Canadian acts beamed into Canadian homes on American airwaves. In Quebec, Mary Travers, known as La Bolduc, became the province's most successful recording artist. Her songs focused on the realities of daily life. Although some of her witty and, for the times, naughty lyrics earned her the disapproval of the church, francophone Quebecers flocked to buy her records.

The classical music tradition was strengthened by the creation of schools of music at the University of Toronto, McGill University, and Université Laval. New symphony orchestras in Toronto, Montreal, and Vancouver gave professional classical musicians an outlet for their talents. In 1939, two immigrant English dance teachers, Gweneth Lloyd and Betty Farrally, launched the Winnipeg Ballet Club, now Canada's oldest ballet company, operating under the name Royal Winnipeg Ballet since 1953.

BIOGRAPHY

Guy Lombardo and His Royal Canadians

North Americans were swept off their feet in this period by a dance band featuring the talents of a tightly knit Italian-Canadian family from London, Ontario. Guy Lombardo and His Royal Canadians were North America's third-best-selling recording act of the first half of the twentieth century, selling more than 100 million records in a career that spanned three decades and nosedived only when rock and roll eclipsed earlier popular music styles in the mid-1950s.

Guy Lombardo (1902-1977), the band leader, and his brother Carmen (1903-1971), singer, songwriter, and alto saxophonist, were the core of the Lombardo entourage. Two other brothers also performed in the band at various times, and Guy's sister Rosemarie was a featured singer for several years in the 1940s. The children of Italian immigrants, the Lombardos were part of an ethnic community in London that trained many musicians. They began performing in the town while still teenagers, and were soon in demand for performances throughout southern Ontario.

Moving to the United States in 1924 and adopting the name Guy Lombardo and His Royal Canadians, they began a recording career that took them to the number one spot on *Billboard* magazine's hit parade 26 times from 1927 to 1950. As the band became popular, Guy Lombardo added more musicians to create the most successful "big band" of the Great Depression era. Composers assiduously courted the Lombardos, and the band introduced some of the major English-language standards of the twentieth century, including "Red Sails in the Sunset," "September in the Rain," and "Managua, Nicaragua." Their radio performances from the Roosevelt Grill in New York, beginning in 1929, were a top draw for two decades, and they also enjoyed some success in the early years of television. They were widely credited with making Scottish poet Robert Burns's "Auld Lang Syne" the classic New Year's tune in North America. Starting with "Many Happy Returns" in 1934, the Lombardo boys were featured in a number of popular movies. Guy also won trophies as a speedboat racer and invested heavily in oil and uranium properties in the United States.

The Lombardo band advertised its music as "the sweetest music this side of heaven," and critics often panned them as a formula orchestra that failed to innovate. Record buyers, however, liked their sound, and their legion of fans included major jazz figures such as Louis Armstrong and Ella Fitzgerald.[12]

Guy Lombardo and His Royal Canadians. SOURCE: FRIENDS OF LOMBARDO/ GUY LOMBARDO MUSIC CENTRE

THE CULT OF THE FOLK

As Canadians contemplated the rapid changes that had occurred since Confederation, they often viewed the past through a romantic haze, inventing traditions and imagining golden ages. The National Museum of Canada, created by an Act of Parliament in 1927, and the Historic Sites and Monuments Board, established in 1919, symbolized this new interest in the past. Upon the advice of the board, the government designated national historic sites. Most of the sites recognized by the board in the interwar period—for example, Port Royal and Queenston Heights—related to military and political developments in the nation's past.

With a long recorded history of European settlement, Maritimers and Quebecers eagerly embraced historical approaches to identity creation. The pre-Confederation pioneers were increasingly depicted as happy folk, living in farming and fishing communities untouched by the materialism of the industrial age. In Quebec, Lionel Groulx's

historical writings emphasized the purity and virtuousness of the settlers in New France. Researchers sought descendants of the folk still living in the "traditional" way, claiming to find in these people the essence of regional identities. In the late 1930s, for example, American anthropologist Horace Miner chose to study the French-Canadian parish of Saint-Denis-de-la-Bouteillerie, free of urbanization, economic diversification, and English Canadians, in order to elucidate "the old rural French-Canadian folk culture in its least-altered existent form."[13]

The "cult of the folk" sold well to consumers of culture and tourism in the modern age. In Nova Scotia, many of the symbols of provincial identity—Peggy's Cove, the *Bluenose*, and the Scottish bagpiper—emerged in the interwar years. Historian Ian McKay underlines the contradictions embodied in the cult of the folk: in upholding their pre-modern, quaint, therapeutic otherness, he argues, it was simultaneously drawing the folk into the commercial and political webs of modern society.[14]

SPORTS IN THE MODERN AGE

In the interwar years, interest in professional sporting events increased among all social classes. Hockey's reputation as the national sport was cemented, as indoor stadiums, artificial ice, and the expansion of the National Hockey League to American cities gave the game new prominence. The Montreal Forum opened in 1924, followed by Maple Leaf Gardens in 1931. After the Ottawa Senators folded in 1934, the only Canadian teams in the NHL were the Montreal Canadiens and the Toronto Maple Leafs, but all four American teams in the league had a majority of Canadian-born players.

Baseball remained a popular participant sport, as did softball, the latter regarded as an acceptable sport for women. There was also a semi-professional baseball league in Quebec, and both Montreal and Toronto had teams in the International League, headquartered in the United States. Although the sports world was still largely a male preserve, Canadian women fared well in international competitions. Fanny Rosenfeld stands out among women athletes of the period, having won the silver medal in the 100-metre dash at the 1928 Amsterdam Olympics. She was also lead runner for the 1928 gold-medal relay team, and was Canada's leading woman broad jumper and discus thrower. In basketball, the Edmonton Grads pursued a remarkable career through the interwar period. When they disbanded in 1941, they left a record that has yet to be equalled, winning 93 percent of their games and 49 out of a possible 51 domestic titles.

Throughout the country, sportswomen faced sexist opponents who claimed that participation in sports was unladylike. In Quebec's Catholic schools, the introduction of physical education programs for girls was delayed until the end of the interwar period because of church concerns that team sports were unseemly for future mothers and involved girls wearing clothes that did not cover their entire bodies. Cécile Grenier, director of physical education programs for girls for the Montreal Catholic School Board from 1938 to 1951, attempted to placate church concerns by focusing on individual sports for recreational purposes rather than team sports.

SERVICE ORGANIZATIONS

Spurred by increased urbanization and a shorter work week, voluntary organizations proliferated in the interwar years. Churches, fraternal associations, and the militia continued to provide men with opportunities to bond on the basis of religious, ethnic, or patriotic inclinations. In English Canada, community-service organizations such as the Rotary Club, Kiwanis, Gyros, and the Elks, which had no ethnic or religious affiliation, raised funds for local facilities such as libraries, swimming pools, community halls, and parks, as well as participating in parades to boost community spirit and supporting community groups such as the Boy Scouts.

Women remained active in church groups and secular voluntary organizations. In 1919, women who had university degrees founded the Canadian Federation of University Women and involved themselves in both social reform and charitable activities. The Canadian Federation of Business and Professional Women's Clubs was organized in 1930 to convince business leaders that better training and fairer treatment for women were ultimately in the interests of business. In 1920, Halifax hosted the first Congress of Coloured Women in Canada, testimony to the growing

One of Canada's outstanding sports stories was supplied by a female basketball team, the Edmonton Grads, students and alumnae of that city's Commercial High School. Beginning in 1915 and continuing for 25 years, the Grads put together an unrivalled record of wins over domestic and international opponents. They are pictured here in 1922 as First Dominion Champions. SOURCE: PROVINCIAL ARCHIVES OF ALBERTA A-11428

The Farming Community

The farming community of the interwar years was anything but unified. While some farmers saw themselves as allies of the working class, others increasingly viewed themselves as middle-class business people. Historians also take opposing sides on the issue. In the classic work *The National Policy and the Wheat Economy* by economist Vernon Fowke, Prairie farmers are presented as a rather uniform group of individuals oppressed by national tariff and railway policies.[15] C.B. Macpherson's study of the Social Credit movement, *Democracy in Alberta*, presents a similar though less sympathetic view of the farmers of that province. Macpherson portrays farmers as "independent commodity producers" who were, in fact, dependent on market forces over which they exercised little control. Still, as individuals who owned modest farmsteads and employed few labourers, their self-image did not allow them to identify with the cause of working people.[16]

Other historians present the farming community as more diversified and call into question the notion of "independent commodity producers." David McGinnis indicates that off-farm labour was required by most farmers in the interwar period to make ends meet; they might have viewed themselves as independent commodity producers, but this perspective was largely an illusion.[17]

Jeffery Taylor argues that false views of farmers' true position were not accidental, but in large part were the creation of agricultural colleges and other institutions in Canadian society that shaped the view that farmers held of themselves.[18] The Manitoba Agricultural College, for example, rejected the older language of agrarianism in which farmers joined workers as an exploited producing class whose problems were the result of greedy monopolists. Instead, its professors encouraged farmers to see themselves as scientific managers of a producing property who could, if they behaved intelligently, make market forces work to their advantage.

John Herd Thompson notes that many farmers employed labourers on a seasonal basis, and that they often proved to be very harsh employers.[19] In a study that focuses on farm labourers, Cecilia Danysk details the increasing stratification of the farm community in the interwar period. As the costs of farming soared, only the farmers who developed large land holdings could survive. The lifestyles of these farmers were quite different from those of farmers who eked out a living from small homesteads. They were even more at variance with the lives of farm labourers. While farm labourers had once been a group comprising men saving money to buy their own farms and transients who did not remain on the Prairies for long, the number of permanent farm labourers was on the rise in the interwar period because the cost of getting into farming had become prohibitive.[20]

---

numbers and organized activism of black citizens in the city. Following the Privy Council ruling on the Persons Case in 1929, Canadian women were deemed equal in rights and privileges as well as pain and penalty, thus opening the door for women to interpret their empowerment in the public sphere as part of a larger movement for human rights, which was gaining momentum internationally.

CONCLUSION

Interwar Canada was a society in transition. Older ways rubbed uneasily against the new mass culture and its commercially oriented values. Self-styled experts on raising children, urban planners promoting suburban living, and birth-control advocates challenged conventional perspectives, while churches led the defence of traditional values. Attracted by American movies, records, magazines, and radio programs, Canadians struggled to establish their own national culture, but it was an uphill battle. The threat of American cultural dominance was balanced by identities that were regional, local, and political. In the 1930s, hard times exposed class and gender differences that had been easier to minimize in the better economic times of the 1920s. With the outbreak of the Second World War in September 1939, Canada's fragile unity would again be tested.

NOTES

1. Cited in Veronica Strong-Boag, *The New Day Recalled: Lives of Girls and Women in English Canada, 1919–1939* (Toronto: Copp Clark Pitman, 1988) 13.

2. Kenneth Coates, *Canada's Colonies: A History of the Yukon and Northwest Territories* (Toronto: Lorimer, 1985) 100.

3. Quoted in Andrée Lévesque, "Deviants Anonymous: Single Mothers at the Hôpital de la Miséricorde in Montreal, 1929–1939," *Historical Papers/Communications historiques* (1984) 178.

4. Quoted in Suzanne Morton, *Ideal Surroundings: Domestic Life in a Working-Class Suburb in the 1920s* (Toronto: University of Toronto Press, 1995) 41–42.

5. Cited in Katherine Arnup, *Education for Motherhood: Advice for Mothers in Twentieth-Century Canada* (Toronto: University of Toronto Press, 1994) 92.

6. "The Dionne Quintuplets: The Birth of an Industry," Special issue of the *Journal of Canadian Studies* 29, 4 (Winter 1994–95).

7. Joy Parr, *The Gender of Breadwinners: Women, Men, and Change in Two Industrial Towns 1880–1960* (Toronto: University of Toronto Press, 1990) 186.

8. Cited in Meg Luxton, *More Than a Labour of Love: Three Generations of Women's Work in the Home* (Toronto: Women's Press, 1980) 29.

9. Translated from Denyse Baillargeon, "La Crise ordinaire: les ménagères montréalaises et la crise des années trentes," *Labour/Le Travail* 30 (Autumn 1992) 156, 158, 144, 146–7.

10. Michael Gauvreau, *The Catholic Origins of Quebec's Quiet Revolution, 1931–1970* (Montreal: McGill-Queen's University Press, 2005) 183.

11. On Prohibition, see Craig Heron, *Booze: A Distilled History* (Toronto: Between the Lines, 2003). The interwar war on drugs is explored in Catherine Carstairs, *Jailed for Possession: Illegal Drug Use, Regulation, and Power in Canada, 1920–1961* (Toronto: University of Toronto Press, 2006).

12. On the life and music of Guy Lombardo, see Guy Lombardo with Jack Altshul, *Auld Acquaintance: An Autobiography* (New York: Doubleday, 1975).

13. Horace Miner, *St. Denis: A French-Canadian Parish* (1939; Chicago: University of Chicago Press, 1963) ix.

14. Ian McKay, "Helen Creighton and the Politics of Antimodernism," in *Myth and Milieu: Atlantic Language and Culture, 1918–1939*, ed. Gwendolyn Davies (Fredericton: Acadiensis Press, 1993) 16.

15. Vernon C. Fowke, *The National Policy and the Wheat Economy* (Toronto: University of Toronto Press, 1957).

16. C.B. Macpherson, *Democracy in Alberta: Social Credit and the Party System* (Toronto: University of Toronto Press, 1962).

17. David McGinnis, "Farm Labour in Transition: Occupational Structure and Economic Dependency in Alberta, 1921–1951," in *The Settlement of the West*, ed. Howard Palmer (Calgary: University of Calgary, 1977) 174–86.

18. Jeffery Taylor, *Fashioning Farmers: Ideology, Agricultural Knowledge and the Manitoba Farm Movement, 1890–1925* (Regina: Canadian Plains Research Center, 1994).

19. John Herd Thompson, "Bringing in the Sheaves: The Harvest Excursionists, 1890–1929," *Canadian Historical Review* 59, no. 4 (December 1978) 467–89.

20. Cecilia Danysk, *Hired Hands: Labour and the Development of Prairie Agriculture, 1880–1930* (Toronto: McClelland & Stewart, 1995).

SELECTED READING

Baillargeon, Denyse. *Babies for the Nation: The Medicalization of Motherhood in Quebec, 1910–1970*. Waterloo: Wilfrid Laurier University Press, 2009

Baillargeon, Denyse. *Making Do: Women, Family, and Home in Montreal During the Great Depression*. Waterloo: Wilfrid Laurier University Press, 1999

Brownlie, Robin Jarvis. *A Fatherly Eye: Indian Agents, Government Power, and Aboriginal Resistance in Ontario, 1918–1939*. Toronto: Oxford University Press, 2003

Campbell, Lara. *Respectable Citizens: Gender, Family, and Unemployment in Ontario's Great Depression*. Toronto: University of Toronto Press, 2009

Carstairs, Catherine. *Jailed for Possession: Illegal Drug Use, Regulation, and Power in Canada, 1920–1961*. Toronto: University of Toronto Press, 2006

Comacchio, Cynthia R. *The Dominion of Youth: Adolescence and the Making of a Modern Canada, 1920–1950*. Waterloo: Wilfrid Laurier University Press, 2006

Duder, Cameron. *Awfully Devoted Women: Lesbian Lives in Canada, 1900–65*. Vancouver: UBC Press, 2010

Heron, Craig. *Booze: A Distilled History*. Toronto: Between the Lines, 2003

Hinther, Rhonda L. and Jim Mochoruk, eds. *Re-Imagining Ukrainian Canadians: History, Politics, and Identity*. Toronto: University of Toronto Press, 2011

Kelm, Mary-Ellen. *Colonizing Bodies: Aboriginal Health and Healing in British Columbia, 1900–50*. Vancouver: UBC Press, 1998

Lévesque, Andrée. *Making and Breaking the Rules: Women in Quebec, 1919–1939*. Toronto: McClelland & Stewart, 1994

Loewen, Royden, and Gerald Friesen. *Immigrants in Prairie Cities: Ethnic Diversity in Twentieth-Century Canada*. Toronto: University of Toronto Press, 2009

Loo, Tina. *States of Nature: Conserving Canada's Wildlife in the Twentieth Century*. Vancouver: UBC Press, 2006

Lux, Maureen K. *Medicine That Walks: Disease, Medicine, and Canadian Plains Native People, 1880–1940*. Toronto: University of Toronto Press, 2001

Mar, Lisa Rose. *Brokering Belonging: Chinese in Canada's Exclusion Era, 1885–1945*. Toronto: University of Toronto Press, 2010

Mathieu, Sarah-Jane. *North of the Color Line: Migration and Black Resistance in Canada, 1870–1955*. Chapel Hill: University of North Carolina Press, 2010

McKay, Ian. *The Quest of the Folk: Antimodernism and Cultural Selection in Twentieth-Century Nova Scotia*. Montreal: McGill-Queen's University Press, 1994

McLaren, Angus. *Our Own Master Race: Eugenics in Canada, 1885–1945*. Toronto: McClelland & Stewart, 1990

Neatby, Nicole and Peter Hodgins, eds. *Settling and Unsettling Memories: Essays in Canadian Public History*. Toronto: University of Toronto Press, 2012

Sandlos, John. *Hunters at the Margin: Native People and Wildlife Conservation in the Northwest Territories*. Vancouver: UBC Press, 2007

Srigley, Katrina. *Breadwinning Daughters: Young Working Women in a Depression-Era City, 1919–1929*. Toronto: University of Toronto Press, 2010

Strong-Boag, Veronica. *The New Day Recalled: Lives of Girls and Women in English Canada, 1919–1939*. Toronto: Copp Clark Pitman, 1988

Swyripa, Frances. *Storied Landscapes: Ethno-Religious Identity and the Canadian Prairies*. Winnipeg: University of Manitoba Press, 2010

Vance, Jonathan F. *Death So Noble: Memory, Meaning, and the First World War*. Vancouver: UBC Press, 1997

Vipond, Mary. *The Mass Media in Canada*. Toronto: Lorimer, 2011

Walls, Martha Elizabeth. *No Need of a Chief for This Band: The Maritime Mi'kmaq and Federal Electoral Legislation, 1899–1951*. Vancouver: UBC Press, 2010

For a comprehensive list of readings for topics covered in this chapter, please visit http://pearsoncanada.ca/conrad.

CHAPTER 11
CANADA'S WORLD WAR, 1939-1945

On 3 March 1943, Joseph Goebbels, Adolf Hitler's minister of Propaganda, noted in his diary: "It drives one mad to think that any old Canadian boor, who probably can't even find Europe on the globe, flies to Europe from his super-rich country which his people don't know how to exploit, and here bombards a continent with a crowded population."[1] Goebbels had reason to be concerned. By 1943, Canada was turning out fighter planes, pilots, and bombs at a rate few could have imagined in 1939, and they all played a critical role in the bombing of Germany. The sad irony of war was recognized by people other than Goebbels. What Canadians seemed unable to do in peacetime they did with surprising ease during the Second World War: they produced their way out of the Great Depression.

Canadians had hoped that the Great War would be the war to end all wars, but it was not to be. In 1939, Canadians were again fighting in Europe against Germany and its allies. There seemed little choice but to try to stop Adolf Hitler, who appeared to be determined to create a new world order in which he and his Nazi followers would reign supreme over peoples they deemed inferior. As in the First World War, Canadians were allied with Great Britain, France, and the United States, but this time Canadians declared war in their own right and emerged from it as a nation to be reckoned with on the world stage.

HITLER'S WAR

When Hitler came to power in 1933, he moved quickly to pursue a fascist program for the reconstitution of a German "homeland," which included destroying other nations and cultures. Italy's fascist leader, Benito Mussolini, gravitated toward Hitler, especially after Great Britain and France tried to thwart plans for an Italian empire in Africa following Mussolini's invasion of Ethiopia in 1935. In 1938, Germany annexed Austria and then gobbled up Czechoslovakia. Italy annexed Albania in the spring of 1939. In August, Hitler signed a non-aggression pact with the Soviet Union under Joseph Stalin, freeing the way for the depredation of their mutual neighbour, Poland. On 3 September, two days after Hitler had invaded Poland, Great Britain and France declared war on Germany. One week later, on 10 September, Canada joined the war against the Nazis. The Japanese, who had already launched a full-scale invasion of China in 1937 and were engaged there in a brutal war of conquest, saw an opportunity to further extend their influence in the Pacific. They

Hitler Youth rally in Nuremberg Stadium on National Socialist Party Day, 1933. SOURCE: STAPLETON COLLECTION/CORBIS

allied themselves with Germany and Italy to form the Axis Powers in 1940 and, in 1941, attacked American and British positions in the Pacific.

Even more than the First World War, this war was easy for most Canadians to see as a struggle between good and evil. It was also a difficult war to avoid. With submarines, fast surface warships, and long-range aircraft capable of spanning great distances, every country in the world was vulnerable. Indeed, the Japanese bombing of Pearl Harbor in Hawaii on 7 December 1941 jarred the United States out of its own isolationism and into the war. The Americans declared war only on Japan, and that led Hitler, under the provisions of the alliance with Japan, to declare war on the Americans.

The Canadian government invoked the War Measures Act to ensure that it had all the powers it needed to fight an all-out war, but it was initially slow to mobilize the nation's military and economic might. Although this policy earned Prime Minister William Lyon King harsh criticism from Premier Mitchell Hepburn of Ontario, among others, it helped reassure francophone Quebecers that this would be Canada's war, not one in which Canada's wartime policy would be dictated by Great Britain. Early in 1939, prompted by his Quebec lieutenant, Ernest Lapointe, and by the Conservative Party's similar pledge, King had promised Quebec that his government would not impose conscription for overseas service in the event of war. It was a pledge that he would have occasion to repeat in two elections held during the early months of the conflict.

CONSCRIPTION, ROUND TWO

After war was declared, Quebec premier Maurice Duplessis hoped to gain an easy victory for his government by calling a snap election and making Canada's involvement in the war the major issue in the campaign. Quebec's ministers in King's cabinet threatened to resign if Duplessis won. Fearing that without its Quebec contingent the cabinet might renege on King's promise not to impose conscription, a majority of Quebecers elected the provincial Liberal Party, led by Adélard Godbout, to office.

Hepburn's stinging criticisms of Ottawa's failure to pursue an all-out war effort prompted King to dissolve Parliament in January and call a national election for March 1940. Campaigning on a policy of voluntary enlistment, the Liberals won a resounding victory, taking over 51 percent of the popular vote and 184 out of 245 seats in the House of Commons.

King was shrewd or just plain lucky to have called an election when he did. In April 1940, Hitler's forces struck down Denmark and Norway and then conducted a blitzkrieg—literally a lightning war—through the Netherlands, Belgium, and France. The surrender of France early in June and the evacuation of the British Expeditionary Force from Dunkirk raised fears that Great Britain might also be defeated. As Great Britain's largest surviving ally, Canada was suddenly forced to consider a much larger contribution to the war effort than King and his cabinet had originally envisaged. The government moved swiftly to enact the National Resources Mobilization Act (NRMA), which provided for the conscription of soldiers for home defence and state control of economic resources.

As the war dragged on, pressures from army commanders, from within cabinet, from opposition members, and from many Canadians caused King to re-evaluate his position on conscription. He decided to hold a national plebiscite on 27 April 1942, which asked Canadians for a "yes" or "no" vote on whether the government should be released from its pledge not to impose conscription for overseas service. Overall, 64 percent of Canadians voted "yes," but at least 85 percent of Quebec francophones demanded that King honour his original promise. King continued to resist imposing conscription, but even the threat of it was enough to spark the formation of the Bloc populaire canadien, a new nationalist political party in Quebec, and to help return the Union nationale to power in a 1944 provincial election.

The provincial wing of the nationalist, anti-conscription Bloc populaire canadien was led by André Laurendeau, a young journalist shown here speaking in Montreal before the 1944 provincial election. The party won four provincial seats, and took several federal seats as well, but disappeared soon after the war. SOURCE: CENTRE DE RECHERCHE LIONEL GROULX P2/T1, 53.4

King did his best to avoid conscription, including firing his pro-conscription defence minister J.C. Ralston in November 1944. Ralston was replaced by General A.G.L. McNaughton, King's choice in 1939 to command the army overseas. When McNaughton failed to secure the necessary voluntary enlistments, the government passed an order-in-council in late November 1944 allowing the armed forces to dispatch 16 000 NRMA men to overseas duty.

Commonly called "Zombies"—a word made fashionable in Hollywood as an African-Caribbean reference to men who had no souls—NRMA men were not pleased about this turn of events. In Terrace, British Columbia, they seized an anti-tank gun to defend themselves against officers trying to send them overseas; in London, Ontario, 600 men of the Oxford Rifles went absent without leave; and in Drummondville, Quebec, 2000 civilians attacked RCMP and military police sent to hunt down deserters. These outbursts went undisclosed in the media, whose war reporting was subject to censorship. In the end, only 13 000 NRMA men were sent overseas.

As in the First World War, conscription strengthened the credibility of Quebec nationalists and added to feelings of betrayal among francophone Quebecers. Unlike Borden and the Conservative Party in the First World War, King avoided a backlash from Quebec in the subsequent election because it seemed clear that he had done nearly everything humanly possible to avoid conscription.

ENLISTMENTS

Canadian participation in the war effort was impressive. Nearly 1.1 million men and women joined the forces, including 100 000 through the NRMA, from a population estimated at 11.5 million in 1941. Most served in the army; about 250 000 joined the Royal Canadian Air Force (RCAF) and nearly 100 000 joined the Royal Canadian Navy (RCN). In addition, a Merchant Navy was established at the beginning of the war to bolster Allied wartime shipping, and the Pacific Coast Militia Rangers (PCMR) was formed early in 1942 to patrol and defend the coastline of British Columbia and the Yukon against a Japanese invasion. About 12 000 served in the Merchant Navy (of whom 2200 died) and 15 000 in the Rangers.

French-Canadian enlistment in the Second World War was significantly higher than in the First World War. Some historians suggest that they accounted for 15 to 20 percent of the volunteers for overseas service, or as many as 160 000 men, a much greater number than in the earlier war. About 37 percent of the men called up for home defence were French Canadians. Like their English-Canadian counterparts, French Canadians who enlisted in the early stages of the war often did so to seek adventure. Others simply wanted employment. Eventually, the wartime economy led to a labour shortage, and recruitment became more difficult.

As in the First World War, Canadians were relatively lucky. More than 42 000 died in service, including about 17 000 members of the RCAF, but these losses paled in comparison to the overall tally. The total dead and wounded in the Second World War, including the Japanese invasion of China that preceded the Asian stage of the war, reached a staggering 70 to 80 million. Many were civilians, killed by bombs, by invading armies, or in concentration camps. The

A member of the Women's Royal Canadian Naval Service (Wrens) operating direction-finding equipment near Moncton, New Brunswick, in August 1945. SOURCE: LIBRARY AND ARCHIVES CANADA PA-142540

Soviet Union alone lost 27 million people, almost 14 percent of its population in 1941, while in China, between 20 and 30 million soldiers and civilians died during the Japanese invasion and occupation. Across Europe, the Nazis, singling out particular groups for total extermination, slaughtered 6 million Jews along with an untold number of Roma, homosexuals, and mentally challenged individuals. Another 14 million people were killed in what are now Poland, Belarus, Ukraine, Estonia, Latvia, and Lithuania as Nazi and Soviet armies crisscrossed their territories.

Although only men were permitted to participate in combat, some 50 000 women served in the Canadian armed forces. The military establishment was reluctant to accept them, but in the face of manpower shortages and the British example, it finally relented to the extent of creating separate female auxiliaries in the various branches of the armed services. In 1941, the army created the Canadian Women's Army Corps (CWAC) and the air force organized the RCAF Women's Division (WD). The navy followed suit in 1942 with the Women's Royal Canadian Naval Service (Wrens). In all, the navy enlisted 7126 women, the army 21 642, and the air force 17 467. There were also 4439 nurses in the Canadian Nursing Service. One nurse and three members of the RCAF (WD) were killed in action.[2]

The military was careful to keep women's divisions separate and subordinate to those of men. Initially slotted into jobs as nurses, clerks, secretaries, drivers, stretcher bearers, and cooks, women gradually took on less traditional roles such as mechanics, truck drivers, technicians, and spies. Margaret Eaton achieved the highest rank of any woman in the services when she was made acting colonel and director-general of the CWAC in April 1944. Nor did women receive the same pay and benefits as men, even when they performed the same job. Women complained about their unequal status and the National Council of Women took up their cause, but the pay gap, while narrowed, was never completely eliminated. When the war ended, all three women's services were abandoned.

While women's usefulness was never really questioned, their morality was. Rumours were rife about their lax morals, especially in the CWAC, where, it was alleged, women had a high incidence of "illegitimate" children and venereal disease. Men were allowed, and indeed encouraged, to vent their sexual energies unless they were directed toward other men. During the Second World War, the senior military brass became increasingly determined to rid the services of those engaged in "disgraceful conduct of an indecent kind," subjecting those accused of homosexual relationships to psychiatric assessments, court-martial proceedings, prison terms, and dishonourable discharges.[3]

DESCENT INTO WAR

Just before the surrender of France in June 1940, Italy entered the war, greatly increasing the pressure on British armed forces in the Mediterranean and North Africa. With the benefit of French air bases, Hitler's Luftwaffe conducted a destructive blitz on London and other British cities beginning in the summer of 1940, and launched a devastating U-boat campaign against Allied shipping in the Atlantic. Instead of invading Great Britain, as was expected, Hitler turned his army on the Soviet Union in June 1941, ignoring his non-aggression pact with Stalin. The United States entered the war at the end of the year, but it took time for its presence to be felt. Meanwhile, in late 1941, Japan destroyed the Far East fleets of the United States and Great Britain, defeated the British and Australians in Malaya and Singapore, and captured the American army in the Philippines. In June 1942, Japanese forces occupied islands in the Aleutian chain of Alaska.

Japanese-Canadian internees packing to leave for camps in the interior of British Columbia in 1942. SOURCE: LIBRARY AND ARCHIVES CANADA C-46350

It is in this context that two incidents in the war, one in Hong Kong and the other in British Columbia, must be understood. In December 1941, two battalions of Canadian troops, totalling nearly 2000 men, were involved in an effort to defend the British colony of Hong Kong against the Japanese. Almost 300 Canadians lost their lives and another 1700 were taken prisoner. Mistreatment in prison camps in Hong Kong and as forced labour in Japanese mines killed nearly 300 before the end of the war. At the time and later, there was much criticism of political and military leaders for allowing Canadians to get involved in such a hopeless campaign.

In February 1942, two months after Japan's attack on American territory at Pearl Harbor, President Franklin Roosevelt announced that people of Japanese ancestry were to be removed from the Pacific coast of the United States. A few days later, the Canadian government followed this example. Over the next few months, more than 22 000 Japanese Canadians—nearly three-quarters of whom had been born in Canada or were naturalized citizens—were removed from the coastal areas of British Columbia. Their homes, businesses, and personal property, initially placed under the "protection" of the federal government, were auctioned to the highest bidders in 1943. Other than suspicions about a few individuals who were already well known to the local RCMP, Ottawa had no evidence of any disloyalty of Japanese Canadians and no one was ever charged with treason. Yet King's government suspended the civil liberties of the entire Japanese-Canadian population, a policy that remained in place until 1949.

Coupled with hysteria created by the war, the long-standing racist attitudes of many British Columbians toward Japanese Canadians made it difficult for the federal government to pursue a more humane policy. About 700 men who had expressed support for a Japanese victory or had protested too vigorously against Ottawa's repressive policies were legally interned in a prisoner-of-war camp in Angler, Ontario, while women, children, the elderly, and the sick were unofficially interned in abandoned mining towns in the interior of British Columbia.

Able-bodied men were separated from their families and sent to work in road camps in the province. Families who wished to remain together were shipped to sugar beet farms in Alberta and Manitoba. Among the children removed from their homes in 1942 were David Suzuki, the future scientist, and Joy Kogawa, whose 1981 novel, *Obasan*, dealt with her family's internment.

Beginning in May 1945, all Japanese Canadians were forced to choose between deportation to war-devastated Japan or relocation east of the Rockies. To make deportation a more attractive option, Ottawa offered money and free passage to those who were destitute or too elderly or infirm to begin life again in eastern Canada. Nearly 4000 people were shipped to Japan between May and December 1946. Starving and desperate in postwar Japan, some of the deportees tried to return to Canada, but found a mountain of bureaucratic red tape blocking their re-entry. It was not until 1988 that the Canadian government officially acknowledged its mistreatment of Japanese Canadians during the war and provided compensation to surviving members of the community in recognition of their suffering.

THE WAR ON LAND

In Europe, the war continued to go badly for the Allies. Although the German army was stalled in its drive to Moscow, Allied efforts to create a division in France ended in dismal failure. An ill-conceived landing on French beaches at Dieppe in August 1942 left 907 Canadians dead and almost 2000 as prisoners. Only in the Middle East was there good news. In November, at El Alamein, Egypt, the British Eighth Army finally broke through the German and Italian lines, forcing Field Marshal Erwin Rommel and his hitherto seemingly invincible Afrika Korps into retreat. At the same time, the Russians were fighting the Germans to a standstill at Stalingrad. A staggering 850 000 Germans and their Italian, Hungarian, and Romanian allies lost their lives in the campaign. In December, the 80 000 survivors surrendered. The war had reached a turning point.

By 1943, the Canadian Army Overseas had expanded into a full field army, the 1st Canadian Army, with two corps, three infantry, two armoured (tank) divisions, and a wide array of additional formations and support units. Aside from the disastrous Dieppe raid and some smaller operations, the army stood guard in Great Britain until

the liberation of western Europe began with the Allied invasion of Sicily and then mainland Italy in the summer of 1943. The 1st Canadian Infantry Division took part in these operations, which became increasingly difficult as the Allies pushed up the boot of Italy against fortified lines the Germans had established in the mountainous terrain. During December 1943, in appalling conditions amid winter rains, more than 2300 men from the 1st Division were killed or wounded in bitter fighting for the town of Ortona, on the Adriatic coast. In early 1944, the Canadian presence in Italy expanded, playing a key role in breaking through the strongly defended approaches to Rome.

Meanwhile, a massive build-up of forces in Great Britain was preparing for an invasion of France at Normandy on 6 June 1944. Among the initial assault force was the 3rd Canadian Infantry Division, which led the assault at Juno Beach, one of the five main landing sites. Several assault companies, notably the Royal Winnipeg Rifles and the Queen's Own Rifles, suffered heavy casualties in the opening minutes of the landing. In addition, more than 100 warships of the RCN formed part of the naval forces that cleared mines, kept enemy warships and submarines at bay, landed troops, and provided artillery support to the soldiers struggling ashore. The huge air armada that forced back the Luftwaffe and saturated the German defences with bombs included many squadrons of the RCAF. It was a daring and costly effort, but it worked. The Allies finally had their long-desired front in northwestern Europe.

During the following weeks, the 1st Canadian Army, under the command of Lieutenant-General H.D.G. Crerar, crossed to France. The push inland from the beaches was a slow-moving, brutal campaign, with the Germans concentrating their strongest armoured forces in the British-Canadian sector. By the last week in August, two German armies had been destroyed, with some 400 000 casualties. The Canadians counted 5000 dead and more than 13 000 wounded, representing some of the heaviest losses of any Allied formation.

After the defeat of the main German forces in Normandy, the 1st Canadian Army moved up the coast of the English Channel, clearing strongholds. The culmination of these operations was a bitter five-week battle in October and early November, which, in the end, opened the Belgian port of Antwerp. The port was essential to maintaining the supplies of all the Allied armies in northwest Europe, but was opened at the cost of more than 6000 killed or wounded Canadians.

THE WAR AT SEA

The Royal Canadian Navy played a significant role in the war effort. After a shaky start, the RCN provided most of the escorts for the North Atlantic convoys that brought essential supplies to Great Britain and the Allied forces. They also had to defend the long coast from Labrador to Nova Scotia, which included the Gulf of St Lawrence, from German U-boats. Both the Battle of the Atlantic and the Battle of the St Lawrence gave people living in eastern Canada a real sense of being on the front lines of the war. Further afield, the RCN participated in the Normandy campaign, helped to protect British waters against U-boat attacks, joined in offensive strikes at German naval bases in Norway, and contributed escort ships to convoys that supplied Russian forces through the Arctic port of Murmansk.

These achievements did not come easily. At the outbreak of the war, the RCN had only six destroyers, a handful of small minesweepers, and no more than 3500 personnel. The plan was to increase this force gradually, primarily for the protection of Canadian waters. The fall of France in 1940 necessitated a different strategy. With access to French ports, "wolf-packs" of German U-boats began to slaughter Allied merchant ship convoys. In response to Great Britain's urgent appeal in May 1941, the RCN rushed the small corvettes, intended for coastal defence, into high-seas service to provide anti-submarine escorts for convoys between Newfoundland and British waters. At the same time, programs to build corvettes and other anti-submarine vessels in Canada were expanded, and recent recruits, ill-trained for their difficult mission, were pressed into service.

The entry of the United States into the war brought U-boats streaming into Canadian and American coastal waters in January 1942. Because the Americans were woefully short of anti-submarine vessels, the RCN was obliged to help the Americans on their east coast and in the Caribbean while maintaining its Newfoundland force and defending Canadian waters. The RCN faced a serious challenge in the Gulf of St Lawrence, where deep waters gave advantage to the U-boats. During the war, two small warships and 19 merchant ships were sunk in the gulf and in the lower reaches of the St Lawrence River. Among them was the Sydney–Port aux Basques ferry, which went down in October 1942 with a loss of 237 lives.

Convoys sailing under the protection of Canadian escorts from Newfoundland to Ireland also suffered heavy losses in 1942. In early November, a convoy bound for the United Kingdom lost 15 of its 42 merchant ships, a tragedy that along with the mounting death toll finally sparked a new approach. The routes of three of the four Canadian mid-Atlantic escort groups were changed in early 1943 so that they could use British base facilities to get improved equipment and advanced training. Soon thereafter, the RCAF acquired long-range bombers that could

MAP 11.1

The European Front, 1944-1945. The map shows the actions of Canadian troops during the Italian Campaign and the Northwest Europe Campaign

provide support for the convoys right across the North Atlantic. In April 1943, Rear-Admiral L.W. Murray, RCN, at Halifax, became commander-in-chief of the Canadian Northwest Atlantic theatre, the only Canadian to command an Allied theatre of war. During the last two years of the war, the RCN and RCAF played a major role in ensuring that thousands of ships and tens of millions of tonnes of cargo safely reached their destinations.

THE WAR IN THE AIR

Shortly after war was declared, Canada agreed to play host to the British Commonwealth Air Training Plan (BCATP), whereby Canadian and other Allied pilots and air crews would be trained for the war effort. Canada was an ideal location for the program. It had ample space

beyond the range of enemy aircraft and was close to vital American aircraft industries, upon which the success of the war in the air depended. At its height, the BCATP employed more than 100 000 ground crew at 231 sites across the country. The program trained over 130 000 pilots, navigators, flight engineers, and other aviation specialists, representing almost half the total air crew supplied by Great Britain and the Commonwealth for the war effort.

Another successful joint venture with the British and the Americans was Ferry Command, which was responsible for delivering planes built in North America to Great Britain. In 1939, the idea of flying planes across the Atlantic rather than sending them by ship was denounced as visionary nonsense by most officials in the British Air Ministry. Fewer than 100 successful transatlantic flights had been made since the first one in 1919. To the surprise of many skeptics, both the idea and the planes flew. Based

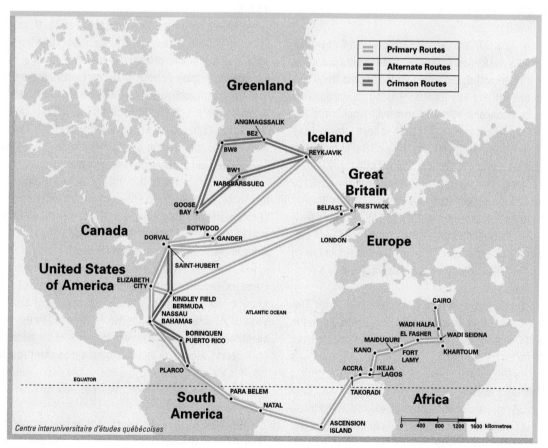

MAP 11.2

Principal Routes Flown by Ferry Command, 1940–1945

in Montreal, Ferry Command flew nearly 10 000 aircraft from enlarged or newly created air bases such as Gander and Goose Bay to Great Britain. At least 500 people lost their lives in Ferry Command, but it was, in the words of historian Carl A. Christie, "one of the most spectacular achievements of the war."[4]

Far more controversial was the Allied bomber offensive against Germany, in which Canadians participated. From its bases in northeastern England, the Royal Air Force's Bomber Command targeted German cities in an effort to disrupt industrial production and reduce German morale. Because the attacks were often on city centres or residential districts rather than industrial areas, critics claimed that the campaign was immoral. The bomber offensive has also been judged by some scholars as ineffective since it continued even when it became clear that the loss of lives among the air crews was unacceptably high.

MORE TO THE STORY
An Enduring Controversy

Canada's participation in overseas wars has often sparked debate, but few topics have generated more controversy than the Allied bomber offensive against Germany. Twice—in 1993 and again in 2007—attempts to interpret Canada's involvement in the bombing campaign were the subject of a Senate committee investigation.[5]

In January 1992, the Canadian Broadcasting Corporation (CBC) and Société Radio-Canada (SRC) aired *The Valour and the Horror*, a three-part documentary on the Second World War written by Brian and Terence McKenna. The second episode, "Death by Moonlight: Bomber Command," emphasized the extraordinary risks to which air crews had been subjected and the questionable morality of targeting civilians. In the weeks following the airing, the CBC was deluged with angry letters, many of them from veterans, who questioned the accuracy and tone of the series, especially the segment on Bomber Command. Critics demanded that the film be withdrawn from circulation. Its defenders argued that the film had been produced in the time-honoured documentary tradition of raising troubling questions and that suppressing it would be a violation of freedom of expression.

Hoping to gain political mileage, members of the Progressive Conservative government denounced the film in the House of Commons, and in 1993 organized a Senate hearing as a platform for critics. Meanwhile, a group of air force veterans launched a $500-million class action defamation suit against the filmmakers and their associates, declaring that their case was "about right and wrong; good and evil; white and black; truth and falsehood."[6] Academic historians, long accustomed to debates about and reinterpretations of the past, were summonsed to support both sides in the controversy, and thus were unable to establish a historical truth that might put an end to the matter. Although the case was eventually settled out of court, it put a "chill" on writers and filmmakers attempting to present revisionist history.

Shortly after the opening of the Canadian War Museum in Ottawa in 2005, a group of veterans, still smarting from the earlier confrontation, objected to the wording on a panel interpreting Bomber Command. The museum's curators had tried to head off controversy by entitling the panel "An Enduring Controversy" and directly raising the issues that sparked debate. This approach was too much for some of the veterans, who felt that the heroism and sacrifice of the young men involved were somehow being called into question.

In an effort to defuse the situation, museum administrators submitted the issue to a blue ribbon committee made up of four historians—David Bercuson, Serge Bernier, Desmond Morton, and Margaret MacMillan. The academics were unanimous in their opinion that the panel was accurate and balanced in its interpretation, but two of the four committee members—Bercuson and Bernier—suggested changes to the wording and images used in the panel that might assuage some of the veterans' concerns. Morton, alarmed by the precedent that would be set in making the changes demanded by the veterans, argued, "A museum is not a monument to opinion. It is a place of learning, argument, and of struggling to understand the truth. Truth does not emerge from the suppression of facts."[7]

Since the museum was reluctant to be seen as caving in to one group or another on a matter of interpretation, it initially decided to maintain the panel as it was originally conceptualized. This time, a Senate committee convened by Liberal members of the Senate in May 2007 heard testimony from the aggrieved veterans and their supporters. Ultimately, the museum panel was expanded to provide more information on Bomber Command, but neither side was entirely happy with the outcome.

The controversy over the interpretation of the Allied bombing offensive against Germany raises the larger question of who has the authority to interpret the past and what role the public in general–and the actors in an event in particular–have in determining how public commemorations of the past are presented. Although the search for an elusive historical truth motivates many people, including academic historians, many are beginning to understand that history is never really past and that it will continue to generate new interpretations and controversy as long as humans have historical memory.

MORE TO THE STORY
War Artists

During the First World War, Lord Beaverbrook commissioned artists to record Canada's war effort. It was the first large official commission for Canadian artists. Men with well-established reputations, such as Maurice Cullen, and promising unknowns, such as David Milne, were hired for the task. So, too, were four men who would later be known as members of the Group of Seven: A.Y. Jackson, Fred Varley, Arthur Lismer, and Frank Johnston.

In 1943 the war art program was reactivated, and artists were commissioned into the three divisions of the armed services. For the first time, female artists were included to document women's contributions: Molly Lamb eventually received a lieutenant's commission in the CWAC; Pegi Nicol MacLeod painted many aspects of the women's forces; and Paraskeva Clark and Alma Duncan recorded women's work in the war industries.

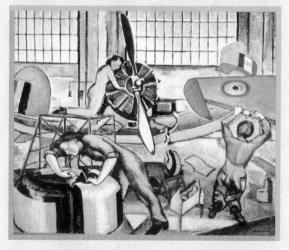

Alex Colville, *Tragic Landscape* (1945). Colville's painting shows a young German paratrooper killed by Canadian troops in April 1945 near Deventer, in the Netherlands. SOURCE: BEAVERBROOK COLLECTION OF WAR ART, CANADIAN WAR MUSEUM 19710261-2126

Paraskeva Clark, *Maintenance Jobs in the Hangar* (1945). Clark documents the activities of the RCAF Women's Division. SOURCE: BEAVERBROOK COLLECTION OF WAR ART, CANADIAN WAR MUSEUM 19710261-5678

Artists captured on canvas some of the worst horrors of the war. Charles Goldhamer painted RCAF flyers at a plastic surgery hospital in England; Aba Bayefsky and Alex Colville had the difficult job of documenting the Belsen concentration camp; Charles Comfort captured impressions of the Dieppe Raid and the Italian Campaign. Confronted with a larger-than-life situation, Canadian war artists produced some of their finest, if most disturbing, work during the war.[8]

Charles Comfort, *Via Dolorosa, Ortona*. Comfort shows soldiers of the 2nd Canadian Infantry Brigade fighting their way through the streets of Ortona, Italy, in December 1943. SOURCE: BEAVERBROOK COLLECTION OF WAR ART, CANADIAN WAR MUSEUM 19710261-2308

Charles Goldhamer, *Burnt Airman with Wig* (1945). This painting of Sergeant James F. Gourlay is one of a series by Goldhamer depicting burned airmen undergoing plastic surgery at the RCAF's plastic surgery wing in the Queen Victoria Hospital in Sussex, England. SOURCE: BEAVERBROOK COLLECTION OF WAR ART, CANADIAN WAR MUSEUM 19710261-3067

There is little doubt that the Allied bomber attacks were deadly. In all, some 560 000 Germans were killed and even more injured, most of them men over military age, women, and children. Although Bomber Command initially lacked the electronic and navigational aids to hit industrial sites with precision, even when more precise attacks became possible, the Royal Air Force chose to continue with area raids directed against German civilians. Bomber Command was doing what it set out to do—hit back at Germany, whose Luftwaffe had killed more than 13 000 civilians in London and other British

cities—but sinking to the level of the enemy in no way justified the strategy.

On the question of efficiency, Allied bombing, at least initially, spurred the Nazis to greater productivity, just as the bombing of London in 1940 had made the British determined to carry on. Only in the final months of 1944 did German production of war materiel begin a rapid decline. Allied bombing seems to have made a contribution to this outcome. Germany was obliged to employ more than half a million workers to repair bomb damage and almost a million men to operate the flak defences around their cities, personnel who could otherwise have been used in factories or on the battlefields.

As for the wisdom of the British air marshals who oversaw the bombing offensive, the evidence is mixed. There is little doubt that the head of Bomber Command, Sir Arthur Harris, was a single-minded individual, but his views on the strategic importance of air power to the war effort were shared by other Allied commanders. Nor is there any question that the bombing offensive was pressed in spite of the high casualty rates among the bomber crews themselves. Only one airman in three survived a 30-mission tour of duty in 1942.

Losses increased the following year when the Canadian government convinced the Air Ministry to form an RCAF group—No. 6 Group—in Bomber Command. As a junior unit, 6 Group, which eventually totalled 14 squadrons, was assigned inferior aircraft and equipment and was stationed in the Vale of York, farther from their targets than any other group in England. The results were predictable. From 5 March to 24 June 1943, 6 Group lost 100 aircraft, morale sagged, and an increasing number of missions were aborted or failed to reach their objectives.

In February 1944, Air Vice-Marshal C.M. McEwan was appointed to bring his professional energy to bear on 6 Group. Better training, new aircraft, and a reprieve from missions in Germany while Bomber Command supported the Normandy invasion netted better results. By the end of 1944, 6 Group boasted the highest accuracy and the lowest casualty rate of any group in Bomber Command. Such achievements do little to counter critics, who argue that the money and manpower committed to Bomber Command would have been much better spent on the understaffed and poorly equipped convoy service or in maintaining army ranks so that conscription could have been avoided.

VICTORY AT LAST

Early in 1945, the Canadians in Italy joined their comrades in the Netherlands for the final campaign. On the eastern front, the Red Army from the Soviet Union advanced on Germany, while the western front crumbled fast under Allied assault. Overrun from all sides, with their leader dead by his own hand, the Germans surrendered on 5 May.

The war in the Pacific dragged on for three more months and became the occasion for another embarrassing incident for the navy. When Canada agreed to provide support for a final drive against Japan, the crew members of HMCS *Uganda*, already in Okinawa, refused to participate on the grounds that the war with Germany was over and they had not enlisted to fight Japan. Since only volunteers were authorized for the Pacific front, the men claimed they were not obliged to fight and had the right to come home. Before *Uganda* reached Canadian shores, the war had come to an abrupt halt following the dropping of atomic bombs on Hiroshima and Nagasaki. On 14 August, the Japanese surrendered. Canada and the world had entered the atomic age.

Rich in uranium, a necessary ingredient of atomic energy, Canada played a major role in the production of the first atomic bomb. Early in the Second World War, a team of British, European, and Canadian scientists under the umbrella of the National Research Council had begun working on aspects of the atomic energy puzzle in laboratories based in Montreal. Canada also supplied the uranium for the Manhattan Project, the code name for top-secret research, based in the United States, on the deadliest weapon ever produced. The Combined Policy Committee, consisting of three Americans, two British, and one Canadian—Minister of Munitions and Supply

An Allied correspondent stands amid the rubble in the aftermath of the Hiroshima bombing of 1945. SOURCE: STANLEY TROUTMAN, CP PHOTO ARCHIVE

C.D. Howe—was established to oversee the project. In September 1945, Canada's first nuclear reactor facility was up and running at Chalk River, but, by that time, the military's use of atomic energy had already demonstrated its effectiveness.

THE BUSINESS OF WAR

On the surface, the Second World War had much the same impact on the Canadian economy as the First World War. It pulled the nation out of an economic slump, expanded production in all sectors of the economy, and dramatically increased export sales. On closer inspection, it was obvious that the country that had declared war on Germany in 1939 was vastly different from the one that had ridden to war on Great Britain's coattails in 1914.

Following a decade of increasing intervention in the economy, the government was better equipped in 1939 than it had been in 1914 to coordinate a major war effort. The system of planning, rationing, taxation, and wage and price controls imposed by the federal government early in the Second World War prevented the devastating inflation that had seriously disrupted the economy in the First World War. From April 1940, the Department of Munitions and Supply, under its energetic minister C.D. Howe, was given sweeping powers to bring wartime production to new heights of efficiency. With the help of members of Canada's business community, who were seconded to Ottawa, Howe expanded existing industries, created new ones, and focused the total resources of the country on the successful prosecution of the war.

The federal government's role in the war economy was pervasive. Its 28 Crown corporations produced everything from airplanes to synthetic rubber. In 1943, Ottawa made the Canadian Wheat Board the exclusive international sales agent for the nation's precious wheat crop. Under the auspices of the Wartime Prices and Trade Board, an army of controllers, regulators, and trouble-shooters fanned out across the country allocating output, rationing consumer purchases, and cutting through red tape. The federal civil service more than doubled, from 46 000 in 1939 to 116 000 in 1945. Ottawa would never return to its prewar size and sleepy pace.

In the First World War, federal spending represented 10 to 15 percent of the GNP. By 1944, Ottawa's expenditures accounted for nearly 40 percent of GNP. Extensive

As this wartime poster of female participants in the military (c. 1944) indicates, women were targeted by the government to invest in the war effort to ensure a prosperous future. SOURCE: LIBRARY AND ARCHIVES CANADA C-91584

taxation of corporate and personal incomes, the sale of Victory Bonds, a new willingness to countenance debt levels that exceeded GNP by the end of the war, and careful regulation of the money supply through the Bank of Canada enabled Canadians to finance their war without massive foreign borrowing.

Despite the impressive record, Canada's wartime economy encountered problems. Britain imposed exchange controls, including restrictions on the convertibility of sterling into dollars. As Britain's wartime purchases in Canada escalated and Canada came to depend on the United States for war supplies, Canadians faced the prospect of having a huge surplus of sterling and a crippling deficit in American currency. Ottawa responded with stringent exchange controls, monitored by the Foreign Exchange Control Board. Imports were permitted only under licence. By 1940, there were restrictions on travel to the United States and an embargo on the importation of many commodities from countries outside the

Sterling Bloc (countries that tied their currencies to Britain's pound sterling). Still, the Canadian trade deficit with the United States mounted alarmingly.

Canada could do little to solve the problem. During the interwar years, Canadian and American industry had become so integrated that virtually everything Canada produced included American components. Parts for Canadian automobile factories, coal for Stelco's furnaces, and machinery for mining companies all came from the United States. The problem was eventually solved when the United States entered the war in 1941. By that time, North America already functioned as a unit in defence production, and the problem for Canada became too much, rather than too little, American exchange.

The Second World War tended to reinforce Canadian economic geography. Wartime production was initially expanded in existing industries, and virtually all plants built and operated by the government were located in the industrial heartland of the country. There were some notable exceptions. Winnipeg became a centre for munitions and communications industries. Adjacent to Alberta's oil and natural gas reserves, Calgary was the obvious site for nitrogen and high-octane fuel production. Vancouver sprouted a Boeing aircraft factory and a modern shipbuilding industry. New military bases quickened the economic pace in communities from Summerside to Esquimalt, while such projects as Ferry Command brought development to the northern territories and Newfoundland and Labrador. Nevertheless, the bias in favour of central Canada was blatant in decisions relating to shipbuilding and repair. The ice-free ports of Halifax and Saint John were treated as secondary to Montreal, which was ice-bound during the winter and whose narrow access was infested with German U-boats. The failure to develop repair facilities in the Maritime provinces consolidated regional disparity and impeded the effectiveness of the Canadian navy.

Traditional attitudes toward labour were challenged during the war. By 1941, the labour pool had dried up and a shortage of workers loomed. In 1942, the government began a campaign to recruit women into the paid labour force. Before the war, only 21 percent of women between the ages of 15 and 65 worked outside the home, and of these, less than 13 percent were married. At first only unmarried women were recruited, but by 1943 even married women with children were strongly encouraged to do their patriotic duty. In Quebec and Ontario, a government-sponsored daycare system offered support for a handful of mothers. The

Daycare was a problem for mothers who took jobs in the paid labour force. This Mi'kmaw woman, identified as Mrs Martin Malti, brought her child with her to the Pictou, Nova Scotia shipyards in 1943.
SOURCE: LIBRARY AND ARCHIVES CANADA PA-116154

number of women in the workforce increased from 638 000 in 1939 to over a million by 1944, some 255 000 of whom were engaged in what were defined as war industries. When the war ended, the prewar sex-typing of jobs resumed.

THE ENEMY WITHIN

As in the First World War, the Canadian government took measures against enemy aliens and others perceived as potential troublemakers. The Defence of Canada Regulations included sweeping powers to curb freedom of expression and arrest anyone who might threaten public safety or recruitment efforts. Besides Japanese Canadians, several other groups also experienced the heavy hand of government control.

Among the first targets were members of political organizations associated with enemy nations. The RCMP, in charge of public security, arrested 358 known supporters of Nazi organizations and sent them to camps at Petawawa, Ontario, and Kananaskis, Alberta. Another sweep after the fall of France and the entrance of Italy into the war netted over 850 more. Canada's official Nazi party was banned and its leaders interned. On 4 July 1940, the government passed an order-in-council declaring the Jehovah's Witnesses illegal. The order made 7000 Canadian Jehovah's Witnesses subject to surveillance and arrest, while their meeting halls and property were handed over to the Custodian of Enemy Property.

The treatment of the Jehovah's Witnesses, like the evacuation of the Japanese, demonstrates how prewar prejudices were acted upon in the wartime context. The Witnesses had been confronting the Roman Catholic Church since the early 1930s, especially in Quebec. Cardinal Jean-Marie-Rodrigue Villeneuve used the excuse of the war effort to appeal to Justice Minister Ernest Lapointe to curb their activities. With similar demands coming from elsewhere in Canada, Lapointe promptly had the ban issued and enforced. It lasted until 1943.

Even refugees were treated with suspicion. Canada accepted only about 3500 refugees from enemy countries between 1939 and 1945. Although strong opposition to Jewish immigration among conservative nationalists in Quebec contributed to Ottawa's minimal compliance with Britain's request to admit German and Austrian refugees, many of them Jews, anti-Semitic views were widely held in Canada, including at the highest level of the civil service. Jewish refugees were initially put in prison camps with German prisoners of war. Although they were eventually housed separately, many remained under guard in rough internment camps. Not even reports of Nazi extermination camps, widespread by 1943, changed official or public sentiment.

The treatment of refugees became a major concern of the Canadian National Council on Refugees (CNCR), whose president was Senator Cairine Wilson. Under pressure from the CNCR, the government passed an order-in-council in December 1943 releasing enemy alien refugees from internment and granting them one-year permits to stay in Canada. The CNCR tried to find work for these unfortunate people, many of whom eventually made major contributions to their adopted country as scientists, university professors, and artists.

Anti-war dissidents also came under surveillance. Since the Communist Party spoke out against the war, it was outlawed in June 1940, and 133 suspected Communists were arrested, including many of the party's leaders. Most Communist internees were released after Hitler invaded the Soviet Union in 1941. Apart from political dissidents, an estimated 12 000 Canadians, mainly Quakers, Mennonites, and Brethren in Christ, declared themselves conscientious objectors. Many were required to work in rural camps or factories, on pain of being interned in labour camps.

No internees were deported after the war ended. The Canadian government planned to deport the Japanese evacuees, but the legality of the policy was soon called into question. By the time the courts had handed down their decision, Canadians and much of the world were beginning to adopt a new attitude toward cultural minorities and refugee populations. The increasingly popular concept of human rights was reflected in the human rights codes banning discrimination in hiring and accommodation passed by the governments of Ontario and Saskatchewan in 1945.

THE WELFARE STATE

Almost as soon as the war started, Canadians began to worry about the nation's postwar agenda. Government planning of the economy during wartime had resulted in a higher standard of living for ordinary people. Why, they asked, could governments not continue such a role in peacetime?

The two major parties appeared at first to ignore such concerns, but they would soon change their tunes. In early 1942, Arthur Meighen, recently re-elected as the federal Conservative leader, sought a parliamentary seat in a by-election in the supposedly safe Conservative riding of York South. King, who feared Meighen's pro-conscription campaign, decided not to run a Liberal candidate, leaving the Co-operative Commonwealth Federation (CCF) to challenge Meighen. Throughout the by-election, Meighen talked of the need to impose conscription, while the previously unknown CCF candidate, Joseph Noseworthy, spoke of the need to plan employment and social insurance programs for the postwar era. The majority of constituents liked Noseworthy's message. Meighen's defeat and subsequent resignation as

Conservative leader had repercussions throughout the political system.

Reform-minded Conservatives argued that the country could not be allowed to fall to the socialists. In 1942, the Conservatives chose John Bracken, the Liberal-Progressive premier of Manitoba, as national leader. Convention delegates also adopted a platform that went beyond Bennett's New Deal to embrace universal pensions, medical insurance, equality for women, and union rights. At Bracken's insistence, the party changed its name to "Progressive Conservative" in the hope of shedding its reactionary image.

Despite attempts to steal its thunder, the CCF advance continued. In 1943, the party captured 34 of the 89 seats in the Ontario legislature and became the official opposition. Provincial Conservative leader George Drew was obliged to promise a comprehensive social security program in an attempt to blunt the CCF advance. Meanwhile, in Saskatchewan, the CCF under the leadership of the dynamic Tommy Douglas won the 1944 provincial election. Douglas capitalized on the popular policies of the CCF and the widespread disenchantment among Saskatchewan farmers with Ottawa's price controls on grain. In Quebec, the Liberal government of Adélard Godbout also advanced progressive measures, such as free, compulsory schooling for children under 14, the partial nationalization of the province's hydroelectric industry to form Hydro-Québec, the adoption of a provincial labour code, and most importantly of all, in 1940, voting rights for women in provincial elections.

The shift in public opinion toward the left was not unique to Canada. In Great Britain, voters elected a Labour government in 1945 to preside over postwar reconstruction. A report published in Britain in 1942 by Sir William Beveridge, a distinguished social planner, argued for a government-sponsored social security system from the cradle to the grave.

BIOGRAPHY

Tommy Douglas

Born in Scotland in 1904, Tommy Douglas immigrated with his family to Winnipeg in 1919, where he witnessed the General Strike. After serving as a printer's apprentice, in 1924 he decided to enter the Baptist ministry. He attended Brandon College for six years, where he was exposed to social gospel teachings. Following his ordination in 1930, he moved to Weyburn, Saskatchewan. There he witnessed first-hand the suffering of farmers during the Depression. Douglas soon became deeply involved in politics, establishing a local association of the Independent Labour Party in 1931 and attending the founding convention of the CCF.

In 1935, Douglas was elected to the House of Commons and soon developed a reputation as a skillful and witty debater. He resigned his seat to lead the CCF to victory in Saskatchewan in 1944, launching the first socialist government in North America. Although the CCF victory made some people nervous, Douglas brought a pragmatic approach to social reform that won widespread approval. Under his leadership, Saskatchewan earned a reputation for innovative and efficient government. Indeed, Douglas pioneered many of the social welfare programs that would eventually be implemented in other provinces of Canada. Douglas remained premier of the province until he resigned in 1961 to become the first leader of the federal New Democratic Party.[9]

Tommy Douglas at work in Regina around 1940, while he was a CCF MP. SOURCE: GLENBOW ARCHIVES NA-5096-79

Ever vigilant of trends that might undermine his power, King decided the time had come to implement major reforms. The government had introduced a national unemployment insurance program in 1940, but it was a cautious initiative. An insurance plan rather than a welfare scheme, the program required earners and employers to make contributions to a fund from which employees could draw if they were laid off from work. As it was initially designed, unemployment insurance covered only a small proportion of the labour force, and even that unequally. Some exemptions, such as farm labourers, were testimony to the influence of special interest groups. Other exemptions reflected patriarchal notions of women's place in the economy. Married women were excluded from coverage, as were domestic workers. Benefits were tied to wages and weeks of continuous work, provisions that discriminated against low-wage and part-time workers.

Many Canadians felt that Ottawa's plans to stabilize the economy should go beyond insurance policies for a small proportion of the labour force. Their perspective was supported in a report prepared for government by a committee generally known by the name of its principal author, Leonard Marsh. A McGill economist, Marsh brought his CCF sensibilities and the insights of the Beveridge Report to the problems of reconstruction. The Marsh Report argued that full employment should be a major goal of the postwar industrial state; to that end, the government and the whole society should play a role in ensuring that people find work, remain healthy, and are properly fed, housed, and educated. Although the cost of programs such as universal old-age pensions and family allowances was high, Marsh argued that such spending constituted a necessary investment for human well-being and economic efficiency.

Conservative critics were appalled by such thinking. Charlotte Whitton, one of Canada's leading social workers, claimed that Marsh's schemes would make Canadians dependent on the state, destroy initiative, and encourage the "feeble-minded" to procreate. Finance Minister J.L. Ilsley was also reluctant to embrace the Marsh proposals, which were costly to implement. Proponents of new social programs responded that maintaining the high taxes of the war period would be the key to financing peacetime social schemes.

Provincial cooperation would be necessary because the courts had ruled that provinces had jurisdiction over social policy. To proceed with national unemployment insurance, the federal government had been obliged to secure an amendment to the British North America Act. The King government had established a Royal Commission on Dominion-Provincial Relations in 1937 to explore ways of reforming the constitution to permit the federal government to intervene directly in the field of social welfare. When the proposals of the royal commission were unveiled in 1940, they were strongly opposed by the premiers of Ontario, Alberta, and British Columbia, who refused to concede their taxation powers so that the federal government could establish a national policy to create full employment and social services.

Most Canadians were unconcerned about constitutional niceties. They wanted reform and they wanted it right away. At a meeting of the National Liberal Federation in September 1943, the party followed the CCF and the Progressive Conservatives in adopting a platform supporting social security. King moved quickly to establish three new departments—Reconstruction, National Health and Welfare, and Veterans Affairs—to preside over government postwar planning. His administration introduced family allowance legislation by which mothers of children under age 16 received a monthly stipend. The first cheques, amounting to between five and eight dollars per child, were mailed in July 1945.

In the last two years of the war, the government focused on policies that would help cushion the shock of returning to peace. It passed the National Housing Act to generate construction, established the Industrial Development Board to help companies retool for peacetime production, created the Veterans' Charter to provide benefits for those who served in the war, and developed policies to help primary producers survive the transition to peacetime markets. In all, the government appropriated $3.12 billion for reconstruction, a remarkable sum even in today's dollars. These policies went some distance in helping the Liberals ward off the CCF threat and win the 1945 election.

LABOUR AND THE STATE

Another reason for the Liberal government's success in fending off socialism was its change of heart on trade union rights. King's initial wartime response to labour alienated the unions. The Industrial Disputes Investigation Act was vastly extended under the War Measures Act to allow the government to use conciliation to avoid strikes. If managers fired workers attempting to form unions, the government looked the other way.

Under wartime conditions, workers were no longer forced to submit silently to the dictates of government and hostile managers. Recognizing that labour shortages prevented employers from firing them for union activities, workers joined industrial and craft unions in droves and resorted to strikes and work slowdowns when companies refused to accept the unions formed by the democratic votes of their employees. In 1943, there were over 400 strikes involving more than 200 000 workers.

Eager to keep war industries functioning smoothly and his political popularity high, King felt compelled to act. In February 1944, Order-in-Council PC 1003 ushered in a new era of labour policy in Canada. The order guaranteed workers the right to organize and bargain collectively, established procedures for the certification and compulsory recognition of trade unions, defined unfair labour practices, and created an administrative apparatus to enforce the order.

The move to accommodate labour and a massive anti-socialist campaign by business interests reduced support for left-wing parties. In 1945, the Ontario Conservatives decisively won a provincial election that reduced the CCF to third place in the legislature. On 11 June, the CCF won only 28 of 245 seats in the federal election, with 15 percent of the popular vote. Although they received a reduced parliamentary majority, the Liberals were given a mandate to govern the country in peacetime. King had proven his ability to stay in the middle of the political road, no matter what direction that road took.

THE NEW WORLD ORDER

King also presided over a government that took a new road in international affairs. Even more obvious in retrospect than at the time, the Second World War reinforced Great Britain's long decline from its dominant role in world affairs. Its mantle passed to the United States. During the Second World War, Canada moved closer to the Americans economically, politically, and militarily. Critics such as the distinguished scholar Harold Innis, who

taught political economy at the University of Toronto, would later claim that in this period Canada moved from "colony to nation to colony" in its efforts to maintain good relations with the superpower next door—that is, that it had achieved independence from Great Britain only to lose it to the United States.

As Hitler's armies erased national borders with ease, King recognized that Canada was increasingly dependent on the United States for its defence. American president Franklin Roosevelt was equally conscious of this fact and was afraid that Canada's involvement in the war made the whole North American continent vulnerable to the fascist dictators. In August 1940, Roosevelt invited King to meet him at Ogdensburg, New York. As a result of their meeting, the Permanent Joint Board on Defence was established to prepare for mutual assistance in defence of North America. The notion of permanency gave King few qualms and the board was established without prior reference to Parliament. In the crisis atmosphere of the late summer of 1940, few people in Canada voiced any objection.

The United States also made adjustments to its wartime policies to ensure that Canada's economy would not suffer unduly. In March 1941, Great Britain and the United States concluded a lend-lease arrangement whereby $7 billion was made available to Great Britain for the purchase of equipment and supplies from the United States. Canada was initially excluded from the agreement, an "oversight" that was rectified at another meeting between Roosevelt and King at Hyde Park, New York, in April 1941. The Americans would increase purchases in Canada and would charge many of the components bought by Canada in the United States to the British account, thereby helping to solve the balance of payment difficulties.

King told Parliament that the Hyde Park declaration "involves nothing less than a common plan for the economic defence of the western hemisphere" and "the enduring foundation of a new world order."[10] King was given to rhetorical exaggeration, but in this instance he was strikingly prophetic. Valuable wartime arrangements as they were, Ogdensburg and Hyde Park were less important in themselves than as symbols of an intimate Canada–United States relationship that was becoming a dominant fact of life for Canada.

Once the United States had officially entered the war following the Japanese attack on Pearl Harbor in December 1941, Canada no longer figured very prominently in American calculations. King hated to be taken for granted, but he had to accept that Canada was a minor player in a world of super-powers. Notwithstanding diplomatic rhetoric about their close alliance, the United States resisted Canadian efforts to have a military mission in Washington to learn more about American military strategy. The United States also protested loudly when Canada quietly supported the successful efforts of Charles de Gaulle's Free French forces to seize Saint-Pierre and Miquelon—two French islands off the coast of Newfoundland—from the Vichy government. King refused to dislodge de Gaulle's forces because he suspected Vichy—the pro-German government in that part of France unoccupied by the Nazis—of using the islands as a base from which to report to the Germans on Allied convoy movements.

When British prime minister Winston Churchill (right) and American president Franklin Roosevelt (left) met in Quebec City in 1943, William Lyon Mackenzie King (centre) was on hand for a photo opportunity, even though he participated little in the discussions between the two world leaders. SOURCE: LIBRARY AND ARCHIVES CANADA C-31186

Canadians took the practical route and developed what became known as the "functional principle" in war-time planning. When Canadian interests were at stake, they would insist on having a voice in determining international policy. This approach was most clearly expressed in the words of Hume Wrong, a senior officer in the Department of External Affairs, in 1942: "The principle . . . is that each member of the grand alliance should have a voice in the conduct of the war proportionate to its contribution to the general war effort. A subsidiary principle is that the influence of the various countries should be greatest in connection with those matters with which they are most directly concerned."[11] Canadians used such arguments to win a seat on the Allied Combined Food Board, which allocated food resources for the war effort, but had less success in gaining influence in organizations established to manage international relations in peacetime.

The American presence loomed ever larger as the war dragged on. Roosevelt had arranged for American bases in Newfoundland, still a dependency of Great Britain but one in which Canada had a considerable interest and had agreed to protect for the duration of the war. When the Japanese occupied the Aleutian Islands in the summer of 1942, the United States, with Canada's permission, built an overland route through Canada to Alaska. The Alaska Highway was a marvel of American efficiency. Between March and October 1942, civilian workers and seven engineer regiments, together totalling 11 000 people, began carving a highway from Alaska, a total of more than 2000 kilometres, at a cost of nearly $150 million. To ensure oil supplies, the Americans built the Canol pipeline from Whitehorse in the Yukon to Norman Wells in the Northwest Territories. The Americans also developed northern staging routes of rough airstrips to transport bombers and fighter planes to Europe and the Soviet Union. By 1943, 33 000 Americans were working in the Canadian North.

King and officials in the Department of External Affairs were troubled by the increasing American presence in Canada's northern territories. In an effort to establish sovereignty over the area and reduce Canada's balance of American dollars, the government announced in December 1943 that the United States was to be paid in full for all permanent military installations they built in Canada. Canada ultimately paid $123.5 million for 28 airfields, 56 weather stations, and a variety of other facilities. In 1943, the Canadian government decided to upgrade its diplomatic presence in Washington. The Canadian legation took on embassy status, and Leighton McCarthy, the Canadian minister to the United States, became an ambassador, the first Canadian diplomat to hold that rank.

Ultimately, cooperation, more than conflict, characterized Canadian–American relations throughout the war. At American request, Canadians agreed to

Waving "the flag" (both the British Union Jack and the American Stars and Stripes) to celebrate victory over Japan, Smoky Lake, Alberta, 14 August 1945. SOURCE: PROVINCIAL ARCHIVES OF ALBERTA G-1293

participate in an expedition to dislodge the Japanese from the Aleutians in 1943, and Canadians adopted American army organization for the 16 000 Canadian Army Pacific Forces assembled for the final campaign against the Japanese in 1945.

The new world order that was put in place after the Second World War was also largely dominated by American policy. In the spring of 1945, meetings were held in San Francisco to establish the United Nations, an organization designed to replace war with negotiation as a vehicle for settling international disputes. Although Canadian diplomats had their own ideas about the economic structures that should govern the postwar world, they went along with American plans for the International Monetary Fund and the World Bank. Only time would tell whether this blueprint for peace and prosperity would be any more successful than the one put in place by the League of Nations following the Great War.

The prospects for a peaceful world were not encouraging. When the war in Europe came to an end, the leaders of the Soviet Union, Great Britain, and the United

States met in Potsdam, Germany, in July 1945 to discuss how to manage the peace process. It was a different group of leaders than had met to plot strategy during the war. Joseph Stalin was the only constant player. Roosevelt had died in April 1945, succeeded by his vice-president, Harry Truman. Great Britain was in the process of holding an election even as the Potsdam conference was in progress. A Labour victory meant that Clement Attlee replaced Winston Churchill at the bargaining table. The conference revealed the growing tension between the Soviet Union and the West, tension that ultimately led to the partition of Germany and the Cold War that was to characterize international relations for decades to come.

DEMOBILIZATION AND POSTWAR RECONSTRUCTION

In Canada, the people planning demobilization during the Second World War were determined not to repeat the mistakes that had created the unrest among veterans following the Great War. In January 1940, the government created the General Advisory Committee on Demobilization and Reconstruction under Great War veteran H.F. McDonald. A new Department of Veterans Affairs was established in 1944 to help soldiers make a successful transition to civilian life. The Veterans' Charter of the same year offered veterans more generous benefits than those available in 1919, including gratuities totalling $752.3 million to help them get re-established. In 1942, the government passed an act requiring companies to rehire veterans in their former jobs under conditions "not less favourable" than if they had never enlisted. Nearly 200 000 veterans benefited from this injunction, and only four charges were brought against uncooperative employers under the Reinstatement Act. A slightly smaller number, about 150 000, had their re-entry into the labour market postponed for several years by a provision that helped veterans attend university or college. Others took up land offered by the Veterans' Land Act and settled into farming.

While it was all well and good to plan for the end of the war, victory in Europe brought the predictable problem of getting the forces home. Repatriation went faster than expected, but nothing could solve the problem of too few ships for too many soldiers. In theory, repatriation followed a point system allowing those with the longest service and who were married to come back first, with ex-prisoners of war, the wounded, and service women being given top priority. In practice, there were problems and unrest. The worst disorder took place in Aldershot, England, in July 1945, when Canadian forces erupted in a two-night riot. By the end of 1945, only half of the nearly 350 000 Canadians in Europe were home. A division of 25 000 troops and 11 air force squadrons was committed to the occupation of Germany. When few Canadians volunteered for this tour of duty, Canada informed the Allied command that it would pull its forces out of Germany by the spring of 1946.

Most ships arriving from Europe docked at Halifax. The city did its best, under difficult circumstances, to welcome "the boys" home, but not before VE day (victory in Europe) celebrations blew the city apart. As news of the German surrender spread, Haligonians closed their offices, stores, and restaurants while throngs of service people and civilians celebrated in downtown streets. Seamen were free to come and go,

but there was nothing for them to do. Liquor stores were looted, a tram trashed, and chaos reigned in the streets of Halifax. Neither the naval patrols nor the city police were strong enough to keep the peace, and Rear-Admiral Leonard W. Murray was at a loss as to how to restore order among his men. The two-day riot caused $5 million worth of damage and left civilians and military authorities pointing fingers at each other for causing the fracas. In the legal proceedings following the riot, 41 soldiers, 34 sailors, and 19 airmen were among the 211 indicted for offences. Murray was relieved of his command because of the affair, and the navy took most of the blame for the damage.

Among those returning on the big ships from Europe were more than 47 500 war brides (and a few war husbands) and their children, numbering nearly 22 000. The vast majority of war brides were British (44 886), although Canadian soldiers also married Dutch, Belgian, French, Danish, Italian, and German women. Once in Canada, war brides faced a difficult adjustment to new families, new communities, and a new country. Some, such as Betty Oliphant, divorced their husbands but ended up staying in Canada anyway. Oliphant became the founder of the National Ballet School.

Canadian soldiers left behind an estimated 23 000 so-called war children, the result of relationships—some brief, others longer term, some even bigamous—with local women. These children and their mothers were abandoned by their Canadian fathers and faced a postwar world where having children "out of wedlock" and being an "illegitimate" child carried a debilitating social stigma. Although 414 child maintenance orders were served on Canadians by authorities in Great Britain, most women received no assistance other than from family and friends. Many war children were given up for adoption. In the postwar period, the plight of the war children was conveniently forgotten.[12]

As in the First World War, the re-establishment of family life was difficult for many veterans. The number of marriages and births increased after the war, but so too did divorces (see Table 11.1). For many veterans, it was impossible to pick up the threads of civilian life. Some women resented being pushed out of civilian jobs and encouraged to stay at home. Others responded enthusiastically to state and business propaganda to establish homes in the suburbs and raise children

TABLE 11.1

Marriages, Divorces, and Births in Canada, 1939-1948

YEAR	MARRIAGES	DIVORCES	BIRTHS
1939	106 266	2073	237 991
1940	125 797	2416	252 577
1941	124 644	2462	263 993
1942	130 786	3091	281 569
1943	113 827	3398	293 967
1945	111 376	5101	300 587
1946	137 398	7757	343 504
1947	130 400	8213	372 589
1948	126 118	6978	359 860

Source: Adapted from F.H. Leacy, ed., *Historical Statistics of Canada* (Ottawa: Minister of Supply and Service, 1983), cited in Desmond Morton and J.L. Granatstein, *Victory 1945* (Toronto: HarperCollins, 1995) 119

in what was regarded as one of the world's luckiest democracies.

Much of the responsibility for establishing Canada's postwar economy on a peacetime footing fell on the shoulders of C.D. Howe, who was appointed minister of reconstruction in 1944. With his usual energy, he set about reducing rationing, converting war industries to peacetime purposes, and re-establishing Canada's export sales. Canada's Merchant Navy was disbanded, and most Crown corporations were sold or closed down. To meet 15 years of pent-up civilian demand, companies were given tax breaks to get their factories producing consumer goods. The loss of overseas markets was in part compensated for by sales made possible under the Marshall Plan.

When it looked as if communism might sweep war-ravaged European countries, the United States agreed in 1947 to a generous aid program, named after American secretary of state George C. Marshall, who proposed it to help Western European nations restore their capitalist economies. Funds were initially tied to purchases in the United States, but soon Canada was included and sold a billion dollars' worth of its products overseas by 1950. With policies such as these, Canada managed to weather the adjustment to peacetime production reasonably well. Instead of the postwar slump predicted by many economists, Canada experienced rapid growth, its GNP rising from $11.8 billion in 1945 to $18.4 billion in 1950.

A wave of strikes followed in the wake of the Second World War. In 1945 and 1946, proportionately more time was lost in strike activity than in 1919. A major strike was conducted at the Ford Motor Company plant in Windsor in 1945, and a national steel strike shut down plants in Sault Ste Marie, Hamilton, and Sydney in 1946. The results of arbitration by Chief Justice Ivan Rand at Ford and the willingness of federal and provincial governments to enshrine the principles of PC 1003 in postwar legislation helped prevent the stand-off between labour and capital that had characterized the aftermath of the Great War. The so-called "Rand formula," which required employers to deduct union dues from all members of a bargaining unit whether they were members or not, offered union security and helped to bring unions and their employers into the bureaucratic processes that increasingly prevailed in most areas of Canadian life.

CONCLUSION

Canada came out of the war a different country from the one that went into it in 1939. With a stronger federal state and the beginnings of a social welfare system, the nation was in a position to avoid returning to the misery experienced during the Great Depression. The booming economy seemed to be holding its own in a peacetime context. In comparison to the devastated cities and countrysides of Europe and Asia, Canada was an untouched utopia and the destination of choice for many European refugees. Canadians were also assuming a new place among the nations of the world. Although not a major player like Great Britain or the United States, Canada began to embrace the term "middle power," a small nation no more, and one with an expanding role to play in international affairs. It was also a country in the process of creating its own identity independent from the British Commonwealth. In 1946, Secretary of State Paul Martin introduced a bill, passed the next year, to establish a distinct Canadian citizenship, since up to that point Canadians still carried British passports. There was some discussion in the media about adopting a Canadian flag—Canadians still waved the Red Ensign, the Union Jack, or the Stars and Stripes during victory celebrations. Issues of Canadian identity were clearly on the agenda as Canada entered the atomic age.

Origins of the Welfare State

Social scientists generally agree on the various factors contributing to the evolution of the welfare state in Canada, but the relative weight of these factors is in dispute. In identifying the groups pressing for the creation of federal social insurance programs, scholars list the following: the unemployed; business groups; municipalities and provinces; liberal churches; and elements within the state bureaucracy. They also note the support of key politicians. Is there evidence to suggest that one group more than another left its mark on the kind of welfare state that emerged in Canada? The contours of the debate can be understood by looking at how scholars explain the emergence of the unemployment insurance program in 1940.

Alvin Finkel suggests that pressure from big business was largely responsible for producing an unemployment insurance program.[13] According to Finkel, business people felt that unemployment insurance would help prevent public finances from being besieged by unplanned expenditures when unemployment rose. Business leaders wanted the scale of payments to be modest so that people would be encouraged to find work. They also wanted the cost to be borne by working people themselves rather than by companies or the government. To a considerable degree, their views prevailed in the program that was introduced in 1940.

James Struthers argues that this scenario is too one-sided, suggesting that popular pressures, both from the unemployed and from liberal-minded citizens, generally played a role in securing unemployment insurance.[14] Some argue that the business community, though divided, was largely opposed to the idea. According to sociologist Carl Cuneo, unemployment insurance was an example of the state implementing reforms to save capitalism from itself. By providing a social safety net for workers, the state was helping prevent widespread social unrest that might lead to revolution and the total destruction of the market economy.[15]

Still others stress the role of specific politicians. R.B. Bennett's need to appear reform-minded before the 1935 election is often mentioned.[16] Since Bennett had promised unemployment insurance as early as 1931, it is not surprising that it emerged as an item in his "New Deal" package of reforms in 1935. J.L. Granatstein attributes William Lyon Mackenzie King's introduction of unemployment insurance in 1940 to his desire to plan for expected postwar unemployment.[17] Struthers also sees the war as the major catalyst for the welfare state. "When King finally pushed for speedy passage of the Unemployment Insurance Act, it was out of his own fear of postwar unrest," Struthers argues. "No one expected that veterans or unemployed war workers would queue up meekly in front of local relief offices. In the final analysis it was war and not the depression which destroyed the poor-law heritage."[18]

Most scholars concede the degree to which state bureaucracy shaped the character of Canada's unemployment insurance program. While admitting that a variety of forces caused politicians to accept the need for some form of social insurance, political scientist Leslie Pal suggests that a state-centred, rather than a society-centred, perspective explains the character of the program itself. In its formative years, he argues, unemployment insurance became grounded in administrative logic when it came to determining contributions, benefits, duration, and coverage. Whereas employee groups tended to view unemployment insurance in terms of rights and employers saw it in terms of costs and the effect on the labour supply, officials were preoccupied with administrative feasibility, actuarial soundness, and strict insurance principles. This led to a similarity of views between employers and officials, particularly on the abuse question, but the similarity was coincidental in that the official view was arrived at independently. It was not the result of "pressure."[19]

When examined from the perspective of gender, there is also a remarkable coincidence of views between state bureaucrats, businessmen, and union leaders on the treatment of female workers under the unemployment insurance program.[20] Indeed, as Ruth Roach Pierson points out, neither progressives nor conservatives, labour nor management, organized to defend the right of married women workers to receive fair compensation when they lost jobs.

The return of the veterans to their old jobs generally meant the dismissal of women who had been recruited to non-traditional jobs in the workforce during the war. In her recent study, Jennifer A. Stephen documents the policies put in place by the federal government to discourage married women who had lost their wartime jobs from seeking new employment. Ottawa coordinated a massive campaign to persuade women that their place was in the home, closed subsidized daycare facilities, and changed wartime tax rules to penalize two-income families. Meanwhile, the new family allowance was promoted as a program that made it unnecessary for married women to seek an income in the labour force.[21]

NOTES

1. Joseph Goebbels, Diary, 3 March 1943, cited in *Challenge and Survival: A History of Canada*, eds. H.H. Herstein, L.J. Hughes, and R.C. Kerbyson (Scarborough: Prentice Hall, 1970) 376.

2. Enlistment and casualty figures vary widely. The figures cited in this chapter are taken from Desmond Morton and J.L. Granatstein, *Victory 1945: Canadians from War to Peace* (Toronto: HarperCollins, 1995) 19.

3. Jackson, *One of the Boys: Homosexuality in the Military During World War II*, 2nd ed. (Montreal: McGill-Queen's University Press, 2010) and Ruth Roach Pierson, *"They're Still Women After All": The Second World War and Canadian Womanhood* (Toronto: McClelland & Stewart, 1986).

4. Carl A. Christie, *Ocean Bridge: The History of RAF Ferry Command* (Toronto: University of Toronto Press, 1995) 3.

5. David J. Becuson and S.F. Wise, eds., *The Valour and the Horror Revisited* (Montreal: McGill-Queen's University Press, 1994).

6. Cited in Graham Carr, "Rules of Engagement: Public History and the Drama of Legitimation," *Canadian Historical Review* 86, 2 (June 2005) 320.

7. Desmond Morton, "Comments on the Controversy Over the Bombing Offensive," typescript, 5.

8. Dean Frederic Oliver and Laura Brandon, *Canvas of War: Painting the Canadian Experience, 1914 to 1945* (Vancouver: Douglas & McIntyre, 2000).

9. Walter Stewart, *The Life and Political Times of Tommy Douglas* (Toronto: McArthur, 2003).

10. J.L. Granatstein and Norman Hillmer, *For Better or for Worse: Canada and the United States to the 1990s* (Toronto: Copp Clark Pitman, 1991) 147.

11. Cited in Morton and Granatstein, *Victory 1945*, 234.

12. Olga Rains, Lloyd Rains, and Melynda Jarratt, *Voices of the Left Behind: Project Roots and the Canadian War Children of World War Two* (Fredericton: Project Roots, 2004) 1–3.

13. Alvin Finkel, *Business and Social Reform in the Thirties* (Toronto: Lorimer, 1979).

14. James Struthers, *No Fault of Their Own: Unemployment and the Canadian Welfare State, 1914–1941* (Toronto: University of Toronto Press, 1981).

15. Carl J. Cuneo, "State, Class and Reserve Labour: The Case of the 1941 Canadian Unemployment Insurance Act," *Canadian Review of Sociology and Anthropology* 16 (May 1979) 147–70.

16. See, for example, Larry A. Glassford, *Reaction and Reform: The Politics of the Conservative Party Under R.B. Bennett, 1927–1938* (Toronto: University of Toronto Press, 1992).

17. J.L. Granatstein, *Canada's War: The Politics of the King Government, 1939–1945* (Toronto: Oxford University Press, 1975).

18. Struthers, *No Fault of Their Own* 213.

19. Leslie Pal, *State, Class and Bureaucracy: Canadian Unemployment Insurance and Public Policy* (Montreal: McGill-Queen's University Press, 1975) 109.

20. Ruth Roach Pierson, "Gender and the Unemployment Insurance Debate in Canada, 1934–1940," *Labour/Le Travail* 25 (Spring 1990) 77–103.

21. Jennifer A. Stephen, *Pick One Intelligent Girl: Employability, Domesticity, and the Gendering of Canada's Welfare State, 1939–1947* (Toronto: University of Toronto Press, 2007).

SELECTED READING

Avery, Donald. *The Science of War: Scientists and Allied Military Technology During the Second World War.* Toronto: University of Toronto Press, 1998

Bernier, Serge et al., eds. *La participation des Canadiens français à la Deuxième Guerre mondiale: mythes et réalités.* Special issue of the *Bulletin d'histoire politique* 3, 3/4 1995

Greenhous, Brereton et al. *The Crucible of War, 1939–1945.* Toronto: University of Toronto Press, 1994

Donaghy, Greg and Patricia E. Roy, eds. *Contradictory Impulses: Canada and Japan in the Twentieth Century.* Vancouver: UBC Press, 2008

Granatstein, J.L. *Canada's War: The Politics of the King Government, 1939–1945.* Toronto: Oxford University Press, 1975

Granatstein, J.L. and Desmond Morton. *A Nation Forged in Fire: Canadians and the Second World War.* Toronto: Lester and Orpen Dennys, 1995

Granatstein, J.L. and Peter Nearly, eds. *The Good Fight: Canadians and World War II.* Toronto: Copp Clark, 1995

Hillmer, Noman, Bohdan Kordan, and Lubomyr Luciuk, eds. *On Guard for Thee: War, Ethnicity, and the Canadian State, 1939–1945.* Ottawa: Canadian Committee for the History of the Second World War, 1988

Keshen, Jeffrey A. *Saints, Sinners, and Soldiers: Canada's Second World War.* Vancouver: UBC Press, 2004

Morton, Desmond and J.L. Granatstein. *Victory 1945: Canadians from War to Peace.* Toronto: HarperCollins, 1995

Oliver, Dean Frederic and Laura Brandon. *Canvas of War: Painting the Canadian Experience, 1914 to 1945.* Vancouver: Douglas & McIntyre, 2000

Pierson, Ruth Roach. *"They're Still Women After All": The Second World War and Canadian Womanhood.* Toronto: McClelland & Stewart, 1986

For a comprehensive list of readings for topics covered in this chapter, please visit http://pearsoncanada.ca/conrad.

PART IV
REINVENTING CANADA, 1945-1975

In the 30 years following the Second World War, Canada emerged as one of the world's great industrial nations, with all the benefits and problems associated with its new status. Wealth continued to be unequally distributed, but the state assumed increasing responsibility for ensuring the basic welfare of all Canadians. No longer tied to the apron strings of Great Britain, Canadians developed a stronger sense of their own identity. The arts flourished, buoyed by the new prosperity and government grants. As the centennial of Confederation approached, many Canadians felt that at long last they had something to celebrate, and Ottawa hosted a birthday party worthy of a great nation. Yet the country's survival remained at risk, threatened by internal divisions and the overwhelming impact of the United States on Canadian economic, political, and cultural life. The Cold War, which periodically threatened to become hot, helped impress the American view of the world on the consciousness of Canadians. Regional fissures made the assertion of a "Canadian identity" elusive, and the expansion of the state at all levels prompted conflicts between provincial and federal governments. Nowhere were tensions more bitter than between Ottawa and the province of Quebec, where a growing sovereignty movement raised the prospect of a breakup of Canada.

CHAPTER 12
REDEFINING LIBERALISM: THE CANADIAN STATE, 1945–1975

In 1972, letters exchanged between Eric Harrington, president of Canadian Vickers Ltd., and Grace MacInnis, New Democratic Party (NDP) Member of Parliament for Vancouver-Kings, demonstrated the poles of political debate in postwar Canada. Taking exception to her speech in Parliament, Harrington wrote, in part:

> Could you please tell me what on earth "day centres" of which you claim we need 130 000 and "family planning centres" of which you claim we need 700 have to do with "equal rights for women"?
>
> Surely family planning and day-care centres for children are purely a family responsibility and a personal matter and don't have a damn thing to do with equal rights.
>
> Please all of you, stay out of our family affairs and our bedrooms, leave our children alone and do some planning that might help the economy, the unemployment situation and a hundred other more important problems on which to date you have been ineffectual.

MacInnis replied pointedly:

> The fact that you can believe that family planning and daycare centres for children are purely a family responsibility and a personal matter indicates very clearly that you enjoy an income standard where you and those who surround you are well able to handle such matters from your own resources. Such, I regret to have to tell you, is not the case for a very large percentage of the Canadian people.[1]

Before the Second World War, few people viewed a decent income, good medical care, pensions, public child care, and a minimum standard of housing as rights of citizenship. Instead, they were goals that people could set for themselves and work individually to attain. Scarred by the economic devastation of the 1930s and impressed by their government's ability to plan for war, Canadians increasingly argued that planning for peacetime purposes could prevent another depression and improve the quality of living for everyone. This ideal inspired a transformation of the nation-state and the peoples it represented.

THE POSTWAR LIBERAL CONSENSUS

In the period from 1945 to 1975, Canadians embraced what is often described as a "postwar liberal consensus." Liberalism once meant freedom from state intervention: it endorsed such principles as freedom of trade, freedom of speech, and freedom of worship. The new liberalism, while confirming support for such goals, also emphasized freedom from want. Rather than being the enemy of liberalism, state intervention became its essence, provided that the state limited its intervention to the economic sphere. As the Harrington–MacInnis exchange demonstrates, there was much debate about the limits of that sphere.

The term "welfare state" is often used to describe government programs designed to give cradle-to-grave security to citizens. As initially conceived, it included the broad set of programs by which the state ensured a guaranteed minimum income and social opportunities for all citizens as a matter of right. Minimum wages and programs for employment creation, farm subsidies, and public education were included in the definition; so, too, were universal programs, such as medical insurance, and narrower programs, such as social assistance, family allowances, and old-age pensions, that targeted certain groups.

Opponents of government intervention for the purpose of redistributing wealth viewed the welfare state differently. Although they rarely attacked spending on education or pensions, they derided social assistance and unemployment insurance as programs that robbed people of initiative and cost too much. These arguments tended to fall on deaf ears in times of prosperity, but they

never completely disappeared. When economic clouds appeared on the horizon in the 1970s, advocates of less ambitious welfare-state policies gained more influence in policy circles.

FEDERAL PARTIES AND LEADERS

In the 1945 federal election, both the Liberals and Conservatives embraced the welfare state, which enabled them to turn back the wartime growth in support for the socialist CCF. Tariffs and relations with Britain, the hot-button issues of prewar elections, became largely irrelevant in an age of international trade agreements and Britain's loss of status on the international stage. The result was that, for a generation, little differentiated the two major political parties. Both supported the basic premise of the Cold War, namely that the world was polarized between supporters of "evil" communism, led by the Soviet Union, and democratic capitalism, led by the United States. This world view caused both political parties to support closer continental ties in foreign and defence policy. Both favoured the cautious addition of programs to appease public demands for social security. Neither condoned a degree of state intervention that might alarm private investors. Personalities and regional interests, rather than overarching ideologies, determined the public image of the main parties.

The Liberal victory in the 1945 election demonstrated that most Canadians trusted King's programs to prevent a postwar depression. Facing opposition from the provinces, King remained fiscally conservative and was cautious about moving too quickly with a social policy agenda. King stepped down as prime minister in 1948 and was succeeded by Louis St-Laurent. A successful Quebec City lawyer with a string of corporate directorships, St-Laurent had been recruited to King's cabinet in 1941. Pleased with their relative postwar prosperity, Canadians gave the avuncular "Uncle Louis" resounding election victories in 1949 and 1953.

Support for the Liberals eroded in 1956 when the government invoked closure on debate in the House of Commons over its controversial bill to support a private gas pipeline. Tiring of Liberal arrogance after 22 years in power, Canadians shifted their allegiance to the Progressive Conservatives, led by John Diefenbaker. He formed a minority government in 1957, and then went on to win

John F. Kennedy, Governor General Georges Vanier, John Diefenbaker, Jacqueline Kennedy, and Olive Diefenbaker in front of Rideau Hall in Ottawa in 1961. SOURCE: LIBRARY AND ARCHIVES CANADA PA-154665

the biggest electoral majority held by any government to date—208 out of 265 seats—in 1958.

Diefenbaker was a Saskatchewan lawyer with a burning ambition to succeed in politics. As a Member of Parliament since 1940, he had become a leading figure in his party but was twice rejected in national party leadership contests. After Conservative leaders John Bracken and George Drew failed to defeat the Liberals, the party turned to the ambitious Saskatchewan MP. Sixty-one when he became party leader in 1956, Diefenbaker was a powerful orator. His calls for a larger old-age pension, huge expenditures to open up Canada's North, and subsidies to the economically challenged Atlantic provinces demonstrated that the postwar Conservative need not be a fiscal conservative.

Diefenbaker's pursuit of closer trade and foreign policy ties between Canada and Britain suggested that old-style Tory imperialism might not be dead, but in practice he was powerless to divert trade to Britain or to influence its foreign policy. Despite his eventual defiance of the Americans on nuclear weapons policy, Diefenbaker and his cabinet were forced, like their Liberal predecessors, to govern in a world dominated by the political and economic

power of the United States. Their options blunted by the context in which they operated and their largely unexamined liberal values, Diefenbaker and his cabinet appeared to waffle on most issues and to represent little ideological difference from the Liberals they had defeated.

Lester Pearson became Liberal leader shortly before the 1958 election that so humbled his party. A long-time bureaucrat in the Department of External Affairs, Pearson was deputy minister when his former boss, St-Laurent, became prime minister and asked him to become minister of external affairs. Pearson proved highly effective in international affairs, and in 1957 he won the Nobel Peace Prize for his role in defusing the Suez Crisis in 1956.

As leader of the opposition, Pearson recommitted his party to implementing the social programs it had promised in 1945 but never fully delivered. Pearson formed minority governments in 1963 and 1965, dependent on NDP support. The Pearson period represented the heyday of social reform in twentieth-century Canada, with a system of national medical care capping a series of new programs designed to provide Canadians with a social safety net. By the time he left office, Pearson could boast that he had taken the reins of power in a country whose social programs paralleled American policy, and in five short years had left the Americans in the dust.

When Pearson stepped down early in 1968, Pierre Elliott Trudeau was elected Liberal leader and then prime minister. The son of a Montreal millionaire, Trudeau was an intellectual and world traveller who entered politics in the 1965 federal election. Associated with progressive causes in his home province, Trudeau maintained this image in the federal arena. As minister of Justice in the Pearson administration, he was responsible for laying the groundwork for legislation that decriminalized homosexual relations, liberalized divorce laws, and made abortion legal under some circumstances. He also championed constitutional reform while remaining firmly opposed to granting any special status to Quebec.

In the 1968 election campaign, Trudeau captured the public imagination with his promise to create a "just society." Cosmopolitan and debonair by Canadian political standards, he projected an image of a vigorous, trendy, forward-looking leader. The spellbound media lapped it

Pierre Elliott Trudeau cultivated his modern, trendy image by hobnobbing with the likes of John Lennon and Yoko Ono, as in this 1969 picture in Ottawa. SOURCE: LIBRARY AND ARCHIVES CANADA PA-110805

up, and "Trudeaumania" was born. In 16 years of government, Trudeau consolidated existing social and regulatory programs, but as the economy stalled in the early 1970s, his reform efforts faced new challenges and Trudeaumania no longer ensured easy election victories.

THIRD PARTIES IN POSTWAR CANADA

Between 1945 and 1975, third parties remained important in the nation's politics. CCF support declined after the 1945 election, and the party was reduced to an eight-member rump in Parliament in the Diefenbaker sweep of 1958. The CCF then joined forces with organized labour in 1961 to create the New Democratic Party. In an attempt to shake off paranoid Cold War allegations that linked the party with communism, the CCF largely abandoned its commitment to public ownership. Instead, it accepted private enterprise as long as it was regulated by a strong state that implemented extensive social programs and progressive taxation to redistribute wealth. Despite its third-party status, the CCF–NDP exerted a significant impact on public policy because the two main parties feared losing support if they failed to implement progressive social programs.

On the political right, Ernest Manning, the Social Credit premier of Alberta from 1944 to 1968, denounced

the federal Progressive Conservative Party's embrace of the liberal postwar consensus. In the 1960s, he called without success for a realignment of Canada's political parties to unite the Conservatives and Social Credit behind a truly conservative program. The unpopularity of such an idea was obvious during the 1967 Conservative leadership race to replace John Diefenbaker. The two leading candidates, Robert Stanfield and Duff Roblin, the former premiers of Nova Scotia and Manitoba, respectively, were both liberal-minded and had expanded the role of the state in the lives of the residents of their respective provinces. Stanfield's early championing of the idea of a guaranteed annual income made him at least as liberal as most of the Liberal ministers he faced as leader of the opposition in the federal Parliament from 1967 to 1976.

Social Credit had faded as a force in federal politics in English Canada by the 1960s, but the Créditistes, the Quebec wing of the party, carried 26 of its 74 federal seats in 1962. The charismatic leadership of Réal Caouette, resentment of the power of big banks over people's lives, and Diefenbaker's perceived indifference to francophones aided the Créditiste breakthrough. They remained a political force in Quebec until the mid-1970s.

PROVINCIAL POLITICS

Social Credit's power base was essentially provincial. Its Alberta bastion was finally assaulted when Peter Lougheed's Progressive Conservatives upset 36 years of continuous rule in 1971. Between 1952 and 1972, Social Credit, led by the popular W.A.C. Bennett, also reigned in British Columbia. Bennett's Social Credit Party was mainly an alliance of right-wingers against a strong provincial CCF that replaced an earlier alliance of Conservatives and Liberals formed to prevent the CCF from winning enough seats to form a government. Bennett and his ministers had virtually no interest in the original Social Credit philosophy with its focus on monetary policy.

While Alberta's Social Crediters maintained their obsession with the power of bankers in the postwar period, the Social Credit governments in both provinces were friendly to big business despite a front of populist rhetoric.

The West also provided provincial strongholds for democratic socialism. In Saskatchewan, the CCF–NDP governed from 1944 to 1964 and pioneered universal state hospital insurance and medical care. NDP governments elected in Manitoba in 1969, Saskatchewan in 1971, and British Columbia in 1972 were responsible for a degree of social policy experimentation well exceeding that of other provinces.

In Quebec provincial politics, Maurice Duplessis's Union nationale provided a conservative, anti-Ottawa administration, focused on provincial autonomy and economic development, until the death of *le chef* in 1959. Quebec voters elected the Liberals in 1960 and 1962, a party that proved both reformist and nationalist. When the pace of reforms left many behind, the Union nationale was returned to office in 1966 on an avowedly nationalist platform. Thereafter, Quebec politics were increasingly polarized between the more

federalist Liberals and the sovereignist Parti Québécois, founded in 1968.

Politics in the Atlantic provinces mirrored national politics: indistinguishable reform-minded Liberal and Progressive Conservative parties were differentiated in the public mind by the personalities of their leaders. With the lowest standard of living in the country and a shrinking proportion of House of Commons seats, Atlantic Canadians felt the need to ally with a national party that could throw some policy and patronage crumbs their way. Meanwhile, the region's political leaders began cooperating across party lines to pressure Ottawa for special regional subsidies and development projects that would jumpstart their economies. Although their tactics brought some concessions, the region continued to lag behind the rest of the nation.

Ontario politics seemed the most predictable, with the Progressive Conservatives in power without interruption from 1943 to 1985, usually with a comfortable majority of legislative seats. The Conservatives were sometimes called "Red Tories" because of their willingness to spend lavishly on education and health in an effort to maintain public support. While the Ontario government was no

MORE TO THE STORY
Symbols of Independence

In the period after 1945, Canada moved quickly to break many ties that smacked of colonial subordination. The Canadian Citizenship Act, which came into effect in 1947, enabled immigrants to become citizens of Canada instead of "British subjects." In 1949, Canada's Supreme Court finally became "supreme" in legal matters, when appeals to the Judicial Committee of the Privy Council in Great Britain were abolished. In 1952, Vincent Massey became the first governor general to be nominated by the government of Canada rather than by the British government. He was also the first native-born Canadian to hold the post.

The emotional attachment to Great Britain died hard. In 1964, the Pearson government decided to adopt a distinctive Canadian flag to replace the British Red Ensign and the Union Jack, which had been used on ceremonial occasions. Controversy erupted not only about the decision to adopt a new flag,

but also about its design. In the end, the government proposed a red maple leaf as the least controversial symbol of the nation. After six months of debate in the House of Commons, the government finally invoked closure and a new Maple Leaf flag was hoisted over the Parliament Buildings in Ottawa on 15 February 1965. Public opinion polls suggested that Canadians were ready for this move, especially francophones and younger citizens, but John Diefenbaker led a crusade on behalf of a vocal minority—including many veterans who had fought under the Red Ensign. Pearson had also planned to adopt "O Canada" as the official national anthem, but this was not accomplished until 1980. Outside of Quebec, "The Maple Leaf Forever," with its triumphant imperialist lyrics, remained popular, while "God Save the King/Queen" was played on official occasions.

more eager than administrations in poorer provinces to increase social assistance to the poor and was slow to move on minimum wage legislation and environmental regulation, the level of state intervention seemed to satisfy a voting majority. The well-funded, efficiently run Ontario party, commonly known as the "Big Blue Machine," also exercised enormous influence on the direction of national policy.

NEWFOUNDLAND ENTERS CONFEDERATION

Newfoundland's entry into Confederation illustrates the impact of both the welfare state and the Cold War on postwar developments. While Canada's social programs enticed many people in the old dominion, the demands of the Cold War stoked Canadian eagerness to accept the new province. Newfoundland sat astride the sea lanes of the North Atlantic, and therefore played an important role in Cold War strategy.

For the people of Newfoundland, many of whom had experienced unprecedented prosperity during the Second World War, the first order of postwar business was to replace the British-dominated commission. In June 1946, they elected delegates to a National Convention to recommend future forms of government. While some people, especially in the outports, favoured Confederation with Canada, others, including many leaders of the Roman Catholic Church, wanted Newfoundland to regain the status of a self-governing dominion. A few wanted to retain commission government.

Through radio broadcasts of the convention, Joseph "Joey" Smallwood emerged as the principal proponent of joining Canada. Journalist, trade unionist, and farmer, the colourful Smallwood promised that Confederation would banish economic uncertainty forever, thanks to the social safety net provided by family allowances and unemployment insurance. Anti-Confederationists, by contrast, suggested that closer economic ties to the United States would make a self-governing Newfoundland prosperous.

The convention majority opposed including the Confederation option on the referendum ballot, but the British, who favoured Newfoundland joining Canada, ignored its wishes. It took two referenda to get a majority vote for one of the options for Newfoundland governance.

Only 52.4 percent voted in favour of Confederation with Canada, but this was enough. On 31 March 1949, Newfoundland became the tenth province of Canada, rounding out the nation from the Atlantic to the Pacific. Smallwood's Liberals won the first provincial elections in May 1949, and he remained premier of the province until forced to resign in January 1972 after the Conservatives, under the leadership of Frank Moores, finally toppled "the only living Father of Confederation."

POLITICS AND REPRESENTATION

The federal parliament and provincial legislatures remained largely the arena of privileged white males of British and, in the case of Quebec, French extraction. The upper levels of the civil service were staffed with men from the same backgrounds. Although women were almost entirely absent from elected positions, a few managed to score political success. In 1951, Thérèse Casgrain became leader of the Quebec CCF. Grace MacInnis

Ellen Fairclough holding the Great Seal of the Secretary of State after her appointment to cabinet in 1957. SOURCE: CITY OF OTTAWA ARCHIVES, OTTAWA JOURNAL COLLECTION CA-19893

was the only woman in Parliament from 1968 to 1972, but five women were elected in 1972 and eight in 1974. In 1957, Ellen Fairclough became Canada's first female cabinet minister when Diefenbaker appointed her secretary of state, and Judy LaMarsh held major portfolios in the Pearson administration, but political leaders appeared to be of the opinion that one woman in the cabinet was enough.

Not all politicians came from French or English backgrounds. Diefenbaker was partly of German-Canadian extraction, as was Ed Schreyer, who became Manitoba's first NDP premier in 1969. Herb Gray was appointed to Trudeau's cabinet, becoming the first Jew to hold such a position; Dave Barrett, elected in 1972 as the first NDP premier of British Columbia, was also of Jewish descent. The successes of ethnic immigrants were especially noticeable at the civic level. Steven Juba served as mayor of Winnipeg for two decades, William Hawrelak was mayor of Edmonton for several terms between the 1950s and the 1970s, and Nathan Phillips, who was Jewish, served as mayor of Toronto. Visible-minority Canadians fared less well, although Dave Barrett's cabinet included one Native and his caucus included two African Canadians. One of these was Rosemary Brown, who won 37 percent of the ballots for the NDP federal leadership in 1974 in a contest with Ed Broadbent.

SHAPING THE WELFARE STATE

The postwar welfare state had an inauspicious start. After the 1945 election, King convened a Dominion-Provincial Conference on Reconstruction and tabled a comprehensive national program to care for the old, the sick, and the unemployed. To fund these costly endeavours, Ottawa suggested it would require exclusive rights to income and corporate taxes and to succession duties. The provinces, led by Ontario and Quebec, argued that they could not surrender all major taxes and still fulfil their responsibilities. After nine months of meetings, King announced that the talks had collapsed. The pace of social reform would be slower than the parties had promised in 1945.

Conservative forces in Canadian society urged caution with respect to welfare-state measures. The social radicalism of the Great Depression and the war had jarred many pro-business groups, such as the Canadian Chamber of Commerce, into supporting a degree of social reform, but they reverted to conservative positions once the predicted postwar depression failed to materialize. The country could not afford to implement a variety of social programs at once, critics argued, warning that if corporate taxation were to be the source of revenues for welfare, private investment would quickly dry up. Instead of a comprehensive program of welfare measures, governments implemented reforms in a piecemeal manner. Nowhere was this more evident than in medical care.

THE ORIGINS OF MEDICARE

The Canadian Medical Association, a wartime supporter of national prepaid medical insurance, recognized that a return to Depression conditions, in which even middle-class Canadians could not pay their doctors, was unacceptable, but it rejected the idea of a state-run program that forced all doctors and patients to enrol. Many physicians argued instead that doctor-controlled and voluntary private insurance schemes were preferable. National public opinion disagreed. In 1944 and again in 1949, 80 percent of Canadians endorsed a federal health plan to cover complete medical and hospital care for a monthly flat rate. Governments also initially rejected the call for universal medical and hospital insurance, but took steps to improve medical services. They put more money into hospitals, and most provinces paid medical bills for the poorest of the poor. In 1957, a hospital insurance program with costs shared by the provincial and federal governments was implemented.

Prosperity allowed more people to consult doctors and to access hospital services, but prosperity was uneven. The regional distribution of medical personnel paralleled regional patterns of wealth. Although Canadians collectively had one doctor to serve every 938 people in 1959, Ontario, British Columbia, and Alberta residents were even better served. Newfoundland had only one doctor for every 2190 residents. The gap in dental services, which were generally deemed inadequate everywhere in the country, was more extreme—one dentist to every 2400 British Columbians, but only one for every 11 000 in Newfoundland. If St John's and Corner Brook were excluded, the figure for dental care in the province was one dentist for every 30 859 people. The lack of local medical services caused the Newfoundland

Federation of Labour to mock the posters that Ontario public health organizations sent to schools:

> "Brush your teeth three times a day and see your dentist twice a year" say posters in the school. The dentist is 150 miles away.
>
> "Fight cancer with a checkup and a cheque." The checkup means a trip by coastal boat to a doctor with no training or equipment to diagnose cancer.
>
> "Prize your eyes" says the CNIB. But on the coast of Labrador or at the head of Bay d'Espoir, there has never been an eye specialist, not even in transit.[2]

By 1960, almost half of Canadians had purchased private medical insurance, but most plans covered only diagnostic and curative services and not dental care, prescription drugs, preventive services, or mental health care. Given the level of poverty in Atlantic Canada, it is not surprising that coverage in the region was 50 percent less than for the country as a whole. In the Prairie provinces, coverage was much lower in rural areas than in cities. People in the North often remained without professional medical services of any kind.

Diefenbaker established a Royal Commission on Health Services in 1961. Its report, submitted in 1964, called for a universal Medicare scheme embracing hospital, physician, dental, and prescription costs. The Liberals promised Medicare in the 1965 election and, on their return to office, announced the first stage of a national health insurance program. While to some extent a response to the royal commission, the government's action also owed much to the province of Saskatchewan, which had introduced Medicare in 1962, despite a strike by its doctors.

The federal Medicare plan, implemented in 1968, added physician care and the services of some non-physician specialists to the earlier federal–provincial hospital insurance scheme. Ottawa would share costs with the provinces if provincial programs adhered to four principles: universality of coverage, coverage of most medical treatment, portability of benefits, and provincial administration. Although every province except Saskatchewan and British Columbia criticized the federal plan, all provinces soon established programs embodying the four federal principles.

WELFARE REFORM

Apart from universal Medicare, there were other significant Pearson-era reforms, beginning with the introduction in 1965 of the Canada Pension Plan (CPP).

MORE TO THE STORY
Canada's Welfare State in Perspective

How did Canadian efforts in the social policy arena compare with those of other countries? Critics of big government point to the rapid increase in Canadian social expenditures. According to the Organisation for Economic Co-operation and Development (OECD), the cost rose from 12.1 to 21.7 percent of gross domestic product (GDP) from 1960 to 1981. Less publicized was the modest extent of government spending on social programs relative to other OECD countries, including some of the world's most competitive trading nations. West Germany had the OECD's largest per capita social expenditures in 1960, yet it continued to post the greatest productivity gains of any OECD country. Sweden, Italy, Austria, and the Netherlands, all successful in global trade, also exceeded Canada in growth and volume of social expenditures.

Pensions are a case in point. By 1981, Canada devoted less of its GDP to public pensions than any other industrialized country. The CPP had, from the beginning, kept rates low to appease private insurance companies. Even with the Guaranteed Income Supplement, pensioners could not maintain a decent standard of living unless they had other income. Private pensions failed to make up the difference: among Western democracies, only the United States had less private pension protection than Canada. In 1980, 44 percent of paid workers in Canada had private pension plan coverage. Lack of portability of most plans meant that many workers nominally covered by pension plans would never collect from them. It was not surprising, then, that Statistics Canada reported in 1980 that 27 percent of seniors lived on "limited incomes" and that the percentage for elderly women was even higher.[3]

The earnings-related pension was implemented in all provinces save Quebec, which in keeping with its increasingly autonomist approach, set up its own plan. The CPP did not supplant the modest old-age pension that all seniors received, regardless of income, beginning in 1951. Recognizing that it was impossible to live on the old-age pension alone and that many pensioners had no other resources, Pearson introduced the Guaranteed Income Supplement in 1966. Low-interest loans for post-secondary students began in 1966. The Canada Assistance Plan (CAP) of the same year built upon the 1956 cost-sharing agreement on welfare and assured all Canadians the right to receive social assistance. The CAP established national guidelines that provinces were obliged to incorporate in their welfare programs to receive federal assistance.

WOMEN AND THE WELFARE STATE

The Canadian version of the welfare state generally treated women unfairly. CPP pensions, which were calculated on the basis of individual earnings, penalized women on two fronts: first, women workers earned on average far less than men; second, many women withdrew completely from the labour force to raise their children. Unemployment insurance policy was also discriminatory. Men could leave jobs for any reason and, if they had worked the required number of weeks, collect unemployment insurance, provided they demonstrated that they were making reasonable efforts to find new work. Women who quit or were forced to leave a job during a pregnancy or after giving birth were deemed ineligible to collect unemployment insurance, even if they were looking for work. Women's organizations and the labour movement successfully campaigned to have this exclusion lifted.

The CAP was less discriminatory. It made state assistance, however modest, available to all women without male partners, including single and divorced mothers, rather than leaving provinces and municipalities the right to determine which "undeserving" women did not qualify for welfare. "Man-in-the-house" rules persisted in most jurisdictions, and a woman could be cut off social assistance if it was discovered that a man was spending the night at her home. In Ontario, volunteers from charitable organizations carried out surveillance of the moral behaviour of mothers' allowance recipients. Welfare

rights groups protested the assumption that suggested that a man must be providing economic support to a woman who was his sexual partner, but the rules for assistance changed slowly.

The 1970 Report of the Royal Commission on the Status of Women argued that a major barrier to women's economic equality was the lack of affordable daycare. Women were assigned the responsibility for child care, but had little government support except for family allowances, whose value over time had been eroded by Ottawa's failure to peg rates to inflation. If a mother of young children worked outside the home, she generally found that the costs of good private child care were prohibitive. The royal commission concluded: "Parents require supplementary help, and society may legitimately be called upon to contribute to community services for its younger generation. The equality of women means little without such a programme, which should include . . . day-care centres."[4]

In some countries, notably Sweden and France, state programs of free daycare for all children had contributed to dramatic reductions in the rates of poverty for single mothers and a fairer distribution of income between men and women. The royal commission recommended a more modest national program, funded in part by user fees geared to income. Concern about rising social costs and a general indifference to gender equality led most governments to shelve this recommendation.

Public opinion on the daycare issue was divided because many Canadians continued to believe that a woman's place was in the home. Speaking to the Canadian Chamber of Commerce in October 1946, Laura Hardy, president of the National Council of Women of Canada, stated: "As women, we want to live in a Canada in which we can raise our children in our own homes and in the schools of our choice, not in public institutions under the guidance of the State."[5] Such phraseology reflected the Cold War rhetoric of opponents of reform: reformers, they often implied, were trying to impose a totalitarian Communist state in which individual choice disappeared. A Gallup poll in 1960 indicated that 93 percent of Canadians opposed the idea of mothers of young children working outside the home; 10 years later, 80 percent remained opposed.

For both economic and personal reasons, many married women with children worked outside the home. The old liberalism dictated that the state should not intervene

BIOGRAPHY

Elsie Gregory MacGill

One of the strong voices within the Royal Commission on the Status of Women for a welfare state more attuned to women's needs was Elsie Gregory MacGill (1905–1980). MacGill was the daughter of British Columbia's first woman judge, Helen Gregory MacGill, a lifelong campaigner for women's rights. Refusing to be held back by a bout of childhood polio, Elsie MacGill embarked on a brilliant career as an aircraft designer. After becoming the University of Toronto's first female graduate in engineering, she earned a master's degree in aeronautical engineering at MIT in 1929, a North American first for a woman. From 1938 to 1943, MacGill was chief aeronautical engineer at the Fort William plant of Canadian Car and Foundry. In this position, she helped design the Hawker Hurricane plane, one of the best Second World War fighter aircraft. Responsible for the production of over 2000 planes, she headed a staff of 4500 at the peak point of Hawker fabrication.

After the war, Elsie MacGill set up her own consulting practice, continuing to work in aircraft design for most of her life. She became an activist in women's groups, serving for a time as president of the Canadian Federation of Business and Professional Women's Clubs. She fought for paid maternity leave, liberalized abortion laws, and publicly supported daycare. Appointed to the Royal Commission on the Status of Women, Elsie MacGill, as one of Canada's best-known feminists and scientists, was regarded by many as almost a co-chair to the official Commission chair, broadcaster Florence Bird.[6]

Elsie Gregory MacGill in 1938. SOURCE: LIBRARY AND ARCHIVES CANADA PA-148380

in a family's decision about how to care for children, but the new welfare-state liberalism suggested that the government had an obligation to ensure affordable, quality daycare for the children of working parents. In practice, in the 1950s, only Ontario had developed systematic licensing of daycare centres, and only Ontario and British Columbia had modest programs of subsidized daycare. Even in these two provinces, most working parents relied on private arrangements for child care.

Studies by women's groups and social agencies pointed to the inadequacies of such haphazard arrangements. Forced by economic desperation to work yet unable to find affordable and reliable child-care centres, women sometimes left very young children with abusive, neglectful, or alcoholic caregivers. Social policy researchers documented a variety of cases of children warehoused in quarters infested with parasites, in facilities without toys or play areas, and in spaces so cramped that closets became sleep areas. Families often kept school-age children home to look after younger siblings. A disturbing number of children, including pre-schoolers, spent much of the day alone. Social workers and women's groups maintained that it was time to stop arguing about whether it was desirable that mothers work, recognize that many were working, and insist that the state help them to find quality, affordable daycare.

By the end of the 1960s, several provincial governments had begun to provide child-care subsidies for the neediest families, but the provinces proved as unwilling as the federal government to fund universal public dayare. While none of Canada's political parties made child care a priority, the NDP was more sympathetic than others to the issue. When Social Credit was voted out of office in British Columbia in September 1972, 2600 children received subsidized daycare in the province. By the end of 1973, the new NDP administration was providing subsidies for 9500 children.

HOUSING POLICY

Discussions about the cost of state-sponsored social programs tended to assume that the poor were the main recipients, but this was not always the case. In 1954, the Central Mortgage and Housing Corporation (CMHC), a government body, agreed to guarantee mortgages from private financial companies with the goal of encouraging more private initiative. To reduce the potential for default, the CMHC limited its loan guarantees to middle- and upper-income Canadians. Little government aid was available to renters, despite campaigns by trade unions, women's groups, and the Canadian Legion. Although the beginnings of state-subsidized senior citizens' housing were in evidence by the late 1950s, few public-housing units were built for families before the 1960s.

Gradually and grudgingly, federal and provincial governments began to admit that the market economy would not adequately house all Canadians. The Ontario Housing Corporation was established in 1964; by 1972, it managed 50 000 units of public housing, including publicly and privately funded developments. Other provinces had similar, if less ambitious, programs. Federal funds made available to the provinces for social housing on a cost-sharing basis were not fully tapped, except by Ontario and by Manitoba once the NDP came to power in that province. Most of the public-housing developments built in the 1960s and 1970s were notable for overcrowding, cheapness of construction, and lack of green space. Residents created committees to complain about pipes that froze every winter, inadequate heating systems, and cracking plaster. Their homes were a stark contrast to

suburban houses whose mortgages were guaranteed and subsidized by state funds. Yet only the homes of the poor were referred to as "welfare housing."

PROVINCES AND THE NEW LIBERALISM

The provinces remained the main direct providers of social services. In addition to providing funds for new schools, universities, hospitals, highways, and public housing, provincial governments established vocational programs to train young people in the skills demanded in the new economy. Provinces also funded bursary programs to enable bright children from lower-income families to pursue post-secondary education. The new liberalism motivated provincial governments to make social services and education opportunities available on a more equitable basis throughout provincial jurisdictions rather than allowing local councils and school boards to determine what services their area could afford. One of the most sweeping programs of municipal reform was undertaken in New Brunswick under the leadership of Louis J. Robichaud, who held office from 1960 to 1970. While his Program of Equal Opportunity brought howls of a "French takeover" from many anglophones, it helped improve conditions in the poor, rural municipalities where most Acadians in the province lived.

To allow poorer provinces to provide education, health, and social services comparable to those in the wealthier provinces, generous equalization payments were built into the tax system beginning in 1957. All provinces received per capita grants from Ottawa based on the average revenues of the two wealthiest provinces, British Columbia and Ontario. The percentage of federal corporate and personal income taxes that was rebated to provinces rose gradually from five percent in 1945 to 24 percent by the early 1960s. Federal cost-sharing programs and grants enriched provincial coffers, but created the threat of federal interference. Alberta's Social Credit government, for example, objected to federal financial penalties against the province for charging hospital user fees. The Atlantic provinces, with their lagging economies, had little choice but to become dependent on federal largesse. In 1958, the federal government established subsidies in the form of Atlantic Provinces Adjustment Grants in recognition of the region's difficult position.

Transfer payments were not the only federal schemes to help "have-not" provinces; Ottawa also implemented targeted development programs. For example, in the early 1960s, the government passed the Agricultural Rehabilitation and Development Act, which poured money into rural areas to improve efficiency in the development of local resources and to create alternative employment in depressed regions. Prince Edward Island became the focus in 1969 of a 15-year Comprehensive Development Plan that promised an investment of $725 million to help restructure farming and fishing activities, improve infrastructure, and diversify the economy, most notably in the area of tourism.

Both the federal and provincial governments attempted to lure industries into depressed provinces and into the poorer regions of wealthy provinces. Unwilling to have the state itself take an entrepreneurial role, governments searched for private investors who, with the help of public funds, would agree to establish new industries. The major recipients of regional assistance grants were corporations. In the 1960s and 1970s, garment firms that set up low-wage sweatshops in rural areas of Manitoba received a dizzying array of federal, provincial, and municipal subsidies. These included grants to introduce new technologies, "forgivable loans" from the federal government, federal wage subsidies, tax concessions, government-paid training for employees, subsidized hydroelectricity rates, and reduced tariffs on fabrics.

Programs by have-not provinces to lure corporate investment were equally wasteful, encouraging, it appeared, a take-the-money-and-run attitude on the part of investors. Manitoba threw away $150 million to attract mysterious foreign investors, who later proved to have Mafia connections, to develop a forestry complex. Saskatchewan developed a partnership with a multinational forestry company that siphoned off provincial money as efficiently as the Mafia did in Manitoba. In Nova Scotia, millions of dollars were lost in efforts to establish a heavy-water plant in Glace Bay and an electronics company in Stellarton. Both communities had been seriously affected by the decline in the coal industry that had previously sustained them, but the new industries failed to take root. Millions of dollars were poured into New Brunswick premier Richard Hatfield's pet project to build a luxury automobile, the Bricklin, but that company, too, went into receivership. In Newfoundland, Premier Smallwood attracted a variety of entrepreneurs willing to gamble with taxpayers' money, but few of his industrial ventures paid off. An oil

refinery at Come-by-Chance that had been opened with great fanfare in October 1973—the *Queen Elizabeth II* was chartered at a reported fee of $97 000 a day for the occasion—went bankrupt within three years.

Regional assistance incentives generally failed in their stated objectives: they served to maintain rather than change the relative distribution of wealth in the country. The Atlantic region, Manitoba, and Saskatchewan became dependent on federal transfer payments for much of their income. By 1975, fully half of the Atlantic region's income was derived from federal transfer payments. The failure of regional development programs encouraged Atlantic Canadians to fight to at least hold on to what they already had. When DOSCO abandoned its steel mill in Sydney and coal mines at Glace Bay, popular pressures forced the province to operate the mill and the federal and provincial governments to work together to keep the mines open.

Public money was also wasted in central Canada as the federal government lavished funds on an unneeded second international airport for Montreal and on high-technology firms in the Ottawa region that failed to live up to their advance publicity. Quebec seemed the most successful in using provincial subsidies to attract new industries. The investment arm of the Quebec Pension Plan offered competing incentives to companies planning to build new plants or move existing ones. Wealthier provinces had the luxury of focusing on indirect subsidies. Ontario stepped up existing infrastructure programs, while British Columbia and Alberta used low provincial taxes to encourage diversification. W.A.C. Bennett, the long-serving Social Credit premier in British Columbia, proved less dogmatic in his reliance on private enterprise than Ernest Manning, his Alberta counterpart. Bennett created a publicly owned ferry corporation, eliminating private operators, and placed the privately owned BC Electric under provincial government ownership in his drive to create an infrastructure that would attract more industry. Huge dams and new highways also attested to Bennett's ambition to turn British Columbia into an industrial powerhouse.

Secondary industry nonetheless continued to concentrate mainly in central Canada. In the mid-1970s, Alberta made a highly publicized, though largely unsuccessful, effort to use its energy wealth to challenge this pattern. In 1975, Premier Lougheed created the Heritage Trust Fund, into which a portion of oil royalties was committed to provide moneys to stimulate new economic activity. Saskatchewan's NDP government followed a different tack, buying shares for the state in private companies to encourage economic development. It was responsible for establishing a steel-manufacturing firm in Regina, but the province's limited resources relative to the Heritage Trust Fund restricted achievements of these kinds.

The energy-producing provinces responded bitterly when the federal government attempted to increase its revenues from oil and gas developments in the wake of the huge increases in oil prices undertaken by the Organization of Petroleum Exporting Countries (OPEC) in 1973. Resource policy was added to a roster of western grievances against the federal government, including monetary policy, the promotion of bilingualism, the introduction of the metric system, and indifference to the plight of farmers. Ironically, while Lougheed and the other premiers of western Canada and the Atlantic region accused the federal government of following policies that negated provincial development strategies in favour of central Canadian economic development, the province most alienated from Ottawa was in central Canada: Quebec.

MODERNIZATION AND NATIONALISM IN QUEBEC

The new liberalism almost guaranteed a collision between Ottawa and Quebec City. With Ottawa insisting that the federal government have a larger role in all areas of social and economic development, Quebec's longtime premier, Maurice Duplessis played the autonomist card, which was popular politically. In 1947, Duplessis pulled out of the wartime arrangement whereby Ottawa collected taxes for the provinces, and in 1954 he set up Quebec's own income tax system. He established a royal commission on constitutional issues, the Tremblay Commission (1953–56), which recommended a profound reshaping of Canadian federalism. Duplessis also spurned federal money seen as interference in Quebec's jurisdictions, such as grants for universities and funds for the Trans-Canada Highway. On a more symbolic level, in 1948 the Duplessis administration passed a law adopting the fleur-de-lys as the province's official flag.

While Duplessis was bolstering Quebec's autonomy, other social changes were sweeping the province. Following the Second World War, francophones in Quebec,

particularly in the cities, increasingly embraced secular values and the new ideas about the role of government that underlay the broader Canadian turn toward the welfare state. This ran counter to the dominant anti-statist ideology of Duplessis, who encouraged increased government support for church-run charities and educational institutions or private initiatives such as housing cooperatives. The Duplessis government's harsh repression of workers during incidents such as the Asbestos strike of 1949 and the Radio-Canada strike in 1958–59 also fostered popular discontent. Many francophone intellectuals became increasingly dissatisfied with the subsidiary role francophones played in the province's economy and with what they saw as Duplessis's servile subordination to Anglo-Canadian and American big business.

Two main currents emerged in intellectual circles to contest Duplessis. Some thinkers, such as Pierre Elliott Trudeau and others who gravitated around the progressive journal *Cité libre*, were leery of linking their struggles for social justice with French-Canadian nationalism, which they saw as retrograde and dominated by the conservative Catholic values of a traditional Quebec francophone elite that had betrayed its people. The Citélibrists called instead for an increasingly interventionist federal state (though one which respected provincial jurisdiction), and rejected any special status for Quebec. Other thinkers, such as journalist and former Bloc populaire MP André Laurendeau, editor of *L'Action nationale* and *Le Devoir*, and Université de Montréal historian Michel Brunet, argued for a reformulation of Quebec nationalism. For them, the Quebec state was the political expression of the French-Canadian nation and should become the lever for improving the lot of francophone Quebecers. This latter current is often referred to as neo-nationalism.

The collapse of the Union nationale after Duplessis's death provided opportunities for neo-nationalists. They expected the provincial government to follow policies that reflected the new liberal consensus in Quebec, which demanded the preservation of the francophone majority while encouraging francophone economic development. They were instrumental in the 1960 election of the Liberals under Jean Lesage, a former federal cabinet minister under St-Laurent. This election ushered in the Quiet Revolution.

The Quiet Revolution refers to the period of change beginning in the early 1960s, during which Quebec's institutions, and Quebec society as a whole, underwent rapid modernization and secularization. It was initially seen as a radical break with the "grande noirceur," or great darkness, of the Duplessis era. Although historians now recognize that change was already underway in Quebec in the years preceding the election of the Lesage government, few scholars deny that the 1960s and 1970s were a period of fundamental transformation in Quebec.

Initially, the Lesage administration's main thrust was increasing francophone control of the province's economy. One means of achieving this goal was through a significant expansion of the role of the state. Using the slogan "maîtres chez nous," René Lévesque, a former Radio-Canada journalist and a member of Lesage's cabinet, led a campaign to nationalize private hydro companies and create Hydro-Québec, which hired francophone managers and engineers. The government also established the Caisse de dépôt et placement in 1965 to manage the investment of provincial pension funds. The desire by Quebec to run its own social programs initially led to confrontation with Ottawa, but the Pearson government eventually allowed provinces to opt out of federal programs, retaining their share of funding as long as they established similar provincial programs. In practice, only Quebec availed itself of this option.

The Quiet Revolution saw the expansion of the Quebec government's role in such sectors as education, culture, and health care, areas in which the Roman Catholic Church had exercised considerable power. Even in international relations, Quebec's government argued that it should be able to enter into international agreements in its areas of jurisdiction without the involvement of the federal government. In part because of the increasing activity and visibility of the Quebec state, a growing number of francophones in the province began to question their attachment to the rest of Canada. Why not separate from Canada and become an independent nation-state?

Such questioning was fuelled by the social ferment of the 1960s, which emphasized colonial liberation and the struggle against anglophone capitalists, reflected in works such as Pierre Vallières's 1968 book, *Nègres blancs d'Amérique* (*White Niggers of America*). Even Daniel Johnson, the Union nationale premier elected in 1966, had written a book arguing that Quebec's choice was between equality and independence. Resistance by the federal government and most English Canadians to special status for Quebec strengthened the hand of

sovereignists. In 1967, René Lévesque resigned from the Liberal Party and cobbled together an alliance of pro-sovereignty forces that in 1968 became the Parti Québécois (PQ). A key plank in its platform was sovereignty-association—the creation of a separate Quebec state with close economic ties to Canada.

English Canadians initially welcomed the election of the Lesage Liberals and the changes wrought by the Quiet Revolution as a sign that Quebec was throwing off the shackles of Duplessis and of the Catholic Church. However, this was soon tempered by increasing pressure from successive Quebec provincial governments for special status for Quebec and by the growth of the Quebec independence movement. While most *indépendantistes* sought change through democratic means, others argued for more direct action. These included the Front de libération du Québec (FLQ), which drew inspiration from radical resistance movements elsewhere in the world to advocate for the achievement of Quebec independence through revolutionary means. Although never consisting of more than a few dozen members, the FLQ was associated with more than 80 terrorist bombings between 1963 and 1970.

THE MOVE TO OFFICIAL BILINGUALISM

The federal government was at a loss as to what to do to address the "Quebec problem." In 1963, the Pearson government established the Royal Commission on Bilingualism and Biculturalism under co-chairs André Laurendeau and Davidson Dunton. The commission revealed that the rate of assimilation of French Canadians outside Quebec and northern New Brunswick was so alarming as to support Quebec nationalist claims that Confederation had failed to protect French culture. Trudeau, with his distrust of Quebec nationalism, was determined to make francophones feel "chez nous" throughout the country, and thus counter what he saw as the growing threat of the Quebec independence movement.

In 1969, Parliament passed the Official Languages Act, which placed French on an equal footing with English throughout the federal government. The bill created an official languages commissioner responsible for ensuring that federal departments served the public equally well in both languages. A significant percentage of new hires required functional bilingualism. In addition, the federal government tried to expand the use of French nationally by providing funds for French-language schools, French immersion programs for anglophones, and organizations for francophones outside Quebec. The success of these programs in strengthening either the French community or national unity is debatable. Most francophones outside Quebec complained that economic realities still forced them to become proficient in English to get well-paying jobs.

Acadians experienced their own quiet revolution. As in Quebec, education was identified as a key to maintaining cultural identity. Acadians pushed for more French-language instruction and for institutions of higher learning to prepare their children for the new opportunities of the service economy. In New Brunswick, where nearly one-third of the population was francophone, sheer numbers made these goals viable. The election in 1960 of an Acadian, Louis J. Robichaud, as premier of New Brunswick ushered in a period of extensive reform. In addition to establishing a francophone university in Moncton in 1963, the Robichaud government launched a massive overhaul of antiquated municipal governance that improved conditions in poor, rural areas where most Acadians lived. Confrontations with Moncton's anglophone mayor, student sit-ins at the Université de Moncton, and a well-attended Day of Concern over unemployment in January 1972 brought attention to Acadian demands for programs that would protect their culture and improve their economic conditions. In 1969, New Brunswick became Canada's only officially bilingual province, its status confirmed in the Constitution of 1982.

Opposition to official bilingualism ran deep in English Canada, though polls suggested majority support. While many middle-class families were placing their children in immersion programs, other Canadians resented the notion that they had to speak French in order to get federal jobs. In popular thinking, particularly in western Canada, all civil service jobs had become bilingual, the only people wanted for bilingual jobs were francophones, and most federal grants went to Quebec, the spoiled child of Confederation. Canadians whose backgrounds were neither French nor English wondered where they fit into the Canadian mosaic. The Trudeau government established a secretary of state for multiculturalism in 1971 to stem criticism from ethnic minorities, but by that time acts of

terrorism in Quebec were calling Canada's peaceable image sharply into question.

THE OCTOBER CRISIS

Within Quebec, official bilingualism and Trudeau's vision of renewed federalism did nothing to address the demands of sovereignists or to curb the radicals. On 5 October 1970, James Cross, the British trade commissioner in Montreal, was kidnapped by members of the FLQ. Five days later, Pierre Laporte, the Quebec minister of Labour and Immigration, was abducted by another FLQ cell. In return for release of the hostages, the kidnappers demanded, among other things, the freeing of imprisoned FLQ members and the broadcasting of the group's manifesto, which called for a workers' revolution to ensure complete independence for Quebec and the liberation of its people from Anglo-Saxon "big bosses."

The kidnappings provoked outrage and fear in English Canada and in large parts of francophone Quebec, although there were significant demonstrations of support for the kidnappers by some prominent Quebecers, including labour leader Michel Chartrand. Many more moderate Quebec nationalists called for negotiation with the kidnappers, while at the same time distancing themselves from the FLQ's actions. Trudeau, meanwhile, was determined to take the hard line, and was supported in this by newly elected Liberal premier Robert Bourassa.

On 16 October, following a request from the mayor of Montreal and from Bourassa, the federal government proclaimed the War Measures Act (WMA), under which it banned the FLQ and suspended civil rights. Roundly condemned in many progressive circles inside and outside Quebec, the WMA played little role in the apprehension of the revolutionaries and the release of the trade commissioner in early December. It may well have precipitated the murder of Laporte, whose body was found in the trunk of an abandoned car on 17 October, the victim of the only political assassination in twentieth-century Canada. The murder of Laporte disgusted many Quebecers and turned them against the FLQ, but the use of the WMA to round up and detain more than 450 people, most of whom were never charged, became another example for Quebec nationalists of the injustice imposed by a Parliament dominated by English Canadians.

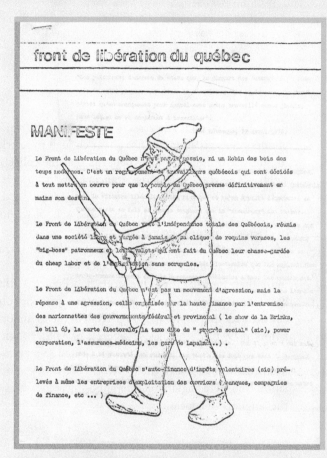

First page of the Front de libération du Québec's 1970 manifesto.
SOURCE: WILLIAM READY DIVISION OF ARCHIVES AND RESEARCH COLLECTIONS, McMASTER UNIVERSITY LIBRARY

As demanded, the FLQ manifesto was broadcast over Radio-Canada/CBC radio and television. These translated extracts give some flavour of the revolutionary ideology that underlay the FLQ's actions and that terrified those in power.

> The Front de Libération du Québec is neither the Messiah, nor a modern-day Robin Hood. It is a group of Quebec workers who are committed to doing everything they can to ensure the people of Quebec take their destiny into their own hands, once and for all. The Front de Libération du Québec wants the total independence of the Québécois, brought together in a free society, purged forever of its band of voracious sharks, the patronage-dispensing "big bosses" and their henchmen, who have made Quebec into their private preserve of cheap labour and of unscrupulous exploitation.

> . . .

> We believed, once, that it was worth the effort to channel our energies, our impatience as René Lévesque put it so well, into the Parti Québécois, but the Liberal victory shows clearly that what is called democracy in Quebec is, and always has been, nothing but the "democracy" of the rich. . . . As a result, British parliamentarism is finished for us, and the Front de Libération du Québec will never let itself be distracted by the electoral crumbs that the Anglo-Saxon capitalists toss into the Québécois barnyard every four years.

> . . .

> We, like more and more Québécois, have had our fill of a government of hand-puppets which performs a thousand and one acrobatics to charm U.S. millionaires, begging them to come and invest in Quebec, "La Belle Province," where thousands of square miles of forests full of game and fish-filled lakes are the exclusive property of those same all-powerful Seigneurs of the twentieth century.

> . . .

> We have had enough of promises of jobs and prosperity, when we will always be the faithful servants and bootlickers of the "big shots" as long as there are Westmounts, Town of Mount Royals, Hampsteads, Outremonts, all those strongholds of high finance of St. James Street and Wall Street, as long as all of us, Québécois, have not driven out by any means necessary, including dynamite and guns, those "big bosses" of the economy and of politics who are ready to stoop to anything in order to screw us better.

> . . .

> We must fight, no longer one by one, but together, until victory, with all the means at our disposal, as did the

Patriotes of 1837-1838 (those whom our Holy Mother the Church hastened to excommunicate, the better to sell out to British interests).

...

We are Québécois workers and we will go all the way. We want, with all the people, to replace this slave society with a free society, functioning of itself and for itself, a society open to the world. Our struggle can only be victorious. Not for long can one hold in misery and scorn, a people once awakened.

Vive le Québec libre!
Vive les camarades prisonniers politiques!
Vive la révolution québécoise!
Vive le Front de Libération du Québec![7]

THE "SPECIAL STATUS" DEBATE

Although Robert Bourassa worked closely with Trudeau to destroy the small revolutionary separatist movement, the two disagreed about how to react to the surging Parti Québécois. Trudeau continued to reject Quebec's affirmations of its special status as the homeland of a French-Canadian nation. Wishing to appease nationalist sentiment, Bourassa followed his predecessors in calling for Quebec to have absolute control in many areas increasingly dominated by Ottawa, particularly social programs, communications, and immigration.

At a federal–provincial conference in Victoria in 1971, Trudeau offered Bourassa a veto for Quebec over constitutional change in return for the premier's support of patriation from Britain of the Canadian Constitution. Bourassa spurned the Prime Minister, warning that Quebec would not support patriation until it was given extra powers. In particular, Bourassa wanted Pearson's "opt-out" principle to be applied to all social programs, present and future, for which federal funds were provided. Trudeau refused.

Bourassa's language legislation also appalled the Prime Minister. Language had long been a hot-button issue in Quebec and had led to incidents such as violent clashes in 1968 in the Montreal suburb of Saint-Léonard between francophones and Italian Quebecers over the rights of the latter to send their children to English schools. In 1974, the Quebec legislature passed Bill 22, making French the only official language in Quebec and promoting its use in the workplace. All children were to be educated in French unless they had a "sufficient" knowledge of English, meaning that immigrant children wishing to enrol in English-language schools would have to pass a language test. Unilingual English signs were banned. Quebec anglophones criticized the bill for infringing on civil liberties. For nationalist francophones, the legislation did not go far enough in restricting the use of English. They believed that the collective rights of a people—in this case, francophone Quebecers—outweighed the individual rights of those who wished to choose their language of business and school without interference by the state.

Given the city's unique demography, Montreal emerged as an epicentre of resistance to Bill 22. While more than four-fifths of Quebecers had French as their first language, on the island of Montreal francophones constituted little more than 60 percent of the total population in 1971. Allophones, Quebecers of neither francophone nor anglophone ancestry, constituted 23 percent of Montrealers, and joined the 16 percent of the city's population who were anglophones in opposing restrictions on the language of education.

INTERNATIONAL RELATIONS AND THE NEW LIBERALISM

If the new liberalism was reflected in federal social welfare programs and the Quiet Revolution in Quebec, it was also evident in international affairs. The image that Canada cultivated was that of a peacekeeper and benevolent donor of foreign aid. Like its American counterpart, the Canadian government subscribed to the view that poverty in the so-called Third World was the result of "underdevelopment" rather than the effects of colonialism and a vastly uneven distribution of wealth. Foreign aid, liberals argued, would allow the governments of poor countries to build the infrastructure, including transportation systems and schools, necessary to encourage industrial development and agricultural improvement.

In 1950, Canada was a signatory of the Colombo Plan, designed to provide assistance to former British colonies in Asia as they gained their independence. Over the next two decades, aid was extended to Commonwealth nations in other parts of the world, to francophone Africa, and, in 1970, to Latin America. The Canadian International Development Agency (CIDA) was established in 1968 to coordinate the nation's foreign aid efforts. Critics of the foreign aid program lamented its lack of generosity and its heavy reliance on "tied aid": countries received funds on condition that they spent specified amounts of their grants to acquire Canadian goods or services.

Canada was perhaps more successful in its role as international peacekeeper. In 1956, Canadian diplomacy was instrumental in finding a solution to the Suez Crisis after British and French troops attacked Egypt following its nationalization of the Suez Canal. Canada was a member of the United Nations Emergency Force that kept the peace between Egypt and Israel from 1956 until 1967, when Egyptian president Gamal Abdel Nasser expelled the UN forces. Among other hot spots where Canadian peacekeepers served were the Congo, Yemen, and Cyprus.

The importance of peacekeeping as opposed to warfare was rarely in question in Canada, but the nation's tendency to follow the United States in many of its foreign policy decisions did not always find favour. Much of Canada's domestic and foreign policy in the post-1945 period reflected the influence of the United States, which had replaced Great Britain as the world's most powerful nation.

THE COLD WAR

After 1945, the Cold War, in which capitalist democracies vied globally with the communist states for resources, trade, and political allies, dominated Canada's foreign policy. This fierce ideological battle created a simplified view of the political and economic options available to nations on either side of the capitalist–communist divide.

In the wake of the Second World War, leaders in the Soviet Union insisted upon establishing friendly regimes in eastern Europe as a protection against Germany, which had devastated their country during two world wars. The Western countries, particularly the United States, rejected such concerns, insisting that the Soviet Union's neighbours had the right to military and economic independence. The Soviets responded by tightening the screws on eastern Europe and imposing Communist-dominated regimes. Each side then declared that the other was bent on world domination, but both sides tried to avoid a direct confrontation—a "hot war"—instead limiting themselves to virulent rhetoric and to support for either pro-Soviet or pro-Western forces in localized conflicts.

In this situation, Canada tended to follow the American lead. The Permanent Joint Board on Defence, established during the Second World War, remained in operation to coordinate the defence policies of the two nations. In 1949, Canada became a founding member of the North Atlantic Treaty Organization (NATO), a military pact that included the United States and Britain as

MORE TO THE STORY
The Gouzenko Affair

The revelation that the Soviets had operated a spy network in Canada in which Canadians spirited classified information to the Soviet government created a sensation when it became public news in February 1946. By then, Western-Soviet relations had deteriorated and many Canadians were prepared to view their wartime ally as a bogeyman.

How damaging were the leaks to the Soviets? In practice, both the Canadian and Soviet governments agreed that what the Soviets had gleaned from their Canadian spies was not particularly significant. Much of it was public information they could have obtained without resorting to espionage. The government's concern was less with the actual information that had been passed to the Soviets than with the potential for real secrets to fall into the hands of the "enemy," such as research relating to nuclear weapons.

The government established a commission to investigate the Gouzenko files and determine what charges should be laid against the individuals fingered in them. The commission was allowed to detain individuals without formal accusations. It recommended charges against 22 individuals, but only half were found guilty, usually of lesser charges than the commission had initially made. The sensationalism of the commission's accusations, which often smacked of guilt by association, received far more publicity than the eventual court cases.

On the basis of the evidence provided by Igor Gouzenko, scientist Raymond Boyer and Fred Rose, Canada's only Communist MP, were found guilty of conspiracy for passing scientific information to the Soviets in 1943. Boyer had been involved in improving a chemical explosive and wanted to share the discovery with Canada's Soviet-allies. But the Canadian government, after consultation with the Americans, decided to withhold this scientific advance from the Russians. Boyer, believing the Soviets needed to know about the discovery in order to strengthen their defence effort against the invading Nazis, gave the information to Fred Rose, who passed it on to Soviet embassy officials. Ironically, a year later, the Canadian government passed on the same information, unaware that the Soviets already knew.

Rose and Boyer's defence that they were aiding the anti-Nazi cause counted for nothing in the atmosphere of the Cold War. They had, after all, knowingly given the Soviets information their government wanted kept secret; therefore, they were traitors. But, as civil libertarians protested, the Canadian state seemed to want to crucify these men not for having consorted with an enemy, but for lacking the foresight to realize that Canada's wartime friend would become its postwar enemy. Rose received a jail sentence. As a criminal, he was ejected from his parliamentary seat.

In the aftermath of the Gouzenko affair and the resulting court cases, a chill fell over political activity on the part of Canada's scientists. State authorities branded the Canadian Association of Scientific Workers, a pacifist-minded organization, as Communist, prompting most of its members and supporters to leave. The organization collapsed and was not replaced.

Gouzenko himself was given a new identity and resettled with his family by the Canadian government, living under police protection for the rest of his life. He went on to write two books, and made occasional appearances in the media, his face and identity protected by a white hood.[8]

Igor Gouzenko in 1954, promoting his prize-winning novel while wearing his trademark white hood.
SOURCE: CP IMAGES

well as continental western European nations. Both organizations were designed to contain the Soviet threat.

Canada also bitterly denounced the Soviets for maintaining a spy network in Canada. In 1945, Igor Gouzenko, a cipher clerk in the Soviet embassy in Ottawa, defected. His revelations, that a Soviet spy ring had been in operation in Canada throughout the war, caused a sensation when they became public in early 1946, and made the leaders of Western nations nervous. Canada had played an important role in the early research leading to the invention of the nuclear bomb, and any possibility that key scientific information could leave government labs and end up in the hands of the Soviet political and scientific establishment was unthinkable in the context of the emerging Cold War.

MORE TO THE STORY
Red Baiting: Anti-Communism in Canada

The Cold War was an ideological battle, and its participants, hoping to impose their values on other countries, were intolerant of dissenting views. The Soviets and their allies crushed dissent ruthlessly. Although Western countries claimed that they were champions of freedom of expression and association, their behaviour often indicated otherwise. In the United States, the House Un-American Activities (HUAC) Committee had harassed Communists since the 1930s. In the early 1950s, the anti-Communist campaign was ramped up by Senator Joseph R. McCarthy of Wisconsin, who used his chairmanship of a Senate subcommittee to investigate a wide spectrum of American citizens, including government bureaucrats, university professors, writers, and popular entertainers.

Anti-communism in Canada was less virulent than in the United States, but it nonetheless infected Canadian institutions. It became a key ingredient in immigration policy. While restrictions on former Nazis were lifted to the point that the RCMP complained that war criminals were being admitted to Canada, no such tolerance was extended to Communists and ex-Communists. Communists were not only deported and kept out as immigrants, but they were also prevented from even visiting Canada.

Following the Gouzenko affair, the federal government attempted to root radicals out of the civil service. A security panel was established with broad powers to determine which state employees might be a threat to national security, a charge that led to either firing or demotion with no chance of appeal. The RCMP infiltrated popular movements, including trade unions, to report on the activities of Communist sympathizers. The National Film Board came under close scrutiny in this period, as did universities. Homosexuals, regardless of their political beliefs, were excluded from government employment on the grounds that Soviet agents might blackmail them into becoming spies by threatening to disclose their sexual orientation. In such an environment, the civil libertarian argument that individuals ought to be judged by their actions and not their beliefs or associations was rejected out of hand. The RCMP kept files on 800 000 individuals and organizations from 1945 to 1980, with the Unitarian Church of Canada, feminist groups, the National Gay Rights Coalition, organizations of Chilean immigrants, and the Parti Québécois all facing infiltration of their organizations by the authorities.

Communists and Communist sympathizers who had been democratically chosen to head unions were denounced so stridently in the media and by their non-Communist union opponents that the state confidently persecuted them and, in some cases, destroyed their unions. Anti-Communist paranoia cost as many as 10 000 Canadian seamen their jobs between 1949 and 1962. The Canadian government, concerned that the democratically elected leaders of the Canadian Seamen's Union (CSU) were Communists, brought Hal Banks, an American union leader linked to organized crime, into Canada to establish a rival union. Although the American and Canadian governments were aware that Banks was ineligible for immigration to Canada because of a criminal record, they cooperated to destroy the CSU, which they feared would call strikes at the behest of the Soviets and interrupt shipments to North America's allies.

Lives could be ruined if individuals were suspected of being Communists or even of being soft on communism. Members of peace groups, such as the Women's International League for Peace and Freedom, founded in 1915, also suffered from red baiters, who smeared anyone who opposed them. In such an atmosphere, those leery of the Cold War philosophy or of particular actions that flowed from such a philosophy generally kept their mouths shut. In both Canada and the United States, fundamental criticism of foreign policy or of red baiting was rare.

THE KOREAN WAR

In 1950, Canada agreed to contribute troops to the United Nations forces sent to hold the line against communism in Korea. Korea had been divided after the war into two zones, North Korea, under Soviet supervision, and South Korea, under American control. Cold War antagonism stalled the amalgamation planned for the two Koreas by the UN. When troops from North Korea invaded South Korea in June 1950, the United States manoeuvred the UN into sending a peacekeeping force into the region. The conflict threatened to escalate when the People's Republic of China became involved. Canada worked behind the scenes to restrain its aggressive ally, but with little success. As the war progressed, United Nations troops under American general Douglas MacArthur, having driven the Communists out of South Korea, entered North Korean territory. This foray led to a military response from China, and the war grew in length and intensity.

Fighting in the Korean War finally came to an end in 1953 with a truce between the two sides, though Korea remained permanently divided between the North and the South. In total, about 25 000 Canadians participated in the hostilities, and 300 lost their lives. Again, war proved a boon to the Canadian economy. The federal government poured money into defence production, and the United States invested in Canadian resources to replace those rapidly being depleted by its expanding Cold War economy. By contrast, the two Koreas, both controlled by ruthless dictators, experienced economic devastation and the loss of millions of lives.

THE NUCLEAR ISSUE

Canada and the United States poured billions of dollars into an elaborate defence program designed to protect North America from a Soviet air attack. Between 1949 and 1957, three radar defence systems—the Pine Tree, Mid-Canada, and Distant Early Warning (DEW) lines—were built. The DEW Line stretched from Alaska to Baffin Island, and cooperation on this project helped pave the way for the North American Air Defence Command (NORAD) agreement of 1958, which produced a unified air command for North America.

America's exclusive possession of nuclear weapons from 1945 to 1949, followed by a decade of clear nuclear superiority over the Soviet Union, encouraged political leaders in the United States to enunciate a policy of "deterrence": the Americans threatened to use "nukes" against Communist states if they intervened in other countries' affairs. In 1954, NATO members, hoping to avoid the expense of large conventional armed forces, adopted nuclear deterrence as the mainstay of their defence strategy. Canada agreed to play a role in surveillance of possible military strike plans by the Communists and purchased a variety of aircraft and missiles from the United States meant to help serve this objective. Canada also agreed to permit storage of American nuclear weapons at Goose Bay and Harman air force bases, which, though on Canadian territory, were controlled by the Americans. When it became clear that Canada's balance of payments was being seriously undermined by expenditures on American military equipment, the United States acceded in 1956 to a Defence Production Sharing Agreement that led to more American purchases from Canadian-based firms.

SUPPORTING DEMOCRACY?

Close ties to the Americans sometimes compromised Canada's vaunted peacekeeping role. This was the case in policy relating to Vietnam, which, like Korea, became a Cold War hot spot. In 1954, French colonizers of Vietnam had been forced to recognize Communist control over the northern half of Vietnam and to cede South Vietnam to anti-Communist Vietnamese landlords and businessmen. Negotiations in Geneva that year produced an accord calling for reunification of North and South Vietnam after elections to be held in 1956. An International Control Commission (ICC) with Canada, Poland, and India as its members was established to monitor implementation of provisions of the Geneva accord.

Fearing that the Communists would win, the United States refused to call a nation-wide election. Instead, the Americans supported a permanent division of the two Vietnams, and appeared to approve of the South Vietnamese government's reign of terror, including the murder of suspected Communist sympathizers and the uprooting of peasant villages. As an ICC member, Canada seemed to see only North Vietnamese violations, while Poland saw only South Vietnamese violations. A report in 1962 prepared by Canada and co-signed by India, desperate for American goodwill because of border wars with China, was regularly brandished by American officials during their undeclared war in Indochina (1965–75) to demonstrate North Vietnamese atrocities.

Canada made one effort to counsel reason to the Americans during the Vietnam War. In April 1965, Prime Minister Pearson, addressing students at Temple University in Philadelphia, cautiously advocated that the American government temporarily cease bombing North Vietnam in an effort to seek diplomatic solutions in Indochina. American president Lyndon Johnson, who in February had stepped up bombing in the divided country, was furious, berating Pearson at a luncheon following his speech. Pearson was careful not to issue another indictment of American policy in Indochina, admitting candidly to journalists in 1967 that open criticism of American foreign policy could lead to American economic retaliation that might be disastrous for Canada.

Such thinking likely led to Ottawa's silence as repressive military dictatorships, supported by the Americans, overthrew a string of democratic governments that the United States considered too leftist or too nationalist, including those of Iran (1953), Guatemala (1954), Brazil (1964), Dominican Republic (1965), Greece (1967), and Chile (1973). It would, however, be misleading to overstate the extent to which Canadian foreign-policy makers cowered in fear of American economic retaliation. Canada's leaders, like their American counterparts, were supporters of international capitalism and wanted to see the defeat of communism at any cost. In practice, it was not a government's democratic character but rather its support for Western investment and trade that became the criterion for American and NATO approval. Fascist Spain and Portugal were included in NATO, and the United States supported a variety of thuggish regimes in Asia and Latin America. Many Canadians were troubled by the apparent contradictions that resulted from Canada's special relationship with the United States. Even at the height of the Cold War in the 1950s, campaigns for nuclear disarmament, human rights, and a more balanced assessment of various Communist regimes were waged. University professors began warning people of the dangers associated with nuclear testing, and in 1960, women from across Canada formed the Voice of Women to promote disarmament and peace.

Dissenting voices soon grew louder, stimulated by the student rebellions that swept North America and western Europe in the 1960s. Dissent was also fuelled by one of Canada's most purposeful immigrant groups: Americans evading the draft, military deserters, and others opposed to the Vietnam War. Estimates of the numbers of American war resisters who immigrated to Canada vary, but range as high as 100 000. Most of them were young and well-educated. They settled all over the country, but were concentrated in Montreal, Toronto, and Vancouver, where the peace movement was most vocal. Outraged by atmospheric testing of nuclear bombs and Cold War brinkmanship, the new generation of pacifists focused on dismantling nuclear weapons and establishing peaceful forums for settling international conflicts.

THE RESPONSE FROM OTTAWA

Governments in Ottawa apparently had no such liberty to criticize American foreign policy. Attempting to chart a separate course on defence proved fatal to one Canadian administration. Influenced by the growing support for nuclear disarmament, Howard Green, Secretary of State for External Affairs from 1959 to 1963, encouraged the Diefenbaker government to reconsider Canada's agreement to acquire nuclear warheads as part of its commitment to NATO and NORAD defence strategies. His cabinet divided by this and other issues, Diefenbaker vacillated on defence policy, causing consternation in Washington.

The Cuban missile crisis brought matters to a head. In October 1962, Diefenbaker received an urgent demand from President John F. Kennedy to put Canada's NORAD forces on alert during an American–Soviet showdown over the installation of Soviet missile bases in Cuba. In 1961, the United States had tried to overthrow a Communist regime in Cuba, the product of a revolution led by Fidel Castro, who took power in 1959. Castro responded to the Bay of Pigs invasion by accepting Soviet missiles, but Kennedy demanded that the missile build-up in Cuba be stopped. The two superpowers eventually settled the matter peacefully, but Diefenbaker's lack of cooperation infuriated the Americans.

In the months following the crisis, statements from the American State Department and from a retiring American NATO leader drew attention to Diefenbaker's about-face on defence policy. The Americans revealed that Diefenbaker's earlier agreement to purchase weapon systems associated with NORAD and NATO commitments necessitated acquisition of nuclear warheads, notwithstanding public statements by Diefenbaker to the contrary. The uproar resulted in the withdrawal of Social

Credit support for Diefenbaker's minority government in February 1963. In the ensuing election, the Liberals won enough seats to form a minority government, and they repaired the breach with the Kennedy administration by acquiring the controversial nuclear warheads.

When he came to power in 1968, Trudeau, who had publicly criticized Pearson for bowing to the Americans, initiated a reassessment of Canada's NATO and NORAD commitments. His government announced plans to cut Canada's NATO troops in Europe by half, and the obsolescence of the nuclear weapons allowed Canada to return to its non-nuclear status. Trudeau also tried to move away from the United States in some areas of foreign policy. In 1970, two years before the Americans took the same step, Canada recognized the People's Republic of China.

CONCLUSION

The postwar liberal consensus in Canada embraced several contradictory threads. While postwar prosperity was to be guaranteed by extensive state regulation of the economy and new programs of social spending, it was sustained by American military expenditures resulting from the Cold War. Similarly, although Canada was striving to be an independent nation with an influence in world councils, it often felt the need to defer to the Americans in foreign and defence policies. At home, the desire to create national programs conflicted with regional demands for greater local control and Quebec's growing desire for nationhood. As we will see in the following chapter, these contradictions also had an impact on the Canadian economy.

A HISTORIOGRAPHICAL DEBATE
Quebec Nationalism from Duplessis to the Quiet Revolution

What were the causes of growing support for Quebec nationalism and, ultimately, Quebec sovereignty in the 1960s and early 1970s? Most specialists acknowledge a shift in this period from a notion of French-Canadian nationalism, which included francophones beyond the province's borders, to neo-nationalism, which increasingly identified Quebec–and especially francophone Quebec–as the nation that needed protecting. What caused this change?

One view at the time linked class and ethnicity and drew on theories of decolonization elaborated in the developing world. According to writers such as sociologist Marcel Rioux, echoing the views of writers in leftist journals such as *Parti pris*, Quebec francophones were relegated to working-class status. They therefore began to develop the view of themselves as an ethnic class that must break free not only from domination by English Canada, but also from the capitalist ethos that pervaded anglophone North America.[9] Similarly, William D. Coleman situates the rise of the Quebec independence movement in the increasing integration of Quebec into North American capitalist structures after the Second World War, with the accompanying decline of traditional French-Canadian culture and the loss of control that this implied for leaders in Quebec society. He emphasizes the differing economic orientations and interests of the various interest groups that made up the independence movement, but ultimately underscores the "class character of the struggle."[10]

Political scientist Kenneth McRoberts offers a more focused economic explanation. The Quiet Revolution, he argues,

raised francophone hopes that they would take over the levers of economic power in the province and experience a measurable increase in their standard of living. When this failed to occur, the upwardly mobile professional middle classes were disappointed. They provided the impetus for the Parti Québécois, as well as movements that preceded its founding.[11] In contrast, political scientist André Bernard rejects purely economic explanations, suggesting that the struggle to preserve the French language united secessionists regardless of social class. Emphasizing the importance of language as the defining factor of the French-Canadian nation, he suggests that "the idea of a unilingual French-speaking people in the territory populated and dominated by French Canadians is more a reflection of ideology than a formula prompted by narrow economic interests."[12]

Other scholars have sought to trace the roots of Quebec neo-nationalism further back than the Quiet Revolution of the 1960s. Political scientist Herbert Quinn characterized the Union nationale under Maurice Duplessis as nationalist, and traced a direct line from Duplessis's defence of provincial rights to René Lévesque's call for independence.[13] Historian Michael Gauvreau sees the origins of the Quiet Revolution in changes within Catholic social movements in the 1940s and 1950s.[14] Historian Michael Behiels points out that neo-nationalism was already on the rise among Quebec intellectuals in the 1940s and 1950s, a reaction to the perceived stranglehold of traditional nationalism in Quebec, with its emphasis on conservative, religious values and its rejection of state intervention.[15] Political scientist Louis Balthazar suggests it was a natural step from there to focusing on Quebec itself and, eventually, Quebec independence. The shift was a gradual one though, aided among other things by an increasing emphasis on Quebec culture in the 1960s and 1970s and on the ongoing conflicts with Ottawa.[16] Some scholars have also sought to rehabilitate the role of Maurice Duplessis in the rise of Quebec-centred nationalism. Sociologist Jacques Beauchemin, for example, credits Duplessis's autonomist battles against Ottawa for providing the impetus for a more nationalist approach.[17] With no recent scholarly overview of the history of nationalism in Quebec, the question remains open to debate.

NOTES

1. Library and Archives Canada, MG 32, C 12, *Grace MacInnis Papers*, vol. 19, File "Women, Status of, 1972," J. Eric Harrington, president, Canadian Vickers Ltd., to MacInnis, 9 May 1972; MacInnis to Harrington, 18 May 1972.

2. Canada, *Royal Commission on Health Services*, brief presented by the Newfoundland Federation of Labour, Oct. 1961.

3. The OECD figures are found in OECD Bulletin, No. 146 (January 1984), reprinted in Andrew Armitage, *Social Welfare in Canada: Ideas, Realities and Future Paths*, 2nd ed. (Toronto: McClelland & Stewart, 1988) 22. The evolution of Canadian pensions is discussed in Alvin Finkel, *Social Policy and Practice in Canada: A History* (Waterloo, ON: Wilfrid Laurier University Press, 2006) 151–167.

4. Report of the Royal Commission on the Status of Women in Canada (Ottawa: Information Canada, 1970) 261.

5. Quoted in Alvin Finkel, "'Even the Little Children Cooperated': Family Strategies, Childcare Discourse, and Social Welfare Debates, 1945–1975," *Labour/Le Travail* 36 (Fall 1995) 105.

6. Richard I. Bourgeois-Doyle, *Her Daughter the Engineer: The Life of Elsie Gregory MacGill* (Ottawa: NRC Research Press, 2008).

7. Adapted by Donald Fyson from the translation by Simma Green in *Canadian Dimension* 7 (December 1970) 5–6.

8. John Sawatsky, *Gouzenko: The Untold Story* (Toronto: MacMillan, 1984); Reg Whitaker and Gary Marcuse, *Cold War Canada: The Making of a National Insecurity State, 1945–1957* (Toronto: University of Toronto Press, 1994); Mark Kristmanson, *Plateaus of Freedom: Nationality, Culture and State Security in Canada, 1940–1960* (Toronto: Oxford University Press, 2003); Reg Whitaker, Gregory S. Kealey and Andrew Parnaby, *Secret Service: Political Policing in Canada from the Fenians to Fortress America* (Toronto: University of Toronto Press, 2012).

9. Marcel Rioux, *Quebec in Question* (Toronto: J. Lorimer, 1978).

10. William D. Coleman, *The Independence Movement in Quebec, 1945–1980* (Toronto: University of Toronto Press, 1984) 226.

11. Kenneth McRoberts, *Quebec: Social Change and Political Crisis,* 3rd ed. (Toronto: McClelland & Stewart, 1988) 173–208.

12. André Bernard, *What Does Quebec Want?* (Toronto: Lorimer, 1978) 45.

13. Herbert Quinn, *The Union Nationale: Quebec Nationalism from Duplessis to Lévesque,* 2nd ed. (Toronto: University of Toronto Press, 1979).

14. Michael Gauvreau, *The Catholic Origins of Quebec's Quiet Revolution, 1931–1970* (Montreal: McGill-Queen's University Press, 2005).

15. Michael D. Behiels, *Prelude to Quebec's Quiet Revolution: Liberalism versus Neo-nationalism, 1945–1960* (Montreal: McGill-Queen's University Press, 1985).

16. Louis Balthazar, *Bilan du nationalisme au Québec* (Montreal: Éditions de l'Hexagone, 1986).

17. Jacques Beauchemin, "Politisation d'un nationalisme ethniciste dans le Québec duplessiste," in Michel Sarra-Bournet, ed., *Les nationalismes au Québec du 19e au 21e siècle* (Quebec: Presses de l'Université Laval, 2001) 117–29.

SELECTED READING

Barnhart, Gordon L., ed. *Saskatchewan Premiers of the Twentieth Century.* Regina: Canadian Plains Research Center, 2004.

Behiels, Michael D. *Prelude to Quebec's Quiet Revolution: Liberalism versus Neo-Nationalism, 1945–1960.* Montreal: McGill-Queen's University Press, 1985.

Blake, Raymond B. and Jeffrey A. Keshen, eds. *Social Fabric or Patchwork Quilt: The Development of Social Policy in Canada.* Peterborough: Broadview Press, 2006.

Blake, Raymond B. *Canadians at Last: The Integration of Newfoundland as a Province.* Toronto: University of Toronto Press, 2004.

Bothwell, Robert. *Alliance and Illusion: Canada and the World, 1945–1984.* Vancouver: UBC Press, 2007.

Bryden, P.E. *Planners and Politicians: Liberal Politics and Social Policy, 1957–1968.* Montreal: McGill-Queen's University Press, 1997.

Dickerson, Mark. *Whose North? Political Change, Political Development, and Self Government in the Northwest Territories.* Vancouver: UBC Press, 1992.

English, John. *Just Watch Me: The Life of Pierre Elliott Trudeau, volume 2, 1968–2000.* Toronto: A.A. Knopf Canada, 2009.

Ferguson, Barry and Robert Wardhaugh, eds. *Manitoba Premiers of the 19th and 20th Centuries.* Regina: Canadian Plains Research Center, 2010.

Fingard, Judith and Janet Guildford, eds. *Mothers of the Municipality: Women, Work and Social Policy in Post-1945 Halifax.* Toronto: University of Toronto Press, 2005.

Finkel, Alvin. *Social Policy and Practice in Canada: A History.* Waterloo: Wilfrid Laurier University Press, 2006.

Gagnon, Alain-G., ed. *Québec: State and Society,* Third edition. Peterborough: Broadview Press, 2004.

Gagnon, Alain-G. and Michel Sarra-Bournet, eds. *Duplessis: entre la grande noirceur et la société libérale.* Montreal: Québec/Amérique, 1997.

Hayday, Matthew. *Bilingual Today, United Tomorrow: Official Languages in Education and Canadian Federalism.* Montreal: McGill-Queen's University Press, 2005.

Henderson, T. Stephen. *Angus L. Macdonald: A Provincial Liberal.* Toronto: University of Toronto Press, 2007.

Hillmer, Norman, ed. *Pearson: The Unlikely Gladiator.* Montreal: McGill-Queen's University Press, 1999.

Johnson, A.W. with Rosemary Proctor. *Dream No Little Dreams: A Biography of the Douglas Government of Saskatchewan, 1944–1961.* Toronto: University of Toronto Press, 2004.

Levant, Victor. *Quiet Complicity: Canadian Involvement in the Vietnam War.* Toronto: Between the Lines, 1986.

Mackenzie, David. *Inside the Atlantic Triangle: Canada and the Entrance of Newfoundland Into Confederation, 1939–1949.* Toronto: University of Toronto Press, 1986.

Martel, Marcel. *Le deuil d'un pays imaginé: rêves, luttes et déroute du Canada français. Les rapports entre le Québec et la francophonie canadienne, 1867–1975.* Ottawa: Presses de l'Université d'Ottawa, 1997.

McRoberts, Kenneth. *Quebec: Social Change and Political Crisis,* Third edition. Toronto: Oxford University Press, 1999.

Mitchell, David J. *W.A.C. Bennett and the Rise of British Columbia.* Vancouver: Douglas & McIntyre, 1983.

Porter, Ann. *Gendered States: Women, Unemployment Insurance, and the Political Economy of the Welfare State in Canada, 1945–1997.* Toronto: University of Toronto Press, 2003.

Rennie, Bradford J., ed. *Alberta Premiers of the Twentieth Century.* Regina: Canadian Plains Research Center, 2004.

Stanley, Della M.M. *Louis Robichaud: A Decade of Power.* Halifax: Nimbus, 1984.

Struthers, James. *The Limits of Affluence: Welfare in Ontario, 1920–1970.* Toronto: University of Toronto Press, 1994.

Teigrob, Robert. *Warming Up to the Cold War: Canada and the United States' Coalition of the Willing, from Hiroshima to Korea.* Toronto: University of Toronto Press, 2009.

Thompson, John Herd and Stephen J. Randall. *Canada and the United States: Ambivalent Allies,* Fourth edition. Montreal: McGill-Queen's University Press, 2008.

Whitaker, Reg and Gary Marcuse. *Cold War Canada: The Making of a National Insecurity State, 1945–1957.* Toronto: University of Toronto Press, 1994.

For a comprehensive list of readings for topics covered in this chapter, please visit http://pearsoncanada.ca/conrad.

CHAPTER 13
GROWTH AT ALL COSTS: THE ECONOMY, 1945-1975

In 1964, Cominco began operating a lead-zinc mine in the Northwest Territories, creating the instant community of Pine Point. About $100 million of federal money was invested in the project, which included developing the town site and building highways, hydroelectric plants, and a railway to haul minerals to markets. By 1975, about 1800 people, mainly from southern Canada, lived at Pine Point. Their high wages and modern homes were evidence of the good lives that many Canadians attained in the postwar period.

Sixty-five kilometres west of this new town created by business and government was the long-established Native community of Fort Resolution. Speaking to a federal inquiry established in 1974 to determine whether energy pipelines should be built across the Mackenzie Valley, Mike Beaulieu of Fort Resolution provided a view of the mine's economic benefits that differed from Cominco's.

> We, the Dene people, do a lot of hunting and trapping and fishing. Our hunting has decreased a lot due to the construction of the highway, the building of the mine, and the increase of the people from the South. . . . Our traditional grounds are slowly being overtaken by these [mine] employees. There is virtually no benefit to be spoken of from the mine.[1]

The impact of the Pine Point mine on the environment and on Native peoples provides an example of the other side of the equation of the unprecedented economic growth that characterized the period from 1945 to 1975. Dramatic improvements in overall living standards were accompanied by environmental degradation, uneven distribution of the new wealth, and destruction of many communities. This chapter traces the economic history of the period when the American dream of unlimited prosperity became a realistic goal for many Canadians, but an unattainable–even undesirable–illusion for others.

THE WELFARE STATE AND WARFARE ECONOMY

Canada's longest relatively uninterrupted boom owed a great deal to widespread acceptance after the Great Depression and the Second World War that government involvement in the economy was necessary to smooth out the business cycle and maintain investor confidence. Following the advice of the influential British economist John Maynard Keynes, governments developed monetary and fiscal policies to ensure that any decline in private investment was balanced by more public investment. Governments would not run businesses, but they would expand the money supply and their own expenditures when the private sector was contracting, easing up on both when private investment recovered. Big business, while not always enthusiastic about this philosophy, mounted little opposition to state intervention as long as it promoted only economic growth and not a major redistribution of wealth. The government–business agreement of the postwar years is often referred to as the "postwar compromise."

When the war ended, the federal government drew on this new economic thinking about the role of the state in the economy to ensure that peacetime was also a prosperous time. Canada's national debt was 1.25 times the annual gross national product in 1945, but Minister for Reconstruction C.D. Howe produced a White Paper on postwar reconstruction that proposed a delay in repaying debts until the economy was on an even keel. Moving quickly to jettison wartime price controls and to privatize Crown corporations, the federal government expanded the money supply to finance the debt and increased spending on social programs. Factories were quickly converted from war production to making cars, clothes, appliances, and housing materials. When production slowed, exports contracted, and inflation soared, Ottawa stoked the economy with tax incentives to industry and programs targeted at veterans, the private housing market, and municipalities. As was predicted, consumer demand soon became the driving engine of the economy. If growth in output and productivity are the measures of success, the government's strategy worked well.

Since Canada's economic prosperity depended on exports, trade liberalization became a cornerstone of Canadian postwar foreign policy. In November 1947, Canada signed the General Agreement on Tariffs and Trade (GATT), aimed at reducing trade barriers. Canada also benefited from the Marshall Plan, a program introduced by the United States in 1947 to help European countries recover from the devastation of the war. With Marshall Plan dollars available for European purchases from Canada as well as the United States, export markets

slowly began to improve. The cyclical upswing was reinforced by massive military spending, sparked by the escalating Cold War. Between 1949 and 1953, defence expenditures rose from 16 to 45 percent of the federal budget, and a new ministry was created to orchestrate the business of war. C.D. Howe became the minister of defence production, and in this guise he continued to play godfather to the business community.

With more than $1 billion spent annually on defence in the 1950s, many aspects of the Canadian economy were shaped by military considerations. As late as 1960, when defence had slipped back to a quarter of federal budgetary expenditures, military purchases accounted for 89 percent of the shipments in the aircraft industry, 41 percent in electronics, and 21 percent in shipbuilding. Research and development in both Canada and the United States was increasingly related to defence priorities. In the United States, the term "military-industrial complex" was coined to describe this new era of defence-induced growth.

American military concerns fuelled continental economic integration. As the Americans became concerned that they were running out of the raw materials required to fuel their military and civilian economy, they invested heavily in Canadian minerals, oil, and lumber. The need for uranium for atomic bombs and nuclear reactors allowed Canadian uranium companies to sell their product at fabulous prices to the United States Atomic Energy Commission. With Canada supplying a third of the world's military and civilian requirements for uranium in the 1950s, Uranium City, Saskatchewan, and Elliot Lake, Ontario, were added to the pantheon of boom towns on Canada's resource frontier.

In 1952, Atomic Energy of Canada Limited (AECL) was created as a Crown corporation to develop peaceful uses of atomic energy. It sold CANDU (CANada Deuterium Uranium) reactors at home and internationally. Ontario was the first province to enter into an agreement with AECL to build nuclear power stations, and the first demonstration plant at Rolphton came into operation in 1962. Of the 29 commercial reactors built, 22 were located in Ontario.

Defence production, particularly after Canada and the United States signed a Defence Production Sharing Agreement in 1958, further encouraged continental economic integration. Stimulated by the Vietnam War, armaments production accounted for an estimated 125 000 Canadian jobs by the late 1960s. Shells, military aircraft, and radio relay sets poured out of Canadian factories while metal-mining companies received record orders for minerals required in military industries.

In cooperation with provinces and private corporations, the federal government supported several megaprojects, including the Trans-Canada Highway and the TransCanada Pipeline. Impressive as an engineering and construction project, the St Lawrence Seaway, built between 1954 and 1959, was co-funded with the Americans. Its purpose was to enlarge the canals and develop the power potential along the inland waterway. Allowing vessels to travel from Anticosti Island to Lake Superior, the seaway cost the Canadian government more than $1 billion. Canadian communities along the St Lawrence were flooded to build the seaway, and it also had a significantly negative impact on Montreal's role as

MORE TO THE STORY
A Modest Prosperity

For most working people, the postwar economic boom brought tangible changes but not wealth. Historian Craig Heron describes his parents' lives during this period.

In May 1945, a young Canadian couple exchanged wedding vows and began a half-century of life together. Harold, age 23, was still in his Royal Canadian Air Force uniform, but would soon be donning the work clothes of a manual worker in a series of relatively low-skill jobs. Marg, age 21, gave up her position as a telephone operator and started to set up the family household before Harold was finally released from the Air Force. Over the next few years they helped launch the Baby Boom by having two sons, whom they raised in a small house perched on the outer edge of suburban Toronto. Once the boys were both in school in the late 1950s, Marg returned to the paid workforce and spent some 20 years as a secretary. Like a declining majority of Canadians in the postwar period, Harold, Marg, and the boys were anglo-Canadian, English-speaking, Canadian-born, and white. They were also working class. . . .

Leaving the family farm with only a Grade Nine education and no marketable skills, Harold's job prospects and earning ability were restricted. Marg's background in a shopkeeping family and a Grade Eleven education constrained her employment opportunities to lower-end clerical work at best. These were limited jobs, not expanding careers. What they earned restricted the family's living standards. They lived most of their married lives in a small, five-room frame house, rarely bought new furniture, ate simple meals, rarely went out to restaurants or movies, relied on older, used cars, had no money for expensive dental work, limited their summer vacations to a visit to Marg's mother's cottage and later to short, inexpensive family camping expeditions, and worried constantly about debt. By the end of the 1950s, in fact, they found they could not survive on Harold's wages alone, and, like thousands of other Canadian working-class housewives at that point, Marg went out to work full time (as employers finally rejected the longstanding taboo on hiring married women). Even with two pay cheques coming in pennypinching was a way of life. Only in the 1970s, when both boys had moved out and established independent households, did Harold and Marg's living standards begin to improve to any great extent.

Indeed, Marg could also have explained how, in the face of ever-present economic vulnerability, she managed the family household as effectively as possible to sustain what historians have come to call a family economy. Economical shopping to stretch wages, along with family labour to avoid cash outlays, were still crucial in the 1950s and 1960s. As a small investment strategy, Harold and Marg also bought two acres of land with no water or sewer connections and a half-finished house, which they spent many years fixing up (in a suburban neighbourhood where such owner-built houses were numerous). Eventually, they made small sums by selling off four lots for new housing, and, many years later, in the late 1980s, sold the remaining land for a substantial sum. Many working-class families had similar survival

strategies in this period, much as they had done for generations in Canada in response to the economic uncertainty of their material situation.[2]

central Canada's maritime hub. But the search for national military and economic security overrode these more local concerns.

Owing to the booming economy, the unemployment rate for 1956 was only 3.2 percent, the lowest rate for the rest of the century. Wages increased faster than prices throughout the postwar decade, while consumption increased on average by 5.1 percent each year. The government's debt as a proportion of gross national product halved from 1946 to 1956 because a wealthier population was paying enough taxes to cover both increased spending and debt reduction.

Technological innovation also stimulated postwar productivity. New products such as synthetic fibres, plastics, and pesticides had been stimulated by wartime demand, while television, the self-propelled combine harvester, and the snowmobile, developed before the war, became commercially viable only in the improved postwar economic climate. The pharmaceutical industry could hardly keep up with the demand for new products,

including such miracle drugs as penicillin, polio vaccines, anti-depressants, and the birth-control pill.

Stimulated by government spending and strong export markets, multinational economic empires bloomed in Canada, including the Macmillan-Bloedel forestry complex headquartered in British Columbia, Ontario's investment giant, Argus Corporation, and K.C. Irving's New Brunswick–based conglomerate. Times had never seemed so good, but in 1957, the American economy went into recession, and the Canadian economy, so closely integrated with its southern counterpart, followed suit.

PRIMARY INDUSTRIES

In the postwar period, farming, once viewed as a way of life, became a business. Marketing boards revolutionized agriculture by establishing quotas, setting prices, and defining market boundaries, and a larger percentage of farm products was destined for canning and, increasingly, freezing. While Canadian and multinational companies prospered, many farmers were squeezed in the corporate goal of increasing profits. Producers were obliged to increase their operations or get out of farming altogether.

The trends in agriculture were similar across the country. In Saskatchewan, average farm size increased from 432 acres to 845 acres between 1941 and 1971, while the farm population fell from 514 677 to 233 792. Prince Edward Island farms also doubled in size, and the farm population tumbled from 144 000 to 27 000. Mechanization, herbicides, and pesticides increased farm outputs, but they added to the costs. In western Canada, operating expenses increased fivefold from 1956 to 1976, while farm net income only tripled. In Quebec, Premier Maurice Duplessis expanded government farm credit, opened up new areas for farmers, and provided electricity to 90 percent of farms by 1955; but the number of farmers dropped from one in five Quebecers to one in 20 between 1951 and 1971.

TABLE 13.1

Canada's Economic Growth, 1945–1976

YEAR	GNP*	GNP IN 1971 DOLLARS*	GNP PER CAPITA IN 1971 DOLLARS
1945	11 863	29 071	2 401
1951	21 640	35 450	2 531
1956	32 058	47 599	2 960
1961	39 646	54 741	3 001
1966	61 828	74 844	3 739
1971	94 450	94 450	4 379
1976	191 031	119 249	5 195

* Millions of dollars

Source: Adapted from F.H. Leacy, ed., *Historical Statistics of Canada,* 2nd ed. (Ottawa: Statistics Canada, 1983), Catalogue 11-516, tables A1, F 13, and F 15

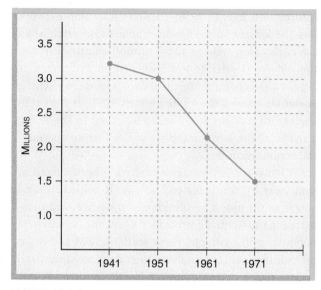

FIGURE 13.1

Farm Populations in Canada, 1941-1971

Source: Adapted from F.H. Leacy, ed., *Historical Statistics of Canada,* 2nd ed. (Ottawa: Statistics Canada, 1983), Catalogue 11-516, Series M1–M11

With families abandoning their farms throughout Canada, the small towns that had provided schools, clinics, and recreational facilities for farm communities struggled to survive, and their inhabitants soon joined the farmers in the exodus to cities.

The transformation of the east coast fishing industry in the postwar decade paralleled that of agriculture. As European markets for saltfish disappeared, sales of fresh and frozen fish were increasingly geared to an oversupplied North American market. At the same time, technology revolutionized productivity in the fisheries. By the 1960s, 1400 trawlers were engaged in the Grand Banks fishery, netting an unprecedented 2.6 million metric tonnes of fish. The trawlers sealed the fate of inshore fishers. By the 1950s, the real choice for most fishers was between becoming a labourer on a corporate trawler or changing occupations. Cooperative fishing organizations founded before the war lost control of

processing and marketing structures as the fishery on both coasts became part of the continental corporate universe.

Impressive growth also occurred in mining and hydroelectric power generation, benefiting from the booming North American domestic and military economies. Companies developed copper deposits at Murdochville on the Gaspé Peninsula, lead-zinc-copper ores in the Dalhousie-Bathurst region of New Brunswick, and potash in Saskatchewan. In 1949, the Iron Ore Company was formed to bring the vast deposits on the Ungava–Labrador border into production. Uranium from the Northwest Territories, Ontario, and Saskatchewan was brought into production.

Canada's energy resources seemed endless. On 3 February 1947, Imperial Oil's Leduc No. 1 well struck oil, and energy discoveries in Alberta soon became regular fare. From 1945 to 1960, Alberta's annual production of crude petroleum increased sixteenfold while natural gas production increased tenfold. Saskatchewan also made promising finds of energy resources. By 1952, pipelines in

Oil well at Leduc, Alberta, 1947. SOURCE: GLENBOW ARCHIVES IP-6G-6

which Imperial Oil was a major shareholder funnelled oil from Alberta either to Vancouver or through Wisconsin to Sarnia, Ontario.

In 1956, the Canadian government entered an agreement with an American company, TransCanada Pipelines, to build a gas pipeline from Alberta to Montreal. In addition to providing a generous loan to the company, Ottawa agreed to create a Crown corporation to build the uneconomical section of the pipeline through northern Ontario. The United States absorbed about half of the Canadian output of oil and gas, but cheap imports of crude oil from the Middle East and Venezuela kept the industry lean until the early 1970s.

Other provinces struggled to keep pace with the burgeoning economies of Ontario and Alberta. In Newfoundland, Premier Joseph Smallwood convinced overseas capitalists to develop the mighty Churchill Falls in Labrador, while New Brunswick premier Hugh John Flemming wrung $30 million out of the federal government to help complete the Beechwood Power complex on the St John River. Nova Scotia developed coal-generated thermal power plants. In the early 1950s, Alcan built a huge generating station at Kemano, British Columbia, to supply its $450 million aluminum smelter at Kitimat. Saskatchewan's premier, Tommy Douglas, with generous subsidies from Ottawa, planned an ambitious power-generating project on the South Saskatchewan River.

THE POSTINDUSTRIAL ECONOMY

The increasing importance of communications in determining the pace of economic change in the second half of the twentieth century led analysts to coin the term *Information Age* to describe the new phenomenon. While industrial and service industries remained significant players in the economy, communications technologies, represented by computers and satellites, contributed to quantum leaps in productivity. Satellite communications developed in the late 1950s and 1960s allowed radio and television signals to be transmitted around the world in a split second. Computers were linked to telecommunications systems in the early 1970s, permitting vast quantities of information to be sent over telecommunications networks.

Canada was among the first nations to experiment with the communication technologies that defined the Information Age. In 1958, Canada's television network was the longest in the world. Canada also established cable-television systems ahead of most countries. When the *Alouette 1* satellite was launched on 29 September 1962, Canada became the third nation in space after the Soviet Union and the United States. With its *Anik* (the Inuit word for "brother") series launched in the 1970s, Canada led the world in the use of satellites for commercial communications.

Virtually every human activity has been altered in some way by computer technology. It helped to send people to the moon, revolutionized the office, and automated manufacturing processes. Once the commercial potential of the computer was realized, IBM and other big multinational corporations soon dominated the field. A Canadian-based corporation, Northern Electric (later renamed Northern Telecom and then Nortel), eventually carved a niche for itself by producing telephone equipment and switching devices for a global telecommunications market. Nevertheless, Canada's trade deficit in electronic goods reached $850 million in 1973 and rose quickly in the years that followed.

In the postwar period, seven of 10 employed Canadians provided services rather than producing goods. A striking feature of Canada's service economy was its link to the growth of the state. Public sector spending increased from five percent of GNP in 1867 to 30 percent by 1960 and 48.2 percent in 1985. Nearly half of government expenditure was on goods and services; the rest involved transfer payments, which moved private income from one group of citizens to another. The federal share of GNP rose only marginally after 1960, but the provinces' shares doubled as their responsibilities grew rapidly. Many people found employment in the burgeoning bureaucracies of municipal, provincial, and federal governments.

The service economy helped to fuel the long-standing trend to urbanization. By 1971, three out of four Canadians were urban dwellers. Most Canadians moved voluntarily and sometimes happily from their rural communities to urban locations where they had better access to jobs and services, but there were exceptions. In Newfoundland, the government offered financial assistance to lure families from their outport communities to anticipated "growth centres." Beginning in 1953, Inuit were coerced by Ottawa to relocate from their traditional communities to Grise Fiord and Resolute Bay in the high Arctic— essentially "northern suburbs"[3]—where their presence would establish Canada's sovereignty. In both cases, the move failed to live up to its promise. Outport Newfoundlanders found few jobs in their new locations, and the Inuit lived in appalling conditions in their new state-sponsored northern communities.

The transformation from a subsistence to a consumer society was evident in every corner of the nation. In the North, the Inuit were integrated into the North American economy through social welfare programs and the sale of their exquisite paintings and sculptures, which had become popular in the art market in southern climes. With factories turning out textiles and clothing at unprecedented rates, women no longer engaged in domestic production. A vacationing antique dealer in the late 1950s bought 1200 spinning wheels in rural areas of Cape Breton. In fashionable middle-class homes, such items now became collectors' items, a happy reminder of the past when almost everyone had to work hard for a living.

Among those who still did back-breaking work, economic growth sometimes meant improved working conditions, but not always. Ontario's lumber industry replaced logging camps—once notorious for their crowded, poorly maintained bunkhouses—with suburban-like accommodations in an effort to retain their workforce. In other industries, employers reckoned that highly paid workers would put up with unsafe or unhealthy conditions. Innovations such as scooptrams used in nickel mining meant whole-body vibrations that caused back and neck injuries and circulatory problems for the workers.

Nuclear plants were among the workplaces where high wages went hand in hand with constant danger. The world's first major peacetime nuclear disaster occurred in 1952 at the experimental nuclear research plant at Chalk River, Ontario, which had another accident that released radioactivity in 1958. In 1974, uranium miners in Elliot Lake, Ontario, went on strike to demand better health and safety provisions as statistics confirmed what the miners had long known: they faced an unusually high incidence of lung cancer and silicosis. Their protests led to Ontario introducing a comprehensive worker occupational health and safety regime, which other provinces also introduced in varying degrees.

Machines that improved productivity not only posed problems for worker safety, but also for maintaining jobs. By the 1970s, the net impact of technology on employment prospects appeared to be negative. Microprocessors, first introduced in 1971, displaced blue-collar workers by controlling systems that automatically cut boards, stitched seams, and assembled parts. "Pink-collar" jobs dominated by women, such as file clerk and records manager, began to fade away as machines took over the recording and reporting of information. At CP Rail headquarters in Montreal, for example, there were 130 fewer clerical positions in Information Systems in 1980 than in 1972, while professional and managerial positions in the area doubled. Only two people moved

Workers in a fluorspar mine at St Lawrence, Newfoundland, in 1962. In his 1975 book *Dying Hard*, anthropologist Elliott Leyton chronicled the slow and painful early deaths from cancer and silicosis afflicting the fluorspar miners in the Burin Peninsula from 1933 onward. The mine finally closed in 1978. SOURCE: LIBRARY AND ARCHIVES CANADA PA-130784

from a clerical position into the professional-managerial ranks. Many workers who lost their jobs proved ill-equipped to take up other available jobs, thus becoming victims of "structural unemployment."

Many projects proceeded without any concern for the environment or local communities. In the English–Wabigoon River system near Kenora, effluent from the Reed paper mill made it unsafe for Natives to fish. Not only was their major food supply affected, but the tourism that had brought a modest level of prosperity to the reserves outside Kenora (and that depended on good local fishing) also dried up. Moreover, mill operators rarely hired Native labour, adding chronic unemployment to environmental degradation. Every northern hydroelectric and mining project told a similar story.

Even when companies did hire Native workers, benefits were generally short-lived. In the 1950s, Noranda Mines opened a plant on the reserve property of the Anishanabek of the Serpent River First Nation to process sulphuric acid created in the mining of uranium. They delivered on a promise to hire First Nations workers, but closed the plant in 1963 after less than a decade of operation, leaving wastes in nearby soil and water. The plant was not properly decommissioned until Native pressures forced the province to act in 1969. Meanwhile, the quantity and quality of the fish on Aird Bay in Lake Huron and on the Serpent River declined because of the pollution from the uranium mines and the sulphuric acid plant.

Native fisheries were threatened elsewhere as well. When Pacific salmon stocks declined in the postwar period, the federal government responded with restrictive regulations that favoured industrial fishing interests over smaller-scale fishers, including Native fishers. The government acted similarly in the Maritimes in response to depleted salmon habitat. On the St John River, the culprits were hydroelectric development and a barrage of pesticides, herbicides, and fertilizers used to maximize productivity of the forest and soils. Although the Native peoples were largely innocent in this assault on salmon habitat, they were victimized by a five-year ban on commercial netting in New Brunswick rivers beginning in 1970, a ban that exempted the sport fishery.

Native peoples were not alone in feeling that economic growth occurred at their expense. Growing cities with shiny skyscrapers and rural ghost towns were reverse images created by an inexorable drive toward economic growth and a consumer society. In Cape Breton, the Sydney Tar Ponds—a toxic brew of chemicals produced as waste by the coke ovens and furnaces in the city's steel-making industry—created health hazards for those living in the surrounding area. Meanwhile, pollution levels from the many chemical industries in the Sarnia area were beginning to raise concerns. State policies that supported growth at all costs ignored human health and the health of the biosphere, the latter only dimly coming into view for most Canadians by the early 1970s.

MORE TO THE STORY
Cars, Economic Growth, and the Environment

Cars were the emblem of the postwar good life for Canadian families. Between 1952 and 1959, imports of foreign-built cars increased from 38 000 to 165 000, contributing to an escalating trade deficit. John Diefenbaker's Progressive Conservative government tried to bridge the gap by offering the Big Three automakers tariff rebates on imported transmissions in return for a commitment from the companies to export more of other parts from Canada. The subsequent Liberal government extended the rebates to all imported car parts in return for guarantees of increased exports of parts.

Opposition from the United States government to unilateral Canadian government deals with American automakers led to the negotiations that produced the Canada-U.S. Automotive Products Trade Agreement of 1965. Under the Auto Pact, duties on cross-border trade on cars and car parts were eliminated, as insisted upon by the American government, but the Canadian government managed to secure the content requirements and production goals that would ensure the long-term viability of the industry in Canada.

Chrysler plant in Windsor, Ontario, 1954 (above), and a White Rose gas station on Highway 2 between Edmonton and Lacombe in 1951 or 1952 (below). The automobile industry seemed omnipresent in the postwar Canadian economy. SOURCE: LIBRARY AND ARCHIVES CANADA NA 112635 (ABOVE) AND PROVINCIAL ARCHIVES OF ALBERTA A12236 (BELOW)

Due in large measure to the Auto Pact, the number of Canadian-assembled cars sold in the United States soared from 46 000 to 723 000 in 1975. Parts production employed 51 600 Canadians in 1974 compared to 31 800 in 1964. The concentration of the automobile industry in southern Ontario contributed to that province's relative wealth. Elsewhere in the country, the

Auto Pact seemed to confirm Ottawa's favouritism toward Ontario. Since jobs in automotive assembly plants were usually unionized, well-paid, and offered job security and good retirement pensions, they attracted workers from across Canada.

There were downsides to the North American automotive industry even in its heyday. In the 1950s, more than 27 000 Canadians died in automobile accidents. American consumer activist Ralph Nader provided compelling proof in his book *Unsafe at Any Speed*, published in 1965, that faulty design rather than personal error accounted for a significant number of automobile deaths. These revelations forced the Canadian government to regulate car safety in the 1970s, largely by imposing rules adopted earlier in the United States. Canada also followed the United States in imposing emissions standards and giving in to industry lobbyists for longer periods to introduce pollution controls. Hydrocarbon, carbon monoxide, and nitrogen oxide emissions were all higher in Canada than in the United States in 1975, and for more than a decade afterwards. In both countries, reluctance to impose fuel-emission standards on vehicle manufacturers eased considerably after OPEC price increases in 1973 raised the strong likelihood of oil shortages for the future.[4]

ECONOMIC DISPARITY

Age, class, ethnicity, gender, and geography remained important factors in determining how one fared in the quest for economic well-being in postwar Canada. In 1965, John Porter published *The Vertical Mosaic*, an impressive analysis of stratification in Canadian society. Porter showed that an economic elite of fewer than 1000 men—mostly of British and Protestant background, and graduates of private schools—dominated the Canadian economy.

In Quebec, where more than 80 percent of the population was French-speaking, francophone employers controlled only 47 percent of the province's jobs in 1961, mainly in the service and agricultural sectors. Francophones were particularly absent from ownership in the manufacturing sector, where the companies they owned produced only 15 percent of the province's manufacturing output. Quebec's largest private companies were under anglophone control. While it is inaccurate to assert, as Quebec nationalists increasingly did, that francophones in the province were workers while anglophones were bosses, wage disparities were striking. The average annual wage of francophone Quebecers in 1961 was only two-thirds that of their anglophone compatriots.

Women figured prominently in the ranks of Canada's economically disadvantaged. As services moved from the domestic economy into the market economy, women often moved with them, but their wages failed to match those of men. Paid domestic work declined under the impact of household appliances, but teaching, nursing, secretarial, clerical, and cleaning jobs expanded and remained dominated by women. Overall, women's labour force participation in Canada increased from 23.4 percent in 1953 to 48.9 percent in 1979, while the male participation rate fell from 82.9 percent to 78.4 percent. Pay scales were blatantly sexist. In 1971, women with full-time jobs made on average less than 60 percent of what men with full-time jobs earned. Women were also far more likely to be employed in part-time work.

Visible minorities, especially First Nations, Métis, Inuit, and African Canadians, remained at the bottom of the economic scale throughout the nation. Immigrants, many of them living illegally in the country, also suffered exploitation by factory owners and farmers. In Montreal, immigrants from the Caribbean, Latin America, India, Pakistan, Greece, Portugal, and Italy worked 12-hour days for subsistence wages. According to one journalist writing in 1974, they "man the clanging textile and clothing factories which line St. Lawrence and Park . . . clean toilets in glittering high-rises, wash dishes in grimy restaurant kitchens, pull switches and operate machinery in fuming plastics and chemical factories, abattoirs, machine shops."[5] At the time, about 100 000 illegal immigrants worked in Canada, generally in sweatshops in Montreal and Toronto. Intimidated by the threat of discovery and deportation, they often had to accept work at less than the legislated minimum wage.

Far from industrial sites, farm workers also often laboured under substandard conditions and wages.

Native dwellings contrast sharply with houses in Fort George (Chisasibi), Quebec, 1973. SOURCE: LIBRARY AND ARCHIVES CANADA PA-130854

Excluded from minimum-wage protection, immigrant orchard workers in British Columbia and Ontario and Native sugar-beet pickers in Manitoba worked long hours for negligible pay and slept in miserable accommodations provided by the employers. Many farm workers were illegal immigrants; still others were contract workers for the growing season, hired under the Seasonal Agricultural Workers' Program that began in 1966 and required to return home to Latin America or the Caribbean once the growing season ended. Canada wanted their labour power, but did not want them as citizens.

Despite economic growth and the advent of the welfare state, the overall distribution of wealth in Canada remained remarkably static. The Economic Council of Canada, an advisory group to the government on economic planning, calculated in 1961 that 27 percent of Canadians received incomes low enough to qualify them as poor. Both Status Indians and farmers, groups with high rates of poverty, were excluded from the calculation. Eight years later, the federal government, using the same measures, announced that poverty had been cut in half as a result of economic growth and the increase in the number of two-income families. The poverty rate would rise again in the slow-growth seventies.

Whether the national economy was booming or in recession, some areas lagged well behind the national average. Southern Ontario generally prospered far more than the rest of the country, while northern Ontario suffered high rates of unemployment and poverty, particularly in Native areas. Even within southern Ontario, there were large pockets of poverty in the southeast. Montreal had a vibrant mixed economy, but northern Quebec and the Gaspé experienced grinding poverty even during economic upswings. In wealthy Alberta and British Columbia, northern residents had little to show for the resource boom that created high average incomes in their provinces.

In the postwar period, the Atlantic region, Quebec, Saskatchewan, and Manitoba constituted the country's have-not provinces. Dependent on equalization grants after 1957 to provide reasonable levels of service to their citizens, they lacked sufficient economic diversification to create more jobs. Ontario strengthened its economic lead over Quebec because of a stronger resource base,

MORE TO THE STORY
The American Fast-Food Industry

The fast-food industry was one example of an American-dominated service industry that made its entry into Canada in the postwar period. Franchise operations, such as Colonel Sanders' Kentucky Fried Chicken, Burger King, and, after 1968, McDonald's, defined the eating-out experience for teenagers and two-income families seeking occasional relief from having to prepare a meal.

Sociologist Ester Reiter worked at a Toronto Burger King in the early 1980s and interviewed fellow employees as part of a thesis project. Each Burger King is operated by a franchisee, who pays Burger King's Miami headquarters a large fee for the right to operate a firm with the Burger King name. Every outlet is required by Miami to unswervingly follow the procedures laid out in the Manual of Operating Data. "Burger King University" in Miami trains managers to implement these procedures uniformly. Headquarters is linked by computer to each franchise and monitors performance daily. The result is that the

"Burger King experience" is the same for workers and customers whether one is in New Orleans or Halifax. For employees, this means a rigid work schedule in which the time allowed to take an order, prepare a specific item, or deliver food to a customer is measured in seconds.

Reiter's fellow workers were teenagers, often working part-time, and immigrant women for whom better jobs were unavailable. Few liked the work, which paid minimum wage, and many felt like robots, waiting for their breaks in the "crew room" for a chance to listen to rock music and talk about plans for the weekend. On the job, "hamburgers are cooked as they pass through the broiler on a conveyor belt at a rate of 835 patties per hour. Furnished with a pair of tongs, the worker picks up the burgers as they drop off the conveyor belt, puts each on a toasted bun, and places the hamburgers and buns in a steamer. The jobs may be hot and boring, but they can be learned in a manner of minutes."[6]

proximity to the American industrial heartland, and a prewar advantage resulting from international capitalists preferring its better-educated, English-speaking work force. Having lagged behind Ontario and Quebec in attracting manufacturing in earlier periods, the Atlantic provinces, Saskatchewan, and Manitoba faced difficulties in convincing investors to establish plants in areas that had smaller populations and were a greater distance from the major population centres in North America.

TAXATION AND THE DISTRIBUTION OF WEALTH

An assessment of the taxation system helps to explain why there was little redistribution of the nation's wealth. Before the war, most working Canadians earned less than the minimum income required to be subject to income taxes. After the war, most workers became income taxpayers. Corporations and the wealthy also paid taxes, but taxes on corporate profits were ameliorated by generous capital cost (depreciation) allowances and by an ever-increasing variety of loopholes. By 1953, dividend holders received a 20 percent tax credit in recognition of dividends forgone because of corporate tax assessments.

Nevertheless, by today's standards, corporations contributed generously to federal and provincial treasuries. The effective tax on business profits, that is, the taxes that governments collected after all loopholes had been applied, averaged 38.2 percent of all profits earned from 1961 to 1987. The comparable figure for 2011 was 24 percent. The highest nominal federal corporate tax, that is the rate before exemptions were applied, was 41 percent in 1960, 40 percent in 1970, and 15 percent for 2014.

In 1962, the Diefenbaker government established a Royal Commission on Taxation, headed by Kenneth Carter, a leading chartered accountant. The commissioners concluded that "The present system does not afford fair treatment for all Canadians. People in essentially similar circumstances do not bear the same taxes. People in essentially different circumstances do not bear appropriately different tax burdens."[7] Commission studies revealed that the poorest Canadians paid proportionately more taxes than well-off citizens. Carter recommended that indirect taxation be substantially reduced and that the base for personal and corporate income tax be broadened by removing most loopholes. The poor would benefit most, and would also receive income support to ensure that all Canadians had a sufficient income to enjoy a decent standard of living.

The Carter Commission's report, which was submitted in 1966, had little impact in a country increasingly dominated by corporate elites. The Liberal government led by Lester Pearson delayed its response to the Carter recommendations, and Pearson's successor, Pierre Elliott Trudeau, largely ignored the report, taxing capital gains at only half the rate of other income, repealing the federal Estate Tax Act, and making only token efforts to provide income guarantees for all households.

THE TRADE UNION MOVEMENT

The trade union movement was the most vocal opponent of the liberal consensus in the postwar period. Although legislation recognized the right of workers to organize, the Industrial Relations Disputes Act of 1948, which applied to federal workers, and its provincial equivalents also attempted to co-opt union leaders into the planning mechanisms of corporations and governments. Under the new labour laws, workers found their rights to negotiate limited to wages and narrowly defined working conditions. Unions were expected to enforce contracts and to keep their members in line. Decisions to reduce the size of the workforce, to speed up production, or to use hazardous materials in the workplace were rarely covered by contracts. Even when management appeared to violate a contract, workers were not allowed to strike. Instead, drawn-out grievance procedures had to be followed to seek redress.

Despite such constraints, workers were not prepared to return to prewar conditions. Long-time United Electrical Workers staffer and Communist activist Bill Walsh recalled:

> We had just won the war, freed the world from fascism. . . . There was a whole new spirit in the world. Returning soldiers were not looking for jobs but they weren't going to sit around waiting for handouts. They talked with new authority. They had been through hell and they weren't going to accept the world they had left behind—including the depression wages still being paid at Westinghouse and the other big companies.[8]

When better wages and working conditions could not be won at the bargaining table, unionists resorted to strikes. Wartime wage freezes created pent-up demands for increases at war's end. In 1946 and 1947, about 240 000 workers struck for a total of almost seven million workdays. Automobile, steel, rubber, textile, packing, electrical manufacturing, forestry, and mining companies all felt the sting of such action. Average wages rose from 69.4 cents per hour in 1945 to 91.3 cents per hour in 1948.

Women in the labour force were generally not unionized and failed to share in the wage gains. In 1948, the Retail, Wholesale, and Department Store Union (RWDSU), supported by the Canadian Congress of Labour, initiated a three-year drive, headed by Eileen Talman, to organize Toronto's Eaton's store. The company pulled out all the stops to oppose the union, linking unions with communism, raising wages just before the vote on unionizing took place, and warning part-time workers that unionism would cost them their jobs. When only 40 percent of the workers supported affiliation with the RWDSU, the CCL leadership, almost exclusively male, concluded that women were too passive to unionize

and ceased its attempts to organize sectors dominated by female labour.

Such stereotypical views were being exploded in Quebec, where women endured a bitter and ultimately successful strike at Dupuis Frères department store in 1952 to win better pay and working conditions. Members of the increasingly secular Confédération des travailleurs catholiques du Canada, these women were a harbinger of things to come in postwar Quebec, where the Union nationale government of Premier Duplessis often came to the armed defence of strike-bound employers. In 1949, workers in the town of Asbestos, unwilling to delay a strike until a government-appointed board of arbitration reported on their grievances, struck so that the company would not have time to stockpile asbestos before the inevitable walkout. During the five-month strike, the workers faced a large contingent of provincial police who protected replacement workers hired by the company. Many strikers were arrested or beaten in clashes with Duplessis's police.

The brutal state response to the strike galvanized considerable resistance to the Union nationale. Liberal and nationalist intellectuals, including future prime minister Pierre Elliott Trudeau, were increasingly united on the need to defeat Duplessis and to protect workers' interests. Even within the church, there were dissenters against Duplessis's heavy-handed tactics. Rank-and-file clergy who supported the Asbestos strikers briefly had a champion in Archbishop Joseph Charbonneau of Montreal, but his ecclesiastical superiors, closely associated with Duplessis, transferred him out of the province.

It was not only in Quebec that striking workers were confronted by police. In November 1945, the Ontario government sent provincial police and reinforcements from the RCMP into the gates of the Ford plant at Windsor to end a five-week-old strike. The strikers responded by blockading the plant with cars. The federal government appointed Justice Ivan Rand to mediate the conflict. Rand had to face the thorny issue of whether the state could force

While their labour force participation continued to expand, women remained concentrated in poorly paid occupations. These typists at the Dominion Bureau of Statistics in 1952 are using Varityper machines, an alternative to traditional typesetting, which allowed institutions to save money by shifting the work to lower-paid employees. SOURCE: LIBRARY AND ARCHIVES CANADA PA-133212

individuals to pay union dues even if they opposed unions for religious reasons. Since everyone in a workplace benefitted from a successful union negotiation, Rand ruled affirmatively but he softened that decision with a provision allowing individuals to apply to divert their union dues to a designated charity. A less happy conclusion greeted the loggers of Newfoundland, who struck in 1959 only to have Premier Smallwood use the RCMP to enforce his decision to decertify the International Woodworkers' Association as the bargaining agent of the loggers.

Opposition by employers to unions meant that the rate of unionization of private sector workers stalled after the 1950s. By contrast, public sector workers increasingly joined unions. Because women were heavily concentrated in the lower echelons of the public service, they made up four-fifths of Canada's new unionists from 1966 to 1976. Women in the "caring" professions, such as nursing, social work, and teaching, also questioned the stereotype that "women's work" was mainly community service rather than remunerative professional labour. Strikes by teachers, social workers, and civil servants, unheard of before the 1970s, began to become commonplace by the end of the decade.

An increase in militancy was especially noticeable in Quebec. In 1960, there were 38 strikes in the province; in 1975, there were 362. The Confédération des travailleurs catholiques du Canada formally ended its affiliation with the church in 1960, renaming itself the Confédération des syndicats nationaux (CSN). The CSN played a major role in the Common Front formed by Quebec public sector unions in 1972, conducting general strikes to improve the position of the lowest-paid public sector workers, most of whom were women. The Common Front provoked much opposition. Quebec's Liberal government, led by Premier Robert Bourassa, passed legislation to end the labour disruption, and jailed the leaders of the province's three largest labour federations when they encouraged their members to defy back-to-work orders.

VOICES FROM THE PAST
Factory Women on Strike

The predominantly young female labour force of Lanark Manufacturing Company, a firm in Dunnville, Ontario, making wire harnesses for the automobile companies, went on strike in August 1964. On strike for six months, their militancy countered popular stereotypes of women as passive workers. Here are some of their reflections about why they struck, what they faced during the strike, and what they gained by striking. Worker Rosemary Cousineau described factory conditions as

> just total exhaustion and stress. Sometimes you'd come home and the tightness in your back felt like you were all in knots.... You had to work so hard and so fast. If you made a mistake, the verbal abuse you'd get.... Predominantly young women were put on the rotary because, as one worker described it, "you had to hurry up. That's why we had more energy than the older girls, because we were young."

One young woman recounted the struggles on the picket line.

> It broke our hearts when we saw people still going in ... and they did everything they could to stop the scabs from

working. The police used to protect the scabs going in and out.... So we'd fight back—even with the police. We'd do anything to get back at 'em. They're supposed to be protection for the public, right? They're not supposed to be biased. But they sure were.... It was all one-sided.... I was in court every week for something or other.

Striker Yvette Ward sized up the results of the strike years later.

> A lot of times I sit and think about it. Lanark, to me, was a landmark in the history of labour because these kids weren't afraid. They went ahead and did it, even though they knew they might lose their jobs forever....
>
> I can't help but remember the unity and the courage and the knowledge that all of the girls from that time had—and the few men that were working there. We were bound together so tight. These girls were working for peanuts, and didn't have much to fight for, but they did. They fought for six months steady without a stop and never gave up for one minute.... It was the experience of a lifetime.[9]

FOREIGN TRADE AND INVESTMENT

The structure of trade as it emerged in the postwar period had one enduring characteristic: exports, which made up a quarter of GNP, consisted primarily of unprocessed and semi-processed products, while imports were mainly manufactured goods, most of them from the United States. In 1946, when the war-wrecked economies of most countries provided little for Canada to import, 75.3 percent of all Canadian imports were from the United States; in 1975, the figure was still 68.1 percent. Meanwhile, Canada's dependence on the American market for its exports grew from 38.9 percent in 1946 to 64.7 percent in 1975.

Capital as well as goods moved easily across the border. Canadians invested heavily in American companies, but not to the extent that Americans invested in Canada. As a result, the American dominance—already established before the Second World War in the ownership of key sectors of the Canadian economy, including manufacturing, petroleum and natural gas, and mining and smelting—grew dramatically.

Although service industries were less likely to be foreign owned, American capital penetrated the retail sector and dominated the burgeoning fast-food industry. Not all fast-food chains were American owned. In the 1960s, a Hamilton-based doughnut shop founded by hockey player Tim Horton made its humble debut; under other owners, it would gradually expand from the

TABLE 13.2

Destination of Domestic Exports (excluding gold), 1946-1975 (in millions of dollars)

AREA	1946	1955	1965	1975
United States	884	2 548	4 840	21 074
Americas Other than U.S.	202	216	433	1 583
United Kingdom	594	768	1 174	1 795
Other western European	189	261	626	2 347
Japan	1	91	316	2 130
Centrally planned (Communist) economies	91	12	418	1 049
Other	312	363	717	2 571
Percentage of exports to U.S.	38.9	59.8	56.8	64.7

Source: F.H. Leacy, ed., *Historical Statistics of Canada,* 2nd ed. (Ottawa: Statistics Canada, 1983), Series G, 401–7

TABLE 13.3

Origin of Canadian Imports, 1946-1975 (in millions of dollars)

AREA	1946	1955	1965	1975
United States	1 387	3 331	6 045	23 641
United Kingdom	137	393	619	1 222
Japan	–	37	230	1 205
Other western European	14	143	514	2 074
Other American	164	409	548	1802
Centrally planned (Communist) economies	5	8	59	234
Other	134	246	618	4 537
Percentage of imports from U.S.	75.3	72.9	70.0	68.1

Source: F.H. Leacy, ed., *Historical Statistics of Canada,* 2nd ed. (Ottawa: Statistics Canada, 1983), Series G, 408–14

mid-1970s to become Canada's largest fast-food service by the end of the century.

Canadians were ambivalent about this transformation in their economic relations. In 1955, the Canadian government appointed chartered accountant Walter Gordon to chair a Royal Commission on Canada's Economic Prospects. The commission report, submitted in November 1957, expressed concerns that American branch plants in Canada hired few Canadian managers, did little exporting, and devoted little attention to research and development. The commissioners suggested that foreign corporations be required to employ more Canadians in senior management positions, and sell an "appreciable interest" in their equity stocks to Canadians.

Some Canadians disagreed with Gordon's concerns. Economist Harry Johnson spoke for many conservatives in arguing that economic nationalism was "a narrow and garbage-cluttered *cul-de-sac*."[10] He wanted all restrictions on foreign trade and investment removed. At the time, few heeded his advice. The major trade agreement between Canada and the United States in this period, the Auto Pact of 1965, suggested there were advantages to Canada in negotiating sector deals that violated free-trade principles. Only seven percent of Canadian-made vehicles were shipped to the United States in 1964, a figure that rose to 60 percent by the end of the century, making automobiles the largest single item in Canada's GDP. (The Auto Pact was abrogated in 2001 because it contravened free-trade agreements that

TABLE 13.4

Percentage of Foreign Control of Selected Canadian Industries, 1939-1973

INDUSTRY	1939	1948	1958	1968	1973
Manufacturing	38 (32)*	43 (39)	57 (44)	58 (46)	59 (44)
Petroleum and natural gas†	–	–	73 (67)	75 (61)	76 (59)
Mining and smelting	42 (38)	40 (37)	60 (51)	68 (58)	56 (45)
Railways	3 (3)	3 (3)	2 (2)	2 (2)	2 (2)
Other utilities	26 (26)	24 (24)	5 (4)	5 (4)	7 (4)
Total**	21 (19)	25 (22)	32 (26)	36 (28)	35 (26)

* Numbers in parentheses indicate percentage controlled by American residents
† Petroleum and natural gas combined with mining and smelting to 1948
** Total includes merchandising, not shown separately

Sources: F.H. Leacy, ed., *Historical Statistics of Canada*, 2nd ed. (Ottawa: Statistics Canada, 1983), Series G, 291-302; John Fayerweather, *Foreign Investment in Canada: Prospects for National Policy* (Toronto: Oxford University Press, 1974) 7

had been negotiated while the automobile agreement had remained in effect.)

With Walter Gordon as finance minister, the Pearson government introduced legislation to protect Canadian financial companies from foreign control, and took steps to reduce American dominance of the Canadian media. Gordon was fighting an uphill battle in a cabinet where many ministers were reluctant to offend the United States. By the time he resigned as finance minister in late 1965, his influence had waned. Nevertheless, Pearson agreed with Gordon's proposal to establish a task force on the structure of Canadian industry to examine whether it really mattered who owned industry in Canada. Gordon's choice for its head was a respected economist, Mel Watkins, of the University of Toronto.

The Watkins Report, formally entitled *Foreign Ownership and the Structure of Canadian Industry*, appeared in 1968 and challenged the misconception that Canada remained short of capital and needed foreign investment. If Canadians who invested abroad had kept their money at home, it argued, they would have reduced the need for foreign capital by half. The task force painted a picture of an inefficient branch-plant manufacturing economy geared to serving the Canadian market alone, leaving international markets to American-based plants.

Released at a time of growing nationalism in Canada and misgivings about the United States, the Watkins Report led to action on the part of the Trudeau government. The Canada Development Corporation (CDC) was created in 1971 to encourage Canadian ownership and

management in vital sectors of the economy. In 1974, the Foreign Investment Review Agency (FIRA) was established to screen proposals for foreign takeovers of existing Canadian businesses. In 1975, the federal government created Petro-Canada, a Crown corporation with a broad mandate to develop a Canadian presence in the petroleum industry.

Apart from the revelations of the Watkins Report, pressure on the government to control foreign investment came from reactions to a number of high-profile plant closings by foreign-owned companies. British-based Dunlop Tire's decision to close its Toronto factory in 1970, putting 597 people out of work, led to campaigns both to limit foreign ownership and to ensure that all companies provide workers with adequate notice and compensation before closing. Trade union campaigns that focused on economic nationalism, argues historian Steven High, obliged "Canadian politicians . . . to legislate advance notice of layoffs, severance pay, pension reinsurance, job placement assistance, and preferential hiring rights."[11]

Not surprisingly, the American oil giants responded with considerable hostility to Canada's nationalistic economic initiatives. American oil companies operating in Alaska claimed the right to have their supertankers travel across the Arctic passage to transport their product to eastern American markets. In 1969 and 1970, the American tanker *Manhattan* carried several cargoes across the Arctic. Canada responded with the Arctic Waters Pollution Prevention Act, meant to protect the fragile northern environment and assert Canadian sovereignty in the North.

Such confrontations with the Americans help explain why President Richard Nixon, introducing import controls on manufactures in 1971, failed to exempt Canada as American governments had in the past. The Trudeau government's response was to seek a reduction of Canada's vulnerability to American actions by expanding global political and economic links. The government branded its new round of diplomacy to achieve new trading partnerships the "Third Option." The first option, maintaining Canada's prior relationship with the United States, had been tried and found wanting. Option two, closer integration with the Americans,

Walter Gordon: Canadian nationalist

Walter Lockhart Gordon was born in Toronto in 1906 into a life of privilege. His grandfather had made a fortune in Ontario's lumber industry and his father was a founding partner in a major Toronto chartered accounting firm. After attending Upper Canada College, a British boarding school, and Royal Military College, he joined his father's firm as a chartered accountant, becoming a partner in Clarkson, Gordon and Company in 1935.

Although Gordon was an unlikely candidate to be a leading economic nationalist, several factors encouraged him in his willingness to challenge pro-American views held by many business leaders in postwar Canada. His father, who served as a colonel in the Canadian army during the First World War, was an ardent British imperialist who resented the late entry of the United States into that war. Gordon's father-in-law, also a wealthy lawyer, became an activist in Communist causes during the Depression.

Gordon opposed communism, but he supported reform and was one of the owners of the CCF-leaning *Canadian Forum* magazine during the 1930s. He had also become a firm Canadian economic nationalist even before he was appointed chair of the Royal Commission on Canada's Economic Prospects in 1955. As a consultant to the Tariff Board during an investigation of the automobile industry in 1935-36, he urged the federal government to resist American efforts to remove stiff Canadian-content requirements necessary for the Americans to ship Canadian-assembled vehicles throughout the British Empire.

When the federal Liberals were defeated in 1957, Gordon became involved in efforts to rebuild the party by focusing on policies to help needy individuals and regions. Rewarded in 1963 by his friend Lester Pearson with the position of minister of finance, Gordon attempted to use his first budget to promote greater Canadian ownership of the economy. His budget proposed a 30 percent takeover tax on foreign investors who acquired Canadian corporate assets, along with a large penalty on non-Canadians receiving dividends from companies operating

Walter Gordon during his election campaign in Toronto's Davenport constituency in 1962. SOURCE: YORK UNIVERSITY ARCHIVES, TORONTO TELEGRAM FONDS FO 433

in Canada that had failed to keep at least 25 percent of their assets in Canadian hands. An organized business outcry caused Pearson to eliminate both of these budget measures.

Gordon supported Trudeau's bid for the Liberal leadership in 1968, and Trudeau offered him a Cabinet post, but Gordon decided to return to the private sector. As a private citizen, he joined with *Toronto Star* editor-in-chief Peter C. Newman and University of Toronto economist Abe Rotstein to launch the Committee for an Independent Canada in 1970. In 1971, the CIC presented a petition with 170 000 signatures to Prime Minister Trudeau calling on his government to legislate limits to foreign investment and ownership. The CIC is given credit for much of the nationalist legislation implemented in the early 1970s.

By the time of his death in 1987, Walter Gordon had witnessed first the legislative enforcement of a degree of economic nationalism, and then its impending demise as the Progressive Conservative government of Brian Mulroney carried out negotiations with the United States for a free-trade agreement.[12]

was unacceptable to Canadian nationalists and appeared, in any case, impossible in the age of Nixon. Although diplomatic efforts to expand Canada's trade with other nations bore some fruit, Canada remained overwhelmingly dependent on the American economy for its imports and exports.

Federal efforts to control American investment in Canada often met with a hostile response from the provinces. Since the provinces had constitutional jurisdiction over resources and could earn much-needed income from their development, they increasingly resisted the use of the federal power over trade and taxation to shape patterns of resource exploitation. Alberta governments opposed any "discriminatory" treatment of foreign capital, to which they attributed their energy boom.

Provincial pressures broke down the long-standing federal resolve to prevent large-scale hydroelectricity exports as a means of ensuring Canadian self-sufficiency in electricity. British Columbia, exploiting the American Northwest's need for more power, persuaded the Pearson government in 1964 to sign the Columbia River Treaty and Protocol, which committed Canada to sell power to the western American states. Soon Manitoba was signing deals with the Americans to deliver power from the province's North. In the 1970s, the Quebec government's James Bay project was meant to meet not only provincial power needs, but also considerable demand from the state of New York.

VOICES FROM THE PAST
Views of Foreign Ownership

In the 1950s and 1960s, Canada's political and business leaders expressed conflicting views regarding the benefits of foreign ownership of Canadian industries. The following excerpts provide a hint of the debate's flavour.

With an enormous area still of almost virgin country to be opened, Canadians need and welcome foreign investments and with their own healthy stake in the national development they have no fears of any domination.

–G.K. Sheils, president of the Canadian Manufacturers' Association, in the *Financial Post*, 1953

The free and unhampered flow of foreign investment into Canada has brought so many benefits to this country that it certainly is entitled to a fair and unbiased hearing from the Canadian people.

. . . If one allows for Canadian investment abroad and the use of foreign resources as a percentage of net capital formation, it turns out that not more than 6 per cent of Canadian investment in the postwar world depended on foreign resources.

. . . Canada's economy has been growing at such a rapid rate that the role of foreign investment in relation to our productive capacity has diminished and will continue to do so.

–C.D. Howe, Minister of Trade and Commerce, in the House of Commons, 1956

No other country in the world with something like our relative state of development has ever had such a degree of foreign domination, or even one half or one quarter the degree of foreign domination. Canada is being pushed down the road that leads to loss of any effective power to be masters in our own household and ultimate absorption in and by another.

–James Coyne, president of the Bank of Canada, to the Canadian Chamber of Commerce, 1960

During the two-and-one-half years I held that office [minister of finance], the influence that financial and business interests in the United States had on Canadian policy was continually brought home to me. On occasion, this influence was reinforced by representations from the State Department and the American Administration as a whole. It was pressed by those who direct American businesses in Canada, by their professional advisors, by Canadian financiers whose interests were identified directly or indirectly with American investment in Canada, by influential members of the Canadian civil service, by some representatives of the university community, and by some sections of the press.

–Walter Gordon, *A Choice for Canada*, 1966[13]

THE END OF THE ECONOMIC MIRACLE

By the early 1970s, there were dark clouds on the economic horizon. The American government had failed to raise taxes to offset expenses associated with the unpopular Vietnam War. Allowing the economy to overheat, it then attempted vainly to reduce inflation by cutting spending and tightening credit. American unemployment increased, and the government responded with trade restrictions, which had repercussions for Canadian trade and therefore Canadian rates of employment and inflation.

Then the OPEC oil price shocks late in 1973 roiled Western economies, which had relied throughout the postwar boom on cheap energy. In 1974, unemployment was a manageable 5.3 percent, but inflation stood at 14.5 percent. A year later, inflation was down to 9.9 percent, but unemployment had reached a postwar high of 6.9 percent. The combination of high unemployment and high inflation was labelled *stagflation*, a short form for stagnation plus inflation.

A political debate ensued about how to combat this unsettling phenomenon. In the August 1974 federal election, Progressive Conservative leader Robert Stanfield called for wage and price controls. Prime Minister Trudeau won re-election after vigorously opposing this prescription. In October 1975, Trudeau reversed himself, announcing a three-year program of controls. Trudeau's economic policies to deal with stagflation proved contradictory. Government spending increased substantially in accordance with Keynesian prescriptions for a stagnating economy, but beginning in 1975, the money supply was severely restricted.

Concerned about profit margins, business leaders began to abandon the postwar consensus on economic policy. Low rates of unemployment and generous unemployment insurance benefits, they complained, were forcing employers to pay wage increases that hurt profits. To stop inflation and create long-term stability, they demanded tight money policies and a scaling back of the welfare state, policies that would lead the way to a new leaner and meaner economic order.

CONCLUSION

The postwar liberal compromise assumed an important role for governments in directing the economy, but troubling contradictions soon surfaced. From the beginning, the business community resented the extent to which popular pressures caused governments to follow directions that were deemed detrimental to the market economy. Although the policies that produced growth brought increased prosperity to many, they left others behind and caused great harm to the environment. There was also a conflict between policies that supported growth and policies that sustained Canadian sovereignty. By the mid-1970s, the postwar liberal compromise seemed in tatters, as oil prices and inflation made a mockery of state planning and social activists were pitted against the business community on the degree and direction of state economic intervention. Economic policy in Canada and elsewhere was about to enter a period of noisy debate.

A HISTORIOGRAPHICAL DEBATE
Was Foreign Direct Investment Beneficial to Canada?

In the early postwar period, Canadians generally regarded foreign direct investment (FDI) as a factor in Canada's rapid economic growth. Although it meant that many companies were controlled by investors outside of Canada, it was assumed that they would respect Canadian sovereignty and follow Canadian laws. By the 1960s, this assumption no longer seemed to hold. The Report of the Royal Commmssion on Canada's Economic Prospects (1957) had alerted Canadians to American dominance over major sectors of the Canadian economy, and by the 1960s fears were being widely expressed that it was undermining both Canadian sovereignty and Canadian economic performance. Economists inevitably waded into the contentious debate that ensued.

In 1966, A.E. Safarian, an economist at the University of Toronto, published an exhaustive study of the performance of foreign-controlled firms in Canada. He concluded that their overall impact was beneficial to both the Canadian economy and the treasuries of Canadian governments. Safarian's evidence for his conclusion was that the level of exports and the quantity of research and development by such firms paralleled that of domestically controlled firms.[14]

The Watkins Report submitted in 1968 challenged Safarian's empirical evidence, suggesting that foreign investment resulted in too many competitors in many sectors of the economy, discouraging innovation and efficiency. American firms were efficient at home in a market ten times the size of Canada's, but their "branch plants" in Canada focused on serving only the Canadian market and gave little thought to export strategies or to research and development. Facing tight markets, domestic competitors were unable to provide a different economic model, which explained why their record in terms of exports, research, and development was no better than the record of branch plants.

Watkins charged that Canada's foreign policies and trade initiatives were compromised by the presence of American multinational corporations, which obliged their branch plants to follow American trade laws when American and Canadian trade laws conflicted. American branch plants had allegedly turned down orders for trucks for China, pharmaceuticals for North Vietnam, and flour for Cuba, all countries that Canada traded with but which the United States rejected as trading partners under its Trading with the Enemy Act.[15]

In 1970, economist Kari Levitt published *Silent Surrender: The Multinational Corporation in Canada*, which affirmed Watkins's conclusions but went further, suggesting that a Canadian addiction to American investment and trade limited Canada's ability to set its own foreign policy goals. Levitt claimed that Canada's economy was distorted by the large-scale presence of foreign ownership, with the country becoming a net importer of capital and focusing on resource

exports to balance imported manufacturing goods, particularly machinery.[16]

Pressures from economic nationalists caused the Trudeau government to place limits on foreign investment, which were mostly reversed after Canada signed a free-trade agreement with the United States in 1989. Writing in 1993, A.E. Safarian suggested that the evidence was unclear as to whether FIRA and the CDC had made any contribution to Canadian economic growth. In general, he argued, the evidence remained that foreign direct investment and an industrial policy that favoured market forces worked best to produce economic growth.[17]

Safarian's views had some unexpected supporters on the political left. In 2005, political scientist Paul Kellogg argued that the focus on national ownership versus foreign ownership obscured the more important issue of the division of spoils between capital and labour, and between Western capitalist countries and the poor countries of the developing world. According to Kellogg, the nationalists, and especially Levitt, exaggerated the extent of foreign ownership by focusing on the manufacturing sector where foreign investment was greatest. Levitt and other nationalists portrayed Canada as a country exploited by the United States and ignored its considerable and highly profitable investments in Latin America, the Caribbean, and elsewhere around the world.

Levitt's prediction that Canada's dependence on natural resources would rise had proven incorrect. Finally, the nationalists were wrong in their predictions that Canada was about to become a net exporter of capital. Kellogg mentions and rejects the view of his critics that the Trudeau legislation had turned the tide, asserting that the levels of foreign investment had begun to decline before the economic legislation was implemented.[18]

In practice, the Canadian economy remained heavily dependent on the export of natural resources before and after the economic nationalist legislation was introduced. Since the legislation was short-lived, it remains debatable whether it had the potential, on its own, to induce a restructuring of the Canadian economy.

NOTES

1. Quoted in Mr Justice Thomas R. Berger, *Northern Frontier, Northern Homeland: The Report of the Mackenzie Valley Pipeline Inquiry* (Ottawa: Minister of Supply and Services Canada, 1977) 1: 123.

2. Craig Heron, "Harold, Marg, and the Boys: The Relevance of Class in Canadian History," *Journal of the Canadian Historical Association,* n.s., 20.1 (2009) 1–4. Reprinted by permission of the Canadian Historical Association and Dr. Craig Heron.

3. Frank James Tester and Peter Kulchyski, *Tammarniit (Mistakes): Inuit Relocation in the Eastern Arctic, 1939–1963* (Vancouver: UBC Press, 1994) 7.

4. The history of automobiles in their period of economic leadership in Canada is traced in Dimitry Anastakis, *Autonomous State: The Struggle for a Canadian Car Industry from OPEC to Free Trade* (Toronto: University of Toronto Press, 2013).

5. Sheila Arnopolous, "Immigrants and Women: Sweatshops of the 1970s," in *The Canadian Worker in the Twentieth Century,* eds. Irving Abella and David Millar (Toronto: Oxford University Press, 1978) 204.

6. Ester Reiter, "Life in a Fast-Food Factory," in *On the Job: Confronting the Labour Process in Canada,* eds. Craig Heron and Robert Storey (Montreal: McGill-Queen's University Press, 1986) 317–18.

7. Canada, *Report of the Royal Commission on Taxation, vol. 1, Introduction, Acknowledgements and Minority Reports* (Ottawa: Queen's Printer, 1966) 1.

8. Quoted in Cy Gonick, *A Very Red Life: The Story of Bill Walsh* (St John's: Canadian Committee on Labour History, 2001) 171.

9. Quoted in Ester Reiter, "First Class Workers Don't Want Second-Class Wages: The Lanark Strike in Dunnville," in *A Diversity of Women: Ontario, 1945–1980,* ed. Joy Parr (Toronto: University of Toronto Press, 1995) 179, 186, 194.

10. Harry Johnson, *The Canadian Quandary* (Ottawa: Carleton University Press, 1963) 11–12.

11. Steven High, *Industrial Sunset: The Making of North America's Rust Belt, 1969–1984* (Toronto: University of Toronto Press, 2003) 12.

12. On the life of Walter Gordon, see Stephen Azzi, *Walter Gordon and the Rise of Canadian Nationalism* (Montreal: McGill-Queen's University Press, 1999); Denis Smith, *Gentle Patriot: A Political Biography of Walter Gordon* (Edmonton: Hurtig, 1973); and Walter Gordon, *Walter Gordon: A Political Memoir* (Toronto: McClelland & Stewart, 1977).

13. Quoted in Philip Resnick, *The Land of Cain: Class and Nationalism in English Canada, 1945–1975* (Vancouver: New Star Books, 1977) 79, 102, 114, 115.

14. A. E. Safarian, *Foreign Ownership of Canadian Industry* (Toronto: University of Toronto Press, 2011; orig. pub. 1966).

15. Melville H. Watkins, *Foreign Ownership and the Structure of Canadian Industry: Report of the Task Force on the Structure of Canadian Industry* (Ottawa: Queen's Printer, 1968).

16. Kari Levitt, *Silent Surrender: The Multinational Corporation in Canada* (Montreal: McGill-Queen's University Press, 2002; orig. pub. 1970).

17. A.E. Safarian, *Multinational Enterprise and Public Policy: A Study of the Industrial Countries* (Aldershot, England: Edward Elgar Publishing, 1993).

18. Paul Kellogg, "Kari Levitt and the Long Detour of Canadian Political Economy," *Studies in Political Economy,* 76 (Autumn 2005) 31–60.

SELECTED READING

Anastakis, Dimitry. *Autonomous State: The Struggle for a Canadian Car Industry from OPEC to Free Trade.* Toronto: University of Toronto Press, 2013

Bourque, Gilles L. *Le modèle québécois de développement: de l'émergence au renouvellement.* Sainte-Foy: Presses de l'Université du Québec, 2000

Breen, David. *Alberta's Petroleum Industry and the Conservation Board.* Edmonton: University of Alberta Press, 1993

Castonguay, Stéphane. *Protection des cultures, construction de la nature: agriculture, foresterie et entomologie au Canada, 1884–1959.* Sillery: Septentrion, 2004

Evenden, Matthew D. *Fish versus Power: An Environmental History of the Fraser River.* New York: Cambridge University Press, 2004

Finkel, Alvin. *Our Lives: Canada After 1945,* 2nd ed. Toronto: James Lorimer, 2012

High, Steven. *Industrial Sunset: The Making of North America's Rust Belt, 1969–1984.* Toronto: University of Toronto Press, 2003

Levitt, Kari. *Silent Surrender: The Multinational Corporation in Canada.* Montreal: McGill-Queen's University Press, 2002

Matsui, Kenichi. *Native Peoples and Water Rights: Irrigation, Dams, and the Law in Western Canada.* Montreal: McGill-Queen's University Press, 2009

McDowall, Duncan. *The Sum of the Satisfactions: Canada in the Age of National Accounting.* Montreal: McGill-Queen's University Press, 2008

McInnis, Peter S. *Harnessing Labour Confrontation: Shaping the Postwar Settlement in Canada, 1943–1950.* Toronto: University of Toronto Press, 2002

Norrie, Kenneth, Douglas Owram, and J.C. Herbert Emery. *A History of the Canadian Economy.* Toronto: Nelson Thomson, 2008

Parr, Joy. *Sensing Changes: Technologies, Environments, and the Everyday, 1953–2003.* Vancouver: UBC Press, 2010

Piper, Liza. *The Industrial Transformation of Subarctic Canada.* Vancouver: UBC Press, 2009

Sangster, Joan. *Transforming Labour: Women and Work in Post-War Canada.* Toronto: University of Toronto Press, 2010

Savoie, Donald. *Visiting Grandchildren: Economic Development in the Maritimes.* Toronto: University of Toronto Press, 2006

Thiessen, Janis. *Manufacturing Mennonites: Work and Religion in Post-War Manitoba.* Toronto: University of Toronto Press, 2013

Willow, Anna J. *Strong Hearts, Native Lands: Anti-Clearcutting Activism at Grassy Narrows First Nation.* Winnipeg: University of Manitoba Press, 2012

Wright, Miriam. *A Fishery for Modern Times: The State and the Industrialization of the Newfoundland Fishery, 1934–1968.* Toronto: Oxford University Press, 2001

For a comprehensive list of readings for topics covered in this chapter, please visit http://pearsoncanada.ca/conrad.

CHAPTER 14
COMMUNITY, NATION, AND CULTURE, 1945–1975

On 29 January 1969, students occupied the computer centre at Sir George Williams University (now part of Concordia) after the administration dragged its feet in responding to accusations of racism against a biology professor. A negotiated agreement between the two sides collapsed on the evening of 10 February. As protesters wrecked equipment and threw debris out the window, the administration summoned the police. Ninety-seven people were arrested. Among them was Roosevelt "Rosie" Douglas, later elected prime minister of his homeland Dominica, and Anne Cools, originally from Barbados, who became the first black person to be appointed to the Canadian Senate. "We were not about any violence," Douglas later recalled. "We were about the demands of the black community in terms of their human rights, their civil rights, and their full equality."[1]

The movement for human rights and social justice that had been gaining momentum for two centuries became more focused in the decades following the Second World War. In 1948, the United Nations adopted a Universal Declaration of Human Rights, penned with the assistance of Canadian legal scholar John Peters Humphrey. It asserted that everyone, "without distinction of any kind, such as race, colour, sex, language, religion, political or other opinion, national or social origin, property, birth or other status," was entitled to life, liberty, and security; to freedom of speech, thought, and assembly; and to "security in the event of unemployment, sickness, disability, widowhood, old age or other lack of livelihood."[2] When authorities were slow to pursue these goals, many people were no longer willing to wait patiently for conditions to improve.

In the early years of the Cold War, movements for social reform faced daunting challenges. The United States was particularly enthusiastic about rooting out "subversives," but Canada was also prepared to purge the civil service, trade union leadership, universities, and publicly funded media of anyone deemed Communist or too radical in calling for reform. By the 1960s, civil rights, peace, and liberation movements of various kinds taking root in the United States and around the world began to find resonance in Canada. As they worked their way through society, Canada was fundamentally changed. Historian Bryan Palmer has argued that "Canada as it had been known ceased, for all practical purposes, to exist in the 1960s."[3]

POPULATION

The dizzying pace of social change in postwar Canada was orchestrated in the context of a rapidly growing population. By 1975, nearly 23 million people called Canada home, up from about 12 million in 1945. This growth was fuelled in part by a baby boom that followed in the wake of the Second World War. In 1959, the fertility rate of women in their childbearing years was nearly 50 percent higher than in 1941. The large cohort of young people who came of age in the 1960s and 1970s inevitably dominated many social trends.

Immigrants also changed the fabric of Canadian society. When it became clear that the Second World War would not be followed by a recession, Canada began to welcome newcomers. From 1946 to 1962, almost 1.8 million people moved to Canada. Early postwar immigrants were primarily European; only four percent came from Asia and Africa, and many of these were white South Africans and Israelis. Overseas offices of the Department of Immigration were confined to Europe, as were visa offices, and the minister of citizenship and immigration enjoyed substantial discretionary power in keeping out people deemed undesirable.

Initially, there was also some resistance to opening doors to immigrants from countries that had been Canada's enemies during the Second World War. About 10 000 Germans and 20 000 Italians were permitted entry from 1946 to 1950, but the explosion in labour needs led to the acceptance of 189 705 Germans and 166 397 Italians from 1951 to 1957. In contrast to earlier periods, Canada also opened its doors to European refugees, among them 37 500 of the 200 000 Hungarians fleeing their homeland after a 1956 uprising against the Soviet-dominated Communist regime failed.

As the economic boom of the 1960s began, it became clear that western Europe, back on its feet after postwar rebuilding, would no longer produce the steady stream of immigrants required to support Canada's expanding economy. To attract the well-educated technical and professional people that Canada most wanted, immigration regulations were changed to open the door to skilled people from regions other than Europe and the United States. Domestic servants, always in short supply, were also granted entry to Canada, even if they came from non-European countries. Revisions to the Immigration Act in 1962 and again in 1967 reduced the colour bias that had once kept Canada's gates largely closed to non-whites. As a result, immigrants began arriving from all over the world—the Caribbean, India, Pakistan, and China, in particular—to find work and well-being.

With the United States offering better salaries in many areas of employment, Canadians continued to find opportunities across the border, contributing to what critics called the "brain drain." Out-migration slowed by the end of the 1960s and briefly reversed, but immigration remained a significant factor in Canada's population growth. During the height of the Vietnam War (1965 to 1975), at least 50 000 American draft dodgers, military deserters, and opponents of American foreign policy sought refuge in Canada, and many of them eventually became Canadian citizens.

As Table 14.1 suggests, immigration accounted for a dramatically larger proportion of the population increase in the early 1970s than in the late 1950s, although immigration levels were almost the same. This is explained by the decline in the birth rate

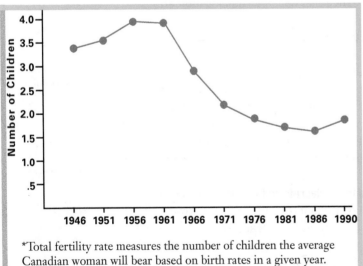

*Total fertility rate measures the number of children the average Canadian woman will bear based on birth rates in a given year.
**Newfoundland, Yukon, and the Northwest Territories are excluded in the 1946 figure.

FIGURE 14.1

Total Fertility Rates, 1946-1990

Sources: Adapted from F.H. Leacy, ed., *Historical Statistics of Canada,* 2nd ed., (Ottawa: Statistics Canada, 1983), Catalogue 11-402, Series B1–14; and *Canada Year Book,* various years

TABLE 14.1
A Growing Population, 1941–1976

PERIOD	POPULATION INCREASE	BIRTHS	POPULATION INCREASE DUE TO BIRTHS (%)	NET IMMIGRATION	POPULATION INCREASE DUE TO IMMIGRATION (%)	POPULATION AT THE END OF PERIOD
1941-51	2141*	1972	92.1	169	7.9	13 648
1951-56	2072	1473	71.1	594	28.9	16 081
1956-61	2157	1675	77.7	482	22.3	18 238
1961-66	1777	1518	85.4	259	14.6	20 015
1966-71	1553	1090	70.2	463	29.8	21 568
1971-76	1425	934	65.5	491	34.5	22 993

Population figures in thousands
* Excludes Newfoundland

Source: Adapted from Statistics Canada, *Canada Year Book* (1994) 113

from 28.3 newborns per 1000 population in 1959 to 15.7 in 1976. While the drop can largely be attributed to the introduction of the birth control pill in 1960, other factors, including the changing status of women and new notions of the good life, contributed to the view that families should be much smaller than they had been in the past. Meanwhile, better nutrition, preventive medicine, and medical breakthroughs such as antibiotics increased both infant survival and life expectancy generally. The dramatic decline in infant deaths since the beginning of

MORE TO THE STORY
Who Is Fit to Have a Baby?

Canadians continued to frown on women who had children out of wedlock. Eligibility provisions in provincial mothers' allowance legislation that excluded never-married mothers remained on the books in all provinces except British Columbia in 1945. They were gradually removed, though in the case of Nova Scotia, only in the 1970s. Social workers continued to pressure unmarried women to give up their children for adoption. In Quebec, thousands of "illegitimate" Catholic children, the so-called "Duplessis orphans," were placed in homes for the mentally ill, regardless of their condition, to hide them from society.

Single mothers were not the only Canadians deemed unworthy to have children. People labelled mentally unfit were also discouraged from reproducing. The province of Alberta had a particularly shameful track record in this regard. From 1929 to 1972, the provincial Eugenics Board ordered the sterilization of 2822 people deemed "mentally defective." The board interpreted this category broadly: adult sexual offenders,

young women considered promiscuous or potentially promiscuous, and school-aged children whose parents could not cope with them and whose intelligence appeared to be less than average. The children were placed in the Provincial Training School for Mental Defectives in Red Deer.

Most of the men and boys ordered sterilized by the board received vasectomies, but some sexual offenders were castrated. Girls in the school were routinely sterilized at puberty. Among them was Leilani Muir, an inmate of the school from 1955 to 1965. An abused child at home, Muir suffered developmental delays and scored poorly on an IQ test. School officials had her Fallopian tubes tied during an unnecessary appendectomy. Muir left the school when she was 21. At the age of 45, after her mother informed her of the sterilization, she sued the provincial government. In 1996, the Court of Queen's Bench awarded Muir $750 000 in compensation. Two years later, the province agreed to substantial financial compensation for other living victims of its eugenics policy.[4]

the century meant that in 1976, only 13.5 infants per 1000 failed to reach their first birthdays, compared with 88.1 in 1921. Children born in 1976 could expect to live 13 years longer than children born in 1931. By the late 1970s, the average life expectancy had reached 70 years for men and 77 for women.

As always, these figures mask demographic differences within the larger Canadian population. Wealthy Canadians still tended to live longer than the poor, and Native peoples were the most likely to suffer early deaths. Although infectious diseases in Native communities were less common than in earlier periods and medical care facilities and personnel were more accessible, poverty-related diseases such as tuberculosis continued to thrive. Despair produced disastrous rates of alcoholism and drug addiction, leading to an array of health problems. Natives between the ages of 20 and 39 had a risk almost four times that of the general population of dying a violent death, the result of either homicide, suicide, or accident.

This new suburb in Lethbridge, Alberta, in 1951 followed the model that was common in bigger cities. Planned as a neighbourhood of about 1500 homes around an elementary school (in the foreground), it featured curved streets and cul-de-sacs meant to break the monotony created by similar-looking boxy homes. SOURCE: GLENBOW ARCHIVES NA 5327-293

CITIES AND SUBURBS

Rapid urban growth in the postwar period left municipal governments scrambling to build new roads, sewers, and other services for their expanding populations. In 1946, the federal government established the Central Mortgage and Housing Corporation to help veterans and middle-class Canadians buy homes. This program helped to fuel the growth of suburbs on the fringes of Canada's major cities. With more people owning cars, "urban sprawl," defined by superhighways, large enclosed shopping malls, and cookie-cutter housing projects, became a feature of many city landscapes.

Portrayed as areas of open space, privacy, and modernity, the suburbs often lacked the sense of community that prevailed in inner cities and rural areas. In most cases, new suburbs initially lacked shopping areas, community centres, theatres, taverns, sport complexes, and other recreational areas. Residents found entertainment in the city centre and friendship through workplace, church, and community organizations that were only sometimes located in their new subdivisions. Many suburbanites, and, indeed, increasing numbers of Canadians generally, either sought privacy or had it thrust upon them in anonymous settings that brought the term "community" sharply into question. Instead of attending community events, people watched television, and even built their homes to accommodate a "TV room." Impersonal supermarkets, department stores, and malls eventually replaced neighbourhood shops where customers and merchants all knew each other.

Stay-at-home moms experienced this new privacy most directly, sometimes with devastating psychological consequences. Often well-educated, suburban women suffered from what American feminist Betty Friedan, in her groundbreaking book *The Feminine Mystique* (1963), called "the problem that has no name." A surprisingly large number developed nervous disorders for which a male-dominated medical profession prescribed tranquilizers that left the underlying problems unresolved. Still, not all women remember the suburbs in a negative way. For some, voluntary work in community leagues and church auxiliaries was a fulfilling experience. Many women formed close friendships with neighbours and shared shopping and child care. Toronto suburbanite Anne Lapp recalled fondly: "Nearly all of us had small children and it was a daylong job keeping them out of the mud and excavated house sites. . . . It was like a small village and we knew almost everyone."[5]

Suburban life, at least as it was portrayed in advertisements, stood in sharp contrast to the experience of the poor living in remote rural areas or inner-city slums. Although electricity and telephone lines had reached most areas of Canada by the end of the 1960s, many Canadians could not afford these services and continued to live without indoor plumbing and central heating. Most cities still harboured hideous slums where landlords paid little heed to municipal housing standards—and got away with their negligence as city governments focused their attention on demands from the suburbs. When programs for urban renewal were eventually adopted, it often meant levelling existing homes and replacing them with fancier houses that only the well-off could afford.

Although public housing programs developed slowly, it was not due to the failure of early experiments. Toronto's Regent Park, Canada's first large-scale public housing development, was completed in 1947. Eleven years later, a study suggested that its 1200 families— low-income people whose former neighbourhoods were plagued by crime, alcoholism, poor health, and school absenteeism—had established a relatively peaceful, healthy neighbourhood. While residents complained of a lack of recreational facilities and about the bureaucratic management of the project, their lives had improved as a result of their relocation to apartments and row houses with good sewage and sanitary services.

Inner-city residents sometimes had success in fending off efforts to build expressways through their neighbourhoods designed to connect new suburbs with the downtown. In the 1960s, defenders of Edmonton's river and ravine valley network of parks persuaded the city to jettison plans for several expressways that would have destroyed natural areas, while Vancouverites prevented construction of a proposed expressway through Chinatown. In Toronto, a broad coalition stopped the Spadina Expressway from being completed in 1971, and caused the city to abandon other planned highway projects in favour of new subway lines. Successes of this kind sparked urban reform movements with a wider agenda of saving older neighbourhoods and creating denser cities less dependent on cars.

THE IMMIGRANT EXPERIENCE

If the postwar suburbs appeared colourless, inner-city areas were often reinvigorated by the influx of immigrants. The majority of postwar immigrants settled in urban areas, and by the 1970s, Toronto, Montreal, and Vancouver were the initial destinations of more than half of all immigrants to Canada. The colourful, multilingual storefronts, the smells of a variety of cuisines, and the preference for streets and cafés over privatized living transformed these cities into cosmopolitan metropolises.

More than half a million Italians came to Canada between 1951 and 1971, the majority of them sponsored by their Canadian relatives in Montreal and Toronto. Maria Rossi's experience was typical of many women who came from Italy. In November 1956, she and her daughter arrived in Toronto. Her husband had emigrated one year earlier from their peasant farm in southern Italy. The family rented a basement flat in the home of another Italian émigré family. Four days after her arrival, she began work as a steam press operator at a local laundry. For the next 20 years she worked continuously in a variety of low-paying jobs that included sewing, cooking, and cashiering.

Within a generation, many immigrants were involved in voluntary organizations designed to sustain their communities. Businessmen's clubs, community centres, and sports teams created a feeling of home away from home and helped to transmit ethnic culture to the next generation. Political organizations, with ties to the "old country," emerged in ethnic enclaves. Ukrainian Canadians, for example, continued to pit pro-Soviet Communists against supporters of an independent Ukraine. With 80 000 mostly nationalist immigrants arriving after the war, the nationalists, who enjoyed financial support from the Canadian government, emerged as the main voice of the Ukrainian community. Zionism, the movement to create a Jewish homeland in Israel, became a uniting cause for Canadian Jews in the aftermath of the Holocaust. Led by the Canadian Jewish Congress, Jews in Canada stepped up their campaigns for legal sanctions against open manifestations of anti-Semitism and other forms of racism.

Efforts by immigrants to preserve their culture led to the federal decision in 1971 to appoint a secretary of state for multiculturalism and to fund ethnic organizations and festivals. In provinces with large ethnic minorities, heritage-language instruction was introduced in the schools. Such developments muted, though failed to eliminate, racism and bigotry in Canadian society.

ASIAN-CANADIAN COMMUNITIES

While Canadians of Asian heritage were finally granted the right to vote in 1947, they had good reason to feel embattled in Canadian society. They had difficulty finding employment outside of their own communities, and rarely rose to positions of authority. With little thought for the consequences, the city of Toronto bulldozed two-thirds of Toronto's Chinatown to build a new city hall in the 1960s. In Vancouver, the situation was no better. As author Denise Chong recalled:

> Vancouver's city council enacted bylaws to sanitize the squalor and ordered commerce off the side-walk—gone were the squawking chickens in cages, the barbecued pork and duck that once hung for the customer's perusal. The gambling dens that used to be my grandmother's livelihood and entertainment had also disappeared; the last one had been pad-locked long ago by city police.[6]

After Canada officially recognized the Communist government of the People's Republic of China in 1970, new Chinese immigrants began to arrive in Canada, reinvigorating Chinese-Canadian communities and giving them more clout to resist the redevelopers.

Immigration from India and Pakistan increased dramatically following the reform of immigration laws in the 1960s. Their numbers included much-in-demand doctors, engineers, and teachers, but those without university degrees were often ghettoized in low-wage work. Eyeing the bottom line, companies recruited South Asian women to perform the lowest-paying and most difficult tasks on the worst shifts. South Asians also provided

Events such as this Chinese dragon parade in Vancouver's Chinatown in 1960 celebrated the cultural diversity of Canadian society. SOURCE: VANCOUVER PUBLIC LIBRARY 79795-A

much of the farm labour force in British Columbia, picking pesticide-sprayed crops without protective clothing or masks, and living in converted barns without running water or electricity. Even those with professional degrees often faced employment difficulties.

AFRICAN CANADIANS

Canada's restrictive immigration laws permitted entry to only a small number of blacks in the 1950s, about half of whom were Caribbean domestics needed to fill a shortage of maids for hotels and wealthy homes. In Nova Scotia, where 30 percent of Canada's deeply rooted black population lived in 1961, blacks fought for their rights through the Nova Scotia Association for the Advancement of Coloured People (NSAACP), founded in 1945. One of its first actions was to raise money to help Viola Desmond fight segregation in movie theatres. Desmond, a Halifax beautician, was arrested in a New Glasgow theatre in 1946 for sitting downstairs rather than in the balcony, to which blacks were usually restricted. She was thrown in jail and fined for attempting to defraud the government of one cent in amusement tax—seats in the balcony were less expensive than those downstairs. Sentenced to 30 days in jail or a $20 fine, she paid the money but appealed the decision. She lost her appeal, but the incident resulted in so much negative publicity that such discriminatory laws were soon abandoned.

Discrimination on the basis of racialized differences was common everywhere in postwar Canada and was even upheld by the courts. In 1949, the Appeal Court of Ontario ruled that there was nothing illegal about a clause in property deeds that barred Jews and blacks from buying property in Beach O'Pines near Sarnia. In Dresden, Ontario, where blacks made up 17 percent of the town's 2000 people in 1950, restaurants, poolrooms, and barber and beauty shops refused patronage from non-whites.

In theory, such victimization of minority groups should have abated considerably with the passage of the Canadian Bill of Rights by the Diefenbaker government in 1960. The bill declared Parliament's commitment to equality of Canadians regardless of race, religion, colour, national origin, or sex. But provincial authority over civil rights and property meant that without a constitutional amendment, the Canadian Bill of Rights applied mainly in areas covered by federal laws. The provinces moved slowly to protect minority rights, and only after considerable political protest from minorities.

Encouraged by the Civil Rights and Black Power movements in the United States, African Canadians in the 1960s became more assertive in their struggle against discrimination. A new generation of black leaders, many of them recent immigrants from the West Indies and Africa, refused to accept discrimination in employment, housing, and services. Numbers contributed to a greater community confidence. Between 1971 and 1981, more than 140 000 West Indian immigrants came to Canada. Their concentration in southern Ontario allowed them to establish a rich institutional culture, including social clubs, newspapers, the annual Toronto Caribbean Carnival (commonly known as Caribana), and anti-racist organizations. Black immigrants were also highly active in decolonization and anti-racist movements in Montreal, of which the Sir George Williams student protest was but one manifestation.

In the 1960s, the plight of blacks in Nova Scotia received international attention when the city of Halifax decided to demolish Africville, a black community on the outskirts of the city. Africville had been shamefully neglected by city authorities, who provided no public services and had located the municipal dump nearby. In 1962, the city council decided to relocate the 400 citizens of Africville to make way for an industrial development. Despite protests, the relocation proceeded and the community was levelled by bulldozers. The demolition of Africville spurred an organized response. In 1968, the Black United Front (BUF) was founded to advance the struggle for reform in Nova Scotia.

In an effort to defuse a growing militancy among blacks in Canada—American Black Panther leader Stokely Carmichael had made much-publicized visits to Halifax and Montreal in 1968—the federal government offered to fund BUF and other black organizations.

Africville in the 1960s. SOURCE: NOVA SCOTIA ARCHIVES 1983-310 NO. 47660 (N-4264)

Beginning in the late 1960s, provincial human rights legislation, backed by human rights commissions with powers to investigate and prosecute cases of clear discrimination on the basis of race, sex, or religion, demonstrated a greater desire on the part of authorities to reduce systemic racism in Canada. Nevertheless, visible minorities continued to struggle against social exclusion.

NATIVE PEOPLES FIND A VOICE

Aboriginals also took strength from the general movement for human rights. For the first time in more than four centuries, demography was on their side. Contrary to expectations, Canada's indigenous peoples did not die out or become assimilated. Instead, they grew in numbers and maintained their culture. Revisions to the Indian Act in 1951 gave elected band councils more powers, awarded women the right to vote in band elections, and lifted the ban on potlatch and sun dance ceremonies. But residential schools continued to operate, and assimilation remained the goal of federal policy. As provinces adopted human rights codes, the franchise was extended to Status Indians, who finally received the vote federally in 1960. The rates of poverty, unemployment, life expectancy, and suicide among Canada's Native peoples suggested that much more was needed.

As part of the Trudeau government's promise to implement a "Just Society," the Minister of Indian Affairs, Jean Chrétien, unveiled a White Paper on Indian policy in June 1969. While it included a number of significant reforms, the White Paper's main proposal was to abolish Indian status and transfer responsibility for Indian Affairs to the provinces. The National Indian Brotherhood (NIB), founded in 1968 to represent Status Indians, was outraged, demanding Aboriginal self-government and respect for Aboriginal treaty rights. In a stinging critique published as *The Unjust Society* (1969), the young Cree chief Harold Cardinal made it crystal clear that assimilation was not on the agenda.

Ottawa withdrew the White Paper and embarked on the long, difficult process of addressing Aboriginal grievances. During the 1970s, pressures from the NIB—reorganized as the Assembly of First Nations in 1982—led the government to abolish residential schools. The last residential school was closed in 1996, but the scars remained. In 1990, the head of the Manitoba Association of Chiefs, Phil Fontaine, stated publicly what had frequently been heard privately: Native children in residential schools had not only been offered inferior education, they had also been victims of physical and sexual abuse. Native youth who left their reserves for towns and cities, Fontaine argued, were rarely assimilated into the larger society. Instead, they succumbed to lives in urban ghettos marked by poor housing, poverty, and alcoholism.

The conditions on many of Canada's more than 600 reserves were a serious blot on Canada's human rights record. Although many First Nations families struggled to provide caring environments, their children often grew up in abusive situations. On some reserves, sniffing gas or glue and other forms of drug dependency became common among Native children, resulting in a high number of substance-related deaths and suicides. In an effort to heal the wounds of oppression, Natives increasingly turned to traditional practices, once suppressed by governments and churches, so that their children could grow up with positive images of Aboriginal culture.

Berger Commission hearings in the Northwest Territories in 1975. SOURCE: NORTHERN NEWS SERVICES LTD

In the early 1970s, almost every resident of Alkali Lake, a Shuswap community of 400 people in the British Columbia interior, was an alcoholic. Phyllis Chelsea and her husband, Andy, were typical. He had been hospitalized on several occasions after binge drinking, and Phyllis had twice required medical care after being beaten by her drunken husband. One evening, after again drinking heavily, Phyllis stopped to pick up her children at their grandmother's house. There she was confronted by her eldest daughter, then only seven, who refused to go home, accusing her parents of being violent drunks. Phyllis was shocked and resolved to stop drinking. Andy was initially unwilling to follow her example until, one day, he was deeply struck by the many bruised, hungry faces among local children on the way to school, a reflection of the effects of alcohol on families in the community.

The Chelseas began to encourage others on the reserve to stop drinking alcohol and managed to persuade the band council to make treatment for alcoholism a condition for receiving financial help. As people sobered up, it became clear that alcohol was a symptom, not the primary cause, of the sad conditions on the reserve. Many of the residents had attended the nearby Catholic-run St John's Mission residential school where they had been victims of sexual abuse, which then became common in the households of Alkali alcoholics.

With the help of healing circles, people moved beyond the shame that had caused generations of local residents to seek comfort in alcohol. By the early 1980s, Phyllis Chelsea could point proudly to a community in which 95 percent of the adults were sober. The children attended a new school built by the band and where elders "came to share prayers, pipe ceremonies, and songs in Shuswap," thus renewing the traditional culture that had all but died out in the wake of poverty, abuse, and despair.[7]

Canadian courts played an important role in addressing Native rights. In a landmark decision relating to the Nisga'a in British Columbia, the Supreme Court ruled in 1973 that Aboriginal title existed before European colonization. This led the Trudeau government to concede that Ottawa was obliged to negotiate comprehensive land claims with Aboriginal peoples not covered by treaties. In Quebec, the Cree and Inuit drew upon this principle to insist in court that their rights be recognized before the massive James Bay power development could proceed. The resulting James Bay and Northern Quebec Agreement of 1975 provided significant compensation for Native groups. Local authorities throughout Canada also increasingly faced direct action, as was the case in Kenora, Ontario, where protesters occupied a park between 1972 and 1974, claiming that it, like much of the town, belonged to the Anishinabek Nation.

As economic development in the North threatened to overwhelm them, Mackenzie Valley First Nations and some Métis declared the existence of a Dene nation and sought independence within the framework of Confederation. A proposed pipeline in the Mackenzie River Valley to bring oil from Prudhoe Bay was postponed after Justice Thomas Berger, appointed in 1974 to conduct an inquiry on the pipeline development, heard eloquent testimony against the project from the Dene and Inuit in the region. Although the government accepted Berger's call for a halt to pipeline developments for a decade, it was slow in pursuing comprehensive land-claims settlements in the North and providing aid to bands seeking to establish local businesses under Native control.

EDUCATION

For many Canadians, the route out of their materially disadvantaged position was through education. Most jobs now required more brain than brawn. As high-paying resource industry and construction jobs declined, a high school diploma became the minimum requirement for many jobs in the service sector. More than half of Canadians had nine grades or fewer of schooling in 1951. Twenty-five years later, only a quarter of the population over 15 years of age had not completed at least nine grades.

University degrees, once limited to a numerically negligible—if influential—elite, became more common, and employers began to expect university degrees or college diplomas for many junior positions. By the mid-1970s, one in 10 Canadians aged 25 to 44 held at least one university degree. The gender balance in higher education also began to change. Although women had been discouraged from attending university in the early years of the twentieth century, they were increasingly found in undergraduate classrooms by the mid-1970s. Gender still governed what programs students pursued. Fields such as engineering, law, and medicine remained male bastions, while schools of social work and nursing had a largely female clientele. Men dominated graduate programs, outnumbering women 8.5 to 1 in receipt of doctorates in 1975, but these trends too were changing.

Provincial governments invested heavily in education after the Second World War. In rural areas, the one-room schoolhouses, where poorly paid teachers taught eight grades at once, gave way to modern, centrally located, well-equipped facilities. By the 1970s, most public school boards required that new teachers hold a university degree in education. Powerful teachers' associations began demanding professional wages for their members, sometimes using strike action to achieve their demands. Schooling practices, meanwhile, became more humane, as corporal punishment and rote learning was replaced by child-centred education and attempts to encourage critical thinking.

With an eye to the changing demands of the labour market, the federal government introduced programs to improve post-secondary education. University enrollment briefly doubled as a result of federal grants to encourage veterans to pursue higher education. In the early 1950s, Ottawa began supplementing provincial grants to universities. When the "baby boomers" began graduating from high school in the 1960s, Canada's university system expanded to accommodate them. New universities—among them Trent in Peterborough, York in Toronto, Simon Fraser in Burnaby, the University of Regina, and the Université de Moncton—were founded. Church-affiliated universities, particularly prominent in post-secondary education in the Maritimes, secularized their governing structures to become eligible for government grants.

The transformation of education was most dramatic in Quebec, where schooling in the 1950s was still heavily influenced by religious authorities. In Catholic-controlled schools, the curriculum focused on classical thought for boys, while girls were taught "preparation for family life, the beauty of the home, its virtues, and its unique position in society."[8] This approach had limited appeal and helped to contribute to a high drop-out rate. There was also a significant divide between anglophones and francophones. In 1960, 11 percent of anglophones in the province aged 20 to 24 attended universities, while only 2.9 percent of francophones enjoyed this privilege.

Dissatisfaction with the conservative, clerically run educational institutions of Quebec revealed itself in the phenomenal success of *Les Insolences du Frère Untel* (*The Impertinences of Brother Anonymous*), which was published in 1960. Written by Brother Jean-Paul Desbiens, it was a stinging indictment of Quebec education by someone within the ranks of the Roman Catholic Church. The Jean Lesage government appointed a commission to examine the state of Quebec education and make recommendations for improvement. Although the commissioners decided that schools should remain organized along religious lines, they recommended that the state play a larger role in administration and curriculum development. In 1964, for the first time since 1875, the provincial government established a Ministry of Education. It introduced new curricula to bring Quebec schools in line with education systems in the rest of North America, and in 1967 it established a network of secular junior colleges—Collèges d'enseignement général et professionnel (CEGEPs)—to provide post-secondary vocational and academic training. In 1968, Quebec's National Assembly created the Université du Québec, with campuses in Montreal and in four smaller cities. Between 1960 and 1970, enrollment in Quebec's secondary schools rose 101 percent, college enrollment rose 82 percent, and university enrollment rose 169 percent.

The creation of the Centrale de l'enseignement du Québec, a militant teachers' union, out of the old Catholic teachers' association reflected the continued secularization of education—and unions—in Quebec. Leaders of the new union issued manifestos inspired more by Marx than by Jesus, and easily overwhelmed the rapidly declining numbers of priests and nuns in their ranks who clung to traditional Catholic perspectives. Nevertheless, conservatives could still mobilize the support needed to win school board elections, for which voter turnout was notoriously low, and fought off attempts to formally secularize the school system. In this goal, they had the support of the Protestant boards, which believed that the dual system defended anglophone rights and the superior schools developed by the wealthier non–Roman Catholic community.

Everywhere in Canada, formal education increasingly became a lifelong experience. Men working in primary industries such as fishing, forestry, and mining were obliged to learn new technical skills to perform their increasingly mechanized jobs, and women re-entering the labour force required training if they hoped to avoid the poorly paid cleaning and caring work to which they were traditionally assigned. In 1960, the federal government introduced a Technical and Vocational Training Assistance Act to support efforts by the provinces to construct new vocational high schools, institutes of technology, and adult training centres.

THE SEXUAL REVOLUTION

Improved levels of education, income, and material well-being were accompanied by a dramatic transformation of attitudes toward sex and family life. While the nuclear family, consisting of a husband, a wife, and several children, remained the ideal for most Canadians, it accounted for a noticeably smaller proportion of households. Divorce laws were liberalized in 1969, allowing unhappy marriages to be dissolved and increasing the number of single-parent households. Common-law marriages, once associated with the poorer classes, became popular across the economic spectrum, particularly among young adults. Divorce and remarriage substantially increased the number of "blended" families: a couple's biological children and the offspring from earlier marriages.

The baby boomers, children of a prosperous and media-dominated age, rejected much of what they perceived as the stuffy Victorian values of their elders. Pushing at the edges of what became known as the "generation gap," they developed a youth culture characterized by rock 'n' roll music, blue jeans, premarital sex, mind-altering drugs, unisex clothing and hairstyles, and political protest. This culture was most evident among middle-class students enrolled in expanding liberal arts programs at universities, but it gradually became the new normal. In schools across the country, teachers battled against long hair on men, short skirts on women, and blue jeans on everyone—but then adopted these symbols of liberation themselves. Surveys among Canadian young people showed that by the mid-1960s, a majority of university students were sexually active; a decade later, the same was true for high school students.

While the sexual revolution alarmed traditionalists, it was here to stay. Men had experienced increased sexual freedom during the war and found licence for their sexuality in American magazines such as *Playboy*, founded in 1953, which circulated in Canada. Women, meanwhile, still agonized about being virgins when they married and often paid the price if they were not, forced by pregnancy into an unwanted marriage or single motherhood. The widespread availability of contraceptives by the 1960s separated sex from pregnancy, and "the pill" gave women more agency. Nevertheless, it soon became clear that values relating to sexuality were, as writer and activist Myrna Kostash suggests, "scripted by men for men's benefit."[9] Women often felt compelled by peer pressure to have sex with their boyfriends, and were sometimes deemed "frigid" and subject to physical force when they were reluctant to consent.

GAY RIGHTS

Despite laws against homosexuality, gays and lesbians established their own bars and other social gathering spots in the postwar period. In 1964, Jane Rule published *Desert of the Heart*, a novel of lesbian love, while the Association for Social Knowledge, a same-sex organization, was formed in Vancouver and the tabloid *Gay* began publication in Toronto. The unwillingness of gays and lesbians to hide their sexual orientation forced the government to consider whether it should enforce anti-gay legislation or accept that sex between consenting adults should be legal, regardless of whether those adults were of the same or different sexes.

While homosexuality was decriminalized in 1969, it did not lose its stigma. In the postwar period, under the influence of psychology, the view that sex with someone of the same gender was conscious criminal behaviour gave way to the view that homosexuality was a pathology that psychotherapy could cure. If it was an advance for gays and lesbians to have their sexual orientation viewed as within the laws of the land, they still had to fight the view that their sexual preference violated the laws of nature. As long as they were regarded as mentally deranged, they remained the target of discrimination in employment and housing and were denied rights of adoption and spousal benefits available to opposite-sex couples. Fledgling gay rights organizations pressed for an end to such discrimination and for recognition of sexual orientation as largely biologically determined rather than the result of reversible mental traumas.

They had their work cut out for them. As late as 1963, the RCMP persuaded the Diefenbaker government, still convinced that homosexuality and communism were perversions and therefore related, to allow it to use a "fruit machine" to root out homosexual applicants for civil service jobs. Only the apparent unreliability of the machine in measuring erotic responses resulted in this experiment's demise.

THE WOMEN'S MOVEMENT

Few postwar developments went as deep and had such a profound impact as the changing status of women. The public–private gender divide never made much sense, but it quickly dissolved in a society where equality was highly prized. Ignoring all swings in the business cycle, women's labour force participation rate doubled between 1951 and 1981. Wage-earning women soon discovered that they were working a "double day"—at home and on the job— and facing a "double standard" in the workplace. Not only were they barred from many lines of employment and most managerial positions, they received less pay than men for doing the same work. Even unemployment insurance benefits were less generous for women whose "real" job was assumed to be in the home.

Inspired by the feisty women's liberation movement in the United States, Canadian women began forming organizations to fight for equality. In Quebec in 1966, Thérèse Casgrain, a long-time feminist activist, helped to found the Fédération des femmes du Québec (FFQ), an umbrella group of women's organizations, to fight for women's rights. In English Canada, women's groups, led by Laura Sabia, president of the Canadian Federation of University Women, and *Chatelaine* magazine editor Doris Anderson, pressured Ottawa for action. In 1967, the Pearson government, prodded by its only female cabinet minister, Judy LaMarsh, established a Royal Commission on the Status of Women. Chaired by broadcaster and journalist Florence Bird, the commission reported in 1970. When Ottawa was slow to respond, women's groups established the National Action Committee on the Status of Women (NAC) in 1972 to ensure that the commission's 167 recommendations—which included calls for reform in education, employment,

immigration, criminal and family law, and child care— would not be ignored.

Like other groups seeking justice, women sometimes resorted to direct action to make their voices heard. Restrictions on abortion rights remaining in the 1969 reforms to the Criminal Code prompted 500 women to join an Abortion Caravan. It began in British Columbia and ended in Ottawa, where protesters shut down Parliament in May 1970 by chaining themselves to seats in the visitors' gallery and shouting "Abortion on Demand!" A month later, Dr. Henry Morgentaler, who had emerged as the champion of the pro-choice movement in Canada, was jailed for performing illegal abortions at his Montreal clinic. Morgentaler continued to play cat and mouse with authorities until 1988, when the Supreme Court struck down the restrictions in the abortion law.

Who owns the streets? "With it" young people from across Canada, who like their American counterparts were known as "hippies," made the Yorkville area of Toronto their meeting place. It soon became a popular tourist attraction, with cars parading night and day through the Yorkville neighbourhood. In this "taking it to the streets" demonstration in 1967, hippies were confronted by police while protesting the laws that gave the streets to people behind the wheels of automobiles, not to pedestrians. SOURCE: DICK DARRELL/GETSTOCK.COM

In the early 1970s, Native women organized to campaign against discriminatory treatment under the Indian Act. Sandra Nicholas Lovelace, a Maliseet from the Tobigue First Nation in New Brunswick, who had lost her Indian status when she married a white man, took her case to the United Nations. In 1981, the UN found Canada in breach of the International Covenant on Civil and Political Rights. By then, feminism in all its manifestations had become one of the most widespread and powerful social movements in Canada.

THE CULTURE OF PROTEST

Canada's young people were central to many of the protest movements that swept across the country in the 1960s. On expanding university campuses, students and professors, some of them recent immigrants from the United States, introduced "New Left" thinking and drew strength from youth uprisings in Europe in 1968. A number of organizations, including the Union générale des étudiants du Québec (1964) and the Student Union for Peace Action (1965), emerged to raise youth consciousness of the injustices that continued to prevail in an allegedly liberal democratic society. Through marches, sit-ins, and information sessions,

students demanded greater democratization of society, beginning with the university itself. Students supported efforts to root out racism and they joined the ranks of the peace movement, which gained momentum as the United States became increasingly mired in the Vietnam War.

Students were often involved in helping the unemployed and working poor to find a voice. By the 1970s, groups representing tenants, welfare rights advocates, single mothers, the unemployed, and other categories of the poor and powerless had been organized. Demonstrations at provincial legislatures, city halls, and the homes of slumlords brought increased media attention to those who lived destitute lives within a prosperous society. In 1971, thousands attended a conference in Ottawa that led to the creation of the National Anti-Poverty Organization to fight for a guaranteed annual income and other legislation that would benefit the country's poorest citizens. In Quebec, where both nationalist sentiment and social grievances spurred tens of thousands to join community groups, a close alliance developed between grassroots movements and the powerful trade unions. Across Canada, "social animators," often university-educated facilitators paid by the unions, mobilized citizens and provided a link between the protests of radical baby boomers, organized workers, and the poor.

MORE TO THE STORY
Marijuana and a New Generation

Before the Second World War, illegal drug use in Canada was largely associated in the public mind with the lower classes and non-whites. Social prejudices, rather than scientific knowledge, often dictated the legislation that made some intoxicants illegal while others, such as alcohol, were legal but regulated after Prohibition ended in various provinces. Marijuana was first included in legislation banning certain substances in 1923; in 1961, it was placed under the Narcotic Control Act, and stiffer penalties were introduced for possession and "trafficking."

Despite its illegality, marijuana became the recreational drug of choice for many teenagers and young adults during the 1960s. Even at the conservative University of Alberta, where only one percent of students in residence had used

drugs in 1965, fully a quarter of residence students in 1971 had experimented with illegal drugs, usually marijuana. Police arrested more than 1500 people in Alberta for cannabis possession in 1971, more than the number of arrests for this act in the entire country just four years earlier.

Police forces presented their arrests of marijuana sellers and users as a victory for the forces of social good. The RCMP commissioner warned in 1968 that "the lawless 'beat' generation will create a mounting fear of anarchy in Canada unless it is met firmly by police with massive public and governmental support."[10] They singled out hippies—mainly young people who had dropped out of society, condemning materialist social values that they regarded as empty, and whose use of marijuana to free minds stifled by social repression was well advertised.

Arrests for marijuana possession and threats by university administrations to expel students convicted on drug charges fuelled pressures from student groups to remove marijuana from the Narcotic Control Act, or even to get rid of the act altogether. Pierre Trudeau responded by establishing the Commission of Inquiry into the Non-Medical Use of Drugs, headed by Gerald Le Dain, dean of York University's Osgoode Hall Law School.

The Canadian medical profession was divided in its response to the rise of marijuana use. While some physicians echoed the British Advisory Committee on Drug Dependence, which said that marijuana use was no more harmful physically than alcohol consumption, others were unwilling to advocate legalization because the long-term effects of its use were unknown. Supporters of legalization pointed out that studies of marijuana's effects were not possible until marijuana ceased to be an illegal substance.

The Le Dain Commission attempted to balance the conflicting voices regarding marijuana. In their 1972 report, the commissioners called for the removal of possession of marijuana from the Criminal Code and weaker penalties for producers and sellers of the substance. The government, pressured by conservative forces within the country and abroad—particularly by the American government, which was increasing penalties for drug use and sales—was unwilling to change its narcotics legislation. Instead, the Department of Justice quietly instructed prosecutors in 1972 to seek an absolute discharge for anyone convicted of simple possession.

THE ENVIRONMENTAL MOVEMENT

The environmental movement in North America reached a new level of awareness in 1962 when Rachel Carson published *Silent Spring*. In this highly publicized book, Carson provided stunning revelations about the dangers posed by the "tide of chemicals born of the Industrial Age." Rivers and oceans, the air and soil, and animal and human species, she argued, were being rapidly destroyed. "We stand now where two roads diverge," Carson concluded. "The road we have long been traveling is deceptively easy, a smooth superhighway on which we progress with great speed, but at its end lies disaster. The other fork of the road offers our last, our only chance to reach a destination that assures the preservation of our earth."[11]

As the environmental movement gained momentum, public and private institutions began to alter their behaviour. The Soviet Union, Great Britain, and the United States signed a treaty to ban atmospheric testing of nuclear weapons in 1963, and industries built higher smokestacks to diffuse their polluting emissions. Consumers contributed to the environmental cause by avoiding the use of chemical-laden detergents, foods laced with pesticides, and leaded gasoline.

Despite such well-meaning efforts, the environmental problem would not go away. Scientists discovered that polychlorinated biphenyls (PCBs), a family of highly toxic chemicals used in electrical equipment, continued to poison the food chain after their use had been discontinued. No one knew how to dispose of the hazardous waste from nuclear power plants. Even the emissions released into the atmosphere by tall smokestacks came back to earth hundreds of kilometres away as acid rain and snow, which ravaged lakes and forests.

Concern for the environment inspired action on a number of fronts. In 1970, a group of American and Canadian activists collaborated to protest nuclear testing by the United States in the Aleutian Islands. Two years later, the activists adopted the name Greenpeace, expanding their protests to include the dumping of toxic wastes into lakes and oceans and the slaughter of whales, dolphins, and baby seals. Campaigns against acid rain and workplace hazards attracted widespread support. The CBC Television program *The Nature of Things*, which began airing in 1960, helped to focus public attention on environmental issues and found a powerful spokesman in David Suzuki, who began hosting the show in 1979. Governments were obliged to pay attention. A United Nations Conference on the Human Environment met in Stockholm in 1972 to discuss the decaying state of the planet. Chaired by a Canadian, Maurice Strong, the conference produced a declaration of environmental rights and established a program to fund and coordinate investigations into environmental problems.

RELIGION IN A SECULAR AGE

In the rampantly secular context of the second half of the twentieth century, many church leaders had their work cut out for them. Weekly church attendance declined precipitously following the Second World War—from more than 60 percent in the late 1940s to 41 percent by 1975—and many churches began having difficulty finding enough clergy to minister to their declining membership.

In the 1950s and early 1960s, most mainstream Protestant denominations tried to strike a balance in their views, supporting social programs such as Medicare while maintaining conservative positions on homosexuality, abortion, divorce, and the role of women. Ironically, while they opposed greater social opportunities for women, Protestant churches offered women opportunities to demonstrate leadership skills in social and charitable activities and missionary roles. In keeping with their notions of distinct gender roles, the churches generally reserved their paid positions and their senior decision-making bodies for men. A committee established by the Presbyterian Church in the 1950s found little support for the ordination of women or even the election of female elders.

By the 1970s, the growing women's movement began to have an impact. While progress, particularly in the ordination of women, was slow—the Anglican Church agreed to ordain women in 1976—most Protestant churches joined with other social groups in calling for state-subsidized quality daycare and for greater economic equality between the sexes. Others supported community groups active in combating child abuse and violence against women.

The Roman Catholic Church in Canada experienced its own soul-searching, spurred by liberalizing trends in Rome that culminated in the Second Vatican Council (1962–65). Although liberals in the church supported the ordination of women and relaxing celibacy requirements for priests, conservatives dominated the official position on moral questions. Church members, it seems, paid little attention. Despite the church's condemnation of effective contraception, the birth rate among Catholics paralleled the rate for non-Catholics. Quebec, though nominally overwhelmingly Catholic, had the country's lowest birth rate by the 1970s. Pollsters found that most Catholics, like most Canadians generally, supported a woman's right to abortion, despite the official position of their church.

Catholics abandoned the church in droves. In Montreal, church attendance dropped by half in the 1960s. Despite reforms designed to appeal to the secular generation, the church had difficulty recruiting enough priests and nuns to minister to their congregations. In 1946, there were 2000 new priests in Quebec; in 1970, only 100. Convents, the mainstay of the religious workforce, were deserted as jobs in teaching, nursing, and social work opened up for women in the paid labour force and feminist ideology challenged the church's teachings on gender roles. Although Protestant churches gradually opened their ministries to women, the Roman Catholic Church successfully resisted movements from within to end its long-standing practice of maintaining an all-male celibate priesthood.

THE CANADIANIZATION MOVEMENT

Many Canadians regarded the increasing secularism of their society as one of many reflections of Americanization. Concerns about the overwhelming influence of the United States on Canadian culture, particularly in anglophone Canada, led to the creation in 1949 of the Royal Commission on National Development in the Arts, Letters, and Sciences, or the Massey Commission. Headed by Vincent Massey—scion of the farm-implements giant Massey-Harris—the commission recommended government programs to strengthen Canadian cultural production, including state control over television stations, federal grants to universities, establishment of a national library, and increased funding to cultural institutions such as the National Film Board, the National Museum, and the Historic Sites and Monuments Board.

Determined to foster a uniquely Canadian culture, the St-Laurent government acted on many of the commission's recommendations. CBC-TV began broadcasting in 1952, initially with a monopoly over television in Canada, and in 1953 the National Library of Canada was founded. The creation in 1957 of the Canada Council, using the windfall estate taxes of two recently deceased entrepreneurs, Isaak Walton Killam and Sir James Dunn, helped to fulfil the commission's recommendation for state support to cultural production in art, ballet, drama, music, and publishing.

One of the Massey Commission's most influential recommendations concerned the role of the CBC in the new medium of television. It recommended putting the CBC's board of governors in charge of licensing television stations and making national productions in the arts a prime responsibility of CBC Television. By 1960, nine CBC stations and 38 affiliates were on the air. CBC-TV produced Canadian dramas and variety shows that provided an outlet for many Canadian actors, musicians, and entertainers, but the stations gave over much of their prime time to American shows.

Although American sitcoms and teleplays proved more popular than their Canadian equivalents, there were a number of successes in the early years of Canadian television programming. *Front Page Challenge*, a sedate guess-the-name-in-the-news show, was introduced in 1956 and remained on the air until 1995 with the same host, Fred Davis, and original panelist Pierre Berton still in harness. *Country Hoedown* introduced a generation of country music entertainers, notably Tommy Hunter, and *Don Messer's Jubilee*, which first aired in 1959, earned a devoted following. *La Famille Plouffe*, a sitcom focusing on the lives of a working-class Montreal family, was a huge success in both its French and English versions.

In 1958, the federal government responded to pressure from private broadcasters to end the CBC monopoly over television. Under new legislation, private channels became eligible for licences and the Board of Broadcast Governors (BBG) was set up to license radio and television stations. After the first private stations went on the air, featuring almost non-stop American entertainment, nationalist pressures forced the BBG to establish a 55 percent Canadian-content guideline in the 1960s. Cheaply produced game shows, modelled on American programs, were the private stations' answer to the rule, and hopes that content regulations would stimulate a viable Canadian television production industry were largely unrealized.

As the centennial of Confederation approached, the Canadianization movement gained momentum. Expo 67 in Montreal, developed around the theme "Man and His World," drew huge crowds and helped to bolster a sense of national pride. In the context of the Vietnam War and their own considerable postwar achievements, Canadians began to imagine themselves as a better version of the North American dream. The goal was now to maintain and promote that superiority. To slow the Americanization of university faculties, the federal government supported policies to hire qualified Canadians over

foreign applicants. The government also responded to many of the recommendations of *To Know Ourselves: The Report of the Commission on Canadian Studies* (1975), authored by the president of Trent University, Thomas H.B. Symons. With the help of federal government funding, Canadian Studies programs sprouted not only in Canadian universities, but also internationally.

By the 1970s, commemoration of events in Canada's history had become a vehicle for promoting stronger civic identities. Such activities involved all levels of government and were carried out for a variety of reasons. Sometimes the goal was job creation, which was the case in the federally sponsored reconstruction of Louisbourg as a tourist attraction in the early 1960s. Provincial projects, such as the Acadian Historic Village in Caraquet, New Brunswick, and the Ukrainian Village outside Edmonton, represented recognition by provincial governments of the voting power of ethnic groups. At other times, projects involved attempts to invigorate decaying areas of cities, as in the conversion of rundown buildings on the Halifax waterfront and in Winnipeg's warehouse district into fancy shops. The sites at King's Landing in New Brunswick and Upper Canada Village in Ontario were assembled from buildings threatened with demolition when the land on which they had been originally built was flooded for new hydro-electric dams. In some cases, such as the remains of a Viking settlement at l'Anse aux Meadows in Newfoundland and the well-preserved buildings in old Quebec City, historic sites received international recognition. Museums, like historic sites, mushroomed after 1960, most focusing on some aspect of the history of Canada.

Despite these efforts, popular culture remained dominated by American television, magazines, movies, and recordings. At the University of Toronto, Harold Innis and Marshall McLuhan expressed concerns about the technological imperative bearing down on Canada, but there seemed to be little that anyone could do to shape popular media that were controlled by powerful American corporations. In 1965, philosopher George Grant published *Lament for a Nation*, in which he argued that the homogenizing forces of liberalism, modernity, and technology had undermined older conservative values that made Canada distinct in North America. For Grant, Diefenbaker's defiance of Kennedy during the Cuban Missile Crisis represented "the last gasp of Canadian nationalism." Grant's book became a bestseller in a country whose anglophone citizens were searching desperately for a new sense of who they were other than British colonials, and for reasons why they might want a separate identity from the United States.

By the end of the 1960s, the federal government was prepared to step up its support for cultural industries. The Pearson government established the Canadian Radio and Television Commission (CRTC) in 1968 to regulate public and private broadcasting, and founded the Canadian Film Development Corporation to encourage a Canadian-based movie industry. After the adoption of tougher Canadian-content regulations in 1970, Canadian talent had more opportunities to find an audience on radio and television. The combined efforts of the CBC and its francophone counterpart Radio-Canada, the Canada Council, and various federal and provincial regulatory bodies spurred an outpouring of film, music, drama, and print that was one of the remarkable developments in postwar Canada.

By the early 1970s, much of English Canada's artistic community had become ardent Canadian nationalists. Cultural icons such as authors Pierre Berton and Farley Mowat, poet Earle Birney, and artist Harold Town were prominent members of the Committee for an Independent Canada. Celebrated novelist and poet Margaret Atwood wrote *Survival: A Thematic Guide to Canadian Literature* (1972), an outline of the development of Canadian literature that attempted to find a distinct Canadian identity in the resilient, if often cheerless, characters who peopled national writing.

Not every successful Canadian author applauded such developments. Mordecai Richler, one of Canada's best-known authors at home and abroad, argued that cultural nationalism would result in mediocre work, and that Canadians should be willing to have their work judged by international standards. Like many Canadians who were not of British descent, Richler suspected that Canadian nationalism was a plot by white Anglo-Saxon Protestants to impose their version of a national identity on immigrant groups who had their own complex identities, of which being Canadian was but a component.

CULTURE AND QUEBEC SOVEREIGNTY

The question of culture and identity played out differently in Quebec. Before the 1960s, francophone cultural production in the province, though vibrant and open to international influences, had to cope with clerical censorship and social conservatism. In 1948, Paul-Émile Borduas led a group of 16 avant-garde Quebec artists and intellectuals who released *Refus global*, an indictment of what they saw as the narrow orthodoxy that prevailed in the province. Borduas was dismissed from his position at the École du Meuble for his effrontery. Despite the hurdles, Gabrielle Roy, born in Saint-Boniface, Manitoba, won widespread acclaim for her novel *Bonheur d'occasion* (1945), a stark portrayal of life in the working-class neighbourhood of Saint-Henri in Montreal. It was translated into English in 1947 as *The Tin Flute* and sold well in both Canada and the United States.

Paul-Émile Borduas, *Les carquois fleuris* (1947). Borduas had an enormous influence on postwar Quebec painting. He studied at the École des Beaux-Arts in Montreal and later moved to Paris. Borduas opposed all formalism in art, arguing that each painter must experiment by letting individual feeling determine both the subject and style of their work. SOURCE: MONTREAL MUSEUM OF FINE ARTS

By the 1960s, the Quiet Revolution and nationalist sentiment led to an outpouring of creativity. Political commitment, particularly support for sovereignty, marked much of the celebrated literature in Quebec. Hubert Aquin's *Prochain épisode* (1965), a stream-of-consciousness account of an imprisoned sovereignist member of a group much like the FLQ, won widespread acclaim. Its general message was that as long as Quebec remained within Confederation, it would be a colonized society in which individual francophones could find no real identity. Such ideas echoed Jacques Godbout's *Le Couteau sur la table* (*Knife on the Table*), published two years earlier. Godbout's principal character is a young francophone whose life is aimless and who becomes the lover of an equally aimless but wealthy anglophone woman; he begins to discover himself and break from his shallow lover only after he reads of the exploits of the nascent FLQ.

Non-fiction best-sellers also often extolled Quebec's separation from Canada. FLQ activist Pierre Vallières's autobiographic account, *Nègres blancs d'Amérique* (*White Niggers of America*), published in 1969, argued that francophones in Quebec were treated as an underclass in the province much as African Americans were treated in the United States, and would continue to be oppressed until they achieved sovereignty. The plays of Michel Tremblay, the province's most successful playwright, focused on the ways that domination by both the English and the Catholic Church had dampened people's ability to express themselves and develop social solidarity. In *Les Belles-Soeurs* (1968), Tremblay portrayed francophone women as the main victims of a social disintegration resulting from the long suppression of independent thought in Quebec. The play was also one of the first to make extensive use of *joual* (the French dialect used by working-class francophone Montrealers).

Quebec's music industry also blossomed. In the 1950s, French-language radio stations were largely dominated by pop music from France, local attempts to copy the metropolitan sound, and standard North American English fare. Only a few artists, such as Félix Leclerc, a Quebec nationalist whose traditional French-Canadian music also won him an audience in France, stood out as distinctly Québécois talent. By the 1970s Quebec's airwaves were dominated by homegrown talents such as Robert Charlebois, Monique Leyrac, and Pauline Julien. Gilles Vigneault became the major songwriter of the sovereignist movement, with his "Mon pays" and "Gens du pays" becoming anthems of the independence forces.

Locally produced movies in French drew large audiences in Quebec. An early success was Claude Jutra's *Mon Oncle Antoine* (1971), which also drew good crowds for its English-language version. More controversial was Michel Brault's *Les Ordres* (1974), which won prizes at the prestigious Cannes Film Festival but was denounced by the federal and provincial governments as an inaccurate portrayal of the arrests and detentions during the October Crisis in 1970. Denys Arcand, Quebec's most successful director and screenwriter in the twentieth century, also began his filmmaking career in the early 1970s.

Television in Quebec, as elsewhere in North America, became the most important medium for cultural production and political awareness. During the Duplessis years, Radio-Canada, the federally funded francophone wing of the CBC, provided one of the few media sources of criticism of Duplessis. Radio-Canada produced a number of celebrities, including future premier René Lévesque. Both Radio-Canada and Radio-Québec, the Quebec broadcasting service established by the provincial government in 1968, provided Quebec entertainers with important outlets for their creative talents.

Stimulated by the rapidly changing society around them, Quebec anglophones were also culturally productive. Hugh MacLennan, a professor at McGill, examined Canadian social values, including conflicts between francophone and anglophone approaches to life, in his novels. In the 1950s, Dorothy Livesay, F.R. Scott, A.M. Klein, and Louis Dudek were key figures in Montreal-centred social realist poetry. Mordecai Richler emerged as the best-known of Montreal's Jewish novelists, gaining an international reputation with novels that provided vivid portrayals of the Jewish experience in the city. Another product of Montreal's Jewish community, Leonard Cohen, achieved national fame as a poet and novelist and then international recognition as a composer of poetic popular-music lyrics.

CULTURAL DEVELOPMENTS OUTSIDE QUEBEC

For obvious reasons, English-speaking Canadians were more susceptible than Quebecers to the American media onslaught in the postwar period. There was much debate among intellectuals and artists about what, if anything, differentiated Canadian and American cultural identity. Like their francophone counterparts, many anglophone artists struggled to define regional and ethnic identities, and the rate of cultural production in many areas of the arts was impressive.

LITERATURE

By the 1950s, writers from every region—Thomas Raddall and Ernest Buckler from the Maritimes, Ontario's Morley Callaghan and Hugh Garner, and the West's W.O. Mitchell, Sheila Watson, and Adele Wiseman—were gaining a national audience. Minority cultures brought a rich complexity to literary production that was hitherto dominated by the descendants of British immigrants. Although not prolific, Wiseman created a moving account of the experience of Jewish immigrants in the Prairies in her novel *The Sacrifice* (1956). John Marlyn, in *Under the Ribs of Death* (1957), dealt with the experiences of the son of Hungarian immigrants in the north end of Winnipeg. He expressed the confusion of many newcomers as they faced an environment that reviled their native cultures yet denied them a firm place within the dominant Anglo-Canadian culture.

Female writers began to come into their own in the postwar period. In *The Swamp Angel* (1954), Ethel Wilson made a hero of a woman who leaves her husband and wealthy home for a life of adventure in remote areas. Although the book met a mixed critical reception at the time, Wilson's novel would be embraced by feminists in the 1960s. Margaret Laurence's novels and short stories were best-sellers. Her small-town Manitoba characters, searching for moral values that made more sense than the prudishness and bigotry that surrounded them, had resonance for many Canadians, and many women identified with the struggles of her female characters to defy society's stifling restraints. Alice Munro, whose short stories focused on rural Ontario, also became a favourite with many Canadians. Like Laurence, she stripped away the veneer of conventional morality to look at the emotions that women experienced as they tried to find both meaning and passion in their lives. Margaret Atwood even more clearly identified with women's liberation and Canadian nationalism with her novels *The Edible Woman* (1969) and *Surfacing* (1972).

Other Canadian writers also developed international reputations for their work. Timothy Findley's plays, novels, and short stories had political themes, including the horrors of war, the extent of state manipulation in people's lives, and the issue of how and why people are labelled as mad. When his novel *Famous Last Words*

appeared in 1977, it became an instant classic. Findley was Canada's leading openly homosexual writer, and some of his short stories explored homosexual relationships. Less overtly political were the novels of Robertson Davies, which had a more psychological focus. His books, such as *Fifth Business* (1970), won huge audiences.

Among francophone writers outside Quebec, the most distinguished was Antonine Maillet. In 1979, she won France's major literary prize, the Prix Goncourt, for *Pélagie-la-Charrette*, a fictional work examining the theme of Acadian expulsion. An earlier work, *La Sagouine*, had gained a wide audience and provided Canadians with a fictional character as enduring as Longfellow's *Evangeline*.

Few Native authors of fiction developed a national reputation before 1975. Occasionally, white authors made notable efforts to sensitively describe the lives of Canada's Aboriginal peoples. Playwright George Ryga's *The Ecstasy of Rita Joe* (1970) and novelist Rudy Wiebe's *The Temptations of Big Bear* (1973) played a role in drawing mainstream society's attention to the oppression that characterized Canada's treatment of the descendants of its original inhabitants. While fictional works by Natives had yet to receive wide readership, several non-fiction works were influential. Like Harold Cardinal's *The Unjust Society* (1969), Shuswap chief George Manuel's *The Fourth World* (1974) placed before a broad public the perspectives of Natives clamouring for dramatic legislative changes in Canadian–Native relations. In her 1973 best-selling autobiography, *Halfbreed*, Maria Campbell described the dire poverty of her childhood in northern Saskatchewan. While Métis traditions partly compensated for grim living conditions and racial discrimination, the death of Campbell's mother in 1952 put an end to this source of solace. Only 12 years old, Maria struggled to hold together her large family. She drifted across western Canada, becoming a prostitute and drug addict in Vancouver, and later doing low-paid "women's work"—cooking, waitressing, hairstyling. In the late 1960s, she became a militant activist in Alberta.

The increase in the production of serious literature in Canada in the postwar period was more than matched by skyrocketing sales for formula romances. In the 1950s, Harlequin was a struggling Winnipeg publisher. Its empire grew as it convinced booksellers of the vast popularity of its escapist plots, mainly among female consumers. By the late 1980s, Harlequin had sold more than 200 million books in more than 100 countries.

Margaret Atwood

Margaret Atwood was the bestselling Canadian author of the twentieth century. Born in Ottawa in 1939, Atwood's childhood was divided between Toronto, where her father taught biology at the University of Toronto, and northern Ontario, where he conducted research. After completing a bachelor's degree in English at the University of Toronto, Atwood studied in the United States, earning a master's degree at Harvard. Her publishing career began with *The Circle Game,* her first book of poetry, in 1966, which won the Governor General's Award. Her first novel, *The Edible Woman,* appeared in 1969, followed by *Surfacing* in 1972. That year, Atwood also published her first book of Canadian literary criticism, *Survival: A Thematic Guide to Canadian Literature.*

An ardent nationalist, feminist, and defender of civil liberties, Atwood became a public figure in Canada, defending causes raised in both her fictional and non-fictional publications. She was a vocal critic of both the Toronto police raids on gay bath houses in 1981 and the Canada–United States Free Trade Agreement in 1988.

Atwood's international reputation soared with the publication of *The Handmaid's Tale* in 1986, a dystopian account of American society where women were under the total domination of men. The book won the Governor General's Award for fiction in 1986 and the first of Atwood's four nominations for Britain's prestigious Booker Prize, a prize she finally won for *The Blind Assassin* in 2000.

Atwood's work covers a variety of themes and locales, but Canadian history is central to much of it. From her poetry collection *The Journals of Susanna Moodie: Poems* (1970) to her novel *Alias Grace* (1996), the latter dealing with the complexities surrounding a nineteenth-century Ontario murderer, Atwood has demonstrated an abiding interest in uncovering the past of her country, and particularly its women.[12]

Margaret Atwood in the Ontario countryside in 1972, the year she published *Survival: A Thematic Guide to Canadian Literature.* SOURCE: RON BULL/GETTY IMAGES

THEATRE AND DANCE

Although most people increasingly consumed their drama on television, live theatre remained popular. The town of Stratford, Ontario, launched the Stratford Festival in July 1953. Hiring the country's top actors and creating a blend of Shakespeare and other classical playwrights, the festival drew theatre-lovers from home and abroad and helped to advance the hugely successful stage and film career of Christopher Plummer. Professional theatres opened in most Canadian cities, initially concentrating, like Stratford, on the classics.

A growing audience in Canada enjoyed performances by dance companies including Les Grands Ballets Canadiens, the National Ballet, and the Danny Grossman Dance Company. Dancers such as Karen Kain and Frank Augustyn of the National Ballet and Evelyn Hart of the Royal Winnipeg Ballet won prestigious international

Frank Augustyn and Karen Kain dance in The National Ballet of Canada's production of *The Sleeping Beauty*, which premiered in 1972.
SOURCE: ANDREW OXENHAM/NATIONAL BALLET OF CANADA ARCHIVES

competitions. With grants from the secretary of state for multiculturalism, cultural groups began to revive dance traditions that had been pushed aside in the rush to fleeting popular dance styles such as the twist, the monkey, and the mashed potato.

ART

Art also benefited from efforts to encourage Canadian cultural output. Landscape art remained popular, but artistic expression ranged broadly and borrowed extensively from Canadian and international trends. Native art and the British Columbia landscape influenced the work of Vancouver surrealist painter Jack Shadbolt. On the Prairies, William Kurelek's work reflected his attempts to deal with a difficult childhood as a Ukrainian Canadian growing up in rural Alberta and Manitoba. Ontario filmmaker and artist Joyce Wieland produced provocative works that reflected her nationalist and feminist values. Several artists from London, Ontario, among whom Greg Curnoe was best-known, created a regional art celebrating local identity and the Canadian struggle to be free of American control. With the east coast environment as his context, Alex Colville inspired a generation of artists,

including Christopher Pratt, Mary Pratt, and Tom Forrestall, to produce works that collectively became known as Atlantic realism.

A major development in this period was the recognition of Native artistic expression. On the west coast, Bill Reid earned an international reputation for his revival of traditional Haida carving. In the 1950s, Norval Morrisseau, an Ojibwa from Sand Point reserve in Ontario, began to create paintings that incorporated the pictography of rock paintings and Ojibwa spiritual themes. Largely due to the promotional energy of Toronto artist James Houston, what is now known as Inuit art was introduced to southern buyers. Beginning in the late 1940s, he encouraged Inuit artists to develop cooperatives as a vehicle for marketing their prints and carvings.

FILM

English-Canadian films were generally less successful than other aspects of the country's cultural productions. The average Canadian watched 18 movies per year in 1950 before television caused a drop in movie attendance. In 1953, 74.6 percent of the feature films that were distributed in Canada originated in the United States, 16.9 percent in France, and 5.8 percent in Great Britain. There was only one Canadian film in movie houses that year: *Tit-Coq*, written by and starring Quebec playwright Gratien Gélinas.

Nonetheless, the government resisted imposing quotas on Hollywood movies, instead entering an agreement with the major studios to include mentions of Canada in American feature films. It was not until the 1970s that the federal government began to provide tax concessions to financial backers of Canadian films. This resulted in a quantitative leap in the number of films produced in the country, and a few films reached high levels of excellence, though few Canadians saw them. American distributors owned the theatres that remained dominated by Hollywood productions. Nevertheless, classic films on Canadian themes were produced, among them *Goin' Down the Road* (1970) by Toronto-based director Donald Shebib and *The Rowdyman* (1972), directed by Newfoundland-born actor and writer Gordon Pinsent.

RECORDING ARTISTS

Until the late 1960s, English-Canadian radio stations mainly played American recording artists, and only a few Canadians managed to break into the American market. Among them was Nova Scotia's Hank Snow, who eventually moved to Nashville to pursue a successful career. His first major hit, "I'm Movin' On," remained number one on Billboard's country chart for 21 weeks in 1950, an achievement unsurpassed until 2013. In 1949, acclaimed Montreal jazz artist Oscar Peterson made his debut in the United States at Carnegie Hall, but he maintained a Canadian base, moving from Montreal to Toronto in 1958. The two most successful Canadian groups of the 1950s, the Crew Cuts and the Four Lads, consisted entirely of graduates of St Michael's Choir School in Toronto. Turning from sacred music to covers of African-American rhythm and blues songs, the Crew Cuts had the distinction of recording the first rock 'n' roll tune to reach number one on the American charts, "Sh-Boom (Life Could Be a Dream)" (1954). Paul Anka of Ottawa, whose popularity extended over several decades, also began his hit-making career in the 1950s.

Generally, however, there was a drought of Canadian artists on the radio. Major folk artists such as Gordon Lightfoot, Joni Mitchell, Ian & Sylvia (Tyson), and the Travellers received much acclaim but little airplay other than on CBC Radio, which had loyal but small audiences. In 1969, the only Canadians with regular radio airplay nationally were Winnipeg's The Guess Who and Toronto's The Band. The Guess Who's "American Woman," which topped the Billboard chart in the United States in 1970, gave a Canadian spin to anti-war sentiments in the Vietnam War era, warning the "American Woman" to keep her "ghetto scenes" and "war machines" away from Canadian boys. In 1970, the Canadian Radio-television Commission (CRTC), which had been established as the regulatory agency for broadcasters, introduced regulations requiring radio stations to ensure that no fewer than 30 percent of the records they played were of Canadian origin. Within a year, artists such as Anne Murray, Neil Young, Gordon Lightfoot, and Joni Mitchell were common fare on the radio. For an increasing number of Canadian artists, success in Canada spilled over to the American airwaves.

CBC radio and television continued to be the main source of publicity for Canadian artists outside the formulaic world of pop music. Because of CBC exposure, a growing number of Canadian artists could fill concert halls nationally rather than just regionally. John Allan Cameron of Cape Breton, who performed folk music with Celtic roots, was an example. Another was Stompin' Tom Connors, who grew up in Skinners Pond, Prince Edward Island, and appealed to both folk and country audiences with his working-class perspective on Canadian themes. His trademark was a pounding foot, inspired by the need to be heard above noisy crowds. Folk festivals, such as Toronto's Mariposa and the Winnipeg Folk Festival, which attracted an audience of 30 000 during its first year of operation in 1974, also provided showcases for a variety of musical artists.

CENSORSHIP

Although censorship regulations were gradually relaxed in the postwar period, Canadians remained cautious about permitting free access to films and publications. Radicals, such as the French feminist Simone de Beauvoir, were barred from the CBC in the 1950s owing to government apprehension about their corrupting influence. During the same decade, books such as *Peyton Place*, *Lady Chatterley's Lover*, and *The Tropic of Cancer* were seized by customs officials at the border.

Across the country, film censorship boards decided what films could be played in provincial theatres. In Alberta, a British Information Office film extolling the United Nations and condemning racism ran afoul of the anti-Communist witch-hunters, and popular American films *The Wild One* and *The Blackboard Jungle* were banned for not being uplifting. Municipal library boards and school boards also banned books of clear literary merit at various times, usually for having too much explicit sex or too many profane words. Campaigns by the religious right in Canada, influenced by the successes of the well-funded Christian right in the United States, led to book bannings as supposedly secular libraries and schools bowed to pressure from groups who claimed that certain books offended Christian sensibilities.

A Censored TV Producer Speaks

Noel Moore's television documentaries had won awards, and he had no reason to regard a CBC request to produce a feature on the life of Russian revolutionary leader V.I. Lenin as problematic. His version of Lenin's life, in many respects, challenged official Soviet propaganda, but it was not tame enough for some Canadian politicians. As Moore explained:

> When the film was due to be shown on CBC Television some reactionary guy on the back benches of the Conservative Party queried it. He stood up in the House and asked if it was true that a document of revolution was going to be shown tomorrow night? So the CBC cancelled my film in 1971 and showed two other films—one was about the life of Hitler and the other was a skiing film which showed you how to set off dynamite to blow up avalanches and in the process they showed in infinite detail how a bomb was made. And, at the same time, my harmless little film essay

was denounced. That was when the whole October Crisis blew up....

The CBC pulled my film on the weakest of excuses. They claimed it was because of this Conservative backbencher, but the phone call came from the Prime Minister's Office—the PMO....

I was blackballed by the CBC after this film. I never did another job for them even though I had won national and international awards....

Ironically, the CBC had just shown an American documentary about the Hollywood Ten and said, "Look how normal we are in Canada. These kinds of things can't happen here." It was happening in Canada and it was cold-war hysteria. Anyway, my film about Lenin did go on the air eventually. It was aired about six months later. The CBC couldn't afford not to show it this time, there was too much at stake.[13]

PROFESSIONAL SPORTS

Postwar prosperity and urbanization brought larger audiences to professional team sports, and as in other nations, sports became increasingly identified in Canada with the "national identity." This was especially the case with hockey. Aired on Saturday night television as well as on radio, games between teams in the National Hockey League produced popular heroes such as Maurice "Rocket" Richard, whose skills on the ice helped the Montreal Canadiens to win a string of Stanley Cups in the 1950s and 1960s. After the Rocket was suspended for the balance of the season in 1955 as a penalty for brawling, fans at the Forum took to the streets in riotous indignation at what they saw as anti–French-Canadian bias in the NHL, in a demonstration that clearly had nationalist overtones.

The legendary competition between the Montreal Canadiens and the Toronto Maple Leafs also reflected the larger tensions between French and English Canadians and has been immortalized in Roch Carrier's short

story, "Le chandail de hockey" ("The Hockey Sweater"). Professional hockey nevertheless remained a North American enterprise, largely dominated by American interests. In 1967, the size of the NHL doubled, but all the new teams were American. The Vancouver Canucks joined the league in 1970, and four Canadian teams, representing the cities of Ottawa, Winnipeg, Edmonton, and Quebec City, were included in the World Hockey Association, a rival to the NHL, founded in 1972.

Canadians could increasingly take pride in their sports achievements on the international stage. For years, Canadian coaches, players, promoters, and fans had insisted that Canadians were the best hockey players in the world and that their unimpressive showings at the Olympics and other international amateur competitions were due to strict definitions of amateurism that excluded players in the NHL. Thus, when a series of games was arranged between the Soviet Union's national team and the best Canadian players in the NHL in 1972, Canada's reputation was on the line. Paul Henderson's famous series-winning goal for Canada has come to be seen as one of the classic moments in Canadian sports history, and led to nationwide celebrations.

Not all Canadians were equally welcome in professional sports. Racial integration advanced slowly, beginning in 1946 when the Montreal Royals baseball team signed African American Jackie Robinson. Before the mid-1980s, only one black player, Willie O'Ree, had been allowed to play in NHL major-league games. A Fredericton-born left-winger and speed demon, O'Ree was asked to play in two Boston Bruins games in 1958, the first of which was against the Montreal Canadiens. Three years later, he played most of the Bruins' regular-season games, but despite a strong performance, was traded several times after the season and relegated back to the minors for the remaining 14 years of his hockey career.

Football was second to hockey as Canada's national sport. In 1956, the Western Interprovincial Football Union and the Interprovincial Rugby Football Union joined forces to form the Canadian Football Council, later renamed the Canadian Football League. All of the teams in the league were Canadian, and they played with rules different from those of their American counterparts, which helps account for the fact that football did not follow the path of hockey in becoming integrated on a North American scale.

While professional sports teams were almost exclusively male, both female and male Canadian athletes won international honours in individual sports. Barbara Ann Scott won the 1948 Olympic figure-skating title and then skated professionally in ice shows. Marilyn Bell was hailed for her swimming achievements, beginning in 1954 with her 52-kilometre swim across Lake Ontario when she was only 16 years old. She later went on to become the youngest swimmer to cross the English Channel and the Strait of Juan de Fuca.

As with the arts, sports benefited from state assistance. In 1961, the Fitness and Amateur Sports Act was passed to encourage physical fitness and to make a better showing in international competition, and especially in the Olympics. Thereafter, much of what passed as amateur sports in Canada became bureaucratized, presided over by paid administrators rather than enthusiastic volunteers.

CONCLUSION

Canadian society in the postwar decades was both a reflection of and reaction to the American cultural juggernaut. While everything from suburbs to popular protests seemed to be modelled on the United States, tenacious efforts were made to create a distinctly Canadian voice. In the case of Quebec, the sovereignty movement gave a particular poignancy to such efforts. The strength of the Canadianization movement in this period was often due to the efforts of governments, through both subsidies and regulations, to protect the Canadian market for homegrown talents. As Canadians began seeing themselves reflected in cultural productions, they developed a new sense of their own identities and continued a lively debate about what it meant to be a Canadian in an increasingly globalizing world.

Willie O'Ree in the uniform of the Boston Bruins. SOURCE: WILLIE O'REE

The Origins of Canada's Policy of Multiculturalism

What were the origins of the "policy of multiculturalism within a bilingual framework" that Prime Minister Pierre Trudeau announced in the House of Commons in October 1971? The immediate reason seems simple enough: the government was responding to the findings of the Royal Commission on Bilingualism and Biculturalism and especially Book IV of its report, published in 1969, which dealt with the contribution of non-British, non-French ethnic groups to Canadian society. While reaffirming the predominance of Canada's two "founding" cultures (and completely ignoring Native peoples in the process), the Commission also made a series of recommendations on how to foster these "other" cultures. The Liberal government largely followed these recommendations but, instead of adopting the biculturalism policy advanced by the Commission, shifted the focus to official multiculturalism. As Trudeau declared in his speech to the Commons, "although there are two official languages, there is no official culture, nor does any ethnic group take precedence over any other."[14]

What motivated this shift? Political scientist Kenneth McRoberts argues that the adoption of multiculturalism was a deliberate rejection of the Royal Commission's emphasis on cultural dualism, which Trudeau feared could threaten national unity by encouraging Quebec nationalism.[15] Indeed, many Quebec commentators, from the 1970s to today, present multiculturalism as above all an attack on Quebec itself, reducing it to just another minority culture.[16] Other analysts downplay the importance of the Quebec question and emphasize instead the political activism of minority ethnic groups.[17] Right from the establishment of the Royal Commission in 1963, elites from these groups feared that the official entrenchment of bilingualism and biculturalism would permanently mark them as second-class citizens. They pushed instead for recognition of Canada as a "multicultural" nation, a term they coined in the early 1960s. Given their increasing political assertiveness, and the desire of the Liberals to attract their votes, Trudeau conceded official multiculturalism, which also helped them swallow the pill of official bilingualism introduced by the 1969 Official Languages Act.

The role of minority groups in fostering the policy of multiculturalism has been the subject of much scholarly discussion. While multiculturalism is often associated with immigration, analysts have underscored that the initial political pressure for multiculturalism came essentially from long-established "white ethnic" groups, such as Ukrainians, who were mostly made up of people born in Canada. Raymond Breton disputes the extent to which even those communities uniformly pushed for multiculturalism, noting that there was relatively little grassroots mobilization in favour of the policy, while C.P. Champion suggests that even among "ethnic" elites, many supported the British conception of Canada that multiculturalism was supposed to combat.[18]

Recently, historians have also been exploring in more detail the racial underpinnings of the policy of multiculturalism. Historian Aya Fujiwara shows that Ukrainian and Japanese ethnic elites were both active in promoting their respective identities and preparing the ground for Canada's shift to multiculturalism in the decades before 1971. It was nevertheless the Ukrainian view of multiculturalism that had by far the greatest influence over government policy in the 1960s, due in part to their presence in influential political institutions such as the Senate, while the Japanese were marginalized based on their race. Sunera Thobani goes further, and suggests that the official policy of multiculturalism was an adroit response to the "international crisis of whiteness" in the 1960s, when changes in immigration patterns and decolonization movements threatened white supremacy. Multiculturalism allowed white elites in Canada to assuage their guilt over past racism and to present Canada as racially innocent, while at the same time masking the persistence of white privilege and disrupting the contestation of racial hierarchies. Eve Haque emphasizes how Native groups tried to participate in the process of shaping the debates on multiculturalism before the Royal Commission on Bilingualism and Biculturalism, and were largely ignored. These critical studies cast the origins of Canadian multiculturalism in a very different light from Will Kymlicka's view of the policy as an essential value stemming from notions of liberal citizenship and minority rights.[19]

There is also little consensus about Trudeau's role. Many of Trudeau's biographers scarcely mention his multiculturalism policy.[20] Others, such as John English, attribute Trudeau's initiation of the policy largely to short-term political motivations and his liberal individualism. Hugh Donald Forbes, in contrast, argues that Trudeau's commitment to multiculturalism had far deeper roots, stretching back to his general criticism of ethnic nationalism in the early 1960s. For him, official multiculturalism was to be the cornerstone of a new, distinctly Canadian form of national identity. While Trudeau's multiculturalist policy appeared to reject Canadian dualism, Eve Haque suggests that "even as Trudeau disavowed the hierarchy of biculturalism, he smuggled it back in by declaring that there were two official languages," and that his policy was still "a white-settler bilingual and bicultural hegemony, which entrenched a racialized, hierarchical framework of difference and belonging."[21] Finally, some analysts downplay Trudeau's role by pushing the roots of Canada's multicultural policy back before the rise of 1960s liberalism. Instead, they see the ground for official multiculturalism being prepared by the Progressive Conservatives under the leadership of John Diefenbaker. Some have even sought its origins in British imperialism.[22] Overall, just like the policy itself, the origin of Canada's policy of multiculturalism continues to generate intense scholarly debate linked directly to differing conceptions of what Canada was, is, and ought to be.

NOTES

1. Eric Sablin, "Rosie the Red Takes Power," in *Saturday Night*, 27 May 2000, http://www.ericsiblin.com/pages/politics/i_rosie.html.

2. The Universal Declaration of Human Rights (http://www.un.org/en/documents/udhr). On human rights in Canada, see Ross Lamberton, *Repression and Resistance: Canadian Human Rights Activists* (Toronto: University of Toronto Press, 2005) and Christopher MacLennan, *Towards the Charter: Canadians and the Demand for a National Bill of Rights, 1929–1960* (Montreal: McGill-Queen's University Press, 2003).

3. Bryan D. Palmer, *Canada's 1960s: The Ironies of Identity in a Rebellious Era* (Toronto: University of Toronto Press, 2009) 3.

4. Douglas Wahlsten, "Leilani Muir Versus the Philosopher King: Eugenics on Trial in Alberta," *Genetica*, 99.2–3 (1997) 185–98.

5. Veronica Strong-Boag, "'Their Side of the Story': Women's Voices from Ontario Suburbs, 1945–1960," in *A Diversity of Women, 1945–1980*, ed. Joy Parr (Toronto: University of Toronto Press, 1995) 53.

6. Denise Chong, *The Concubine's Children: Portrait of a Family Divided* (Toronto: Viking, 1994) 228.

7. Dan Smith, *The Seventh Fire: The Struggle for Aboriginal Government* (Toronto: Key Porter, 1993) 57.

8. Kenneth McRoberts and Dale Posgate, *Quebec: Social Change and Political Crisis*, 2nd ed. (Toronto: McClelland and Stewart, 1980) 53.

9. Myrna Kostash, "Dissing Feminist Sexuality," *Canadian Forum* (September 1996) 16.

10. Marcel Martel, *Not This Time: Canadians, Public Policy, and the Marijuana Question 1961–1975* (Toronto: University of Toronto Press, 2006) 168.

11. Rachel Carson, *Silent Spring* (Boston: Houghton Mifflin, 1962) 244.

12. Reingard M. Nischik, *Engendering Genre: The Works of Margaret Atwood* (Ottawa: University of Ottawa Press, 2009) and Coral Ann Howells, *The Cambridge Companion to Margaret Atwood* (Cambridge: Cambridge University Press, 2006).

13. Len Scher, *The Un-Canadians: True Stories of the Blacklist Era* (Toronto: Lester, 1992) 75–77.

14. John English, *Just Watch Me: The Life of Pierre Elliott Trudeau, vol. 2, 1968–2000* (Toronto: A.A. Knopf Canada, 2009) 145. For the relationship between the Royal Commission and multiculturalism, see Eve Haque, *Multiculturalism Within a Bilingual Framework: Language, Race and Belonging in Canada* (Toronto: University of Toronto Press, 2012) 224, 236.

15. Kenneth McRoberts, *Misconceiving Canada: The Struggle for National Unity* (Toronto: Oxford University Press, 1997) 123–124.

16. For example, Guy Rocher, "*Multiculturalism: The Doubts of a Francophone,*" *Multiculturalism as State Policy: Report of the Second Canadian Conference on Multiculturalism* (Ottawa: Canadian Consultative Council on Multiculturalism, 1976) 47–53; Fernand Dumont, *Raisons communes* (Montreal: Boréal, 1995) 37–39; or Gérard Bouchard, *L'interculturalisme: un point du vue québécois* (Montreal: Boréal, 2012) 93–94.

17. Evelyn Kallen, "Multiculturalism: Ideology, Policy and Reality," *Journal of Canadian Studies* 17, 1 (1982) 53; Michael Temelini, "Multicultural Rights, Multicultural Virtues: A History of Multiculturalism in Canada," *Multiculturalism and the Canadian Constitution,*ed. Stephen Tierney (Vancouver: UBC Press, 2007) 55.

18. Jean Burnet, "Multiculturalism, Immigration and Racism: A Comment on the Canadian Immigration and Population Study," *Canadian Ethnic Studies, 7, 1* (1975) 37; Will Kymlicka, "The Evolving Canadian Experiment with Multiculturalism," *L'Interculturalisme. Dialogue Québec-Europe, Actes du Symposium international sur l'interculturalisme, Montréal, 25–27 mai 2011,* ed. Gérard Bouchard (on line at http://www.symposium-interculturalisme.com); Raymond Breton, "Multiculturalism and Canadian Nation Building," *The Politics of Gender, Ethnicity, and Language in Canada*, ed. Alan Cairns and Cynthia Williams (Toronto: University of Toronto Press, 1986) 27–66; C.P. Champion, *The Strange Demise of British Canada: The Liberals and Canadian Nationalism, 1964–1968* (Montreal: McGill-Queen's University Press, 2010) 138–145.

19. Aya Fujiwara, *Ethnic Elites and Canadian Identity: Japanese, Ukrainians, and Scots, 1919–1971* (Winnipeg: University of Manitoba Press, 2012); Sunera Thobani, *Exalted Subjects: Studies in the Making of Race and Nation in Canada* (Toronto: University of Toronto Press, 2005); Will Kymlicka, *Multicultural Citizenship: A Liberal Theory of Minority Rights* (Toronto: Oxford University Press, 1995).

20. For example, George Radwanski, *Trudeau* (Toronto: Macmillan of Canada, 1978); Richard Gwyn, *The Northern Magus: Pierre Trudeau and Canadians* (Toronto: McClelland & Stewart, 1980); or Stephen Clarkson and Christina McCall, *Trudeau and our Times* (Toronto: McClelland & Stewart, 1990, 1994).

21. English, *Just Watch Me* 142–147; Hugh Donald Forbes, "Trudeau as the First Theorist of Canadian Multiculturalism," *Multiculturalism and the Canadian Constitution*, ed. Stephen Tierney (Vancouver: UBC Press, 2007) 27–42; Haque, *Multiculturalism Within a Bilingual Framework* 224, 236.

22. Champion, *The Strange Demise of British Canada* 27, 145–152; Garth Stevenson, *Building Nations From Diversity: Canadian and American Experience Compared* (Montreal: McGill-Queen's University Press, 2014) 206–215; Peter Henshaw, "John Buchan and the British Imperial Origins of Canadian Multiculturalism," *Canadas of the Mind: The Making and Unmaking of Canadian Nationalisms in the Twentieth Century,* ed. Norman Hillmer and Adam Chapnick (Montreal: McGill-Queen's University Press, 2007) 191–213.

SELECTED READING

Bibby, Reginald W. *Restless Gods: The Renaissance of Religion in Canada.* Toronto: Novalis, 2004

Biron, Michel, François Dumont, and Élisabeth Nardout-Lafarge. *Histoire de la littérature québécoise.* Montreal: Boréal, 2010

Campbell, Lara, Dominique Clément, and Greg Kealey, eds. *Debating Dissent: Canada and the 1960s.* Toronto: University of Toronto Press, 2012

Carstairs, Catherine. *Jailed for Possession: Illegal Drug Use, Regulation, and Power in Canada, 1920–1961.* Toronto: University of Toronto Press, 2006

Charland, Jean-Pierre. *Histoire de l'éducation au Québec: de l'ombre du clocher à l'économie du savoir*. Saint-Laurent: Éditions du Renouveau pédagogique, 2005

Clément, Dominique. *Canada's Rights Revolution: Social Movements and Social Change, 1937–82*. Vancouver: UBC Press, 2008

Cormier, Jeffrey. *The Canadianization Movement: Emergence, Survival, and Success*. Toronto: University of Toronto Press, 2004

Edwardson, Ryan. *Canadian Content: Culture and the Quest for Nationhood*. Toronto: University of Toronto Press, 2008

Fahrni, Magda, and Robert Rutherdale, eds. *Creating Postwar Canada: Community, Diversity, and Dissent, 1945–75*. Vancouver: UBC Press, 2008

Gerson, Carole, and Jacques Michon. *History of the Book in Canada: Volume 3: 1918–1980*. Toronto: University of Toronto Press, 2007

Hamelin, Jean. *Histoire du catholicisme québecois. Volume III: Le XXe siècle. Tome 2: de 1940 à nos jours*. Montreal: Boréal express, 1984

Howell, Colin D. *Blood, Sweat and Cheers: Sport and the Making of Modern Canada*. Toronto: University of Toronto Press, 2001

Iacovetta, Franca. *Gatekeepers: Reshaping Immigrant Lives in Cold War Canada*. Toronto: Between the Lines, 2006

Kinsman, Gary, and Patrizia Gentile. *The Canadian War on Queers: National Security as Sexual Regulation*. Vancouver: UBC Press, 2010

Kuffert, L.B. *A Great Duty: Canadian Responses to Modern Life and Mass Culture in Canada, 1939–1967*. Montreal: McGill-Queen's University Press, 2003

Martel, Marcel. *Not This Time: Canadians, Public Policy, and the Marijuana Question, 1961–1975*. Toronto: University of Toronto Press, 2006

McLaren, Angus, and Arlene Tigar McLaren. *The Bedroom and the State: The Changing Practices and Politics of Contraception and Abortion in Canada, 1880–1997*. Toronto: Oxford University Press, 1997

Monière, Denis, and Florian Sauvageau, eds. *La télévision de Radio-Canada et l'évolution de la conscience politique au Québec*. Québec: Presses de l'Université Laval, 2012

Palmer, Bryan D. *Canada's 1960s: The Ironies of Identity in a Rebellious Era*. Toronto: University of Toronto Press, 2009

Rutherford, Paul. *When Television Was Young: Primetime Canada 1952–1967*. Toronto: University of Toronto Press, 1990

Sewell, John. *The Shape of the Suburbs: Understanding Toronto's Sprawl*. Toronto: University of Toronto Press, 2009

Taylor, C.J. *Negotiating the Past: The Making of Canada's National Historic Parks and Sites*. Montreal: McGill-Queen's University Press, 1990

Vipond, Mary. *The Mass Media in Canada*, 4th ed. Toronto: Lorimer, 2011

Warren, Jean-Philippe. *Une douce anarchie: les années 68 au Québec*. Montreal: Boréal, 2008

For a comprehensive list of readings for topics covered in this chapter, please visit http://pearsoncanada.ca/conrad.

PART V
POST-MODERN CANADA, 1976–2014

If the first three decades after the Second World War were years of bright hope for many Canadians, the quarter-century that followed had more sombre tones. Economic growth and average incomes stalled. In this context, the old liberal consensus cracked and "neo-liberal" perspectives began to dominate Canadian political strategies. Neo-liberal theorists called for a rolling back of the welfare state and a greater reliance on market mechanisms for achieving economic stability. In an era of globalization, it was argued, concern for economic competitiveness took precedence over efforts to improve the lives of disadvantaged members of society. The results of adopting this approach quickly became apparent. The gap between the rich and poor yawned ever wider, and the disparity between have and have-not provinces increased. Not surprisingly, the new direction sparked angry responses as citizens mobilized to demand more socially conscious policies in a period when concerns for social justice and environmental integrity seemed to be in retreat. The dawn of a new millennium only added to the pressures bearing down on people everywhere. With attacks by Muslim extremists, climate change, economic instability, and pandemics dominating the headlines, Canadians entered a new age of anxiety from which there seemed to be no escape.

CHAPTER 15
CANADA IN THE GLOBAL ECONOMIC VILLAGE, 1976–1999

In 1993, Canadian general Roméo Dallaire was named force commander of the United Nations Assistance Mission for Rwanda (UNAMIR). His assignment was to persuade the combatants to honour their pledges to accept a peace agreement. When it became clear that one side of the agreement, led by Hutu extremists, planned to slaughter the Tutsi minority in Rwanda, he tried to convince the United Nations to send the military support necessary to prevent genocide, but American and French delegates blocked this measure. Although he saved as many lives as he could, Dallaire witnessed the death of 800 000 Tutsis and Hutu moderates before the Tutsi-led armed opposition managed to overpower government forces. "What I have come to realize as the root of it all," he later wrote, "is the fundamental

The Roméo Dallaire Foundation sponsored a conference in May 2014 to mark the twentieth anniversary of the Rwandan genocide. Dallaire appears here with other participants in the conference. SOURCE: ROMÉO DALLAIRE FOUNDATION

indifference of the world community to the plight of seven to eight million black Africans in a tiny country that had no strategic or resource value to any world power."[1]

Dallaire's painful awakening to the greed and callousness that underlay the foreign policies of most Western nations prompted him to call into question their claims to be promoting democracy and human rights. It also showed Canada at its finest in international affairs. Alone among developed nations, Canada agreed to send reinforcements to UNAMIR once the slaughter had begun in April 1994. But Rwanda was an exception. Like other nations in this period, the Canadian government largely pursued self-interest on the international stage. In this chapter we explore changing attitudes about Canada's role in the world between 1975 and 1999, and assess the impact of neo-liberal perspectives on the welfare state consensus that prevailed in the first three postwar decades. Several major developments provide a context for discussions of Canadian foreign policy and economic strategies during the last quarter of the twentieth century: the end of the Cold War, an expansion of international trade, and irrefutable evidence that climate change threatened Earth's future.

END OF THE COLD WAR

The Cold War appeared to be a permanent phenomenon in 1975. A Soviet invasion of Afghanistan in 1979 to support a takeover of its government by Communists produced a hostile reaction from Western nations. Canada joined a boycott of the Olympics held in Moscow in 1980, and the Soviets and their allies responded by boycotting the Olympics held in Los Angeles in 1984. Under Ronald Reagan, elected president in 1980, the United States invested billions in new nuclear and conventional arms, and the Soviet Union responded in kind.

But change was in the offing in the Soviet Union. In 1985, the Soviet Communist Party chose Mikhail Gorbachev as the new general secretary, the most powerful position in the USSR. Gorbachev was a reformer who attempted to decentralize political and economic power in his vast country while negotiating peaceful relations with the West. He gradually pulled Soviet troops out of Afghanistan where they and their local allies were being pulverized by Islamic and other resistance forces, backed by the Americans and Saudis. Tensions between the superpowers eased, but centrifugal forces in the Soviet Union and the resistance of

part of the Communist leadership to Gorbachev's reforms resulted in the collapse of the Soviet Union in 1991. The 15 republics of the former superpower became independent countries, most of them interested in closer trade relations with the West. At the same time, the People's Republic of China began supplementing its Communist system with market strategies that included more trade with capitalist countries and a degree of foreign investment.

The dissolution of the Soviet Union and the spread of capitalism in former Communist countries encouraged some Western political theorists to suggest that the "end of history" was at hand. Henceforth, only one economic system would prevail across the world—capitalism—and one political system—liberal democracy. Nation-states would become less important, while a market economy would enrich everyone on a global scale.

Even as such theories were put forward, they were being disproven in practice. New wars, corporate greed, the undemocratic behaviour of many nations, and a continuing discrepancy in the wealth of nations refuted claims that the end of the Cold War would create global prosperity and international harmony. Moreover, there was growing evidence that climate change, exacerbated by the imperatives of economic growth embraced by both sides of the Cold War, had made the status quo unsustainable rather than a model for world development.

NEO-LIBERALISM

By the mid-1970s, escalating oil prices and inflation became the catalyst for new directions in economic policy described as neo-liberalism. Keynesian notions about government spending had prevailed during the prosperous decades following the Second World War, but now they seemed inadequate to meet the challenge of annual government deficits and dwindling corporate profits. Since governments felt compelled to cut corporate taxes and generally resisted significant increases to the individual tax rate, annual deficits—the result of the imbalance between revenues and expenditures—became commonplace. Deficits compounded from year to year created large debt loads that had to be financed through loans from financiers. As a result, an increased portion of state expenditure went simply to repaying debts, leaving even less money to finance social programs. Many people accepted the argument that governments could not go on spending forever without taking their revenues into account. In this context, the view that it was necessary to increase marketplace control over the economy and reverse the extensive state interventionism of the post-1945 period gained growing support. The term "neo-liberalism" was used to describe this perspective because it harkened back to classical liberal economic theory, which regarded state intervention as harmful to the economy.

In this context, the views associated with the American economist Milton Friedman, largely ignored in the immediate postwar period, gradually gained ascendancy among many world leaders. According to Friedman and his followers (sometimes called *monetarists* because of their emphasis on monetary policy), government intervention—deficit financing, tax incentives, and the expansion of the money supply—had led to rigidities and inefficiencies in Western economies. The oil crisis and welfare state spending, they argued, created an imbalance between government revenues and expenditures that forced stark choices. Should governments continue to search for ways to regulate economic activity to benefit both workers and consumers and to redistribute wealth? Or was the public interest better served by governments admitting defeat and surrendering economic power completely to corporate leaders?

The neo-liberal solution was to encourage efficient production to improve the supply of goods and services rather than to stimulate demand through government spending. If governments simply reduced taxes, controlled inflation, and let the private sector adjust to changing economic conditions, the global economy would right itself soon enough. Those who still subscribed to Keynesian economic thinking noted that such policies had been pursued during the Great Depression with disastrous results, but reminders of this kind, voiced eloquently by the Canadian-born Harvard economist John Kenneth Galbraith, were increasingly ignored by political leaders.

Supply-side economics inspired the policies of conservative governments in Great Britain under Margaret Thatcher (1979–1990), in the United States under Ronald Reagan (1981–1988), and in Canada under Brian Mulroney (1984–1993). With their economies experiencing the worst dislocation since the 1930s, these leaders attempted to reduce spending on social programs, privatize government activities, cut taxes, and exercise tighter control over the money supply. They argued that they had no choice in the current economic climate. Critics complained that neo-liberal governments were starving themselves of revenue and following policies that were redistributing wealth in favour of the richest members of society, but they were unable to prevail in a world where national governments were increasingly falling under the spell of global corporate interests.

GLOBALIZATION

By the closing decades of the twentieth century, most people agreed with Canadian communications theorist Marshall McLuhan that human beings were living in a "global village." Events anywhere in the world could be communicated instantaneously through radio, television, and (beginning in 1990) the Internet. Globalization—defined as the compression of time and space through changes in communication technologies—was increasingly manifested in worldwide networks that called into question many of the institutions established in the Industrial Age, including geographically defined nation-states.

The global reach of giant corporations was one of the most obvious manifestations of accelerated globalization. Following the Second World War, Japan built an extremely efficient industrial sector that often produced cheaper and better-quality goods than those produced in North America and Europe. By the 1970s, Japanese radios, televisions, stereo equipment, appliances, computers, and cars were putting North American factories out of business. A close alliance between business and government had promoted Japan's industrial initiatives, and the "Four Tigers" of Asia—Hong Kong, South Korea, Taiwan, and Singapore—soon benefited from similar strategies to make major strides in industrial development.

Their well-being threatened by new competitors, the energy crisis, and the environmental movement, giant corporations in North America and Europe began moving their production facilities to off-shore locations around the world. Developing countries, desperate for capital investment, offered cheap labour, lower taxes, and fewer regulations that would eat into profits. Able to transfer assets instantaneously around the world, these "transnational" corporations could defy attempts by any government to control their activities. It was not long before corporate managers were extracting favourable conditions from the governments of Western nations eager to prevent jobs from being exported to other countries. Corporate taxes were cut, trade union protection reduced, environmental regulations relaxed, and social programs pared back in an effort to convince corporate leaders that they were welcome.

While governments increasingly capitulated to the view that corporations rather than the state should set the rules for the economy, regional trading blocs were created or strengthened in an effort to secure elusive markets. The European Economic Community, created by six western European nations in 1957, expanded to include almost all of western Europe and in the 1990s parts of eastern Europe in what became known as the European Union (EU). Members of the EU were expected to drop all trade barriers against fellow members and collectively determine protectionist trade policies with the rest of the world. Canada was swept up by this movement for freer trade, beginning in the mid-1980s. The spread of free trade seemed a logical consequence of the economic developments in the postwar period that had gradually made transnational corporations more powerful than most nation-states.

When a recession began in late 1981, corporations undertook a massive program of "restructuring" for a leaner and meaner global economy. Automating production processes, reducing the number of workers, and offering a more flexible response to changing market conditions, it was argued, would allow the fittest to survive and triumph. A wave of mergers and takeovers followed, which further concentrated economic power. By 1986, 32 families and nine corporate conglomerates controlled more than a third of Canada's non-financial assets.

VOICES FROM THE PAST
A Family's Story of Life under Neo-Liberalism

Take away the "nanny state," argued neo-liberals, and families would become more self-reliant. The experience of real families suggested more complicated results when services were cut to the neediest citizens. Sociologist Kate Bezanson traced the stories of Ontario residents affected by the deep cuts made by the provincial government of Mike Harris in Ontario in the second half of the 1990s, cuts that were paralleled in several provinces where elected governments were particularly committed to neo-liberal ideas.

Here is what Anne told Kate Bezanson. Anne was a single mother of four young children in southeastern Ontario. Her family was affected by cuts in medical care and social services, special education, and social assistance rates. Three of her children had severe asthma requiring considerable medication and daily use of ventilators for 40 minutes; one had a bowel disorder as well, and three had attention deficit disorder. Cuts in medical care and social services made it difficult for Anne to get appointments for her children and herself. Some of the asthma medications were no longer covered by the provincial drug benefit plan for social assistance recipients. Anne waited months for her seven-year-old's learning disability to be diagnosed. Meanwhile, he was frustrated and refused to go to school.

Reductions in social assistance rates and medical coverage meant that Anne had to rely on food banks, but several times the family all became ill from the food bank fare. She pawned goods and considered returning to her abusive spouse. Her stress levels increased and her health deteriorated. She did, however, manage to get help from a psychologist for herself and counsellors for her children. Anne budgeted carefully and worked part-time at a retail store to make up for the drop in the handicapped payment she received for her children, from $650 a month to $350.

Although Anne's husband dodged child support, he moved into her place to look after their children when she was hospitalized. Somebody reported her to the mother's allowance hotline, established to snitch on women who violated the man-in-the-house rule (the assumption in the implementation of social assistance that a woman who had sex with a man should be able to get him to pay the major costs of supporting her children and herself). In 1998, Children's Aid agreed to provide her family with a worker for 10 hours a week to help with homework and child care. By then, two of the children had developed serious behavioural problems and one had to be placed in a treatment home the following year.

Commenting on Anne's experiences, Bezanson notes: "Anne's coping strategies—her budgeting, receipt keeping, and tracking of multiple costs and payments—took an enormous amount of time. Staff turnover and lack of response on the part of social service workers intensified her workload. The work of social reproduction in Anne's case expanded, not just because of income fluctuations, but because of fluctuations in formal and informal supports and the amount of unpaid work time it took to coordinate and ensure support."[2]

In the late 1970s, as inflation raged, women workers, even in manufacturing industries, remained poorly paid relative to men. Some, like the women who made automotive wiring for Fleck Manufacturing in Centralia, Ontario, responded by joining unions. In March 1978, 146 women at the Fleck plant, members of the United Auto Workers, went on strike. The strike lasted five months and included large solidarity demonstrations by Ontario unions as well as police intervention and many arrests. In the end, the women, who were paid $2.65 an hour when the strike began, won a 20 cents an hour increase as well as union security. SOURCE: SCHUSTER GINDIN, IN SAM GINDIN, *The Canadian Auto Workers: The Birth and Transformation of a Union* (TORONTO: LORIMER, 1995), CHAPTER 7

FREE TRADE AGREEMENTS

Neo-liberal thinking gradually became the framework for Canadian public policy. In 1982, with the country mired in recession, Prime Minister Pierre Elliott Trudeau appointed a Royal Commission on the Economic Union and Development Prospects for Canada, chaired by Donald Macdonald, a former Liberal finance minister. The commission's report, released in September 1985, argued that Canada had to develop a more flexible economy, capable of adjusting to global economic change and new technologies. Market mechanisms, rather than government intervention, the report maintained, provided the best means of ensuring a vibrant Canadian economy.

To that end, free trade with the United States offered the only hope for continued economic prosperity.

The commission marshalled a broad array of evidence to support free trade. Despite attempts to pursue a "third option" of more diversified trade, especially through an arrangement with the European trading bloc, Canada's dependency on the United States had actually increased in the previous decade. More than three-quarters of Canada's exports were sold to the United States, and half of that trade was between the parent companies and branch plants of multinational corporations. With more than a third of their gross national product (GNP) derived from foreign trade, Canadians would experience a crisis of unthinkable proportions if the flow of goods across the Canada–United States border was disrupted. The time had come, the commissioners claimed, to shake up the industries that remained sheltered behind the old National Policy and lay the foundations for a New Age economy that would serve Canadians in the twenty-first century.

When he campaigned in the federal election of 1984, Brian Mulroney claimed to be opposed to free trade between Canada and the United States. That issue, he suggested, had been settled in the federal election of 1911. Indeed, when he was running for leadership of the Progressive Conservative Party in 1983, Mulroney warned: "Free Trade with the United States would be like sleeping with an elephant. If it rolls over, you're a dead man. And I'll tell you when it's going to roll over. It's going to roll over in a time of economic depression and they're going to crank up those plants in Georgia and North Carolina and Ohio, and they're going to be shutting them down up here."[3]

Ignoring such bold pre-election statements, Mulroney followed the advice of the Macdonald commission and initiated trade negotiations with the United States. The Mulroney government had powerful backers in taking this step. Founded in 1976, the Business Council on National Issues, an organization comprising the chief executive officers of 150 leading Canadian corporations, most of them multinationals, was fully committed to free trade. The venerable Canadian Manufacturers Association, once the bulwark of the protectionist National Policy, came on side. So did the Canadian Federation of Independent Business, which represented the right wing within the increasingly powerful small business community in Canada.

The details of the Free Trade Agreement were ironed out in the fall of 1987. Canada's chief negotiator, along with Trade Minister Pat Carney, was Simon Reisman, a career civil servant who had been instrumental in negotiating the 1965 Auto Pact. Tariffs on primary and manufactured goods would be eliminated over a 10-year period and free trade in services would gradually be introduced. Most non-tariff barriers to trade, such as quotas and content regulations, were also slated for elimination. Following a year of heated debate, Mulroney called an election on 25 November 1988 after the Liberal majority in the Senate made clear their unwillingness to ratify the Free Trade Agreement before the government had received an electoral mandate for its implementation. Leaders of the New Democratic Party (NDP), labour unions, feminists, some church groups, and a variety of nationalist coalitions opposed free trade in principle, while the Liberal Party, which waffled about the concept, rejected features of the actual proposal.

Opponents of the Free Trade Agreement justified their stand by maintaining that it would allow multinational corporations to consolidate their North American operations in locations with better climates and lower wage levels than those prevailing in Canada. Jobs would be lost in the goods-producing sectors, and the wages of those remaining in the labour force would be substantially reduced. Moreover, they argued, Canada's cultural industries would be threatened and Canadians would be forced to tailor their welfare, environmental, and regional development policies to "harmonize" with the goals of the larger economic partner. Under such pressure, Canada as a nation would surely fall apart. Economic nationalists asserted that such a comprehensive trade agreement was unnecessary. Since American industry did not want to lose Canadian resources and markets, it was unlikely that the United States would suddenly pull the plug on trade with Canada.

Mulroney maintained that the agreement merely furthered the work of the General Agreement on Tariffs and Trade (GATT), which had effectively removed tariffs on 80 percent of all goods produced in Canada. Although the government's ability to levy tariffs to protect industries would gradually disappear, he claimed that the opening of the American market to more Canadian-produced goods and services would, overall, benefit workers in the manufacturing and service sectors. He argued that Canadian sovereignty was not threatened by the agreement, and accused his opponents of "scare-mongering" when they suggested that old-age pensions or Medicare might be undermined by free trade. Since the details on which subsidies would constitute unfair trade practices had yet to be negotiated, opponents of the agreement were left with little evidence to back up their claims that government policies in everything from agriculture to regional development might be undermined.

If the 1988 election is taken as a referendum on the issue of free trade, its opponents won, since the Liberals and New Democrats together received more than 52 percent of the total votes cast. Supporters of the agreement, that is the Progressive Conservatives and the fledgling Reform Party, won about 46 percent of the vote, with the remaining vote going to parties whose campaigns were focused mainly on other issues. But elections in Canada do not take the form of a referendum. The Liberals and New Democrats split the votes of opponents of the Free Trade Agreement, while the Progressive Conservatives won most of the votes of free-trade supporters. The large plurality of Progressive Conservative voters returned a second Mulroney majority government. By the end of 1988, the Free Trade Agreement had been approved by both the Commons and the Senate and went into effect on 1 January 1989. Canada was entering a new economic era.

BIOGRAPHY
Mel Hurtig: A Champion of Canadian Independence

Mel Hurtig, a successful Canadian entrepreneur, was one of the leading opponents of the Free Trade Agreement of 1988. In the years that followed, he documented the agreement's negative impact on the Canadian economy and attempted in vain to lead a political struggle to force the Canadian government to tear it up.

SOURCE: MEL HURTIG

Like many of the entrepreneurs who demurred from Canadian industry's support of free trade, Hurtig's investments had mainly been in Canadian cultural enterprises. Born and raised in a Jewish family of furriers in Edmonton in 1932, Hurtig opened Hurtig Books, the city's first independent bookstore, in 1956 and used it as a showcase for emerging Canadian novelists, playwrights, and poets. He later opened two more bookstores on the Prairies, selling all three of his stores in 1972 with a plan to start his own publishing house. Hurtig Publishers had produced more than 200 titles before Hurtig sold his list to McClelland & Stewart in 1991 so that he could devote his time to writing his own books.

Hurtig's great accomplishment as a publisher was *The Canadian Encyclopedia*, which appeared in 1985. He needed about $10 million for the task, but was rebuffed by the Canada Council when he approached them in 1975. He had more luck when he turned to Premier Peter Lougheed. Although Lougheed disagreed with Hurtig's opposition to

foreign ownership and, as a Progressive Conservative, was hardly impressed by Hurtig's run for the federal Liberals in the 1972 election, he paid the costs of research for the encyclopedia ($3.4 million) and of distributing one free copy to every school and library in Canada. Using money from a fund that had been established to celebrate Alberta's 75th year in Confederation in 1980, Lougheed announced that the encyclopedia was Alberta's gift to Canada. For Hurtig, it was a labour of love. When it appeared in 1985, it included three volumes and more than 2000 pages in a comprehensive effort to explore Canadian society and history.

Hurtig's deep attachment to Canadian cultural development and independence from the American goliath led him to become a founding member of the Committee for an Independent Canada in 1973. The CIC had disbanded by the time the Mulroney government began to tout free trade, so Hurtig helped to establish the Council of Canadians in 1985 as a vehicle to oppose North American economic integration. Frustrated that both the Liberals and the NDP had toned down their earlier promises to cancel the Free Trade Agreement if they formed the government, Hurtig founded and led a new party in 1992, the National Party. Neither his party nor the free-trade issue played a prominent role in the 1993 federal election.

The Betrayal of Canada, Hurtig's first book, appeared in 1992. It provided a passionate dissection of the harm that the author believed the FTA had done to both Canadians and to the country's future. It was the bestselling non-fiction book in Canada that year. In the book, Hurtig argued that the agreement had already brought "a big decline in the standard of living of Canadians," and predicted that "the future will be much worse . . . the destruction and disappearance of our country."[4]

Hurtig continued to chronicle the impact of free trade in the years that followed. In 2008, he published *The Truth About Canada,* a scathing account of how Canadian values had changed in the years following the signing of the FTA. Linking foreign investment, business opposition to redistribution of wealth through taxation, and growing poverty and exclusion in Canada, he compared Canada before and after free trade, and also compared Canada on a range of issues of social justice with other industrialized countries. Overall, he argued, other than the United States, Canada had become one of the least caring countries in the developed world.[5]

Pat Carney: A Champion of the American Market

Pat Carney leads British Prime Minister Margaret Thatcher through the Plaza of Nations at Expo 86 in Vancouver, 12 July, 1986. SOURCE: CHUCK STOODY/CP IMAGES

Pat Carney was the first woman to hold major economic portfolios in a Canadian federal cabinet. Between 1984 and 1988, she served as minister of Energy, Mines, and Resources, minister of International Trade, and president of the Treasury Board. As minister of International Trade, she was responsible for negotiating the Free Trade Agreement with the United States.

Carney was a successful entrepreneur and, like many entrepreneurs who actively promoted free trade with the United States, she had been involved with export industries, in her case oil and gas. She was born in 1935 in Shanghai, China; her father and mother were, respectively, a policeman and a writer. They moved to the Kootenays in British Columbia when Carney was four. As an undergraduate student at the University of British Columbia, she graduated in 1960 with a degree in economics and political science. She became one of Canada's first female business journalists, working for the two Southam newspapers in Vancouver.

In 1970, Carney moved to Yellowknife where she established an economic consultancy and public relations firm that she called Gemini North. She developed many contacts in the oil and gas industry, and received contracts to create support for a gas pipeline along the Mackenzie River Valley. Although the Berger report of 1977 stalled development of the pipeline, Carney developed a reputation as a knowledgeable supporter of business interests in the North. She also completed an MA in regional planning at UBC during the 1970s.

Carney was elected as MP for Vancouver Centre in 1980, and four years later, she was named to Mulroney's cabinet. Her appointment as minister of international trade in 1986 came as little surprise since she vigorously defended free trade as the way to stop the American government practice of imposing penalties on British Columbia's softwood lumber exporters. She had developed a reputation for being both articulate and tough in dealing with her political opponents. Carney locked horns with Simon Reisman, Canada's chief negotiator for the FTA, whom she accused of failing to inform her of the state of negotiations. At one point she even offered Prime Minister Mulroney her resignation if the government failed to give her a greater role in negotiations. It did, but Carney decided nonetheless not to run in the 1988 election, and to return to media work.

While Carney was a neo-liberal and free trader who believed that governments over-regulated businesses and thereby stifled entrepreneurship, she was not a social conservative. She supported greater gender equality, and, when she presided over the Treasury Board, she appointed a Task Force on Barriers to Women in the Public Service. Carney also supported reproductive choice. Appointed to the Senate in 1990, she defied the government that had appointed her by voting against their compromise bill on abortion because it placed restrictions on a woman's right to an abortion.

When she stepped down from the Senate in 2007, Carney claimed that free trade with the Americans had proved a success, though she admitted there had been "costs." She took little personal credit for the successes. "The real heroes and heroines of the free trade agreement are those Canadian businessmen and women who took the opportunity to access the huge U.S. market, to the benefit of millions of Canadians. Governments can only provide the framework. Canadians themselves earned the benefits and paid the costs."[6]

THE FREE TRADE ERA

The ink was barely dry on the Free Trade Agreement when many firms, beginning with Gillette, announced that they were closing all or part of their Canadian operations and centralizing their manufacturing in the United States. In every case, they insisted that their plans to vacate Canada were unrelated to the agreement and had been in place prior to its enactment. After 1 January 1989, they could move without fear that Canada would use tariff or non-tariff barriers to restrict their penetration of Canadian markets. Supporters of free trade minimized the importance of the exodus, arguing that tariffs encouraged non-competitive operations with the limited horizon of a domestic market. Canadians, they argued, should turn the companies that survived the restructuring into world-class firms with markets around the globe. Meanwhile, company executives began to renege on their claims that free trade would do little to jeopardize Canadian welfare and environmental programs. Instead they argued that welfare measures and state interventionism more generally were obstacles to attracting and retaining corporate investment.

MORE TO THE STORY
Massey-Harris

The agricultural machinery company founded in 1847 by Daniel Massey went from strength to strength in the late nineteenth and early twentieth centuries. The company moved from Newcastle to Toronto in 1855, and in 1891 merged with its chief competitor to become Massey-Harris, the largest company of its kind in the British Empire. By the first decade of the twentieth century, it had captured a huge share of the rapidly expanding Prairie market for farm machinery and had established branch operations in the United States. When the company ran into difficulties following the Second World War, it was reorganized under the direction of its holding company, Argus Corporation, and continued to prosper. As Massey-Ferguson, it developed a global market and reached annual sales of more than $1 billion in the 1960s.

In the difficult economic climate of the late 1970s, Massey's fortunes again began to slip. Conrad Black, the ambitious young head of Argus, became chair of the troubled company in 1978, but the bottom fell out of the farm machinery market in 1980 and Argus wrote off its Massey-Ferguson shares as worthless. In an effort to save the capital and jobs that Massey represented, banks, governments, and shareholders poured $1.2 billion into the failing firm between 1978 and 1984. By 1987, when Massey-Ferguson changed its name to Varity Corp. (after the Varity Plough Company, which had been acquired in 1892), it was a third of its former size, but nonetheless ranked as the 49th largest firm in Canada with sales and operating revenue of $1.8 billion. Following the signing of the Free Trade Agreement, it moved its head office to the United States.[7]

A deep recession gripped Canada in 1990. Although it affected all Western nations, the recession was more severe in Canada than in most other countries, lasting for three years and followed by a "jobless recovery." Mel Hurtig claimed in *The Betrayal of Canada* (1992) that, in its first two years, the Free Trade Agreement was responsible for the loss of 264 000 manufacturing jobs as branch plants closed and new operations were located in the United States and elsewhere. Supporters of the agreement accused the nationalists of blaming free trade for job losses that

In his 1992 cartoon "Oh please, Oh please," cartoonist Bruce MacKinnon offers an Atlantic Canada perspective on the North American Free Trade Agreement. SOURCE: THE HALIFAX HERALD LIMITED

and vicious form of imperialism that was producing poverty in most countries and creating a race for the bottom in such areas as environmental standards and working conditions.

This view appeared to be confirmed by the creation in 1995 of the World Trade Organization (WTO), whose mission was to break down barriers to transnational trade. When the WTO met in Seattle in 1999, well-orchestrated protests publicized opposition to the brand of globalization endorsed and promoted by the WTO. The Canadian government was represented at the official WTO meetings, while other Canadians were among the tens of thousands in Seattle protesting against what they regarded as the undemocratic activities of the governments and corporations that ran the WTO. In the years following the Seattle confrontation, huge demonstrations and street theatre continued to greet meetings of international trade and finance organizations, though the media tended to trivialize the opposition by focusing on a small subset of anarchists who glorified violence in their attack against the kingpins of the new global order.

were purely the result of the recession. Even without free trade, they argued, Canadians would have been victims of the restructuring and downsizing policies that were now part of global economic strategies. They had their own statistics to throw at the doomsayers, including a 16 percent increase in the volume of Canadian exports between 1989 and 1992, the continued success of the government in fighting inflation, and the drop in the value of the Canadian dollar, all of which suggested that the Canadian economy was making the necessary adjustments to survive in an increasingly competitive economic environment. Those supporting the global movement for free trade had further cause for celebration when Mexico joined the United States and Canada as a partner in the North American Free Trade Agreement (NAFTA) of 1992.

By the end of the century, an equally global movement had developed that called into question the type of globalization being imposed on nation-states. Its leaders argued that there was no reason why globalization should be controlled exclusively by transnational corporations and by the governments of a few wealthy nations, led by the United States. Such an approach was nothing more than a new

Demonstrations against the free trade version of globalization became common after the Seattle demonstration of 1999. Two years later, tens of thousands demonstrated in Quebec City as the Summit of the Americas proposed erasing economic borders within North and South America. Here, protesters dismantle the chain-link fence with which police had ringed the Old City. SOURCE: TOM HANSON/CP IMAGES

THE JOBLESS RECOVERY

Although moderate economic growth had succeeded the recession, Canada, like many Western nations, could not find work for about a tenth of its labour force. Profitable businesses such as major banks, the energy giants, and Bell Canada joined less successful employers and governments in reducing their workforces. Business leaders justified cutbacks by asserting that trade liberalization was forcing companies to be more competitive. That meant mergers, factory shutdowns, and the introduction of technology, particularly computers, all of which reduced the economy's demand for human labour. Robots began to replace assembly-line workers; traditional "women's jobs" vanished as electronic communications did the work formerly performed by secretaries; and automated banking reduced the need for tellers. The unemployed remained out of work for longer periods of time than had their counterparts even a decade earlier.

Between 1990 and 1998, the after-tax income of Canadian families fell seven percent in constant dollars. The majority of households still had a comfortable income, but a growing number of Canadians were living below the poverty line as the recessions of the early 1980s and early 1990s took their toll. While 3.5 million Canadians were classified as poor in 1987, an additional 1.4 million impoverished Canadians were added just six years later. About 1.4 million children under the age of 18 were among the poor in 1993, representing 21 percent of all Canadian children. Sixty percent of poor children lived in homes headed by single mothers, whose ability to find work or daycare, never mind both, had been undermined first by the recession and then by the jobless recovery.

Women's labour-force participation nonetheless continued to rise. By 1994, women made up 45 percent of the workforce, an increase of eight percent from 1976. Fewer women believed it was either desirable or likely that they could depend entirely on the income of a man to maintain them and their children. Men's wages and job security, meanwhile, were on the decline, making it imperative in most families for women to seek paid work. Although women increasingly unionized and fought successfully for better wages, there was still a considerable degree of inequality in income. In 1994, women working full-time earned 72 percent of the incomes of men working the same number of hours. Far more women than men were trapped in part-time work, with the result that women's incomes overall were only 58 percent of men's.

Apart from gender, colour was a factor in labour-force earnings. Members of visible minorities earned 30 percent less than other Canadians in the labour force in 1998, with African-Canadian males and most Aboriginal peoples encountering the greatest income disparities. Ultimately, the so-called "new world order" redistributed wealth in favour of the rich. In 1973, the wealthiest 10 percent of families in Canada had 6.77 times the income of the poorest 10 percent after the impact of taxes and social transfers was factored in. The comparable figure in 1998 was 7.24 percent.

INFLATION VERSUS UNEMPLOYMENT

Federal economic policies, both under the Progressive Conservatives and their Liberal successors, elected in 1993, continued to emphasize the battle against inflation and government debt rather than the battle against unemployment. Yet high unemployment drained the federal treasury as unemployment insurance and social assistance costs mounted and revenue from the income taxes paid by working people decreased.

Jean Chrétien's Liberals hinted in the 1993 election that there might be some return to employment creation as a priority, but shortly after the election, Finance Minister Paul Martin, a leading member of the corporate community, made clear that the new government would follow substantially the same financial policies as its predecessor. Social programs would be cut and the Bank of Canada's monetary policies would not be fundamentally altered. Unemployment insurance, rather than unemployment, became a target of government policy. It was made much harder to get, and in 1997–1998 only a third of the unemployed received what was now called "employment insurance" versus 80 percent in 1990–1991.

Young people were disproportionately the victims of the new unemployment. In an economy that was producing few new jobs, experienced workers were favoured over newcomers, making it difficult for young people to get a start in the labour market. In contrast to the generation of the 1960s, young people in the 1990s were unlikely to find well-paying manufacturing jobs after high school. They were in a somewhat better position to find employment if they had post-secondary education, but even this achievement provided no guarantee. Life-long employment with a single company became

MORE TO THE STORY

MORE TO THE STORY
Research Institutes: A New World of Corporate "Spin"

From 1945 to 1975, as the interventionist state grew in Canada, business interests attempted to shape public opinion against expensive social programs, corporate taxes, and state regulation of industry through campaigns by traditional business organizations such as the Canadian Chamber of Commerce and the Canadian Manufacturers Association. They had little success in swaying public opinion. A survey presented to the 1965 Canadian Chamber of Commerce convention suggested that most people discounted what business organizations had to say as self-interested propaganda.

Gradually, the leaders of large corporations in Canada began following their American and British counterparts in establishing allegedly non-partisan, non-profit "research institutes" and "think tanks" to conduct and disseminate research meant to create public support for state policies that corresponded with the corporate agenda. Such efforts began modestly with the creation of the National Citizens Coalition (NCC) in 1967 by Colin M. Brown, a London Life insurance agent who opposed universal medical insurance. The NCC was incorporated in Ontario in 1975 and expanded its focus to include campaigns against many government programs and unions. Between 1998 and 2002, Stephen Harper, who later became prime minister, was president of the NCC.

While the NCC focused primarily on political campaigns, the Fraser Institute, founded in Vancouver in 1974, styled itself as an independent research group with a focus on market-oriented solutions to social issues. Its founder, Michael Walker, an economist at the University of Western Ontario, received financial support from MacMillan-Bloedel, the forestry giant, which was at loggerheads with British Columbia's NDP government from 1972 to 1975. Walker claimed that the Fraser Institute, as a non-profit research organization, was controlled by its staff and not its funders. In practice, its well-paid staff knew that their research results had to conform to the funders' interests. The organization received charitable status, making contributions to its work tax-free. In 1975, the Institute generated

revenues of $421 389, which would explode to almost $11 million by 2010.

The Fraser Institute published studies of its research results along with a monthly magazine and a bi-monthly newsletter. It also sponsored student essay contests, held seminars for students, and created internships. Most importantly, it created close relationships with the media, which often published the Institute's results without raising issues about its funders or underlying ideology, and without reporting the views of scholars or public figures who took issue with the Fraser Institute's assumptions and research methodologies.

Before long, the Fraser Institute inspired copycats. The Montreal Economic Institute was founded in 1987, followed by the Canadian Taxpayers Foundation in 1990, the Atlantic Institute for Market Studies in 1995, and the Frontier Centre for Public Policy, a Prairies grouping, in 1997. The C.D. Howe Institute, which had its origins in the work of the C.D. Howe Memorial Foundation, became an independent organization in 1982, with funding from major corporations and investors. The previous year, the Conference Board of Canada emerged from its former incarnation as a wing of an American business think tank, and by the early 2000s employed about 200 people. Each of these organizations had public relations departments that made use of sophisticated communications techniques to shape public opinion. Supporters and detractors alike credited the seemingly objective corporate-sponsored research institutes for a major shift in public attitudes regarding the relative roles of government and the private sector. They also played an important role in encouraging support for free trade.

Opponents of neo-liberalism, particularly in the labour movement, funded competing research institutes such as the Canadian Centre for Policy Alternatives, which began work in Ottawa in 1980, and Alberta's Parkland Institute, founded in 1997. These organizations had modest funding relative to their corporate counterparts and far less coverage for their findings in the corporate-controlled media.[8]

increasingly uncommon, and young workers often had to be content with short-term contracts followed by new intensive job searches.

"McJobs" in the service industry appeared to be the fate of large numbers of people in their twenties, even if they had excellent qualifications for professional employment.

While some young people beat the odds and either found good jobs in the profession for which they had trained or created their own fortunes through entrepreneurial ventures, it was clear that opportunities were limited. The term "Generation X" entered the language to denote a generation of young people who some pessimists suggested could only live well if they remained in their parents' homes throughout their adult lives. In 1995, despite a large decline in the labour participation rate of young people owing to longer periods of study, fully 20 percent of those between the ages of 15 and 25 who were out of school and actively seeking work could not find even part-time jobs. The rate for high school graduates was the same as for dropouts.

AN ECONOMIC TURNAROUND

As the new millennium approached, rates of economic growth picked up, government deficits began to fall, and the federal and most provincial governments were well on their way to becoming deficit-free and making some progress in paying off their accumulated debts. With federal surpluses piling up by the end of 1999, the policy focus of high income earners became tax reduction. Neo-liberals claimed that high taxes penalized entrepreneurship, blunted innovation, and threatened Canada's ability to compete in a globalized environment.

The turnaround at the end of the twentieth century was due to a robust export trade, most of it the result of a booming American economy and its demand for Canada's primary resources. Increases in resource prices, particularly for energy, fish, forest products, and minerals, were only part of the story. Canada's high-technology sectors, especially transportation and communications, were winning large contracts abroad. Bombardier of Valcourt, Quebec, was a prime example. Before the 1970s, Bombardier had both Canadian and international markets for its recreational equipment, led by snowmobiles. By the 1990s, it had established itself firmly as an international player in the aerospace, defence, and mass transit sectors. In the latter, it had large contracts in Turkey, New York, Malaysia, and Germany. With production facilities in 19 countries, Bombardier seemed the picture postcard for those arguing that Canada was a net beneficiary of globalization. Various federal and Quebec industry grant programs quietly aided this allegedly private-enterprise success story.

Canada's telecommunications sector, and especially firms like Nortel, benefited from the communications revolution that was epitomized by the rapid development of the Internet and more especially the World Wide Web. The Web, which had become part of everyday life for many Canadians by the end of the millennium, had begun in 1990 as a project in a physics laboratory in Geneva, Switzerland. Two computer scientists combined the concepts of the "Internet" and hypertext to revolutionize communications with a new system of information storage and exchange. Soon governments, including Canada's, were talking about an "information highway" that would connect all citizens, and corporations were using "the net" to lure new customers for everything from books to stocks. While Canadians initially proved less willing than Americans to use the Internet for more than retrieval of information, the Web was touted as the wave of the future for everything from receiving information from governments to buying groceries.

THE ENVIRONMENT

While economists and politicians debated the best ways to achieve economic growth, environmentalists began sounding the alarm. Disasters such as those that occurred at Three Mile Island in Pennsylvania (1979), Bhopal, India (1984), and Chernobyl, Ukraine (1986) underscored the difficulty of controlling technology. "Acid rain," produced by sulphur dioxide and nitrogen dioxide mixing with natural moisture, imperilled nature, humans, and buildings alike. The destruction of the ozone layer by chlorofluorocarbons (CFCs), used in aerosols, foam insulation, and super-cleaners for electronic equipment, and the rapid disappearance of tropical rain forests caused further deterioration of the atmosphere. Although the major world powers reduced their stocks of nuclear weapons in the aftermath of the Cold War, the weapons that remained were capable of wreaking irreparable environmental damage.

In 1987, a United Nations World Commission on Environment and Development, chaired by Norwegian politician Gro Harlem Brundtland, published a report (*Our Common Future*) calling for a global strategy of sustainable development rather than growth at all costs. The following year, an Intergovernmental Panel on Climate Change (IPCC) was formed by two United Nations bodies: the World Meteorological Organization and the UN Environment Program. It brought together hundreds of scientists to prepare and review the climate data. The IPCC's first report on climate change, issued in 1990, was a sobering document, noting that the burning of fossil fuels, intensive agricultural practices, and deforestation had contributed to dangerous levels of global warming. The panel called for an immediate reduction of 60 percent of long-lived gases such as carbon dioxide, chlorofluoro-carbons, and nitrous oxide to halt a projected rise of world temperatures by three degrees before 2100. A second report by the IPCC in 1995 elaborated on the potential havoc that such a rise in temperatures could have on sea levels, storms, and food supplies.

The Brundtland Report provided the momentum for the Mulroney government to pursue a more ambitious environmental agenda, shaped with the help of environmental activist Elizabeth May. In addition to adopting an Environmental Assessment Act and an Environmental Protection Act, Ottawa signed a bilateral acid rain treaty with the United States, and Canada was the first industrialized country to embrace the Framework Convention on Climate Change and the Convention on Biological Diversity proposed at the United Nations Earth Summit in 1992.

In 1997, the United Nations held a convention on climate change in Kyoto, Japan. It resulted in an "Accord" committing advanced industrial nations to modest reductions in the production of greenhouse gases, the first steps toward the more serious reductions called for by the IPCC. Two hundred and six nations, including Canada, united to produce the Kyoto Accord. Canada agreed to reduce its greenhouse gas emissions by 2012 to six percent less than emissions in 1990. More concerned with economic growth and trade liberalization, the United States refused to endorse the Accord.

The Chrétien government signed the 1997 Kyoto protocol, but Canada's greenhouse gases actually rose in the following decade as economic growth continued to trump efforts to develop a new relationship between people and their planet. Despite some successes, Canada remained a global laggard on environmental policy as the twentieth century ended. A University of Victoria study, using end-of-century data in 25 environmental categories, ranked Canada 28th of the 29 developed countries in the Organisation for Economic Co-operation and Development (OECD). On a per capita basis, only the United States had a worse record.[9]

Ongoing environmental disasters highlighted the growing imbalance of power between big corporations and everyone else. The collapse of East Coast cod stocks in 1992 was dramatic proof of environmentalists' arguments that there were limits to growth. A spate of international conferences resolved little because the governments whose representatives were in attendance refused

Cover of the first report of the Intergovernmental Panel on Climate Change.
SOURCE: INTERGOVERNMENTAL PANEL ON CLIMATE CHANGE

to challenge the power of multinational corporations, which did not attend.

CANADIAN FOREIGN POLICY AND THE ECONOMY

In the late twentieth century, the impact of economic concerns on foreign policy continued to be evident. Arms sales provide an example of economic activities with a foreign-policy overlay. Although Canada proclaimed its support of human rights and peace among nations, it cheerfully sold arms to Iraq and Iran as the two countries waged a territorial war in the 1980s. In 1985, Canada sold $1.9 billion in military supplies, a sixfold increase since 1970. Almost 90 percent of those arms were sold to the United States. The federal government continued to subsidize defence industries, despite studies suggesting that the expenditures would create more jobs in other areas of the economy.

In the 1990s, as the Soviet Union dissolved, it became clear that the end of the Cold War would not necessarily usher in an era of peace. Iraq's invasion of Kuwait, an American ally, in August 1990 marked the first major post–Cold War military conflict. Canada supported a tough United Nations embargo on and then an American invasion of Iraq despite claims by critics that the embargo had not been given a chance to work. The Gulf War was enormously popular in the United States but less so in Canada, particularly in Quebec, where a majority opposed Canadian participation. Nonetheless, Mulroney lent his full support to President George H. W. Bush, extending him a hero's welcome when he visited Ottawa after the war.

Canada's role in peacekeeping remained the aspect of foreign policy that made Canadians proudest. Although only 1149 Canadian military personnel served in United Nations peacekeeping missions in 1991, they accounted for more than 10 percent of all UN peacekeepers in the world. The nation's long record of service in Cyprus and the Middle East drew praise from many quarters of the globe. That record was supplemented by Canada's peacekeeping efforts in the chaotic and dangerous atmosphere of Yugoslavia, which had descended into chaos in 1991, leaving a variety of competing ethnic-based groups to vie for territory in a series of bloody civil wars.

In the post-Cold War era, Canada's image as a peacekeeper began to lose some of its lustre. Missions in Iraq, Somalia, Croatia, and Rwanda proved largely unsuccessful in what had essentially become peacemaking rather than peacekeeping efforts. In 1993, Lieutenant-General Roméo Dallaire lacked the resources to prevent a bloodbath in Rwanda, and the mission to Somalia in the same year was badly tainted by the murder of a young intruder into a Canadian camp, which led to the disbanding of the Canadian Airborne Regiment following a high-profile inquiry.

The neo-liberal context put economic considerations above all others in determining foreign policy, and the replacement of the federal Progressive Conservatives by the Liberals in 1993 did nothing to change that. In the mid-1990s, Prime Minister Chrétien and most of the provincial premiers conducted trade missions in the People's Republic of China, demonstrating an unwillingness to apply more than token pressures on China's government to respect human rights. The government also rejected calls to suspend defence orders for such countries as Turkey, Vietnam, and Thailand because of their questionable

Police used pepper spray to break up demonstrations at the site of the APEC Summit meetings in Vancouver in November 1997. Here, a demonstrator receives help after getting pepper spray in her eyes. SOURCE: DAN LOH/CP IMAGES

human rights records, and was slow to respond to concerns over the use of child labour by some of its Asian trading partners. In 1997, the Canadian government resisted pressures to exclude Indonesia's President Suharto, responsible for the murder of hundreds of thousands of his fellow citizens, from the Asia-Pacific Economic Cooperation (APEC) summit in Vancouver. Outside the meeting of the political and economic leaders of the Pacific Rim countries, protesters denounced Suharto's presence. RCMP officers pepper-sprayed protesters, and evidence suggested that the Prime Minister's Office had directed much of the security strategy for the conference.

Although Canada's overall record in opposing dictators when trade was at stake was spotty, the Progressive Conservative government under Brian Mulroney played a leadership role in boycotting trade with South Africa's apartheid regime. The boycotts precipitated an economic crisis that forced South Africa's whites-only government to negotiate with liberation forces for a transition to a non-racial democracy.

CONCLUSION

In 1975, Canadian nationalists exercised considerable influence on trade and foreign policy issues. That influence was far weaker by the end of the twentieth century. Fear of American economic domination gave way to fear of American protectionism. Efforts to find other markets for Canadian goods or to make the Canadian economy more self-sufficient had been abandoned as unrealistic. The focus on exports and an integrated North American economy had important implications for decision-making about the role of the state in the economy and the welfare of the nation's citizens. Only an intrepid few questioned the long-established view that economic growth was necessary, though a wider dissemination of the science on climate change caused some environmentalists to argue that economic restructuring was necessary to limit or even reverse growth and to better distribute what was produced. The next chapter examines the policy changes that resulted as the neo-liberals increasingly dominated political decision-making.

A HISTORIOGRAPHICAL DEBATE

Was the Free Trade Agreement a Success?

Scholars disagree about whether the Free Trade Agreement with the United States proved beneficial for Canada. While the Mulroney government and much of the Canadian business community argued in 1988 that it would produce more jobs and have no negative impact on social policy, those opposing the agreements predicted dire consequences for workers and Canadian society generally.

Like other scholars who judge the FTA a success, economist Richard Lipsey distances himself from the rosy picture painted during the 1988 election. He suggests that "Prime Minister Mulroney promised 'Jobs jobs and more jobs' in spite of the fact that trade liberalization is about replacing low quality jobs with higher quality ones, not about creating more jobs in total."[10] Worker productivity, Lipsey maintains, increased during the first decade of the agreement, as tariff-protected, labour-intensive companies were gradually replaced with more specialized, capital-intensive operations.

As for the social implications of the FTA, Lipsey is blunt: "an FTA was seen as part of a policy package of liberalising the whole Canadian economy, exposing it more fully to market forces."[11] That included "reforming" unemployment insurance, reducing regional subsidies, and privatizing Crown corporations. In Lipsey's view, all of these reforms, necessitated by the FTA, were beneficial to Canada's long-term productivity and were not an attack on Canada's sovereignty. Because of the restructuring of Canadian industries resulting from the agreement, Lipsey argues, Canada's recovery from the 1990s recession was export-led: Canadian exports expanded from around 25 percent of GDP before the FTA to 40 percent 10 years later. Further, foreign direct investment in Canada increased significantly, while Canadian direct investment in the United States increased only modestly. For the most part, the new disputes mechanism worked and reversed a trend toward penalizing Canadian companies selling in the American marketplace if they had government subsidies by taking into account whether the competing American firms had equivalent or greater subsidies.

Another economist, Daniel Trefler, also sees free trade in a positive light. Commenting after the FTA had been in operation for more than 15 years, he admitted that the workers in formerly tariff-protected industries bore the "short-term adjustment costs" (i.e., they lost their jobs), but suggests that consumers, efficient plants, and the Canadian economy as a whole recorded long-term gains.[12]

Labour economist Andrew Jackson disputes the claims made by Lipsey and Trefler, judging the FTA as a complete failure for Canada and a gift to the United States. Jackson argues that Trefler's calculations of improvements in labour productivity per hour simply disguise the fact that full-time jobs gave way to part-time jobs. Indeed, he argues, productivity per worker barely changed at all. Between 1989 and 1998, Canada's real economic growth averaged only 1.8 percent annually compared to 2.5 percent in the United States. While American unemployment dropped below five percent and most jobs were full-time, Canadian unemployment bolted from 7.5 percent to 11 percent in the early 1990s, and was still eight percent in 1999, with many of the new jobs being part-time. Although the productivity gap in manufacturing between the two countries was expected to close, it actually widened, and the predictions that the FTA would speed up Canada's transition to a knowledge-based economy and bolster development of its capital goods sector, Jackson claims, also proved to have no foundation.[13]

These less-than-impressive trends have not deterred the enthusiasm of most FTA supporters. Instead, political scientist Duncan Cameron argues, they see them as an argument for "deep integration." "Deep integration," Cameron explains, "includes measures in the areas of defence, foreign policy, immigration, human rights, and social policy—as well as trade, investment and industrial and economic policy."[14] Still eager to implement their neo-liberal utopia, supporters of deep integration seek to impose market constraints on all government decisions in an effort to achieve the productivity gains that the FTA promised but failed to deliver.

NOTES

1. Roméo Dallaire, *Shake Hands with the Devil: The Failure of Humanity in Rwanda* (Toronto: Random House, 2003) 6.

2. Kate Bezanson, *Gender, the State, and Social Reproduction: Household Insecurity in Neo-Liberal Times* (Toronto: University of Toronto Press, 2006) 159.

3. Marjorie Griffin Cohen, "The Lunacy of Free Trade: A Look at the Structure of Canada's Economy and International Trade Shows Why Free Trade Can't and Won't Work for Canada," in *Crossing the Line: Canada and Free Trade with Mexico*, ed. Jim Sinclair (Vancouver: New Star, 1992) 16.

4. Mel Hurtig, *The Betrayal of Canada*, rev. ed. (Toronto: Stoddart, 1992) 339.

5. Mel Hurtig provides his autobiography and delineates his nationalist views in *At Twilight in the Country: Memoirs of a Canadian Nationalist* (Toronto: Stoddart, 1996).

6. Canada, *Debates of the Senate (Hansard)*, 22nd Session, 39th Parliament, Vol. 144, Issue 23. On the life of Pat Carney and her views on public issues, see her autobiography, *Trade Secrets: A Memoir* (Toronto: Key Porter Books, 2000).

7. For the history of Massey-Harris and the agricultural implements industry in Canada more generally, see Peter Cook, *Massey at the Brink: The Story of Canada's Greatest Multinational and Its Struggle to Survive* (Toronto: HarperCollins, 1981); Michael Bliss,

Northern Enterprise: Five Centuries of Canadian Business (Toronto: McClelland & Stewart, 1987); and Graham D. Taylor, *The Rise of Canadian Business* (Toronto: Oxford University Press, 2009).

8. On think tanks and research institutes in Canada, see Murray Dobbin, *The Myth of the Good Corporate Citizen: Canada and Democracy in the Age of Globalization* (Toronto: James Lorimer, 2003). Their impact in other countries is explored in Richard Cockett, *Thinking the Unthinkable: Think-tanks and the Economic Counter-Revolution* (London: Fontana, 1995).

9. David R. Boyd, *Unnatural Law: Rethinking Canadian Environmental Law and Policy* (Vancouver: UBC Press, 2003) 6.

10. Richard G. Lipsey, "The Canada–U.S. FTA: Real Results Versus Unreal Expectations," *Free Trade: Risks and Rewards*, ed. L. Ian MacDonald (Montreal and Kingston: McGill-Queen's University Press, 2000) 104.

11. Lipsey, "The Canada–U.S. FTA" 102.

12. Daniel Trefler, "The Long and Short of the Canada–United States Free Trade Agreement," *American Economic Review*, 94 (September 2004) 870–95.

13. Andrew N. Jackson, "From Leaps of Faith to Lapses of Legacy," *Free Trade: Risks and Rewards* 107–17.

14. Duncan Cameron, "Free Trade Allies: The Making of a New Continentalism," *Whose Canada? Continental Integration, Fortress North America, and the Corporate Agenda*, ed. Ricardo Grinspun and Yasmine Shamsie (Montreal and Kingston: McGill-Queen's University Press, 2000) 56.

SELECTED READING

Bashevkin, Sylvia. *Women on the Defensive: Living Through Conservative Times.* Chicago: University of Chicago Press, 1998

Bavington, Dean. *Managed Annihilation: An Unnatural History of the Newfoundland Cod Collapse.* Vancouver: UBC Press, 2010

Brandt, Deborah, ed. *Women Working the NAFTA Food Chain: Women, Food and Globalization.* Toronto: Sumach, 2000

Cameron, Duncan, Daniel Drache, and Mel Watkins, eds. *Canada Under Free Trade.* Toronto: Lorimer, 1993

Chorney, Harold, John Hotson, and Mario Seccarecia. *The Deficit Made Me Do It!* Ottawa: Canadian Centre for Policy Alternatives, 1992

Clarkson, Stephen. *Uncle Sam and Us: Globalization, Neoconservatism, and the Canadian State.* Toronto: University of Toronto Press, 2002

Cohen, Marjorie Griffin. *Free Trade and the Future of Women's Work: Manufacturing and Service Industries.* Toronto: Garamond, 1987

Dallaire, Roméo. *Shake Hands with the Devil: The Failure of Humanity in Rwanda.* Toronto: Random House, 2003

Grinspun, Ricardo and Yasmine Shamsie, eds. *Whose Canada? Continental Integration, Fortress North America, and the Corporate Agenda.* Montreal and Kingston: McGill-Queen's University Press, 2000

Hurtig, Mel. *The Betrayal of Canada*, rev. ed. Toronto: Stoddart, 1992

Inwood, Gregory J. *Continentalizing Canada: The Politics and Legacy of the Macdonald Royal Commission.* Toronto: University of Toronto Press, 2004

Marchak, M. Patricia. *The Integrated Circus: The New Right and the Restructuring of Global Markets.* Montreal: McGill-Queen's University Press, 1991

Panitch, Leo and Samuel Gindin. *The Making of Global Capitalism: The Political Economy of American Empire.* London: Verso, 2013

Robinson, Ian. *North American Trade as if Democracy Mattered: What's Wrong with NAFTA and What Are the Alternatives?* Ottawa: Canadian Centre for Policy Alternatives, 1993

Razack, Sherene. *Dark Threats and White Knights: The Somalia Affair, Peacekeeping and the New Imperialism.* Toronto: University of Toronto Press, 2004

For a comprehensive list of readings for topics covered in this chapter, please visit http://pearsoncanada.ca/conrad.

CHAPTER 16
THE POLITICS OF UNCERTAINTY, 1976–1999

Many Canadians sat glued to their televisions on the evening of 30 October 1995. The previous year, the Parti Québécois, led by Jacques Parizeau, had won the Quebec election and proceeded with a promised second referendum on sovereignty. As the sovereignty option gained momentum, Prime Minister Jean Chrétien made an emotional plea to Quebec not to throw away the benefits of Confederation, American president Bill Clinton delivered a message expressing his preference for a united Canada, and some First Nations in Quebec staged their own separate referenda. In the week before the vote, a pro-Canada rally in Montreal, sponsored in part by airline and railway companies offering deeply discounted fares, drew an estimated 100 000 Canadians from outside Quebec. Political theatre continued as the votes were counted. With the outcome uncertain until the early hours of the morning, the "No" side won by the slimmest of margins: 50.58 percent to 49.42 percent. Bitterly disappointed by the near-unanimous opposition to sovereignty on the part of anglophones and allophones, Parizeau declared: "It's true, we were beaten, yes, but by what? By money and ethnic votes, essentially."[1]

The second referendum on Quebec sovereignty was conducted in a vastly different political landscape than the first referendum in 1980. By 1995, the Canadian government had implemented North American free trade and neo-liberal social policies that reduced federal monies to the provinces for social programs. Corporate threats to move their operations to developing countries to avoid taxes, labour contracts, and environmental regulations promoted the growth of fear-based conservatism. In the face of these developments, civil society organizations representing Natives, women, and other disadvantaged groups became more vocal in demanding reforms. Bitter conflicts between advocates of market fundamentalism and proponents of social justice became the hallmark of Canadian political life in the last quarter of the twentieth century.

TRUDEAU'S CANADA

The Liberal Party had been the chief political beneficiary of postwar prosperity. Given credit by Canadians for implementing welfare state policies, the Liberals governed the country for 32 of the 39 years from 1945 to 1984, drawing support primarily from Ontario and Quebec. The Liberal Party was weak in western Canada, where competition between the right-wing Progressive Conservatives and the left-wing New Democrats squeezed out a party that was seen not so much as centrist but as central Canadian. By contrast, the party was strong in Quebec, in part because the Progressive Conservatives and New Democrats were viewed as being too dominated by anglophones. The selection of francophone leaders from Wilfrid Laurier and Louis St-Laurent to Pierre Trudeau served to reinforce the view that the Liberal Party was the most sympathetic to the interests of francophone Quebec.

Trudeau managed to win a majority of seats in the 1974 election, but his flip-flop on wage and price controls and the deteriorating state of the economy left voters in a cranky and cynical mood. Nowhere was this mood more obvious than in the western provinces, where the federal government's efforts to control energy policy and foreign investment were interpreted as only more examples of eastern Canadian domination of the national agenda.

Capitalizing on western alienation, the Progressive Conservative Party chose Joe Clark, a young MP from Alberta, to succeed Robert Stanfield as their leader in 1976. Clark understood the growing discontent in the West, but he was a "progressive" Conservative—often described as a "Red Tory"—and thus offered no major threat to the postwar liberal consensus. Although he led his party to just a few seats short of a majority in the May 1979 election, his government was defeated in December on a budget that included an increased tax on gasoline. Trudeau, who had planned to step down as leader of the Liberal Party, was thrust into another election, which he won handily, but only two ridings west of Ontario elected Liberal members.

Claude Ryan and René Lévesque, leaders of the "No" and "Yes" sides in the 1980 referendum, had been major nationalist figures in Quebec since the 1960s. They had even collaborated during the 1970 October Crisis, as shown in this picture, but disagreed over Quebec sovereignty. SOURCE: LIBRARY AND ARCHIVES CANADA PA-117480

In the fall of 1980, the Trudeau government introduced the National Energy Program (NEP), designed to establish lower-than-world prices for oil in Canada, increase Canadian ownership of the precious resource, and enhance federal government revenues. The Canadian petroleum industry had expanded rapidly in the 1970s, not only in Alberta, but also in Saskatchewan and increasingly off the Atlantic coast, where the declaration of a 200-mile limit (about 370 kilometres) in 1977 added significantly to Canada's resource endowment. Although it could be argued that the NEP was initiated in the spirit of earlier equalization measures designed to spread wealth beyond the producing provinces, Ottawa's assertion of control over natural resources angered provincial premiers.

When the price of oil began to drop with the onset of a recession in the early 1980s, bankruptcies ensued, especially in the Alberta oil patch. A separatist party, the Western Canada Concept (WCC), held huge rallies in Calgary and Edmonton in the wake of the announcement of the NEP and elected a rural MLA in a provincial by-election in 1982.

QUEBEC SOVEREIGNTY

Quebec separation became more than just a threat after the Parti Québécois (PQ) won the 1976 provincial election. With the purposeful and popular René Lévesque at the helm, it seemed possible that Quebec might declare independence from Canada. An increasing number of Quebecers, especially francophones, dreamed of achieving sovereignty and argued that only by taking their destiny into their own hands could they become a prosperous, entrepreneurial people, no longer dependent on outsiders who were trying to assimilate them.

In what was increasingly being called "the rest of Canada" (abbreviated as ROC), this threat to national unity caused consternation and much soul-searching. Had Ottawa not made every effort to address Quebec's concerns? The federal bureaucracy had become more reflective of the linguistic balance in the nation, and cost-sharing programs and equalization grants ensured that poor provinces, including Quebec, could keep pace with other jurisdictions. What else did they want? Trudeau took a tough line against separatist sentiment but he had met his match in Lévesque, who won the hearts of many Québécois.

The PQ came to power promising to hold a referendum on the status of Quebec. Recognizing that a majority of Quebecers remained reluctant to make a complete break with Canada, the referendum question posed to voters on 20 May 1980 simply asked whether citizens were prepared to give their provincial government the authority to negotiate political sovereignty while maintaining an economic association with Canada.

Fresh from its recent election victory, the Trudeau administration actively campaigned for the "No" side led by Quebec Liberal Party leader Claude Ryan. Nearly 60 percent of voters, including half of francophones and an overwhelming majority of anglophones and allophones, voted "No." Lévesque had hoped to convince "soft nationalists"—people prepared to support a sovereign Quebec only if it did not have negative economic consequences for them—that a declaration of independence would produce a soft landing for Quebec because the new nation would remain in an alliance of economic interest with Canada.

Such hopes were challenged during the referendum campaign by many premiers, most notably Saskatchewan's Allan Blakeney, who indicated that his province would have no interest in giving a departing Quebec a special relationship with the provinces that remained in the federation. Ironically, Lévesque may have harmed his chances of winning a referendum by passing legislation—Bill 101—which built on efforts by his provincial Liberal predecessors to reinforce the status of the French language in the province. Many fence-sitters believed that this legislation demonstrated that the provincial government had sufficient powers to defend French, making moot the sovereignist argument that leaving Canada was essential in order to preserve Quebec's francophone character. The sovereignist cause was also harmed by drastic predictions of economic doom from Quebec's business leaders, and gaffes on the part of the "Yes" side, such as the statement by a female PQ cabinet minister that any woman who voted "No" was an "Yvette," a stereotypically submissive woman. A number of women opposed to sovereignty banded together as the "Yvettes" and helped turn the tide against the "Yes" cause.

PATRIATING THE CONSTITUTION

Building on the federalist momentum, Trudeau announced immediately after the referendum that his government would introduce constitutional reform. It was a bold move, especially since decades of negotiations had produced no consensus on the matter. As in the past, most provinces resisted the initiative—only Ontario and New Brunswick were initially onside. The Trudeau cabinet then agreed to proceed without unanimous provincial support and won the right to do so in a court challenge mounted by the provinces. Fearing that constitutional reform would be achieved without the provinces winning concessions, nine premiers came to terms with Trudeau in November 1981, leaving Lévesque to claim betrayal.

Pierre Trudeau and Queen Elizabeth II completing the patriation of Canada's Constitution in Ottawa on 17 April 1982.
SOURCE: LIBRARY AND ARCHIVES CANADA PA-140705

sufficient revenues to provide reasonably comparable levels of public services at reasonably comparable levels of taxation."

The Charter guaranteed Canadians, within "reasonable limits," freedom of speech, association, conscience, and religion, and prohibited discrimination on the basis of colour, sex, or creed. Provinces could also override constitutional rights by specifically exempting pieces of legislation from the Charter's reach. Dubbed the "notwithstanding clause," it allowed legislatures to

By the Canada Act, 1982, the British Parliament ended its power to amend the British North America Act and replaced it with the Constitution Act, which included the renamed British North America Act, an amending formula, and the Charter of Rights and Freedoms. The amending formula allowed the federal government to introduce changes in the Constitution with the approval of the federal Parliament plus two-thirds of the provinces representing a combined population of at least 50 percent of all Canadians. Unanimous consent of the provinces and both houses of Parliament was required for amendments affecting representation in the House of Commons, Senate, and Supreme Court, and for changes affecting bilingualism.

To provide some flexibility, any province that considered its legislative rights compromised by a constitutional amendment could declare that amendment null and void within its boundaries. Provinces were also granted the right to opt out of federal programs established by amendment that affected educational or cultural matters, with full financial compensation. As a concession to the poorer provinces, section 36 of the Constitution Act committed Canadian governments to the principle of equalization to "ensure that provincial governments have

assert that a law would apply notwithstanding Charter provisions. Section 28 declared that Charter rights "are guaranteed equally to male and female persons." This section was added as a result of coordinated pressures from women's groups, which sprang into action when the first draft of the Charter remained silent on gender equality. Feminist lobbying also succeeded in exempting section 28 from the override provisions of the Charter.

Aboriginal lobbies failed to win the right to self-government, but the Charter guaranteed that nothing in the document would affect "existing aboriginal and treaty rights" or prejudice later land settlements. As prescribed by the Constitution Act, Ottawa convened meetings with Aboriginal leaders to discuss this matter, but little was accomplished. The three westernmost provinces refused to surrender control over resources to Native peoples, and Quebec boycotted all Constitution-related conferences.

NEO-LIBERALISM FINDS A CHAMPION

In February 1984, Trudeau announced his plans to retire. He was succeeded as prime minister and Liberal Party leader by John Turner, who had resigned from the

Trudeau cabinet in 1975 to become a corporate lawyer in Toronto. Turner took power at a particularly inauspicious moment for the Liberal Party. After almost three years of a bruising recession and increasing government deficits, Canadians were ready to change governments. After holding office for less than three months, Turner became leader of the opposition when Brian Mulroney led the Progressive Conservative Party to a landslide victory in a federal election early in September.

Born to an Irish Catholic family in Baie-Comeau, a small community on Quebec's North Shore, Mulroney was a labour lawyer for major Quebec corporations when he ran unsuccessfully for the Progressive Conservative Party leadership in 1976. After Joe Clark stumbled in 1979, Mulroney worked behind the scenes to replace him, forcing a leadership convention in 1983, which he won by a close margin. Mulroney promised not to enter a free trade agreement with the United States, a promise on which he later reneged. He also promised Canadians that he would restore employment and reduce deficits without touching Canada's social programs, which he labelled a "sacred trust." During the campaign, he took advantage of a televised forum on women's issues to announce that his party would implement a national daycare program if he won the election. While he did not deliver on the promise, his willingness to make it suggested that he did not believe the Progressive Conservatives could be elected on a program of cutting back the state's obligations.

Once in power, Mulroney increased the pace of federal retreat from earlier commitments to improve access to quality education and health services that began under previous Liberal administrations. In 1977, Trudeau replaced equal federal–provincial sharing of Medicare and post-secondary education costs with block funding. The new arrangement was called "Established Programs Financing," and gave the provinces a percentage of federal income and corporate taxes plus a cash grant. While cash grants were initially increased by the annual rate of inflation, the Trudeau government set limits to increases in federal spending on post-secondary education for 1982 and 1983.

In 1986, the Mulroney government went further, announcing that federal cash grants for Medicare and post-secondary education would be reduced by two percent annually. Four years later, it introduced a bill to speed up the federal withdrawal from Established Programs Financing so that by 2004 the government's cash transfer for medical and education spending, which was $9 billion in the 1989–1990 fiscal year, would be zero.

CONSTITUTIONAL WRANGLING

Taking most of the seats in his home province in 1984, Brian Mulroney hoped to upstage Pierre Trudeau by "bringing Quebec into the Constitution." Robert Bourassa, the Liberal leader who returned to power as Quebec premier in 1985, was equally determined to win constitutional concessions that could blunt the sovereignist movement. He presented five requirements for Quebec's signature on the Constitution: recognition of Quebec as a distinct society; a Quebec veto for constitutional amendments; a greater role for provinces in immigration policy; the right for provinces to remain outside of all new cost-sharing programs without financial penalty; and provincial input into the selection of Supreme Court judges.

A first ministers' conference held at Meech Lake, near Ottawa, in April 1987 tentatively approved a package that met Quebec's demands. To win support from premiers who balked at Quebec having a veto over constitutional change, Mulroney granted all provinces a veto. Hoping to avoid efforts to amend the agreement, Mulroney announced that not one word of the document could be changed.

The three-year time limit set for debate on constitutional amendments provided ample opportunity for provincial support to unravel. Although polls showed that the majority of Quebecers favoured the Meech Lake Accord, most sovereignists rejected it as insufficient to meet Quebec's demands. So, too, did Trudeau, who emerged from retirement to denounce the agreement. The accord flew in the face of Trudeau's vision for Canada, not only by granting Quebec a poorly defined "distinct society" status, but also by greatly strengthening the powers of the provinces at the expense of the federal government. Apart from the distinct society clause, which caused considerable anxiety outside Quebec, the two aspects of the accord that drew the most fire were its cost-sharing provisions and the unanimity required for constitutional amendments.

Women's groups, trade unions, and anti-poverty organizations argued that the provincial right to opt out of shared-cost programs would create a patchwork of social policies leading to inequalities across the country, and that the requirement for unanimity would almost certainly prevent new national programs from being implemented. Aboriginal leaders also despaired of ever advancing their agenda if unanimity was required for constitutional amendments. Residents of the Yukon and the Northwest Territories largely rejected an accord that would virtually preclude them from ever becoming provinces. Without provincehood, they would have no voice in the Senate and no right to nominate Supreme Court judges, and they would have no say at constitutional conferences or regarding constitutional amendments.

Despite the opposition, Meech Lake might have succeeded had three elections not changed the provincial arithmetic. Newly elected Liberal premiers Frank McKenna in New Brunswick and Clyde Wells in Newfoundland, and Progressive Conservative Gary Filmon in Manitoba, all sought changes to the accord. Just weeks before the ratification deadline in 1990, Mulroney reassembled the premiers and offered a statement accompanying the accord that granted a degree of Senate reform and clarified the scope of the distinct society clause. The New Brunswick and Manitoba governments were won over. Clyde Wells, who opposed Meech Lake because it weakened the federal government and failed to recognize the concept of the equality of the provinces, agreed to have a free vote on the revised accord. Meanwhile, Elijah Harper, the lone Native member in the Manitoba legislature, protesting the accord's failure to enhance Native rights, used procedural methods to prevent the passage of the accord before the deadline. When it became clear that Manitoba could not pass the accord in time, Clyde Wells called off the Newfoundland vote.

The Meech Lake Accord died in June 1990, leaving many francophones in Quebec outraged. As the anger mounted, Lucien Bouchard, a popular minister in Mulroney's cabinet, resigned to become leader of the Bloc Québécois. The Bloc was a breakaway group of nationalist MPs, elected as Progressive Conservatives and Liberals, who became disillusioned with what they perceived as Canada's failure to accommodate Quebec's demands for greater autonomy. The Bloc's stated goal was to defend Quebec's interests in Ottawa until independence was achieved.

Elijah Harper in his seat in the Manitoba legislature in 1990, during debates on the Meech Lake Accord. As a Cree traditionalist, Harper is holding an eagle feather. For the Cree and other Aboriginal peoples, the eagle is a sacred bird that carries the prayers of the faithful to the Creator. When an eagle dies, its powers live on in its feathers if they are removed via the proper rituals and granted to deserving individuals.
SOURCE: WAYNE GLOWACKI/WINNIPEG FREE PRESS/CP IMAGES

In an effort to regain the momentum, Mulroney convened a marathon session of the premiers and Native leaders at Charlottetown in August 1992. The resulting Charlottetown Accord offered Quebec much of what it had been promised during the Meech Lake discussions but, to achieve agreement on special status, Bourassa conceded equal provincial representation in the Senate. Quebec was also guaranteed that its representation in the House of Commons would not fall below 25 percent, its approximate percentage of the population of Canada in 1992. The premiers recognized Native rights to self-government but, again, the parameters were to be determined in subsequent negotiations.

When several provinces, including Quebec, decided to test support for the accord in binding referenda, Mulroney decided to hold a national referendum. Sovereignists opposed the accord on the grounds that it failed to recognize Quebec's need for control over such matters as communications and banking. In the rest of Canada, many felt that Quebec had been given too much power. Issues regarding what the accord did or did not offer Aboriginals, women, and other groups also divided Canadians. On 26 October 1992, voters in three provinces—Newfoundland, Prince Edward Island, and New Brunswick—supported the accord in the hope that constitutional bickering could be put to an end. Ontario voters were split down the middle. In the remaining six provinces, including Quebec, the accord suffered a clear defeat.

THE WEST WANTS IN

By this time, alienation in western Canada had coalesced into the Reform Party. Established in 1987, it was led by Preston Manning, the son of the long-serving Social Credit premier of Alberta. The western provinces had been the bulwark of the Progressive Conservative Party since the 1950s, but under Brian Mulroney the focus had shifted back to Quebec. Although Mulroney put an end to the hated National Energy Program, his alleged failure to exercise fiscal restraint troubled many Progressive Conservatives in the West. Mulroney had implemented a variety of program cuts, but persistent high unemployment made it difficult for him to make much headway in reducing annual deficits. The tipping point for western discontent came in 1986 when the Montreal-based firm Bombardier was awarded the contract for maintenance of Canada's CF-18 military aircraft, despite Winnipeg's Bristol Aerospace having submitted what, to many people, seemed to be a superior bid.

Positioning themselves to the right of the Progressive Conservatives, Reformers demanded a more rigorous neo-liberal economic agenda and were prepared to let Quebec leave Confederation rather than receive special status. In 1988, the party campaigned with the slogan "The West Wants In," signalling that the region now had the political muscle to influence the national agenda. Other than lower taxes and balanced budgets, major planks in the party's platform included an elected Senate with equal provincial representation, privatization of Crown corporations such as the CBC, Canada Post, and Petro-Canada, and an immigration policy based "solely on economic need." The last issue hinted that the party

had also become a home for social conservatives, people deeply troubled by everything that Canadian liberalism stood for: bilingualism, multiculturalism, feminism, gay and lesbian rights, and secular values. The Reform Party elected its first MP, Deborah Grey, in a 1989 by-election in Alberta.

Mulroney further alienated westerners and many other Canadians in 1992 when his government decided to replace a hidden Manufacturers' Sales Tax with a seven percent Goods and Services Tax (GST), which registered in the wallets of every Canadian. The Liberal-dominated Senate tried to block this move, but Mulroney appointed enough new senators to achieve his goal.

With public opinion turning resolutely against his government, Mulroney stepped down in June 1993. He was succeeded as party leader and prime minister by Kim Campbell, an MP from Vancouver who had proven her mettle as minister of Indian and Northern affairs and minister of justice. Campbell had little hope of success in the October 1993 election, but few predicted the final outcome. The Progressive Conservatives were reduced to only two members, while the Bloc Québécois took 54 seats, two ahead of the Reform Party, to become the official opposition. The Liberals, led by Jean Chrétien, marched down the middle, taking 177 seats and forming a majority government with 41 percent of the popular vote. Their promises to end austerity and reinvest in social programs rallied progressive voters. Abandoned by many progressives, on the one hand, and angry westerners, on the other, the NDP was almost obliterated, falling from 44 seats before the election, to only nine MPs. With the federalist party to their left appearing to be on life support, the Liberals felt that they had a great deal of latitude to appease both industry and supporters of the Reform Party by abandoning their election promises.

THE BORN-AGAIN LIBERAL PARTY

Few politicians had as much staying power as Jean Chrétien. The eighteenth of 19 children born to a family of modest means in Shawinigan, Quebec, Chrétien studied law at Laval and won a seat in the House of Commons in 1963 at the age of 29. Holding a variety of portfolios during his long parliamentary career, he was Trudeau's trusted lieutenant through the War Measures Act, the 1980 Quebec referendum, and the constitutional

Cartoonist's view of Brian Mulroney in 1992, turning his attention from the Constitution to the economy. SOURCE: THE GLOBE AND MAIL

campaign. After losing the Liberal Party leadership to John Turner in 1984, Chrétien retired from politics to work in the private sector, but returned to the political arena when Turner stepped down in 1990.

As heir to Trudeau's legacy, "the little guy from Shawinigan" had more popular appeal than his rival for leadership, Paul Martin. Long-time president and CEO of Canada Steamship Lines, based in Montreal, Martin was in tune with neo-liberal thinking in corporate boardrooms. Appointed minister of finance in the Chrétien government, Martin continued along the path laid down by Mulroney, but much more successfully. Budget deficits were replaced by surpluses, and the national debt was reduced thanks to major cuts in accessibility to unemployment insurance and in Established Program Funding for the provinces. Even the Canada Assistance Plan, one of the pillars of the welfare state, was abolished. Much of this program was achieved through the 1995 federal budget, a neo-liberal document that removed $25 billion in federal spending over a three-year period, mostly at the expense of

the provinces. Although there were minor tax increases as well, the Liberal goal was clearly to make reduced government expenditure the major contributor to deficit-fighting, and by 1998, overall federal spending was about nine percent lower than it had been before the 1995 budget.

Jean Chrétien appeared ambivalent about his party's embrace of austerity, and promised that once deficits were eliminated his government would reinvest in social programs. Federal reductions in social transfers to provinces translated into less money in the pockets of the poorest Canadians, disproportionately women. Cuts in social welfare hit single mothers and their children hardest, and the federal Liberal government's abandonment of its promise of a national daycare program in the 1993 election meant that monies available in most provinces for childcare for women seeking employment did not increase. With wages rising slower than inflation, and part-time jobs often replacing full-time employment, many working women and men also joined the ranks of the poor.

Private initiatives arose in an effort to deal with poverty as it became clear that governments were uninterested in dealing with the problem. Food banks started modestly in the early 1980s in some urban centres. By 1992, 150 000 people were served each month by the Daily Bread Food Bank in Toronto alone, and an estimated two million Canadians relied on food banks at some point that year.

The federal government made a commitment in 1989 to end child poverty. At the time, 14.4 percent of Canadian children were being raised in poverty. Although some programs were implemented to direct cash to the poorest households with children, cuts in social assistance and unemployment insurance, along with inflation, resulted in an increase in the child poverty rate to 21.1 percent by 1996.

QUEBEC'S SECOND REFERENDUM

Federal cutbacks proved auspicious for advocates of Quebec independence. Less than nine months after the federal government announced its neo-liberal budget, Quebec voted for a second time on the issue of sovereignty. Although intially in favour of a question that focused only on Quebec independence, Jacques Parizeau was convinced by other sovereignist leaders to promise voters that a "Yes" victory would lead to negotiations with Canada on an economic partnership, to be followed by a second referendum after such negotiations concluded. The "Yes" campaign got off to a sluggish start, despite major blunders by the "No" side, but the pace quickened after the economic partnership came to the fore. The assumption of leadership of the "Yes" campaign by the popular Lucien Bouchard also gave sovereignist forces a major boost. As discussed in the historiographical box at the end of this chapter, political scientists, historians, and other analysts still disagree as to the reasons for the surge in support for the "Yes" side, which brought them to the brink of victory, and ultimately for the failure of the "Yes" side to garner the few tens of thousands of extra votes that it needed to win.

After the narrow "No" victory, the Chrétien government introduced a resolution declaring Quebec a distinct society, sponsored federal projects in Quebec, and, in late 1999, introduced the Clarity Act, which required any future referendum on sovereignty to be "clear," both in the wording of the question and the size of the majority

necessary for Quebec's separation from Canada. It was passed by both houses of Parliament in 2000. Critics noted that the legislation was itself ambiguous on what constituted a "clear question" and a "clear majority." Despite the near-win by the sovereignists in 1995, the growing weariness in Quebec regarding constitutional issues meant that the sovereignty issue was temporarily put on the back burner.

ONTARIO'S INTERRUPTED PROSPERITY

Southern Ontario, the country's traditional industrial heartland, was hardest hit by the economic uncertainty that had descended in the 1970s. Manufacturing jobs disappeared, particularly during the recessions of 1982–1985 and 1990–1993, and companies declared bankruptcy at an alarming rate. In the postwar years, high-paying jobs in such sectors as steel, automobiles and automobile parts, aerospace, and electrical appliances had been the sources of envy by much of the rest of the country. Now people working in these industries were being laid off with little prospect of finding jobs for which they were qualified.

The succession of Progressive Conservative administrations that had governed Ontario from 1943 to 1985 came around slowly to the business view that the state could no longer afford the full range of services it was providing. In 1985, when the newly chosen premier, Frank Miller, put forth this message, the Conservative dynasty came crashing down. The Liberals formed a minority government with NDP support and won a big majority in 1987. By then, the Ontario economy was booming again and the Liberals, led by David Peterson, stood squarely against the federal Mulroney government's program of social spending cuts and free trade with the United States. The government eliminated patient billing by physicians who wanted more income than their Medicare payments provided, and extended full funding to separate schools up to Grade 13, but the mood of voters proved volatile. A party fundraising scandal weakened the Liberals and voters reacted angrily to an election call in 1990, just three years into the government's mandate. They replaced Peterson with the NDP, headed by Bob Rae.

The NDP proved unable to adopt a consistent policy. In their first budget in 1991, they defied the neo-liberal logic that had gripped most governments in Canada, producing a stimulative budget with a $10-billion deficit. The business community and media condemned this return to Keynesianism. Over the next four years, the NDP largely recanted its first budget and reined in social spending. Rae alienated much of the union movement when he imposed an across-the-board wage cut of five percent on all public sector workers in provincial or municipal institutions. Those whose annual salaries were under $30 000 were spared, and the government's "social contract" attempted to compensate for wage cuts with job security guarantees and greater worker involvement in implementing programs. Nevertheless, unionists were appalled by a supposedly pro-labour government violating union-negotiated contracts.

One area where the NDP government had considerable success was in bailouts of large private companies that had run into trouble because of changing economic circumstances, poor management, or international corporate strategies. Spruce Falls Power and Paper, Algoma Steel, de Havilland Aircraft, Mitel Corp., Provincial Papers, St. Mary's Paper, Algoma Central Railway, Urban Transportation Development Corp., and Ontario Bus Industries, among others, rebounded with state aid, saving many jobs. Still, unemployment remained high.

In the 1995 election, Ontario voters punished the hapless Bob Rae, who had the misfortune to govern during five years of economic stagnation. Mike Harris's Progressive Conservatives received 45 percent of the vote, almost double their previous total, running on a campaign of cutting the public service, slashing social assistance, privatizing government services, and cancelling employment equity programs.

The Harris government wholeheartedly embraced a neo-liberal agenda, reducing taxes for the middle and upper classes while slashing health, education, and welfare expenditures to pay for it. Programs to aid battered women, the disabled, and the mentally ill were targeted for reduced subsidies, dozens of hospitals throughout the province were closed, and environmental regulations were weakened. The Harris government also initiated extensive reform at the municipal level, attempting to offload welfare expenditures onto the municipalities and initiating plans to create a "megacity" in Metro Toronto.

All of these policies provoked vocal resistance. The megacity plan was decisively rejected in local referenda, and ongoing "Days of Action" were organized by a coalition of labour and community groups. The Tories dismissed the opposition as "special interest groups" and continued to pursue their neo-liberal agenda. By the 1999 provincial election, the Ontario economy was booming and Harris was talking about reinvesting in the province, particularly in health and education. He was re-elected, but with a reduction in seats and the popular vote.

THE NEW WEST

Battles over control of natural resources in the early 1970s marked the return of western alienation as a major factor in national politics for the first time since the Second World War. The energy-producing provinces rejected the philosophy of the National Energy Program. They wanted Canadians to pay international prices for energy, claiming that the made-in-Canada price simply deprived them of revenues and drove away projects to develop Northern Alberta's tar sands (now rebranded oil sands by publicity-conscious corporations). The costs of removing oil from the tar sands with existing technology could not be justified if the price of oil were kept artificially low. This debate pitted the three most westerly provinces and the oil-producing "wannabes" in the east—Newfoundland and Nova Scotia—against energy-poor provinces and the federal government, at least while international oil prices were high. When prices began a steep decline in 1982, major projects in Alberta came unglued. By the time prices revived in the 1990s, cheaper processes for the extraction of oil from tar sands had become available.

Trudeau claimed that the NEP was an instrument of nationalism, but in the West it was viewed as simply a manifestation of central Canadian control of the national agenda. It would harm the energy sector while benefiting the manufacturing sector that was mainly located in Ontario and Quebec. It was also regarded as costly and untimely because the grants and tax incentives offered to Canadianize the industry proved expensive for the public purse at a time when deficits were beginning to soar. Unlike transfer payments to individuals, these incentives had no obvious stimulative impact on the economy.

Although the NEP was modified sufficiently to enable a truce between Trudeau and Alberta premier Peter Lougheed in 1981, it would be blamed by many westerners—perhaps most—for an economic downturn, beginning in 1982, in which many people lost their homes and savings. While the NEP was a key factor in the rise of western alienation and led to movements such as the separatist Western Canada Concept, it was not the only source of resentment in the West. There was a perception that the West was ignored when federal contracts were awarded, as the award of the federal military aircraft maintenance program to Bombardier appeared to demonstrate. At the same time, grain farmers were angry at the decision of the Trudeau government in the early 1980s to phase out the historic Crow rates, which had kept the cost of shipping grain competitive with American farmers' transportation costs. While the right-wing Reform Party was the big gainer federally from western discontent, provincial politics in the West proved more complicated.

BRITISH COLUMBIA

Before the 1990s, the divide between right and left remained fairly wide in British Columbia. The NDP took between 39 and 46 percent of the vote in provincial elections, but repeatedly lost to the Social Credit Party in what was essentially a two-party province. The Socreds, under Bill Bennett, demonstrated the shift away from the postwar consensus after the 1983 provincial election when, despite their marginal victory in the popular vote, they implemented a program of massive cuts in education and social spending and the privatization of a large variety of government services.

In response, public servants and state employees such as teachers, nurses, and social workers joined with client groups to form Operation Solidarity. They shut down most state operations in the province for a week to protest the cuts. Leaders of the private sector unions shunned a request to make the shutdown a general strike, and in the end Solidarity had to be content with fairly minimal concessions on the part of Bennett's government.

The Social Credit Party became a spent force after Bennett's successor, William Vander Zalm, a charismatic millionaire, resigned over allegations of conflict of interest in his sale of the family firm. Vander Zalm was replaced by Rita Johnson, Canada's first female premier. In the election that followed, the NDP won a large majority without increasing their traditional vote. Much of the Social Credit vote had gone to the Liberals, who formed the official opposition. Mike Harcourt, the NDP premier, resigned in late 1995 after a flurry of criticism about his feeble attempts to deal with a party fundraising scandal.

The Harcourt government also had a difficult time trying to balance the demands of environmentalists and unionized forest workers, both traditional NDP supporters in the province. Clear-cutting at Clayoquot Sound on Vancouver Island became a defining issue for the organized environmental movement not only in British Columbia, but also across the country. Hundreds of protesters, including NDP MP Svend Robinson, were arrested as they tried to prevent loggers from clear-cutting. Forestry workers protested that the environmentalists were unconcerned about the economic devastation that would affect families and communities if logging stopped with nothing to replace it.

The triumph of the right wing in a power struggle within the Liberal Party gave Harcourt's replacement, Glen Clark, a chance to revive a government battered by scandal. Unlike voters in Ontario and some other provinces, British Columbia voters were not yet prepared to elect a party that focused on tax cuts and seemed suspect in its commitment to social spending. The NDP were re-elected in 1996.

ALBERTA

In Alberta, the Conservatives remained in office continuously after 1971, but underwent an ideological sea change as prosperity oozed away in the 1980s and 1990s. While the Conservatives had initially invested generously in social programs, they began to make cuts in social spending in the 1980s. The election of Ralph Klein as premier in 1993 escalated the shift toward less state responsibility for citizens. Klein slashed the costs of government, with social programs taking most of the punishment. Nurses, schoolteachers, welfare recipients, and the elderly suffered the most in a program that attracted national attention. Within the province, the most controversial move was the closing down of a large number of intensive care units in hospitals and the encouragement of private medical entrepreneurs to make up for deficiencies in a slimmed-down public health system. As provincial energy revenues soared in the late 1990s, the "Klein Revolution" gave way to generous spending on health and education once again. But true to their new right-wing ideology, the Conservatives also passed legislation that permitted a degree of privatization of hospitals.

SASKATCHEWAN AND MANITOBA

In the 1980s, Saskatchewan replaced the NDP administration of Allan Blakeney with a free-enterprise Conservative government under Grant Devine. The Tories privatized some Crown corporations and attempted unsuccessfully to lure businesses with subsidies and loans. Floundering in a sea of corruption, the Conservatives lost the 1991 election to the NDP, led by Roy Romanow, but much of its populist zeal was gone. Although the new government used a combination of taxes and cuts to deal with declining revenues and developed a reputation for prudent fiscal management, it had few ideas about how to diversify the Saskatchewan economy.

Manitoba's political parties were perhaps more sharply divided than Saskatchewan's. Following the NDP government led by Ed Schreyer in 1977, Sterling Lyon's Conservatives, unlike other Tory administrations of the prosperity era, were dedicated to cutting programs for the poor and health and education spending. In the 1980s, NDP premier Howard Pawley reversed direction again and, despite the province's relative poverty, ignored the growing neo-liberal campaign of the business classes. Tax increases necessary to maintain public expenditures eventually led to a tax revolt that deposed Pawley's government. The Conservatives under Gary Filmon, initially vague about the direction in which they would take the province, had clearly joined the neo-liberal camp by the mid-1990s. But in 1999, provincial voters, angry with health care cuts, put the NDP back into office, this time under Gary Doer.

ATLANTIC CANADA

During the era of postwar prosperity, the Atlantic provinces had depended on federal equalization grants and transfer payments to offset the poor economic performance of the region. Development programs, sponsored by federal and provincial governments, failed to usher in a period of sustained prosperity, and people continued to leave the region to find work. When the federal government began trying to rein in national deficits in the 1990s by cutting back on unemployment insurance and other forms of transfer payments, the four eastern provinces faced challenges at a level not seen since the 1920s.

In 1977, when Canada declared a 200-mile exclusive fishing zone in the northwest Atlantic, it looked as if the fortunes of Atlantic Canadians were at last looking up. Rich in oil, natural gas, and fish, the offshore banks promised untold riches. From the beginning of the new era in the fishing industry, there were tensions between inshore fisheries and large corporations as to how best to manage the fisheries in light of Canada's weak efforts to prevent foreign overfishing within the 200-mile limit. Predictably, given the extent of overfishing by the North Atlantic nations, the fisheries boom of the 1970s quickly turned into a bust. By the early 1980s, east coast processing companies were in trouble, and two corporate giants, Fishery Products International and National Sea, swallowed up their competitors. As fish stocks began to collapse in the late 1980s, Canadian quotas were cut, fish plants were shut down, and many fishing communities faced extinction.

In July 1992, the federal government announced that there would be a two-year moratorium on northern cod fishing. This meant unemployment for many Atlantic Canadians, but people from Newfoundland and Labrador were hit particularly hard. At least 19 000 fishers and plant workers in that province were thrown out of work, and the survival of dozens of communities on Newfoundland's east coast was threatened.

Meanwhile, in the late 1970s, the large Hibernia oil field was discovered off Newfoundland. Brian Peckford, Newfoundland's Progressive Conservative premier, insisted that the province have equal control with Ottawa over offshore developments. Trudeau was reluctant to relinquish federal control of offshore resources, and in 1984 the Supreme Court upheld his view that Ottawa had exclusive jurisdiction.

The election of the Mulroney Progressive Conservatives in 1984 resulted in a victory for Peckford. With the assistance of John Crosbie, the colourful and outspoken Newfoundland member in the Mulroney cabinet, the Canada–Newfoundland Atlantic Accord was signed in 1985. While it offered fewer benefits from offshore developments than Crosbie had hoped, it seemed to signal a less rigid attitude in Ottawa toward accommodating the interests of have-not provinces.

Expectations in Newfoundland and Nova Scotia that they might follow Alberta's lead to become energy-rich provinces from an offshore oil bonanza proved slow to materialize. While stimulating economic growth, the

Hibernia development provided few jobs after the construction phase ended, and the clawback provisions on equalization payments meant that the federal government rather than the provinces received the lion's share of the royalties.

The tendency of capital investment to gravitate toward established centres of economic growth resulted in provincial governments resorting to desperate measures to accommodate corporate interests. When Michelin, the French-owned tire manufacturer in Nova Scotia, threatened to quit the province if one of its three sites was unionized, the province quickly passed legislation requiring that a majority of the workers from all three sites had to vote for the union before it could be legally recognized. Since two plants were in areas without a strong union tradition, the bill effectively killed chances for the union to gain a toehold. The government that was so willing to accommodate corporate concerns seemed deaf to complaints about rock slides, cave-ins, and dangerous levels of methane gas from miners at the Westray coal mine in Pictou County. When an explosion destroyed the mine in 1993, eight months into its operation, 26 men were left dead beneath the surface.

Economic uncertainty helped fuel political volatility. In New Brunswick, voters unhappy with flamboyant Conservative premier Richard Hatfield gave every seat in the province to Frank McKenna's Liberals in 1987. McKenna was particularly aggressive in trying to attract call centres to his province, but these low-paying operations did little to change the overall economic picture in New Brunswick. Following McKenna's resignation in 1997, his party collapsed and a reorganized Progressive Conservative Party swept back to power in 1999 under the youthful Bernard Lord.

Prince Edward Island experienced a similar swing from the Liberals to the Progressive Conservatives. Catherine Callbeck led the provincial Liberal Party to victory in the 1993 election, but Callbeck's victory was short-lived. Forced to deal with drastic federal cutbacks, she was blamed for the pain they caused in a province where the small tax base gave finance ministers little room to manoeuvre. In 1996, the Liberals were turned out of office by the Progressive Conservatives led by Pat Binns. A native of Saskatchewan, Binns was a farmer who proved successful in maintaining voter confidence in the primarily rural province through two more provincial elections.

Nova Scotia's politics, dominated by the Conservatives from 1978 to 1990, entered a period of fierce three-party competition in the late 1990s. Disillusioned by the cutbacks of both Conservative and Liberal governments, a large number of provincial voters decided they had had enough of Tweedledum and Tweedledee and gave their votes to the New Democratic Party, though the NDP failed to form a government.

THE NORTH

Canada's territorial North experienced enormous changes in the late twentieth century. In both the Yukon and Northwest Territories, people with southern roots employed in government, military, mining, and service activities gradually began to outnumber indigenous inhabitants. The population base nevertheless remained small, with no more than 100 000 people claiming the Canadian North as their home in the 1980s.

By the end of the twentieth century, considerable progress had been made on Aboriginal land claims and governance in the North. The Inuit living in the Mackenzie Delta and the Yukon First Nations reached agreements on land rights in 1984 and 1988 respectively. In 1992, the Inuit of the eastern Arctic signed an agreement with Ottawa that gave them subsurface mineral rights to 350 000 square kilometres of land and that established a process for the eastern Arctic to become a separately administered territory. On 1 April 1999, Nunavut (meaning "the people's land" in the Inuktitut language) became Canada's third territorial jurisdiction. Eighty-five percent of Nunavut's population of about 27 000 was Inuit.

Achieving more political power remained a constant concern of people living in Canada's North. As territories, the Yukon, Northwest Territories, and Nunavut have fewer rights than provinces. The head of state in the territories is a commissioner, appointed by the federal government. Beginning in the late 1970s, commissioners reduced their executive functions and elected assemblies began operating much like their provincial counterparts. The Inuit Circumpolar Council, founded in 1977 to represent the interests of Inuit living in Canada, Greenland, Alaska, and Russia, quickly became a major player in the environmental movement.

With airborne toxins from the south poisoning the food chain in Arctic regions and rising temperatures threatening disaster for sea animals and birds dependent on the rapidly melting sea ice, the environment became a dominant issue for territorial governments. The melting ice also made the Northwest Passage a viable transportation route and opened primary resources such as oil and gas to intense exploitation. By the end of the twentieth century, sovereignty over the passage and the seabed beyond the 200-mile limit was increasingly called into question by the United States, Russia, Norway, and Denmark, countries that also claimed a stake in the rush for spoils in an ever-warming Arctic.

THE TRADE UNION MOVEMENT

Canada's trade union movement was under attack in the age of neo-liberalism, but fared much better than its American counterpart from 1976 to 1999. In the United States, southern and western states passed "right to work" legislation that banned the closed shop. As northern firms moved south to take advantage of cheap labour and poor environmental standards, workers in the northeast often abandoned their unions to preserve their jobs, albeit at a high cost in terms of wages and working conditions. By the mid-1990s, only about 15 percent of American workers were unionized, about half the rate of 20 years earlier.

In Canada, by contrast, the fall-off was less steep—from 37.2 percent of the non-agricultural labour force in 1984 to 32.5 percent in 1998. Nevertheless, in the era of free trade, Canadians were not immune to trends south of the border. As many Canadians were learning in the age of globalization, local governments had little ability to protect citizens against the often take-it-or-leave-it demands of mobile multinational corporations. In Quebec, governments often neglected to enforce the law against replacement workers that had been enacted by Premier Lévesque in 1977. Ontario's NDP government passed similar legislation, but it was repealed by Harris in 1995. Both the PQ and the NDP, supposedly friends of organized labour, had at one time or another imposed wage rollbacks on public employees. Conditions were worse for organized labour in

provinces where the social democratic parties had never been in power. Alberta, though a rich province, boasted of its American level of unionization to companies looking to establish in a low-wage, no-union environment in which to establish themselves.

ABORIGINAL EMPOWERMENT

Status Indians, Métis, and Inuit, all defined officially as Aboriginal peoples by the Constitution Act, drew on a series of Supreme Court rulings in their favour and various United Nations declarations on the rights of Aboriginal peoples to improve their status in Canada. Mounting frustration with Ottawa's reluctance to deal with Aboriginal and treaty rights reached new levels when the Mulroney government agreed to recognize Quebec as a distinct society while denying a similar concession to Aboriginal peoples. In 1990, Phil Fontaine, national chief of the Assembly of First Nations, made it crystal clear why such a concession was important: "Like Quebec, we want to be recognized as a distinct society, because recognition means power."[2]

Establishing sovereignty and self-government, along with asserting land rights, became top priorities for Aboriginal peoples in their relations with Ottawa, but the diversity of conditions across Canada made negotiations daunting for both sides. Rights to much of the territory in British Columbia, the North, Quebec, and the Atlantic provinces were called into question, as were those to areas throughout Canada that had been expropriated by governments for everything from golf courses to military bases. In some cases, unresolved land issues dating back centuries suddenly became relevant again, and earlier interpretations of treaties, especially if they were negotiated in bad faith, also came under scrutiny.

In 1984, the Supreme Court ruled that Ottawa had fiduciary responsibility for Aboriginal peoples. Three years later, pre-treaty land rights were confirmed. In 1997, in a landmark decision involving the Gitxsan-Wet'suwet'en Nation of British Columbia, the Supreme Court not only reconfirmed Aboriginal rights but also argued that those rights went beyond hunting and fishing to the broader rights relating to their traditional lands. In addition, the ruling validated oral testimony as a source of evidence in claims cases.

This seeming reversal of power relations brought complaints and sometimes violence. Following a 1999 Supreme Court ruling confirming that Donald Marshall Junior had a treaty right to "make a moderate living" by catching and selling fish, violence erupted in the Maritimes, where Mi'kmaq and Maliseet suddenly had access to resources that had long been denied them. By this time, a series of confrontations had brought international attention to Canada's "Aboriginal problem." In 1990, a long-standing dispute over land near Oka, Quebec, being expropriated for a golf course provoked a 78-day standoff between the Mohawk Warriors and the provincial police, who called upon the Canadian army for assistance. To defuse the situation, Ottawa agreed to buy the disputed territory for the Mohawk. The intensity of the conflict, which

A masked Mohawk Warrior tends to his weapon during the 1990 Oka crisis. SOURCE: RYAN REMIORZ/CP IMAGES

included the death of a police officer, finally forced the Mulroney government to pay attention. In 1991, Ottawa re-established an Indian Claims Commission and appointed a Royal Commission on Aboriginal Peoples, which reported in 1996.

As was required by the Charter of Rights and Freedoms, the Canadian government amended the Indian Act in 1985 to remove the discrimination against Native women who married non-Aboriginal men. About 100 000 women and children had their Indian status reinstated by 1997. While a human rights victory, the new policy created tensions over who was "Indian enough," culturally or genetically, to be reinstated, and brought complaints about overcrowding and pressure on band resources by a sudden influx of people.

More than a century of patriarchal power under the Indian Act had greatly reduced women's status in their communities. Only granted the vote in band elections in 1951, women were a minority of chiefs and councillors and suffered even more than Canadian women generally from male violence. When they tried to bring their issues to authorities, they were often denied a fair hearing. The Native Women's Association of Canada, founded in 1974, took the Canadian government to court for refusing to include them in the talks leading to the Charlottetown Accord. They lost their case, and they were excluded from constitutional negotiations.

Native Canadians remained a diverse people, the majority of whom belonged to more than 600 bands attached to over 2600 reserves. For every story in the media about dysfunctional communities riven by disease, drug addiction, pollution, unemployment, and violence, there was another highlighting a success story. The business-school ideal of success has been adopted in some Aboriginal communities. With the support of the Toronto-Dominion Bank, a First Nations Bank was established in Saskatoon in 1997, and others followed. This initiative emerged from the recommendations of the Royal Commission on Aboriginal Peoples, which made 440 specific recommendations and identified four key issues: the need for a new relationship between Aboriginal and non-Aboriginal peoples; self-determination through self-government; economic self-sufficiency; and healing for Aboriginal peoples and communities.[3]

British Columbia Natives and the Struggle for Self-Determination

The history of British Columbia's dealings with First Nations is arguably the most shameful in the country. After British Columbia entered Confederation, its government insisted that treaties not be signed in that province. For more than a century, Native lands were seized for industrialization and urban expansion without negotiating with the landowners. In 1985, the Supreme Court of Canada awarded the small Musqueam band $10 million in compensation for Indian Affairs having duped them into granting an unfair golf course lease on their land. Meanwhile, Natives in the province began to actively resist developers, even if it meant breaking Canadian law, and clashed with loggers harvesting trees on their traditional lands.

In 1990, British Columbia finally agreed to negotiate land rights, but a year later, British Columbia Supreme Court judge Allan McEachern issued a verdict in the Delgamuukw case that called those rights into question. That ruling was invalidated in 1997 when the Supreme Court of Canada, hearing an appeal of this case involving the Gitxsan-Wet'suwet'en Nation, rejected McEachern's logic. The federal court decision placed some pressure on British Columbia's NDP government to negotiate agreements with Native peoples, if only to counter the economic uncertainty that business representatives claimed the court's ruling created for them.

Perhaps fittingly, the Nisga'a of the Nash Valley negotiated the first successful comprehensive land claims treaty in Canada. For more than a century, the Nisga'a had asserted their land claims even as the provincial government, with tacit federal support, handed away their territory to forestry and mineral companies. Nisga'a leader Frank Calder pursued the issue in the courts and, in 1973, the Supreme Court agreed that Natives held Aboriginal rights to land, but split three to three on the issue of whether those rights had been extinguished in British Columbia. The deciding vote went against Calder on a technicality, but the recognition of Aboriginal rights had ramifications for all Canadian Natives and ensured that the Nisga'a struggle for self-determination would continue.

In 1998, the government of British Columbia and the Nisga'a people reached agreement on a treaty, which was subsequently ratified by a referendum of the Nisga'a and a vote of both the British Columbia legislature and the Parliament of Canada. The opposition parties in British Columbia made exaggerated claims about the treaty, which became law in 2000, and played upon non-Aboriginal fears of being displaced by the original owners. Opponents of the treaty among the Nisga'a, meanwhile, pointed out what they had lost. The Nisga'a received 1930 square kilometres as a territory in which they would exercise law-making authority in such areas as land use, cultural practices, and employment policies. The various benefits and monetary grants that accompanied the treaty were worth $487.1 million. In return, they gave up all claims to 80 percent of their traditional territory and accepted the Canadian Criminal Code and the Canadian Charter of Rights and Freedoms rather than the right to exercise complete sovereignty within their lands.[4]

THE WOMEN'S MOVEMENT

The women's movement continued to play an important role in Canadian society, where the conditions of women changed but their status remained the same. Although the National Action Committee on the Status of Women and other women's organizations worked hard to keep their concerns in the public eye, the media and political leaders seemed to pay less attention in the closing years of the twentieth century. The demonization of feminism by increasingly vocal right-wing groups made many young women reluctant to take up causes focusing exclusively on women, while the diversity of women's interests made it difficult to focus the agenda.

In the 1970s, the number of women elected to the House of Commons began to rise, reaching nearly 21 percent by the end of the century. Gains were also made in female participation at the provincial and municipal levels. In 1989, the NDP's Audrey McLaughlin became the first woman to lead a major federal party. Two years later, the

Social Credit Party in British Columbia chose Rita Johnson as party leader and premier. When provincial Liberal Party leader Catherine Callbeck won the 1993 election in Prince Edward Island, she made history as the first woman in Canada to be elected to a provincial premiership.

Despite these achievements, women remained rare at the top of political, military, and corporate hierarchies. Instead they formed the majority among the ranks of the poor, their average income remaining at about 70 percent that of men. With the liberalization of divorce laws, women could escape unhappy marriages, but those who did so often faced penury. By the 1980s, one marriage in three ended in divorce, and about 85 percent of single-parent families were headed by women. In 1998, Statistics Canada reported that nearly 60 percent of children raised only by mothers were growing up poor.

MORE TO THE STORY
Women on the March

In the 1990s the Fédération des femmes du Québec made the struggle against women's poverty a priority on their feminist agenda. Led by their new president, Françoise David, the Fédération organized a march on Quebec City in 1995 to pressure the governing Parti Québécois government of Premier Jacques Parizeau to address the growing problem of female poverty. Nearly 4000 women completed a 10-day March for Bread and Roses. With an eye to the upcoming autumn referendum on sovereignty, Parizeau told the women that their demand for a program of social infrastructure could only be met when Quebec was independent from Canada, though he conceded a small increase in the minimum wage. The opposition Liberals ignored the women, associating them with sovereignist efforts to discredit Canadian federalism.

Two years later, Parizeau's successor, Lucien Bouchard, announced that his government would take steps to implement one of the marchers' key demands: universal, affordable daycare. The policy was rolled out slowly, but Quebec's five-dollars-a-day program marked it out as the most progressive jurisdiction in North American on the issue of child care.

Rather than rest on their laurels, the Fédération des femmes du Québec continued to sponsor mass public events to shine the spotlight on the economic injustice and violence that marked the lives of women. The results were far-reaching. Recognizing that these problems went well beyond Quebec and Canada, they took the lead in 1998 in organizing a World March of Women Against Poverty and Violence. Coordinated marches were held in 157 countries in October 2000. In some countries, these were the first mass mobilizations of women for feminist demands. There were marches 30 000 strong in both Montreal and Ottawa, the largest mobilization of women for public protests to that time in Canadian history.

Broadcaster and long-time feminist activist Judy Rebick noted that the Canadian media outside Quebec largely ignored this explosion of global women's solidarity and the role of Quebec women in initiating it. Here was a movement that was publicizing the fact that the majority of the world's poor, including in Canada, were women and children. Why was their cause not newsworthy? Rebick observed sarcastically: "I forgot feminism is dead and nothing good ever happens in Quebec."[5]

In 1996, a year after the Bread and Roses march, about 2000 women took part in a 24-hour anti-poverty vigil before the Quebec National Assembly, an activity organized by a coalition of Quebec women's groups led by Françoise David. These women were part of a human chain formed around the building.
SOURCE: CLEMENT ALLARD/CP IMAGES

The women's movement had more success in its demand for a woman's right to choose to terminate a pregnancy. After the relaxation of the abortion law in 1969, access to abortion was uneven across the country, leading the Supreme Court to rule in 1988 that the law, which required an abortion to be approved by a three-doctor panel, violated the guarantees in the Charter of Rights and Freedoms of equal rights for all Canadians. After the court decision, Parliament grappled unsuccessfully with this divisive issue, leaving Canada with no law restricting rights to an abortion.

Violence against women became a more urgent concern after 6 December 1989, when a deranged young man fatally shot 14 female engineering students at the École Polytechnique de Montréal while shouting his hatred of feminists. In the wake of this tragedy, women's groups pressed for battered women's shelters, rape crisis centres, counselling for abusers and their victims, gun control, and increased court charges and convictions for rapists, batterers, and harassers.

In an era of budget-cutting, federal support for women's organizations was gradually whittled away. The Mulroney government cut back on funding for the National Action Committee on the Status of Women (NAC), which had actively opposed the Charlottetown Accord. Both the NAC and the Canadian Advisory Council on the Status of Women were among the first victims of Paul Martin's budget reforms.

THE ENVIRONMENTAL MOVEMENT

Environmental groups were also rarely the recipients of government funding. They persisted nonetheless, and added many new organizations, national and local, to their ranks. In the 1980s, the Canadian Coalition on Acid Rain was responsible for the research and publicity that persuaded Brian Mulroney to seek an agreement on acid rain with the Americans. Campaigns by Ducks Unlimited resulted in the conservation of threatened wetlands, while the World Wildlife Fund, among other groups, convinced governments to open new parks and wilderness reserves. The Friends of Clayoquot Sound, along with local First Nations, held protests during the summer of 1993 that brought the arrests of almost 1000 people, but that also resulted in a government decision to put a moratorium on logging in the region. That same summer, protesters in Pictou County, Nova Scotia, began an organized and long-standing campaign to end the forestry companies' use of chemical sprays on woodlands.

Disillusionment with the overall slow pace of progress on the environmental front caused some ecological activists to create a national Green Party in 1983. It had no electoral success by the end of the century, and most environmentalists of the period preferred to lobby all governments and political parties rather than pin their hopes on electing a party whose main focus was on the environment. Such non-partisanship was particularly the case for Aboriginal movements, which regarded suspiciously the motives of political parties and even their non-Aboriginal allies.

GAY RIGHTS

Lesbian, gay, bisexual, and transgendered (LGBT) Canadians continued to struggle for acceptance in Canadian society and for legal protection from discrimination. While gays and lesbians won the right to be ordained ministers in the United Church in 1988, the Roman Catholic Church joined evangelical Protestants in continuing to denounce homosexuality, along with abortion and divorce, as threats to the traditional family. Intolerance against homosexuality sometimes manifested itself in violence. Homophobic thugs beat up and in some cases killed gay men, while police raids on gay bars and bathhouses indicated a continuing willingness to harass gays in the name of public morality.

Not surprisingly, LGBT Canadians were cautious about expressing their sexuality openly for fear of reprisals. Nonetheless, about 3000 people marched in Toronto in 1981 to protest the arrest of over 300 men at four bathhouses. The community's caution peeled away even more when the acquired immune deficiency syndrome (AIDS) pandemic descended on the world in the early 1980s. While by no means confined to homosexuals, AIDS spread quickly in the gay community, encouraging an organized and public response. The LGBT community came together to develop support networks for people infected with AIDS, to conduct education campaigns to encourage safe sexual practices, and to pressure government for a wide range of reforms.

Elizabeth May

Many Canadians develop political skills while working in civil society organizations. A good example is Elizabeth May, who became leader of the Green Party in 2006. She was born in Hartford, Connecticut, in 1954; her mother was a prominent peace activist and her father worked in the insurance business. In 1972, the family decided to leave the United States, moving to Cape Breton Island, where they barely eked out a living by running a restaurant and gift shop in the community of Margaree Harbour.

Elizabeth May cut her political teeth in 1975 when she joined a local group opposed to spraying the now-banned chemical fenitrothion to combat a spruce budworm infestation in the region. An inspired activist, she stood up to the Swedish multinational corporation Stora Kopparberg, which threatened to close its Nova Scotia pulp mill if the government refused to conduct a spraying program. When the company launched a lawsuit against the protesters, May travelled to Sweden with Ryan Googoo, Grand Chief of the Mi'kmaq, to raise support for her cause. She also became involved in protests against uranium mining in Nova Scotia and against Scott Paper's plans to spray Agent Orange to kill hardwood trees and shrubs to make it easier to harvest softwood for their pulp and paper operations.

Eager to see improvements in environmental policy, May agreed in 1986 to work as an advisor to Tom McMillan, Minister of the Environment in the Mulroney administration. She resigned two years later when the Minister granted permits for the Rafferty-Alameda Dams in Saskatchewan without an environmental assessment. In 1989, she became the founding executive director of the Sierra Club of Canada.

Elizabeth May in 2011. SOURCE: CARLOS OSORIO/GETTY IMAGES

From this position, she lobbied for a variety of environmental causes and continued to draw media attention. In 2001, she conducted a 17-day hunger strike on Parliament Hill to demand the relocation of families living next to Canada's largest waste site, the Sydney Tar Ponds, reservoirs for a toxic brew of chemicals from 80 years of steel production in the city.

May easily bested her rivals for leadership of the Green Party of Canada in 2006, but she was unable to win the riding of Central Nova against the Conservative Party's Peter MacKay in the 2008 election. In the 2011 election, she won the riding of Saanich–Gulf Islands and sat as the only Green Party member in the House of Commons.[6]

Meanwhile, governments gradually began to reconsider their exclusionary policies. In 1977, sexual preference was removed as a criterion for rejecting potential immigrants, and the Parti Québécois government added sexual orientation to the non-discrimination section of Quebec's human rights code, making Quebec the first major jurisdiction in the world to enshrine equality based on sexual orientation. Similar legislation was passed in Ontario in 1986 and in Manitoba in 1987. Activists won court battles that gave same-sex partners benefits similar to those of heterosexual spouses. In 1992, the Mulroney government lifted the ban on homosexuals in the armed forces, and three years later the Supreme Court ruled that "sexual orientation" should be read into the non-discrimination sections of the Constitution. In 1998, the Supreme Court ruled in favour of Delwin Vriend, a laboratory instructor at a Christian college in Edmonton, whom the college had fired because his sexual orientation clashed with their anti-gay statement of religious belief. Effectively, that added sexual orientation to the list of prohibited grounds for exclusion for employment purposes throughout the country, even when provincial human rights legislation was silent on the subject.

By the end of the century, most gays were no longer closeted. They published newspapers and magazines and participated in a highly creative gay culture. The highlight was annual Pride events, including a 10 day festival in Toronto, well-attended summer events that were often proclaimed by city councils. Pride festivals began modestly in Toronto in 1981 as part of an effort by the local gay community to make its presence known after the bathhouse arrests. LGBT community groups in other cities, buoyed by the enthusiastic reception that Pride received in Toronto, began to sponsor their own events, including annual Pride Day parades, drag shows, costume events, and rainbow flag–raising ceremonies.

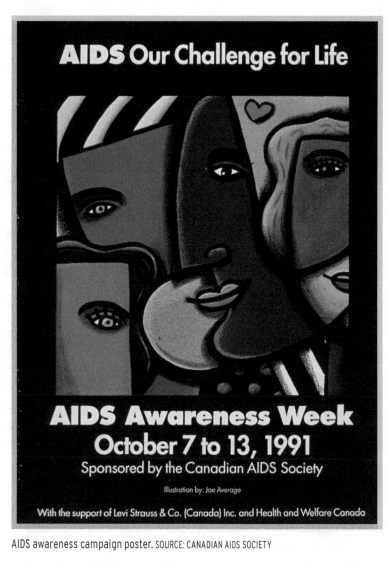

AIDS awareness campaign poster. SOURCE: CANADIAN AIDS SOCIETY

CONCLUSION

As the postwar liberal consensus was called into question, a new pessimism about the ability of successive governments in Ottawa to solve the nation's problems began to set in. New regionally based parties offered solutions, provinces demanded that their rights be respected, and extra-parliamentary groups, often with little patience for the political games that prevailed in Ottawa, became more assertive. What was lost in this process was an attachment to the larger nation-state. As the twentieth century ended, it was clear that neo-liberalism had not created a new consensus among Canadians, and that battles between old liberals who supported extensive government programs and neo-liberals would characterize Canadian politics for some time to come.

Why did the "Yes" Side Lose, but Almost Win, the 1995 Quebec Referendum?

The close defeat of the Yes side in the 1995 Quebec referendum was galling for sovereignist forces. Jacques Parizeau's speech blaming "money and ethnic votes" was just the first in a series of attempts to explain the loss by factors beyond the control of the sovereignist camp. Books with evocative titles such as *Le référendum volé (The Stolen Referendum)*, *Les secrets d'Option Canada (The Secrets of Option Canada)*, and *Nos ennemis, les médias (Our Enemies, the Media)* still attract a wide readership.[7] Their authors decry a "campaign of fear" by business leaders and federalist politicians as to the economic consequences of sovereignty, systematic media bias in favour of the No side, and efforts in Montreal to pad voting rolls with recent immigrants. Above all, they denounce illegal campaign overspending by No groups and Canadians from outside Quebec for events such as the pro-Canada "love-in" rally in Montreal just days before the vote. They also single out the overwhelming No vote by anglophones and allophones. Sociologist Pierre Drouilly attributes the referendum result to the long-standing hostility of Quebec's anglophones towards its French-speaking majority: "In the brouhaha of human History, they adamantly pursue their main objective: stopping by any means the emergence of a sovereign French society in North America."[8] As for claims that the voting rights of anglophones and allophones were systematically violated, they are minimized or dismissed out of hand.

Scholarly analysis of the referendum generally takes a different tack, focussing not on why the Yes side lost, but on why it came so close to winning, after trailing badly in the polls.[9] Some point to the "Bouchard effect." As historian Sylvie Beaudreau put it, "The near-victory of the 'yes' side on 30 October had been due to the efforts of one man: Lucien Bouchard."[10] Some political scientists, such as Vincent Lemieux and Maurice Pinard, agreed. Others, while not denying Bouchard's importance, noted that the rise in support for the Yes side began well before he took over the campaign from Jacques Parizeau. Instead, they identified other factors: early gaffes on the No side, especially heavy-handed threats by business leaders; the lack of charismatic and credible No leaders; the absence of any concrete offer of constitutional change from Canadian federalists, except in the dying days of the campaign; and above all, the Yes side's success in convincing Quebecers that economic partnership with the rest of Canada would be easily negotiated.

There is no consensus among analysts as to the relative weight of these different factors, and they disagree over other issues. Many commentators outside of Quebec affirmed that the ambiguity of the referendum question bolstered the Yes vote. Did "Yes" voters think they were voting for an independent Quebec, or rather for renewed federalism? Most who have analyzed polls and interviews suggest instead that Quebecers understood very well the portent of their vote.[11] Similarly, while some suggest that the Montreal "love-in" might just have pushed the No side over the top, others minimize its impact on the vote.[12] In more recent work, these debates have moved in new directions. Thus, historian Jocelyn Létourneau affirms that the question's premise that Quebec could both leave Canada and stay closely affiliated with it was the logical continuation of French Quebecers' long-standing ambiguous relationship with Canada. As for the "love-in," sociologist Jean-Philippe Warren and communications specialist Eric Ronis have examined the rally as an example of the politics of emotions, concluding that "love did not appear very effective in a 'politics of recognition' between the two nations of Quebec and English Canada."[13]

While most of the debates focus on the Quebec population as a whole, other analysts have turned to examining the behaviour of more specific groups, often with a view to attacking stereotypes. Though the Yes side actively courted women voters (despite a notable blunder by Bouchard calling on white Quebec women to have more children), more Quebec women voted No than Yes. Many analysts concluded that there was a gender gap in support for sovereignty in Quebec, but work by feminist scholar Chantal Maillé cautions us against assuming that women's voting choices in the referendum can be reduced to support for sovereignty, and emphasizes instead their search for guarantees of a just society.[14]

The reaction of Quebec's Native population is similarly complex. While Natives as a whole voted massively for the No side, their small population meant that their votes had little effect on the overall tally on referendum night, and their part in the referendum is thus sometimes dismissed as marginal.

Nevertheless, their status as First Nations, their claims to much of Quebec's territory, and their special relationship with the federal government gave particular weight to their actions, such as holding their own referenda with their own questions, refusing entry to Elections Quebec officials, and even threatening to secede themselves. Some writers, such as Robin Philpot, saw their massive rejection of the Yes option as a reflection of the fear tactics of the federal government. Others pointed instead to the Parti Québécois' stance that if Quebec separated from Canada, its Native populations would have no choice but to follow,[15] a position not much different from that of the European diplomats who had negotiated the Treaty of Paris in 1763.

Two recent books underscore the ongoing interest in the 1995 Quebec referendum. Robert Wright's *The Night Canada Stood Still* provides a detailed narrative of the referendum campaign, notable in that it examines in detail the reactions in the rest of Canada. Chantal Hébert's *The Morning After,* based on interviews with many of the leaders of the Yes and No camps, asks what would have been the plan if the Yes side had, in the end, won.[16] Both provide much fodder for future analyses that may go beyond the basic questions of who voted how, and why.

NOTES

1. A video clip of Parizeau's speech can be found in the CBC Archives, http://www.cbc.ca/archives/categories/politics/federal-politics/separation-anxiety-the-1995-quebec-referendum/money-and-the-ethnic-vote.html. The simultaneous translation is erroneous in one key respect: Bouchard said "des votes ethniques" ("ethnic votes") rather than "the ethnic vote."

2. Cited in Olive P. Dickason with David T. McNab, *Canada's First Nations: A History of Founding Peoples from Earliest Times* (Don Mills, ON: Oxford University Press, 2008) 440.

3. *Royal Commission Report on Aboriginal Peoples,* http://www.aadnc-aandc.gc.ca/eng/1307458586498/1307458751962. The five-volume, 3537-page report is usefully summarized and discussed in Dickason and McNab, *Canada's First Nations,* 417–420.

4. On the Nisga'a Treaty, see Tracie Lee Scott, *Postcolonial Sovereignty? The Nisga'a Final Agreement* (Saskatoon: Purich Publishers, 2012).

5. CBC News, *Viewpoint,* Judy Rebick column, 3 January 2001.

6. Elizabeth May provides autobiographical materials and glimpses into her activist strategies in her book *How to Save the World in Your Spare Time* (Toronto: Key Porter Books, 2006).

7. Robin Philpot, *Le référendum volé* (Montreal: Les Intouchables, 2005); Patrick Bourgeois, *Nos ennemis, les médias: petit guide pour comprendre la désinformation canadienne* (Quebec: Éditions du Québécois, 2005); Normand Lester and Robin Philpot, *Les secrets d'Option Canada* (Montreal: Les Intouchables, 2006).

8. Pierre Drouilly, "La polarisation linguistique du vote: une constante de l'histoire électorale du Québec", *Bulletin d'histoire politique* 5, 2 (1997), 41. Authors' translation.

9. Major studies include Denis Monière and Jean Herman Guay, eds., *La bataille du Québec. Troisième épisode: 30 jours qui ébranlèrent le Canada* (Montreal: Fides, 1996); Kenneth McRoberts, *Misconceiving Canada: The Struggle for National Unity* (Toronto: Oxford University Press, 1997); Maurice Pinard, Robert Bernier and Vincent Lemieux, *Un combat inachevé* (Sainte-Foy: Presses de l'Université du Québec, 1997); and Robert A. Young, *The Struggle for Quebec: From Referendum to Referendum?* (Montreal: McGill-Queen's University Press, 1999). On specific issues, see also Vincent Lemieux,

"Le référendum de 1995: quelques pistes d'explication", *Québec-Canada: What is the Path Ahead? / Nouveaux sentiers vers l'avenir,* ed. John E. Trent, Robert Andrew Young and Guy Lachapelle (Ottawa: University of Ottawa Press, 1996); Guy Lachapelle, "The 1995 Quebec Referendum: How the Sovereignty Partnership Proposal Turned the Campaign Around", *Québec Studies* 24 (1997) 180-196; John Fox, Robert Andersen and Joseph Dubonnet, "The Polls and the 1995 Quebec Referendum", *Canadian Journal of Sociology* 24, 3 (1999) 411–424; and Claire Durand, "À qui la faute? Le référendum dix ans après", *D'un référendum à l'autre: le Québec face à son destin,* ed. Alain-G. Gagnon (Quebec: Presses de l'Université Laval, 2008) 27–50.

10. Sylvie M. Beaudreau, "Quebec", *Canadian Annual Review of Politics and Public Affairs 1995,* ed. David Leyton-Brown (Toronto: University of Toronto Press, 2002) 137.

11. Harold D. Clarke, Allan Kornberg and Peter Wearing, *A Polity on the Edge: Canada and the Politics of Fragmentation* (Toronto: University of Toronto Press, 2000) 158–159; Durand, "À qui la faute", 32–33.

12. Pinard, Bernier and Lemieux, *Un combat inachevé,* 274; Durand, "À qui la faute", 34–35.

13. Jocelyn Létourneau, *Que veulent vraiment les Québécois? Regard sur l'intention nationale au Québec (français) d'hier à aujourd'hui* (Montreal: Boréal, 2006) 97–98; Jean-Philippe Warren and Eric Ronis, "The Politics of Love: The 1995 Montreal Unity Rally and Canadian Affection", *Journal of Canadian Studies* 45, 1 (2011) 23.

14. Chantal Maillé, "Quebec Women and the Constitutional Issue: A Scattered Group", *Journal of Canadian Studies* 35, 2 (2000) 95–108. See also Guy Lachapelle, "Le comportement politique des Québécoises lors de la campagne référendaire de 1995: une application de la théorie du dépistage", *Politique et sociétés* 17, 1–2 (1998) 91–120.

15. Philpot, *Le référendum volé,* 99–106; Jill Wherrett, *Aboriginal Peoples and the 1995 Quebec Referendum: A Survey of the Issues* (Ottawa: Political and Social Affairs Division, Library of Parliament, 1996). For a brief analysis of Natives' votes, see Pinard, Bernier and Lemieux, *Un combat inachevé* 311–313; for an overview of their actions, Martin Papillon, "Aboriginal Peoples and Quebec: competing or coexisting nationalisms?", *Quebec Questions: Quebec Studies for the Twenty-First Century,* ed. Stéphan Gervais et al. (Toronto: Oxford University Press, 2011) 117–118.

16. Robert Wright, *The Night Canada Stood Still* (Toronto: HarperCollins Canada, 2014); Chantal Hébert with Jean Lapierre, *The Morning After: The 1995 Quebec Referendum and the Day that Almost Was* (Toronto: Alfred A. Knopf Canada, 2014). An earlier work similarly based on journalistic interviews is Mario Cardinal, *Breaking Point Quebec-Canada: The 1995 Referendum* (Montreal: Bayard Canada, 2005).

SELECTED READING

Behiels, Michael D. and Matthew Hayday, eds. *Contemporary Quebec: Selected Readings and Commentaries.* Montreal: McGill-Queen's University Press, 2011

Blake, Raymond B., ed. *Transforming the Nation: Canada and Brian Mulroney.* Montreal: McGill-Queen's University Press, 2007

Carty, R.K., ed. *Politics, Policy and Government in British Columbia.* Toronto: University of Toronto Press, 1996

Coates, Ken S. *The Marshall Decision and Native Rights.* Montreal: McGill-Queen's University Press, 2000

Gagnon, Alain-G., ed. *Contemporary Canadian Federalism: Foundations, Traditions, Institutions.* Toronto: University of Toronto Press, 2009

Gagnon, Alain-G., ed. *Québec: State and Society.* 3rd ed. Peterborough: Broadview Press, 2004

Harrison, Trevor. *Of Passionate Intensity: Right-Wing Populism and the Reform Party of Canada.* Toronto: University of Toronto Press, 1995

Howlett, Michael, Dennis Pilon, and Tracy Summerville, eds. *British Columbia Politics and Government.* Toronto: Edmond Montgomery Publications, 2009

Jeffrey, Brooke. *Divided Loyalties: The Liberal Party of Canada, 1984–2008.* Toronto: University of Toronto Press, 2010

Kinsman, Gary. *The Regulation of Desire: Sexuality in Canada*. 2nd ed. Montreal: Black Rose Books, 1996

Kulchyski, Peter, ed. *Unjust Relations: Aboriginal Rights in Canadian Courts*. Toronto: Oxford University Press, 1994

Lawrence, Bonita. *Fractured Homeland: Federal Recognition and Algonquin Identity in Ontario*. Vancouver: UBC Press, 2012

McRoberts, Kenneth. *Misconceiving Canada: The Struggle for National Unity*. Toronto: Oxford University Press, 1997

McWhinney, Edward. *Chrétien and Canadian Federalism: Politics and the Constitution, 1993–2003*. Vancouver: Ronsdale, 2003

Miller, J.R. *Compact, Contract, Covenant: Aboriginal Treaty-Making in Canada*. Toronto: University of Toronto Press, 2009

Milne, David. *Tug of War: Ottawa and the Provinces Under Trudeau and Mulroney*. Toronto: Lorimer, 1986

Payne, Michael, Donald Wetherell and Catherine Cavanaugh, eds. *Alberta Formed/Alberta Transformed*. Edmonton and Calgary: University of Alberta Press and University of Calgary Press, 2006

Poitras, Jacques. *Irving vs Irving: Canada's Feuding Billionaires and the Stories They Won't Tell*. Toronto: Penguin, 2014

Thomas, Paul G. and Curtis Brown, eds. *Manitoba Politics and Government: Issues, Institutions, Traditions*. Winnipeg: University of Manitoba Press, 2010

Warner, Tom. *Never Going Back: A History of Queer Activism in Canada*. Toronto: University of Toronto Press, 2002

Wesley, Jared J. *Code Politics: Campaigns and Cultures on the Canadian Prairies*. Vancouver: UBC Press, 2011

White, Randall. *Ontario Since 1985: A Contemporary History*. Toronto: Eastend Books, 1998

Wicken, William C. *Mi'kmaq Treaties on Trial: History, Land, and Donald Marshall Junior*. Toronto: University of Toronto Press, 2002

Winfield, Mark S. *Blue-Green Province: The Environment and the Political Economy of Ontario*. Vancouver: UBC Press, 2012

Wright, Robert. *The Night Canada Stood Still*. Toronto: HarperCollins Canada, 2014

For a comprehensive list of readings for topics covered in this chapter, please visit http://pearsoncanada.ca/conrad.

CHAPTER 17
CANADA IN THE AGE OF ANXIETY, 2000–2014

"Occupation sufficient to ground Aboriginal title is not confined to specific sites of settlement but extends to tracts of land that were regularly used for hunting, fishing or otherwise exploiting resources and over which the group exercised effective control at the time of assertion of European sovereignty."[1] This excerpt from a Supreme Court of Canada ruling on 26 June 2014 reflected a gradual evolution of legal thinking in Canada regarding the extent of Native people's rights to control the future of their traditional lands. It provided a challenge to governments in Canada accustomed to granting permits for land use with little thought to the possible impact on Native peoples, whose ideas regarding human interaction with the environment were often at variance with those of relative newcomers to Canada. In this case, the court was dealing with a conflict between the Tsilhqot'in and the British Columbia government over a logging licence granted by the latter in 1983. The Supreme Court decision was welcomed by most Native peoples and environmentalists.

This ruling was a rare ray of light for opponents of neo-liberalism, which informed many of the decisions of the Conservative Party that held office under Stephen Harper's leadership following the 2006 election. Although the Conservatives were obliged to govern with a minority of seats in the House of Commons after the elections of 2006 and 2008, the party's majority win in 2011 offered more scope for its efforts to transform Canadian society.

Conservative fortunes were bolstered in the twenty-first century by fears of international terrorism after Muslim extremists used hijacked planes to crash into the World Trade Center in New York and the Pentagon in Washington on 11 September 2001. Public fears of terrorism were manipulated, as were fears of communism in the early Cold War period, to justify greater militarism, closer scrutiny of the critics of state policies, and suppression of freedom of speech. The Conservative government did its best to modify Canadians' image of themselves, from socially conscious collectivists to individualists, and to transform Canada into a warrior nation. Events such as the deadly October 2014 attacks on soldiers by young men inspired by religious radicalism made clear the effect of Canada's shift from peacemaker to anti-Islamist ally of the United States. This chapter examines developments in the early years of the new century, which from close range seem to have ushered in a new era of anxiety and set the stage for deep changes in Canadian society.

POLITICAL DEVELOPMENTS

Jean Chrétien's Liberals won another majority in 2000, easily withstanding an attempt by the Reform Party to expand their support by rebranding themselves as the Canadian Alliance Party. Replacing Preston Manning with Stockwell Day, a former Pentecostal school administrator who had served as Alberta's provincial treasurer, the Canadian Alliance managed to gain only six additional seats, prompting yet another party reorganization. Early in 2004, the Canadian Alliance merged with the Progressive Conservatives to form the Conservative Party of Canada, led by Stephen Harper, a neo-liberal ideologue who was determined to bring an end to Liberal Party dominance of Canadian federal politics.

The Liberal Party, meanwhile, took a different tack after the 2000 election, trying to restore its image as a progressive force, a goal now made possible by a series of budget surpluses. Playing to Canadian concern about the erosion of Medicare, Jean Chrétien appointed Roy Romanow, the former NDP premier of Saskatchewan, as a one-man commission to determine how best to ensure the health of Canadians. Romanow proposed a major injection of federal money into provincial Medicare programs to compensate for earlier cuts. In 2003, a federal–provincial agreement provided the provinces with billions of additional federal dollars. There were no strings attached due to an earlier federal–provincial agreement, the Social Union Framework, which reduced the federal role to providing untargeted funds to provincial governments in broad areas such as health and social services.

When Chrétien retired in the fall of 2003, Paul Martin succeeded him as prime minister. The son of a long-time minister in federal Liberal cabinets, Paul Martin Junior

pursued a business career, capping his rise to prominence as sole owner of Canada Steamship Lines. In 1988 he entered the political arena, winning a Liberal seat in Montreal. Although he lost to Chrétien in his bid to become leader of the Liberal Party in 1990, he played an important role as finance minister in slaying the deficit. In 2002 Chrétien fired Martin, who made no secret of his ambition to replace the Prime Minister, but he easily won the party leadership when his nemesis finally stepped down in 2003.

Martin focused on improving Canada's productivity while protecting its social programs, but revelations of irregularities in federal sponsorship programs in Quebec called into question the integrity of the Liberal Party. Following the 2004 election, Martin emerged as leader of a shaky minority government. Governing with NDP support, the Liberals provided additional funding to Medicare, introduced a federal–provincial agreement on child care, and took the lead in negotiating an agreement for a $5.1 billion program (the Kelowna Accord) to improve the lives of Aboriginal peoples in the areas of health, education, and housing. They also legalized same-sex marriage and flirted with the idea of legalizing the use of marijuana. This was not enough for the NDP under its new leader Jack Layton. Hoping to take advantage of Liberal weakness and to gain votes from progressives for having forced Martin to invest more in social spending than he planned, the NDP withdrew its support for the Liberal government and inadvertently opened the door for the Conservative Party to lead a minority government after the January 2006 election.

Stephen Harper arrived at his political position by a circuitous route. Born in Toronto, he excelled at school, where he joined the Young Liberals Club. After graduating, he moved to Alberta to work for Imperial Oil and transferred his political loyalties to the Progressive Conservatives when Trudeau introduced the National Energy Program. Impatient with Mulroney's lack of fiscal restraint, Harper became an early recruit to the Reform Party, serving as its chief policy officer and then legislative assistant to Reform MP Deborah Grey. He won a seat in Calgary West in 1993, but due to differences with Preston Manning, he refused to run in 1997 and became leader of the right-wing National Citizens Coalition. Despite the embrace of neo-liberal policies by both Progressive Conservative and Liberal governments, Harper, as president of the National Citizens Coalition, claimed in 2000 that "Canada appears content to become a second-tier socialistic country, boasting ever more loudly about its economy and social services to mask its second-rate status, led by a second-world strongman appropriately suited for the task."[2] Shortly thereafter, his name appeared on a "firewall" letter to Alberta's premier Ralph Klein calling for the province to become a semi-sovereign state that could stand up to centralizing, socializing Liberal federal governments. A member of the evangelical Christian and Missionary Alliance, Harper is at heart both a neo-liberal and a social conservative. He left little doubt during the 2006 campaign that he was determined to move Canada in a new direction.

Harper often garnered support from the Bloc Québécois, which disagreed with the new prime minister's right-wing agenda but was encouraged by his promises to keep the federal government out of provincial jurisdictions and to increase equalization payments to Quebec. Martin's national child care and First Nations programs were scrapped, the GST was cut from seven to five percent, and military spending was increased. Seeing a financial crisis looming, Harper called a snap election in the fall of 2008, despite legislation passed by his own party that fixed federal election dates every four years. His campaign focused on discrediting a proposal by federal liberal leader Stéphane Dion, to impose a carbon tax. Although the Conservatives increased their number of seats from 124 to 143, they were left in a minority position.

The failure of the Conservatives to respond in a serious way to the global financial crisis that erupted during the election campaign prompted the Bloc, Liberals, and NDP to come together to insist on a vigorous program of government spending to counter the precipitous downturn in the private sector. Harper initially resisted, but came forward with a program of counter-cyclical spending after an effort by the Liberals and NDP to form a government with Bloc support. In the brief constitutional crisis that ensued, Harper insisted on his right to prorogue Parliament to prevent a vote of non-confidence in his government. The Governor General Michaëlle Jean granted the prorogation and, by the time Parliament had reconvened, the agreement among the opposition parties had come unstuck, partly because the Prime Minister had changed course on the economy and agreed to a generous program of public works.

As was the case with the Liberals under Jean Chrétien, the opposition to the government split their votes among contending parties. In the May 2011 election, the Conservatives won a clear majority of seats (166), while the Liberals under their new leader Michael Ignatieff were reduced to third-party status, winning only 34 seats. For the first time in Canadian history, the NDP, under the leadership of Jack Layton, emerged as the official opposition with 103 seats, 59 of them in Quebec. Support for the Bloc Québécois collapsed in the final weeks of the campaign, with the result that the sovereignist party won only four seats and its leader, Gilles Duceppe, was defeated in his own riding. The swing toward the NDP in Quebec was particularly astonishing since Quebecers had previously only ever elected two NDP MPs. While impressive in its results, Harper's parliamentary majority was won with less than 40 percent of the votes cast in the election, in which 7.5 million eligible voters (almost 39 percent of the electorate) failed to cast a ballot.

Following the election, Ignatieff stepped down and Layton lost his battle with cancer. The NDP chose Thomas Mulcair as Layton's replacement in 2012. Having won a by-election for a Montreal seat in 2007, Mulcair had helped Layton lay the groundwork for the NDP's improbable landslide in the 2011 federal election in that province. A year after the NDP leadership race, it was the Liberal Party's turn to find a new leader. They chose Justin Trudeau, who, like Mulcair, was a Montreal MP and whose popularity owed much to his being the eldest son of Pierre Trudeau. Public opinion polls suggested that the Liberals were fast becoming Canada's most popular political party. Although the popularity of the young leader was largely responsible for the rise of Liberal fortunes, scandals involving expenses of senators appointed by Harper caused some former Conservative Party supporters to lose confidence in the government.

Over the course of his mandate, Harper moved aggressively to implement his neo-liberal agenda. Policies were put in place to shrink the civil service, reduce the rate of growth of federal grants to provinces for health and social services, cut corporate tax rates, shut down the Canadian Firearms Agency, and replace Canada's relative neutrality in the Middle East with consistent support for Israel in its conflicts with Palestinians. When his government made compliance with the long-form version of the 2011 decennial census voluntary, the Chief Statistician of Canada, Munir Sheikh, resigned, complaining that the results of a non-mandatory survey would be statistically questionable. The Conservatives also restricted the rights of government scientists and other civil servants to release data that might contradict the rationales the government provided for its policies.

The opposition parties lacked the numbers to break Harper's stride, but the Supreme Court of Canada, determined to protect the Constitution and the Charter of Rights and Freedoms, often stood in his way. When the Conservative government tried to shutter Insite, a safe-injection centre for Vancouver drug addicts, claiming that it condoned illegal activity, the Supreme Court rejected this argument, observing that Insite's harm-reduction approach had saved lives. Similarly, the Harper government's defence of laws that forced prostitutes to work in the shadows despite the legality of their profession was overruled by the Court as unacceptable because the laws put the lives of sex workers in danger. The government's tough-on-crime bills also met opposition from the Supreme Court when they violated the Charter rights of defendants. Even Harper's efforts to reform the Senate without following constitutional processes were dismissed. The Court's decisions regarding Native rights, while not directed against the federal government, put obstacles in the path of a government determined to reduce efforts by First Nations to slow down or stop proposed energy and mining developments.

In frustration, the Harper government attempted in March 2014 to name a reliably conservative Quebec-trained Federal Court judge as one of the Supreme Court's three Quebec members. When the Supreme Court ruled that as a Federal Court judge, he did not qualify, Harper lashed out at Chief Justice Beverley McLachlin, only stepping back from serious allegations against her dealings with his office when it became clear that almost the entire judiciary in Canada was on the chief justice's side.

ENVIRONMENTAL CHALLENGES

In February 2007, the Intergovernmental Panel on Climate Change (IPCC) filed its fourth comprehensive report. It reaffirmed that the planet was experiencing continuous increases in temperatures on land, sea, and permafrost, a result mainly of the increased human production of greenhouse gases. Predicting a rise in sea levels by seven metres with the melting of the Greenland ice cap if humans failed to adapt their behaviour, the report called for global emissions to fall by 90 percent as soon as possible to prevent an environmental tragedy.

Although Canadian governments promised swift action, their commitment to a reduction in global warming was questionable. The Chrétien Liberal government signed the Kyoto Protocol in 1998 and it was ratified by Parliament in December 2002, but under pressure from industrial lobbyists, the Liberals relied mainly on voluntary cooperation by industry to meet Kyoto's goals. Predictably, there was little reduction in greenhouse gas (GHG) emissions. The election of Stephen Harper's Conservatives in January 2006 reinforced inaction. In opposition, Harper had denounced Kyoto as a socialist plot, and once in power he continued to oppose the protocol and advised government scientists that they could not speak publicly on the issue of global warming without clearing their comments with their ministry. At the 2009 United Nations Climate Conference in Copenhagen, Harper followed the Americans in promising to reduce Canada's carbon emissions by 17 percent for the period from 2005 to 2020, but the Americans moved much more purposefully in reaching that goal.

Under Harper, Canada also became even more of a laggard in efforts to forecast and mitigate effects of climate change. In 2014, Natural Resources Canada, in an extensive report entitled "Canada in a Changing Climate: Sector Perspectives on Impacts and Adaptations," praised governments at all levels for beginning to recognize the need to plan for adaptation, but observed that there were "relatively few examples of implementation of specific changes to reduce vulnerability to future climate change, or take advantage of potential opportunities."[3] Natural Resources Canada singled out Australia, Germany, the United Kingdom, and Norway as having developed national plans for adapting to a warming world, but Canada was slow to follow their lead.

In contrast to federal reticence, every Canadian province and territory developed plans to reduce its carbon footprint, focusing on development of renewable energy, refitting energy-inefficient buildings, expanding public transportation, and improving fuel standards in transportation. Many of these plans claimed successes, with seven provinces reducing their fossil fuel emissions from 2005 to 2014, led by Ontario with a 17 percent reduction, closely followed by New Brunswick and Nova Scotia. In contrast, the three Prairie provinces recorded increased emissions. Alberta led the pack with a seven percent increase that was entirely attributable to an

Inuk Environmental Activist: Sheila Watt-Cloutier

Sheila Watt-Cloutier was born in Kuujuaq, Nunavik (northern Quebec), an Inuit community, in 1953. She was raised as an Inuk (the singular for Inuit), hunting and living off the land, by her mother, a healer and interpreter, and father, an RCMP officer. When she was 10, her parents placed her in schools in southern Canada. She then attended McGill University, studying counselling, education, and human development. After graduation, she returned to Nunavik to work as an Inuktitut interpreter for Ungava Hospital. She joined other Inuit community members to press the Quebec government to place Inuit values and language at the core of Inuit communities' educational curricula.

Increasingly involved in land claims and environmental struggles in the 1990s, Watt-Cloutier became president of the Inuit Circumpolar Council from 1995 to 2001 and then its international chair from 2002 to 2006. The ICC speaks for 155 000 Inuit in Canada, Greenland, Alaska, and Russia. Under the leadership of Watt-Cloutier, northerners spearheaded a campaign that resulted in a ban on persistent organic pollutants at the Stockholm convention in 2001. Addressing climate change became the major aim of the council, which sees global warming as both an environmental and a human rights issue for a people dependent on marine life.

In 2005, Watt-Cloutier, on behalf of the council, petitioned the Inter-American Commission on Human Rights, calling for relief for Inuit from the assault on their human rights by fossil-fuel-induced global warming. The council argued that species requiring sea ice, including polar bears, ice-dwelling seals, walrus, and some marine birds, face extinction if global warming is not alleviated. The people of the North face increased danger as marine storms become less predictable and their access to supplies from southern Canada in winter becomes precarious as the ice on winter roads on local waterways melts earlier each year. The council rejected the petition, but the Inuit position was poignant:

Inuit are an ancient people. Our way of life is dependent on the natural environment and animals. Climate change is destroying our environment and eroding our culture. But we refuse to disappear. We will not become a footnote to globalization. Climate change is amplified in the Arctic. What is happening to us now will happen soon in the rest of the world. Our region is the globe's climate change "barometer." If you want to protect the planet, look to the Arctic and listen to what Inuit are saying.[4]

Watt-Cloutier, who lives in Inuvik, Nunavut, continues to campaign for action against global warming. Nominated in 2007 for a Nobel Peace Prize for her ongoing environmental activism, Watt-Cloutier lost to former American vice-president Al Gore, who was the inspiration behind a highly influential 2006 documentary, *An Inconvenient Truth*, warning of the dangers of climate change. She did, however, receive a variety of prestigious awards for her tireless defence of her people, which has become an equally passionate defence of life on the planet.[5]

Sheila Watt-Cloutier. SOURCE: CHRIS WINDEYER/CP IMAGES

80 percent increase in oil sands production that more than erased the province's carbon reductions in other sectors of the economy. Plans for a considerable expansion in the production of bitumen, the tar-like product of

the oil sands whose extraction involved greater GHG emissions than the extraction of conventional oil, were the main reason for projections that Canada would fail to reduce its carbon footprint between 2005 and 2020.

The oil sands became a hot-button issue in the twenty-first century. Environmentalists in other countries zeroed in on the unacceptable carbon foot-print that the tar sands represented, giving Canada a bad name internationally. Even in Alberta, where defenders of the province's main engine of economic growth remained powerful, concerns were expressed that the huge quantities of water required in the extraction of bitumen threatened the province's overall water supply. Native groups in the Fort McMurray area provided evidence that they suffered inordinately high incidences of rare, fatal cancers along with contamination of their water supplies. Outside the landlocked province, there was increased concern about proposed pipelines to carry raw bitumen to Asia (the Northern Gateway Pipeline), to American refineries (the Keystone XL Pipeline), and to projected refineries in Saint John, New Brunswick (the Energy East Pipeline).

Northern Gateway, which passed a Harper government environmental assessment in 2014, met with considerable resistance in British Columbia from Native populations along the route and from environmentalists concerned about the potential damage from spills to plants, water, and wildlife. Rail as a substitute for pipelines also looked increasingly dubious after a train derailment in Lac Mégantic in the Eastern Townships of Quebec in July 2013 resulted in a blast that incinerated 47 people and destroyed half of the town centre. The derailed train carried highly explosive oil from the Bakken oilfield that lies under two American states and Manitoba and Saskatchewan. One partial solution to making pipelines more acceptable, proposed by the trade union movement in Alberta with some support from environmentalists, was to reduce oil sands production but make up the lost jobs through refining more of the bitumen in Alberta, the refined product being less explosive and easier to ship.

Alberta oil sands were not the only unconventional fossil fuel that created controversy. Hydraulic fracturing, the injection of fluid under high pressure into wellbores deep in the earth, permitted the recovery of shale gas and other petroleum products that had once seemed impossible to access. Every part of the country attracted "fracking" projects and opposition from affected communities who were frightened by reports that fracking might cause water contamination, destruction of air quality, and the release into the atmosphere of gases along with chemicals used in the process. Supporters had too little science behind them to allay such fears of dangers to health and environmental sustainability, and focused instead on the riches that fracking could bring. Pressures from opponents forced a moratorium on fracking in Quebec in 2011 and Newfoundland and Labrador in 2013. In Nova Scotia in 2012, the Mi'kmaq Warrior Society partially blockaded the Canso Causeway to publicize their opposition to hydraulic fracturing, and there were violent clashes between Aboriginal people and exploratory drillers in New Brunswick in 2013.

In British Columbia, where opponents of fracking were well organized, the government viewed the process as essential to bringing liquefied natural gas, the province's putative economic ticket to a prosperous future, to market. In the central Mackenzie Valley, despite community opposition, the National Energy Board gave a green light to American-based Conoco Phillips to frack in the Canol shale formation, believed to hold three to five billion barrels of recoverable oil. The governments of the three Prairie provinces remained willing to resist community opposition to fracking, while Ontario and Prince Edward Island had yet to approve any projects by 2014.

Skepticism about climate change gradually retreated as the frequency of weather disasters increased exponentially. In 2011 alone, a wildfire destroyed much of Slave Lake, Alberta, record floods afflicted Manitoba, and New Brunswick, Ontario, and Quebec all were hammered by hurricanes. Newfoundland had experienced a ferocious hurricane the year before. In 2013, flooding in southern Alberta forced 100 000 Calgarians from their homes along with residents of many smaller communities, while Toronto was hit by both a massive rainstorm in July and an ice storm in December that left hundreds of thousands of people without power. New Brunswick also had an ice storm in December 2013, which was followed by a tropical storm in July 2014, both knocking out power in some areas.

The federal government's weak record in the area of climate change reflected an emphasis on economic growth over environmental protection. In 2012, the Harper government removed federal funding from the Experimental Lakes Area in the Kenora district despite its world-renowned record in the study of water pollution, removed most of the protections for lakes in the Navigable Waters Protection Act, and weakened conservation provisions of the Fisheries Act. Harper remarked in June 2014 that "No matter what they say, no country is going to take actions that are going to deliberately destroy jobs and growth in their country. We are just a little more frank about that."[6] Harper's view that countries faced a stark choice between job creation and environmental protection has been challenged by various commentators, including Munir Sheikh, the former Chief Statistician of Canada. Sheikh observed that a number of industrialized countries that had imposed environmental taxes and achieved greater greenhouse gas reductions than Canada had as good or better economic performances as Canada. Environmental, economic, and social goals were compatible with the right mix of policies.[7] Non-conventional fossil fuels, in any case, accounted for only two percent of Canada's output in 2013, though surveys suggested that most Canadians believed that they contributed far more to the national economy.

MORE TO THE STORY
Arctic Sovereignty

In the twentieth century, the chief threat to Canadian sovereignty in the North came from occasional forays of American icebreakers and nuclear submarines in the Northwest Passage. Global warming gradually reshaped the Northwest Passage into a potentially safe seasonal sea lane for commercial ships. In September 2013, the *Nordic Orion*, a Danish-built vessel registered in Panama, became the first commercial bulk carrier to pass through the Northwest Passage. The *Nordic Orion* was carrying 15 000 metric tons of metallurgical coal from Vancouver to Finland as it crossed Canada's Arctic waters and the Passage, seeking the fastest feasible route to ship its large cargo.

Russia and the European Union sided with the American claim that no country could impose laws on transport through the "international" waters of the Passage. Russia also laid symbolic claim to an economic zone in the region of the North Pole, planting its flag by submersible on the seabed of the North Pole in 2007.

While any claim to the barren pole might at one time have seemed pointless, estimates of extensive mineral and energy reserves beneath the Arctic ice, presumably more reachable as the ice thinned, changed the stakes. The United Nations Convention on the Law of the Sea allows nations exclusive control over underwater natural resources for 200 nautical miles (370 kilometres) beyond their shoreline, unless they can demonstrate that the continental shelf extends beyond that limit. Canada spent $200 million to collect data on the sea floor, but the effort did not clearly establish the continental shelf extension. Nonetheless, in December 2013, Canada made a formal application to the United Nations to have 1.7 million square kilometres of the Arctic sea floor recognized as being under exclusive Canadian control.

Successive Canadian governments promised to bolster Canada's claims to the Arctic by building facilities in the region and strengthening Canada's Arctic research. The promises remained largely unfulfilled. In 2006, Stephen Harper pledged to build new Arctic icebreakers capable of dealing with changing ice conditions and a northern deepwater port, but later abandoned the icebreaker promise in favour of more modest patrol ships. Experts on the region suggested that Canada take additional steps to win greater support for its claim of sovereignty by investing in scientific research to establish more clearly its claim to the sea areas bordering on recognized Canadian lands and demonstrating an ability to clean up oil spills, provide security against terrorist attacks, and protect threatened species in northern regions.[8]

This 2013 Globe and Mail editorial cartoon parodies the competing Arctic claims of Canada and Russia. SOURCE: GLOBE AND MAIL/CP IMAGES

CANADIAN FOREIGN POLICY

While North American territory had long been spared war on home soil, this changed on 11 September 2001. The attack by Muslim extremists on New York and Washington left nearly 3000 people dead and helped to change the tone and direction of Canadian foreign policy.

Although Canadians were appalled by these events, their response was relatively restrained. American president George W. Bush immediately declared a "War on Terror" and claimed that terrorists resented the democratic freedoms enjoyed by Westerners. Jean Chrétien, in contrast, suggested in a CBC interview on the first anniversary of the 9/11 attacks: "You cannot exercise your powers to the point of humiliation for the others . . . we're looked upon as being arrogant, self-satisfied, greedy and with no limits. And the 11th of September is an occasion for me to realize it even more."[9]

In October 2001, the United States invaded Afghanistan after its government, led by the Muslim extremist Taliban movement, refused to surrender Osama bin Laden, the leader of al Qaeda, a terrorist organization deemed to be responsible for 9/11. Canada participated in a NATO-led International Security Assistance Force sent to Afghanistan and remained a combatant in that country until July 2011. Canadians paid little attention to the war until the summer of 2005, when Canadian troops shifted their focus from Kabul to the Taliban stronghold of Kandahar. By July 2011, when the Canadian combat role in the war was officially ended, 157 soldiers had come home in body bags—more casualties than had been suffered in the previous half-century of peacekeeping.

Chrétien, however, refused to take Canada into George W. Bush's "coalition of the willing" to wage war on Iraq in 2003. Since the United Nations saw little evidence for the American claim that Saddam Hussein's dictatorship was hiding "weapons of mass destruction" aimed at Western countries, it opposed the invasion of Iraq. Bush, supported by British prime minister Tony Blair, decided to proceed without UN backing. In making the decision not to join the coalition, Chrétien was influenced by Canadian popular opinion, especially in Quebec, where protests in Montreal against the war drew as many as 200 000 participants.

In a security-conscious world, Canada's commitment to human rights was also compromised. The Anti-Terrorism Act, passed three months after 9/11,

Canadian soldiers in Afghanistan in 2006 after hearing that one of their comrades had been killed in a friendly fire incident. SOURCE: LES PERREAUX/ CP IMAGES

increased the powers of the Canadian Security and Intelligence Service (CSIS) and the Royal Canadian Mounted Police to acquire information, detain suspects, and ban organizations believed to be supporting terrorism. Despite protests from civil society groups, the security state remained firmly in place and manifested itself with force during the G20 (Group of 20 finance ministers and central bank governors, established in 1999 at the suggestion of Paul Martin) in Toronto in the summer of 2010.

Alleged terrorist arrests were not limited to Anti-Terrorism Act detentions. Several Canadians were also arrested abroad because of reports from Canadian security organizations to their foreign counterparts. The most publicized case involved Maher Arar, an Ottawa telecommunications engineer. In September 2002, Arar was returning home from a vacation in Tunisia when American security officials took him into custody during a stopover in New York. The Americans, using erroneous information provided by the RCMP, accused Arar of having links to al Qaeda. Though Arar was a Canadian citizen, the Americans deported him to Syria, his country of birth. This was an example of a practice known as "rendition," in which countries that had formally renounced the use of torture to extract information from potential informants contracted the torturing out to countries without such inhibitions. In Syria, Arar was tortured for more than 10 months.

Maher Arar speaks at a news conference in Ottawa in December, 2006.
SOURCE: TOM HANSON/CP IMAGES

While Canada initially offered only a mild protest against Arar's fate, official demands for his release strengthened when Canadian public opinion was mobilized in Arar's favour. A government-ordered commission of inquiry concluded that the RCMP had misinformed the Americans about Arar and that he had never posed a security risk. In January 2007, the Canadian government offered substantial financial compensation to Arar, for whom recovery from the torture and allegations came slowly.

Canada's booming military export industries, subsidized by the federal government, suggested that economic interests played a major role in determining whom Canada regarded as allies. From 2000 to 2006, Canada's second largest buyer—following the United States—of military supplies was Saudi Arabia, a country lacking both democratic institutions and rights for women. Egypt and China, two other countries with limited civil rights, were also customers for Canada's military industries. By 2006, Canada's military exports were about $2 billion, a sevenfold increase over the previous decade. According to the US Congressional Research Service, Canada is the world's sixth largest international exporter of military products in the twenty-first century. In 2014, the arms industry in Canada, according to its spokespeople, was a $12 billion industry responsible for 109 000 jobs.

A NEW CENTURY, A NEW BOOM

While the manufacture of weapons of destruction seemed impervious to booms and busts, Canada's economy in the early twenty-first century lost manufacturing jobs while employment rose in the resources and service sectors. Until the global recession began in the fall of 2008, Canada benefited from a number of international developments. In the wake of 9/11, the Americans stimulated their economy with military expenditures and tax reductions for the wealthy. Rising economic powers such as China, India, and Brazil became investment havens for Western entrepreneurs, and seemed to inject new life into a formerly sagging world economy. In turn, capital from newly rich countries and OPEC nations flowed into the Western countries, including Canada. Soaring commodity prices contributed to a job creation bonanza that helped lower Canada's unemployment rate to 5.8 percent by October 2007, the country's best performance since 1974. The Canadian dollar reached US$1.08 one month later, a 50-year high, due in part to increases in commodity prices, with the price of oil reaching all-time records.

Canada's high-technology sector took a roller coaster ride in the new century. The dot-com boom of the late 1990s turned into a huge crash in 2000. Meanwhile, Nortel, which had grown quickly in the 1990s as markets for its high-tech communication components took off, proved unable to endure the recession that struck the European Union in 2000 and the United States in 2002. Its global workforce fell from almost 95 000 in 2000 to 35 000 two years later, and the firm disappeared in the aftermath of the 2008 recession. High-tech made a comeback as the recession lifted, with the leading success story being that of Research in Motion (RIM) in Waterloo, Ontario. Begun as a small-scale operation manufacturing and selling wireless devices in 1984, the company's market soared in the early 2000s with its BlackBerry smartphone that allowed consumers to receive email messages continuously and much else besides. By 2004 there were a million BlackBerry subscribers, and by 2008, 16 million. Although the company employed 19 000 people internationally, including 9000 in Waterloo, in 2011, fierce competition in the smartphone sector and poor business decisions gradually humbled RIM. By 2014, renamed BlackBerry Limited, the company claimed only 6500 employees worldwide. Kitchener-Waterloo reeled in the face of thousands of job losses, though some of the former RIM employees created high-tech start-ups in the twin cities.

Beneath the surface, the economy was less resilient than the one that had emerged in the aftermath of the Second World War. In that period, manufacturing had grown apace, though narrowly concentrated in central Canada. By contrast, in the early 2000s, the deindustrialization that had slowly begun in the 1970s accelerated, and central Canada bore the brunt of the job losses. From November 2002 to February 2007, about a tenth of all manufacturing jobs in Canada disappeared. Ontario lost 141 600 manufacturing jobs and Quebec lost 124 100, while the rest of the country had a net gain of 18 400 jobs. More than 300 000 jobs in auto assembly, auto parts, steel, electronics, shipbuilding, and other sectors disappeared, many lost to low-wage developing countries. The high Canadian dollar, combined with the prospects of cheap labour abroad, gave many profit-seeking capitalists good reason to close Canadian operations. By 2007, there was more new investment in the Alberta oil sands than in the entire Canadian manufacturing sector.

Due to high nickel prices, the economic picture looked rosy in Sudbury, and Alberta and Saskatchewan were flush with decent-paying, if short-term, jobs for construction workers, including workers flown in from other provinces, to build oil sands projects and heavy oil upgraders. Tens of thousands of "temporary foreign workers" were imported to fill employment gaps created by the boom in the commodities industries, particularly the development of the oil sands. Mining in British Columbia flourished. New Brunswick planned to construct a new liquefied natural gas (LNG) terminal in Saint John and to refurbish the Point Lepreau nuclear plant. Newfoundland and Nova Scotia, still reeling from the loss of much of the fishery in the 1990s, stood to gain billions in economic activity from the Hibernia and Sable Island energy projects, though neither provided more than 1000 jobs in the post-development phase. Quebec's manufacturing losses were partially offset by growth in the province's knowledge industries, including a large research sector in software and bio-pharmaceutical companies.

Foreign ownership of the economy persisted. According to the Corporations Return Act, foreign-based corporations controlled 21.2 percent of corporate assets and 29.2 percent of corporate operating revenues in 2005, earning 30.5 percent of corporate operating profits. Although the numbers had been stable since 2000,

mergers of Canadian corporations with American corporations, including Molson Breweries with Coors and Domtar with Weyerhauser, further complicated the looming question: "Who owns Canada?" More than half of all manufacturing assets and just under half of oil and gas assets were American controlled. Among previously Canadian-owned companies that came under foreign ownership in the early twenty-first century were all the steel companies; metal-mining giants Alcan, Inco, and Falconbridge; Fairmont and Four Seasons Hotels; CP Ships; the Hudson's Bay Company; and Sleeman Breweries. Head office jobs and sometimes local operations disappeared altogether. When Molson Breweries workers went on strike in Edmonton in 2007, American management simply closed the plant.

Canada's total exports in 2000 were equivalent to 45.6 percent of GDP, a steep rise from the period before free trade, to the delight of supporters of NAFTA. But that figure fell to 36.5 percent of GDP in 2006, less than it had been in 1994 when NAFTA was implemented, even though energy exports had risen from 5.6 to 6.5 percent of GDP. The rising value of the dollar had reduced the international attractiveness of Canadian manufactured products and services. Imports declined in turn, but only two-thirds as much as exports. Export industries paid wages 25 percent higher than the rest of the economy, and many lost jobs were replaced by poor-paying service jobs.

Despite the free trade agreement between Canada and the United States, even resource industries sometimes faced restrictions in American markets. The US government heavily subsidized agricultural producers, creating barriers for Canadian exporters of farm products. American lumber producers continued to successfully pressure their government to restrict imports of Canadian softwood lumber with devastating consequences for the Canadian lumber industry, particularly in British Columbia. In 2006, the Americans partially relented, signing an agreement with Canada that accepted free trade as a principle, but contradicted that principle by requiring that Canada impose an export tax on softwood exports when the price of the Canadian product fell below a set dollar value.

While the energy-fuelled economic boom rolled along, Statistics Canada data suggested that average Canadians were receiving few benefits. The rich prospered while the middle class and the poor fell further behind. In 2006, 16.2 percent of Canadians (excluding Treaty Indians), or about five million, lived on incomes

This open-mine pit forms part of the oil sands extraction in the area around Fort McMurray, Alberta, where tens of thousands of hectares of land had been dug up by 2008, with few prospects of dug-up areas ever being restored. SOURCE: BOB ANDERSON/MASTERFILE

below Statscan's low-income cutoffs. Between 1980 and 2005, the top 20 percent of income earners added 16.4 percent to their earnings while the bottom 20 percent lost 20.6 percent. Canada's top chief executive officers had earned $3.5 million on average in 1998; in 2005, that figure rose to $9.1 million. By contrast, the earning power of wages fell 2.85 percent during those years. As during the 1930s Depression, the widening gap between rich and poor laid the groundwork for economic instability and political unrest.

THE BUST

Much of the economic growth from 2002 to early 2008 was based on speculative investment. In the recesses of financial institutions on Wall Street, accountants, using complicated mathematical formulae, developed a whole new range of investment opportunities based more on fiction than fact. One example was mortgage loans to unemployed Americans, creating a housing bubble that engulfed many countries, including Canada. The generally quite young and brash fund managers who were handling these transactions often received millions from the investment companies for which they worked, but bore none of the risk.

While such investments paid handsome dividends, no one wanted to listen to the minority of economists who

suggested that the boom was based on investments no more solid than illegal pyramid schemes. Financial deregulation, introduced in the United States in the late 1990s, meant that the state had few resources to stop unethical risks taken by fund managers. Although Canada had largely resisted financial deregulation, both Canadian banks and individual Canadians invested in these dodgy international schemes.

In mid-September 2008, the global financial edifice came crashing down. First, on September 14, Lehman Brothers, a major New York–based securities firm, filed for bankruptcy protection, and Merrill Lynch, awash in red ink, saved itself from a similar fate by selling off to Bank of America for about $50 billion, far less than it had been worth just months earlier. Within two days, the American government had bailed out AIG, a major insurance company, for $85 billion and bailout plans for Wall Street financial firms more generally sailed through Congress. The United Kingdom, faced with similar financial collapses, along with other European and Asian countries, also committed billions to shore up the companies that were creating a risk to the entire global capitalist edifice. In the face of this financial meltdown, governments collectively invested more than a trillion dollars to protect the perpetrators of the financial crisis, largely ignoring its victims.

The Canadian government quietly provided $114 billion in guarantees and financial aid for Canada's biggest banks between October 2008 and July 2010, using the Bank of Canada, Canada Mortgage and Housing, and the US Federal Reserve as its instruments. While all of the loans were repaid, the Canadian Centre for Policy Alternatives labelled this risky use of funds equivalent to seven percent of the total value of the Canadian economy in 2012 as a "bailout." Federal government spokespeople rejected the word "bailout," and claimed that they had merely provided "liquidity support."

Canada's economy, tied closely to global economic developments, went into recession in October as commodity prices fell and exports tumbled. Following the lead of other countries affected by the recession, the federal government temporarily abandoned its neo-liberalism. In early 2009, Harper announced a two-year stimulus program of $62 billion that raised Canada's deficits to record levels. In the fiscal year 2009–10, the Canadian deficit soared to $55.9 billion, but proportionately Canada's stimulus program was far more modest than those of the United States, the United Kingdom, and most continental European nations. A large part of the stimulus in Canada was the federal government's guarantees to the big three automobile companies, hard hit by the recession, meant to match similar guarantees to these companies by the American government, and to banks and other leading financial institutions, mostly in the form of nearly interest-free loans.

The financial crisis wiped out many of the gains of the previous boom period. Almost 406 000 Canadian jobs vanished from October 2008 to April 2009, as the overall economy shrank by about four percent. Unemployment shot back up to 8.4 percent, about where it was before the boom started, and 1.5 million people were officially unemployed. Another 800 000 Canadians who wanted full-time work could only land part-time employment or, discouraged in their job search, had temporarily withdrawn from the labour force. Exports declined by a third from July 2008 to April 2009. Many Canadians saw their investments shrink mightily. Personal bankruptcies and credit defaults mounted.

By early 2011, the employment picture brightened as commodity prices rebounded. Nevertheless, the global economy remained unsteady. The economies of several countries in the European Union were on the verge of collapse and investors were leery of Wall Street, which seemed to be returning to its fantasy economy based on derivatives. Canada's economy remained sluggish, despite shrinking wages and low wages that, in theory, should have been promoting new investment. Unemployment rarely fell below seven percent in the three years that followed.

THE TRADE UNION MOVEMENT

Those who still had jobs in Canada in the 2010s were less likely to enjoy union protection than their counterparts a quarter century earlier. According to Statistics Canada, 30 percent of the Canadian non-agricultural work force was unionized in 2012, compared to 38 percent in 1981. Canada's trade union movement was under attack in the age of neo-liberalism, but less so than its American counterpart, which had been reduced to 11.2 percent of the labour force in 2012.

In the era of free trade, the flight of manufacturing companies weakened a former stronghold of organized labour. Private-sector unionization dropped precipitously as the union movement proved unable to organize major sources of new employment in the retail, financial, and communications sectors. McDonald's hired opponents to unions to overwhelm or replace supporters. Walmart, unable to prevent the certification of a union in their Jonquière, Quebec, store in 2004, closed that location six months later. In 2011, Walmart also managed to pressure unionized workers at another store in Saint-Hyacinthe to decertify. By contrast, public-sector unionism remained strong and, as a result, women, much better represented in government employment than in the private sector, were slightly more likely to be union members than men, a reversal from a generation earlier.

The challenges of organizing in the private sector led many unions to merge to make more money available for organizing campaigns and for strike funds. In 2013, two unions that were themselves the product of earlier mergers—National Automobile, Aerospace, Transportation and General Workers (CAW) and Communications, Energy and Paperworkers Union (CEP)—joined to create UNIFOR. With 308 000 members, it became Canada's largest private-sector union. Only two

MORE TO THE STORY

Not Quite Canadian: Canada's Temporary Foreign Workers

Alexander Bondorev of Latvia, Aleksey Blumberg of Ukraine, Fayzulla Fazilov of Uzbekistan, and Vladimir Koroshkin of Uzbekistan fell more than 13 storeys to their deaths in Toronto on Christmas Eve 2009. Their suspended scaffold collapsed and they wore no safety harnesses. All four men, along with Dilshod Mamurov of Uzbekistan, who fell with them but miraculously

These women participated in a Toronto candlelight vigil on 7 January 2010 for the four "temporary foreign workers" whose lives ended in a construction tragedy in Toronto on Christmas Eve, 2009. SOURCE: CARLOS OSORIO/GETSTOCK.COM

survived though badly maimed, were temporary foreign workers. They were all sometimes-invisible migrant workers, like the Depression-era Dust Bowl migrants from Oklahoma to California, who, in the words of songwriter Woody Guthrie, "come with the dust and go with the wind."

As the boom began in 2002, the federal government expanded its temporary foreign worker (TFW) program, earlier confined mainly to farm labour, to include building trades, retail clerks, cooks, labourers, and gas station attendants. Even more categories were added in 2007. In 2002, 181 794 legal temporary foreign workers entered Canada; by 2012, that number had increased to 491 547. Many "illegal," that is, undocumented and unapproved foreign workers, were also in Canada doing work that most Canadian-born workers would regard as slave labour.

Alberta soon accounted for more than one-third of the TFWs. In 2007, the Alberta Federation of Labour hired immigration lawyer Yessy Byl as an advocate for this group of largely non-unionized workers. She found that many had been exploited by labour brokers, who charged illegal fees to find jobs for them, and by their employers. It was common for employers of temporary foreign workers to fail to pay the wages initially promised, to refuse to pay mandatory overtime, and to charge exorbitant rents for employer-provided, substandard accommodation. Byl documented that 60 percent of the employers had breached either the Employment Standards Code or the Occupational Health and Safety Act, or both. Penalties for such breaches were rare.[10]

In 2013 and 2014, reports that many banks and restaurants were replacing Canadian employees with temporary foreign workers created negative publicity that caused the Harper government to put more limits on the use of TFWs. Immigration support groups argued that Canada should replace the TFW program with a program that allowed workers from abroad deemed necessary in certain industries to immediately become eligible to become permanent citizens and to have the same rights as Canadian citizens.

public-sector unions, CUPE (Canadian Union of Public Employees) with 630 000 members, and NUPGE (National Union of Public and General Employees) with 340 000 members, were larger.

PROVINCIAL POLITICS

The federal tilt to the right had echoes in some provinces. NDP governments were defeated in British Columbia in 2001 and Saskatchewan in 2007 by neo-liberal parties, and the Parti Québécois was ousted by the somewhat more fiscally conservative Liberals in 2003. By contrast, the Manitoba NDP routed its opponents in successive provincial elections, and the Ontario Liberals rode to power on a socially interventionist platform. While divisions among the major parties in the Atlantic provinces defied traditional notions of left- and right-wing ideologies, the continuing growth of the NDP as a political force in Nova Scotia demonstrated growing polarization in that province. The NDP won Nova Scotia's provincial election in 2009 but, faced with slim revenues, focused as much on cutting government jobs as on preserving social programs, and lost to the Liberals in the provincial election of 2013. New Brunswick continued to alternate Liberal and Conservative governments, while the Progressive Conservatives launched a new reign in Newfoundland and Labrador in 2003 under the highly popular Danny Williams that ran out of steam when Williams stepped down in 2010. Prince Edward Island's long-standing Tory government lost power to the Liberals in 2007, whose hold on power seemed quite strong seven years later.

Provinces with resource-based economies found it easiest to manage as federal transfers shrank. Oil-rich Alberta had paid off its debts by 2005 and began mounting budgetary surpluses. Most voters were pleased, but critics argued that its low taxes, minimal unemployment, and debt-free status hid the government's failure to diversify the economy beyond petroleum. By 2006, Saskatchewan was beginning to take the economic lead from Alberta. A year later, provincial voters gave the reins of power to the Saskatchewan Party, a party formed in 1997 on the ruins of a scandal-plagued provincial Progressive Conservative Party. In British Columbia, Liberal governments after 2001 chopped provincial social programs, sold BC Rail to Canadian National, privatized much of BC Hydro and health-care support, and stripped negotiated contract rights, creating a backlash that allowed the NDP to regain support, although it failed to win in any of the three following provincial elections.

In Ontario, a backlash developed against Mike Harris's "Common Sense Revolution" in the early 2000s after the deaths of seven people in Walkerton, Ontario, from drinking water contaminated with toxins. Spending cuts and contracting out in areas of traditional government regulation, such as the safety of water supplies, clearly carried dangers. A massive power outage in southern Ontario in the summer of 2003, coupled with increasing power bills a year earlier, damaged the campaign of Ernie Eves, Harris's successor, to gradually privatize Ontario Hydro. Dalton McGuinty's Liberals easily defeated the Conservatives in 2003.

After almost a decade in power, McGuinty resigned as premier in 2012, his government having been reduced to a minority in the most recent election and subsequently plagued by spending scandals. His successor, Kathleen Wynne, was not only Ontario's first female premier, but also the first openly gay premier in Canada. In 2014, Wynne reestablished a majority for the Liberals in an election in which she promised to refloat Ontario's troubled economy with generous spending on infrastructure and to strengthen pension protection for the province's residents with a compulsory contributory pension plan that would top up CPP payments to Ontario citizens during retirement. Wynne's re-election, despite the success of her Conservative opponents in painting her as an accomplice in the most egregious decisions of the McGuinty administration, demonstrated that people in Ontario were unprepared to have a second round of Harris-style neo-liberal government.

In Quebec, meanwhile, the provincial Liberals regained power in 2003 after nine years of Parti Québécois rule and promised to rein in public spending and re-engineer the welfare state. Faced with the country's most militant

unions and citizens' movements, Premier Jean Charest, a former federal Progressive Conservative leader, only chipped away at the programs of his PQ predecessors. In 2007, with the rise of a new right-wing populist party, the Action démocratique du Québec (ADQ), the Charest Liberals were reduced to a minority government and the PQ relegated to third place. The Liberals were able to force a new election a year later, and by appealing to voters' economic concerns, once again formed a majority government.

In 2012, an attempt by Charest to raise post-secondary tuition fees in Quebec to levels closer to the rest of Canada led to a full-scale revolt by students and their supporters. This included massive demonstrations, with protesters banging pots and pans to show their displeasure, and severe police repression. The protests reflected not only the narrow issue of tuition fees, but also broader dissatisfaction with a Liberal government tainted by scandals relating to election financing and construction kickbacks. Pauline Marois, the PQ leader, firmly took the side of the protesters. This helped her win an election called later that year by the scandal-plagued Liberals, but only with a minority government. Once elected, Marois kept her promise to annul the Liberal fee hikes, but many of her other progressive policies were blocked by the Liberals and by the Coalition Avenir Québec (CAQ), which had replaced the ADQ as the province's right-wing populist party.

Marois also struggled to reinvigorate a party and a sovereignist movement that many younger people regarded as outdated and populated by aging boomers. In an effort to garner support by appealing to nationalist sentiment, she announced plans to reinforce Québécois identity by promulgating a Quebec Charter of Values. The charter included a ban on employees in the public and para-public sectors, including schools, hospitals, and universities, wearing "ostentatious" religious symbols. This was part of an ongoing debate within the province about the "reasonable accommodation" of religious and ethnic minorities. At the same time, Marois downplayed discussions of Quebec sovereignty and of a future referendum, much to the dismay of many hard-line sovereignists.

With polls showing a surge in PQ support, fuelled by the charter's appeal to right-wing nationalists who would normally have avoided the left-wing PQ, Marois called an election in 2014. The PQ was bolstered by star candidates such as Pierre-Karl Péladeau, one of Canada's wealthiest media magnates. During the campaign, Marois refused to be pinned down on whether she would hold another referendum if elected with a majority, while some of her candidates, including Péladeau, gave the distinct impression that sovereignty was their only goal. The Liberals and the CAQ pilloried the PQ for being obsessed with sovereignty rather than good government, a tactic that usually worked with Quebec voters. The PQ cause was also hindered by a series of outrageously intolerant comments by some supporters of the charter. The Liberals under Philippe Couillard won a resounding victory, and the PQ finished with its smallest percentage of the vote since the 1970 provincial election. Combined with the defeat of the Bloc Québécois at the federal level in 2011, this led the sovereignist movement into a period of intense self-questioning, though it remained far from dead.

NATIVE PEOPLES

The number of Canadians who self-identified as Aboriginal grew 20 percent between the 2006 and 2011 censuses, four times the rate of population increase in the country as a whole. Altogether, 1 400 685 people considered themselves Aboriginal, 4.3 percent of the Canadian population. Of these, 851 560 called themselves First Nations, but only 637 660 were Status Indians eligible for government support. There were also 451 795 Métis and 59 445 Inuit.

The Métis were the fastest growing of all Aboriginal groups in Canada. After a century of being ignored, the new Constitution formally recognized the Métis, who moved quickly to establish their status. Case law followed as did a debate, still not fully resolved, about how people of mixed heritage should be defined. In 2003, the Supreme Court ruled in *R. v. Powley* that three conditions must prevail to achieve Métis status: self-identification as a Métis individual; ancestral connection to a historical Métis community; and acceptance by a Métis community. The Métis won an important victory in the Federal Court of Appeal in 2014 in a case that had been winding through courts for 15 years: as a distinct Aboriginal group, they had the same rights as First Nations and Inuit to receive federal financial support and to negotiate land rights. According to the ruling, non-status Indians had no such rights. The federal government, claiming that rights for Métis might cost them billions of dollars annually, announced that it would appeal the Federal Court of Appeal decision to the Supreme Court.

Native activism in the courts brought the federal government to the table to negotiate a solution to the many court claims that Native peoples had initiated with regard to their treatment in the notorious residential schools. In June 2008, Stephen Harper formally apologized to the estimated 80 000 surviving students of residential schools, provided $1.9 million in "common experience" payments, and established a Truth and Reconciliation Commission to encourage healing around the physical and cultural abuse that occurred in the schools. After dragging its heels in signing the 2007 UN Declaration on the Rights of Indigenous Peoples, the federal government finally agreed in 2010 to sign the document.

Notwithstanding his concession that the establishment of residential schools was an injustice, Prime Minister Harper declared at a press conference after a G20 summit in Pittsburgh in 2009 that Canada had "no history of colonialism," and that this differentiated Canada from great powers who were often criticized for past injustices.[11] In contrast, Native leaders believed that Canada was, at base, a colonial settler state. They continued to use both the courts and militant organizing, such as the women-led "Idle No More" national movement that began a series of marches and teach-ins in 2012, to assert their rights to control the future of lands where they continued to practise traditional economic pursuits linked inextricably with their culture.

The Tsilhqot'in ruling of 2014 noted that provinces could make decisions regarding lands claimed by Native peoples, including treaty lands, as long as they consult with the affected Aboriginal groupings and ensure that the traditional pursuits of these people are protected. A court decision just two weeks later suggested that the Tsilhqot'in decision might not have as far-reaching implications as originally thought. An effort by the Grassy Narrows First Nation to prevent Ontario from granting a commercial licence to a pulp and paper company to clear-cut within Keewatin territory was rejected, although with a caveat that if "the taking up leaves the Ojibway with no meaningful right to hunt, fish or trap in relation to the territories over which they traditionally hunted, fished, and trapped, a potential action for treaty infringement will arise."[12]

Although their full meaning will not be known for some time to come, the Supreme Court's decisions represented a significant victory for First Nations and their environmental allies in conflicts with both governments and corporations that proclaimed that rapid development of Canada's natural resources for export was the best

In the winter of 2006, a standoff erupted in the southwestern Ontario town of Caledonia between Six Nations defenders of their people's traditional lands and non-Aboriginals who supported the development of a proposed subdivision. In this picture, Six Nations protesters stand on top of their barricade moments before taking it down on 23 May 2006 in an effort that proved unsuccessful in persuading the federal government to negotiate Aboriginal demands. They had more success with the government of Ontario. SOURCE: NATHAN DENETTE/CP IMAGES

guarantor of future prosperity. While the Supreme Court was mainly attempting to determine how Canada's common law tradition applied to the country's dealings with Aboriginal peoples and the rights they could claim to have earned by first occupation of the land, its decisions had a bearing on many proposed developments.

MORE TO THE STORY
"I Apologize"

In recent years, apologies by governments to groups that have been victims of injustice at the hands of former governments in Canada have accumulated. Both the campaigns of aggrieved groups and changing social values have resulted in reappraisals of past policies. At the federal level, the apologies began in 1988 when Prime Minister Mulroney apologized to Japanese Canadians for the federal government's wartime actions in interning, dispossessing, and dispersing them from their Pacific coastal homes and communities. In 2003, Prime Minister Jean Chrétien apologized to Acadians for the British deportation in 1755. Paul Martin expressed Canada's regret that it had interned Ukrainian Canadians during the First World War and Italian Canadians in the Second World War. In 2006, Stephen Harper apologized for the head tax that was imposed at the end of the nineteenth century on the Chinese entering Canada, while in 2008, he apologized not only for the residential school policy, but also for the *Komagata Maru* incident of 1914. There were also more local apologies, including a statement of regret from the British Columbia government in 2004 for having seized Doukhobor children from their parents in the 1950s to enforce compulsory schooling laws, and a full apology in 2014 to Chinese Canadians for a long history of anti-Chinese immigration policies at both the federal and provincial levels. In 2010, Mayor Peter Kelly of Halifax apologized to the former residents of Africville for the bulldozing of their community in the 1960s.[13]

CANADIAN WOMEN IN THE TWENTY-FIRST CENTURY

On the surface, the women's movement had made great gains by the early twenty-first century. The premiers of Ontario, Quebec, British Columbia, Alberta, and Newfoundland and Labrador were all women in the opening months of 2014, though palace revolts removed the latter two during the year and the Quebec premier went down to electoral defeat. A few large corporations even had women as their CEO. Women easily outnumbered men in university programs and had made significant inroads in a number of professions, though they still remained in the minority among doctors, lawyers, and university professors.

A deeper analysis suggests that problems remained. For most women, the injustices against which the women's movement had fought, including the double workday of paid work and most of the responsibility for child-raising, lower incomes, exclusion from the higher ranks of most organizations, and the constant threat of violence from loved ones and strangers alike, persisted. In 2008, the average woman's earnings from all sources—wages, salaries, pensions, investments, and government transfers—were $30 100 relative to $47 000 for men. It meant that the average woman had access to only 64 percent of the funds available to men, a huge gap, though an improvement over the 1976 figure of 43 percent. It helped to explain why poverty among adults in Canada continued overwhelmingly to have a woman's face.

Violence against women remained a social epidemic. In British Columbia, Robert "Willie" Pickton boasted to an undercover officer after he was arrested in 2002 that he had butchered 49 prostitutes, most of them from Vancouver's downtown eastside, on his farm in Port Coquitlam. Many of Pickton's victims were Aboriginal women. In 2010, Sisters in Spirit, a research institute established by the Native Women's Association, reported that it had the names of nearly 600 murdered or missing First Nations, Métis, and Inuit women in its database. That year, the federal government cut the funding that had allowed the database to be assembled.

TABLE 17.1

Women's Inflation-Adjusted Earnings Relative to Men's Earnings in Canada, 1976 to 2008

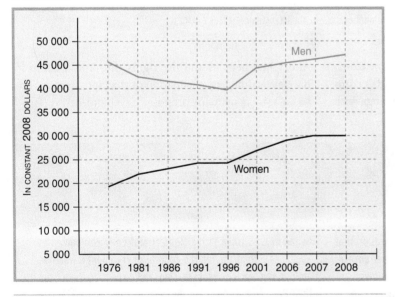

Source: Cara Williams, "Economic Well-Being," in Statistics Canada, "Women in Canada: A Gender-based Statistical Report," n.d. www.statcan.gc.ca/pub/89-503-x/2010001/article/11388-eng.htm

There were increasing calls upon the federal government to set up a royal commission to investigate the murders and disappearances of Aboriginal women, but despite support for such a commission from a range of women's and Native groups as well as the opposition parties, the government refused to respond.

In an era of budget-cutting, federal support for women's organizations was gradually whittled away. Both the National Action Committee on the Status of Women and the Canadian Advisory Council on the Status of Women were among the first victims of Martin's budget reforms in the 1990s. After the Harper government came to power, it withdrew funding from many civil society groups working on behalf of women, including Sisters in Spirit. Women were thus forced to rely on membership fees and private donations to continue their lobbying efforts.

BIOGRAPHY
Maude Barlow: International Activist

Maude Barlow addresses a discussion hosted by Save Our Saugeen Shores in August 2013 in Port Elgin, Ontario. SOURCE: JIM WEST / ALAMY

Maude Barlow exemplified the global activism that became common in the twenty-first century. Born in Toronto in 1947, she grew up in Ottawa, Nova Scotia, and New Brunswick, learning social activism from her parents. Involved in feminist campaigns in the 1970s, Barlow was hired by the City of Ottawa in 1980 to serve as Director of Equal Opportunity for Women. Her public profile, particularly on campaigns against pornography, attracted the attention of Pierre Trudeau, who hired her as his adviser on women's issues in 1983.

In 1988, Barlow was persuaded by Mel Hurtig to replace him as the national chairperson of the Council of Canadians, which he had founded in 1985. While she initially followed Hurtig in focusing on the threat posed to Canadian livelihoods and Canadian identity from foreign investment and trade, she gradually came to believe that Canadian activists would achieve little without working with activists in other countries.

Social justice activism on a global scale, she argued, needed to be nourished as a counterbalance to capitalist globalization, with corporate profit as its sole goal.

Barlow played a major role in exposing a proposed Multilateral Agreement on Investment (MAI) among OECD countries in 1997 whose provisions would have protected investors' rights against incursions by national governments. She then rallied resistance to the measure, the first major cross-national effort of defenders of national sovereignty to use the Internet. The Council of Canadians worked with other civil society groups to create a peaceful blockade of the Montreal Conference on Globalized Economies, an event in support of the MAI. Efforts of this kind in a variety of OECD countries caused the governments that had backed the MAI to withdraw their support for such legislation, at least temporarily. In addition to two books on the threat of the MAI to Canadian sovereignty, Barlow produced one for American audiences on the threat of the proposal to "American freedom."

Organizers of the anti-MAI campaign, including Barlow, were among the leaders of the powerful opposition mustered by grassroots groups to the World Trade Organization meetings in Seattle in 1999 and Cancun in 2003 that attempted to achieve MAI-type rules through a different forum. They also participated in the mass rallies against free trade across North and South America at the Summit of the Americas in Quebec City in 2001. Barlow addressed huge crowds at World Social Forums in Porto Alegre and Mumbai regarding the need for civil society groups across the world to stand together against efforts to remove popular democracy in favour of rule by multi-national corporations protected by international agreements that states would not be allowed to change once they signed on.

During the course of her international campaigning, Barlow became convinced that big corporations were attempting to commodify air, earth, and water, which she called "the global commons." She co-founded the Blue Planet Project, an organization meant to protect that commons, and particularly waterways. Her research on the threats to water supplies from industry and global warming was outlined in a trilogy of books that she produced on the subject. That research, along with her active campaign to have the right to water recognized by the United Nations as a universal human right, led to Barlow's appointment as the senior adviser on water issues to the president of the UN General Assembly in 2008-09. In 2014, Barlow was hard at work with other civil society colleagues across the globe to prepare a Universal Declaration of the Rights of Mother Earth for consideration by UN members.

Apart from her continuing work with the Council of Canadians and the Blue Planet Project, by 2014 Barlow had become the chair of the Washington-based Food and Water Watch and councillor with the Hamburg-based World Future Council, while serving as a co-founder of the International Forum on Globalization. Addressing graduates at York University, as she received an Honorary Doctorate of Laws, Barlow commented:

> I swear to you that it is true—the life of an activist is a good life, because you get up in the morning caring about more than just yourself or how to make more money. A life of activism gives hope (a moral imperative in this work), energy and direction. You meet the best people. You help transform systems and ideas and you commit to leaving the earth in at least as whole a state as you inherited it because every generation has the right to breathe clean air and drink sweet clean water.[14]

GAY RIGHTS

Gay rights, which had been gaining ground since the 1960s, still had hurdles to jump, including the right of gays and lesbians to legal marriage. Although efforts to persuade legislators to make gay marriages legal had previously failed, court decisions, beginning with the Court of Appeal for Ontario in 2003, determined that limiting marriage to heterosexuals violated equality provisions in the Canadian Charter of Rights and Freedoms. By the end of 2004, five other provincial and territorial courts had ordered governments to rewrite the definition of marriage to include heterosexuals and homosexuals. Parliament approved legislation in 2005 that redefined marriage to include both heterosexual and homosexual relationships, but allowed individual religious institutions to determine whether or not they would recognize same-sex unions among their congregants. A year earlier, sexual orientation was added to the "hate propaganda" section of the Criminal Code.

The rights of transgender people were also gradually recognized. Provincial governments began to pay for sex reassignment surgery. Ontario's Human Rights Tribunal ruled in 2012 that all transgender people had the right to change their sex designation on government documents, whether or not they had undergone transsexual surgery. In 2014, the Vancouver School Board agreed to train staff so that they were sensitive to the needs of transgender men and women and the language they used to describe themselves.

CONCLUSION

Canada's main challenges as the new century opened would have been unfathomable to the Fathers of Confederation, who had little concern about environmental threats, the politics of Afghanistan, or the rights of women, gays, and Aboriginals. Other issues confronting Canadians today have been present since Confederation, including the balance of powers between the federal and provincial governments, the treatment of immigrants, and foreign versus domestic direction of the economy. Many Canadians seem generally optimistic that despite their divisions, they can build upon their past achievements to create a more sustainable and harmonious society, but they recognize that these goals can only be achieved in cooperation with other peoples in our steadily shrinking global village. Questions regarding the most effective approach for Canada to take as international conflicts arise continue to provoke lively debate and unfortunately sometimes violence as well. Canada's participation in the international military response to radicalized groups such as the Islamic State of Iraq and Syria (ISIS), on the basis of a vote in Parliament by the Conservative majority, brought this particular war right to Canada's doorstep. In October 2014, in separate incidents, two young men who had been recently seduced by the call to arms from ISIS and other similar groups attacked and killed two Canadian soldiers, one in Saint-Jean-sur-Richelieu (Quebec) and another in Ottawa. The Ottawa attack, which occurred in and around Parliament

itself, led to MPs preparing to use flagpoles as spears and the Prime Minister being forced to hide in a closet while the fighting raged. Equally worrisome was the response from some decision-makers and opinion leaders. Prime Minister Harper vowed to reinforce the security powers of agencies such as CSIS, while some public commentators in Quebec (which is where both attackers had roots) blamed a supposed too-great toleration of Islam, citing for example the inflence that veiled daycare workers might have over the children in their care. While such a conclusion was clearly unwarranted, it underscored the tensions that continued to inform public policy in a world fraught with anxiety.

A HISTORIOGRAPHICAL DEBATE
Stephen Harper and the Shaping of Historical Narratives

The Harper government's cuts to government institutions extended to organizations dedicated to the preservation of Canadian history, including Library and Archives Canada and the historical section of Parks Canada. While sidelining such widely respected Canadian institutions, the Conservative government invested $28 million in a celebration of the two hundredth anniversary of the outbreak of the War of 1812 and converted the Canadian Museum of Civilization into the Museum of Canadian History with a greater emphasis on political and military history. The Canadian Citizenship Guide was revised to emphasize Canada's military past and connection with the Crown rather than its multiculturalism and peacekeeping. In 2013, the Conservative-dominated Standing Committee on Heritage announced plans to review what students at all levels in Canada were being taught about Canada's history. What did it all mean?

Quebec historian Jocelyn Létourneau suggests that Harper was responding to a fuzzy national identity for Canadians that public institutions had promoted in the Trudeau era. With their emphasis on multiculturalism, they tended to downplay military events and political conflicts and produced an "antiseptic" view of the country for its citizens. According to Létourneau, while Harper maintains recognition of Canada's multiculturalism, he wants English Canadians in particular to view their country as also being the product of important military events, often linked

with the country's British traditions. First Nations and Quebecers are celebrated for their roles in contributing to this royalist, military-minded Canada.[15]

Other historians have been more forcefully critical of the Harper agenda and have accused the government of manipulating both historical research and its dissemination. Historian Ian McKay and social activist Jamie Swift, in their book *Warrior Nation: Rebranding Canada in an Age of Anxiety*, argue that the Harper government's narrow emphasis on Canada's military history distorts our past for political purposes. Harper, they suggest, is attempting to make Canadians think of their country's history in terms of courageous military actions in an attempt to justify more recent wars such as the one in Afghanistan. These authors accuse the government of viewing foreign and military policy through the lens of anglophone Christian defenders of globalized capitalism with disdain both for peaceful relations among people and for the rights of nations to follow socioeconomic paths of their own choosing. They compare Harper unfavourably with Lester Pearson and his policies of peacekeeping.[16]

Others have also voiced criticisms of the Harper government's interpretation of the nation's past. Political scientists Kiera L. Ladner and Michael McCrossan, defending an Aboriginal historical perspective of Canada, argue: "The narrative of the Canadian nation offered by the Prime Minister is one that selectively omits a history of genocide, territorial dispossession, cultural destruction, and regime replacement in favour of a rendering of history which represents Canada as a primarily British settler society."[17] Building on this argument, feminist historian Veronica Strong-Boag claims:

> In the 21st century, reactionary advocates of diminished rights and expectations have history and evidence-based research in general firmly in their sights. That bull's eye reflects the centrality of modern scholarship and activism in exposing colonialism, capitalism, and patriarchy and in illuminating plural and counter-hegemonic identities. In the last few decades the systemic oppression and the continuing vitality of First Nations, workers, and women have been irrefutably documented and that data has been central to calls for recognition and redress in matters from residential schools and land claims to pay equity and family law. Today's conservatives meet that mother lode of evidence with the same response many have to proof of climate change, namely, deny, deny, deny.[18]

Such views of the importance of placing people's history in the forefront rather than political history and military history have been vociferously attacked by conservative historians as destructive of national unity in Canada. The most passionate defence of a history that emphasizes Canada's military achievements and minimizes the kind of history that Strong-Boag extols was provided in J.L. Granatstein's best-selling polemic *Who Killed Canadian History?*, which appeared in 1998. Granatstein accused social historians of fostering a culture of complaint and undermining national unity and Canadian patriotism.[19]

According to historian Lyle Dyck, the chasm that once existed between conventional military and political historians and social historians has been narrowing in recent years. He notes that "our concepts of military history are also rapidly changing with the emergence of numerous topics unanticipated even a generation ago, such as the role of women and racial minorities in the 20th-century wars, Post-Traumatic Stress Disorder among combatants, and the campaign to root out lesbian and gay soldiers during World War II and the Cold War eras."[20] Although the Harper government's notions of military history are wedded to the earlier "nation-building" military history, historians continue to build on each other's and the public's sense of the past, creating a more complex sense of who Canadians are and how they created a place that, for a time at least, is called Canada.

NOTES

1. Supreme Court of Canada, *Judgments of the Supreme Court of Canada,* "Tsilhqo'tin Nation v. British Columbia," 26 June 2014. http://scc-csc.lexum.com/scc-csc/scc-csc/en/item/14246/index.do

2. "Separation, Alberta-style: It is time to seek a new relationship with Canada," *National Post,* 8 December 2000.

3. Natural Resources Canada, "Canada in a Changing Climate: Sector Perspectives on Impacts and Adaptation" (Ottawa: Natural Resources Canada, 2014) 260. http://www.nrcan.gc.ca/sites/www.nrcan.gc.ca/files/earthsciences/pdf/assess/2014/pdf/Full-Report_Eng.pdf

4. Inuit Circumpolar Council press release, 7 December 2005. http://www.inuitcircumpolar.com/index/php?ID=316&Lang=En

5. Sheila Watt-Cloutier describes her life and her advocacy in "Speech by Sophie Prize Winner Sheila Watt-Cloutier," 15 June 2005, http://www.sofieprisen.no/Articles/23.html; and "Sheila Watt-Cloutier on

Climate Change and Human Rights," http://www.youtube.com/watch?v=GlSh4XeoLBA. Her memoir is scheduled to be published in 2015 by Allen Lane under the title, *The Right to Be Cold: One Woman's Story of Protecting Her Culture.*

6. *The Globe and Mail*, 9 June 2014.

7. Munir Sheikh, "What Do These PMs Know That Economists Don't?" *The Globe and Mail*, 18 July 2014.

8. Jessica Shadian, *The Politics of Arctic Sovereignty: Oil, Ice, and Inuit Governance* (London: Routledge, 2014).

9. "PM slammed, defended for 9/11 remarks" CBC News September 13, 2002. Reprinted by permission.

10. Alvin Finkel et al., *Working People in Alberta: A History* (Edmonton: AU Press, 2012) 234–35.

11. "Every G20 Nation Wants to Be Canada, Insists PM," 26 September 2009. http://www.reuters.com/article/2009/09/26/columns-us-g20-canada-advantages-idUSTRE58P05Z20090926

12. Supreme Court of Canada, *Judgments of the Supreme Court of Canada*, "Grassy Narrows First Nation v. Ontario (Natural Resources)," 7 July 2014. http://scc-csc.lexum.com/scc-csc/scc-csc/en/item/14274/index.do. For the history of the Grassy Narrows struggles, see Anna J. Willow, *Strong Hearts, Native Lands: Anti-Clearcutting Activism at Grassy Narrows First Nation* (Winnipeg: University of Manitoba Press, 2012).

13. Issues regarding redress for historical injustices are explored in Jennifer Henderson and Pauline Wakeham, eds., *Reconciling Canada: Critical Perspectives on the Culture of Redress* (Toronto: University of Toronto Press, 2013).

14. "Maude Barlow's Blog," Council of Canadians, 12 June 2014. http://www.canadians.org/blog/life-activism-gives-hope-energy-and-direction. Barlow provided an early autobiography in *The Fight of My Life: Confessions of an Unrepentant Canadian* (Toronto: Harper Collins, 1998).

15. Jocelyn Létourneau, "L'identité canadienne refaçon-née?," *Labour/Le Travail*, 73 (Spring 2014) 225–27.

16. Ian McKay and Jamie Swift, *Warrior Nation: Rebranding Canada in an Age of Anxiety* (Toronto: Between the Lines, 2012).

17. Kiera L. Ladner and Michael McCrossan, "Whose Shared History?," *Labour/Le Travail*, 73 (Spring 2014) 200.

18. Veronica Strong-Boag, "Limiting Identities: The Conservative Attack on History and Feminist Claims for Equality," *Labour/Le Travail*, 73 (Spring 2014) 206.

19. J.L. Granatstein, *Who Killed Canadian History?* (Toronto: HarperCollins Canada, 1998).

20. Lyle Dick, "Remarks on the Harper Government's Review of History," *Labour/Le Travail*, 73 (Spring 2014) 204.

SELECTED READING

Albo, Greg, Sam Gindin, and Leo Panitch. *In and Out of Crisis: The Global Financial Meltdown and Left Alternatives.* Winnipeg: Fernwood, 2010

Barlow, Maude. *Blue Future: Protecting Water for People and Their Planet Forever.* Toronto: House of Anansi, 2013

Boyd, David R. *Unnatural Law: Rethinking Canadian Environmental Law and Policy.* Vancouver: UBC Press, 2003

Camfield, David. *Canadian Labour in Crisis: Reinventing the Workers' Movement.* Halifax: Fernwood, 2011

Day, Shelagh and Gwen Brodsky. *Women and the Canada Social Transfer: Securing the Social Union.* Ottawa: Status of Women Canada, 2007

Henderson, Jennifer, and Pauline Wakeham, eds. *Reconciling Canada: Critical Perspectives on the Culture of Redress.* Toronto: University of Toronto Press, 2013

High, Stephen, and David W. Lewis. *Corporate Wasteland: The Landscape and Memory of Deindustrialization.* Toronto: Between the Lines, 2007

Kowaluk, Lucia, and Steven Staples, eds. *Afghanistan and Canada: Is There an Alternative to War?* Montreal: Black Rose Books, 2009

Martin, Lawrence. *Harperland: The Politics of Control.* Toronto: Viking Canada, 2010

McKay, Ian, and Jamie Swift. *Warrior Nation: Rebranding Canada in an Age of Anxiety.* Toronto: Between the Lines, 2012

Nikiforuk, Andrew. *Tar Sands: Dirty Oil and the Future of a Continent*. Vancouver: Greystone Books, 2010

Roach, Kent. *September 11: Consequences for Canada*. Montreal: McGill-Queen's University Press, 2003

Shadian, Jessica. *The Politics of Arctic Sovereignty: Oil, Ice, and Inuit Governance*. London: Routledge, 2014

Stasiulis, Daiva K., and Abigail B. Bakan. *Negotiating Citizenship: Migrant Women in Canada and the Global System*. Toronto: University of Toronto Press, 2005

Weart, Spencer. *The Discovery of Global Warming*. Cambridge, MA: Harvard University Press, 2003

Wells, Paul. *The Longer I'm Prime Minister: Stephen Harper and Canada, 2006–*. Toronto: Random House, 2013

_____. *Right Side Up: The Fall of Paul Martin and the Rise of Stephen Harper's New Conservatism*. Toronto: Douglas Gibson Books, 2007

Willow, Anna J. *Strong Hearts, Native Lands: Anti-Clearcutting Activism at Grassy Narrows First Nation*. Winnipeg: University of Manitoba Press, 2012

Yalnizyan, Armine. *The Rich and the Rest of Us: The Changing Face of Canada's Growing Gap*. Ottawa: Canadian Centre for Policy Alternatives, 2007

For a comprehensive list of readings for topics covered in this chapter, please visit http://pearsoncanada.ca/conrad.

CHAPTER 18
COMMUNITY AND CULTURE SINCE 1976

Kids are expensive. If it were just my wife and I, she wouldn't have to work. But at one point when there was five in here. . . . Your kids want everything now. You can't just buy them "adventure" running shoes. They want Adidas or Reeboks. That's the killer. . . . My parents didn't have much. To me, what I wanted and what I got were two different things. I just saw a kid walk by with a $150 starter coat. My son's got one too [laughs] and I'm thinking when does it end? I think I would have been satisfied growing up, to have a decent coat, never mind a starter coat with a Montreal Canadiens logo. Sure, I'd like my kids to have better than what I had or at least better than what my parents could give me, but then we put a gun to our head by doing this. . . . When does it stop?[1]

These comments by "Dom," a Niagara Falls man in his early forties in 1995, reflect the conflicting values of many Canadians as the twentieth century closed. While most adult Canadians worked outside the home, some people looked nostalgically upon earlier times when, supposedly, a single income had supported a family. Participating in the rampant materialism of society, many Canadians nonetheless also viewed consumerism as more of a curse than a blessing. In this chapter, we look broadly at the social and cultural developments in Canada as one millennium ended and another began, providing some context for the hopes and worries of people like Dom.

POPULATION

Canada's estimated population increased from 23 million in 1975 to 35 million at the end of 2013. Natural increase accounted for about 60 percent of the population growth, and immigration the rest (see Table 18.1). Refugees from Indochina and Latin America fleeing persecution and ethnic discrimination in their war-torn countries were among Canada's poorest immigrants.

With the gradual elimination of racist barriers, the countries of origin of immigrants to Canada changed significantly. While only four percent of new immigrants from 1945 to 1962 were from outside Europe or the United States, by 2011, that was the case for 70 percent of those who had immigrated since 2006. Asia was the major continent supplying new residents for Canada, accounting for 57 percent, followed by the Americas at 16 percent, Europe at 14 percent, and Africa at 13 percent.

TIMELINE

1976–2013 8.2 million immigrants arrive in Canada

1977 Parti Québécois passes Bill 101

1980 Terry Fox begins his "Marathon of Hope" run

1984 Edmonton Oilers win their first of five Stanley Cups

1986 Denys Arcand's film *Le Déclin de l'empire américain* released

1988 Ben Johnson is stripped of an Olympic medal after testing positive for banned steroids

1997–2003 Canadian Internet usage more than doubles

2000 CBC begins airing the series *Canada: A People's History*

2010 Vancouver Winter Olympics

2014 Population of Canada estimated at over 35 million

TABLE 18.1

Growth of Canada's Population, 1976–2013

PERIOD	POPULATION AT END OF PERIOD	TOTAL POPULATION GROWTH	BIRTHS	DEATHS	IMMIGRANTS	EMIGRANTS
1976-81	24 820	1370	1820	843	771	278
1981-86	26 100	1280	1872	885	678	278
1986-91	28 037	1937	1933	946	1177	213
1991-96	29 610	1573	1936	1024	1118	338
1996-2001	31 019	1409	1705	1089	1221	376
2001-06	32 576	1557	1682	1129	1410	304
2006-11	34 343	1767	1870	1190	1263	287
2011-13	35 345	1002	763	498	523	114

All numbers in thousands. Population figures corrected to take into account census undercounting.

Source: Statistics Canada, CANSIM tables 051-0001 and 051-0004.

While Canada remained a country in which an overwhelming majority had European origins, that profile began to change dramatically. According to the 2011 census, 1 400 685 Canadians reported Aboriginal origins, including Status and non-Status "Indians," Inuit, and Métis. Another five million were members of non-Aboriginal visible minorities. The South Asian and Chinese-Canadian populations exceeded 1 600 000 and 1 400 000 respectively, and almost 800 000 Canadians were of African origin. Other ancestries within the Canadian mosaic included 600 000 Filipinos, over 400 000 Arabs, and almost 400 000 Southeast Asians.

Visible minorities, largely recent arrivals, flocked to Canada's major cities where jobs were easier to find and where immigrant communities were already established. The result was that more than half of all visible-minority new Canadians settled in Ontario, with British Columbia, a magnet for many South and East Asians, proving the second-most attractive province for non-Europeans. In contrast, Quebec's population was significantly less diverse, with only about a quarter as many visible-minority residents as Ontario. The four western provinces continued to be the home of almost two-thirds of Aboriginal peoples. While visible minorities, other than Aboriginal peoples, made up about 19 percent of all Canadians in 2011, their share of the total population in both the Toronto and Vancouver metropolitan areas was well over 40 percent. In Markham and Richmond, suburbs of Toronto and Vancouver respectively, visible minorities made up over 70 percent of the population. In contrast, in Canada's second largest metropolis, Montreal, only 20 percent of the population belonged to visible minorities.

It was not only visible-minority immigrants who gravitated to major cities and a few provinces in Canada.

Three new Canadians take their citizenship oath. SOURCE: AARON HARRIS/CP IMAGES

VOICES FROM THE PAST

Social Meltdown in Fort McMurray

"I've had problems with alcoholism and I just drank every night for five weeks," Jason Fraser, a 24-year-old iron worker from Nova Scotia, living in Fort McMurray, told a reporter in 2007. "As far as the social atmosphere in the camps, it's not the most healthy environment. There's lots of negativity and built-up misery being shared and communicated. There are a lot of people that are in the situation where they're spending way too much time away from their family to have any kind of semblance of regular family life."

Another chapter in the population story of Canada at the turn of the twenty-first century was internal migration. With its economy booming, Alberta became a popular destination for Canadians looking for a job. Between 2001 and 2006, more than 225 000 Canadians from other provinces moved to Alberta. Many of them worked in the service sector in Calgary and Edmonton. Others found employment in Fort McMurray, a community adjacent to the oil sands that mushroomed from 31 000 people in 1981 to nearly 77 000 in 2010. While the residents of Fort McMurray came from every province, many of them arrived from the Atlantic region, where economic restructuring and the collapse of the fisheries dealt a lethal blow to many communities.

The growth in population outstripped the abilities of the Regional Municipality of Wood Buffalo, which included Fort McMurray, to build housing for workers, whether their jobs were temporary or long-term. Housing prices in Fort McMurray were among the highest in Canada, and rentals were scarce and equally unaffordable. Since they saw their jobs as temporary, many Atlantic Canadians lived in camps and commuted back home on a regular basis at the expense of their employers. Air Canada and WestJet added new flights to Halifax, Sydney, and St John's to accommodate the mobile workforce, while the women who had been left behind added responsibilities such as firefighting and coaching little league teams to their already busy schedules. The men worked 14 days in a row, 12 hours a day, to get a week off in their home province. Exhaustion often led to accidents and deaths, but the wages for tradespeople could not be matched at home.

As Jason Fraser argued, the living conditions in Fort McMurray were not conducive to a healthy lifestyle. The dormitories where the men were housed, he claimed, "basically look like a bomb [dropped on them]." Although there was a shortage of doctors and nurses, the community had 15 escort services, a Boomtown Casino, and easy access to drugs and alcohol. Fraser, moreover, felt uncomfortable in his job. "Nobody ever thought about the environmental impact . . . I had a lot of moral repression. I felt really bad for what I was taking part in."

When jobs in the West began to disappear in 2008 as a result of the financial crisis, many recruits to the reserve army of labour began to return home, and the special flights were cancelled. Some of the charter flights were revived a few years later when oil prices began to rise again, though some companies simply paid for workers to take regularly scheduled flights. Communities in Atlantic Canada, which benefited from the remittance payments of their distant citizens, found themselves vulnerable not only to the ebb and flow of their local economies, but also to that of the western Canadian oil patch.[2]

From 1961 to 2011, more than 90 percent of all immigrants settled in Ontario, British Columbia, and Quebec. In 2011, the foreign-born made up 22 percent of the population of Canada, but there were striking provincial differences. While over a quarter of the people of Ontario and British Columbia were immigrants, about 10 percent of Quebecers and less than two percent of Newfoundlanders had been born abroad. The Atlantic provinces, still leaking population to the rest of the country, offered too few opportunities to attract many immigrants.

The federal government had reduced immigration levels to below 100 000 a year in response to the recession of 1982, but they were allowed to rise once the economy rallied. During the recession of the early 1990s, smaller cuts in immigration were made as it became clear that Canadians were having too few children to maintain the population through natural increase alone. Because of more effective contraception and changing social values, Canadian fertility rates had fallen below the 2.1 children per woman required to maintain current populations, and they remained below that level into the new millennium. The rate in 2011 was only 1.61, meaning that without large-scale immigration, the population of Canada would fall dramatically within a generation.

Infant mortality rates continued to fall, and in 2011, only 4.8 per 1000 children failed to reach their first birthday. Life expectancy for those born in 2007–2009 was 81.1 years, an increase of more than eight years since the early 1970s.

The trends of urbanization and suburbanization continued apace, with farmlands being gobbled up by voracious metropolitan developers. In 2013, almost two-thirds of Canadians lived in the 20 largest census metropolitan areas, and the three largest metropolises—Toronto, Montreal, and Vancouver—accounted for more than a third of the country's population.

EDUCATION

More than ever, formal education became a means to finding satisfying and high-paying work in the last quarter of the twentieth century. As secure blue-collar jobs with good union wages began to evaporate, the doors for young people with limited education shut tight. In 1995, 20 percent of both high-school drop-outs and high-school graduates looking for work were unable to find even part-time positions, and many of those able to find employment worked for the legal minimum wage.

Studies of the career paths of the baby boomers demonstrated that by the 1990s, almost half of university graduates who were in the labour force had reached high-level management or professional positions. Their earnings easily outstripped those of their high-school classmates without post-secondary education, while the income of community college graduates sat between those of university and high-school graduates. University education proved particularly important to immigrant youngsters as a means of improving their economic situation relative to their parents, though social class continued to be the major determinant of which young people would go on to post-secondary education.

While formal education became more important, it also became less affordable. Government cutbacks in grants to post-secondary institutions resulted in higher tuition fees. In the 1960s, tuition fees paid about a fifth of the cost of a university education in most provinces. By 2005, they paid about half. The consequence was that students had to dig deeper to pay for their education. Part-time jobs helped, but they were hard to find in periods of recession. More students lived at home throughout their education years or relied on student loans.

Tales of recent graduates who had accumulated debts of as much as $50 000 but could only find modest jobs abounded in the 1990s. Still, studies suggested that in 2000, university graduates of the early 1990s were out-earning people of their age who had not attended university. And while the high cost of post-secondary education acted as a deterrent to many youth, university and college enrollments nevertheless increased. Full-time university enrollment, which reached about 570 000 in 1992–93, had climbed to almost 940 000 by 2011–12. Community college enrollment also increased over the same period, from about 470 000 to 732 000 full- and part-time students. Part-time university enrollment stagnated, with barely more in 2011–12 (about 325 000) than in 1992–93 (about 316 000).

By the 1996 census, women outnumbered men among university graduates. They made up two-thirds of the graduates in the humanities and social sciences, and three-quarters in education. They also gained greater access to previously male-dominated fields of study such as law and medicine, and made inroads in programs leading to degrees in business, management, and public administration. Gender parity remained more elusive in other high-paying fields such as engineering and architecture (where more than three-quarters of 2011 graduates were men), or mathematics and computer science (where fewer than a third of graduates were women). Despite their educational attainments, women on average reported lower income than men and were less likely to be found in top management positions.

If education in Canada was increasingly seen as a vehicle for providing highly trained workers for industry, it had yet another purpose for Quebec governments: maintaining French language and culture. In 1977, the Parti Québécois government passed Bill 101 which, among other things, permitted only Quebec-born anglophones to educate their children in English. Under this law, all immigrants, regardless of linguistic background, were obliged to send their children to French-language schools. At first, even anglophones born elsewhere in Canada were excluded from English education, but a 1984 Supreme Court decision reversed that policy, much to the anger of Quebec nationalists. The language of education remained a hot-button issue in Quebec, with recurrent controversies surrounding the teaching of English in French schools since 2008.

Some recent immigrants to Quebec initially resisted the francophone majority's imposition of French as the only language of instruction. From their point of view, they had moved to Canada, and they did not see why they had to embrace the cultural aspirations of francophone Quebecers. Immigrants found that Canada's claims to support multiculturalism seemed to be contradicted by prejudices favouring linguistic and cultural conformity to the two largest linguistic groups.

IMMIGRANT EXPERIENCES

Immigrant experiences varied. In the 1980s and 1990s, wealthy Hong Kong residents, skittish about the impending return of their city to the Chinese government in 1997 after a century of British control, were actively courted by the Canadian government because of the capital and expertise they promised to inject into the economy. By contrast, South Asian farm and factory workers continued to experience exploitative conditions. Vietnamese and other Indochinese immigrants, many of them "boat people" fleeing either political repression or economic hardship, began arriving in Canada in the late 1970s. While many prospered in their new home, the rate of unemployment among Canadians of Vietnamese descent in the early 1990s was double the Canadian average. Violent youth gangs in the Vietnamese community reflected the presence of an underclass facing a bleak future. Middle-class Vietnamese resented the media spotlight on the gangs and the limited attention paid both to those who were succeeding despite the odds and to the conditions that caused some youth to turn to gangs.

African Canadians continued to experience a great deal of racism in employment and housing, and they also regarded themselves as victims of police brutality. A series of police shootings of unarmed blacks in Montreal and Toronto led to accusations that many police officers were racists who stereotyped all blacks as criminals. Neo-Nazi skinheads—largely unemployed white male youths—attacked non-whites of Asian and African origin and desecrated Jewish cemeteries.

State and unofficial discrimination against an ethnic minority also surfaced in Canada in the wake of

11 September 2001. Since the perpetrators of the crime had been Muslim fundamentalists, state security checks for potential terrorists often seemed to target people of Arabic origins. Some Canadians of Arab descent lost their jobs, allegedly because they were security risks, without being informed as to how authorities had come to this conclusion. Public hysteria over the American events led to tragic reports of Arab and other Muslim children being stoned on their way to school, to desecration of mosques, and to threats and intimidation of Arabs and those who looked like they might be Arabs. Religious institutions were often key to creating greater acceptance of a diversity of peoples in Canada, but some actually promoted intolerance.

THE CHURCHES

Despite the overall decline in church attendance, two-thirds of Canadians in 2011 still claimed to be Christians; almost one-quarter reported no religion. Although Roman Catholicism continued to lose followers in Quebec, membership increased in Canadian cities where many new immigrants were practising Roman Catholics. As in the United States, some evangelical churches showed marked increases in membership, among them the Christian and Missionary Alliance, Seventh-Day Adventist, and Pentecostal churches, which emphasized spiritual rebirth. The counter-secularization movement also had its followers among the nearly eight percent of Canadians who subscribed to other religions, including Judaism, Islam, Hinduism, Buddhism, Sikhism, and various New Age beliefs (see Table 18.2).

For many Catholics and Protestants, Canada's evolution as a multicultural country began to pose new issues. When new Canadians of non-Christian faiths began protesting that public schools were requiring their children to participate in Christian ceremonies, many school boards agreed to take religion out of Christmas celebrations and to end such practices as prayers and Bible readings in the school. The growing number of atheists and agnostics similarly applied pressure upon schools and other public institutions to end religious observances.

Inevitably, some Canadians began to feel that the pendulum had swung too far in favour of placing all religious practices on an equal footing. A proposal in Ontario in 2005 to allow the use of Islamic sharia law in

TABLE 18.2

Religious Affiliations of Canadians (in percentages)

RELIGIOUS AFFILIATION	1911	1951	2001	2011*
Roman Catholic	39.4	44.7	43.2	38.7
United	—	20.5	9.6	6.1
Anglican	14.5	14.7	6.9	5.0
Presbyterian	15.6	5.6	1.4	1.4
Lutheran	3.2	3.2	2.0	1.5
Baptist	5.3	3.2	2.5	1.9
Pentecostal	—	0.7	1.2	1.5
Other Protestant/ Christian	17.3**	2.5	8.3***	9.5***
Orthodox	1.2	1.2	1.6	1.7
Jewish	1.0	1.5	1.1	1.0
Muslim	†	†	2.0	3.2
Buddhist	†	†	1.0	1.1
Hindu	†	†	1.0	1.5
Sikh	†	†	0.9	1.4
No religion	0.4	0.4	16.2	23.9
Other	2.0	1.4	2.8	0.6

* With a global non-response rate of over 25 percent, the data for 2011 are suspect
** Includes Methodist and Congregationalist
*** Other Christian
† Included in "Other"

Source: Adapted from *Canada Year Book 1994,* 123; Statistics Canada, *Religions in Canada 2001* (2003); and Statistics Canada, *2011 National Household Survey* (2013)

some circumstances raised a chorus of condemnation. In Quebec, a commission of inquiry was struck in 2007 to evaluate the "reasonable accommodation" of religious practices such as requiring women to wear a veil. The 2014 provincial election in Quebec turned in part on the Parti Québécois proposal of a Quebec Charter of Values which would ban the wearing of "overt" religious symbols by public servants and para-public workers. Most of the emphasis was not on Christian symbols, but rather on those of Muslims, Jews, and Sikhs. The PQ plan came to nought when they were voted out of office.

The churches continued to face the dilemma of the extent to which they should become involved in secular issues, and which ones. During the 1980s recession, the Canadian Conference of Catholic Bishops' Social Affairs Commission issued a manifesto entitled *Ethical Reflections* *on the Economic Crisis.* The bishops set forth the ethical priorities that they wanted governments to follow: "The needs of the poor have priority over the wants of the rich; the rights of workers are more important than the accumulation of machines or the maximization of profit; the participation of the marginalized takes precedence over an order that excludes them."[3] With unemployment in double digits, the bishops called on the government to focus on policies that would create jobs rather than continuing to emphasize the battle against inflation, as the business community urged. Anglican and United Church leaders praised the Catholic bishops for their stand, but there were voices against economic radicalism within all three churches. Much of the hierarchy identified with the business leaders, whose corporate sponsorship was essential to the churches' charitable work. In 1988, the limits of the churches' social justice movement were demonstrated by the decision of the Roman Catholic and Anglican churches to take no position on the Canada–United States Free Trade Agreement.

CULTURAL DEVELOPMENTS

Trends from the 1960s and early 1970s in Canadian cultural development continued: Canadian literature blossomed, a respectable recording industry developed, and at least in English Canada, almost no one paid money to watch Canadian films except the rare one that achieved American acclaim. In this period, it became clear that culture, like resource development and manufacturing, was an industry, contributing as much to the GDP as farming or textile production. Although much Canadian culture was divided along linguistic lines, some manifestations, such as the Cirque du Soleil, cut across the linguistic divide to become international cultural phenomena.

Governments at both federal and provincial levels paid close attention to the policies regulating cultural industries. They offered incentives for Hollywood moguls to make their films in Canada, sponsored overseas trips for artists and writers to promote their products, and supported cultural workers through such programs as the Public Lending Right Commission to compensate writers for the availability of their books catalogued in Canadian libraries. In this period, the print medium faced increasing competition from the screens of movie theatres, televisions, computers, and mobile devices, all of which beamed the world's culture to most Canadians.

FILM, TV, AND THE WEB

Francophone cinema maintained a strong profile from the 1970s to the 2000s. Quebec filmmaker Denys Arcand emerged as an international success story with *Le Déclin de l'empire américain* (1986). His film *Jésus de Montréal* won the Jury prize at the Cannes Film Festival in 1989, and in 2004, *Les invasions barbares* garnered many international tributes, including the Academy Award for Best Foreign Language Film. More recently, Xavier Dolan's *J'ai tué ma mère* (2009), *Laurence Anyways* (2012), and *Mommy* (2014) garnered awards at top international film festivals such as Cannes. While films by Arcand, Dolan, and a few others continued to draw large audiences and some even penetrated the English-Canadian market, other French-language filmmakers complained that reduced government subsidies and chain ownership of cinemas made it difficult to make films or find an audience for them. Increasingly, filmmakers had to be content with having their movies screened on television, where they often found large audiences.

The situation for filmmakers in English Canada was even less rosy. National Film Board (NFB) documentaries continued to receive acclaim. A feminist film unit within the NFB, Studio D, was particularly successful, producing *If You Love This Planet*, an Academy Award–winning anti-nuclear documentary; *Not a Love Story*, an anti-pornography film; and *Forbidden Love*, an examination of lesbian relationships. While government programs ensured the survival of an independent Canadian film industry, only a few feature films such as Cynthia Scott's *The Company of Strangers*, Anne Wheeler's *Bye Bye Blues*, and several films by Atom Egoyan received wide distribution in theatres. On the whole, cinema in both English and French Canada continued to be dominated by American products, some of which were filmed in Canada to take advantage of lower labour costs.

English-Canadian television faced new challenges in an era of government cuts and competition from the "200-channel universe" that allowed Canadians to view endless hours of mostly American programs. There were exceptions. Canadians warmed to their political and social humorists, and shows such as *This Hour Has 22 Minutes*, *Royal Canadian Air Farce*, and *Rick Mercer Report* drew audiences in the millions.

Despite the success of the American Cable News Network (CNN) in dominating international newscasts, Canadians continued to watch news programs produced within the country. CBC's Newsworld channel in particular quickly developed a loyal following after it was launched in 1989. The CBC series *Canada: A People's History*, aired in 2000 and 2001 to celebrate the millennium, was popular with most viewers, though it was controversial among historians. Nevertheless, English Canadians increasingly had difficulty distinguishing between the sitcoms, dramas, and game shows produced at home and those beamed in from American channels, and gave far more of their time to the latter than the former. As well, to penetrate the lucrative American market, Canadian shows such as *Rookie Blue* were produced to be generically North American rather than specifically Canadian.

The imperatives of language assured Quebec's television producers of a more loyal audience, both in Quebec and elsewhere in French Canada. In the 1980s and 1990s, hundreds of thousands of francophones watched Pierre Gauvreau's *Le Temps d'une paix* (*Peacetime*), a dramatization of life in Quebec from 1918 to 1930, and *Cormoran*, which highlighted political and class struggles in Rimouski during the Great Depression. Fernand Dansereau's *Le Parc des Braves* focused on the Second World War, while his *Shehaweh* was set in the period of Montreal's founding. Beginning in 1997, Jacques Lacoursière's *Épopée en Amérique*, a series chronicling the history of Quebec, drew large television audiences. Among TV series focusing on modern Quebec, several by the feminist author, broadcaster, and former PQ cabinet minister Lise Payette were particularly successful. Her series *Marilyn*, which began a long TV run in 1991, had as its protagonist a charwoman whose experiences put her in contact with people from all walks of life in Quebec. Other Quebec series adopted more standard formats, such as police dramas, sitcoms, and reality television, but always with a specifically Quebec twist.

By the early 2000s, both film and television in Canada as a whole had to face competition from a new source of entertainment: the World Wide Web. Canadians were early adopters of Internet use. Already by 1997, two years after the generalized launch of the Web, 29 percent of Canadian households reported regularly using the Internet. Only six years later, in 2003, the proportion had more

Denys Arcand

Denys Arcand, one of Quebec's most successful directors and screenwriters in the twentieth century, began making his mark in the early 1970s. In many respects, his life mirrors the larger social changes that have taken place in Quebec since the 1960s.

Born in 1941 in the village of Deschambault, up the St Lawrence from Quebec City, Arcand grew up in a deeply Roman Catholic setting. As he noted in 2012, "I was born and lived for a long while in a sleepy Quebec village . . . a village crushed under the mantle of Catholic silence. Beneath this apparently placid surface frothed brutal violence, adultery and suicides. We never spoke of them."[4]

Arcand studied history at the Université de Montréal under neonationalist thinkers such as Maurice Séguin and Michel Brunet, emerging with a master's degree in 1963 and a critical and sometimes melancholy perspective on Quebec history that would imbue all of his future films. Like many young men of the Quiet Revolution period, he also developed a great deal of skepticism toward religion. His first post-university job was as a filmmaker for the National Film Board, producing historical films. In one of them, his thinly disguised depiction of the nuns of New France as fanatics was emblematic of the change that had occurred from one generation to the next in the fortunes of the church in Quebec.

In 1970, Arcand directed a three-hour documentary on textile workers in Quebec called *On est au coton*. The title had a double entendre, suggesting that it was not only about workers in the cotton trade, but also about people reduced to the level of sheep. The film's scathing indictment of capitalists' treatment of their workers caused the NFB, still reeling from Cold War purges, to halt release of the film after only a few showings. Ironically, NFB intervention gave Arcand a great deal of publicity in Quebec for what otherwise might have been dismissed as an overly long documentary. By 1976, Arcand's growing international reputation as a filmmaker forced the NFB to finally remove all restrictions on the viewing of the film.

Arcand's next film was also a political documentary, *Québec: Duplessis et après* (1972). It interposed shots of recent developments in Quebec with footage of the Duplessis years

Denys Arcand at the 2004 Academy Awards. SOURCE: LAURA RAUCH/AP PHOTO/CP IMAGES

to attempt to burst the bubble of politicians who pretended that the corruption and demagogy of the Duplessis years had evaporated in post-Quiet Revolution Quebec. A year later, Arcand released a feature film, *Réjeanne Padovani*, which went further, presenting Quebec's politicians as the corrupt puppets of Mafia figures who really ran the province. The radicalism of this Quebec director, which might have resulted in his being crushed by the combination of his state and church opponents a decade earlier, had proven by the mid-1970s to be an asset in his quest for artistic and commercial approval. In 1978, Arcand returned to Duplessis with an acclaimed but controversial miniseries on Radio-Canada television. The series provided a remarkably balanced view of Le Chef, which pleased neither Duplessis's former collaborators nor his foes.

Arcand's relationship with Quebec nationalism and the sovereignty movement was complex. He supported Parti Québécois efforts during the referendum of 1980 to win sovereignty for Quebec, but remained skeptical about the future of a people who through history had refused to engage wholeheartedly in the quest for national emancipation. As he noted in 2012, "seeking to portray reality always made me enemies on both sides of the fence: I was never a defender of federalism, I always said that, under certain conditions, Quebec independence was certainly desirable, but that it remained improbable."[5] His 1982 film on the referendum, *Le confort et l'indifférence*, mocked both the "Yes" and "No" sides of the referendum debate for their lack of vision about Quebec's future and their focus on such seeming trivia as whether the price of gasoline would go up or down in an independent Quebec. Disabused sovereignists refer to the film even today as a topical portrayal of the fundamental ills of politics and nationalism in Quebec.

Like a significant number of Quebec artists and intellectuals, Arcand turned further away from the active promotion of sovereignty after the bitter defeat of 1980, and was increasingly condemned as cynical by more idealistic Quebec artists and critics. Symbolic of the increasing maturity and sophistication of Quebec francophone cinema, Arcand's 1986 film *Le Déclin de l'empire américain* (released in English as *The Decline of the American Empire*) became an international commercial success. In the film, a group of Montreal friends, mainly university professors, talk about sexual exploits and politics, touching on themes that appealed to audiences far beyond Quebec. In 2004, Arcand's film *Les invasions barbares* (*The Barbarian Invasions*), a sequel to *Déclin*, became a huge international success, but it also included acerbic commentary on Quebec's state-run health care system. His third film in the *Déclin* trilogy, *L'âge des ténèbres* (*Days of Darkness*), which was also highly critical of the state of contemporary Quebec, was chosen to close the Cannes Film Festival in 2007, but its critical reception was far less enthusiastic. His latest film, *Le Règne de la beauté* (2014), was once again anchored deeply in Quebec culture and history, with broader reflections on the banality of contemporary hedonistic society, though it too met with critical and commercial indifference. Such is perhaps the fate of a filmmaker who has refused to portray reality simplistically.

than doubled, to 64 percent. By 2012, 83 percent of Canadian households had access to the Internet at home. Online gaming, social networking, and other Web-specific activities competed with film and TV for leisure hours, while the traditional film and TV industry also faced direct competition from sites such as YouTube and Netflix. Along with P2P downloading and other services, these Web-based alternatives to traditional broadcast and cable TV also allowed Canadian consumers to bypass Canadian-content rules altogether. By 2014, almost half of Canadians consumed part of their television programming over the Internet, and although traditional television remained the main means by which Canadians accessed their favourite shows, subscription to cable and satellite TV was on the decline. A third of English Canadians were subscribed to Netflix, though the almost exclusively English-language content of the service meant that adoption by francophones was much lower.

The value of film and television production in Canada stagnated in the first decade and a half of the new millennium, and the number of people employed in the sector dropped. In the face of these dramatic changes, some in the industry began to push for greater controls on Canadians' Web activity and for a system of fees on Internet access to support the Canadian TV and film industry, while others called for deregulation.

LITERARY ACHIEVEMENTS

Despite competition from other media, English-Canadian literature continued to appeal to readers at home and abroad. Margaret Atwood, Michael Ondaatje, Carol Shields, Rohinton Mistry, Anne Michaels, and others won major international book awards, and a host of writers such as Wayne Johnston, Alice Munro, M.G. Vassanji, Anne-Marie MacDonald, Alistair MacLeod, Yann Martel, Mordecai Richler, and Guy Vanderhaeghe also topped Canadian and international bestseller lists. French-Canadian literature had less broad international distribution, but like

French TV and films enjoyed a relatively loyal market among francophones and significant subsidies from both the Canadian and Quebec governments, as well as some success in France.

The multicultural character of Canada's contribution to world literature is striking. Mistry is an Indian expatriate, while Ondaatje was born in Sri Lanka. Other key contributors were Trinidad-born Neil Bissoondath, based in Quebec City, and Bengali-Canadian poet and literary social critic Himani Bannerji. Nova Scotia's black community has produced two fine poets in Maxine Tynes and George Elliott Clarke, while Toronto poet Dionne Brand explored the issues of sexism, racism, imperialism, and homophobia in her work.

Native authors were also beginning to be noticed by the broader society. Thomas King's portraits of Native life in works such as *Medicine River* (1990), the powerful novels of Joseph Boyden in the early 2000s, and Tomson Highway's plays, including the critically acclaimed *Dry Lips Oughta Move to Kapuskasing* (1989), represent just a few of the Native attempts to bring their stories to Canadians as a whole. The Mi'kmaq found a voice in the poetry of Rita Joe.

RECORDING ARTISTS

Sales of "Canadian content" recordings increased from $54 million in 1990–91 to $154 million in 1998. By the latter date, 17.3 percent of sales in Canada, compared with 10.5 percent eight years earlier, were of records whose artists, writers, or producers were Canadian citizens. In part, this was simply because Canada produced a number of international superstars in the last decade of the twentieth century, many of them women. Céline Dion, Alanis Morissette, Shania Twain, Sarah McLachlan, and Diana Krall were the world's bestselling female artists in pop, country, folk, and jazz. Among male artists, Bryan Adams, Barenaked Ladies, and The Tragically Hip were English Canada's best-known exports, while Jean Leloup, Garou, and Roch Voisine had major success in France. The vibrancy of the Canadian popular music scene continued in the first decade of the twenty-first century, with artists such as Arcade Fire and Justin Bieber becoming international superstars.

As in other cultural fields, the rise of the Internet posed serious challenges to Canadian music producers. After reaching a peak in the late 1990s, sales of recordings by Canadian artists stagnated and then fell to $108 million by 2008, although their share of all recording sales increased to over 22 percent. As in the film and TV industry, producers and some artists blamed Internet piracy and called for stricter controls and tax-based financing, though at the same time many began to adapt to the new models of distribution via services such as iTunes and Google Play.

Popular music was one of the few occupations that a talented few could use to transform their economic prospects. Céline Dion was the fourteenth child of a working-class Quebec family and became the province's leading francophone pop star. In the 1980s, while a teenager, she rose to stardom in Quebec and established an equally solid reputation in France. At the time she spoke barely a word of English, but in the

Sarah McLachlan. SOURCE: GENE SCHILLING/CP IMAGES

1990s she learned it well enough to become the world's bestselling female artist. Another rags-to-riches story is the career of Shania Twain, who had grown up in poverty in Timmins, Ontario, with her mother and Métis stepfather. When her parents died in a car crash, the teenaged Twain raised her younger brothers and sisters with money she earned as a local singer. By 2000, she was country music's all-time bestselling female artist. Folk-pop singer Sarah McLachlan was the founder of Lilith Fair, a female musicians' summer festival that for several years drew large numbers in the United States and Canada.

While some of these artists might have found success without Canadian-content regulations, the rules encouraged more diversity in the types of music aired by radio and TV stations. Political tunes such as Bruce Cockburn's "Rocket Launcher" and Parachute Club's "Rise Up," which may not have been played in Canada in the period before the "Can Con" rule, proved to be big sellers. Rita MacNeil's "Working Man"—featuring Men of the Deeps, a coal miners' choir from Cape Breton—made every country music station playlist in Canada, and also became a chart-topper in Great Britain. Apart from MacNeil, who hailed from Big Pond, Cape Breton, many other Atlantic artists, including Ashley MacIsaac, Natalie MacMaster, Great Big Sea, The Barra MacNeils, Figgy Duff, and The Rankin Family, performed folk music with Celtic roots. In western Canada, artists such as Connie Kaldor, James Keelaghan, Spirit of the West, and Tom Russell drew on regional themes and often spoke to the lives of the disadvantaged.

Marginalized earlier in the period, some Native artists gained recognition in the 1990s and 2000s. Kashtin, two Innu performers from northern Quebec who sang in their Native language, produced a hybrid of Native music and rock 'n' roll, and played to large audiences of both francophones and anglophones in the south. Susan Aglukark, although singing mainly in English, paid tribute to her Inuit heritage and dealt with social problems of the North. Native dance troupes performed traditional dances in ceremonial costumes before their own people and increasingly before white audiences as well, attempting to reproduce the dances as they had been performed by their ancestors rather than refashioning them for commercial broadcasters.

MEDIA CONCENTRATION AND THE CHALLENGE OF THE WEB

In this period, control over the mass media, which continued to have an enormous impact on Canadian social values, became concentrated in the hands of a few corporations. The Royal Commission on Newspapers reported in 1980 that three chains controlled 90 percent of French-language newspapers and that another three conglomerates controlled more than two-thirds of English-language newspapers in Canada. Since that time, the concentration of ownership has only increased. The Southam chain dominated most large anglophone urban markets outside the Atlantic provinces, though it faced well-established competitors in Toronto. Once owned by the Southam family, the chain was controlled by magnate Conrad Black from 1996 to 2000, when it was bought by I.H. "Izzy" Asper, a Winnipeg entrepreneur and former Manitoba Liberal leader, who had already built a television empire. Then in 2010, a pervasive media empire, Postmedia News, acquired most of the bankrupt Asper conglomerate. Such media concentration, which also occurred in other Western democracies, raised questions about the degree to which the media could be counted on to provide a range of points of view.

The Web posed a major challenge to all earlier forms of media. Providing infinite, unmediated, and easily accessible sources of information, it undermined the subscription-based business model of traditional media, with newspapers being hit especially hard. The rise of Web-based content and ecommerce also brought both challenges and opportunities to Canadian publishers and booksellers. Canadian publishers initially strongly resisted Google's attempt to create a universal digital library under its control, but many later agreed to the international settlement that allowed Google to continue its project. As for booksellers, if Canadians could buy directly from large multinationals such as Walmart or Amazon, with correspondingly lower prices, and in the case of Amazon or Google Play, even have ebooks delivered directly to their mobile devices, what could even a large Canadian player like Chapters-Indigo do to compete? Symbolically, in 2014, Toronto's famed World's Biggest Bookstore, owned by Indigo, closed its doors for good. As for small and independent bookstores, their fate was often sealed. In some circles, there were proposals to reverse these trends. In Quebec, for example, a movement emerged in 2013 to impose price regulation in the book market to sustain small bookstores in the face of cut-throat competition from massive international corporations. But so far, capitalist imperatives and free-market ideology have won the day.

PROFESSIONAL SPORTS

Hockey continued to be the most popular spectator sport in Canada. When the World Hockey Association faced bankruptcy in 1979, all of the WHA teams but Ottawa joined the NHL, and the transfer of the NHL's Atlanta franchise to Calgary increased the number of Canadian teams to seven. The Edmonton Oilers won five Stanley Cups from 1984 to 1990, and Oiler Wayne Gretzky became almost synonymous with the game. To the chagrin of most Edmontonians, Gretzky was sold to the Los Angeles Kings in 1988 by Oilers owner Peter Pocklington for $18 million. It was a reminder that hockey, like most professional sports, had become big business, and that a franchise belonged to owners rather than a particular city. By the mid-1990s, Quebec City and Winnipeg could not afford the cost of signing star players, and their teams headed south of the border. In 2011, Winnipeg got its Jets back, and Quebec City was so determined to regain an NHL team that it built a brand-new arena at great expense to municipal taxpayers without even the guarantee of an eventual NHL franchise.

Football fans proved resistant to the high ticket prices necessitated by the 1990s to pay lucrative players' contracts. Although the ownership of Ontario teams was private, the western teams were owned and operated by non-profit community organizations. An attempt to increase interest in the Canadian Football League by expansion of franchises to the United States in the mid-1990s flopped. American football fans proved uninterested in the Canadian version of the game, and soon the CFL was once again made up of only Canadian teams. The league also faced competition from its larger American counterpart, the National Football League, which was increasingly popular in both English and French Canada.

Professional baseball in Canada was represented by American major league teams based in the two largest cities. The Montreal Expos had difficulties filling the ill-suited Olympic stadium and moved to Washington, D.C., in 2004. The Toronto Blue Jays attracted large crowds in their hometown, even though no member of the team was a Torontonian or even a Canadian. After spending almost $50 million on player salaries, the Blue Jays won the World Series in 1992 and 1993.

While professional sports teams were almost exclusively male, both female and male athletes won international honours in individual sports, bringing home medals in a variety of events at Olympic, Commonwealth, and Pan-American Games, as well as world championships in individual sports. Competitive figure skating in particular drew spectators in large numbers.

SPORTS AND SOCIETY

For many Canadians, even amateur sports were becoming big business, and the desire to win often led athletes and coaches to cheat. A steroids scandal rocked Canada after sprinter Ben Johnson was stripped of a gold medal at the Seoul Olympics in 1988. In the media circus and official inquiry that followed, Canadians learned that many athletes used performance-enhancing steroids. Questions of amateurism that had plagued earlier international competition seemed rather quaint as sports took on a big-business atmosphere where millions of dollars in endorsements could await Olympic gold medallists. Canada's reputation in running rebounded with Donovan Bailey's convincing 100-metre win in the 1996 Olympics. National sporting pride grew further when Vancouver hosted the Winter Olympics in 2010 and Canada won a record 14 gold medals, including in both men's and women's hockey.

While many young Canadians dreamed of becoming sports celebrities, their chances were best if they were Anglo-Canadian males with professional or white-collar parents. The costs involved in training athletes who could compete in national and international events excluded most working-class children. Girls faced particular challenges as sexual segregation continued to make sports a largely male preserve. Attempts by girls and women to share the same opportunities as boys were mightily resisted. In 1985, the Ontario Hockey Association barred 13-year-old Justine Blainey from participating on a leading boys' hockey team. Several courtrooms and thousands of dollars later, Justine got her wish in 1987, but the OHA continued

Terry Fox

For many Canadians, the country's most inspiring athlete had never attempted to win any competition. Born in Winnipeg in 1958 to working-class parents, Terry Fox moved with his family to British Columbia in 1966, eventually settling in Port Coquitlam. A keen athlete both in high school and at Simon Fraser University, he seemed destined for a career in physical education, a profession then on the rise with Canadians' new interest in fitness. Then his prospects dimmed. In 1977, Fox was diagnosed with bone cancer in his left knee, and his left leg was amputated. Fitted with an artificial limb, and with encouragement from disability advocates such as the wheelchair athlete Rick Hansen, Fox was determined to remain an athlete and "conquer" his disability. He played wheelchair basketball and also competed in a marathon. In 1979, he decided to take on a larger challenge: a cross-Canada run to raise funds for cancer research, baptized the "Marathon of Hope."

Fox began his run in Newfoundland in April 1980. He was sponsored by major corporations such as Ford and Adidas, though he refused to endorse their products, and received initially lukewarm support from the Canadian Cancer Society. The enterprise started slowly, and he faced particular challenges in Quebec, because, among other reasons, neither he nor his team spoke French. Coming just after the painful episode of the 1980 referendum, his pan-Canadian enterprise found little echo among the Quebec public or in the French-language media.[6] In Ontario, however, Fox was transformed into a national hero by media attention and through the revitalized efforts of the Canadian Cancer Society. At a time when economic uncertainty and political instability left many Canadians feeling rudderless, Fox made people "feel good," although some criticized the media's heavy focus on his heroic individualism.

After five months of running almost 40 kilometres per day, Fox was forced to give up his run near Thunder Bay on 1 September 1980 when doctors found that the cancer had spread to his lungs. His run raised almost $2 million, and fundraisers in the immediate aftermath brought in another $20 million. Until his death in June 1981, he remained a Canadian media superstar, and was made a Companion of the Order of Canada.[7] As well as raising awareness of cancer, his refusal to give in also dramatized the oft-ignored capabilities of people with disabilities and helped change Canadians' attitudes toward them. Fox's legacy was continued by a foundation established in his name, which has since raised hundreds of millions of dollars. The Terry Fox Run, an annual fundraising event for cancer research, became one of the major participatory sports events in English Canada. Fox also inspired others to emulate him: Steve Fonyo, who had also lost a leg to cancer, accomplished the entire trans-Canada run in 1984-85, while Rick Hansen circled the globe in his wheelchair in 1985-86 to raise awareness about disabilities.

Terry Fox during his Marathon of Hope. SOURCE: CP IMAGES

to grumble that the body checking and slapshots of the boys' league made the inclusion of girls inappropriate.

While sports for youngsters was supposed to be about fun, it sometimes became a nightmare. In 1997, Sheldon Kennedy, a former member of the Swift Current Broncos, a junior team, who had made it to the NHL, revealed that in the late 1980s the Broncos coach had persistently sexually abused him. It soon became clear that Kennedy was not his only victim, and that coaches of other teams had sexually abused players as well. The hockey scandal followed revelations about sexual abuse of both boys and girls in other sports, alarming parents and sports authorities at a time when more and more children were becoming involved in organized sporting activities.

Canadians in the postwar period spent a great deal of money and time as sports spectators, both at children's and professional games, but attending sports activities and participating in them were two different stories. In the early 1970s, it was estimated that 90 percent of adults did not do the minimum amount of exercise recommended for protection against heart disease and stroke. While Canadians were living longer, poor nutrition habits, lack of exercise, and smoking were ending many lives prematurely and causing many other Canadians, who survived cancer surgery, heart attacks, or strokes, to live restricted lives.

The federal government, aided by campaigns of nutritionists, physical education specialists, and physicians, increasingly encouraged Canadians to rethink their lifestyles. Urged on by a federal body called Participaction, which placed clever ads on radio and television, previously indolent Canadians took up jogging, enrolled in aerobics classes, swam, or at least took the occasional long walk. The physical fitness craze meant new business for leisure industry operators, from ski hills to fitness clubs.

Anti-smoking campaigns also had an impact. By the 1990s, the intrepid smoker stood out in the snow or rain during a coffee break at most workplaces, public buildings, and halls of education. Airlines banned smoking altogether, and intercity buses, once thick with smoke, became havens for the non-smoker as well. In most cities, restaurants were divided by law into smoking and non-smoking sections, and some city councils legislated smoking out of all establishments where food was served. By 2009, all provinces and territories had banned smoking entirely in all enclosed public places and workplaces. The percentage of Canadians over 15 who smoked dropped by almost two thirds between the mid-1970s and 2012, from 44.5 percent to 16.1 percent.

The diets of many Canadians have changed and are now more likely to meet Nutrition Canada's requirement for "balanced" eating, but problems arose among those who ate too little or too much. In the consumer-oriented media, social images, especially for young women, created the view that the ideal body was fat-free. This unhealthy suggestion led to a rise in anorexia and bulimia, with risks of death by starvation. More commonly, unhealthy diets led to obesity as people gorged on calorie-laden fast foods and drank too much alcohol. When physicians linked the consumption of red meat to cancer and cardiovascular problems, most people took notice and the cattle industry changed breeding habits to develop leaner meats.

Social class was a major factor in the response to new ideas about healthy living advanced by nutritionists. Surveys suggested that the working class and the poor had less money to devote to good dietary choices, less time to engage in regular exercise, and, in any case, often regarded the advice against smoking, drinking, and sedentary relaxation as an attack on the few pleasures in their lives. This perspective, not surprisingly, was encouraged by the companies that produced the foods that contributed to the obesity epidemic.

CONCLUSION

The anxiety and conflict that characterized formal political and economic developments over the past three and a half decades stood in sharp contrast to the effervescence that marked Canadian community and cultural life. In this period, Canada had become a more multicultural and pluralist society, and the creativity of its diverse peoples seemed to know few boundaries. The dominance of American culture remained an issue that preoccupied many Canadian critics, at least in English Canada, but ordinary people seemed comfortable with the fact that Canada was a North American nation with access to the markets of the world's richest nation for their films, books, and recordings. In the early twenty-first century, living next door to the United States promised to continue to provide the creative tension that has long been a stimulus to Canadian cultural production, while the rise of the Web increasingly exposed Canadians to a culture that seemed more and more globalized, though ultimately still very American.

Being Canadian

Until 1946, Canadians carried British passports. The Canadian Citizenship Act, which came into effect on 1 January 1947, recognized Canadian citizenship in its own right, while still recognizing Canadians as British subjects. In 1977, a new Citizenship Act allowed Canadians to hold multiple citizenships. Canadian citizenship is typically achieved by birth in Canada, birth abroad when at least one parent is a Canadian citizen, adoption abroad by at least one Canadian citizen, or permanent residence (living in Canada for three out of four years and meeting Canada's citizenship requirements).

It was in this context that the Canadian government, at the cost of $94 million, evacuated 15 000 Canadian citizens (out of a total of 40 000) living in Lebanon when violence between Israel and Hezbollah escalated in 2006. Canadian-born Omar Ahmed Khadr received less sympathetic treatment when he was incarcerated by the Americans at their prison in Guantanamo Bay in Cuba for his involvement in attacks on Americans in Afghanistan. Unlike other Western nations that repatriated their citizens detained at Guantanamo, the Canadian government repeatedly delayed repatriating Khadr, even when the Supreme Court ruled in 2010 that his constitutional rights had been violated. He was finally repatriated to Canada in 2012, serving out his prison term in a Canadian penitentiary.

Other Canadians have also felt the sting of second-class citizenship. When a bomb exploded on Air India Flight 182 in June 1985, it killed all 329 passengers and crew on board, most of them Canadian citizens. The slow and inadequate response to the disaster prompted Indo-Canadians to wonder if the political and judicial system saw the tragedy as India's, not Canada's, problem.

At the time of the 2006 crisis in Lebanon, the historian J. L. Granatstein published an opinion piece in the *Globe and Mail*, stating bluntly what many Canadians were thinking: ". . . obviously, the government has some responsibility to assist Canadians caught up in a conflict. But those holding this country's passport for convenience's sake, who renew every five years without visiting, let alone living in Canada?"[8] Meanwhile, long-time Canadian residents born elsewhere, including war brides and their children, and children born out of wedlock or to a father who took a second citizenship before 1977, discovered that they were not Canadian citizens and were therefore denied Canadian passports.

In response to criticism arising from the Lebanon evacuation and the desperation of Canadian residents needing passports to enter an increasingly security-conscious United States, the Canadian government launched a review of Canada's citizenship laws. Amendments to the Citizenship Act in 2009 (Bill C-37) awarded citizenship to most "lost Canadians," and denied the right of citizenship to the foreign-born grandchildren of Canadians living abroad. It also restored Canadian citizenship to those who had lost their citizenship as a result of becoming a citizen of another country before 1977 and to people born outside of Canada who are first-generation descendants of Canadian citizens.

Currently, up to three million Canadian citizens live outside the country. A majority of them are Canadian-born, and more than a third reside in the United States. While nearly 70 percent of Canadians living abroad indicate that they plan to return to Canada at some point in their lives, the rest plan to remain elsewhere. A few choose to live in tax havens that spare them from paying Canadian taxes. What is the role of these expatriates in Canadian society?

In his book *Who We Are: A Citizen's Manifesto*, Rudyard Griffiths argues that Canadian citizenship should be "earned through physical settlement" and active contribution to the "economic and social betterment" of the country.[9] Jennifer Welsh, self-described as a "full-fledged member of the Canadian diaspora," in her position as a professor at Oxford University, suggests that his assumption that individuals are capable of sustaining only one social identity needs to be tested in our increasingly mobile world. While Canadians lose their right to vote in federal elections after they have lived outside the country for five years, countries such as Italy and Poland, she points out, encourage their expatriates to participate in elections. Finland has even created an expatriate parliament to make collective decisions on issues of importance.

Welsh leave us with an intriguing question. Is it not time, she asks, that Canadians begin thinking of their country in human rather than geographic terms? By linking more directly with the diaspora, she argues, Canada becomes "wherever Canadians are," which "makes it a very big nation indeed."[10]

NOTES

1. Quoted in Paul Anisef, Paul Axelrod, Etta Balchman-Anisef, Carl James, and Anton Turritin, *Opportunity and Uncertainty: Life Course Expectations of the Class of '73* (Toronto: University of Toronto Press, 2000) 239–40.

2. Stuart Neatby, "Hard Times Sold in Vending Machines: Worker Migration from Atlantic Canada to the Tar Sands," *Oil Sands Truth*, 8 January 2008, http://oilsandstruth.org/hard-times-sold-vending-machines and "More on the Social Meltdown of Fort McMurray," *Oil Sands Truth*, 4 December 2007, http://oilsandstruth.org/more-social-meltdown-fort-mcmurray.

3. Cited in Tony Clarke, *Behind the Mitre: The Moral Leadership Crisis in the Canadian Catholic Church* (Toronto: HarperCollins, 1995).

4. Carl Bergeron, *Un cynique chez les lyriques: Denys Arcand et le Québec* (Montreal: Boréal, 2012) 111 (authors' translation). For a complete biography of Arcand, see Réal La Rochelle, *Denys Arcand, l'ange exterminateur: biographie* (Montreal: Leméac, 2004).

5. Bergeron, *Un cynique chez les lyriques*, 113 (authors' translation).

6. Francine Saillant, *Cancer et culture: produire le sens de la maladie* (Montreal: Éditions Saint-Martin, 1988).

7. Leslie Scrivener, *Terry Fox: His Story*, rev. ed. (Toronto: McClelland & Stewart, 2000).

8. J.L. Granatstein, "Conflicted Over Citizenship," *Globe and Mail*, 31 July 2006, A13.

9. Rudyard Griffiths, *Who We Are: A Citizen's Manifesto* (Toronto: Douglas & McIntyre, 2009) 161.

10. Jennifer Welsh, "Our Overlooked Diaspora," *Literary Review of Canada* (March 2011) 5.

SELECTED READING

Adria, Marco. *Technology and Nationalism.* Montreal: McGill-Queen's University Press, 2010

Bibby, Reginald W. *Restless Gods: The Renaissance of Religion in Canada.* Toronto: Novalis, 2004

Biron, Michel, François Dumont, and Élisabeth Nardout-Lafarge. *Histoire de la littérature québécoise.* Montreal: Boréal, 2010

Dorland, Michael. *So Close to the State/s: The Emergence of Canadian Feature Film Policy.* Toronto: University of Toronto Press, 1998

Driedger, Leo, and Shiva S. Halli, eds. *Race and Racism: Canada's Challenge.* Montreal: McGill-Queen's University Press, 2000

Edwardson, Ryan. *Canuck Rock: A History of Canadian Popular Music.* Toronto: University of Toronto Press, 2009

Friesen, Gerald. *Citizens and Nation: An Essay on History, Communication, and Canada.* Toronto: University of Toronto Press, 2000

Halli, Shiva S., and Leo Driedger, eds. *Immigrant Canada: Demographic, Economic, and Social Challenges.* Toronto: University of Toronto Press, 1999

Hayday, Matthew. *Bilingual Today, United Tomorrow: Official Languages in Education and Canadian Federalism.* Montreal: McGill-Queen's University Press, 2005

Howell, Colin D. *Blood, Sweat and Cheers: Sport and the Making of Modern Canada.* Toronto: University of Toronto Press, 2001

Kallen, Evelyn. *Ethnicity and Human Rights in Canada*, 3rd ed. Toronto: Oxford University Press, 2010

Kelley, Ninette, and Michael Trebilcock. *The Making of the Mosaic: A History of Canadian Immigration Policy*, 2nd ed. Toronto: University of Toronto Press, 2010

Leach, Jim. *Film in Canada*, 2nd ed. Toronto: Oxford University Press, 2011

Li, Peter S. *Destination Canada: Immigration Debates and Issues.* Toronto: Oxford University Press, 2003

Melnyk, George. *One Hundred Years of Canadian Cinema.* Toronto: University of Toronto Press, 2004

Mensah, Joseph. *Black Canadians: History, Experience, Social Conditions*, 2nd ed. Halifax: Fernwood, 2010

Nischik, Reingard M., ed. *History of Literature in Canada: English-Canadian and French-Canadian*. Rochester: Camden House, 2008

Pike, David L. *Canadian Cinema Since the 1980s: At the Heart of the World*. Toronto: University of Toronto Press, 2012

Vance, Jonathan F. *A History of Canadian Culture*. Don Mills: Oxford University Press, 2009

Vipond, Mary. *The Mass Media in Canada*, 4th ed. Toronto: Lorimer, 2011

For a comprehensive list of readings for topics covered in this chapter, please visit http://pearsoncanada.ca/conrad.

INDEX